THE INTERPRETATION OF
PLURILINGUAL TAX TREATIES

The Interpretation of Plurilingual Tax Treaties

Theory, Practice, Policy

by:

Richard Xenophon Resch

Ph.D., LL.M., D.B.S., B.A.

Doctoral Dissertation
submitted to

LEIDEN LAW SCHOOL

LEIDEN UNIVERSITY
THE NETHERLANDS

Doctorate awarded on
October 10, 2018

Supervisors:
Prof. Dr. Kees van Raad (Leiden University)
Prof. Dr. John Avery Jones (London School of Economics, UK)

Doctorate Committee:
Prof. Dr. Nico Schrijver (Leiden University)
Prof. Dr. Hugh Ault (Boston College Law School, Newton MA, USA)
Prof. Dr. Frank Engelen (Leiden University)
Prof. Dr. Sigrid Hemels (Erasmus University Rotterdam and Lund University, Sweden)
Prof. Dr. Frank Pötgens (Free University Amsterdam)
Prof. Dr. Koos Boer (Leiden University)

Cover: Lara Sips
Editing and Layout: Richard Resch

Publisher: tredition, Hamburg, Germany
ISBN Hardcover: 978-3-7439-0208-4

Bibliographic information of the German National Library: The German National Library records this publication in the German National Bibliography; detailed bibliographic data is available on the Internet at http://dnb.d-nb.de.

Dedicated to the loving memory of my parents.

'Man acts as though he were the shaper and master of language,
while in fact language remains the master of man.'

— MARTIN HEIDEGGER[†]

[†] *Philosophical and Political Writings* (New York: Continuum, 2003), 267.

Contents

Contents

Contents

List of Tables

List of Figures

Case Law

Arbitral Tribunals. *Aron Kahane Successeur v Francesco Parisi and the Austrian State.* Romanian-Austrian Mixed Arbitral Tribunal. Recueil des décisions des tribunaux arbitraux mixtes institués par les traités de paix, 1929. *The Kingdom of Belgium, the French Republic, the Swiss Confederation, the United Kingdom and the United States of America v The Federal Republic of Germany.* Arbitral Tribunal for the Agreement on German External Debts. Reports of International Arbitral Awards, 1980.

European Court of Human Righs. *Golder v United Kingdom.* European Court of Human Rights. Application no. 4451/70, 1975. *Colozza v Italy.* European Court of Human Rights. Application no. 9024/80, 1985.

European Court of Justice. *Van Schijndel and van Veen v SPF, Opinion of Advocate General Jacobs.* Joined Cases C–430/93 and C–431/93. ECR I–4705, 1995.

Inter-American Court of Human Rights. *Hilaire, Constantine and Benjamin et al. v Trinidad and Tobago.* Inter-American Court of Human Rights, 2002.

International Centre for Settlement of Investment Disputes. *Kiliç İnşaat İthalat İhracat Sanayi ve Ticaret Anonim Şirketi v Turkmenistan.* ICSID, Case No. ARB/10/1. Washington, D.C.: International Centre for Settlement of Investment Disputes, 2012.

International Court of Justice. *Conditions of Admission of a State to Membership in the United Nations (Article 4 of the Charter), Advisory Opinion.* ICJ. Annual Reports of the International Court of Justice, 1948. *Rights of Nationals of the United States of America in Morocco (France v United States of America).* ICJ. Annual Reports of the International Court of Justice, 1952. *Anglo-Iranian Oil Co. (United Kingdom v Iran).* ICJ. Annual Reports of the International Court of Justice, 1952. *Ambatielos (Greece v United Kingdom), Preliminary Objection.* ICJ. Annual Reports of the International Court of Justice, 1952. *Temple of Preah Vihear (Cambodia v Thailand), Preliminary Objections.* ICJ. Annual Reports of the International Court of Justice, 1961. *South West Africa (Ethiopia v South Africa).* ICJ. Annual Reports of the International Court of Justice, 1962. *North Sea Continental Shelf (Federal Republic of Germany/Denmark; Federal Republic of Germany/Netherlands).* ICJ. Annual Reports of the International Court of Justice, 1969. *Fisheries Jurisdiction (United Kingdom v Iceland).* ICJ. Annual Reports of the International Court of Justice, 1974. *Continental Shelf (Libyan Arab Jarnahiriya/Malta).* ICJ. Annual Reports of the International Court of Justice, 1985. *Nicaragua v United States of America – Military and Paramilitary Activities in and Against Nicaragua.* ICJ. Annual Reports of the International Court of Justice, 1986. *Arbitral Award of 31 July 1989 (Guinea Bissau v Senegal).* ICJ. Annual Reports of the International Court of Justice, 1991. *Territorial Dispute (Libyan Arab Jamahiriya/Chad).* ICJ. Annual Reports of the International Court of Justice, 1994. *Maritime Delimitation and Territorial Questions between Qatar and Bahrain (Qatar v Bahrain), Jurisdiction and Admissibility.* ICJ. Annual Reports of the International Court of Justice, 1994. *Legality of the Threat or Use of Nuclear Weapons, Advisory Opinion.* ICJ. Annual Reports of the International Court of Justice, 1996. *Gabčíkovo-Nagymaros Project (Hungary/Slovakia).* ICJ. Annual Reports of the International Court of Justice, 1997. *Kasikili/Sedudu Island (Botswana/Namibia).* ICJ. Annual Reports of the International Court of Justice, 1999. *LaGrand (Germany v United States of America).* ICJ. Annual Reports of the International Court of Justice, 2001. *Sovereignty over Pulau Litigan and Pulau Sipidan (Indonesia v Malaysia).* ICJ. Annual Reports of the International Court of Justice, 2002. *Avena and Other Mexican Nationals (Mexico v USA).* ICJ. Annual Reports of the International Court of Justice, 2004.

Permanent Court of International Justice. *Netherlands Workers Delegate to the ILO.* PCIJ. Publications of the Permanent Court of International Justice, 1922. *The Mavrommatis Palestine Concessions.* PCIJ. Publications of the Permanent Court of International Justice 1922–1946, 1924. *Treaty of Neuilly (Bulgaria v Greece).* PCIJ. Publications of the Permanent Court of International Justice 1922–1946, 1924. *Polish Postal Service in Danzig.* PCIJ. Publications of the Permanent Court of International Justice, 1925.

WTO Appellate Body. *United States — Final Countervailing Duty Determination with Respect to Certain Softwood Lumber From Canada.* WT/DS257/AB/R. Report of the WTO Appellate Body, 2004. *United States — Subsidies on Upland Cotton.* WT/DS267/AB/R. Report of the WTO Appellate Body, 2005.

Australia. *Thiel v Federal Commissioner of Taxation.* [1990] 171 CLR 338.

Austria. VwGH. '2210/60 VwSlg 2707 F/1962'. RIS, September 1962. VwGH. '2013/15/0266'. RIS, June 2015.

Canada. *Gladden v Her Majesty the Queen.* [1985] 85 DTC 5188. *The Queen v Crown Forest Industries Ltd. et al.* [1995] 95 DTC 5389. *Wolf v Canada.* [2002] 4 F.C. 396. *Conrad M. Black v Her Majesty the Queen.* [2014] TCC 12.

France. Conseil d'État. *Société Schneider Electric,* 2002. Conseil d'État. *Société Natexis Banques Populaires v France,* 2006. Conseil d'État. *Ministre du Budget c Ragazzacci,* 2012. Conseil d'État. *9ème et 10ème sous-sections réunies,* 25/02/2015, 366680. *Inédit Au Recueil Lebon,* 2015.

Germany. BFH. 'I 244/63'. BStBl 1966 III, February 1966. BVerfG. '1 BvR 112/65'. BVerfGE 34, February 1973. FG Düsseldorf. 'VII 484/77'. EFG 1980, January 1980. BFH. 'I R 241/82'. BStBl 1984 II, August 1983. BFH. 'I R 63/80'. BStBl 1986 II, August 1985. FG Köln. 'II K 223/85'. EFG 1987, December 1986. BFH. 'I R 369/83'. BStBl 1988 II, February 1988. BFH. 'I R 74/86'. BStBl 1990 II, February 1989. BFH. 'I R 20/87'. BStBl 1989 II, March 1989. FG Köln. '2 K 3928/09'. EFG 1853, April 2012. BFH. 'I R 48/12'. BStBl 2014 II, June 2013.

India. *Fugro Engineering BV v ACIT. TTJ.* Vol. 122. Delhi Income Tax Appelate Tribunal, 2008. *Ram Jethmalani v Union of India.* Supreme Court of India, 2011. *Director of Income Tax v New Skies Satellite BV.* ITA 473/2012, 2016.

Norway. Høyesterett. *PGS Geophysical AS v Government of Norway.* 2004-01003-a, (Sak Nr. 2003/1311). Amsterdam: IBFD, *Tax Treaties Case Law Database 2016,* 2004.

Poland. *Archdukes of the Habsburg-Lorraine House v The Polish State Treasury. Annual Digest of Public International Law Cases (1929–1930), Case No. 235.* Supreme Court Poland. Cambridge University Press, 1930.

United Kingdom. *Quinn v Leatham.* [1901] AC 45. *Best v Samuel Fox & Co. Ltd.* [1952] AC 716. *Buchanan (James) & Co. Ltd. v Babco Forwarding and Shipping (UK) Ltd.* [1978] AC 141, HL. *Fothergill v Monarch Airlines Ltd.* [1981] AC 251, HL. *Bank of India v Trans Continental Commodity Merchants Ltd. & J. N. Patel.* [1982] 1 Lloyd's Rep. 427. *Singh Butra v Ebrahim.* [1982] 2 Lloyd's Rep. 11, C.A. *United City Merchants v Royal Bank of Canada.* [1983] AC 168, HL *Inland Revenue Commissioners v Commerzbank.* [1990] STC 285. *Pepper v Hart.* [1993] AC 593. *Memec Plc v Inland Revenue Comissioners.* [1996] STC 1336. *Memec Plc v Inland Revenue Comissioners.* [1998] STC 754. *Sportsman v IRC.* [1998] STC (SCD) 289. *R v Secretary for the Home Department, Ex Parte Adan.* [2001] AC 477. *Czech Republic v European Media Ventures SA.* [2007] EWHC 2851 (Comm). *R (on the Application of) Federation of Tour Operators v HM Treasury.* [2007] EWHC 20622 (Admin).

United States. *Penhallow et al. v Doane's Administrators.* 3 U.S. 54 (1795). Dallas's Reports. *Rose v Himeley.* 8 U.S. 241 (1808). *Foster & Elam v Neilson.* 27 U.S. (2 Pet.) 253 (1829). *United States v Percheman.* 32 U.S. (7 Pet.) 51 (1833). *Lochner v New York.* 198 U.S. 45 (1905). *Johnson v Olson.* 92 Kan. 819 142 P. 256

(1914). *Maximov v United States.* 299 F.2d 565 (2d Cir. 1962). *TWA v Franklin Mint Corp.* 466 U.S. 243 (1984). *Air France v Sacks.* 470 U.S. 392 (1985). *O'Connor v United States.* 479 U.S. 27 (1986). *Volkswagenwerk Aktiengesellschaft v Schlunk.* 486 U.S. 694 (1988). *Eastern Airlines, Inc., Petitioner v Rose Marie Floyd, et vir., et al.* 499 U.S. 530 (1991). *United States v Alvarez-Machain.* 504 U.S. 655 (1992). *Itel Containers Int'l Corp. v Huddleston.* 507 U.S. 60 (1993). *Fujitsu Ltd. v Federal Exp. Corp.* 247 F.3d 423 (2d Cir. 2001).

Abbreviations: General

AEAO	*Anwendungserlass zur Abgabenordnung* (administrative directive concerning the application of the German general tax act)
AF	Africa without AW countries
AO	*Abgabenordnung* (German general tax act)
AS	China (People's Rep.), Indonesia, Iran, Japan, Korea (Dem. People's Rep.), Korea (Rep.), Laos, Mongolia, Myanmar, Nepal, Philippines, Taiwan, Thailand, Turkey, and Vietnam
ASEAN	The Association of South East Asian Nations
AW	Arab World
BAO	*Bundesabgabenordnung* (Austrian federal tax act)
BFH	*Bundesfinanzhof* (German federal fiscal court)
BGB	*Bürgerliches Gesetzbuch* (German civil code)
BIT	Bilateral Investment Treaty
BMF	Bundesministerium der Finanzen (German federal ministry of finance)
BStBl	*Bundessteuerblatt* (German federal fiscal gazette)
BVerfG	*Bundesverfassungsgericht* (German federal constitutional court)
BVerfGG	*Bundesverfassungsgerichtsgesetz* (German federal constitutional court act)
CFER	Common European Framework of Reference for Languages
CETA	Comprehensive Economic and Trade Agreement between Canada and the European Union
CIS	Commonwealth of Independent States plus former members and associate states
CISG	United Nations Convention on Contracts for the International Sale of Goods
CW	Commonwealth of Nations including former members, prospective members, and other former British colonies that have never been Commonwealth members
DARS	Draft Articles on Responsibility of States for Internationally Wrongful Acts
ECJ	European Court of Justice
ECHR	European Court of Human Rights
EU	European Union plus EFTA countries but excluding France, Ireland, Malta, and the UK
FG	*Finanzgericht* (German fiscal court of first instance)
FGO	*Finanzgerichtsordnung* (German fiscal procedure act)
GAAR	General anti-abuse rule
GG	*Grundgesetz* (German constitution)
ICJ	International Court of Justice
ICSID	International Centre for Settlement of Investment Disputes
ILC	International Law Commission

ITAT	Income Tax Appelate Tribunal (India)
ITLOS	International Tribunal for the Law of the Sea
JN	*Jurisdiktionsnorm* (Austrian legal act regulating the jurisdiction of courts in private law matters)
LA	Latin America excluding CARICOM (Caribbean Community)
MAP	Mutual agreement procedure
MLI	OECD BEPS multilateral instrument
OECD	Organisation for Economic Co-operation and Development
OECDKP	OECD key partners invited by the OECD to strengthen cooperation through 'Enhanced Engagement' programmes: Brazil, India, Indonesia, China (People's Republic), and South Africa
PCIJ	Permanent Court of International Justice
PE	Permanent establishment
RIS	*Rechtsinformationssystem Bundeskanzleramt* (legal information system of the Federal Chancellery of the Republic of Austria)
SADC	Southern African Development Community
TOW	Type of wording
UNCLOS	United Nations Convention on the Law of the Sea
VCLT	Vienna Convention on the Law of Treaties
VwGH	*Verwaltungsgerichtshof* (Austrian supreme administrative court)
ZPO	*Zivilprozessordnung* (German civil procedure act)

Abbreviations: Figures and Tables

%X	As percentage of X; X may be any combination of other abbreviations, e.g. %PL w PT, reading 'as percentage of plurilingual treaties with prevailing text'
AF	Africa without AW countries
AL	Authentic languages
AS	China (People's Rep.), Indonesia, Iran, Japan, Korea (Dem. People's Rep.), Korea (Rep.), Laos, Mongolia, Myanmar, Nepal, Philippines, Taiwan, Thailand, Turkey, and Vietnam
AW	Arab World
CIS	Commonwealth of Independent States plus former members and associate states
CM	Cumulative
CW	Commonwealth of Nations including former members, prospective members, and other former British colonies that have never been Commonwealth members
EOL	English as official language
EU	European Union plus EFTA countries but excluding France, Ireland, Malta, and the UK
g	Good English proficiency
global	Entire sample including terminated treaties
l	Low English proficiency
LA	Latin America excluding CARICOM (Caribbean Community)
lang	Language
m	Medium English proficiency
n	Native English-speaking
NAF	Not AF
NAS	Not AS
NAW	Not AW
NC	No change in type UL or PL by replacement
NCIS	Not CIS
NCW	Not CW
NEU	Not EU
NLA	Not LA
NOECD	Not OECD
NOEL	Not EOL
No.	Number of treaties
NR	Not replaced terminated treaties
OECD	Organisation for Economic Co-operation and Development

OECDKP	OECD key partners invited by the OECD to strengthen cooperation through 'Enhanced Engagement' programmes: Brazil, India, Indonesia, China (People's Republic), and South Africa
PD	Per decade
PL	Plurilingual treaties
PT	Prevailing text
R	Replaced terminated treaties
term	Terminated treaties
total	Entire set/group analysed
TOW	Type of wording
UL	Unilingual treaties
vg	Very good English proficiency
vl	Very low English proficiency
w	With
w/o	Without

Abbreviations: Language Codes

afr	Afrikaans
alb	Albanian
ara	Arabic
arm	Armenian
aze	Azerbaijanian
bel	Belarusian
ben	Bengali
bos	Bosnian
bul	Bulgarian
bur	Burmese
cat	Catalan
chi	Chinese
cro	Croatian
cze	Czech
dan	Danish
dut	Dutch
dzo	Dzongkha
eng	English
est	Estonian
fao	Faroese
fin	Finnish
fre	French
geo	Georgian
ger	German
gre	Greek
gro	Greenlandic
heb	Hebrew
hin	Hindi
hun	Hungarian
ice	Icelandic
ind	Indonesian
iri	Irish
ita	Italian
jap	Japanese
kaz	Kazakh
kor	Korean
kyr	Kyrgyz
lao	Lao
lat	Latvian
lit	Lithuanian

may	Malay
mol	Moldovan
mon	Mongolian
mtg	Montenegrin
nep	Nepali
nor	Norwegian
per	Persian
pol	Polish
por	Portuguese
rum	Romanian
rus	Russian
scr	Serbo-Croatian
ser	Serbian
sin	Sinhala
slo	Slovak
slv	Slovenian
spa	Spanish
swe	Swedish
tgk	Tajik
tha	Thai
tkm	Turkmen
ukr	Ukrainian
uzb	Uzbek
vts	Vietnamese

Editorial Notes

i. **Punctuation and Style.** Punctuation and style follow suggestions in the *Oxford Style Manual*, the *Chicago Manual of Style*, Butcher's *Copy-editing*, and Strunk-White.[1]

ii. **Quotations.** Quotations follow British practice in using single quotation marks for verbatim quotations, double quotation marks for nested quotations, and no quotation marks for block quotations.[2] Square brackets indicate interpolations. Dots enclosed in parentheses indicate an omission or placeholder in the original: three dots indicate an omission, five dots a placeholder for insertions, and two dots a placeholder for digits (year).

iii. **Citations.** Citations are rendered in note format, based on the *Chicago Manual of Style*. Tax treaties are cited as Country-Country (year) or, when the other country is obvious from the context, Country (year). Unless specified otherwise, all references to Article 31, Article 32, and Article 33 (including paragraph numbers and letters in parenthesis) refer to Articles 31, 32, and 33 of the VCLT.[3] The specification 'VCLT' is omitted to avoid cluttering the text and added only when other VCLT articles are cited for purposes of disambiguation.

iv. **Spelling and Grammar.** Spelling follows Fowler's *Dictionary of Modern English Usage* and the Oxford Dictionary.[4] The word 'data' is a plural, but use as a singular is gaining acceptance. Depending on the context, both forms are used by me.

v. **Translations.** Unless otherwise noted, translations are my own.

---

[1]E. M. Ritter, ed., *The Oxford Style Manual* (Oxford: Oxford University Press, 2003); Russell David Harper, ed., *The Chicago Manual of Style*, 16th ed. (Chicago, IL: University of Chicago Press, 2010); Butcher, Judith, *Butcher's Copy-editing: The Cambridge Handbook for Editors, Copy-editors and Proofreaders*, 3rd ed. (Cambridge: Cambridge University Press, 1992); Strunk, William Jr., *The Elements of Style*, ed. White, E.B., 4th ed. (Harlow, Essex: Pearson Education Limited, 2014).

[2]See Ritter, *The Oxford Style Manual*, 148, s. 5.13; 194, s. 8.1.2

[3]UN, *Vienna Convention on the Law of Treaties*, May 23, 1969, Treaty Series I-18232 (United Nations, 1980), Articles 31–33. Appendix A.1 contains their full text.

[4]Burchfield, R. W., ed., *The New Fowler's Modern English Usage*, 3rd ed. (Oxford: Oxford University Press, 1996); https://en.oxforddictionaries.com.

vi. **Other.** References to sections in the chapter on treaty interpretation of the online IBFD Commentary refer to a version available in 2016.[5] In the meantime, its outline and thus section numbering has been changed. Where applicable, I have added the corresponding new section numbers in square brackets, referring to the state of affairs as updated on 1 May 2018. The reader is alerted that, depending on the IBFD's editorial policy, those numbers may be outdated again in the future.

---

[5]John F. Avery Jones, 'Treaty Interpretation', in *Global Tax Treaty Commentaries* (IBFD, 2016).

Preface

This study has been submitted as a dissertation to receive a doctorate from the University of Leiden Law School in the Netherlands. It is the result of research conducted under the supervision of Prof. Dr. Kees van Raad and Prof. Dr. John F. Avery Jones between 2014 and 2018.

The research leading to this book has been inspired by the author's reading of an article discussing the concepts of tax sparing and matching credit,[6] in the course of which the Conseil d'État decision in *Natexis*[7] is analysed in great detail. At least in the opinion of the present author and the article authors Arruda Ferreira and Trindade Marinho, a difference in meaning between the French and Portuguese texts may have contributed to a wrong interpretation by the court and a misapplication of the tax treaty between France and Brazil. Although this difference in meaning is touched on only as a side issue in the cited article, it remained with the present author as an unresolved puzzle and fundamental problem of tax treaty interpretation and application requiring solution, thereby inspiring this study.

I would like to thank my supervisors Kees van Raad and John Avery Jones for all their support and guidance. In addition, I would like to thank Ksenia Levushkina, Roberto Bernales, Ridha Hamzaoui, Antoine Reillac, and Tian Xu for their help with the Russian, Spanish, French, and Chinese texts of the Vienna Convention, Ksenia Levushkina for her additional help with the Russian Model Convention and several treaties in Russian, Ridha Hamzaoui for his additional help with several treaties in Arabic and French, Vanessa Arruda Ferreira and Anapaula Trindade Marinho for their initial inspiration, and Vanessa Arruda Ferreira for her additional input. Finally, I would like to thank Wim Wijnen for his help with the Dutch summary.

---

[6]Vanessa Arruda Ferreira and Anapaula Trindade Marinho, 'Tax Sparing and Matching Credit: From an Unclear Concept to an Uncertain Regime', *Bulletin for International Taxation* 67, no. 8 (2013): 397–413.

[7]Conseil d'État, *Société Natexis Banques Populaires v France*, 2006.

Note on Style

Writing a doctoral dissertation in English as a foreign language is a challenge, even for someone who has received most of his university education in English and spent most of his career to date in English speaking environments. Nevertheless, the choice for English has been a conscious one. English is undeniably the *lingua franca* of international tax law, and anybody who wants reception of his arguments beyond national borders has to employ it. Given the subject of this thesis, writing it not in English would have defeated its purpose.

But, writing in a foreign language remains a handicap the reader must endure, not the author. In order to reduce the gap between being able to write in English and being able to write well in English, I have looked for guidance to improve the readability of this book. The most relevant advice comes from Karl Popper: 'Anyone who cannot speak simply and clearly should say nothing and continue to work until he can do so.'[8] Regarding specific guidelines to improve on clarity, I have found Orwell's six elementary rules helpful but in need of adjustment because not written with academic writing in mind:

1. Never use a metaphor, simile, or other figure of speech which you are used to seeing in print.
2. Never use a long word where a short one will do.
3. If it is possible to cut a word out, always cut it out.
4. Never use the passive where you can use the active.
5. Never use a foreign phrase, a scientific word, or a jargon word if you can think of an everyday English equivalent.
6. Break any of these rules sooner than say anything outright barbarous.[9]

The first three I have tried to implement rigorously, also in terms of avoiding pleonastic terminology commonly employed by other authors on the subject.[10] Not being a native English speaker, I have occasionally found myself confronted with a trade-off between elegance and precision. In such

---

[8] Karl R. Popper, *In Search of a Better World: Lectures and Essays from Thirty Years* (London: Routledge, 2012), 83.

[9] The Economist, *Style Guide*, 11th ed. (London: Profile Books Ltd., 2015), 1.

[10] See Chapter 1, s. 1.5.2.

case I have opted without exception for the latter as a matter of general principle even when risking clumsy formulation. Such choice is imperative in view of the methods I employ.[11] Some authors emphasise the necessity to use symbolic expressions when applying logic to avoid this problem;[12] however, use of symbols and logical operators is helpful only if everyone who participates in the discourse is familiar with them – otherwise it constitutes an obstacle. For this reason I dispense with any use of logic operators and only use symbols in their most obvious application not entirely uncommon in legal or economic scholarship, such as denoting propositions with a letter.

Traditionally, use of active voice is discouraged in academic writing; however, this iron principle seems to slowly soften. Personally, I much prefer articles written in active voice for being less strenuous to follow and not portraying a false sense of objectivity. On the other hand, using first person mode for an entire thesis would surely stand out, and not necessarily in a good way. Rather than opting for either extreme, I have chosen a balance in favour of passive voice with injections of active voice, all with rule six in mind. First person singular is used sparsely or replaced by something like 'this study'. First person plural is sometimes used to imply the reader and myself. For purely stylistic reasons, third person singular not referring to any specific person is used exclusively in male form – of course without implying any gender primacy.

Rule five would defeat its own purpose if applied to academic writing. Scientific jargon is important because it communicates complex ideas with concise pre-defined notions, which allows condensation of text. Hence, using jargon gives preference to rules two and three over five. For the same reason I occasionally use Latin phrases (with translations provided in parenthesis). They are not only synonymous for what they literally express, but also for an entire theory or principle they condense in one short expression.

These style considerations affect the structure of this thesis. Most importantly, the individual chapters will not contain separate conclusion sections, but the conclusions are part of the flow of argument. This may seem un-

---

[11]See Chapter 2, s. 2.2.1.

[12]See, e.g., Ilmar Tammelo, *Modern Logic in the Service of Law*, 1st ed. (Wien; New York: Springer, 1978), x.

usual to the academic reader but is only conclusive: if I have done a good job in making my point, repeating it is redundant. In the same vein, although providing a brief synopsis of the previously drawn conclusions, Chapter 10 does not summarise all points in detail again; its job is rather to distil further conclusions at the macro level. With regard to synoptic observations, I refrain from pleonastic referencing throughout Chapter 10 (and the Annex); only verbatim quotations as well as points not previously quoted will be fully referenced.

1. Introduction

1.1. Scientific Contribution

This study makes the following contribution to the field of tax treaty interpretation:

1. It refutes the current orthodoxy that courts may rely on a single text for cases of routine interpretation, by showing that such approach necessarily produces cases of treaty misapplication in violation of the VCLT when the text relied on is not designated as prevailing. In addition, it refutes the commonly held view that courts may rely on the original text by virtue of it being the text of initial negotiation and drafting. Conversely, it shows that a valid combination of the VCLT principles obliges courts to compare all authentic language texts when none of them is designated as prevailing.

2. It shows that the VCLT permits courts to rely solely on a text designated as prevailing whether or not a divergence between the texts has been raised and established; all counterarguments brought forward by the critics of such approach are refuted, while any limitations to its applicability are outlined.

3. Based on all tax treaties concluded between 1960 and 2016 as recorded in the IBFD Tax Treaties Database, it provides an empirical survey of the global tax treaty network with respect to its lingual properties, together with an analysis concerning the interpretation and application of all types of final clause wordings employed.

4. Finally, it assumes the perspective of a technical strategy paper and, on the basis of all findings, issues policy recommendations on how to best eliminate residual interpretational complexity induced by plurilingual form, together with its economic cost.

In summary, the insights generated by this study may help to reduce misapplication of plurilingual tax treaties, by way of increased awareness about the pitfalls of the current orthodoxy and, in consequence, its abandonment. The alternative submitted (sole reliance on prevailing texts), if adopted, will reduce global resource costs of tax treaty interpretation and, at the same time, increase its overall consistency via elimination of unintended deviations caused by language idiosyncrasies. To support this goal, this study seeks to provide useful arguments and data to policy makers, treaty negotiators, judges, practitioners, and scholars.

1.2. Motivation

Although there is plenty of academic literature concerned with treaty interpretation, the volume of material concerned with the specific issues posed by plurilingual form is fairly manageable. As far as comprehensive studies exclusively focussed on the topic are concerned, only four come to mind with respect to the discourse on tax treaties, namely, the works of Arginelli, Maisto, Tabory, and Hilf.[1]

Arginelli's thesis is fairly recent, whereas the studies of Maisto, Tabory, and Hilf date back to 2005, 1980, and 1973, respectively. Only Arginelli and Maisto incorporate a special tax treaty perspective, whereas Tabory and Hilf are concerned with plurilingual treaties in general. In addition, Maisto's volume is divided in focus: it deals in part with European law and is not a systematic study but a collection of chapters by several authors on various issues and specific country perspectives, albeit methodically arranged.

Neither of the four contains a comprehensive empirical study investigating plurilingual form of tax treaties. Maisto's volume discusses a limited data set as part of the selective country chapters, but the sample only comprises 512 treaties from the treaty networks of a few OECD members ex-

---

[1]Paolo Arginelli, *The Interpretation of Multilingual Tax Treaties* (Leiden: Leiden University Press, 2013); Guglielmo Maisto, *Multilingual Texts and Interpretation of Tax Treaties and EC Tax Law* (Amsterdam: IBFD, 2005); Mala Tabory, *Multilingualism in International Law and Institutions* (Alphen aan den Rijn: Sijthoff & Noordhoff, 1980); Meinhard Hilf, *Die Auslegung mehrsprachiger Verträge: eine Untersuchung zum Völkerrecht und zum Staatsrecht der Bundesrepublik Deutschland.* (Berlin, New York: Springer-Verlag, 1973).

clusively from the EU/EFTA region. Therefore, it is not representative of the global tax treaty network and insufficient to draw unbiased conclusions from. Moreover, it provides no comprehensive information about the treaty final clause wordings concerning implementation of lingual form.

The number of articles devoted to the subject is again fairly manageable compared to the number of articles dealing with other topics of tax treaty interpretation. Of the prominent academics in international tax law, only Michael Lang has taken up the topic recently in two articles.[2] All in all, it seems as if the community of legal scholars engaged in the discourse on tax treaty interpretation considers plurilingual form a side issue not of central importance that may be ignored safely until it imposes itself.[3] This attitude has manifested itself as orthodoxy in doctrine.[4] In reality, however, plurilingual form is hardly a minor feature of tax treaties that would justify such disproportion in discussion: almost three-quarters of the well over 3,000 concluded tax treaties currently in force or yet to come into force are plurilingual.

Arginelli's recent thesis is of almost encyclopaedic breadth, making it a valuable resource; however, my reservations concerning his views are fundamental. They are based on the fact that he does not question established theories and therefore only helps to solidify a harmful practice, just because he does not want to argue against the mainstream:

> Against this background, drawing a normative legal theory of treaty interpretation affirming principles that conflicted with the generally accepted constructions of Articles 31–33 VCLT, or that lie to a significant extent outside the generally accepted borders of a perceived reasonable interpretation of such articles, would be equal to sustaining a legal theory of interpretation that, in the best case, could establish itself only in the very long run

---

[2]See Michael Lang, 'The Interpretation of Tax Treaties and Authentic Languages', in *Essays on Tax Treaties: A Tribute to David A. Ward*, ed. Guglielmo Maisto, Angelo Nikolakakis, and John M. Ulmer (Amsterdam: IBFD, 2013), 15–30; Michael Lang, 'Auslegung von Doppelbesteuerungsabkommen und authentische Vertragssprachen', *Internationales Steuerrecht* 20, no. 11 (2011): 403–10.

[3]The BEPS multilateral instrument, which has equally authoritative English and French texts, is currently reviving general sensitivity for the issue because it modifies a large number of treaties having texts in various languages. Since it was released only after conclusion of this study, it will be dealt with separately in the Annex.

[4]See Chapter 3, s. 3.3.2.

and would cause a protracted period characterized by more legal uncertainty than in the current state of affairs and, in the worse case, would be generally regarded as utopian, since too detached from Articles 31–33 VCLT to be considered a reasonable interpretation thereof, thus lacking the legal status to be applied in practice as long as those articles remained in force. However, since the purpose of the present research is to suggest how the interpreter should *now* tackle and disentangle the most common types of issues emerging from the interpretation of multilingual tax treaties under public international law, the author is not willing to accept the above-described drawbacks of a normative legal theory infringing the generally accepted rules and principles of treaty interpretation derived from Articles 31–33 VCLT. In the author's intention, his normative legal theory should be shaped so as to fit within the generally accepted borders of a perceived reasonable interpretation of such articles; where the inferences drawn from the semantic analysis appeared to lie outside those outer borders, such inferences should be disregarded for the purpose of setting up the author's normative (semantics-based) theory of treaty interpretation. Hence, from a theoretical perspective, the author's normative legal theory of interpretation must be regarded as a non-ideal normative theory, as opposed to ideal normative theories.[5]

This seems tantamount to saying his entire research project is intended merely to confirm conventional wisdom, and whenever the results according to his adopted methodology contradict general opinion, they should be ignored. I do not share Arginelli's standpoint but rather agree with Popper that 'orthodoxy is the death of knowledge, since the growth of knowledge depends entirely upon disagreement.'[6] Moreover, Arginelli fails to provide a comprehensive empirical study of the global tax treaty network concerning plurilingual form but draws conclusions based on the Maisto sample,[7] which is problematic for said reasons.

Given all this, I submit my study in the good old tradition of academic dispute as a response to all scholars who have so far merely reproduced and bolstered the mainstream position I consider misguided; however, my aim is not just to refute a theory I regard erroneous and in support of a harmful practice that promotes divergence rather than uniformity of interpretation, but also to submit a sound approach in its place that is consistent with the

---

[5] Arginelli, *The Interpretation of Multilingual Tax Treaties*, 17–18.

[6] Karl R. Popper, *The Myth of the Framework: In Defence of Science and Rationality* (New York: Routledge, 1994), 34.

[7] See Arginelli, *The Interpretation of Multilingual Tax Treaties*, 131–34.

VCLT principles and can be implemented easily to resolve the problems caused by plurilingual form in practice.

With respect to the dangers of such approach pointed at by Arginelli, I do not share his concerns. To the extent my approach is adopted, the period of adoption would be characterised by more legal certainty than the current state of affairs, increasing in proportion with the rate of adoption. Given its feasibility, I do not consider it utopian. Certainly not to the extent it is readily available without requiring modification of operative provisions in actual treaties, which is the case for almost two-thirds of all plurilingual treaties in the global tax treaty network. Whether it will be adopted is another matter, of course. That is a question for policy makers, treaty negotiators, and judges. I have no influence on them, but that shall not prevent me from presenting my views. My hope is simply that my readers, whoever they may be, will find something of value for their own tasks in this book.

1.3. Research Question

The overarching research question of this study is whether courts are legally required to compare all authenticated language texts when interpreting a plurilingual tax treaty. The question is considered both in the context of all texts being equally authoritative and of one text being designated as prevailing. Over the course of the study, the issue is divided into five general questions, which are then subdivided by the individual chapters into several individual issues to develop my answer and extend the contribution of my study in terms of practical applicability and policy recommendations:[8] (1) Are judges legally obliged to compare all authentic language texts in the absence of a prevailing one? (2) If so, how is the comparison performed correctly? (3) To what extent can we eliminate the need for a comparison with the help of prevailing texts without risking treaty misapplication? (4) To what extent can we rely solely on prevailing texts in actual practice? (5) What can/should be done to further extend practical applicability of sole reliance on prevailing texts?

---

[8]Since chapters three and five present my fundamental answers to the overarching research question for treaties with and without prevailing text, they are formulated to proceed from hypotheses rather than questions.

1.4. **Structure**

Conceptually, this study is divided into several parts. The introductory part consists of chapters one and two, which introduce and scope the project, explain the meaning of key terminology, and outline the methodology applied.

The theoretical part is made up of chapters three to seven and subdivided into several subparts: chapters three and four deal with interpretation in case of all equally authoritative texts, whereas chapters five and six are concerned with the case of one text being designated as prevailing. Chapter seven is its own subpart, reversing the perspective from international to domestic law.

The empirical part consists of chapters eight and nine. They share a common methodological framework but have different functions: chapter eight is concerned with practical applicability of the theoretical approach developed to actual tax treaties, whereas chapter nine investigates implementation of English as *lingua franca* throughout the global tax treaty network.

The concluding part is made up of chapters ten and eleven: the first provides overall conclusions and policy recommendations while the latter deals exclusively with the BEPS multilateral instrument. The following list provides a more detailed overview:

- Chapter 2 outlines my methodology.

- Chapter 3 contains my argument refuting the currently prevailing view that judges may rely on a single text in isolation for cases of routine interpretation. In addition, it refutes the view that judges may rely on the original text by virtue of it being the text of initial negotiation and drafting.

- Chapter 4 deals with practical implementation and additional issues concerning tax treaties in particular, an in-depth consideration of which has been postponed by Chapter 3 for structural reasons in order to avoid detours from the main line of argument.

- Chapter 5 makes the case for sole reliance on prevailing texts. In addition, it sketches any limitations to this approach.

- Chapter 6 reviews and refutes all counterarguments submitted by the most adamant opponents to sole reliance on prevailing texts.

- Chapter 7 frames the issue from the viewpoint of domestic procedural law. This is necessary because tax proceedings are conducted under the jurisdiction of national courts. In consequence, domestic procedural law and legal culture influence results in practice and must be taken into account.

- Chapter 8 quantifies the extent to which sole reliance on actual prevailing texts may be applied in practice with respect to all treaties in the global tax treaty network. In addition to an empirical survey of treaty lingual properties, it examines policies of individual countries and certain groupings concerning implementation of prevailing texts. Moreover, it contains its own theoretical subpart concerning interpretation of all final clause wordings found in actual tax treaties.

- Chapter 9 investigates use of English as *lingua franca* for unilingual tax treaties and prevailing texts. Because such use enforces the approach proposed in the theoretical part and affects the decisions by countries concerning lingual form of their treaties, it is an essential factor to consider when formulating policy recommendations.

- Chapter 10 aggregates the conclusions of the individual chapters and discusses them from a macro perspective. In addition, it formulates policy recommendations on the basis of all findings.

- Chapter 11, the Annex, evaluates the policy implemented by the OECD BEPS multilateral instrument in terms of authentic languages, and sketches possible approaches to remedy its deficiencies.

- Finally, the appendices provide auxiliary information that may prove useful to the reader, as well as the sample data.

1.5. Terminology

This section explains the meaning of some key terms used by me in a technical sense.

1.5.1. Plurilingual versus Multilingual

Curiously, although the ILC Commentaries on the VCLT Draft Articles exclusively use 'plurilingual',[9] most academic literature on plurilingual treaties uses 'multilingual' instead.[10] The implied concepts prove difficult to distinguish,[11] and use of terminology remains diverse even among linguists, although 'multilingual' seems to have established itself as standard in English academic literature across disciplines.[12]

The Oxford Dictionary defines multilingual as 'In or using several languages' and plurilingual as 'Relating to, involving, or fluent in a number of languages; multilingual.' The Common European Framework of Reference for Languages (CEFR) draws a more pronounced distinction:

> Plurilingualism differs from multilingualism, which is the knowledge of a
> number of languages, or the co-existence of different languages in a given
> society. ...Beyond this, the plurilingual approach emphasises the fact that
> ...he or she does not keep these languages and cultures in strictly separated
> mental compartments, but rather builds up a communicative competence to

---

[9] ILC, *Draft Articles on the Law of Treaties with Commentaries 1966. Documents of the Second Part of the Seventeenth Session and of the Eighteenth Session Including the Reports of the Commission to the General Assembly*, vol. II, Yearbook of the International Law Commission 1966, A/CN.4/SER. A/1966/Add.1 (United Nations, 1967), 219, para. 7; 224, paras. 1, 3; 225–226, paras. 6–9. Henceforth, the Commentaries on the Draft Articles will be referred to as VCLT Commentary.

[10] See, e.g., Tabory, *Multilingualism in International Law and Institutions*; Maisto, *Multilingual Texts and Interpretation of Tax Treaties and EC Tax Law*; Arginelli, *The Interpretation of Multilingual Tax Treaties*.

[11] See Daniel Coste, Danièle Moore, and Geneviève Zarate, 'Plurilingual and Pluricultural Competence: Studies Towards a Common European Framework of Reference for Language Learning and Teaching' (Strasbourg: Language Policy Division, Council of Europe, 2009), 10 et seq.

[12] See Charlotte Kemp, 'Defining Multilingualism', in *The Exploration of Multilingualism: Development of Research on L3, Multilingualism and Multiple Language Acquisition* (Amsterdam; Philadelphia: John Benjamins Publishing Co., 2009), passim.

which all knowledge and experience of language contributes and in which languages interrelate and interact.[13]

The same distinction is made by the European Observatory for Plurilingualism in its charter, in which plurilingualism is defined as 'the use of several languages by the same individual' and distinguished from multilingualism as follows:

> This concept [plurilingualism] differs from that of multilingualism, which means the coexistence of several languages within a social group. A plurilingual society is composed mainly of individuals capable of expressing themselves at various levels of proficiency in several languages, …whereas a multilingual society may be predominantly made up of monolingual individuals ignoring the language of the other.[14]

In summary, plurilingual implies equal competence in several languages, whereas multilingual implies their coexistence.

Whatever terminology is chosen in the treaty context does not matter because the meaning is strictly defined: there is only one treaty made up of one set of terms, that is, only one text although available in several languages.[15] Notwithstanding, 'plurilingual' seems somewhat closer to the idea of one text in several languages, whereas 'multilingual' inspires an image of several coexistent language texts. For this reason – *nomen est omen* (the name is a sign), and in order to comply with the original terminology employed by the ILC, I shall use 'plurilingual'.

1.5.2. Text(s)

The plural 'texts' is misleading in view of the treaty as one set of terms, because it may inspire the idea that there could be more than one text. During the drafting period of the VCLT the ILC discussed use of the plural extensively, and several voices argued in favour of 'versions' in order to refer to the different language versions of the one treaty text; however, use

---

[13]Language Policy Division, 'Common European Framework of Reference for Languages: Learning, Teaching, Assessment' (Strasbourg: Council of Europe), 4.

[14]Observatoire européen du plurilinguisme, 'Charte européenne du plurilinguisme', June 2015, *Préambule*.

[15]See ILC, *Draft Articles on the Law of Treaties with Commentaries*, II:225, para. 6.

of 'texts' prevailed while 'version' and 'versions' were reserved for texts of non-authentic status.[16]

This convention has been implemented in Article 33(2) and will be adhered to here: throughout, 'text' refers to an authenticated language version of the text while 'texts' refers to more or all authenticated language versions. Occasionally, however, the singular will refer to the treaty text in the abstract as one set of terms, not to any language text in particular and irrespective of the total number of language texts. Such double meaning is unavoidable because of the ILC terminology; I trust the intended meaning will be obvious from the context.

Despite its own convention, the ILC frequently adds the adjective 'authentic' in the VCLT Commentary.[17] Even the VCLT does so in paragraphs (3) and (4) of Article 33. Most academic literature on the subject adopts this terminology. Although this does not hurt, it is superfluous. Therefore, I do not follow the example but refrain from adding 'authentic' every single time. Occasional exceptions are made to benefit a sentence with precision or the reader with ease of understanding.

1.5.3. Clear

Most of the academic literature on the subject applies the adjective 'clear' to treaties and texts as a matter of course without explicit definition. This is problematic because it may ingrain a wrong understanding of clarity in a colloquial sense – the reader might read on without much contemplation. The Oxford Dictionary defines clear as 'Leaving no doubt; obvious or unambiguous.' A treaty text may indeed be clear in this sense, but only after interpretation, not before.[18] This is the essence of the VCLT general rule

---

[16]See Frank A. Engelen, *Interpretation of Tax Treaties under International Law: A Study of Articles 31, 32, and 33 of the Vienna Convention on the Law of Treaties and Their Application to Tax Treaties* (Amsterdam: IBFD, 2004), 351, 356, 358–59; Richard K. Gardiner, *Treaty Interpretation* (Oxford: Oxford University Press, 2010), 356–58.

[17]See ILC, *Draft Articles on the Law of Treaties with Commentaries*, 195, para. 1; 224, paras. 1, 3–4; 225, paras. 6–8; 272, para. 5; 273, para. 9.

[18]See J. Wouters and M. Vidal, 'Non-Tax Treaties: Domestic Courts and Treaty Interpretation', in *Courts and Tax Treaty Law* (Amsterdam: IBFD, 2007), s. 1.3.2; L. Oppenheim, *Oppenheim's International Law*, ed. R. Jennings and A. Watts, 9th ed. (Harlow: Longman, 1992), 1267; Brian J. Arnold, 'The Interpretation of Tax Treaties: Myth and Reality', *Bul-*

aimed to arrive at a textual not literal meaning.

Furthermore, it is not necessary for a treaty to be unequivocal to be clear. As Larenz and Canaris observe, no legal text will be unequivocal unless 'drawn up exclusively in a symbolised sign language',[19] but it is the purpose of interpretation to establish the manifest meaning versus other interpretations that are less manifest.[20] To the extent it is possible to establish such manifest meaning, the text is clear. Otherwise, it remains ambiguous or obscure. All this will be argued in depth later on; for the moment it is sufficient to record that, throughout this study, 'clear' is used in a technical sense when referring to texts and treaties.

1.5.4. Analytic and A Priori

The terms 'analytic' and 'a priori' will be used occasionally because of their relevance with respect to the methods employed.[21] Analytic propositions are true a priori because of the meaning of the terms used and their relationship via the sentence structure, with a negation necessarily implying

---

letin for International Taxation, no. 1 (2010): 3–4; Conseil d'État, *Société Schneider Electric*, 2002, per M. Austry, *commissaire du gouvernement*: 'the text of an international treaty, even when clear, must always be interpreted taking into account its object', as translated by Eirik Bjorge, '"Contractual" And "Statutory" Treaty Interpretation in Domestic Courts? Convergence Around the Vienna Rules', in *The Interpretation of International Law by Domestic Courts: Uniformity, Diversity, Convergence*, ed. Helmut Philipp Aust and Georg Nolte (Oxford; New York: Oxford University Press, 2016), 49–71, 57; Emilio Betti, *Allgemeine Auslegungslehre als Methodik der Geisteswissenschaften* (Mohr Siebeck, 1967), 251, in terms of texts in general; cf. Emer de Vattel, *The Law of Nations* (Indianapolis, IN: Liberty Fund, Inc., 1797), s. 263.

[19] Karl Larenz and Claus-Wilhelm Canaris, *Methodenlehre der Rechtswissenschaft*, 3rd ed. (Berlin: Springer-Verlag, 1995), 26.

[20] By manifest I mean the result of an interpretation under Article 31 that is not ambiguous, obscure, absurd, or unreasonable and, in view of the wording, context, and object and purpose, more reasonable than any other suggested meaning, i.e., one or more meanings can be discerned, and a decisive choice can be made on the basis of the means provided by Article 31 in case several interpretations are possible. Although, colloquially speaking, an absurd or unreasonable reading may be manifest in the sense of being unequivocal – the text really says so – such is factored out from the meaning of the term as used here unless the contrary is indicated explicitly.

[21] See Chapter 2, s. 2.2.1.

a contradiction in terms. Therefore, they are of special interest in logic as fundamental building blocks.

The classic sources with respect to their meaning are Leibniz and Kant. Leibniz distinguishes truths of reason from truths of experience, the former combining the ideas of analytic and a priori. He classifies truths of reason as necessarily true, their opposite being impossible, and truths of experience as contingently true, their opposite being possible. Necessary truths may be split via analysis into simpler ideas until one arrives at some primitive truth at their basis. At the end of this process remain only simple notions of which no further definition is possible, as well as first principles of which further proof is neither necessary nor feasible because they are essentially statements of identity, negations of which would entail explicit contradictions.[22]

In contrast to Leibniz, Kant distinguishes explicitly between the analytic and the a priori.[23] Accordingly, an analytic proposition is one in which the subject entails the predicate, and an analysis of the subject establishes that the predicate is included in it.[24] Kant uses the specific example of extended versus heavy bodies. The former constitutes an analytic proposition because all bodies are by definition extended in space, so the predicate 'extended' does not go beyond the boundaries of what is included in the subject 'body'. Conversely, the latter constitutes a synthetic proposition because

---

[22]See Gottfried Wilhelm Leibniz, *Monadologie*, trans. Robert Zimmermann (Wien: Braumüller und Seidel, 1847), ss. 33, 35.

[23]See Immanuel Kant, *Kritik der reinen Vernunft* (Köln: Anaconda, 2009), *Einleitung*.

[24]The German *Urteil* used by Kant is to be translated with 'judgement' rather than 'proposition'. I use the latter because 'judgement' may be misinterpreted to imply a mental process leading from the premises to the conclusion, which is contrary to the conception of inference in modern logic, see Chapter 2, s. 2.2.1. Kant's terminology may indicate that he was influenced by Antoine Arnauld and Pierre Nicole, *Logic or the Art of Thinking*, trans. Jill Buroker (Cambridge: Cambridge University Press, 1996), published anonymously in 1662 as *La Logique ou l'art de penser* and commonly regarded as 'the most influential logic text from Aristotle to the end of the nineteenth century', see Jill Buroker, 'Port Royal Logic', in *The Stanford Encyclopedia of Philosophy*, ed. Edward N. Zalta, Spring ed. (Stanford University, 2017). It founded the middle phase in the development of logic as a discipline (between classical Aristotelian and modern logic), which was characterised 'by a prevalence of epistemological and psychological issues', see Ernst Tugendhat and Ursula Wolf, *Logisch-semantische Propädeutik* (Stuttgart: Reclam, Philipp, jun. GmbH, Verlag, 1993), 7.

the predicate is not included in the subject by definition but constitutes an addition to it.

The notions of a priori and a posteriori are classified as epistemological concepts denoting ways of cognition via reason or experience.[25] All analytic propositions are necessary and as such a priori, that is, discoverable purely by reason, whereas all empirical, a posteriori propositions are synthetic. Kant draws these explicit distinctions because he wanted to introduce a third category of synthetic truths discoverable purely by reason, that is, while all empirical propositions are synthetic, not all synthetic propositions are, in his view, empirical.[26]

1.5.5. All Treaties and Global Tax Treaty Network

'All treaties' is used as a proxy for the entire sample defined in Chapter 2 and listed in Appendix E. 'Global tax treaty network' is used as a proxy for the entire sample without terminated treaties. Occasionally, 'all treaties' will be used colloquially to imply all treaties of a certain group or country, including or excluding terminated treaties; I trust the intended meaning will be obvious from the context. It has to be borne in mind that all generalising references imply the status quo at the cut-off date for the sample (15 August 2016).

1.5.6. Lingua Franca and (True) Diplomatic Language

I use the term *lingua franca* because it is commonly understood.[27] The Oxford Dictionary defines it as 'A language that is adopted as a common language between speakers whose native languages are different.' Here it is used in a slightly wider sense, not only to imply cases in which two countries adopted a third language for a prevailing text or unilingual treaty, but

---

[25] See Steup, Matthias, 'Epistemology', in *The Stanford Encyclopedia of Philosophy*, ed. Edward N. Zalta, Fall ed. (Stanford University, 2016).

[26] Kant's argument in this respect is not relevant here, so I shall not elaborate it any further; the interested reader is referred to Anthony Quinton, 'The "A Priori" and the Analytic', *Proceedings of the Aristotelian Society* 64 (1963): 31–54.

[27] See John King Gamble and Charlotte Ku, 'Choice of Language in Bilateral Treaties: Fifty Years of Changing State Practice', *Indiana International and Comparative Law Review* 3 (1993): 236, 10n.

also to imply cases in which two countries concluded a treaty with a prevailing text in the official language of one of them, because some aggregated data comprises all three scenarios. 'Diplomatic language' will be used to denote only the latter, while 'true diplomatic language' will be used to refer to cases of two countries having concluded a unilingual treaty in a third language.

2. Methodology

2.1. Preliminary Considerations

2.1.1. General Approach

Every scholar submitting a thesis has to answer the question in which way his contribution is original and scientific, that is, how and to what extent he is creating new knowledge instead of saying something purely descriptive or, worse, offering mere opinion. In contrast to other scholars who have dealt with the topic of plurilingual treaty interpretation, and in particular Hardy,[1] whose treatment of the subject has substantially influenced the currently prevailing view, I employ axiomatic-deductive reasoning. The fundamental axiom on which I build my theory is the principle of unity of the treaty:

> [I]n law there is only one treaty – one set of terms accepted by the parties and one common intention with respect to those terms – even when two authentic texts appear to diverge.[2]

In addition, I use the methodology of interpretation provided by the VCLT to help derive the premises and deduct the conclusions put forward. In the same vein, the arguments put forward by the most adamant supporters of the opposite view are evaluated in respect of their validity and soundness against the background of the VCLT principles. Finally, I conduct an empirical analysis of the global tax treaty network to quantify the applicability of my theoretical findings and formulate policy recommendations. In summary, the quest of this study is to derive conclusions of logic and

---

[1] Jean Hardy, 'The Interpretation of Plurilingual Treaties by International Courts and Tribunals', *The British Year Book of International Law*, 1961, 73–155. His approach will be discussed in detail in Chapter 6.

[2] ILC, *Draft Articles on the Law of Treaties with Commentaries*, II:225, para. 6. Henceforth referred to as principle of unity.

good sense from the VCLT 'principles of logic and good sense'.[3] On their basis I shall submit a pragmatic approach to solve the problem of additional interpretational complexity induced by plurilingual form.

My choice of methods is utilitarian – I do not maintain that the methods I employ for purposes of this study are generally sufficient as methods of jurisprudence,[4] but my objective is to use the methods needed to solve the problems addressed. I stress this in particular for readers coming from a common law background, to whom my approach focussed on axiomatic-deductive reasoning may appear outlandish. Doctrine plays a different role in common law for historical and systematic reasons, wherefore the overall methodical approach is different as well, focussed on tracking the evolution of case law concerned with specific fact patterns, rather than the logical and systematic structure of legislation and consistent application of general principles, as is the focus of civil law.[5]

Oliver Wendell Holmes's famous dictum of law being characterised by experience rather than logic has become an iconic and often misused refer-

---

[3]Ibid., II:218–19, para. 4.

[4]Jurisprudence is defined by the Oxford Dictionary as 'The theory or philosophy of law.' The English 'science' predominantly implies natural sciences, wherefore it is etymologically more narrow than the German *Wissenschaft*. The Oxford Dictionary defines science primarily as 'The intellectual and practical activity encompassing the systematic study of the structure and behaviour of the physical and natural world through observation and experiment.' As Kaufmann writes, 'The German *Wissenschaft* does not bring to mind only – perhaps not even primarily – the natural sciences but any serious, disciplined, rigorous quest for knowledge', Nietzsche, Friedrich, *The Gay Science: With a Prelude in Rhymes and an Appendix of Songs*, trans. Walter Kaufmann (New York: Random House, Inc., 1974), Translator's Introduction, 5. The German *Kulturwissenschaften* (cultural sciences) and *Sozialwissenschaften* (social sciences) would be classified as humanities or arts in English. The German *Rechtswissenschaft* (traditionally *Jurisprudenz*) finds its English counterpart in 'jurisprudence' or simply 'law' as listed among the humanities. 'Law' is too general including the law proper, wherefore I resort to 'jurisprudence'. Concerning the ambiguity of the former, see Raoul Charles van Caenegem, *Judges, Legislators and Professors: Chapters in European Legal History*, revised ed. (Cambridge: Cambridge University Press, 2008), 2–4. The literal translation of *Rechtswissenschaft* as 'legal science' feels constructed impromptu and conceptually transgressive, suggesting jurisprudence to be a science in a sense I want to avoid and consider misguided because it distracts from the real issue and only engages in a futile argument that is ultimately harmful to the discipline.

[5]This will be discussed at length in Chapter 7, s. 7.2.

ence to voice distrust in theory and logic in particular[6] – a sentiment common among English jurists: 'By and large, English lawyers and writers have
tended to think of it as almost a virtue to be illogical, and have ascribed that
virtue freely to their law; "being logical" is an eccentric continental practice,
in which commonsensical Englishmen indulge at their peril.'[7]

Although an examination of English case law over a decade has 'revealed
that on every occasion on which the judges referred to "strict logic" it was
to reject its conclusions',[8] English judges have been shown to regularly use
deductive logic in their reasoning.[9] An overly indiscriminate understanding
of the dismissal of logic by common law judges may therefore be based
on a misunderstanding and carry strange fruits in form of a 'general anti-
rationalism'.[10] What is rejected by the common law judge is the syllogistic
approach of his civil law colleagues,[11] not deductive logic in general:

> So it is not simply a matter of recognising that the word 'logic' is often used
> in different senses by judges and lawyers; it is also necessary to appreciate

---

[6] See Herbert L. A. Hart, *Essays in Jurisprudence and Philosophy* (Oxford; New York: Oxford University Press, USA, 1984), 129; P. S. Atiyah, *Pragmatism and Theory in English
Law* (London: Stevens & Sons, 1987), 8; Lord Macmillan, 'Two Ways of Thinking', in
Law and Other Things (Cambridge: Cambridge University Press, 1937), 80. Read out
of context, Holmes's remark is misleading. To fully appreciate what he is saying, it is
necessary to read the passage surrounding the remark in full. He is not denouncing
the usefulness of logic but merely points to logic alone being insufficient to grasp a
cultural product like law: 'It is something to show that the consistency of a system
requires a particular result, but it is not all. The life of the law has not been logic: it
has been experience. The felt necessities of the time, the prevalent moral and political
theories, intuitions of public policy, avowed or unconscious, even the prejudices which
judges share with their fellow-men, have had a good deal more to do than the syllogism
in determining the rules by which men should be governed', Oliver Wendell Holmes,
The Common Law, ed. Paulo J. S. Pereira and Diego M. Beltran, 1881 edition (Toronto:
University of Toronto Law School Typographical Society, 2011), 5.

[7] Neil MacCormick, *Legal Reasoning and Legal Theory* (Clarendon Press, 1978), 40, quoting
the then Regius Professor of Public Law at Edinburgh.

[8] Atiyah, *Pragmatism and Theory in English Law*, 12.

[9] See MacCormick, *Legal Reasoning and Legal Theory*, 19–32.

[10] Atiyah, *Pragmatism and Theory in English Law*, 90: 'English lawyers …sometimes make
a positive virtue of their skill in "muddling through" to some hopelessly irrational compromise or pragmatic solution to a problem.'

[11] See ibid., 13, discussed in more detail in Chapter 7, s. 7.2.

that even the strictest of strict logic can be 'used' in two different senses. It can be and is very regularly 'used' in the sense of being *applied,* as in the many examples which Professor MacCormick gives in his discussion of this question. But in these cases the real arguments are never about the logical deductions themselves: they are always about the premisses. Once the premisses have been finally determined or agreed, the conclusions do follow inexorably, of course, and are usually seen to follow inexorably. So judges often apply logic, but they rarely 'use' logic in the sense of reasoning their way to a conclusion which is not otherwise obvious by a process of logic.[12]

Nothing else is suggested here by using logic as method (see below). The criticism of axiomatic-deductive reasoning as a method of jurisprudence from the perspective of common law pragmatism is that it may be of limited help in legal practice:

It is sometimes possible to justify legal decisions by deductive arguments whose premisses are valid rules of law and propositions of 'proven' fact. Given certain presuppositions about the nature of legal systems and the obligations of legal officials such justifications are conclusive. But we can run out of rules without running out of the need for legal decisions – because rules are unclear, or because the proper classification of relevant facts is disputable, or even because there is dispute whether there is or is not any legal ground at all for some claim or decision at law. The really interesting question about legal argumentation is: how can it proceed when in this sense we do 'run out of rules'?[13]

My point, however, is that in the above quoted principle of unity we have a valid rule of law that provides clear guidance as fundamental and indisputable premiss concerning the issue at hand, and my methodical approach in this respect does not intend to give up pragmatism in favour of theory – quite to the contrary. The ultimate test of pragmatism is whether it leads to a result that, colloquially speaking, 'works'.[14] As will be argued in detail in the following chapters, the approach to interpretation of plurilingual tax treaties currently supported by most scholars does not work as intended

---

[12]Ibid., 14–15.

[13]MacCormick, *Legal Reasoning and Legal Theory*, 100.

[14]The Oxford Dictionary defines pragmatism as 'An approach that evaluates theories or beliefs in terms of the success of their practical application.'

when examined up close. Therefore, it is necessary to rethink the matter. In the words of Kurt Lewin: 'There is nothing so practical as a good theory.'[15] Hence, concerning the following, I kindly request my readers from the common law sphere to bear with me through the sections that seem overly continental to them, as they may see the virtue of my approach once they have appreciated all my substantive arguments in full – or so I hope.

2.1.2. Jurisprudence as a Science

The aim of science is knowledge. The classic conception of knowledge as reasoned true opinion has been provided by Plato.[16] Although this conception has evolved over time,[17] it already comprises both the objective (truth) and the fundamental methodology to attain it (reasoning). To qualify as knowledge, something must be at the same time true and the outcome of a rational process – mere belief the content of which happens to be true incidentally without being the product of well-founded reasoning cannot be considered knowledge.[18]

Jurisprudence is not concerned with truth in this sense because it is a normative discipline: juridical judgements are generally not conceptualised as being true but rather as correct, proper, appropriate, or justified.[19] Thus, jurisprudence is not a science alike natural sciences. The objects of natural sciences are the laws of nature, whereas the object of jurisprudence is law, a cultural construct created to serve a specific purpose;[20] hence, jurispru-

---

[15]Kurt Lewin, 'Problems of Research in Social Psychology', in *Field Theory in Social Science; Selected Theoretical Papers*, ed. D. Cartwright (New York: Harper & Row, 1951), 169.

[16]See Plato, *Theaetetus* (Perseus Digital Library, Tufts University, 380 B.C.), 201a et seq.; Sophie Grace Chappell, 'Plato on Knowledge in the Theaetetus', in *The Stanford Encyclopedia of Philosophy*, ed. Edward N. Zalta, Winter ed. (Stanford University, 2013).

[17]See Jonathan Jenkins Ichikawa and Matthias Steup, 'The Analysis of Knowledge', in *The Stanford Encyclopedia of Philosophy*, ed. Edward N. Zalta, Spring ed. (Stanford University, 2014); Hanne Andersen and Brian Hepburn, 'Scientific Method', in *The Stanford Encyclopedia of Philosophy*, ed. Edward N. Zalta, Summer ed. (Stanford University, 2016).

[18]See Plato, *Theaetetus*, 201a et seq.

[19]See Ulli F. H. Rühl, 'Ist die Rechtswissenschaft überhaupt eine Wissenschaft?' (Bremen: Universität Bremen, 2005), 1–2.

[20]See Popper's distinction between natural and normative laws, Karl R. Popper, *The Open Society and Its Enemies* (London: Routledge, 2011), 55–57. Accordingly, a natural law

dence may be classified as a cultural science.[21] Anybody eager to present it as a science alike natural sciences will fall into Kirchmann's trap: 'As jurisprudence makes the arbitrary its object, it becomes arbitrary itself – three corrective words from the legislator and whole libraries turn into wastepaper.'[22]

Erroneous theories in natural sciences violating the laws of nature will be falsified by those laws. Scientists can channel this process by devising experiments deliberately set up to disprove their theories, thereby progressing in knowledge through demarcation from false beliefs.[23] In contrast, theories in cultural sciences may exist – and even co-exist with their antitheses as antinomies[24] – without being falsified by the external world. They may even shape the external world as self-fulfilling prophecies in the sense that a theory adopted by agents operating in a socio-cultural system may shape the system through their behaviour in accordance with that theory.[25]

If anything, this amplifies the need for scientific method. It seems obvious that in such context sound rational thought is of prime importance to

---

may be described as a 'strict, unvarying regularity which either in fact holds in nature (in this case the law is a true statement) or does not hold (in this case it is false)' and therefore is unalterable, whereas normative laws, 'i.e. such rules as forbid or demand certain modes of conduct', are social conventions and therefore alterable. Since the latter do not describe facts but only lay down directions for behaviour, they may be called true or false only in a metaphorical sense, implying judgements such as 'good or bad, right or wrong, acceptable or unacceptable'.

[21]See Heinrich Rickert, *Kulturwissenschaft und Naturwissenschaft*, 1st ed. (Berlin: Celtis Verlag, 2013), passim; Rühl, 'Ist die Rechtswissenschaft überhaupt eine Wissenschaft?', 11 et seq.

[22]Julius von Kirchmann, 'Die Werthlosigkeit der Jurisprudenz als Wissenschaft' (Berlin: Julius Springer, 1848), 23. The German original reads *Wissenschaft* but refers to jurisprudence, as is obvious from its context.

[23]See Karl R. Popper, *The Logic of Scientific Discovery*, reprint 2004 (Routledge, 2002), passim.

[24]Meaning a 'contradiction, real or apparent, between two principles or conclusions, both of which seem equally justified', Encyclopedia Britannica, 'Antinomy'.

[25]See Oskar Morgenstern, 'Descriptive, Predictive and Normative Theory', *Kyklos* 25, no. 4 (1972): 707. Soros has theorised this as 'reflexivity', see George Soros, *The Alchemy of Finance: Reading the Mind of the Market by George Soros* (Hoboken, New Jersey: John Wiley & Sons, Inc., 1987), 27–45. He elaborates on the concept more comprehensively in his later writings, but *Alchemy* is particularly interesting in the way he tests the theory on financial markets.

disprove erroneous theories. Therefore, the real issue at stake is not whether jurisprudence could be regarded a science alike natural sciences, but 'how to determine which beliefs are epistemically warranted'[26] within the man-made system of law in the context of the purpose of jurisprudence to not only describe the law but also to interpret and help develop it into a sound and consistent system.[27] Since it is a fundamental requirement of any scientific endeavour to be as objective and rational as possible, science may be conceived of as consisting in the collection of knowledge and its ordering into a coherent system of thought that is free of contradictions, based on Kant's understanding of science as 'a coherent whole of knowledge ordered according to principles'.[28] The element of coherence in this regard consists in the connection of the parts by conclusive reasoning: 'Thus *science* signifies a *system* of notions, in other words, a totality of connected, as opposed to a mere aggregate of disconnected, notions. …The very thing distinguishing every science from the mere aggregate is the fact that its notions follow from one another as from their ground or reason.'[29] In summary, jurisprudence may be conceptualised as a science in terms of method, and this is the understanding underlying this study.

2.2. Methods Employed

To satisfy this conception, I use three methods. First and foremost: logic. Adherence to the principles of logic fosters scientific endeavours as defined,

---

[26]Steve Fuller, 'The Demarcation of Science: A Problem Whose Demise Has Been Greatly Exaggerated', *Pacific Philosophical Quarterly* 66, nos. 3 – 4: 331.

[27]See Karl Larenz, *Über die Unentbehrlichkeit der Jurispridenz als Wissenschaft*, vol. 26, Schriftenreihe Der Juristischen Gesellschaft e.V. (Berlin: Walter de Gruyter & Co., 1966), 12 et seq. Common lawyers may disagree with such contention, see Chapter 7, s. 7.2.

[28]Immanuel Kant, *Metaphysische Anfangsgründe der Naturwissenschaft* (Riga: Johann Friedrich Hartknoch, 1786), *Vorrede*; see Klaus Tipke, 'Steuerrecht als Wissenschaft', in *Festschrift für Joachim Lang: Gestaltung der Steuerrechtsordnung*, ed. Roman Seer et al. (Köln: Schmidt, Otto, 2010), 26–27; Emil Kraus, *Der Systemgedanke bei Kant und Fichte* (Berlin: Verlag von Reuther & Reichard, 1916), Einführung. Accordingly, the Oxford Dictionary expands its definition of science by 'A systematically organized body of knowledge on a particular subject.'

[29]Arthur Schopenhauer, *On the Fourfold Root of the Principle of Sufficient Reason*, trans. E. F. J. Payne (New York: Open Court Classics, 2001), 5, s. 4.

because it ensures a consistent and ordered system of thought free of contradictions. As pointed out by Tarski, 'Logic is justly considered the basis of all other sciences, even if only for the reason that in every argument we employ concepts taken from the field of logic, and that ever correct inference proceeds in accordance with its laws.'[30]

Some have argued that because of their normative content, laws (like questions and orders) are not accessible to logic but require a specially designed deontic logic.[31] I do not share this opinion but agree with Philipps that such deontic logic is by no means indispensable, albeit occasionally useful.[32] Much alike questions and orders, laws can be divided into a normative and a propositional part, which can then be subjected to logical considerations.[33] Even if laws themselves pose some difficulties in this respect that can be overcome by appropriate construction, theories of and about law are subject to standard logic.

Although logic may be helpful as a tool to disprove erroneous theories and construct valid ones, it may be insufficient on its own.[34] As Bunikowski points out, 'Logic only tells you hypothetically that if you give a certain term a certain interpretation then a certain conclusion follows. Logic is silent on how to classify particulars – and this is the heart of a judicial decision.'[35] Jurisprudence as a science of rationally analysing legal texts[36] – in our particular case the VCLT – requires an additional methodology of inter-

---

[30] Alfred Tarski, *Introduction to Logic: And to the Methodology of Deductive Sciences* (Courier Corporation, 2013), 108.

[31] See Paul McNamara, 'Deontic Logic', in *The Stanford Encyclopedia of Philosophy*, ed. Edward N. Zalta, Winter ed. (Stanford University, 2014).

[32] See Lothar Philipps, 'Braucht die Rechtswissenschaft eine Deontische Logik?', in *Rechtstheorie: Beiträge zur Grundlagendiskussion*, ed. Günther Jahr and Werner Maihofer (Frankfurt am Main: Vittorio Klostermann, 1971), 367.

[33] See Richard M. Hare, *The Language of Morals*, reprint (London; New York: Oxford University Press, USA, 1991), passim; Nicholas Rescher, *The Logic of Commands* (London: Routledge & Kegan Paul PLC, 1966), passim.

[34] See Robert Alexy, *Theorie der juristischen Argumentation* (Frankfurt am Main: Suhrkamp Verlag, 1983), passim.

[35] Dawid Bunikowski, 'The Origins of Open Texture in Language and Legal Philosophies in Oxford and Cambridge', *Oxford Journal of Legal Studies*, August 2015, 5, 7n.

[36] See Larenz and Canaris, *Methodenlehre der Rechtswissenschaft*, 26.

pretation, that is, *hermeneutics*,[37] because of what Hart famously theorised as the 'open texture' of law and 'a penumbra of debatable cases in which words are neither obviously applicable nor obviously ruled out.'[38]

Finally, since the purpose of this study is not only to disprove erroneous theories currently accepted as orthodoxy, but also to solve the problem of additional interpretational complexity induced by plurilingual form in practice, the extent to which the solution developed on the basis of my theoretical analysis can be applied to existing tax treaties needs to be examined in order to support formulation of appropriate policies. For this reason, a quantitative analysis is required to measure applicability and develop a 'numerical expression of confidence'[39] in policy formulation. In the following sections I shall outline more precisely what is implied by these three methods and why I consider them most useful to achieve the goals I set for myself.

2.2.1. Logic

The explicit focus of this study on logic deserves elaboration – surely all scientific work in the field of law and, indeed, any legal reasoning in general first and foremost claims to be a rational endeavour based on logical thinking, without any need for special mentioning.[40] This default assump-

---

[37]Used here exclusively in the sense of the Oxford Dictionary, the American Heritage Dictionary of the English Language, and the Merriam-Webster Dictionary as 'The branch of knowledge that deals with interpretation', 'The theory and methodology of interpretation', and 'the study of the methodological principles of interpretation', respectively, not in the sense of an ontological theory of understanding, cf. Martin Heidegger, *Ontology – The Hermeneutics of Facticity*, trans. John van Buren (Bloomington, IN: Indiana University Press, 1999), 6–16. As pointed out by the Merriam-Webster and Oxford Dictionaries, 'hermeneutics' is 'plural in form but singular or plural in construction' and 'usually treated as singular'.

[38]Herbert L. A. Hart, *The Concept of Law* (Oxford: The Clarendon Press, 1961), 123; Herbert L. A. Hart, 'Positivism and the Separation of Law and Morals', *Harvard Law Review* 71, no. 4 (1958): 593–629, III; see Bunikowski, 'The Origins of Open Texture in Language and Legal Philosophies in Oxford and Cambridge', passim.

[39]Andersen and Hepburn, 'Scientific Method', s. 4.

[40]This is not only a question of scientific rigour but also crucial to the legitimacy of judicial decisions, see Alexy, *Theorie der juristischen Argumentation*, 15. The German Federal Constitutional Court has stated in this respect that 'the judge must rid himself of

tion applies the term logic in a wider colloquial sense than implied here, including all sorts of rational procedures. Legal reasoning is not exhausted entirely by logic but necessarily includes material aspects in which the role of purely logical thinking is only subsidiary.[41]

Here 'logic' implies the more narrow meaning of modern logic,[42] which started in the late nineteenth century with Gottlob Frege[43] and is sometimes also referred to as formal or symbolic logic because of its focus on formal validity and the propensity of its protagonists to use symbols in their analysis of expressions. Modern logic builds on classical Aristotelian logic,[44] and its defining characteristic is the strict separation of logical considerations from psychological questions. Both classical Aristotelian and modern logic concern themselves rather with the laws of being and the operations of language, with the latter being the primary focus of modern logic.[45]

Understood in this sense, logic concerns itself only 'with the principles of valid inference' as applied to the linguistic form of propositions and their relations,[46] allowing formally valid conclusions in turn. The notion of inference is not intended to imply a mental process leading from the premises to the conclusion, but only that the premises necessarily imply the conclusion, that is, it is impossible for the conclusion not to be true when the premises are. In the words of Aristotle: 'A syllogism is discourse in which, certain things being stated, something other than what is stated follows of necessity from their being so. I mean by the last phrase that they produce the consequence, and by this, that no further term is required from without in order to make the consequence necessary.'[47] This does not necessarily have to mean that the premises and conclusion are indeed true, but only

---

arbitrariness; his decision must be based on rational reasoning', BVerfG, '1 BvR 112/65' (BVerfGE 34, 269, February 1973), C, IV, 1.

[41] See Tammelo, *Modern Logic in the Service of Law*, ix, 2.

[42] See Tugendhat and Wolf, *Logisch-semantische Propädeutik*, 8 et seq.

[43] Gottlob Frege, *Begriffsschrift: Eine der arithmetischen nachgebildete Formelsprache des reinen Denkens* (Halle: Louis Nebert Verlag, 1879).

[44] Comprised in Aristotele's six works on logic written 350 B.C., see Aristotle, *The Organon*, ed. Harold P. Cooke and Hugh Tredennick (Andesite Press, 2015).

[45] See Tugendhat and Wolf, *Logisch-semantische Propädeutik*, 9–10.

[46] See William Kneale and Martha Kneale, *The Development of Logic*, revised ed. (Oxford; New York: Oxford University Press, USA, 1985), 1.

[47] Aristotle, *Prior Analytics* (The Internet Classics Archive, 350 B.C.), Book I, Part 1.

that if the premisses are true, the conclusion must be true as well and cannot be false.[48] All logic is essentially formal in this sense, implying that an argument is valid because of its logical form regardless of the particular content of its premisses and conclusions. The commonly used label 'formal logic' is therefore pleonastic.[49]

The principal logical tool used to evaluate the validity of an inference is the principle (or law) of non-contradiction,[50] that is, the proposition that it is impossible for an expression that contradicts itself to be true or, more precisely, that two contradictory propositions *a* and *not-a* cannot both be true in the same sense at the same time.[51] Thus, in its proclaimed logical necessity, the validity of an inference rests on the validity of the principle of non-contradiction.[52] Although it is common to simply presuppose the principle of non-contradiction as a fundamental axiom,[53] such is not entirely unproblematic because the principle itself is not self-evident in the sense that we cannot use it as an argument against someone who denies its universal validity in form of a dialectic rationality that includes the possibility of contradictions as a fundamental part of reality.[54] Hence, it is important to clarify wherein precisely the proclaimed necessity of the validity of the principle of non-contradiction lies.

In principle, the answer to this question has been provided already by

---

[48]See MacCormick, *Legal Reasoning and Legal Theory*, Ch. 2.

[49]See Tammelo, *Modern Logic in the Service of Law*, 2.

[50]See Bertrand Russell, *The Problems of Philosophy* (Oxford: Oxford University Press, 2001), Ch. 7 – sometimes (particularly in German literature) also referred to as the principle (or law) of contradiction (*Satz vom Widerspruch*), see Tugendhat and Wolf, *Logisch-semantische Propädeutik*, 50.

[51]See ibid., 51 et seq. The principle can be traced back to Plato and Aristotle. Whereas Plato derives it empirically, see Plato, *Republic* (Perseus Digital Library, Tufts University, 380 B.C.), 4.436b, Aristotle is the first to formulate it as a fundamental logical axiom a priori, see Aristotle, *Metaphysics* (The Internet Classics Archive, 350 B.C.), Book IV, Parts 3–5.

[52]See Kant, *Kritik der reinen Vernunft, Das System der Grundsätze des reinen Verstandes. Erster Abschnitt. Von dem obersten Grundsatze aller analytischen Urteile.*

[53]John Paul II declared it a 'fundamental premiss of human reasoning' at the core of 'a body of knowledge' belonging to the 'spiritual heritage of humanity', even if sometimes possessed only in a 'general and unreflective way', John Paul II, *Encyclical Letter Fides et Ratio*, 1998, Introduction.

[54]See, e.g., Georg Wilhelm Friedrich Hegel, *Wissenschaft der Logik* (Berlin: Hofenberg, 2016), passim.

Aristotle,[55] and its most significant further development has been brought forward by Strawson.[56] According to Aristotle, stating something means saying something definite, otherwise we really state nothing and do not deserve argument. According to Strawson then, the purpose of applying a predicate to a subject is differentiation. That certain predicates mutually exclude each other is not necessarily attributable to their ontological reality but a man-made function of speech so intended:

> But must a language have incompatible predicates in it? And what makes predicates incompatible? I want to answer the first question by saying, not that a language has incompatible predicates in it; only that it is very natural that it should. And I want to answer the second question by saying that it is we, the makers of language, who make predicates incompatible. One of the main purposes for which we use language is to report events and describe things and persons. Such reports and descriptions are like answers to questions of the form: what was it like? What is it (he, she) like? We describe something, say what it is like, by applying to it words that we are also prepared to apply to other things. But not to all other things. A word that we are prepared to apply to everything without exception (such as certain words in current use in popular, and especially military, speech) would be useless for the purposes of description. For when we say what a thing is like, we not only compare it with other things, we also distinguish it from other things. (These are not two activities, but two aspects of the same activity.) Somewhere, then, a boundary must be drawn, limiting the applicability of a word used in describing things; and it is we who decide where the boundaries are to be drawn.[57]

In short, any predicate depends on how we delineate and intend to apply it. By applying a certain predicate in a certain sense to a subject x we create an 'incompatibility-range' that defines when y is to count as an instance of x and when not.[58] The extent of any such incompatibility-range is itself a function of the precision with which we define the scope of the predicate: any two predicates A and B belong to the same incompatibility-range as long as the statement 'x is A' at the same time implies 'x is not B', as a result

---

[55] See Aristotle, *Metaphysics*, Book IV, Part 4.

[56] See Peter Frederick Strawson, *Introduction to Logical Theory* (London: Methuen, 1952), 1 et seq.

[57] See ibid., 5.

[58] See ibid., 6.

of which A and B are equally as incompatible as A and not-A. Consequently, by stating both 'x is A' and 'x is B' we are not saying anything of informative value, because we state something and take it back at the same time by stating the opposite – the statements 'x is A' and 'x is B' cancel each other out by virtue of our definitions of A and B. In summary, the proclaimed validity of the principle of non-contradiction merely implies that by not adhering to it we utter nothing of informative value, not that we violate some eternal law of nature.[59]

At this point we can return to the choice of methodology and reason for it: the greater danger of accepting contradictions is not that we ultimately fail to say anything of informative value, but that we may say and argue anything, unchecked, also known as the fallacy *ex contradictione sequitur quodlibet* (from contradiction, anything follows).[60] Hence, the importance of specifying wherein precisely the validity of the principle of non-contradiction lies and strict reliance on it is given by the necessity to guard against ill-conceived arguments brought forward under the label of 'common sense'.[61]

The Oxford Dictionary defines common sense as 'Good sense and sound judgement in practical matters', and there is nothing wrong with that. Common sense so defined has its place in legal reasoning and, arguably, may even have its place as a methodology of epistemology;[62] however, it goes

---

[59]See Tugendhat and Wolf, *Logisch-semantische Propädeutik*, 60–64.

[60]See Karl R. Popper, 'What is Dialectic?', *Mind* 49, no. 196 (1940): 408–10. Popper criticises Hegel sharply for accepting contradictions and, therefore, having contributed to pave the way for twentieth century anti-rationalism and ideological dogmatism by providing an intellectual strategy of immunisation against criticism. He reiterated and extended his criticism in Karl R. Popper, 'Facts, Standards, and Truth: A Further Criticism of Relativism', in *Moral Relativism: A Reader*, ed. Paul K. Moser and Thomas L. Carson (New York, NY: Oxford University Press, USA, 2000), 32–52; Popper, *The Open Society and Its Enemies*, Ch. 12.

[61]Colloquially, the label is often used to declare something as simply obvious; however, for a reasoning to be considered scientific, it has to provide sufficient grounds for its conclusions, which cannot merely consist in the latter corresponding to 'common sense' by way of declaration. For proper scientific reasoning, it is at the same time superfluous and insufficient to refer to common sense; any explicit invocation is therefore suspect of merely attempting to turn one's own opinion into an *argumentum ad verecundiam* (appeal to authority) while lacking sufficient reasons apart from personal conviction.

[62]See Thomas Reid, *Essays on the Intellectual Powers of Man* (Cambridge: Cambridge University Press, 2011); George Edward Moore, 'A Defense of Common Sense', in *Contem-

without saying that a necessary precondition for any argument to claim the property of being commonsensical under this definition is for it to adhere at minimum to the principles of logic, which demarcate the boundaries of what can be qualified as good sense and sound judgement. Any self-proclaimed common sense argument transgressing the principles of logic must be considered ill-conceived. In the words of Tammelo:

> It is to be emphasized that modern legal logic can have no substitute in a non-logic. This is not to deny that there are good habits or patterns of lawyers' reasonings whose logical structure is not obvious, but which nevertheless conform to logically sound reasoning. This implicit, 'common-sense' logic may be sufficient for most practical purposes. However, when there is any doubt as to the formal validity or solidity of instances of legal reasoning, there is no escape from recourse to appropriate methods of modern logic in order to attain a certainty about this validity or solidity. ...Formal impeccability is a precondition of self-consistent reasoning. It is indisputable that in the field of law, as elsewhere, self-consistency is a most important aim – a standard for all aspects of lawyers' work performed in the spirit of their professional ethics.[63]

Unfortunately, the complex subject matter examined by this study brings with it all sorts of in the above sense ill-conceived arguments in doctrine, the quest of this study is to debunk. Unravelling the conceptual knot requires a sharp tool. This tool is provided by logic as the sum of 'principles and methods for tracing and displaying self-consistent thought.'[64]

The choice of method is also by no means arbitrary in view of the scope of our topic as posed by the VCLT: the principles supplied by it for the interpretation of treaties are qualified by its drafters as 'principles of logic and good sense'.[65] Although this terminology is not extensively explained in the VCLT Commentary, it is noteworthy that not only the term 'good sense' alone has been used, but that it is coupled with the term 'logic'. Use of 'good sense' alone would bear the danger of opening the doors to all sorts of arguments, whereas its explicit combination with 'logic' makes clear that

---

porary British Philosophy (second series), ed. J. H. Muirhead (London: George Allen & Unwin, 1925), 192–233.

[63]Tammelo, *Modern Logic in the Service of Law*, 2.

[64]Ibid., vii.

[65]ILC, *Draft Articles on the Law of Treaties with Commentaries*, II:218, para. 4.

the principles of interpretation enshrined in the VLCT are not only amenable to logical considerations, but that logical considerations are essential to the establishment of their rationale.

In the course of my analysis I shall use the logical tool of a thought experiment,[66] devised on the basis of the *Natexis* case.[67] Thought experiments are devices most commonly used in physics and philosophy and, to some extent, also in other natural and social sciences such as Biology and Economics. They are less common in jurisprudence but not unknown.[68] Several types of thought experiments may be distinguished,[69] but their common idea consists in the consideration of a hypothesis in a logically structured way to deliberate its consequences and arrive at universally valid conclusions without having to actually perform the experiment in reality. I use this device in order to abstract from specific facts of case law and focus on design features of tax treaties that allow generalisations.

2.2.2. Hermeneutics

In order to ascertain appropriate application of the VCLT principles when interpreting plurilingual treaties, we have to interpret Article 33 and establish its meaning. In particular, we will have to establish the meaning of the terms 'divergence', 'reconcile', and 'prevailing'. Being a multilateral treaty, the VCLT falls under its own scope.[70] Therefore, its text must be interpreted drawing on the principles and means codified in it.[71] The VCLT is a plurilingual treaty with texts in Chinese, English, French, Russian, and Spanish, none of which is designated as prevailing. As argued by this thesis, all texts have to be compared in such case to ensure correct interpretation.

---

[66] See James Robert Brown and Yiftach Fehige, 'Thought Experiments', in *The Stanford Encyclopedia of Philosophy*, ed. Edward N. Zalta, Spring ed. (Stanford University, 2016).

[67] Conseil d'État, *Société Natexis Banques Populaires v France*.

[68] As quoted by Fredrick Kennard, *Thought Experiments: Popular Thought Experiments in Philosophy, Physics, Ethics, Computer Science & Mathematics* (Lulu.com, 2015), 9, the Catholic Encyclopedia (1913)/Pandects states that 'every logical rule of law is capable of illumination from the law of the Pandects.'

[69] See Brown and Fehige, 'Thought Experiments'.

[70] UN, *Vienna Convention on the Law of Treaties*, Articles 1–2.

[71] Ibid., Article 31–33.

Interpretation of terms has to start somewhere, which raises the question to what extent dictionaries may be used in order to establish their meaning. Dictionaries provide the meaning of words as used by people in their most common contexts; they have the aim to explain the ordinary, non-technical meaning applicable in everyday use.[72] Therefore, resorting to dictionaries in order to elucidate the meaning of tax treaty terms is problematic. Legal language is crammed with jargon used in a technical sense different from dictionary meanings.[73] The language of tax treaties is no exception in this regard, and such special meanings become the ordinary meanings in the tax treaty context.[74]

In addition, tax treaties usually feature *renvoi* clauses modelled on Article 3(2) of the OECD and UN Model Conventions.[75] Accordingly, terms that have no explicit treaty definition are to be given the meaning they have under the domestic laws of the contracting states 'unless the context otherwise requires'. Such domestic law meanings may also form part of an otherwise incomplete treaty definition.[76] In summary, since the treaty ordinary meaning of terms always depends on their context and object and purpose, we must be cautious about both resorting to dictionary definitions divorced from the treaty context and applying domestic law definitions if they defeat the object and purpose of the treaty.[77]

Notwithstanding, recourse to dictionaries still has its place in the interpretation of treaty terms. Legal language is not a symbolised formal language but uses ordinary language as its medium. Even its technical terminology consists mostly of terms borrowed from ordinary language, the mean-

---

[72] See Jonas Pfister, *Werkzeuge des Philosophierens* (Stuttgart: Reclam, Philipp, jun. GmbH, Verlag, 2013), 52–53. Usually, they also provide etymological information about the origin of words and how their meaning has changed over time.

[73] See Deborah Cao, *Translating Law* (Channel View Publications Ltd., 2007), 53–54.

[74] See Avery Jones, 'Treaty Interpretation', s. 3.4.11, and s. 9.3.2 [5.2.3.2] for a discussion of liable and subject to tax as examples.

[75] OECD, *Model Tax Convention on Income and on Capital: Condensed Version* (Paris: OECD Publishing, 2017); UN, *United Nations Model Double Taxation Convention Between Developed and Developing Countries* (United Nations, 2011).

[76] See Avery Jones, 'Treaty Interpretation', s. 7.2.2 [4.3.2.2].

[77] See Engelen, *Interpretation of Tax Treaties under International Law*, 137 et seq., 149 et seq; Avery Jones, 'Treaty Interpretation', s. 3.4.4; *Gladden v Her Majesty the Queen*, [1985] 85 DTC 5188, para. 14.

ing of which is then contextually charged and formed into the intended technical meaning. The choice of words for this operation is not arbitrary but correlates to their ordinary language meaning, which shares basic connotations with the legal meaning and lends itself to the intended modification. The same is true for tax treaty terms as a special category of legal language. For example, the permanent establishment (PE) concept has a defined treaty meaning,[78] which overrides any defined domestic law and dictionary meaning. Yet, this treaty meaning builds on and modifies the dictionary meanings of the employed terms 'permanent' and 'establishment'.

In extreme situations, such modification may lend itself to departures far away from the basic connotation of the dictionary meaning, particularly when the added technical connotation modifying the dictionary meaning provides some leeway for courts in their interpretation. According to the decision of the ITAT in the *Fugro* case, for example, the permanence test for the existence of a PE in India is satisfied when there exists a place of business for the time in which the business operation can be completed.[79] This constitutes a far stretch not only in terms of the dictionary meaning of permanence but also considering its tax implications against the background of the intentions behind the PE concept.[80] As a result of this interpretation, any short-term project or operation could constitute a PE as long as the non-resident company has a place of business in India long enough for the project or operation to be concluded, even if it lasts only for a couple of days.[81]

Therefore, despite being faced with a similar set of facts like the ITAT in the *Fugro* case and Norway being a country with a treaty policy geared towards a low PE threshold, the Norwegian supreme court decided in the *PGS* case against the existence of a PE, on the basis that 'permanent establishment' as defined by the treaty being modelled on the OECD Model implies a certain duration with respect to the natural understanding of the terms employed and the practice of OECD countries suggesting six months as a

---

[78] OECD, *Model Tax Convention on Income and on Capital: Condensed Version* (Paris: OECD Publishing, 2014), Article 5.

[79] *Fugro Engineering BV v ACIT, TTJ*, vol. 122, Delhi Income Tax Appelate Tribunal, 2008.

[80] See OECD, *Model Tax Convention*, 2017, Commentary on Article 5.

[81] See Editor's Note, Case Summary *Fugro Engineering B.V.*, *Tax Treaty Case Law Database* (Amsterdam: IBFD, 2016).

consensus minimum for that duration test to be satisfied.[82]

Although both interpretations may be based on arguments derived from the same paragraph of the OECD Commentary at the time,[83] the *PGS* decision takes into account that the initial choice for the words 'permanent' and 'establishment' as building blocks of the PE concept is not arbitrary, but that their dictionary meanings provide the basis for arriving at the finally intended tax treaty meaning and, therefore, may help to shed some light on the boundaries of the concept implied in controversial cases. Indeed, the intuitive reservations we might have concerning examples like the decision of the ITAT in the *Fugro* case are a direct result of this relationship.

In summary, dictionary meanings remain useful for the textual interpretation of treaty terms because they illuminate the boundaries of the concepts employed. They provide the ordinary language context and connotation of any word, which should be examined always to grasp the general conceptual limits of what is and what is not included in the notion, unless they are explicitly transgressed by a different defined or contextual meaning. Of course, this applies in particular when the terms to be interpreted do not have a technical treaty or applicable domestic law definition; however, even when terms with a technical legal meaning are at issue, dictionary meanings may prove helpful and are used by courts to hedge the textual treaty meaning.[84] As Lord Wilberforce has put it, 'There is no reason why he [the judge] should not consult a dictionary, if the word is such that a dictionary can reveal its significance.'[85]

---

[82]Høyesterett, *PGS Geophysical AS v Government of Norway*, 2004–01003–A, (Sak Nr. 2003/1311) (Amsterdam: IBFD, *Tax Treaty Case Law Database 2016*, 2004).

[83]Commentary on Article 5, para. 6, up to OECD, *Model Tax Convention*, 2014 (updated to paras. 28–30 in 2017). For a discussion of the PE permanency test and the *PGS* and *Fugro* cases, see Andreas Perdelwitz, 'A Certain Degree of Permanence Between Temporary and Everlasting Business Activities', in *Taxation of Business Profits in the 21st Century*, ed. Andreas Perdelwitz and Carlos Gutiérrez (Amsterdam: IBFD, 2013).

[84]See, e.g., *Wolf v Canada*, [2002] 4 F.C. 396, as discussed by Jacques Sasseville, 'The Canadian Experience', in *Multilingual Texts and Interpretation of Tax Treaties and EC Tax Law*, ed. Guglielmo Maisto (Amsterdam: IBFD, 2005), 35–62, 50–61; Jacques Sasseville, 'The OECD Model Convention and Commentaries', in *Multilingual Texts and Interpretation of Tax Treaties and EC Tax Law*, ed. Guglielmo Maisto (Amsterdam: IBFD, 2005), 133.

[85]*Fothergill v Monarch Airlines Ltd.*, [1981] AC 251, HL, 273. Explicitly supported by Lords

2.2.3. Quantitative Analysis

Concerning the applicability of sole reliance on the prevailing text to actual tax treaties, I conduct an empirical analysis of the global tax treaty network with respect to lingual form and final clause wordings. The global perspective is differentiated via time-series analysis, per country analysis, and categorisation of the data into meaningful groups in order to investigate policy. The wordings of actual final clauses are catalogued, categorised, and analysed against the background of the interpretative framework provided by the VCLT and the theory developed in the theoretical chapters.

The sample analysed consists of all tax treaties concluded between 1 January 1960 and 15 August 2016 insofar as they have been recorded by the IBFD,[86] independent of their status, that is, not only treaties in force are taken into account but also terminated treaties and treaties not yet in force or still to be ratified. Treaties reported as merely initialled, under negotiation, or abandoned have been excluded. The same goes for mere exchanges of notes, memoranda of understanding, dominion double taxation relief rules, and agreements concerning the provisional abolition of double taxation prior to a treaty.

All types of tax treaties have been included (mainly income and capital and inheritance and gift tax treaties), whether separate, combined, or only covering specific types of income. One hundred and forty-six treaties that satisfied the above criteria for inclusion had to be excluded from the final sample because either their texts could not be retrieved at the cut-off date or the wordings of their final clauses could not be established beyond doubt.[87] Transport tax treaties have not been included by convention, as many of them are only concluded via an exchange of notes, which precludes a consistent investigation of their linguistic outlook in the current context.

Not included in the survey from the outset have been exchange of inform-

---

Tullybelton (286), Scarman (293), and Roskill (300).

[86] *Tax Treaties Database* (Amsterdam: IBFD, 2016). Treaties concluded before 1960 have been excluded in order not to bias the data, as several old terminated treaties are difficult to obtain. According to the data observed, treaties concluded before 1960 make up less than 5% of all tax treaties and are therefore insignificant regarding the overall conclusions.

[87] See Appendix E.1.

ation treaties, social security treaties, economic relations treaties, FATCA agreements, friendship and fiscal co-operation agreements, friendship and commerce treaties, and mutual assistance agreements.[88] Although these treaties may be considered closely related to the international tax universe, this has been done on purpose because of the focus of this study on tax treaties and their specific properties. Given the different subject matters of the listed other treaties, their linguistic properties may differ, and their objects and purposes may not suffer from the same interpretation issues identified by this study, wherefore their addition could bias the data and analysis because many of them (exchange of information and FATCA) are in their magnitude fairly recent phenomena. A separate evaluation of them has been left to future research.

In total, the sample analysed in this study comprises 3,844 tax treaties concluded between January 1960 and August 2016.[89] All percentage numbers concerning the sample presented in tables are rounded to two decimal points, whereas percentage numbers in the running text are mostly rounded to integers.

---

[88]Unless not stand-alone but coupled with a tax treaty in one single instrument, see, e.g., Denmark-Greenland (1979).

[89]See Appendix E.

3. Routine Interpretation: A Refutation

3.1. Research Question

This chapter concerns itself with the question whether courts are legally required to compare all authenticated language texts when none of them is designated as prevailing.[1] In this context, it will also discuss the commonly held view that judges should give preference to the text of initial negotiation and drafting when they are faced with a divergence between the texts. The hypothesis put forward in this chapter may be split into the following four elements: (1) Articles 31–33 in combination with Articles 26–27 VCLT put courts under an obligation to compare all texts of a plurilingual tax treaty in the absence of a prevailing one; (2) this obligation is independent of domestic procedural law; (3) the currently prevailing view maintaining the opposite rests on an erroneous interpretation of Articles 31–33; and (4) Articles 31–33 do not sanction giving preference to the original text merely in virtue of it being the text of negotiation and drafting. Before we can discuss these propositions, it is necessary to clarify the meaning of the fundamental notions of treaty and text as well as their relationship.

3.2. Preliminary Considerations

3.2.1. The Treaty and Its Text

What constitutes the treaty? Must the treaty be considered an underlying agreement of concurring wills that exists independently from the text as legal instrument being merely the expression of such agreement, or does the text as legal instrument constitute the treaty as its formal embodiment?

---

[1]Parts of this chapter have been presented in embryonic form in the following peer reviewed publication: Richard Xenophon Resch, 'Not in Good Faith – A Critique of the Vienna Convention Rule of Interpretation Concerning Its Application to Plurilingual (Tax) Treaties', *British Tax Review*, no. 3 (2014): 307–28.

Or, is this a misleading dichotomy and a treaty is essentially and insepar-ably both, an agreement in the form of a written text? The consequences of an answer to this question are non-trivial. If we were to arrive at the con-clusion that, in short, the text is the treaty, then any interpreter has only the text itself as a reference to establish its meaning, that is, the treaty's content. As a corollary, if there are more language texts, the meaning of each can be established only by reference to itself and/or the others, not by any reference to an agreement behind all texts that is not accessible except for what is expressed by them. Hence, we need to answer two questions: (1) What is the relationship between the treaty and its text? (2) In view of the answer to (1), does the and/or default to *and* or *or*?

What constitutes a treaty was discussed by the ILC over a period of six-teen years on the basis of the Brierly, Lauterpacht, Fitzmaurice, and Wal-dock reports.[2] One of the main sources used by Special Rapporteur Brierly for his initial report and draft was the Harvard Draft Convention, which had defined a treaty as 'a formal instrument of agreement'.[3] In contrast, the Draft Convention on the Law of Treaties presented by Brierly defined a treaty as 'an agreement recorded in writing'.[4] In Brierly's view, the writ-ten record did not require a particularly formal instrument,[5] such being no more than evidence for the existence of a treaty he considered to be an agreement existing before the act of its conclusion.[6] Therefore, his Com-mentary emphasised the underlying agreement as constituting the essence

---

[2]See Mark Eugen Villiger, *Commentary on the 1969 Vienna Convention on the Law of Treat-ies* (Leiden; Boston: Martinus Nijhoff Publishers, 2009), 75–76.

[3]ILC, *Documents of the Second Session Including the Report of the Commission to the Gen-eral Assembly*, vol. II, Yearbook of the International Law Commission 1950, A/CN. 4/SER.A/1950/Add.1 (United Nations, 1957), 243, Appendix A, Article 1(a). For a his-torical appraisal of the Harvard Draft Convention see Gardiner, *Treaty Interpretation*, 56–57.

[4]ILC, *Documents of the Second Session Including the Report of the Commission to the Gen-eral Assembly*, II:226, Article 1(a). Brierly's intention was not to provide an independent definition of 'treaty', but only to define treaties for the limited scope of the draft con-vention, see ibid., 226, para. 14.

[5]See ibid., II:227, para. 23.

[6]See ILC, *Summary Records of the Second Session, 5 June – 29 July 1950*, vol. I, Yearbook of the International Law Commission 1950, A/CN.4/SER.A/1950 (United Nations, 1958), 82, paras. 88, 92.

of treaties, with the written record being merely a matter of practical necessity.[7]

Brierly's view was criticised by the majority of the ILC members, who preferred a definition of treaties that reverted to the wording of the Harvard draft.[8] In essence, the difficulty underlying the discussion consisted in the inseparability of both constituents.[9] In the words of Rapporteur Alfaro, 'The agreement could no more be separated from the instrument than the body from the soul. The soul of a treaty was the unanimity of intent. The body was the formal written instrument. The agreement without the instrument was nothing, and vice versa. ...What constituted a treaty was an agreement converted into an instrument.'[10] In contrast to Brierly, the discussion in the meetings placed more importance on the formal instrument constituent, not considering any 'agreement recorded in writing' but only a 'formal instrument of agreement' to be a treaty.[11] In the end the ILC voted in favour of the Harvard Draft wording by six votes to four, with one abstention.[12]

When we fast-forward to the VCLT, we see that the wording of Article 2(1)(a), which defines treaties for purposes of the convention, appears closer to Brierly's conception:

> For the purposes of the present Convention: ...'treaty' means an international agreement concluded between States in written form and governed by international law, whether embodied in a single instrument or in two or more related instruments and whatever its particular designation.

According to the VCLT Commentary, the scope of what constitutes a treaty is relatively broad, 'covering all forms of international agreements in writing concluded between States', subject to relatively low formal require-

---

[7]See ILC, *Documents of the Second Session Including the Report of the Commission to the General Assembly*, II:227, para. 19.

[8]See ILC, *Summary Records of the Second Session, 5 June – 29 July 1950*, 65, para. 73a; 68, paras. 8–8b; 69, para. 14; 71, paras. 33–34; 72, paras. 39a–c; 75, para. 14; 76, para. 26; 77, para. 33; 82, paras. 90–91, 94; 82–83, paras. 3–3a, 6, 7–7b; 84, para. 9.

[9]See ibid., I:82, para. 94.

[10]Ibid., I:83, para. 6.

[11]See ibid., I:84, para. 9.

[12]See ibid., I:84, para. 17.

ments regarding the respective instruments.[13] The wording 'concluded' seems to suggest stronger formal requirements than merely 'recorded in writing'; however, there is no fixed meaning of 'concluded' in international law, but the term simply implies a set of distinctive procedures that make a treaty binding.[14] As long as the objective intentions of the parties to create rights and obligations governed by international law are evident from the wording, the form is of secondary relevance.[15] Nevertheless, the scope of what constitutes a treaty under the VCLT is confined to agreements 'in written form', even if only for practical reasons and not to deny the legal force of oral agreements and the applicability of the same principles to them.[16] In summary, treaties are to some degree necessarily textual for purposes of the VCLT, with both constituents 'agreement' and 'instrument' being essential to constitute a treaty. This leaves the question of the exact

---

[13]See ILC, *Draft Articles on the Law of Treaties with Commentaries*, II:188, paras. 2–3; Engelen, *Interpretation of Tax Treaties under International Law*, 19–31.

[14]See Villiger, *Commentary on the 1969 Vienna Convention on the Law of Treaties*, 78–79.

[15]See Engelen, *Interpretation of Tax Treaties under International Law*, 21–24. The ICJ has made clear that all kinds of documents may constitute a treaty. Given clear language in the document at issue regarding obligations entered into, the court rejected otherwise declared intentions to the contrary as irrelevant: 'The 1990 Minutes refer to the consultations between the two Foreign Ministers of Bahrain and Qatar, in the presence of the Foreign Minister of Saudi Arabia, and state what had been "agreed" between the Parties. …Thus the 1990 Minutes include a reaffirmation of obligations previously entered into. …Accordingly, and contrary to the contentions of Bahrain, the Minutes are not a simple record of a meeting, …they do not merely give an account of discussions and summarize points of agreement and disagreement. They enumerate the commitments to which the Parties have consented. They thus create rights and obligations in international law for the Parties. They constitute an international agreement. …The Court does not find it necessary to consider what might have been the intentions of the Foreign Minister of Bahrain or, for that matter, those of the Foreign Minister of Qatar. The two Ministers signed a text recording commitments accepted by their Governments, some of which were to be given immediate application. Having signed such a text, the Foreign Minister of Bahrain is not in a position subsequently to say that he intended to subscribe only to a "statement recording a political understanding", and not to an international agreement', *Maritime Delimitation and Territorial Questions between Qatar and Bahrain (Qatar v Bahrain), Jurisdiction and Admissibility*, ICJ (Annual Reports of the International Court of Justice, 1994), 121–122, paras. 24–25, 27.

[16]See ILC, *Draft Articles on the Law of Treaties with Commentaries*, II:189, para. 7.

relationship between a treaty and its text open.[17]

An indirect answer may be obtained from examining the way how we are supposed to treat the text. Concerning this we know that we have to give priority to objective considerations based on the text:

> The article as already indicated is based on the view that the text must be presumed to be the authentic expression of the intentions of the parties; and that, in consequence, the starting point of interpretation is the elucidation of the meaning of the text, not an investigation *ab initio* into the intentions of the parties.[18]

Thus, when interpreting a treaty, we ought to follow a textual but not literal approach, based on the ordinary meaning, context, and object and purpose,[19] whereas teleological interpretations of the text in violation of its wording must not be given effect.[20] This intrinsic, text-based approach is not absolute but complemented by a limited extrinsic approach if the former

---

[17]Presumably, the purpose of the VCLT definition is to limit it to written treaties while recognising the existence of subsidiary agreements, instruments, and practice in Article 31, paras. 2a, 2b, 3a, and 3b, which need not (or, in the case of practice, will not) be in writing, leaving the force of oral agreements and the applicability of the VCLT principles to them unaffected, as is explicitly specified by Article 3(b) VCLT, see Jan Klabbers, *The Concept of Treaty in International Law* (The Hague: Kluwer Law International, 1996), 49–50.

[18]ILC, *Draft Articles on the Law of Treaties with Commentaries*, II:220, para. 11, repeated in substance at 223, para. 18.

[19]UN, *Vienna Convention on the Law of Treaties*, Article 31(1); see *Temple of Preah Vihear (Cambodia v Thailand), Preliminary Objections*, ICJ (Annual Reports of the International Court of Justice, 1961), 32; *Anglo-Iranian Oil Co. (United Kingdom v Iran)*, ICJ (Annual Reports of the International Court of Justice, 1952), 104: 'But the Court cannot base itself on a purely grammatical interpretation of the text. It must seek the interpretation which is in harmony with a natural and reasonable way of reading the text, having due regard to the intention of the Government of Iran at the time when it accepted the compulsory jurisdiction of the Court.' For a comprehensive discussion of the textual approach prescribed by the VCLT, see Ian Sinclair, *The Vienna Convention on the Law of Treaties* (Manchester: Manchester University Press, 1984), 114 et seq.; Engelen, *Interpretation of Tax Treaties under International Law*, Ch. 5. For a demarcation of the textual versus a literal approach in case law, refer to the summary elaborations of Mummery J. in *Inland Revenue Commissioners v Commerzbank*, [1990] STC 285, 297–298; *Fothergill v Monarch Airlines Ltd.*, 272, 279, 285, 290, 294; *Gladden v Her Majesty the Queen*, 519.

[20]See Engelen, *Interpretation of Tax Treaties under International Law*, 429.

leaves the meaning ambiguous or obscure, or leads to a result that is manifestly absurd or unreasonable, in which case recourse may be had to supplementary means in order to determine the meaning;[21] apart from that, the latter may be used only to confirm but not contest a manifest meaning established under Article 31.[22] Consequently, the will of the parties manifested in the agreement and its expression in the text converge for purposes of interpreting and applying the treaty, because 'law cannot take into consideration anything that remains buried away in the minds of the parties. ...[T]he expressed will is the only will upon which the parties have been able to reach an agreement.'[23] In summary, since it has only itself as a reference, the text must be treated *as if it were* the treaty – the main task of interpretation being 'to give effect to the *expressed* intention of the parties.'[24]

3.2.2. The Meaning of Text and Its Implications

What constitutes the text? The answer to this question is more straightforward: the text comprises all authenticated language versions of the text, and the procedures establishing authentic status are defined by Article 10 VCLT and its Commentary:

> Authentication is the process by which this definitive text is established, and it consists in some act or procedure which certifies the text as the correct and authentic text.[25]

> The text of a treaty is established as authentic and definitive: (a) by such procedure as may be provided for in the text or agreed upon by the States participating in its drawing up; or (b) failing such procedure, by the signature, signature ad referendum or initialling by the representatives of those States of the text of the treaty or of the Final Act of a conference incorporating the text.[26]

---

[21]The terminology of intrinsic versus extrinsic, which is appropriated for its suitability here and also by Sinclair, *The Vienna Convention on the Law of Treaties*, 118, was originally introduced by Charles de Visscher, *Problèmes d'interprétation judiciaire en droit international public* (Paris: Pedone, 1963).

[22]UN, *Vienna Convention on the Law of Treaties*, Article 32(a) and (b).

[23]Paul Reuter, *Introduction to the Law of Treaties* (Kegan Paul Intl, 1995), 30, para. 65.

[24]Lord McNair, as quoted by John F. Avery Jones, ed., 'Interpretation of Tax Treaties', *Bulletin for International Taxation*, no. 2 (1986): 76.

[25]ILC, *Draft Articles on the Law of Treaties with Commentaries*, II:195, para. 1.

[26]UN, *Vienna Convention on the Law of Treaties*, Article 10.

The immediate implication for the interpretation of treaties with their text in more than one language is that all language texts form part of the context definition under Article 31(2).[27] If we neglect the existence of Article 33 for the moment, this implies that all texts have to be considered authentic means of interpretation to which more relative weight must be attributed than to supplementary means.[28] Therefore, a legal obligation to compare all language texts as part of the context could be construed from Article 31 in the absence of Article 33.[29]

During the drafting period of the VCLT the Israeli government proposed that Article 31 should explicitly codify a comparison of all texts because the utility of such comparison extended beyond the decider function in case of textual differences.[30] This suggestion was not implemented in the VCLT, which raises the question how multiple language texts relate to each other for purposes of interpretation: Do all considered together constitute the text, or each considered by itself? Once more, the consequences of the answer are non-trivial: the former implies that considering one text in isolation can never make the treaty accessible in its entirety, whereas the latter implies that such is possible in principle.

To answer the question, a look under the hood of Article 33 is necessary. Its construction rests on two basic propositions. The first, henceforth denoted as *p*, is the fundamental principle of unity:

---

[27] See Engelen, *Interpretation of Tax Treaties under International Law*, 544.

[28] See ibid., 390.

[29] In addition to all texts forming part of the context, the requirement to interpret a treaty 'in light of its object and purpose' enshrined in Article 31(1) also implies a legal obligation to compare the texts if such must be presumed to be necessary to appreciate the full object and purpose, see Christopher B. Kuner, 'The Interpretation of Multilingual Treaties: Comparison of Texts Versus the Presumption of Similar Meaning', *International & Comparative Law Quarterly* 40, no. 4 (1991): 963, 73n, with reference to Hans van Loon, 'The Hague Conventions on Private International Law', in *Further Studies in International Law*, ed. Francis Geoffrey Jacobs and Shelley Roberts, vol. 7, United Kingdom Comparative Law Series (London: Sweet & Maxwell, 1987), 221, 238; Frederick A. Mann, 'Uniform Statutes in English Law', in *Further Studies in International Law* (Oxford: Clarendon Press, 1990), 284–85.

[30] See ILC, *Documents of the Second Part of the Seventeenth Session and of the Eighteenth Session Including the Reports of the Commission to the General Assembly*, vol. II, Yearbook of the International Law Commission 1966, A/CN.4/SER. A/1966/Add.1 (United Nations, 1967), 92, 301, para. 16(h).

3. Routine Interpretation: A Refutation

> [I]n law there is only one treaty – one set of terms accepted by the parties and one common intention with respect to those terms – even when two authentic texts appear to diverge.[31]

This principle is a presumption of law that cannot be rebutted.[32] It constitutes the fundamental axiom from which all further analysis must depart. In essence, it is a statement of numerical identity: A = A, A being the treaty.

As we have seen above, we ought to treat the text *as if it were* the treaty. Given that there may exist several language texts each of which has been established as definitive through the process of authentication, we can now better classify this *as if it were* relation between the treaty and its text, namely, as a relation of qualitative identity, because numerical identity is an analytic one-one relation a priori, whereas the relation between a treaty and the language of its text is potentially one-many.[33]

To say that a text is qualitatively identical to the treaty implies that both equally feature certain relevant properties as a result of which they may be qualified as the same. With respect to the treaty and its text, the relevant property for sameness consists in the text expressing the full content of the treaty, which must be presumed to be the case once a text in a particular language has been authenticated.[34]

---

[31] ILC, *Draft Articles on the Law of Treaties with Commentaries*, II:225, para. 6.

[32] See Jörg Manfred Mössner, 'Die Auslegung mehrsprachiger Staatsverträge', *Archiv des Völkerrechts*, Bd. 15, no. 3. H. (1972): 282; Ulf Linderfalk, *On the Interpretation of Treaties: The Modern International Law as Expressed in the 1969 Vienna Convention on the Law of Treaties* (Springer, 2007), 356.

[33] Aristotle is the first to elaborate on the difference between numerical and qualitative identity extensively, see Aristotle, *Topics* (The Internet Classics Archive, 350 B.C.), Book 1, Part 7; Aristotle, *Metaphysics*, Book IV, Part 4; Book V, Part 9. For refined considerations, see Gottfried Wilhelm Leibniz, *Metaphysische Abhandlung*, ed. Ulrich Johannes Schneider (Hamburg: Felix Meiner Verlag, 2002); Ludwig Wittgenstein, *Tractatus Logico-Philosophicus* (London: Kegan Paul, 1922); Gottlob Frege, 'Über Sinn und Bedeutung', *Zeitschrift für Philosophie und Philosophische Kritik*, 1892, 25–50; Saul A. Kripke, 'Identity and Necessity', in *Identity and Individuation*, ed. Milton K. Munitz, 1st ed. (New York: New York University Press, 1971); Saul A. Kripke, *Naming and Necessity* (Cambridge, Mass: Harvard University Press, 1980).

[34] The same applies to unilingual treaties: the *as if it were* relation between the treaty and its text in only one language is also one of qualitative not numerical identity. This is embodied by the VCLT allowing for the correction of errors under Articles 48(3) and

As a corollary, the variable *language* must be regarded as explicitly excluded by p from the sum of properties rendering the text qualitatively identical to the treaty, or else there could not be multiple language texts. On the basis of p, multiple language texts imply that language is irrelevant for the essential property of expressing the full content of the treaty: once authenticated, any language text must be presumed to express the full content of the treaty and therefore any other text until proven otherwise.[35]

In summary, there is only one treaty with one set of terms, the text represents the treaty, and each text constitutes the definitive text by way of authentication, wherefore all texts must be considered the same in their content even though the wordings in the different languages may differ. Hence, on the basis of p, the answer to the above question must by means of a logical tautology be that each text constitutes the text (that is, treaty).[36]

The second proposition on which the VCLT rules are based, henceforth denoted as q, is that discrepancies between the texts attributable to language are a material reality:

> Few plurilingual treaties containing more than one or two articles are without some discrepancy between the texts. The different genius of the languages, the absence of a complete *consensus ad idem*, or lack of sufficient time to co-ordinate the texts may result in minor or even major discrepancies in the meaning of the texts.[37]

This raises the question whether the point made is one of logical necessity or merely a fact of life. The former would mean that the practice of states to

---

79 VCLT. Such errors constitute defects of the text in its intended relation of qualitative identity with the treaty, and their correction does not imply a change or amendment of the agreement in substance (the corrected text applies *ab initio* under Article 79(4) VCLT) but merely a correction of the identified failure of the text to properly display the intended property of expressing the full content of the treaty, see ILC, *Draft Articles on the Law of Treaties with Commentaries*, 273, para. 6.

[35]Identity is a transitive relation: if A = B and B = C, then A = C, viz., if A = B and A = C, then B = C.

[36]In the technical sense of an analytical truth a priori but essentially redundant statement. To say that each of the authentic language texts is the text provides no new information; it states something true while saying nothing really meaningful (in the sense that we learn nothing new from that statement about the treaty), see Wittgenstein, *Tractatus Logico-Philosophicus*, passim, by analogy.

[37]ILC, *Draft Articles on the Law of Treaties with Commentaries*, II:225, para. 6.

conclude treaties in plurilingual form is fundamentally flawed, whereas the latter implies that it is only corrupted by practical implementation. From the presumption that the genius of every language is different, discrepancies seem to follow as a logical necessity.[38] We may safely leave this discussion to the linguists because the corollary of *p*, that is, all texts are qualitatively identical, can only be reconciled with *q*, that is, most texts differ, if differences between the texts can be reconciled by way of interpretation. Otherwise *q* would amount to *not-p*, and *p* and *q* would contradict each other.

If *q* would indeed have to be considered true as a logical necessity, the exclusion of language as a material factor by *p*, that is, the practice of states to conclude treaties in plurilingual form, would have to be questioned as fundamentally flawed. Hence, the premiss of language being an immaterial factor implicit in *p* is challenged by *q* as unsound. In the face of *q*, it has to be reformulated into *language ought to be an immaterial factor*, because the principle of unity contained in *p* requires that there is only one treaty with one set of terms. Since *p* may not be immaterial by definition, *q* must be shown to be immaterial by way of interpretation, in the sense of *although the expression differs, the meaning is the same*.

In summary, we first of all ought to treat any text *as if it were* the treaty, because we have no separate underlying agreement at our disposal against which the text could be gauged other than the one expressed by the texts themselves. Secondly, based on the principle of unity, we ought to depart from the assumption that all texts must equal each other in meaning even if they differ from each other in expression. Crucially, however, both the content of each text and the sameness of all texts in this respect can be established only by way of interpretation in view of *q*. There is a fundamental tension between *p* and *q* that requires dissolution because *p* and *q* contradict each other if *q* holds true and the difference in expression cannot be shown to be immaterial in view of *p*, while *q* also implies that any text may single-handedly fail to convey the full content of the treaty (and the other

---

[38] According to Ajulo, 'linguists are unanimous in the view that no language can express fully any idea primarily conceived in another language', Sunday Babalola Ajulo, 'Myth and Reality of Law, Language and International Organization in Africa: The Case of African Economic Community', *Journal of African Law* 41, no. 1 (1997): 40.

texts) because of linguistic ambiguities or mistakes in the authentication process.

As a corollary, because *p* requires that 'every effort should be made to find a common meaning for the texts before preferring one to another',[39] *q* requires that all texts are considered together for purposes of interpreting the treaty, because to establish whether *p* holds true, that is, whether *q* amounts in fact to *not-q* after careful consideration, there is no exogenous variable against which the texts could be gauged, but the texts can only be gauged against each other and therefore have to be considered together in order for the interpreter to safely arrive at their common meaning constituting the true content of the treaty.[40]

Apart from the Israeli government cited above, this view was strongly endorsed by Rosenne, who argued for an explicit inclusion of a comparison of texts among the means of interpretation and concluded that the general rule of interpretation would be deficient without.[41] His proposal has not been implemented, and its underlying rationale is not supported by the majority of scholars to date. From the prominent academics in international tax law, only Klaus Vogel seemed to have adhered to it initially:

> With respect to **bilingual or multilingual** agreements, Art. 33 VCLT provides …that the original versions in **each language are equally binding**. …The domestic judge, therefore, when interpreting treaties cannot and may not limit

[39] ILC, *Draft Articles on the Law of Treaties with Commentaries*, II:225, para. 7.

[40] See Hardy, 'The Interpretation of Plurilingual Treaties by International Courts and Tribunals', 126, 133–34, however, wrongly applied to cases in which a prevailing text exists, see Chapter 6, s. 6.2; Engelen, *Interpretation of Tax Treaties under International Law*, 545–46; Mössner, 'Die Auslegung mehrsprachiger Staatsverträge', 282; Kuner, 'The Interpretation of Multilingual Treaties', 961, with reference to M. Hudson, *International Legislation* (1971), vol. V, x; Michael Edwardes-Ker, *Tax Treaty Interpretation*, 1994, Ch. 20, 215, forcefully: 'Because Article 33 of the VCLT provides that each authenticated version of a plurilingual treaty is equally authoritative, all such versions should always be interpreted – because they all comprise one composite treaty.' This view has also been held by the Supreme Court of Kansas in *Johnson v Olson*, 92 Kan. 819 142 P. 256 (1914): 'The treaty must not only be construed as a whole, but where it is executed in two languages both are originals and must be construed together', as quoted by Kuner, 'The Interpretation of Multilingual Treaties', 955, 11n.

[41] ILC, *Summary Records of the Eighteenth Session, 4 May – 19 July 1966*, vol. I, Part II, Yearbook of the International Law Commission 1966, A/CN.4/SER.A/1966 (United Nations, 1967), 208–10, paras. 7–16.

himself to the version of the treaty written in his mother tongue; he must always refer to the foreign version as well.[42]

But, with reference to Engelen's research and position, he qualified his view in the 5th edition of his Commentary by inserting 'as soon as doubts arise' between the 'must' and the 'always'.[43]

In the preliminary general part of his Commentary, Wassermeyer seems to take the position that always all language texts have to be considered as long as they are authenticated;[44] however, he qualifies his view by stating

---

[42]Klaus Vogel, *Klaus Vogel on Double Taxation Conventions: A Commentary to the OECD, UN and US Model Conventions for the Avoidance of Double Taxation of Income and Capital; with Particular Reference to German Treaty Practice*, 3rd ed. (London: Kluwer, 1997), 38, para. 72.

[43]Klaus Vogel and Moris Lehner, eds., *Doppelbesteuerungsabkommen der Bundesrepublik Deutschland auf dem Gebiet der Steuern vom Einkommen und Vermögen: Kommentar auf der Grundlage der Musterabkommen*, 5th ed. (München: Beck, 2008), 141, para. 111, referring to Engelen, *Interpretation of Tax Treaties under International Law*, 384. This has been continued by the 6th German version, edited by Moris Lehner after Klaus Vogel's death, see Moris Lehner, ed., *Doppelbesteuerungsabkommen der Bundesrepublik Deutschland auf dem Gebiet der Steuern vom Einkommen und Vermögen: Kommentar auf der Grundlage der Musterabkommen (begründet von Klaus Vogel)*, 6th ed. (München: Beck, 2015), 196, para. 111. In contrast, the new 4th English edition still implements the wording of the 3rd English edition quoted above, equivalent to the 4th German edition, see Ekkehart Reimer and Alexander Rust, eds., *Klaus Vogel on Double Taxation Conventions*, 4th ed. (The Netherlands: Wolters Kluwer Law & Business, 2015), 40, para. 87; Klaus Vogel and Moris Lehner, eds., *Doppelbesteuerungsabkommen der Bundesrepublik Deutschland auf dem Gebiet der Steuern vom Einkommen und Vermögen: Kommentar auf der Grundlage der Musterabkommen*, 4th ed. (München: Beck, 2003), 151, para. 111. Whether this material difference of the new 4th English edition to the 5th and 6th German editions is intentional or merely the result of translating the respective paragraph in the introduction to the 4th German edition is not entirely obvious. In view of what the editors state in their preface, the latter seems more likely, however, not guaranteed: 'As from the 4th edition, the time for exact translations of the German book has elapsed, Klaus decided to separate the English from the German version and asked us to strive for a new Commentary – in the tradition of his previous English editions, but as an international endeavour with a higher degree of equidistance to national treaty practice and case law. ...The result is an almost entirely new book. With the exception of Klaus's *Introduction*, which of course has gained the status of a classic and has undergone only careful but minor updating, we have started anew. All important developments since 1997 have been integrated.'

[44]See Franz Wassermeyer, ed., *Doppelbesteuerung: Kommentar zu allen deutschen Doppel-*

in his Commentary on Article 3 of the OECD Model that because of the general presumption of all texts being congruent, it is justified to rely only on the text in the official language of the state applying the treaty as long as there is no concrete evidence for a divergence.[45]

3.3. The VCLT Framework

3.3.1. The Content of Article 33

Article 33 comprises four paragraphs. Paragraphs (1) to (3) enshrine the principle of unity. Paragraph (1) stipulates equal authority of all authenticated texts unless parties agree otherwise, while paragraph (2) provides that non-authenticated versions have equal authority only if parties agree so. Paragraph (3) is a presumption that the terms of the treaty have the same meaning in each text. The presumption is not based on empirical evidence but on the principle of unity; however, in contrast to the underlying principle itself, the presumption is fully rebuttable in view of q and paragraph (4), in the sense that the presumption ceases to be effective when there is a divergence between the texts.[46] In light of q and paragraph (4), paragraph (3) must be read as stating that the terms of the treaty ought to be assumed to have the same meaning except when, as a matter of fact, they do not. In the latter case some further interpretative effort is necessary to reconcile the texts and establish a common meaning under paragraph (4), which provides that the meaning that best reconciles the texts with regard to the object and purpose shall be adopted when a divergence cannot be resolved under the general rule of interpretation.[47]

In terms of a comparison of texts, this essentially implements the position of Special Rapporteur Sir Humphrey Waldock. Based on both conceptual and practical considerations, he argued against an explicit inclusion of

---

besteuerungsabkommen, vol. I (München: Beck, 2016), MA, Vor Art. 1, 37, para. 47.

[45]See ibid., MA, Art. 3, 54–55, para. 83.

[46]See Kuner, 'The Interpretation of Multilingual Treaties', 955; Peter Germer, 'Interpretation of Plurilingual Treaties: A Study of Article 33 of the Vienna Convention on the Law of Treaties', *Harvard International Law Journal* 11 (1970): 414; Mössner, 'Die Auslegung mehrsprachiger Staatsverträge', 300.

[47]Article 33(4) will be dealt with in detail in the next chapter.

such comparison among the principal means of interpretation. According to him, including it would be 'undermining the security of the individual texts' and for the most part only contribute to distort interpretation because of the inherent differences in languages. For this reason, each text should be interpreted in the context of its own language, and a comparative interpretation should be conducted only if in the course of such separate interpretation a problem in form of an ambiguity or divergence arises. In addition, he argued that the inclusion of a comparison would introduce additional practical difficulties and create an extra burden to the disadvantage of countries lacking the needed resources.[48]

Noteworthy, his conceptual argument emphasises p by pointing to the reality of q. It argues that in order to avoid two-way distortion of each text's meaning by idiosyncrasies of the other language transplanted out of context, it is essential to first interpret the texts separately according to their own idiomatic construction:

> It is one thing to admit interaction between two versions when each has been interpreted in accordance with its own genius and a divergence has appeared between them or an ambiguity in one of them. But it is another thing to attribute legal value to a comparison for the purpose of determining the ordinary meaning of the terms in the context of the treaty; for this may encourage attempts to transplant concepts of one language into the interpretation of a text in another language with a resultant distortion of the meaning.[49]

This does not reject the need for a comparative interpretation altogether, but only excludes it from the principal elements of interpretation and confines it to the point in time when interpretation of each text separately has been concluded and a problem between the outcomes remains. Thus, it is much more an argument concerning the mechanics of comparing texts than one against the necessity of such comparison in principle.

---

[48]See ILC, *Documents of the Second Part of the Seventeenth Session and of the Eighteenth Session Including the Reports of the Commission to the General Assembly*, II:100, para. 23; ILC, *Summary Records of the Eighteenth Session, 4 May – 19 July 1966*, I, Part II:211, para. 35.

[49]ILC, *Documents of the Second Part of the Seventeenth Session and of the Eighteenth Session Including the Reports of the Commission to the General Assembly*, II:100, para. 23.

3.3.2. The Prevailing View

Engelen has formulated the currently prevailing view in his seminal study on tax treaty interpretation.[50] Its fundamental proposition is that courts are not obliged to compare all texts but, based on Article 33(3), may rely on a single one for purposes of 'routine interpretation'.[51] Yet, this reliance should be exercised in good faith, that is, a single text may be relied on only until either an inclarity in the text used arises or a divergence between the texts is discovered.[52]

Engelen's own position seems to be more advanced. He recognises the risk that, as a consequence of the routine interpretation approach, textual divergences may be overlooked easily, which leads to misapplication of treaties. Therefore, contracting states may find themselves in the position of having violated their international obligations if it is established subsequently that the text relied on did not accurately reflect the treaty's meaning.[53]

Noteworthy, this risk is particularly high for tax treaties. In a normal state-state dispute under the jurisdiction of an international court each state will likely argue on the basis of the text in its own language, and the court will have to deal with the language issue automatically. A taxpayer-state dispute, however, arises within one state under the jurisdiction of that state's domestic courts. Hence, as a practical matter, if either party wants to gain support for its arguments from the other language text, it may have to bring it to the attention of the court. Engelen more or less ends with a warning in this respect and draws no further conclusions concerning the application of the VCLT rules to the interpretation of plurilingual tax treaties.

The question arises what exactly we are to understand by 'routine interpretation'. Neither the VCLT nor its Commentary distinguishes between different modes of interpretation according to which different principles would apply. There is only one combined 'General rule of interpretation' – the singular is declaratory in terms of substance.[54] In essence, the notion of 'routine interpretation' does not relate to any category of interpretation

---

[50]See Engelen, *Interpretation of Tax Treaties under International Law*, 384–88, 419, 546.
[51]Henceforth referred to as routine interpretation approach.
[52]See ibid., 388–90, 546.
[53]See ibid., 389–91.
[54]UN, *Vienna Convention on the Law of Treaties*, Article 31.

under international law but is a construct introduced by scholars.

Several authors echo the terminology explicitly,[55] whereas others merely paraphrase the theory behind it.[56] Waldock's argument in favour of relying on a single text until a 'difficulty arose' or, more precisely, until 'a divergence has appeared between them or an ambiguity in one of them' serves as the common point of departure.[57] Tabory refers to the 'absence of a specific problem' and provides a scheme of interpretative steps for which she distinguishes between a 'problem or lack of clarity' and a 'difference of meaning'.[58] Kuner points to the necessity of an 'allegation' to be made in terms of 'an ambiguity in one version or a difference among versions',[59] whereas Germer refers to an 'alleged divergence between the different authentic language versions of the treaty' only.[60] Gardiner contrasts scenarios 'where there is no reason to believe that there is any issue affected by the choice of language of the text which is being interpreted' to those when a 'difference or dispute over interpretation is presented to a court or tribunal', in which case a 'comparison of texts is likely to be essential.'[61] Hilf refers to 'inclarities' that appear and have to be resolved, or 'divergences' between the texts that appear in 'whatever way', have become 'visible', the party

---

[55]See Tabory, *Multilingualism in International Law and Institutions*, 198, 'routine understanding' at 196; Gardiner, *Treaty Interpretation*, 361; Kuner paraphrases the theory behind it, making use of the word 'routine', see Kuner, 'The Interpretation of Multilingual Treaties', 954; Arginelli summarises the arguments of a number of scholars quoting their terminology, see Arginelli, *The Interpretation of Multilingual Tax Treaties*, 248 et seq.

[56]See Hilf, *Die Auslegung mehrsprachiger Verträge*, 77; Germer, 'Interpretation of Plurilingual Treaties', 412.

[57]See ILC, *Summary Records of the Eighteenth Session, 4 May – 19 July 1966*, I, Part II:211, para. 35; ILC, *Documents of the Second Part of the Seventeenth Session and of the Eighteenth Session Including the Reports of the Commission to the General Assembly*, II:100, para. 23. This immediately begs the question how a divergence – in contrast to an ambiguity – can 'arise' or 'appear' without it being raised by someone if only one text is looked at. The vague language and passive form often found with the proponents of the routine interpretation approach merely hides the underlying presupposition that the issue is essentially one of procedural law (discussed in depth below).

[58]Tabory, *Multilingualism in International Law and Institutions*, 196, 177.

[59]Kuner, 'The Interpretation of Multilingual Treaties', 954.

[60]See Germer, 'Interpretation of Plurilingual Treaties', 412.

[61]Gardiner, *Treaty Interpretation*, 360.

'stumbles on', or is 'confronted with'.[62] In his comprehensive treatment of the issue, he most thoroughly elaborates the crucial argument at the core of the routine interpretation approach, namely, that a state may be considered to have acted in line with its international obligations in good faith as long as it does not wilfully risk misapplication of the treaty by continuing to rely on a single text in the face of either inclarities or divergences.[63]

Drawing on Hilf, Engelen concludes that a single text can be relied on as long as its interpretation leads to a 'clear' and 'reasonable' result and no divergence 'has come to light', albeit under the risk that actual divergences between the texts may stay undetected, which bears the danger of treaty misapplication.[64] In this context, he implicitly connects the criterion of clarity to the wording of Article 32(a) and (b) for defining its scope and concludes that when the interpretation of a single text under the general rule of interpretation leads to an ambiguous, obscure, absurd, or unreasonable result, the interpreter first has to refer to the other text(s) before having recourse to supplementary means:

> In conclusion, it is submitted that, when the interpretation of any one au-
> thentic text in accordance with Article 31 VCLT leaves the meaning ambigu-
> ous or obscure or leads to a manifestly absurd or unreasonable result, the
> Vienna Convention system of interpretation and, in particular, the principle
> of good faith requires the interpreter to first have recourse to the other au-
> thentic texts in order to determine the meaning before recourse is had for
> this purpose to the supplementary means of interpretation mentioned in
> Article 32 VCLT.[65]

In summary, the fundamental proposition of the routine interpretation approach is that any party to a treaty may in good faith rely on any single text in isolation as long as the following two conditions are fulfilled:

c_1: The text relied on is clear.
c_2: There is no divergence between the texts.

---

[62]Hilf, *Die Auslegung mehrsprachiger Verträge*, 72, 77, 80, 82.

[63]See ibid., 77–82, discussed in more detail in Chapter 7, s. 7.6, in the context of state responsibility.

[64]See Engelen, *Interpretation of Tax Treaties under International Law*, 390–91.

[65]Ibid., 390.

3. Routine Interpretation: A Refutation

Regarding condition c_1, I agree with Engelen that clarity is to be defined in terms of an interpretation under Article 31 not leaving the meaning ambiguous or obscure or leading to a result that is manifestly absurd or unreasonable, that is, the scope of clarity is demarcated by Article 32(a) and (b), or else the attribution of different weights by the VCLT to the different means of interpretation would be upset. A wider colloquial definition of inclarity that would imply a treaty could be classified as unclear before all texts have been consulted to elucidate its meaning, and that recourse to supplementary means to determine the treaty meaning could in consequence be had before looking at the other texts, does not find representation in Articles 31–33.[66] All texts are per definition of context under Article 31(2) authentic means of interpretation, and supplementary means may be used to establish the treaty meaning only in case an interpretation considering all authentic means leaves the meaning ambiguous or obscure, or leads to an absurd or unreasonable result. Apart from that, supplementary means may be used only to confirm but not contest the meaning arrived at under Article 31.

Regarding condition c_2, some authors stress the importance of a divergence being alleged by a party to the dispute. Engelen refers to the ICJ decision on the territorial dispute between Libyan Arab Jamahiriya and Chad, which seems to follow this rationale:

> The Treaty was concluded in French and Arabic, both texts being authentic; the Parties have not suggested that there is any divergence between the French and Arabic texts. ...The Court will base its interpretation of the Treaty on the authoritative French text.[67]

For additional support he quotes the American Law Institute, according to which courts 'may consider any convenient text unless an argument is addressed to some other text'.[68] This line of argument will be subject to in-

---

[66] This will be discussed in detail in the next chapter, s. 4.4.2.

[67] *Territorial Dispute (Libyan Arab Jamahiriya/Chad)*, ICJ (Annual Reports of the International Court of Justice, 1994), 6; Engelen, *Interpretation of Tax Treaties under International Law*, 388–89.

[68] The American Law Institute, *Restatement of the Law Third: The Foreign Relations Law of the United States*, vol. 1, 1987, 199, para. 2; see Engelen, *Interpretation of Tax Treaties under International Law*, 384–85. Noteworthy, this stance marks a departure by the American Law Institute and US Secretary of State from their previously held views, see

depth considerations below; however, we may record already that the suggestion does not necessarily correspond to the wordings of Article 33(1) and (4), which only refer to cases of divergence in general and differences in meaning disclosed by a comparison of the texts, that is, to instances when some kind of divergence exists, without delimiting the ways this has been established or specifying who has instigated a comparison.

3.3.3. Critique of the Prevailing View

In the opinion of the proponents of the routine interpretation approach, Article 33 as a whole contains no obligation to conduct a comparison when the text interpreted is clear, but the interpreter may rely in such case on the presumption in Article 33(3) as long as no divergence rebuts it. The argument rests on the absence of any divergence but remains silent as to how that condition has been established. Unlike an inclarity, however, a divergence might not come to the attention of the interpreter without a comparison of texts.[69] In order for the argument of the routine interpretation approach to be valid, it must be the case that the presumption actually gets rebutted whenever a divergence rebutting it exits, or else reliance on the presumption does not work as presupposed by the routine interpretation approach. Hence, we may test its validity for the case of tax treaties with the help of a simple thought experiment. The fundamental theorem looks as follows:

> **Proposition r_1:** Based on the presumption in Article 33(3), states may in good faith rely on any single text in isolation if no cases exist or can be conceived in which a divergence necessarily stays undisclosed while interpretation of the text chosen leads to a clear result.
> **Proposition r_2:** Such cases exist or can be conceived for tax treaties.
> **Conclusion r_1+r_2:** States cannot in good faith rely on any single text in isolation; for tax treaties the presumption in Article 33(3) is rebutted by default, and courts are obliged to compare all texts under Article 31(1) and (2), as they are part of the context.

Kuner, 'The Interpretation of Multilingual Treaties', 955, with reference to *Restatement (Second) of Foreign Relations Law of the United States*, §147(1)(i), 1965, and G. Hackworth, *Digest of International Law* (1927), vol. V, 265.

[69]See Tabory, *Multilingualism in International Law and Institutions*, 199; Kuner, 'The Interpretation of Multilingual Treaties', 958.

3. Routine Interpretation: A Refutation

If we accept r_1, the argument hinges on r_2. For purposes of the following discussion, it is assumed that the reader will agree with r_1, so that an extensive discussion of the principle of good faith and its application, which lies beyond the scope of this study, is unnecessary.[70] It is difficult to delineate the scope of good faith in its application as a legal principle, because it rests on the broader and less tangible moral concepts of honesty, fairness, and reasonableness.[71] Hence, there may be room to contest r_1. Notwithstanding, interpretation in good faith is an essential element of the *pacta sunt servanda* rule if that rule 'is to have any real meaning'[72] – all rights and obligations under the treaty must, in their spirit as well as according to their letter, be put into effect by the parties to the best of their abilities.[73]

Rejecting r_1 would result in a softening of this legal obligation if we must concede that correct interpretation is a matter of chance. As acknowledged by the drafters of the VCLT themselves, divergences between texts of plurilingual treaties are not a remote contingency but a considerable empirical reality, if not even to be assumed a necessary result of the 'different genius of the languages' a priori.[74] This implicitly rejects Hilf's and Engelen's argument that states must be considered to conform to their international responsibilities in good faith unless they wilfully ignore divergences, in the sense that they might have a point if undetected divergences were a remote contingency, but not when the existence of undetected divergences must be considered systemic, in which case not consulting the other texts is as good as wilfully ignoring divergences.

On the basis of the *Natexis* case discussed by Arruda Ferreira and Trindade Marinho,[75] the thought experiment conceived above can be conducted to show that r_2 is fulfilled for tax treaties. Imagine a bilingual

---

[70]For in-depth considerations, see Engelen, *Interpretation of Tax Treaties under International Law*, 33–34, 124 et seq.; Arginelli, *The Interpretation of Multilingual Tax Treaties*, 154–58; Joseph F O'Connor, *Good Faith in International Trade* (Aldershot: Dartmouth Publishing Co. Ltd., 1991), Ch. 8.

[71]See Engelen, *Interpretation of Tax Treaties under International Law*, 123.

[72]ILC, *Draft Articles on the Law of Treaties with Commentaries*, II:219, para. 5.

[73]See Villiger, *Commentary on the 1969 Vienna Convention on the Law of Treaties*, 363–68.

[74]See ILC, *Draft Articles on the Law of Treaties with Commentaries*, II:225, para. 6.

[75]Conseil d'État, *Société Natexis Banques Populaires v France*; Arruda Ferreira and Trindade Marinho, 'Tax Sparing and Matching Credit'.

treaty the two texts of which are based on the OECD Model, but one says 'subject to tax' where the other says 'liable to tax', all other things being equal. Both wordings are sufficiently unambiguous but mean different things, namely, a tax is effectively paid versus a tax may potentially be paid. This divergence between the texts will not disclose itself by looking at one text in isolation, because the avoidance of double taxation as object and purpose is not unequivocal in this respect: both subject and liable to tax avoid double taxation. Therefore, interpretation of each text in isolation under Article 31 may lead to two conflicting meanings, each of which may be regarded as manifest and applicable by the judge if considered only by itself.

Natexis may be considered a case exemplifying this. The issue raised by it, that is, the difference in meaning between the Portuguese *incidido* and the French *supporté*, is akin to the issue of difference in meaning between liable and subject to tax in the OECD Model.[76] Arguably, what happened in *Natexis* is that the divergence resulted in the French text failing to convey the full scope of the treaty's object and purpose. Alternatively, the conclusion may be that the Conseil d'État simply made a mistake by missing the true point of the object and purpose when interpreting the tax sparing clause,[77] provided that one agrees with the contention of the present author and the authors Arruda Ferreira and Trindade Marinho that the court interpreted the treaty wrongly.[78] In any case, it is safe to assume that there

---

[76]See Arruda Ferreira and Trindade Marinho, 'Tax Sparing and Matching Credit', 411, 92n.

[77]See ibid., 413.

[78]*Natexis* is not a case for which the position of the court could be defended by the reasoning that if one of two texts has a wider meaning, the court should adopt the narrower one that harmonises with both texts and is doubtless in accordance with the common intention, as applied by the PCIJ in *The Mavrommatis Palestine Concessions*, PCIJ (Publications of the Permanent Court of International Justice 1922–1946, 1924). First, in *Mavrommatis* the court did not intend to lay down a general rule, but the restrictive interpretation applied was considered appropriate only for that particular case, see ILC, *Draft Articles on the Law of Treaties with Commentaries*, 225, para. 8. Second, the reasoning per se is hardly appropriate in a case of subject versus liable to tax. The more restrictive subject to tax does not necessarily harmonise the intentions of the parties: although it is included in the wider liable to tax, it sometimes means the opposite. This will be discussed in more detail in the next chapter, s. 4.3.2. In respect of Conseil d'État, *Ministre du Budget c Ragazzacci*, 2012, which may serve as a counterexample to *Natexis*,

would have been a bigger chance for a different interpretation of the treaty if the court had looked into the Portuguese text. In the same vein, it is safe to assume that a Brazilian court interpreting the treaty would have reached a different conclusion from the Conseil d'État merely by departing from the Portuguese text. Such outcome is not in line with the objective of common interpretation,[79] which is inherent in the principle of unity.[80] Since the Portuguese text was not considered in *Natexis*,[81] the question arises as to what might happen if another French taxpayer claims the tax sparing credit in a French court, now based on the divergence disclosed by the authors Ar-

---

the object and purpose may be considered to have satisfactorily solved the issue of liable versus subject to tax. With reference to the object and purpose being the avoidance of double taxation, the Counsel d'Etat applied the English text and denied a refund of the *avoir fiscal*, a granting of which would have led to double non-taxation because the taxpayer would not have been subject to any tax in the UK on non-remitted dividends. This differs from the *Natexis* scenario because there is still a difference between unintended double non-taxation and intended double exemption, which is particularly important in the context of *Natexis* and the respective tax sparing clause, the meaning of which does not necessarily disclose itself if only the text saying 'subject to tax' is considered, because the object and purpose of a treaty is primarily to be obtained from the text of the treaty, consistent with the textual approach to interpretation prescribed by the VCLT, see Sinclair, *The Vienna Convention on the Law of Treaties*, 118. Even if the treaty also states avoidance of abuse to be its goal, not all cases of double non-taxation must necessarily be considered avoidance cases, see Ingo Jankowiak, *Doppelte Nichtbesteuerung im internationalen Steuerrecht* (Baden-Baden: Nomos, 2009), passim.

[79]See OECD, *Model Tax Convention*, 2017, 'Introduction', para. 5; Vogel and Lehner, *Doppelbesteuerungsabkommen der Bundesrepublik Deutschland auf dem Gebiet der Steuern vom Einkommen und Vermögen: Kommentar auf der Grundlage der Musterabkommen*, 142–45, paras. 113–120; Philip Baker, *Double Taxation Conventions: A Manual on the OECD Model Tax Convention on Income and on Capital* (Sweet & Maxwell, Limited, 2001), pt. E. 26.

[80]See Vogel, *Klaus Vogel on Double Taxation Conventions*, 41, para. 75a; Reimer and Rust, *Klaus Vogel on Double Taxation Conventions*, 43, para. 93.

[81]It should be mentioned that France is not a signatory to the VCLT. Notwithstanding, the principles of treaty interpretation enshrined in the VCLT may be considered part of the corpus of customary international law. Consequently, they may be considered applicable also to countries that are not a party to the VCLT, see Philippe Martin, 'Courts and Tax Treaties in Civil Law Countries', in *Courts and Tax Treaty Law* (Amsterdam: IBFD, 2007), 4; Avery Jones, 'Interpretation of Tax Treaties', 75; *Fothergill v Monarch Airlines Ltd.*, 282; *Thiel v Federal Commissioner of Taxation*, [1990] 171 CLR 338, 356. This will be discussed in more detail in Chapter 5, s. 5.5.

ruda Ferreira and Trindade Marinho. If this taxpayer – unlike *Société Natexis Banques Populaires* – would receive the credit with reference to the Portuguese text, the result would be two differing court decisions and two different tax treatments for taxpayers in the same situation on exactly the same issue, that is, there would be a fragmentation of jurisprudence and, likely, a breach of domestic principles of equality.

Now, although we may indeed argue that an ambiguity of a single text necessitates reference to the others (as is acknowledged by the proponents of the routine interpretation approach),[82] we cannot make the *argumentum a contrario* (argument from the contrary). It does not necessarily follow from the mere fact of the text used being clear that we may regard its meaning as the applicable one, because that mere fact alone tells us nothing about the other texts and their meaning. The Young Loan Arbitration tribunal has established in this regard that we may not rely on the clearer text automatically because the meaning of the clearer text may not be the correct one in the light of the object and purpose.[83] Hence, without investigation whether it portrays the correct meaning, giving primacy to one text from the outset on grounds of it being more clear violates the principle of unity.[84]

It also violates the principle of effectiveness enshrined in the maxim *ut res magis valeat quam pereat* (it is better for a thing to have effect than to be made void), which has a double implication: teleological interpretations rendering the text ineffective must be ruled out; however, because the treaty must be understood to be intended to achieve some purpose, any interpretation failing to achieve that purpose is equally incorrect.[85] Thus, if there are divergences between the texts of a treaty, we may not automatically assume that the clearer one more accurately reflects the intended meaning.

---

[82]See Engelen, *Interpretation of Tax Treaties under International Law*, 388–90; Gardiner, *Treaty Interpretation*, 360.

[83]See *The Kingdom of Belgium, the French Republic, the Swiss Confederation, the United Kingdom and the United States of America v The Federal Republic of Germany*, Arbitral Tribunal for the Agreement on German External Debts (Reports of International Arbitral Awards, 1980), 110, para. 40.

[84]See Sinclair, *The Vienna Convention on the Law of Treaties*, 150–51.

[85]See ILC, *Draft Articles on the Law of Treaties with Commentaries*, II:219, para. 6; Malgosia Fitzmaurice, 'The Practical Working of the Law of Treaties', in *International Law*, ed. Malcolm D. Evans (Oxford; New York: Oxford University Press, 2003), 202.

The clearer meaning may be more unequivocal with respect to static semantics, that is, it may be well-formed regarding syntax and have *a* clear meaning; however, that meaning may not necessarily be the true semantic meaning because there is a difference between meaning and reference: the meaning of a term is not necessarily congruent with its referent.[86]

Article 16 of the OECD Model may serve as an example: texts based on the English version of the Model will use the term 'board of directors', whereas texts based on the French version will read *counsel d'administration ou de surveillance* instead. Similarly, texts based on the German translation will read *Verwaltungs– und Aufsichtsrat*. The French and German terminology corresponds to the respective French and German two-tier board systems of corporate organisation, whereas the English wording corresponds to Anglo-Saxon style one-tier board systems. Hence, if each text is considered only by itself without a comparative perspective, they may be understood to refer to two distinct realities. If we assume treaties with English and French or English and German texts with precisely these properties and underlying one-tier and two-tier board systems, each seems to have a clear meaning in terms of static semantics when considered only by itself, because the terms 'board of directors', *counsel d'administration ou de surveillance,* and *Verwaltungs- und Aufsichtsrat* refer to clearly defined sets of persons under domestic law;[87] however, they do not necessarily refer to the same set, and their referents may not correspond to the meaning to be established by reconciling the meaning of the texts under Article 33(4).[88]

Now, if we may not assume that the clearer text more accurately reflects the meaning when divergences between the texts have arisen, we may also not assume that the text we are looking at conveys the one true meaning of

---

[86]See Frege, 'Über Sinn und Bedeutung', 25–50; Hilary Putnam, 'Meaning and Reference', *The Journal of Philosophy* 70, no. 19 (August 1973): 699–711. Reference merely consists in 'a relation that obtains between certain sorts of representational tokens (e.g. names, mental states, pictures) and objects', Marga Reimer and Eliot Michaelson, 'Reference', in *The Stanford Encyclopedia of Philosophy*, ed. Edward N. Zalta, Summer ed. (Stanford University, 2016), before Introduction.

[87]The term 'member of the board of directors' is not defined in the OECD Model; therefore, it has to be interpreted according to domestic law 'unless the context otherwise requires', OECD, *Model Tax Convention*, 2017, Article 3(2).

[88]See Vogel, *Klaus Vogel on Double Taxation Conventions*, 956–57.

the treaty merely because it is clear, even if no divergence has been raised. Therefore, all texts must be compared to ensure that they provide the same meaning even though each of them may convey *a* clear meaning when considered only by itself.[89] With its interpretation of the presumption in Article 33(3), the routine interpretation approach creates a kind of interpreter's paradox concerning the interpretation of plurilingual treaties, analogous to Erwin Schrödinger's famous thought experiment colloquially known as 'Schrödinger's cat':[90] without a comparison, the interpreter cannot know whether a divergence exists and, consequently, cannot know whether he is required to conduct a comparison because the presumption in Article 33(3) must be considered rebutted. This fundamental indeterminacy of the treaty meaning resolves only when the interpreter makes the comparison and discovers the meaning of all texts, that is, the interpreter's action determines the outcome. Therefore, the meaning of a single text interpreted in isolation may not be considered clear in the sense of conveying the one true meaning of the treaty. It may appear clear, but it remains indeterminate as long as all texts have not been compared.[91] In the words of Lord Wilberforce (by analogy but nevertheless pertinent):

> There it is not only permissible to look at a foreign language text, but obligatory. What is made part of English law is the text set out 'in the First Schedule', i.e. in both Part I and Part II, so both English and French texts must be looked at. *Furthermore, it cannot be judged whether there is an inconsistency between two texts unless one looks at both.*[92]

In summary, the fundamental proposition of the routine interpretation approach may be considered valid and sound only when c_1 and c_2 are both true. As formulated by its proponents, its stronger form presupposes that 'if c_1, then c_2', while its weaker form considers it sufficient for the fundamental proposition to be valid when c_1 is true as long as nobody contests c_2. Both forms suffer from failure to acknowledge that c_2 does not follow

---

[89]See Lang, 'Auslegung von Doppelbesteuerungsabkommen und authentische Vertragssprachen', 405.

[90]See Erwin Schrödinger, 'Die gegenwärtige Situation in der Quantenmechanik', *Die Naturwissenschaften* 23, no. 48 (1935): 807–12.

[91]See Mössner, 'Die Auslegung mehrsprachiger Staatsverträge', 301.

[92]*Fothergill v Monarch Airlines Ltd.*, 272 (emphasis added).

analytically from c_1 a priori, but whether c_2 is true is a matter independent from c_1 and subject to empirical evidence. Therefore, the implicit presumption of the routine interpretation approach in terms of the stronger form is invalid as long as c_2 is not established empirically by a comparison of all texts. As regards the weaker form, such would treat the proposition 'if c_1, then c_2' as a natural assumption subject only to a contingency of c_2 to be false, justifying not to look into the matter of whether c_2 is true as long as nobody contests it. But, as is also established case law,[93] c_1 is not sufficient to justify the fundamental proposition of the routine interpretation approach by itself, because clarity of a single text considered in isolation is not a sufficient criterion under the VCLT framework of interpretation. In addition, the thought experiment conducted has shown that, at least for tax treaties, failure of c_2 to be true cannot be considered a mere contingency to be safely neglected in good faith until proven otherwise, but must be considered a systemic problem. Therefore, an assumption for c_2 to be true without further investigation cannot be considered sound practice in view of Article 26 VCLT.

3.4. The Impact of Domestic Procedural Law

The question arises whether procedural law has any bearing on the matter, that is, whether the argument brought forward may depend to some extent on the legal system from which one is departing.[94] In a state-state dispute under the jurisdiction of an international court, both parties are prone to argue on the basis of their own language text. Tax proceedings, however, are taxpayer-state disputes under the jurisdiction of the national courts of one contracting state. Therefore, both parties have an incentive to argue on the basis of the text in that state's official language and, if the routine interpretation approach is accepted, are less prone to look at the other text(s).

---

[93] See *Young Loan Arbitration*, 110, para. 40.

[94] In this section, the issue is discussed from the perspective of international law. Regardless of the conclusions, the anatomy of the current international tax system with national courts presiding over disputes that include international aspects remains to have an important impact on the application of tax treaties in practice. Therefore, Chapter 7 will return to the matter from the domestic law perspective.

In consequence, it less likely that divergences are raised while it is not less likely that they exist.

Given this, the issue in question is whether the presiding court is under an obligation to compare all texts, under no obligation but free to do so or not, or prevented from comparing all texts. Based on all the aforesaid, my conclusion has been strongly in support of the first. The view traditionally advanced by scholars (which underlies the routine interpretation approach) is that the answer depends on domestic procedural law and, in particular, on whether and to what extent the court has to apply the law *ex officio* (by right of office) subject to the principle of *iura novit curia* (the court knows the law).[95]

The role of courts and the implementation of *iura novit curia* differs between jurisdictions and, in particular, between civil and common law.[96] In common law countries, the job of courts seems to be to decide disputes on the basis of the arguments put before them. Although courts are not precluded from raising arguments about something that the parties have not pleaded and will do so concerning matters of public interest,[97] it seems

---

[95]Parties do not need to plead the law, but it is the duty of the court to apply the appropriate legal rules to the dispute brought before it, irrespective of what is pleaded by the parties, see Mattias Derlén, *Multilingual Interpretation of European Union Law* (Kluwer Law International, 2009), 315 et seq; Lisa Spagnolo, 'Iura Novit Curia and the CISG: Resolution of the Faux Procedural Black Hole', in *Towards Uniformity: The 2nd Annual MAA Schlechtriem CISG Conference*, ed. Lisa Spagnolo and Ingeborg Schwenzer (The Hague: Eleven International Publishing, 2011), 183; Lang, 'The Interpretation of Tax Treaties and Authentic Languages', 20–21.

[96]See Frederick A. Mann, 'Fusion of the Legal Professions?', *Law Quarterly Review* 93 (1977): 369; Derlén, *Multilingual Interpretation of European Union Law*, 315. According to Jacobs, however, a stark contrast between civil and common law in this respect is misplaced, but the issue is rather one of degree between different jurisdictions, both civil and common law, see *Van Schijndel and van Veen v SPF, Opinion of Advocate General Jacobs*, Joined Cases C–430/93 and C–431/93 (ECR I–4705, 1995), paras. 33–35, 41. Spagnolo suggests that 'some version of *iura novit curia* exists in all jurisdictions. Judges are presumed to know and empowered to apply the law, or at least the domestic law. A "strict" approach to *iura novit curia* obliges the court to *ex officio* identify and apply the substantive law it considers applicable to the case. A "soft" approach to *iura novit curia* authorizes this, but does not demand it', Spagnolo, 'Iura Novit Curia and the CISG', 185–186.

[97]For example, courts will refuse to enforce illegal contracts, see *Bank of India v Trans*

not to be meaningful to suggest that they are legally obliged in this respect.

We may reformulate the routine interpretation approach accordingly: Since the VCLT contains a presumption that 'The terms of the treaty...have the same meaning in each authentic text',[98] but no explicit instruction for the judge to establish the truth of that presumption – only directions what to do once the presumption has been rebutted, the duty to rebut the presumption is not covered by the VCLT but an issue to be determined under domestic procedural law.[99] Consequently, as long as domestic procedural law attributes a passive role to the court presiding, failure of the parties to the dispute to claim not-c_2 is as good as c_2 being true, and the judge may in good faith rely on c_1 alone to justify application of the routine interpretation approach, that is, Article 33(3) may be understood to sanction treaty interpretation on the basis of a single text in isolation as long as that text is clear and nobody comes along to displace the presumption.

Formulated like this, the proposition appears valid, however, disturbing on several accounts. As has been acknowledged by the drafters of the VCLT, divergences must be expected to constitute the rule not the exception.[100] Therefore, such reliance on the presumption contained in Article 33(3) downplays q and the need to defuse it via interpretation, basing itself on the exception rather than the rule, which per se does not inspire confidence in the interpretation effort. As we have seen, clarity of a single text by itself is not a sufficient criterion to rely on for purposes of interpretation

---

Continental Commodity Merchants Ltd. & J. N. Patel, [1982] 1 Lloyd's Rep. 427, 429, per Bingham J.; *Singh Butra v Ebrahim*, [1982] 2 Lloyd's Rep. 11, C.A., 13, per Lord Denning; *United City Merchants v Royal Bank of Canada*, [1983] AC 168, HL, 189, per Lord Diplock; *Van Schijndel and van Veen v SPF, Opinion of Advocate General Jacobs*, para. 35; Trevor C. Hartley, 'Pleading and Proof of Foreign Law: The Major European Systems Compared', *International and Comparative Law Quarterly* 45 (1996): 288; Rainer Hausmann, 'Pleading and Proof of Foreign Law – a Comparative Analysis', *The European Legal Forum*, Section I, no. 1 (2008): 6. Hence, according to Spagnolo, it may be more correct to characterise this not as absence but a soft implementation of *iura novit curia*, see Spagnolo, 'Iura Novit Curia and the CISG', 186.

[98]UN, *Vienna Convention on the Law of Treaties*, Article 33(3).

[99]See, by analogy, Spagnolo, 'Iura Novit Curia and the CISG', 184.

[100]See ILC, *Draft Articles on the Law of Treaties with Commentaries*, II:225, para. 6; Hilf, *Die Auslegung mehrsprachiger Verträge*, 24; Hardy, 'The Interpretation of Plurilingual Treaties by International Courts and Tribunals', 82.

under the VCLT framework. The outcome may be that 'the tribunal may find itself interpreting a text on the faulty assumption that it reflects the meaning of the treaty as a whole, when in fact it contradicts the intended meaning.'[101] Consequently, such approach weakens *p* and fails to consistently serve the *pacta sunt servanda* rule in practice.

In addition, since national procedural rules vary, so will outcomes. Depending on whether and to what extent the principle *iura novit curia* is implemented in domestic procedural law, the presiding court may consider itself to be obliged, free, or prohibited to refer to the other texts.[102] Against this state of affairs speaks that if tax treaties must be presumed to be 'intended to reconcile national fiscal legislations and to avoid the simultaneous taxation in both countries',[103] which necessitates some degree of common interpretation,[104] the realisation of such goal cannot be partly imposed on the taxpayer (who is not even party to the treaty) but should be the full responsibility of the courts of the contracting states because it must be considered the duty of the court presiding to prove beyond reasonable doubt that its authoritative interpretation is the correct one.[105] As Kuner observes, 'if states are to see any value in concluding treaties, then the primary goal of interpretation must be to reach a correct evaluation of their intent as

---

[101] Tabory, *Multilingualism in International Law and Institutions*, 199.

[102] See, by analogy, Spagnolo, 'Iura Novit Curia and the CISG', 183–84.

[103] Raoul Lenz, 'Report on the Interpretation of Double Taxation Conventions' (International Fiscal Association, 1960), 294.

[104] See Vogel and Lehner, *Doppelbesteuerungsabkommen der Bundesrepublik Deutschland auf dem Gebiet der Steuern vom Einkommen und Vermögen: Kommentar auf der Grundlage der Musterabkommen*, 142–45, paras. 113–120; Klaus Vogel and Rainer Prokisch, 'Interpretation of Double Taxation Conventions', General Report (Rotterdam: International Fiscal Association, 1993), 62–63; Ekkehart Reimer, 'Seminar F: Die sog. Entscheidungsharmonie als Maßstab für die Auslegung von Doppelbesteuerungsabkommen', *Internationales Steuerrecht*, no. 15 (2008): 554, s. 4.3; Klaus Vogel, 'Über Entscheidungsharmonie', in *Unternehmen Steuern: Festschrift für Hans Flick zum 70. Geburtstag*, ed. Franz Klein et al. (Köln: Dr. Otto Schmidt Verlag KG, 1997), 1055–6; Hans Flick, 'Zur Auslegung von Normen des Internationalen Steuerrechts', in *Von der Auslegung und Anwendung der Steuergesetze*, ed. Günther Felix, Festschrift für Armin Spitaler (Stuttgart: C.E. Poeschel, 1958), 158.

[105] This certainly applies in countries where the court is supposed to apply the law *ex officio* subject to the principle *iura novit curia*, see Lang, 'Auslegung von Doppelbesteuerungsabkommen und authentische Vertragssprachen', 405–6.

expressed in the treaty.'[106]

Not only outcomes will differ but, depending on their domestic procedural law, the burden of interpretation is divided unevenly between countries. Those that do not (or only softly) implement *iura novit curia* are sanctioned to favour the text in their own official language and disregard the others, which in substance violates the equal authenticity of all texts declared by the treaty. If this leads to a situation that each treaty partner applies only its own text and a divergence between the texts is not detected simultaneously by both treaty partners, the treaty will be split into two sets of terms in violation of the principle of unity.

Results will vary not only between the contracting states but also within jurisdictions. Two decisions of the same court on equivalent facts fulfilled by two different taxpayers may differ if the taxpayer in the later procedure raises the issue of a relevant divergence, whereas the taxpayer in the earlier one had failed to do so. Such fragmentation of jurisprudence may be questionable in view of applicable domestic law principles of equality and legal certainty in the context of a general mission of courts to ensure consistency in the application of law, as for example is the case for the Dutch Hoge Raad, the German BFH, the French Conseil d'Etat, the Belgian Cour de Cassation/Hof van Cassatie, and the US Tax Court.[107]

In view of all this, the question arises whether the fundamental proposition of the routine interpretation approach as reformulated above is sound. When deciding the dispute as brought before it by the parties, the court has to ensure that the international obligations covered by the treaty are observed,[108] not only the law as argued by the parties. Failure to correctly

---

[106]Kuner, 'The Interpretation of Multilingual Treaties', 962.

[107]See Peter J. Wattel, 'Tax Litigation in Last Instance in the Netherlands: The Tax Chamber of the Supreme Court', *Bulletin for International Taxation* 70, nos. 1 – 2 (December 2015), s. 2.1; Rudolf Mellinghoff, 'The German Federal Fiscal Court: An Overview', *Bulletin for International Taxation* 70, no. 1/2 (December 2015), ss. 2.2–2.3, 3.2, 3.4, 4.5; Philippe Martin, 'The French Supreme Administrative Tax Court', *Bulletin for International Taxation* 70, no. 1 (2016), s. 3; Martin, 'Courts and Tax Treaties in Civil Law Countries', 7–9; Myriam Ghyselen and Bernard Peeters, 'The Court of Cassation as the Supreme Body of the Judiciary in Belgium', *Bulletin for International Taxation* 70, nos. 1 – 2 (December 2015), s. 1.2; Keith Fogg, 'The United States Tax Court – A Court for All Parties', *Bulletin for International Taxation* 70, no. 1/2 (December 2015), s. 2.

[108]UN, *Vienna Convention on the Law of Treaties*, Article 26.

interpret the treaty will result in a breach of those obligations.[109] Hence, the primary concern for the court should be to apply the correct principles of interpretation. National procedural rules should be evaluated in respect of their compatibility with those principles. If the conclusion is in the negative, they must be discarded under Article 27 VCLT, which prohibits any party to 'invoke the provisions of its internal law as justification for its failure to perform a treaty.'

In other words, national procedural law may not limit the application of the VCLT principles of interpretation, but those principles take precedence. The extent to which domestic procedural rules may be applied legitimately is confined to the extent they do not impair the obligation of the contracting state to perform its duties under the treaty.[110] As pointed out by Lord Scarman (by analogy but nevertheless pertinent), 'We may not take refuge in our adversarial process, paying regard only to the English text, unless and until one or other of the parties leads evidence to establish an inconsistency with the French.'[111]

In summary, the applicable principles of interpretation are provided by the VCLT. If those principles require a comparison of all texts in order for them to be applied correctly, such is the duty of the court presiding over the dispute; absence of argument by the parties to the dispute invoking the other text(s) cannot affect such obligation.[112]

---

[109] Concerning our example based on the *Natexis* case, the real issue at stake is not that as a result of neglecting the other text the taxpayer is unduly taxed, but that the balance of taxing rights agreed on by the treaty partners and implemented via reciprocal restrictions of their sovereign taxing rights under the treaty is upset. In consequence, the tax sparing credit is soaked up by the residence state in violation of the treaty.

[110] See, by analogy, Spagnolo, 'Iura Novit Curia and the CISG', 190–97.

[111] *Fothergill v Monarch Airlines Ltd.*, 293 (emphasis added).

[112] Nollkaemper provides a good summery account of the argument concerning the obligation of national courts to apply the VCLT rules of interpretation: 'A first ground which can provide a justification for the application of international rules of interpretation in domestic courts is that such application may be an intrinsic part of the performance of international obligations. This obligation to perform a treaty in good faith is then extended to the principles of interpretation of treaties. There are two variations of this argument. A strong version would say that there is a freestanding obligation to apply international principles of interpretation (the *pacta sunt servanda* principle would then apply to the Vienna Convention …itself) and that this obligation would rest on

3. Routine Interpretation: A Refutation

Hence, we are back at the question of whether the interpretative framework of the VCLT requires a comparison of all texts in order to ensure the intended result, which has been answered in the affirmative for tax treaties. The VCLT does not explicitly state this requirement, but it follows from a valid combination of the supplied principles. All texts have to be compared to establish the one true meaning of the treaty because of the otherwise inherent indeterminacy attributable to an object and purpose that is not unequivocal in its application, wherefore clarity of any single text considered in isolation is not sufficient to ensure that the meaning so established effects what the parties to the treaty intended.

The fundamental proposition of the routine interpretation approach as reformulated, that the obligation to compare all texts is an entirely exogenous variable to be established under domestic procedural law because the VCLT is tacit in terms of explicit imperative language concerning such obligation, must be rejected as unsound in view of the dictum that every reasonable effort must be made to find a common meaning of all texts and no single text must be preferred over the others until such effort is fully exhausted.[113]

---

national courts. Article 26 of the VCLT stipulates that "every treaty in force" has to be performed in good faith – apparently not excluding the VCLT itself. Though the VCLT is not expressly drafted in terms of "obligations", it would seem that the entire rationale of the treaty is that states are not at liberty to apply or refrain from applying the provisions of the treaty. In that sense, the principles of interpretation, as a matter of obligation, have to be applied by states. …A weaker version of this argument is that while states …may not be obliged to give effect to principles of interpretation as a freestanding obligation, such principles inform the meaning and application of the primary norms. Application of such principles may then not be obligatory as such, but may be required to the extent that this would be necessary to ensure the effective application of the international norm subject to interpretation. A failure to give effect to an international obligation with the meaning and content it has at the international level may constitute a wrongful act, for giving effect to an international norm that is devoid of its international normative context may well be giving effect to a different norm', André Nollkaemper, 'Grounds for the Application of International Rules of Interpretation in National Courts', in *The Interpretation of International Law by Domestic Courts: Uniformity, Diversity, Convergence*, ed. Helmut Philipp Aust and Georg Nolte (Oxford; New York: Oxford University Press, 2016), 37–38. The issue of state responsibility will be discussed in detail in Chapter 7, s. 7.6.

[113] See ILC, *Draft Articles on the Law of Treaties with Commentaries*, II:225, para. 7. Article 2 DARS, which lists the elements of internationally wrongful acts, refers to the

3.5. A Refutation Based on General Hermeneutics

Above I have refuted the routine interpretation approach in respect of the specific principles codified in the VCLT. In this section I shall add a refutation based on general hermeneutics and the fundamental intention of the VCLT to establish the textual meaning of a treaty:[114]

---

breach of an obligation not a rule in letter (b). Its Commentary clarifies that 'What matters for these purposes is not simply the existence of a rule but its application in the specific case. ...The term "obligation" is commonly used in international judicial decisions and practice and in the literature to cover all the possibilities', ILC, *Draft Articles on Responsibility of States for Internationally Wrongful Acts, with Commentaries; Report of the Commission to the General Assembly on the Work of Its Fifty-Third Session,* Document A/56/10, vol. II, Part 2, Yearbook of the International Law Commission 2001, A/CN.4/SER.A/2001/Add.1 (United Nations, 2001), 36, para. 13.

[114] Although concerned with a particular type of texts that, to some extent, have their own logic, Articles 31–33 are not drafted as detailed technical instructions fundamentally different from normal techniques of interpretation, but as general 'principles of logic and good sense', which are merely supplemented by specific conventions regarding canonical means, see ILC, *Draft Articles on the Law of Treaties with Commentaries*, II:218–26. This raises the question whether and to what extent treaty hermeneutics may 'claim any independent systematic significance' from general hermeneutics, or whether the former must be regarded merely 'as a special application of' the latter, see Hans-Georg Gadamer, *Truth and Method*, trans. Joel Weinsheimer and Donald G. Marshall, 2nd ed. (London; New York: Continuum, 2004), 321, by analogy. Treaty hermeneutics displays some particular contours in this regard; however, the particularities that may be identified to distinguish interpretation of treaties from that of texts in general resemble accentuations rather than clear demarcations completely separating treaty from general hermeneutics. As pointed out by Arnold, 'The basic interpretive approach set out in Art. 31(1) should not strike anyone as novel. ...The same three major elements – the ordinary meaning of words (text), context, and purpose – form the foundation for the interpretation of language generally. Tax legislation and tax treaties are no different in this regard', Arnold, 'The Interpretation of Tax Treaties', 5. Therefore, a broader perspective may be instructive: the thought and methodologies generated by general hermeneutics may prove useful in the context of contemplating treaty interpretation, and a historical perspective concerning the development of hermeneutics as a discipline may enable us to better classify scholarly theories and reject overcome ideas. This is particularly so because the VCLT rules provide only a general framework; their application in detail is left to the interpreter, who is still required to apply a solid hermeneutic approach in general, see ILC, *Draft Articles on the Law of Treaties with Commentaries*, II:218, para. 4.

3. Routine Interpretation: A Refutation

> '[T]he ordinary meaning of a term is not to be determined in the abstract but in the context of the treaty and in the light of its object and purpose.'[115]

Accordingly, the meanings of terms in a treaty are not to be confused with their literal meaning but must be considered in their contextual relation to other terms in the text and the purposive structure of both the provisions they are part of and connected with, as well as the treaty as a whole.[116]

In its particular relation to treaty interpretation, this implements the idea of the hermeneutic circle, which has been introduced by Friedrich Schleiermacher in a series of lectures in the beginning of the 19th century.[117]

---

[115] ILC, *Draft Articles on the Law of Treaties with Commentaries*, II:221, para. 12.

[116] See *Temple of Preah Vihear (Cambodia v Thailand), Preliminary Objections*, 32: 'the Court considers that it must interpret Thailand's 1950 Declaration …as a whole and in the light of its known purpose, …words are to be interpreted according to their natural and ordinary meaning in the context in which they occur'; *Anglo-Iranian Oil Co. (United Kingdom v Iran)*, 104; *Inland Revenue Commissioners v Commerzbank*, 297–298, per Mummery J; *Memec Plc v Inland Revenue Comissioners*, [1998] STC 754, 766g; *Fothergill v Monarch Airlines Ltd*, 272, 279, 285, 290, 294, per Lords Wilberforce, Diplock, Fraser and Scarman; *Sportsman v IRC*, [1998] STC (SCD) 289, 293: 'There is no such thing as an abstract ordinary meaning of a phrase divorced from the place which that phrase occupies in the text to be interpreted'; Sinclair, *The Vienna Convention on the Law of Treaties*, 121; Avery Jones, 'Treaty Interpretation', s. 3.4.4. Regarding legal hermeneutics, this may be traced back to Roman law: '*Incivile est nisi tota lege perspecta una aliqua particula eius proposita iudicare vel respondere*' (it is unlawful to pass judgement or expert opinion according to any provision of a law without considering the whole law), see Okko Behrends et al., *Corpus Iuris Civilis II: Digesten 1-10*, 1st ed. (Heidelberg: C.F. Müller, 1995), 114. Concerning language in general, see Gottlob Frege, *Die Grundlagen der Arithmetik: eine logisch mathematische Untersuchung über den Begriff der Zahl* (Breslau: Verlag von Wilhelm Koebner, 1884), s. 62: 'Only in the context of a sentence do words have any meaning', translation by John Wallace, 'Only in the Context of a Sentence Do Words Have Any Meaning', *Midwest Studies in Philosophy* 2, no. 1 (1977): 144–46, 144; Wittgenstein, *Tractatus Logico-Philosophicus*, s. 3.3: 'Only the proposition has sense; only in the context of a proposition has a name meaning.'

[117] Friedrich D. E. Schleiermacher, *Hermeneutik und Kritik: mit besonderer Beziehung auf das Neue Testament* (Berlin: G. Reimer, 1838), 36–37, 39. Mantzavinos provides an English translation of one of Schleiermacher's formulations: 'that the same way that the whole is, of course, understood in reference to the individual, so too, the individual can only be understood in reference to the whole', C. Mantzavinos, 'Hermeneutics', in *The Stanford Encyclopedia of Philosophy*, ed. Edward N. Zalta, Fall ed. (Stanford University, 2016), s. 2. This is not intended to submit logically circular reasoning – the circle is but a

Schleiermacher's deliberations have been pivotal for the development of hermeneutics as a discipline: they mark the historical point at which the division into subject specific theoretical constructions is overcome and a general theory of hermeneutics as a fundamental discipline is developed.[118]

---

metaphor. In Schleiermacher's view, interpretation is a holistic task: all linguistic, psychological, and historical elements have to be considered together in light of each other. Single text passages can be understood only in the context of the text to which they belong, which in turn can be understood only in its overall context. The interpreter cannot consider everything all at once but has to begin somewhere, expand his focus, and work his way towards full comprehension. From reading single text passages he may develop a provisional understanding of them and, in their comparative consideration, the text as whole, which he may then refine by considerations of the psychological and historical context. The result may be reapplied to the individual passages to refine their interpretation, which in turn leads to an improved overall understanding, and so forth. Interpretation is thus a process of approximation that oscillates between contemplation of the parts and the whole in light of each other and gradually increases understanding along a spiral of interactive refinement – hence the image of a circle: 'Such holism introduces a pervasive circularity into interpretation, for, ultimately, interpreting these broader items in its turn depends on interpreting such pieces of text. Schleiermacher does not see this circle as vicious, however. Why not? His solution is not that all of these tasks should be accomplished simultaneously – for that would far exceed human capacities. Rather, it essentially lies in the (very plausible) thought that understanding is not an all-or-nothing matter but instead something that comes in *degrees*, so that it is possible to make progress toward full understanding in a piecemeal way', Michael Forster, 'Friedrich Daniel Ernst Schleiermacher', in *The Stanford Encyclopedia of Philosophy*, ed. Edward N. Zalta, Fall ed. (Stanford University, 2017), s. 4. The VCLT conception is very similar: treaty interpretation is to be regarded a holistic 'single combined operation' – all means are to be thrown into the 'crucible' and weighed by the interpreter in light of each other, see ILC, *Draft Articles on the Law of Treaties with Commentaries*, 219–220, para. 8. Of course, the court has to start somewhere. Typically, it begins with a consideration of the words, which are then analysed in an 'interactive process' in light of the other means, see ILC, 'Report of the International Law Commission on the Sixty-fifth Session, 6 May – 7 June and 8 July – 9 August 2013', Doc. A/68/10 (United Nations, December 2013), Ch. 4, 18, para. 14.

[118] Although important efforts to establish a *hermeneutica generalis* may be traced back several centuries before him to Dannhauer and others, Schleiermacher's work may be seen as the culmination of this process, see Böhl, Meinrad, Wolfgang Reinhard and Peter Walter, *Hermeneutik: die Geschichte der abendländischen Textauslegung von der Antike bis zur Gegenwart* (Böhlau Verlag Wien, 2013), passim; Joisten, Karen, *Philosophische Hermeneutik* (Berlin: Akademie Verlag GmbH, 2009), 17–18, 82, 96–97; Mantzavinos, 'Hermeneutics', Introduction.

3. Routine Interpretation: A Refutation

Schleiermacher distinguishes between a lax and a rigorous approach to interpretation. The lax approach departs from the idea that understanding happens automatically; its goal is merely the avoidance of misunderstanding. Conversely, the rigorous approach departs from the idea that misunderstanding happens automatically, whereas understanding must be actively pursued.[119] In consequence, the lax approach is content with an exegesis of single text passages that appear obscure and therefore remains an agglomeration of unconnected sporadic observations,[120] whereas the rigorous approach investigates texts in a systematic manner from the start, considering the meanings of all terms in their entire context.

Schleiermacher concludes that the lax approach does not qualify as a scientific method, but methodical interpretation must begin from the moment a reader wants to understand the content of a text, not only once he encounters passages that make him lose confidence about the level of his understanding, because when understanding blurs concerning specific passages, it is a sign that efforts to understand have been neglected beforehand in a more fundamental way. The ultimate goal of interpretation is to understand a text first as good as and finally better than its author.[121]

---

[119]Schleiermacher, *Hermeneutik und Kritik*, 29 et seq.

[120]An example of such approach in the legal context would be Vattel's view: 'The first general maxim of interpretation is, that *It is not allowable to interpret what has no need of interpretation.* When a deed is worded in clear and precise terms, – when its meaning is evident, and leads to no absurd conclusion, – there can be no reason for refusing to admit the meaning which such deed naturally presents. ...Since the sole object of the lawful interpretation of a deed ought to be the discovery of the thoughts of the author or authors of that deed, – *whenever we meet with any obscurity in it, we are to consider what probably were the ideas of those who drew up the deed, and to interpret it accordingly.* This is the general rule for all interpretations. It particularly serves to ascertain the meaning of particular expressions whose signification is not sufficiently determinate', de Vattel, *The Law of Nations*, ss. 263, 270. It is obvious how such would fail in the context of plurilingual treaties when interpreting a single text in isolation, mistaking its interpretation for the meaning of the treaty. As established above, clarity of a single text in isolation is no definitive criterion for the meaning of a plurilingual treaty in the absence of a prevailing text, see also *Young Loan Arbitration*, 110, para. 40.

[121]See Schleiermacher, *Hermeneutik und Kritik*, 32. According to Schleiermacher, every text is conceived and must be understood from a double perspective, namely, the totality of language and the totality of the author's thought process. From this he deduces two fundamental hermeneutic methods he labels 'grammatical' and 'psychological'. The

This conception resonates with the VCLT general rule of interpretation. The stipulation that the meaning of the treaty is not the literal but the ordinary meaning arrived at under an interpretation of its terms in good faith in their context and in the light of their object and purpose paraphrases Schleiermacher's rigorous approach to interpretation. Larenz and Canaris submit a similar conception concerning legal texts in general when they conclude that

> It would be a misconception to assume that legal texts would require interpretation only where they appear to be particularly 'dark', 'unclear', or 'contradictory'. Rather, *all* legal texts are, as a cardinal rule, both capable of being interpreted and in need of interpretation. Their need for interpretation is not a 'shortage' that could be remedied by efforts to draft an as precise as possible final version, but will remain for as long as not all legislation, court rulings, and even contracts will be drawn up exclusively in a symbolised sign language.[122]

Also Schleiermacher's formulated goal of understanding the text first as good as and finally better than its author resonates. Treaties are drafted in general terms to be applied to a wide variety of scenarios, which are not all imagined by the drafters in detail. When applying the treaty to the facts of a particular case, the judge first has to understand the intentions of the contracting states as expressed in the treaty text(s) as good as the contracting states themselves and finally better in the sense that he has to judge how these intentions should apply to particular circumstances the

---

first concerns understanding of an expression in relation to the language it is part of, while the second understands any utterance as part of a speakers life process. The grammatical method then attempts to understand a text on the basis of the total use of language by a given lingual community, employing linguistic and literary knowledge, while the psychological method attempts to duplicate the thought process of the author from a historical perspective, employing knowledge of the author's entire work as well as the work of his contemporaries in order to comprehend the entire background of the author's thinking. Both are equally important in understanding a text and, therefore, have to be employed on an equal footing in the interpretative process, as a result of which understanding a text better than its author becomes possible from a historical vantage point.

[122]Larenz and Canaris, *Methodenlehre der Rechtswissenschaft*, 26, with reference to Hart's 'open texture' argument, see Hart, *The Concept of Law*, 123.

contracting parties did not foresee.[123]

In contrast, the currently prevailing view concerning plurilingual treaty interpretation, that it is save to ignore the other language texts as long as no problem in form of an ambiguity or divergence arises, appears like a formulation of the lax approach. Certainly, any comparable suggestion would not be accepted as a sound method of interpretation in the discourse on general hermeneutics since Schleiermacher.[124]

3.6. Reliance on the Original Text

When judges are faced with a divergence between the texts of a treaty, the natural reflex may be to give preference to the one they can identify as the text of negotiation and drafting.[125] Scholars who have engaged in comparative studies of court decisions have identified such practice and provided comprehensive argument in its favour. Hardy leads the way: based on imperative reasoning, he concludes that in the case of incompatible texts there must be an obvious drafting error. Such would not justify declaring the treaty as defective, but only the text with the error. It would then be normal

---

[123]See Gadamer, *Truth and Method*, 324: 'The judge who adapts the transmitted law to the needs of the present is undoubtedly seeking to perform a practical task, but his interpretation of the law is by no means merely for that reason an arbitrary revision. Here again, to understand and to interpret means to discover and recognize a valid meaning. The judge seeks to be in accord with the "legal idea" in mediating it with the present.'

[124]In respect of its theoretical conception, the routine interpretation approach may be placed historically within the corpus of hermeneutic approaches that had focussed predominantly on the interpretation of single dark passages, before the holistic turn effected by Schleiermacher, see Böhl, Meinrad, Wolfgang Reinhard and Peter Walter, *Hermeneutik*, passim; Joisten, Karen, *Philosophische Hermeneutik*, passim. Even so it seems unlikely that its reasoning (by analogy) would have been accepted by the prominent hermeneutic theorists preceding Schleiermacher. For example, Saint Augustine, who according to Heidegger provided 'the first "hermeneutics" in grand style', Heidegger, *Ontology – The Hermeneutics of Facticity*, 9, forcefully rejected interpretation of a single translation in isolation as an unsound method and source of errors, see Saint Augustine, *On Christian Doctrine: A Select Library of the Nicene and Post-Nicene Fathers of the Christian Church*, ed. Philip Schaff, vol. 2 (Buffalo: The Christian Literature Company, 1887), Book II, Ch. 11–12, paras. 16–18.

[125]Henceforth referred to as the original text.

in such case to rely on the meaning of the original text because of it most closely implementing the agreement of the contracting parties; however, this would depend on the circumstances of the treaty's conclusion, that is, if (and to what extent) the negotiators were directly involved in the drafting of the other texts, or whether those happened to be mere translations by translators.[126]

Although supported by many scholars, this approach is not in line with the VCLT.[127] Before discussing this in detail, it is important to note that Hardy's pre–VCLT reasoning does not convince based on its own construction. His conclusion contradicts his own premiss that the point of agreement on the common intention is the time of the treaty's conclusion.[128] If at that time the treaty does not confer any superiority to the original text, granting it decisive power over the others violates that clear common intention. As Hardy himself admits, the two principles of the superiority of the original text and the equivalence of texts are mutually exclusive by definition.[129]

His supporting arguments of clear drafting errors and translation shortcomings also fail to convince. Such would have been identified and, if at all possible, corrected by applying the means provided by Articles 31–33 before concluding that the meanings of the texts are incompatible. Once we

---

[126]See Hardy, 'The Interpretation of Plurilingual Treaties by International Courts and Tribunals', 105, 151–52. Similar suggestions are made by Sinclair, *The Vienna Convention on the Law of Treaties*, 152; Arginelli, *The Interpretation of Multilingual Tax Treaties*, 231–32, 241; Anthony Aust, *Modern Treaty Law and Practice* (Cambridge; New York: Cambridge University Press, 2000), 205–6; Lang, 'The Interpretation of Tax Treaties and Authentic Languages', 21–22; Dinah Shelton, 'Reconcilable Differences? The Interpretation of Multilingual Treaties', *Hastings International and Comparative Law Review* 20 (1997): 637; Josef Schuch and Jean-Philippe Van West, 'Authentic Languages and Official Translations of the Multilateral Instrument and Covered Tax Agreements', in *The OECD Multilateral Instrument for Tax Treaties: Analysis and Effects*, ed. Lang, Michael et. al. (Wolters Kluwer Law & Business, 2018), 84.

[127]See ILC, *Draft Articles on the Law of Treaties with Commentaries*, II:226, para. 9; Avery Jones, 'Treaty Interpretation', s. 3.7.1.3; Giorgio Gaja, 'The Perspective of International Law', in *Multilingual Texts and Interpretation of Tax Treaties and EC Tax Law*, ed. Guglielmo Maisto (Amsterdam: IBFD, 2005), 92.

[128]See Hardy, 'The Interpretation of Plurilingual Treaties by International Courts and Tribunals', 104.

[129]See ibid., 106.

arrive at the conclusion that the texts are incompatible after exhaustion of all interpretative means provided by the VCLT, the suggestion that there is a clear drafting error or translation mistake is unhelpful because a criterion on the basis of which the defective text could be identified without doubt is lacking, especially in the case of only two texts contradicting each other without a third or more texts as additional context.

The argument that a choice must be made in all cases between texts with incompatible wordings is invalid when the texts are equivalent concerning the provision granting equal authority to all texts. Any other provision the wording of which turns out contradictory between the texts cannot render the provision granting equal authority to all texts defective, but must be considered defective itself in view of such provision, that is, the provision granting equal authority to all texts cannot at the same time be the reason for and the object of the deficiency of other provisions. The conclusion cannot be that because another provision is defective in view of the provision granting equal authority to all texts, the equal authority of all texts must be modified. Rather, if no obvious error is identified in one text under the application of Articles 31–33 and healed by interpretative means or via agreement of the contracting states under Articles 48 and 79 VCLT, the conclusion must be that the contradictory provision itself is defective and the parties either failed to agree on the matter of the provision or failed to properly express their agreement.[130]

Nevertheless, Arginelli picks up Hardy's reasoning and goes as far as to proclaim that because of it being the text in the language of negotiation and drafting, it would be 'illogical, unreasonable and unfair' not to give the original text special relevance, wherefore it should be treated as a 'proxy for the *travaux préparatoires*' to reconcile apparent differences in meaning.[131]

---

[130]See Vogel, *Klaus Vogel on Double Taxation Conventions*, 39, para. 72a. The 6th German edition erroneously abandons this view still held by the 4th and 5th German editions (Lehner, *Doppelbesteuerungsabkommen der Bundesrepublik Deutschland auf dem Gebiet der Steuern vom Einkommen und Vermögen: Kommentar auf der Grundlage der Musterabkommen (begründet von Klaus Vogel)*, 197, para. 112a), see next chapter, 30n. In contrast, the new 4th English edition upholds Vogel's earlier view (Reimer and Rust, *Klaus Vogel on Double Taxation Conventions*, 41, para. 88). Whether this is intentional or the result of translating the 4th German edition is not entirely obvious, see above, 43n.

[131]See Arginelli, *The Interpretation of Multilingual Tax Treaties*, 231–32.

In order to argue his suggestion, he conducts a survey of the arguments of other scholars in support of this view, the *travaux préparatoires* of the VCLT, and case law.[132]

He acknowledges that during the discussions at the ILC's 874th meeting the proposal of Mr Verdross to include an explicit provision giving preference to the original text in case reconciliation of texts proved impossible did not gather support.[133] Yet, he contends that the idea of a treaty being negotiated and drafted in a certain language conferring special weight to the text in that language was generally recognised by the ILC, from which he concludes that such a fact should be taken into account to the effect that the intentions of parties 'should be derived *primarily* from the drafted texts and the supplementary means of interpretation'.[134] As most grave argument in support of his view he postulates a deficiency of translation by definition citing Hardy and Rosenne,[135] according to whom there is 'all the difference in the world between a negotiated version and one produced mechanically by some translation service, however competent'.[136] A similar view has been put forward by the joint dissenting opinion in the *Young Loan Arbitration*,[137] which has influenced many scholars such as Sinclair.[138]

The argument deserves some consideration. Advocates of this view seem to equate the proposition 'X is a translation of Y' with the proposition 'X fails to properly portray the meaning of Y in an equivalent manner'. But unless one is convinced that there is no such thing as a proper translation guaranteeing equivalence in meaning, the latter does not necessarily follow

---

[132]See ibid., 231–40.

[133]See ILC, *Summary Records of the Eighteenth Session, 4 May – 19 July 1966*, 208, para. 5; 210, para. 22; 210–211, paras. 33–34, 37.

[134]Arginelli, *The Interpretation of Multilingual Tax Treaties*, 232–36 (emphasis added).

[135]See ibid., 232.

[136]Shabtai Rosenne, 'The Meaning of "Authentic Text" in Modern Treaty Law', in *An International Law Miscellany* (Leiden; Boston: Martinus Nijhoff Publishers, 1993), 450.

[137]See *Young Loan Arbitration*, 140, paras. 40–41.

[138]See Sinclair, *The Vienna Convention on the Law of Treaties*, 152. A similar position is taken by Lang, 'The Interpretation of Tax Treaties and Authentic Languages', 23–24; Mössner, 'Die Auslegung mehrsprachiger Staatsverträge', 290; Shelton, 'Reconcilable Differences? The Interpretation of Multilingual Treaties', 637; Schuch and West, 'Authentic Languages and Official Translations of the Multilateral Instrument and Covered Tax Agreements', 84–85.

from the former, that is, the latter does not qualify as an analytic proposition a priori. Of course, translation is a process that may result in errors; however, their existence may only be established in the light of empirical evidence on grounds of the criteria laid down in the VCLT, that is, a yardstick to identify and measure the error is necessary. The view that there is no such thing as a proper translation is not compatible with the accepted international practice of states to conclude treaties with equally authoritative texts in different languages, the principle of unity, and the presumption of equal meaning in Article 33(3). If one would subscribe to it, one would in consequence be compelled to change the common practice concerning the conclusion of treaty instruments as well as the underlying principles themselves. Thus, any argument conferring general superiority to the original text implicitly based on the supposition that translation into another language cannot create a text of equivalent meaning must be rejected – at least in view of the status quo.[139]

In summary, there is no principle implemented in the VCLT rules that the original text should be given more weight over the others, and the VCLT Commentary explicitly denies such suggestion.[140] As pointed out by Special Rapporteur Sir Humphrey Waldock in the ILC's 874th meeting, the defects of the initially drafted text may be the source of the problem rather than the solution; hence, any notion that the initially drafted text should necessarily

---

[139]For linguists this may of course be a topic of debate, see, e.g., Sergio Bolaños Cuéllar, 'Equivalence Revisited: A Key Concept in Modern Translation Theory', *Forma y Función*, no. 15 (August 2010): 60–88, and Anthony Pym, 'On History in Formal Conceptualizations of Translation', *Across Languages and Cultures* 8, no. 2 (January 2007): 153–66; however, such discussion lies outside the scope of the subject matter at hand. As long as states officially designate translated texts as equally authentic, faulty translation can only be an issue of errors and unwittingly introduced differences on a case by case basis that are identified via the interpretative means provided by the VCLT, and any supposition that translations are by definition inferior must be refused. The mere fact that a text is a translation tells us nothing about whether it correctly conveys the meaning of the treaty or its relative value versus the other texts in this respect, but its value for interpretative purposes is determined by its status as authentic text alone.

[140]See ILC, *Draft Articles on the Law of Treaties with Commentaries*, II:226. para. 9; ILC, *Summary Records of the Eighteenth Session, 4 May – 19 July 1966*, I, Part II:210–11, paras. 22, 33–34.

prevail must be rejected.[141] Like any other text, the original text may have more or less weight depending on further evidence that shows there was an obvious translation problem and the faulty translation does not suit the object and purpose of the treaty; however, what is decisive in such case is that there is indeed an identified particular translation error not in line with the intentions of the contracting parties, not that the text happens to be a translation.

The views of Hardy, Arginelli, and others in respect of the interpretative value of the original text boil down to an implicit *petitio principii* (begging the question) that runs counter to Articles 31–33. They do not interpret but revise them. That courts in practice resort to the original text does not establish its decisive weight as a matter of principle. Such recourse may be justified in any particular case as outcome of an interpretation under Articles 31–33, but not merely because of it being the initially negotiated and drafted text while the others are translations. For example, in the often quoted *LaGrand* case the court observed in the proceedings that the French text, the meaning of which it confirmed as applicable over that of the English text invoked by the US, was the original one; however, it based its decision on Article 33(4) and a corresponding analysis of the object and purpose, which established the prevalence of the meaning as suggested by the French text, not on the mere fact that the French text happened to be the original one.[142]

In his conclusion, Arginelli rephrases his views. The imperative vocabulary used in his analysis is replaced by subjunctive form:

> However, the preceding positive analysis shows that the drafted text (i.e. the text that has been discussed upon during the negotiations and eventually drafted as result thereof) *may sometimes* be given more weight than the other texts for the purpose of construing the treaty, since there is a *reasonable presumption* that it *may* reflect more accurately the common intention of the parties, in particular where the treaty negotiators were not involved in the subsequent drafting and examination of the other authentic texts.[143]

---

[141] See ILC, *Summary Records of the Eighteenth Session, 4 May – 19 July 1966*, I, Part II:210–11, para. 33; Gardiner, *Treaty Interpretation*, 366–69.

[142] See *LaGrand (Germany v United States of America)*, ICJ (Annual Reports of the International Court of Justice, 2001), paras. 100–102; Gaja, 'The Perspective of International Law', 97.

[143] Arginelli, *The Interpretation of Multilingual Tax Treaties*, 241 (emphasis added).

3. Routine Interpretation: A Refutation

In substance, this echoes again the considerations of Hardy, Rosenne, and the joint dissenting opinion in the *Young Loan Arbitration* with respect to the need of taking the individual facts and circumstances of how the authenticity of the texts was established into account; however, the subjunctive form concedes that the value of the original text is an exogenous variable that must be evaluated case by case based on an extrinsic yardstick, and a definite statement in its favour based on existing legal principles is not possible. The conjured up 'reasonable presumption' cannot be a surrogate for a mere ethical judgement but must be filled with considerations based on the principles enshrined in the VCLT, according to which alone the relevance of the original text must be evaluated. The mere consideration that a particular text has been the text of negotiation and drafting is not part of these principles and may therefore not be subsumed under the surrogate 'reasonable presumption'.

On a final note, ascribing special relevance to the original text is in friction also with the routine interpretation approach supported by many of the quoted scholars at the same time. If such special relevance would be conceded, the routine interpretation approach could be applied only asymmetrically with respect to ones own language, namely, by the country the official language of which happens to be the language of the original text, whereas the other country would always be urged to ultimately rely on the, from its perspective, 'other' text. Thus, the combination of both views is fundamentally incompatible with international law in the sense of implicitly allowing one country to prefer its own language while the other is either limited in its choice or at minimum always has to consult the decisive original text as well. This not only violates the equal authenticity of texts, that is, the principle of effectiveness in view of a final clause declaring such equal authenticity, but also the fundamental principle of the sovereign equality of states.[144]

---

[144]UN, *Charter of the United Nations* (United Nations, 1945), Article 2(1). A thorough discussion of the principle lies outside the scope of this study. The interested reader is referred to Ulrich K. Preuß, 'Equality of States – Its Meaning in a Constitutionalized Global Order', *Chicago Journal of International Law* 9, no. 1 (2008): 17–49; Hans Kelsen, 'The Principle of Sovereign Equality of States as a Basis for International Organization', *The Yale Law Journal* 53, no. 2 (1944): 207–20; Hans Kelsen, *The Law of the United Nations: A Critical Analysis of Its Fundamental Problems* (The Lawbook Exchange, Ltd., 1950), 50 et seq.

4. Practical Implications and Additional Issues

4.1. Research Questions

The considerations submitted in the previous chapter raise three questions concerning practical application: First, should recourse to supplementary means be had when interpreting any single text before recourse to the others, or only after a comparison with respect to a common meaning? Second, what weight should be given to supplementary means in relation to Article 33(4) – should recourse to the former be had over the latter, or should the latter take precedence? Third, how does *renvoi* to domestic law implemented by model conventions and tax treaties affect interpretation in plurilingual cases?

4.2. Preliminary Considerations

It is likely that the judge will (have to) consider a problem posed by a particular case from several angles before concluding that there exists a difference between the texts an application of all means provided by the VCLT cannot resolve. The most efficient sequence may to some extend depend on the type of problem faced; however, considerations of how much weight to attribute to what means under what circumstances are a significant structural element of the VCLT – they affect the outcome of every interpretation and need to be taken into account or misinterpretation may result.

The critic may object that because the intention of the drafters of the VCLT has been to codify only a few general 'principles of logic and good sense' and not the exact conditions of their application, the 'unity of the process of interpretation' as a 'single combined operation' is implied: all means have to be thrown into the 'crucible' and evaluated without any suggestion of a rigid mechanical order.[1] I do not dissent – on the contrary, I

---

[1] See ILC, *Draft Articles on the Law of Treaties with Commentaries*, II:218–20, paras. 4–5,

firmly support a holistic approach that comprises considerations of all necessary means, which in my view includes the other language texts as long as they must be considered equally authoritative.

My point, however, is that the VCLT framework establishes different relative weights to be attributed to authentic and supplementary means.[2] This in turn allows for contemplation of the proper sequence to structure the process of interpretation, because the judge cannot read everything at the same time but, as a spatio-temporal being, has to begin somewhere and look at all materials one by one. As the ILC has pointed out, the idea of a 'single combined operation' is not to be understood literally as a consideration of everything all at once, but rather as a consideration of all the different means in a holistic manner attributing appropriate weights to them, which reminds of Schleiermacher's conception of interpretation as a process of gradual approximation:

> Just as courts typically begin their reasoning by looking at the terms of the treaty, and then continue, in an interactive process, to analyse those terms in their context and in the light of the object and purpose of the treaty, the precise relevance of different means of interpretation must first be identified in any case of treaty interpretation before they can be 'thrown into the crucible' in order to arrive at a proper interpretation, by giving them appropriate weight in relation to each other. The obligation to place 'appropriate emphasis on the various means of interpretation' may, in the course of the interpretation of a treaty in specific cases, result in a different emphasis on the various means of interpretation depending on the treaty or on the treaty provisions concerned. This is not to suggest that a court or any other interpreter is more or less free to choose how to use and apply the different means of interpretation.[3]

Now, I do not disagree with the contention that as long as the judge considers all necessary means, keeps the fundamental distinction between authentic and supplementary means in mind, and attributes the appropriate

---

8–9; Arginelli, *The Interpretation of Multilingual Tax Treaties*, 148–54, 164, 203, 231–41.

[2] See ILC, *Draft Articles on the Law of Treaties with Commentaries*, II:220, para. 10 et seq.; Sinclair, *The Vienna Convention on the Law of Treaties*, 117; Engelen, *Interpretation of Tax Treaties under International Law*, 408–13; Tabory, *Multilingualism in International Law and Institutions*, 218. This will be discussed in more detail below.

[3] ILC, 'Report of the International Law Commission on the Sixty-fifth Session, 6 May – 7 June and 8 July – 9 August 2013', 18, paras. 14–15.

emphasis accordingly, he may enter into this process from any angle; how-ever, if he were to begin for example by a consideration of supplementary means, which by their very nature allow for a wider array of conclusions and therefore may be 'misleading',[4] he would run the danger of imposing a conviction formed on their basis on his subsequent reading of the text.[5]

In summary, the suggestion that application of the VCLT principles is not mechanical does not mean it should not be methodical. As Paul Ricoeur has said, 'If it is true that there is always more than one way of construing a text, it is not true that all interpretations are equal.'[6] Before we examine the role of supplementary means in this context, it is useful to demarcate the scope of Article 33(4).

4.3. The Scope of Article 33(4)

Article 33(4) specifies that whenever a difference of meaning between the texts persists after application of Articles 31 and 32, the meaning that must be considered to best reconcile the different meanings on grounds of the object and purpose shall be chosen.[7] This means two criteria must be satis-fied: First, the meaning chosen under application of Article 33(4) must be one considered to in some way reconcile the different meanings established beforehand under application of Articles 31 and 32 even though they could not be made to conform under such application. Second, the criterion re-lied on to gauge the degree of reconciliation is the object and purpose. This raises two questions: What is included in the concept of reconciliation, and how far does the role of the object and purpose extend in this respect?

4.3.1. The Meaning of Reconcile

According to the Oxford Learner's Dictionary, to reconcile something with something means 'to find an acceptable way of dealing with two or more

---

[4]ILC, *Draft Articles on the Law of Treaties with Commentaries*, II:220, para. 10.

[5]This will be argued in more detail below.

[6]Paul Ricoeur, *Interpretation Theory: Discourse and the Surplus of Meaning* (TCU Press, 1976), 79.

[7]The case of prevailing texts will be discussed in the next chapter.

ideas, needs, etc., that seem to be opposed to each other'. Clearly, the emphasis is on 'seem', which implies that the perceived opposition is not contradictory but common elements can be identified and conciliation is to some degree possible or the opposition can be overcome in some other way acceptable. Indeed, we may postulate that the concept of reconciliation necessitates the possibility of concordance and the absence of logical contradiction, because logical contradictions cannot be reconciled by definition. Propositions *a* and *not-a* cannot both be true in the same sense at the same time. Stating both is not a form of reconciliation but merely means uttering something of no informative value, departing from the realm of rationality, and succumbing to the fallacy of *ex contradictione sequitur quodlibet*[8] – the idea of reconciling a contradiction being a perfect case in point.

When interpreting Article 33 according to VCLT rules, the principle of non-contradiction must be adhered to with the principle of unity in mind as fundamental axiom. It follows that divergent texts can by definition only be reconciled if they are not inherently contradictory and a concordant interpretation is in some way possible with the help of the means codified as acceptable by the VCLT. Thus, the wording 'reconcile' implicitly presupposes an inherent property of reconcilability of the divergent texts. If such inherent reconcilability is not immediately given and reconciliation proves impossible under the application of the standard means provided for, decisive reference to the object and purpose is stipulated as acceptable means of last resort to establish the meaning of the treaty,[9] that is, the meaning so chosen must satisfy the requirement of reconcilability in the sense that if the respective meanings of the texts are mutually exclusive, it must be manifest that only it could have been intended.

In summary, the scope of Article 33(4) is delimited by a combined application of the principle of unity and the principle of non-contradiction. Unless there is evidence to the contrary, all texts of a treaty must be presumed to have the same (one true) meaning as stipulated by Article 33(1) and (3). If evidence to the contrary persists, the unity of the treaty is violated unless such violation can be overcome with the help of the object and purpose.

---

[8] See Chapter 2, s. 2.2.1.

[9] See UN, *Vienna Convention on the Law of Treaties*, Article 33(4); Avery Jones, 'Treaty Interpretation', s. 3.7.1.7.

Therefore, Article 33(4) applies in substance only to cases that do not pose contradictions, unless the contradiction can be resolved in the sense that a decision can be made for one text to reflect the true common intention of the parties by recourse to the object and purpose as sole decider, which will depend on whether different degrees of serving the object and purpose can be discerned.

This reasoning is implicit also in the approach taken by the PCIJ in the *Mavrommatis* case:

> [W]here two versions possessing equal authority exist one of which appears to have a wider bearing than the other, it [the court] is bound to adopt the more limited interpretation *which can be made to harmonize* with both versions and which, as far as it goes, is doubtless in accordance with the common intention of the Parties.[10]

Commonly, *Mavrommatis* is discussed by scholars concerning the applicability of a general 'principle of restrictive interpretation',[11] that is, whether a narrower common interpretation must always be preferred to a wider one that is not necessarily common to all texts. In this context, it is crucial to note first and foremost – as the VCLT Commentary indeed does – that 'the *Mavrommatis* case gives strong support to the principle of conciliating – i.e. harmonizing – the texts'.[12] According to the Oxford Dictionary, the meaning of harmonise is to 'Make consistent or compatible',[13] which of course is possible only if the property of compatibility is already inherent and can be brought to bear. Contradictions cannot be made consistent or compatible – that is the very definition of a contradiction. The wording 'can be made' used by the court reflects that the emphasis is primarily on a presupposed possibility of harmonisation, not about the court being bound to choose the more limited interpretation as the better way to effect such harmonisation, which still depends on it being doubtless in accordance with the object and purpose.

---

[10] *The Mavrommatis Palestine Concessions*, 19, as quoted by ILC, *Draft Articles on the Law of Treaties with Commentaries*, 225, para. 8 (emphasis added).

[11] See, e.g., Hardy, 'The Interpretation of Plurilingual Treaties by International Courts and Tribunals', 77–78; Wouters and Vidal, 'Non-Tax Treaties', s. 1.3.5.

[12] ILC, *Draft Articles on the Law of Treaties with Commentaries*, II:225, para. 8.

[13] The definition of conciliate is synonymous: 'Reconcile; make compatible.'

The court's decision is based on the supposition that the more restricted interpretation is a subset of both interpretations, providing for the inherent property of compatibility and allowing for an acceptable choice in the particular case.[14] In terms of a general rule, the *Mavrommatis* approach may be applied only to cases in which the differing interpretations are not mutually exclusive, and only to the extent it would really be the case that the more restricted interpretation necessarily always is the more proper one in respect of the object and purpose, as would be implied by elevating the *Mavrommatis* approach to the status of a principle. The ILC consequently denied it the quality of a general rule,[15] but made reconciliation ultimately a derivative of matching the diverging texts to the object and purpose of the treaty as the acceptable decisive means of last resort in case reconciliation of the diverging texts under the general rule of interpretation turns out impossible.[16]

4.3.2. The Object and Purpose as Decisive Criterion

How can a consideration of the object and purpose, which proved unhelpful when considered during the application of Article 31, be helpful a second time around? Engelen seems to imply that Article 33(4) provides for a teleological expansion of the VCLT interpretative framework, in the sense of opening the textual meaning of 'object and purpose' up to a more liberal investigation into the intentions of the parties *ex post*.[17] In contrast, Avery Jones emphasises the mere decisive force character of the object and purpose criterion, which by itself does not necessarily support any notion of a

---

[14]For in-depth discussions of *Mavrommatis*, see Hardy, 'The Interpretation of Plurilingual Treaties by International Courts and Tribunals', 76–80; Paul A. Eden, 'Plurilingual Treaties: Aspects of Interpretation' (Rochester, NY: Social Science Research Network, March 2010), 6–8; Arginelli, *The Interpretation of Multilingual Tax Treaties*, 201–2, 236–37, 293–94.

[15]See ILC, *Draft Articles on the Law of Treaties with Commentaries*, II:225–26, para. 8; Gaja, 'The Perspective of International Law', 93–94.

[16]UN, *Vienna Convention on the Law of Treaties*, Article 33(4); see Avery Jones, 'Treaty Interpretation', s. 3.7.1.7; Engelen, *Interpretation of Tax Treaties under International Law*, 403–4; Arginelli, *The Interpretation of Multilingual Tax Treaties*, 317–21; Gaja, 'The Perspective of International Law', 94–98.

[17]See Engelen, *Interpretation of Tax Treaties under International Law*, 548.

teleological expansion of the VCLT interpretative framework through the wording of Article 33(4).[18] The idea being that if an interpretation according to the criteria enshrined in Article 31 considered as a whole turns out inconclusive, consideration of the object and purpose alone will enable a decision for one text.[19] In consequence, the object and purpose criterion itself does not need to be more liberally construed, but a textual interpretation of its meaning remains prescriptive.

The view of Avery Jones is more in line with the overall context of the ILC's rejection of purely teleological reasoning in favour of objective textual interpretation on the sole basis of the intentions as expressed by the contracting parties,[20] so to be supported at this point. As a corollary, Article 33(4) does not cover divergences that cannot be reconciled at all in case the object and purpose criterion fails as well, but presupposes reconcilability based on a conclusive textual interpretation of the object and purpose. Another important corollary to keep in mind for the discussion in the next chapter is that because of this, Article 33(4) must be interpreted to only regulate what is supposed to happen when there is no prevailing text, because the VCLT interpretative framework enshrines the idea that a textual interpretation of a single text under Articles 31 and 32 will always lead to the establishment of its meaning,[21] which prevails in case of divergence.

Attributing decisive force to the object and purpose as ultimate criterion is coherent with the supposition that the contracting parties intended to agree, which is a fair presumption given the existence of a treaty and implied good faith on behalf of the parties. This presumption together with the principle of unity justifies resorting to the object and purpose as ultimate criterion, because against this background interpretation must depart from

---

[18]See Avery Jones, 'Treaty Interpretation', s. 3.7.1.7.

[19]The tribunal in the *Young Loan Arbitration* refers to the object and purpose as 'decisive yardstick', *Young Loan Arbitration*, 110, para. 40.

[20]See ILC, *Draft Articles on the Law of Treaties with Commentaries*, II:220, para. 11, 223, para. 18. For a comparison of approaches, see Sinclair, *The Vienna Convention on the Law of Treaties*, 114–119; J.G. Merrils, 'Two Approaches to Treaty Interpretation', in *Australian Year Book of International Law*, 1969, 55–82. For a critical appreciation, see Peter McRae, 'The Search for Meaning: Continuing Problems with the Interpretation of Treaties', *Victoria U. Wellington L. Rev.* 33 (2002): 209.

[21]See Avery Jones, 'Treaty Interpretation', s. 8.2.2.6 [5.1.2.2.6].

the point of view that all texts ought to have the same meaning even if they appear not to and reconciliation proves difficult.[22]

In the event of mutually exclusive interpretations, however, the object and purpose criterion can function only to the extent it can help to identify the text reflecting the true common intention of the parties, which then must be assumed to be the text which 'best reconciles' all texts, so that the mutual exclusion can de facto be overcome by reference to the object and purpose.[23] If the object and purpose for some reason fails to help identification of the one text reflecting the true common intention of the parties and the mutual exclusion cannot be overcome as a consequence, the reconciliatory approach of Article 33(4) fails to provide a solution.[24]

Therefore, the argument of Arginelli in its imperative sense, that 'reconcile' has to be interpreted to mean that the court *must* attribute a common meaning to all texts even though a comparative interpretation under Article 31 failed to establish one, because the expression 'the meaning which best reconciles the texts' in Article 33(4) 'must be read in its context, which first and foremost includes the underlying idea of the unity of the treaty and the connected rule of law, reflected in Article 33(3), that all authentic texts *do* have the same meaning',[25] must be rejected. Such can apply only to cases in which the true intention of the parties can be discerned beyond reasonable doubt with the help of the object and purpose criterion. If that proves impossible, we cannot attribute one single meaning to all texts under the VCLT, as it forbids a choice for one meaning based on other criteria than provided.

In other words, although we have to start from the presumption that all texts ought to mean the same and employ all efforts to establish that common meaning in case they appear otherwise,[26] we may indeed arrive at the conclusion that they do not mean the same once the means provided by the VCLT are all exhausted without success. Article 33(3) only presumes that the terms of the treaty have the same meaning in each text, which may

---

[22] See Hardy, 'The Interpretation of Plurilingual Treaties by International Courts and Tribunals', 105; Arginelli, *The Interpretation of Multilingual Tax Treaties*, 310.

[23] UN, *Vienna Convention on the Law of Treaties*, Article 33(4).

[24] See Engelen, *Interpretation of Tax Treaties under International Law*, 548.

[25] Arginelli, *The Interpretation of Multilingual Tax Treaties*, 310 (emphasis added).

[26] See ILC, *Draft Articles on the Law of Treaties with Commentaries*, II:225, para. 7.

be rebutted by evidence to the contrary. Therefore, any imperative under-standing in the sense of *what must not exist cannot exist* reads into the VCLT and may result in reading into treaties, which runs counter to the VCLT's intended textual approach to interpretation.

Returning to our hypothetical example based on the *Natexis* case, the wording 'liable to tax' includes both cases of liable and subject to tax and liable but not subject to tax, whereas the wording 'subject to tax' excludes all cases of liable but not subject to tax. For the latter subset of cases, liable and subject to tax are by definition mutually exclusive concepts because subject to tax demands that tax is paid, whereas the intention behind liable to tax in such case is that, effectively, no tax is paid. In consequence, the *Mavrommatis* approach would lead to the wrong result every single time, which justifies its rejection as a general rule by the ILC, because it proves that cases may exist for which the assumption that the more limited inter-pretation is always a compatible subset of the wider interpretation, which would be a necessary condition for applying the *Mavrommatis* approach as a general rule, is invalid. Hence, the lowest common denominator may not be relied on generally to effect reconciliation.[27]

When one text says 'liable to tax' while the other says 'subject to tax', the object and purpose fails to decide the case as a means of last resort,[28] as both liable and subject to tax equally conform to the object and purpose of avoiding double taxation, while effective double non-taxation may not necessarily be in conflict with any object and purpose of avoiding fiscal evasion.[29] The mere conclusion that in view of the unity of the treaty there must be an obvious drafting error is of no help because without further evidence it would be impossible to determine which text embodies the er-ror, and the VCLT forbids the designation of a single text as the applicable one if such choice cannot be made on grounds provided by Articles 31–33. Therefore, the only available conclusion is that the treaty is defective in the sense that the parties either failed to agree or failed to properly convey their

---

[27] See ibid., II:225–26, para. 8; Sinclair, *The Vienna Convention on the Law of Treaties*, 149–51; Aust, *Modern Treaty Law and Practice*, 205.

[28] Unless the context and supplementary means allow for further inferences as to the true intentions of the contracting parties, e.g., through formulations obviously aimed at double exemption or clear evidence of drafting errors.

[29] See Jankowiak, *Doppelte Nichtbesteuerung*, passim.

agreement on the point in question.[30]

Vogel has identified real life examples of defective tax treaties.[31] The case of the Agreement on Reparations from Germany quoted by Mr. Bartos in the ILC's 770th meeting may serve also as an example to the extent that mere surveillance and active management are mutually exclusive concepts and no further evidence concerning the true intentions of the contracting parties can be derived from the texts and supplementary means.[32] Another prominent case concerned the Italy-Ethiopia (1889) treaty of Wichale (Ucciali).[33] Article XVII of the Amharic text stated that the Emperor of Ethiopia 'may' use the government of the King of Italy for all dealings with other powers or governments, whereas the Italian text read 'must' instead. Italy proclaimed a protectorate over Ethiopia based on the Italian text. Ethiopia repudiated the claim. This finally led to war, Italian defeat in the battle of Adwa 1896, and acknowledgement of Ethiopian independence.[34] Clearly, *must* is a universal proposition while *may* is not, that is, mandatory and optional are contradictory concepts – there is no middle ground between them.[35]

---

[30]See Vogel, *Klaus Vogel on Double Taxation Conventions*, 39, para. 72a. The 6th edition erroneously abandons this view held until the 5th edition by stating that 'a situation not regulated by the treaty is not to be assumed, not even as *ultima ratio*, but a consideration of the object and purpose will almost always lead to a congruent interpretation, if necessary by relying on the lowest common denominator', Lehner, *Doppelbesteuerungsabkommen der Bundesrepublik Deutschland auf dem Gebiet der Steuern vom Einkommen und Vermögen: Kommentar auf der Grundlage der Musterabkommen (begründet von Klaus Vogel)*, 197, para. 112a. As discussed above, this view rests on an erroneous interpretation of the wording 'reconcile', mistakenly elevating the *Mavrommatis* approach to the status of a general principle, which it has been denied by the ILC. The lowest common denominator may not always represent the true object and purpose, as in our example of liable versus subject to tax.

[31]See Vogel, *Klaus Vogel on Double Taxation Conventions*, 39, para. 72a; Reimer and Rust, *Klaus Vogel on Double Taxation Conventions*, 40–41, para. 88.

[32]See ILC, *Summary Records of the Sixteenth Session, 11 May – 24 July 1964*, vol. I, Yearbook of the International Law Commission 1964, A/CN.4/SER.A/1964 (United Nations, 1965), 319, para. 65.

[33]See Kuner, 'The Interpretation of Multilingual Treaties', 953, 4n.

[34]See Encyclopedia Britannica, 'Treaty of Wichale'.

[35]Contradictions are subject to the logical principle of *tertium non datur* (law of excluded middle), i.e., all universal propositions must either be true or false, see Russell, *The*

During the drafting period of the VCLT, the problem of cases with non-reconcilable meanings had been raised most comprehensively by the American delegation,[36] which also stressed that difficulties in reconciling the texts may not only arise because of differences in wording but also on a conceptual level, namely, when two legal systems are involved in which the same term means something different, or when a term has a particular legal meaning in one system without direct correspondence in the other. As will be discussed in depth in the final part of this chapter, this is particularly relevant in the case of tax treaties.

It is only consistent that the ILC changed the wording of Article 33(4) from the initially proposed 'a meaning which is common to both or all the texts shall be preferred' and the later 'a meaning which as far as possible reconciles the texts shall be adopted' to the final 'the meaning which best reconciles the texts, having regard to the object and purpose of the treaty'.[37] Both rejected draft wordings presuppose that there is always a common meaning that can be chosen to reconcile the texts at least to some degree. They cannot be applied to contradictory texts because they provide no further means to resolve a contradiction, which has been rightly observed by Mr Kearney from the American delegation, who also pointed out that contradictory meanings are a common phenomenon in practice.[38]

To the extent these draft wordings should be understood to state that the meanings of the texts are different (in the sense that the difference cannot

---

Problems of Philosophy, Ch. 7. Aristotle is the first to formulate the principle as a fundamental logical axiom a priori, see Aristotle, *On Interpretation* (The Internet Classics Archive, 350 B.C.), s. 1, part 9.

[36] See UN, *United Nations Conference on the Law of Treaties, First Session Vienna, 26 March – 24 May 1968, Official Records, Summary Records of the Plenary Meetings and of the Meetings of the Committee of the Whole*, A/CONF.39/11 (United Nations, 1969), 188–89, paras. 39–43; 442, para. 38; UN, *United Nations Conference on the Law of Treaties, First and Second Sessions Vienna, 26 March – 24 May 1968 and 9 April – 22 May 1969, Official Records, Documents of the Conference*, A/CONF.39/1 l/Add.2 (United Nations, 1970), 151.

[37] ILC, *Summary Records of the Sixteenth Session, 11 May – 24 July 1964*, I:319, Article 75(2); ILC, *Summary Records of the Eighteenth Session, 4 May – 19 July 1966*, I, Part II:208, Article 73(4); UN, *Vienna Convention on the Law of Treaties*, Article 33(4).

[38] See UN, *United Nations Conference on the Law of Treaties, First Session Vienna, 26 March – 24 May 1968, Official Records, Summary Records of the Plenary Meetings and of the Meetings of the Committee of the Whole*, 188, para. 40.

be resolved, as literally stated) and, at the same time, congruent (implying the difference can be resolved), but without providing any further means to effect that congruency (apart from an implicitly assumed common meaning that can, however, as literally stated, not be observed), they are nonsensical in the sense of being contradictory, as has been rightly pointed out by Mr Paredes in the ILC's 770th meeting.[39] Concerning this, the wording 'a meaning which as far as possible reconciles' is no improvement over the initial 'a meaning which is common to both or all the texts', because with contradictory meanings there is no 'as far as possible' but only an either-or. Therefore, it is invalid to maintain with Sur that the wording 'as far as possible' would allow the interpreter to remove divergences among the texts even when actual reconciliation proves impossible.[40]

The final wording adopted by the VCLT resolves this deficiency to the extent that an evaluation in respect of the object and purpose as single decisive criterion can indeed help to overcome the divergence. Contrary to the earlier draft wordings, which effectively implemented the *Mavrommatis* approach of smallest common denominator as a general principle, the meaning chosen under the final wording does not necessarily have to be the one as far as possible common to all texts but may be the meaning not common to all texts if a final evaluation in respect of the object and purpose would indicate so with decisive force. In our hypothetical example based on the *Natexis* case that meaning would be the one of liable but not subject to tax.

In summary, if one text says A while the other says not-A, and their mutual exclusiveness cannot be overcome by a consideration of the object and purpose as sole decider, the treaty must be considered defective in view of the prescribed textual approach to interpretation, as the interpreter must not read an agreement into the treaty that is not covered by its text. Therefore, such cases fall outside the scope of Article 33(4).

---

[39] See ILC, *Summary Records of the Sixteenth Session, 11 May – 24 July 1964*, I:319, para. 63.
[40] See Serge Sur, *L'interprétation en droit international public*, vol. 75 (Paris: Librairie générale de droit et de jurisprudence, 1974), 274.

4.4. Use of Supplementary Means

Now that the scope of Article 33(4) is defined, we may think about how supplementary means fit into the process. The VCLT wording seems to imply a clear order of steps. Article 33(4) refers to the 'application of articles 31 and 32', and Article 32 refers to the meaning established under 'application of article 31'. Neither Article 31 nor Article 32 mentions Article 33. Therefore, recourse to supplementary means seems to precede application of the latter; however, Article 32 distinguishes between two different uses, thereby delimiting the overall use of supplementary means. Its particular drafting separates the two different uses not via self-contained paragraphs but merely via two parts of the same sentence. This begs the question whether the reference to Article 32 in Article 33(4) extends to the entire article including the second part of its sentence and its letters (a) and (b), or only to the first part.[41] In order to answer this question, a look under the hood of Article 32 is necessary.

4.4.1. Fundamental Principles

Article 32 establishes that the authentic means of interpretation codified in Article 31 are of higher authority in the interpretative process than supplementary means.[42] The latter may be used only to confirm but not contest

---

[41] Henceforth, when only the first part is implied, it will be cited as Article 32_1 for purposes of disambiguation.

[42] Contra: Arnold, 'The Interpretation of Tax Treaties', 7–8. The distinction Arnold draws between weight and use is not convincing. He fails to make clear how exactly weight should be considered different from use in substance and effect. Delimiting the use of something is equal to delimiting its weight in the overall use of everything to be considered. Stating that one may use certain means only in a limited role is synonymous to stating that they have less weight. And this is precisely what Article 32 instructs: supplementary means may be used only to confirm but not contest the meaning established under Article 31 apart from exceptional cases, see ILC, *Draft Articles on the Law of Treaties with Commentaries*, 222–223, paras. 18–19. Arnold's submissions to the contrary are merely speculative: he submits a purposive interpretation of his own that is in flagrant disregard of the wording, context, and object and purpose of Article 32, simply based on his personal observations concerning practice and an invocation of 'common sense'. As the ILC has stressed, the holistic approach to interpretation prescribed by the VCLT means 'not to suggest that a court or any other interpreter is more or less

the meaning established under Article 31,[43] and recourse to them is by no means mandatory but merely 'permissible',[44] as is reflected by the wording 'Recourse *may* be had'.[45] More liberal use to actively determine the treaty meaning is permissible only if Article 31 leaves the meaning 'ambiguous or obscure', or 'leads to a result which is manifestly absurd or unreasonable'.[46]

The VCLT Commentary stresses that Article 32 does not 'provide for alternative, autonomous, means of interpretation but only for means to aid an interpretation governed by the principles contained in article 27'.[47] This implies that even when supplementary means may be used to determine the meaning because the outcome of Article 31 may not be applied for reasons specified in Article 32(a) and (b), the meaning so derived has to remain within the scope demarcated by the principles enshrined in the general rule and cannot be just *any* meaning.

Consequently, judges must apply prudence when having recourse to supplementary means and avoid substituting them for the terms of the treaty.[48] Apart from exceptional cases, supplementary means may be used merely as additional support, and a conclusive interpretation of the text reached on the basis of Article 31 may not be challenged by conflicting alternative inter-

---

free to choose how to use and apply the different means of interpretation', ILC, 'Report of the International Law Commission on the Sixty-fifth Session, 6 May – 7 June and 8 July – 9 August 2013', 18, paras. 14–15.

[43] UN, *Vienna Convention on the Law of Treaties*, Article 32_1.

[44] ILC, *Draft Articles on the Law of Treaties with Commentaries*, II:223, para. 19.

[45] UN, *Vienna Convention on the Law of Treaties*, Article 32 (emphasis added).

[46] Ibid., Article 32(a) and (b). The ICJ had stressed already in 1948 that recourse to the *travaux préparatoires* is not an automatic exercise but requires sufficient reason to be justified: 'The Court considers that the text is sufficiently clear; consequently, it does not feel that it should deviate from the consistent practice of the Permanent Court of International Justice, according to which there is no occasion to resort to preparatory work if the text of a convention is sufficiently clear in itself', see *Conditions of Admission of a State to Membership in the United Nations (Article 4 of the Charter), Advisory Opinion*, ICJ (Annual Reports of the International Court of Justice, 1948), 63; reiterated in *Ambatielos (Greece v United Kingdom), Preliminary Objection*, ICJ (Annual Reports of the International Court of Justice, 1952), 45.

[47] ILC, *Draft Articles on the Law of Treaties with Commentaries*, II:223, para. 19. Draft Article 27 became Article 31 in the VCLT.

[48] See *Fothergill v Monarch Airlines Ltd.*, 276–77, 294–96, per Lords Wilberforce and Scarman.

pretations on the basis of supplementary means.[49] This safeguards correct treaty application and legal certainty because taxpayers may rely on the meaning reflected by the wording officially approved to correctly express the intentions of the contracting states, without that meaning being controlled by extrinsic material that may not even be publicly accessible.[50]

4.4.2. Application to Plurilingual Treaties

In line with the dictum that the fundamental principles of interpretation are to be no different for plurilingual treaties than they are for unilingual ones,[51] the above should also be the guiding principles when interpreting plurilingual treaties. This raises two questions: First, when may we seek rescue in supplementary means – before or after a comparison of texts under application of Article 31? Second, when are we to invoke Article 33(4) – before or after having recourse to supplementary means?

It is not difficult to imagine the situations to which the criteria of ambiguity and obscurity refer in respect of a unilingual treaty, namely, situations in which an interpretation under Article 31 has lead to either several dif-

---

[49]See ILC, *Draft Articles on the Law of Treaties with Commentaries*, II:222–23, paras. 18–19. The *travaux préparatoires* may be misleading because they are a collage of all positions taken by the contracting parties during the negotiation phase; what matters is the final compromise that made it into the text, see ibid., II:220, para. 10; Martin Ris, 'Treaty Interpretation and ICJ Recourse to Travaux Préparatoires: Towards a Proposed Amendment of Articles 31 and 32 of the Vienna Convention on the Law of Treaties', *Boston College International and Comparative Law Review* 14, no. 1 (1991): 112–13; see also the views expressed by the Yugoslavian government during the VCLT discussions, ILC, *Documents of the Second Part of the Seventeenth Session and of the Eighteenth Session Including the Reports of the Commission to the General Assembly*, II:361. The earlier wording 'as far as possible' of Draft Article 73(2), ILC, *Documents of the Sixteenth Session Including the Report of the Commission to the General Assembly*, vol. II, Yearbook of the International Law Commission 1964, A/CN.4/SER.A/1964/Add.1 (United Nations, 1965), 206, is an example that, although it was abandoned in favour of the final wording of Article 33(4) saying something completely different, has nevertheless influenced the views of several authors, see, e.g., Tabory, *Multilingualism in International Law and Institutions*, 202; Sur, *L'interprétation en droit international public*, 75:274.

[50]See *Fothergill v Monarch Airlines Ltd.*, 279–80, 288, per Lords Diplock and Tullybelton; Wouters and Vidal, 'Non-Tax Treaties', s. 1.3.4.

[51]See ILC, *Draft Articles on the Law of Treaties with Commentaries*, II:225, para. 7.

ferent but equally plausible meanings or no clearly discernible meaning at all.[52] The same applies to plurilingual treaties; however, there ambiguity or obscurity may not only be an issue of each or both texts but also arise between texts.[53]

Imagine the following scenario: the text in one language read in isolation means A, although B is a possible but less manifest meaning. For the text in the other language, the situation is exactly reverse. Given that legal language lacks the precision of a purely formal language like mathematics or computer code and any language has its own idiomatic idiosyncrasies, such cases may be common. If any text is interpreted in isolation, there is no problem of ambiguity because each text has a manifest meaning. In consequence, Article 32(a) may not be invoked. If we would adhere to the routine interpretation approach, the result would be different interpretations depending on the text used and, in the worst case, a misapplication of the treaty.

How about if the judge examines the *travaux préparatoires* when interpreting a single text and comes to the conclusion that he needs to apply B? Such approach is problematic because not considering the other texts while having recourse to supplementary means in their active role violates the fundamental principle of different weights to be attributed to authentic and supplementary means. The other texts are part of the context definition in Article 31(2) and thus constitute authentic means to be considered in order to derive the ordinary meaning before it can be dismissed in favour of applying Article 32(a). In other words, all means provided by Article 31 have yet to be exhausted, and it would be premature to claim that the ordinary meaning is ambiguous or obscure. Hence, before basing his decision on supplementary means, the judge must first consult the other texts.

---

[52]See the definitions of ambiguous and obscure in the Oxford Dictionary. For example, because of its wording being 'consistent with either interpretation', the ICJ found Article 95 of the General Act of the International Conference of Algeciras (1906) inconclusive, wherefore it had recourse to the *travaux preparatoires*, see *Rights of Nationals of the United States of America in Morocco (France v United States of America)*, ICJ (Annual Reports of the International Court of Justice, 1952), 209–13; Ris, 'Treaty Interpretation and ICJ Recourse to Travaux Préparatoires: Towards a Proposed Amendment of Articles 31 and 32 of the Vienna Convention on the Law of Treaties', 122–23.

[53]See ILC, *Draft Articles on the Law of Treaties with Commentaries*, II:225, para. 7.

Indeed, the other texts may heal the ambiguity in a way that recourse to Article 32(a) will not become necessary but remain precluded. Imagine that one text employs the grammatically imprecise wording X. X means A, but B could be implied because of the imprecise formulation. Interpretation under Article 31 points to A, but B cannot be ruled out. The other text, however, employs wording Y, which is the grammatically precise formulation of A and rules out B. Optionally, A is confirmed via recourse to the *travaux préparatoires*. Thus, the ambiguity is healed without recourse to supplementary means in their active role; they have not been used to determine the ordinary meaning but merely to confirm the choice made under Article 31.

As regards Article 32(b), the situation is more complex. *Prima facie*, its wording conjures up associations of avoidance scenarios under domestic GAARs: the law is reasonable in general but when stood up on its head and applied to facts that were not foreseen, the outcome may be considered absurd or unreasonable in view of what the law intended. In the VCLT context, however, one may ask how the interpretation of a single text 'in good faith in accordance with the ordinary meaning to be given to the terms of the treaty in their context and in the light of its object and purpose' could ever turn out to be 'manifestly absurd or unreasonable'[54] – the criteria in Article 31 surely cover abusive scenarios violating good faith or the object and purpose.[55]

The wording 'manifestly' emphasises that supplementary means may only play a decisive role in limited situations that in all reasonableness cannot be considered to be what the parties intended.[56] According to the Oxford Dictionary, it means 'In a way that is clear or obvious to the eye or mind', that is, the asserted absurdity or unreasonableness must be obvious for anybody and not merely arguable. Such situations must be considered to be limited to drafting errors or other material defects.[57] In the absence

---

[54] UN, *Vienna Convention on the Law of Treaties*, Articles 31 and 32(b).

[55] See Avery Jones, 'Treaty Interpretation', s. 3.4.3.

[56] See ILC, *Draft Articles on the Law of Treaties with Commentaries*, II:223, para. 19.

[57] See Engelen, *Interpretation of Tax Treaties under International Law*, 540–44. For example, the 'Descriptive Minute' of the Dutch-Belgian Boundary Convention (1843) contained inconsistent language according to which several plots of land were simultaneously assigned to the Netherlands and Belgium. Without elaborating on its methodology,

of such obvious material defect, any suggestion of an unreasonable result seems to amount to a teleological supplementation of the VCLT interpretative framework, as it would require a yardstick beyond good faith, ordinary wording, context, and object and purpose on the basis of which the judgement could be made.[58]

The supplementary means cannot provide that yardstick themselves because they may only confirm but not contest an interpretation under Article 31, that is, they may be used only to determine the meaning once an interpretation under Article 31 has led to a manifestly absurd or unreasonable result. Article 32(b) presupposes that the judgement of the text being absurd or unreasonable has been made already. Under Article 32(b) the interpreter may have recourse to supplementary means only to heal such situation but not to establish its presence, that is, he may not use supplementary means to establish whether he may use them to determine the treaty meaning.[59] Therefore, the only possible conclusion would be to assume an extrinsic yardstick that could then only consist in the intentions of the contracting parties according to which the outcome must be considered absurd or unreasonable but which are not expressed in the text, as otherwise an interpretation under Article 31 could not have turned out manifestly absurd or unreasonable in the first place. Such conclusion runs counter to the clear intentions of the drafters of the VCLT.[60]

---

the ICJ had recourse to the *travaux preparatoires,* see *Sovereignty over Certain Frontier Land (Belgium v Netherlands),* ICJ (Annual Reports of the International Court of Justice, 1959); Ris, 'Treaty Interpretation and ICJ Recourse to Travaux Préparatoires: Towards a Proposed Amendment of Articles 31 and 32 of the Vienna Convention on the Law of Treaties', 123–24.

[58] The wording 'absurd' is less problematic in this respect because its scope is more narrow, providing less argumentative leeway. The Oxford Dictionary defines it as 'Wildly unreasonable, illogical, or inappropriate.'

[59] See ILC, *Draft Articles on the Law of Treaties with Commentaries,* II:223, para. 19.

[60] See ibid., II:220–23, paras. 11, 18–19. *Prima facie,* the wording of the *Polish Postal Service* case cited by the VCLT Commentary seems to suggest that a 'liberal' interpretation may be possible under Article 32(b). Considering the overall VCLT context, however, the wording 'liberal construction' in the judgement and the ILC's reference to it may not be construed to support teleological interpretation, but must be considered only to imply a more liberal use of supplementary means under exceptional circumstances, see *Polish Postal Service in Danzig,* PCIJ (Publications of the Permanent Court of International Justice, 1925), 39–40. Such reading fits with the subordinate role of supplement-

Unless there is an obvious drafting error rendering the text inconsistent, it seems unintelligible how the interpretation of a unilingual treaty under Article 31 could ever lead to an absurd or unreasonable result if the possibility of teleological reasoning is excluded.[61] In any case, recourse to Article 32(b) is subject to the same argument as recourse to Article 32(a) outlined above: if the interpretation of a single text under Article 31 leads to a manifestly absurd or unreasonable result, such judgement cannot be regarded final before the other texts have been consulted. Therefore, the interpreter has to consult all other texts before relying on supplementary means.[62]

Let us return to our example from above. Both texts are compared, but no decision for either A or B can be made. The next step depends on how we classify this situation. If we would classify it as an ambiguity falling under Article 32(a), recourse to supplementary means would be warranted. Against this may be argued that, based on the principle of effectiveness, Article 33(4) should take precedence because the diagnosed problem is one between texts – precisely what Article 33 has been devised for. Applying Article 32(a) renders Article 33(4) an empty provision because the

---

ary means and reinforces it by stressing that liberal use is strictly confined to a limited set of scenarios.

[61] I may simply lack the imagination (or the experience of a judge); however, I challenge the reader to present a case that disproves my conclusion in this respect. The two cases referenced by the ILC as examples do not qualify in my opinion, see ILC, *Documents of the Sixteenth Session Including the Report of the Commission to the General Assembly*, 57, para. 16. As this is not a core issue here, I added my take on these cases in Appendix B to substantiate my assertion for the interested reader. Reference to absurdity in line with Article 32(b) is common in India, see Vik Kanwar, 'Treaty Interpretation in Indian Courts: Adherence, Coherence, and Convergence', in *The Interpretation of International Law by Domestic Courts: Uniformity, Diversity, Convergence*, ed. Helmut Philipp Aust and Georg Nolte (Oxford; New York: Oxford University Press, 2016), 239–64, 247; however, apart from drafting problems mostly in terms of treaty provisions in violation of constitutional law, see, e.g., *Ram Jethmalani v Union of India*, Supreme Court of India, 2011, para. 61: 'However, the fact that such treaties are drafted by diplomats, and not lawyers, leading to sloppiness in drafting also implies that care has to be taken to not render any word, phrase, or sentence redundant, especially where rendering of such word, phrase or sentence redundant would lead to a manifestly absurd situation, particularly from a constitutional …perspective. The government cannot bind India in a manner that derogates from Constitutional provisions, values and imperatives.'

[62] See Engelen, *Interpretation of Tax Treaties under International Law*, 390.

argumentative ground covered by supplementary means is much broader, which makes it unlikely that Article 33(4) could ever be of help after a consideration of them fails to resolve the problem.

Indeed, what is likely to happen in this scenario is that the judge will look for a purposive interpretation on the basis of supplementary means to decide whether A or B has been intended, which is precisely what Article 33(4) prescribes – only by other means. But, recourse to supplementary means in their limited active role is intended only as an aid when consideration of the text alone leaves the judge at a loss. Hence, Article 32(a) should be resorted to only after all authentic means (including the object and purpose as sole decider) have been exhausted, as otherwise the fundamental weight distribution between authentic and supplementary means intended by the VCLT is upset. This conclusion is supported by recourse to supplementary means being merely 'permissible',[63] whereas Article 33(4) forms part of the prescriptive VCLT rules.

Let us consider a variation of the above scenario to make it even more obvious: now one text states A and the other B, both excluding each other. The answer to the question of how to treat this case depends again on how we classify it. Again we may view it as an ambiguity resulting from different manifest meanings of the two texts, which would warrant application of Article 32(a) – the difference to the original scenario is merely a matter of degree. Again this effectively crowds out application of Article 33(4) because it is hardly conceivable that a judge could not to come up with a purposive argument based on supplementary means and, in the unlikely event this would happen, that Article 33(4) could be of any assistance thereafter. Now, it is rather obvious that this is precisely a scenario covered by Article 33(4), and any suggestion to have recourse to supplementary means instead clearly violates the principle concerning their lesser weight as well as the principle of effectiveness.

Such approach would not only render Article 33(4) but also Article 32(b) an empty provision. Article 32(a) already does the job, and Article 32(b) does not apply consecutively because Article 32 refers to an 'interpretation according to article 31' only. Conversely, failure of Article 33(4) to resolve the problem may be considered an absurd or unreasonable result in the face

---

[63] ILC, *Draft Articles on the Law of Treaties with Commentaries*, II:223, para. 19.

of a treaty, which suggests that parties actually intended to agree. Hence, it seems sensible to resort to Article 32(b) after and not before Article 33(4) has failed, because the quest of Article 33(4) is to establish the ordinary meaning on the basis of the textual object and purpose as sole decider, whereas the idea behind Article 32(b) is to allow precedence of an alternative meaning based on supplementary means under exceptional circumstances.[64]

The whole classification problem is merely the result of the particular drafting of the VCLT, which factors the issue of plurilingual form out of the conception of the general rule and confines it to a separate article. In this context, it is important to note that Articles 31 and 32 employ the term 'meaning' in a different sense from Article 33. Article 31 reads 'A treaty shall be interpreted in good faith in accordance with the ordinary meaning to be given to the terms of the treaty in their context and in the light of its object and purpose'. Thus, it refers to the meaning of the treaty. In fact, Article 31 only talks about the treaty, not the text. The term 'text' only appears once as part of the definition of context in Article 31(2).

Article 32 then refers to the meaning of the treaty via its reference to Article 31, that is, 'the meaning resulting from the application of article 31'. Article 33 also implies the meaning of the treaty overall when referring to 'meaning', but it uses the term in a dual sense: as meaning of the treaty and as meaning of each text, which ultimately must be brought in concordance with the meaning of the treaty, that is, the meaning common to all texts.[65] This difference in use results from the different subject matters of the articles and their particular drafting. Articles 31 and 32 are drafted in terms of general principles of interpretation in the abstract, for which the notions 'meaning of the treaty' and 'meaning of the text' implicitly converge as if a unilingual treaty were implied. The topic of plurilingual form, for which the two notions may diverge, is shifted in its entirety to Article 33.

Now, the abstract principles enshrined in Articles 31 and 32 apply irrespective of the number of texts: in the case of a unilingual treaty the term 'meaning' as meaning of the treaty refers to the meaning of the single text, whereas in the plurilingual scenario it refers to the meaning common to

---

[64]See ibid., II:223, para. 19.

[65]As outlined above, the meaning common to all texts is the one true meaning of the treaty, not necessarily a meaning all texts share as lowest common denominator.

all texts. In consequence, when the same definitions of ambiguous, obscure, absurd, and unreasonable applied to treaties in the abstract[66] are applied to plurilingual treaties, we cannot claim to have arrived at a situation in which the meaning of the treaty may be judged as fundamentally ambiguous if we yet have to take the other texts into account, as we still need to consider the full context and, if necessary, the object and purpose as sole decider in order to establish the ordinary meaning of the treaty with final certainty before we can consider the result fundamentally ambiguous.[67] Otherwise, the notions of fundamental ambiguity and divergence blend into each other.

The drafting of the VCLT however suggests that they are demarcated from each other because it dedicates a separate article to plurilingual form: 'ambiguous', 'obscure', 'absurd', and 'unreasonable' are intended to refer to problems of the treaty meaning in general, whereas 'divergence' is intended to refer to problems between texts that need to be resolved first in order to establish the treaty meaning or, in case that remains impossible, a persistent difference in meaning between the texts to which then the individual concepts of fundamental ambiguity may be applied. If the drafters of the VCLT had intended to resolve problems between texts by recourse to supplementary means, having Article 33(4) would be unnecessary except for residual cases in which Article 33(4) is needed analogous to Article 31 as a legal basis the content of which (in the sense of what better fulfils the object and purpose) has to be determined by recourse to supplementary means. Reducing the function of Article 33(4) to this narrow role, however, runs counter to the idea of relying first and foremost on the text when interpreting a treaty.

Article 32 does not reference Article 33 explicitly because it takes over the abstract perspective of Article 31 and regulates merely permissible use of supplementary means as an additional aid to interpretation in general.[68] To

---

[66]Henceforth referred to as fundamental ambiguity.

[67]In essence, we have only established single text not fundamental ambiguity. Concerning the abstract perspective of Articles 31 and 32, single text and fundamental ambiguity implicitly converge; however, one must not lose sight of Article 32(a) and (b) being drafted with the latter in mind, which only equals single text ambiguity in case of a unilingual treaty. The classification confusion arises if the idea of fundamental ambiguity conceived in the abstract is simply transposed to the plurilingual scenario without explicit distinction between single text and fundamental ambiguity.

[68]See ibid., II:222–23, paras. 18–19.

suggest otherwise would imply that a consideration of the authentic means of interpretation should be conducted only up to the point when the operation of Article 33(4) would become necessary. At that point the interpreter would be suggested to switch to a consideration of supplementary means in their active role under Article 32(a) and (b) and return to authentic means under Article 33(4) only if that fails to resolve the problem. The implied back and forth between authentic and supplementary means seems inconsistent with the overall hierarchical weight attribution implemented by the VCLT and, as argued, the principle of effectiveness.

In view of these considerations, the following is submitted: A literal reading of Article 32 and Article 33(4) does not fit with a textual interpretation in the light of their context and object and purpose, since it would suggest reliance on supplementary means of interpretation for the active determination of the treaty meaning before all authentic means are exhausted. An alternative determination of the treaty meaning under Article 32 is according to its own wording only allowed once an interpretation with the help of authentic means has turned out ambiguous or obscure, or has lead to a result which is manifestly absurd or unreasonable. With plurilingual treaties such cannot be declared before recourse to the other texts has been had.

As it is the task of Article 33(4) to establish the ordinary meaning by recourse to the object and purpose as sole decider, it may be regarded as an extension of Article 31 for plurilingual cases, with its explicit reference to Article 32 being only a partial reference to the first part,[69] in the sense that the application of Article 31 has established a common meaning of the *prima facie* diverging texts that has then been confirmed by supplementary means under Article 32_1, that is, the interpretative rule in Article 33(4) does not need to be invoked. This mere partial reference implements a relationship with Article 32 analogous to Article 31, in the sense that supplementary means are supplementary both to the general rule and the interpretative

---

[69] It is noteworthy in this respect that Article 33(4) only cites Article 32 without adding letters (a) and (b). This general reference causes the ambiguity discussed here, because of the particular drafting of Article 32; however, if we assume the omission to be intentional – which is not entirely unreasonable because, at least in principle, the principle of effectiveness implies that drafting is intentionally precise rather than unintentionally vague – the conclusion presented here is even covered by the literal wording of Article 33(4).

rule in Article 33(4), which is consistent with the general intention to permit recourse to supplementary means merely as an aid, whereas Article 33(4) forms part of the prescriptive VCLT rules.

After Article 31 fails to reconcile the texts in a way that can be confirmed by a consideration of supplementary means, recourse should be had first to Article 33(4). If the object and purpose as sole decider fails to resolve the problem, we may resort to supplementary means as an aid to establish a common meaning to the incongruent meanings of the texts, as such situation may be classified as a situation of fundamental ambiguity in view of the existence of a treaty that suggests the parties intended to agree on the issue in question. Conversely, Article 32 should not be applied directly to divergences between texts, because they are first and foremost the domain of Article 33(4). The outcome concerning the overall meaning of the treaty may be classified as fundamentally ambiguous only after Article 33(4) has failed, in which case supplementary means may be resorted to in their active role.

This sequence makes sense from a practical perspective, as the reason for relying on supplementary means is a problem in form of an unresolved divergence between the texts the interpreter is confronted with, which implies that a comparison of them has already taken place. In the course of such comparison, all authentic means including the object and purpose as sole decider should be exhausted before recourse to supplementary means is had, or else the comparison is incomplete. This does not imply a different system of interpretation violating the dictum quoted above, but only adapts the system devised in the abstract to work as intended for the concrete case of multiple texts by establishing the ordinary meaning of the treaty as the meaning common to all texts.

At this point the question may be asked whether depending on the particular facts and circumstances of a case there may be good arguments to support another approach, for example, if the root of the problem is an obvious mistake resulting in two texts being different in a way nobody could have intended as opposed to two texts trying to say the same but failing. Consider the treaty UK-Denmark (1980). Its final clause declares the texts in English and Danish as 'equally authoritative', and its Article 28(3) reads 'Payments made by an individual who is resident in a Contracting State

...to a pension scheme established in and recognised for tax purposes in the other Contracting State may be relieved from tax'. The words 'and recognised for tax purposes in' were, by mistake, omitted from the statutory instrument giving effect to the treaty in the UK,[70] whereas the published Danish text implemented the correct wording.[71] For each single text considered in isolation, there is no problem of ambiguity or unreasonableness; the issue is one of differing personal scopes between the texts of the treaty and the UK statutory instrument implementing the English text.

In a hypothetical scenario in which a UK judge would only draw on the statutory instrument and apply the routine interpretation approach because no party raised the issue, the potential outcome would be a misapplication of the treaty. If the issue is raised, it should automatically resolve via reference to the signed copy. A judge should have no problem referring to the originally signed instrument even though it is not the one implemented in domestic law. Indeed, he is required by international law to apply the provisions of the concluded treaty and cannot invoke the statutory instrument as relieving him of this duty without breaching Articles 26 and 27 VCLT. If he fails to look up the signed copy, the *travaux préparatoires* should immediately resolve the issue because they will document the existence of the missing phrase. Hence, no need to invoke Article 33(4).

Let us suppose the different wording would not only be an error of the UK statutory instrument but also be the wording of the English text. If we assume that the Danish wording is the one intended, a look into the *travaux préparatoires* will, in all likelihood, reveal so. Elaborate object and purpose considerations on the basis of the texts, however, will not prove helpful when dealing with a list of conditions for obtaining relief, as obtaining relief for contributions to a foreign pension scheme is not a question of double taxation. In a tax credit system, double taxation is the normal starting point. The treaty provides relief by referral to domestic law, and double exemption is not normally possible. Under the approach submitted here, the resulting failure of the object and purpose criterion to reconcile the texts could be considered an unreasonable result. This would warrant recourse to supple-

---

[70]S.I. 1980 No. 1960; however, the text published by the Foreign and Commonwealth Office contains the correct wording.

[71]BEK 6 of 12/2 1981.

mentary means under Article 32(b), which, in all likelihood, would produce the proper outcome; however, in view of the particular facts and circumstances, such detour seems like a moot exercise.

Let us consider another example in which the mistake is less obvious. The English text of Article 13(7) in the UK-Netherlands (1980) treaty with equally authoritative English and Dutch texts reads 'to levy according to its law a tax chargeable in respect of gains from the alienation of any property on a person'. In the Dutch text the crucial bit translates to 'levy tax on gains from the alienation of property of a person'.[72] Although a provision the literal wording of which is geared towards the treatment of the tax object placed in a treaty fundamentally drafted to apply to tax subjects is odd and necessarily a source of difficulty, such provisions are not unknown in tax treaties.[73] Therefore, a consideration of the texts alone on the basis of Article 33(4) may turn out to be a moot exercise while the *travaux préparatoires* may quickly reveal that one text happens to be a bad translation; however, the routine interpretation approach to interpret a single text in isolation under Articles 31 and 32 may lead to wrong results, while considering Article 32(a) and (b) after a comparison of texts under Article 31 but before Article 33(4) bears the risk that, erroneously, an interpretation entirely autonomous from the principles contained in Article 31 and Article 33(4) is adopted because supplementary means may allow for a wider array of conclusions.

The ICSID decision on the BIT Turkey-Turkmenistan (1992) in *Kiliç* may serve as an illustration of the latter.[74] Although not necessarily the outcome as such, the reasoning of the court may be rejected. The English text of the BIT implies that submission of disputes by investors to local courts

---

[72] See Stéphane Austry et al., 'The Proposed OECD Multilateral Instrument Amending Tax Treaties', *Bulletin for International Taxation* 70, no. 12 (October 2016), s. 3, 18n.

[73] For example, Germany-US (1989), Article 1(7), based on United States, *Income and Capital Model Convention*, 2016, Article 1(6); see Richard Xenophon Resch, 'Tax Treatment of US S–Corporations under the Germany-US Tax Treaty', *European Taxation* 49, no. 3 (2009): 122–28; Richard Xenophon Resch, 'Case Closed: Tax Treatment of US S–Corporations under the Germany-US Tax Treaty – Treaty Benefits for Hybrid Entities', *European Taxation* 54, no. 5 (2014): 192–97.

[74] *Kiliç İnşaat İthalat İhracat Sanayi ve Ticaret Anonim Şirketi v Turkmenistan*, ICSID, Case No. ARB/10/1 (Washington, D.C.: International Centre for Settlement of Investment Disputes, 2012).

before arbitration are optional, whereas the Russian text implies them to be mandatory, with submission to arbitration being possible only after a final award at the local courts has not been granted within one year. The final clause of the BIT declares both texts as equally authentic. From testimony of linguistic experts the court concluded that 'attempting to interpret the relevant English text in accordance with Article 31 of the VCLT leaves its meaning ambiguous or obscure. In these circumstances, it is appropriate for the Tribunal to consider supplementary means of interpretation as permitted under Article 32 of the VCLT.'[75]

The court then considered the circumstances of the conclusion of the BIT as supplementary means and found that Turkey had entered into several BITs with the Turkic states within the narrow time frame of five days, all of which included substantially identical arbitration provisions requiring mandatory recourse to domestic courts before submission for arbitration. From this the court concluded that the English text of the BIT should be interpreted as requiring mandatory recourse to local courts as well, as such reading 'best reconciles the interpretation of the texts, having regard to the circumstances surrounding their adoption.'[76] With respect to Article 33(4) the court added the following:

> To the extent that it might not be possible to resolve the possible difference in meaning of the English and Russian text through the application of Articles 31 and 32, the Tribunal can, in accordance with the principles reflected in Article 33(4) of the VCLT, adopt the meaning which would best reconcile the two texts.
>
> To the extent that this had been necessary – and the Tribunal concludes that it is not – the Tribunal would have had no hesitation in concluding that the ambiguity of the English text could only be reconciled with the clearly mandatory Russian text by the determination that the English text also required a mandatory recourse to the local courts. This follows, because what is plainly mandatory cannot be optional, but what may either be mandatory or optional, can be seen as mandatory.[77]

---

[75] Ibid., para. 9.17.

[76] Ibid., para. 9.21.

[77] Ibid., paras. 9.22–9.23. Noteworthy, the court seems to interpret the reference to Article 32 in Article 33 as referring to the article in its entirety and, therefore, to consider its letters (a) and (b) as preceding application of Article 33(4). Symptomatically, the latter is

Questions of interpretation are for the court, so the court is right not to straight away follow the suggestions of the linguistic experts to reinterpret the English text according to grammar and phrasing considerations alone, but to declare the necessity of further considerations because the text considered turned out ambiguous.[78] As next step, however, the court went straight away to supplementary means on the basis of Article 32(a), whereas it should have done so only after an interpretation under Article 33(4) would have failed. To suggest that the meaning of the treaty is ambiguous before it has been interpreted in the light of all texts is premature – that the meaning of one text considered in isolation appears ambiguous is not sufficient to establish the truth of such contention. Instead of considering only the wording of a single text ambiguous, the court mistakenly treated the treaty as being fundamentally ambiguous.

It seems likely that considerations based on the object and purpose would not lead to a definite result, because both mandatory and optional submission to local courts before arbitration serve the same general purpose, only in different ways. Hence, it might not be possible for the court to establish the one true meaning given it faces two conflicting texts simply stating the opposite of each other. Therefore, Article 32(a) and (b) would be next in line, and the order of recourse to authentic versus supplementary means based on the hierarchy between them might not have mattered all that much concerning the outcome.

Notwithstanding, we may see from this case how giving preference to supplementary means over Article 33(4) could go wrong in practice. The primary argument of the court based on the circumstances of the BIT conclusion is relatively thin. In particular, it does not pay enough attention to the bilateral treaty relationship between the contracting parties. That the other BITs Turkey concluded at the same time with the other Turkic states

---

found no longer necessary, i.e., Article 33(4) is effectively rendered an empty provision. As a result, the VCLT interpretative framework is stood up on its head: instead of using supplementary means to confirm an interpretation based on authentic means, the court does the opposite, i.e., it confirms an interpretation it derives from what it considers to be supplementary means by an interpretation then to follow supposedly from applying Article 33(4), both of which are, however, questionable in itself besides the inversion (see below).

[78] See ibid., paras. 9.14–9.16.

106

contained equally drafted provisions all implementing mandatory submission to domestic courts before submission for arbitration sure tells us something about Turkey's treaty policy, but nothing much about Turkmenistan. For the argument to be more credible, the court should at least have ventured to gain some insight into Turkmenistan's treaty policy concerning arbitration.[79]

The argument of the court is simply one from analogy and involves no further considerations concerning context and object and purpose, not even from an examination of the *travaux préparatoires*.[80] Notwithstanding, especially the evaluation of the English text by the linguistic experts in combination with some further indications from Turkish official translations not discussed here in detail render the conclusions of the court more plausible than not;[81] however, all these considerations are not of conclusive force and would not qualify if in conflict with an evaluation on the basis of the object and purpose under Article 33(4). Instead of setting itself up to arrive at a meaning 'governed by the principles contained in article 27',[82] which provide the general parenthesis even for a determination of the meaning on the basis of supplementary means, the court's approach led it to arrive at *any* meaning somehow plausible in view of the general circumstances.

The last comment of the court concerning Article 33(4) indicates that it simply chose the meaning it considered more likely rather than doing what Article 33(4) really requires, namely, an in-depth examination of the treaty texts against the background of the expressed object and purpose. Instead of focussing on *how* to reconcile the texts, namely, in the way the VCLT

---

[79] At the time, however, Turkmenistan had only one other BIT with Spain (1990) signed and in force, which would have made deduction of a consistent treaty policy difficult.

[80] It is questionable whether the other BIT's concluded really fall under the scope of Article 32 as 'circumstances of *its* [the treaty's] conclusion' (emphasis added), as is seemingly assumed by the court.

[81] Additional political considerations the court did not explicitly elaborate on to bolster its argument, such as the situation of Turkmenistan being a newly independent state and Turkey being one of the first countries recognising the independence of all Turkic states, which in turn makes it likely that Turkmenistan would have made some concessions to Turkey's treaty policy even if it had a different one itself, may be considered to point in the same direction.

[82] ILC, *Draft Articles on the Law of Treaties with Commentaries*, II:223, para. 19. Draft Article 27 became Article 31 in the VCLT.

prescribes, it treated reconciliation as an end in itself to be effected by any means. Ironically, its reasoning that 'what is plainly mandatory cannot be optional, but what may either be mandatory or optional, can be seen as man-datory'[83] is simply a conceptual mistake. Contrary to its view, the choice for either mandatory or optional in such situation is no reconciliation at all because nothing 'may either be mandatory or optional' at the same time.

In summary, the approach suggested here by me is submitted as a matter of good practice in order to eliminate the pitfalls entailed in any other approach. Consideration of the object and purpose criterion under Article 33(4) before recourse to supplementary means may never lead to an improper result, as the argumentative scope is much narrower than that provided by supplementary means. Either it will lead to a solution based on the object and purpose, which may only be confirmed but not contested by supplementary means, or it will not lead to any solution at all, in which case recourse to supplementary means follows as next step. Recourse to Article 33(4) will in the worst case prove unhelpful, whereas direct recourse to supplementary means both before considering the other texts and applying Article 33(4) may in the worst case lead to improper results. Of course, in a mistake situation the task is to find the cause for it, for which the preparatory materials may prove to be more helpful than Article 33(4); however, unless the result is such that it is obvious nobody could have intended it, the approach suggested here is recommended as a fail-safe method.

The considered examples point again to a critical problem of plurilingual tax treaties. Differences between texts with respect to wordings that define personal scope or types of income may not always affect the avoidance of double taxation, but the issue at stake may be rather the sharing of the tax base between the contracting states. Therefore, considerations of the object and purpose as sole decider on the basis of the text alone may not prove helpful. This is a problem because there is abundant opportunity for such differences to occur, and the reason may not necessarily be careless translation but rooted in the idiomatic properties of language.

Consider the *New Skies* decision of the Delhi High Court concerning roy-

---

[83] *Kiliç İnşaat İthalat İhracat Sanayi ve Ticaret Anonim Şirketi v Turkmenistan*, para. 9.23.

alties under the Netherlands-India (1988) tax treaty.[84] Article 12(4) of the treaty defines royalties as 'payments of any kind received as a consideration for the use of, or the right to use, any copyright of any patent, trade mark, design or model, plan, secret formula or process, or for information concerning industrial, commercial or scientific experience.' The final clause declares the Dutch, Hindi, and English texts as authentic and designates the English text as prevailing in case of a divergence between the Dutch and Hindi texts. Let us disregard the prevalence of the English text for the moment and assume equal authority of all texts. The court only relied on the English text and was led down a track of extensive deliberations by domestic law considerations concerning the meaning of 'secret formula or process'. Sanghavi provides a summary:

> In *Director of Income Tax v. New Skies Satellite BV (New Skies)*, the Delhi High Court belaboured the short issue of whether the adjective "secret" qualifies only the noun 'formula' or the two nouns 'formula' and 'process' in the definition. At the root of the confusion was the very similar term 'royalty', which is very similarly defined in the Indian Income Tax Act, 1961 (ITA 1961) as 'any consideration …for …the use of any …, secret formula or process or trade mark or similar property'. Early decisions in this regard had suggested that a payment for the use of a process – not necessarily a secret process – would be considered to be a royalty for the purposes of the ITA 1961. This interpretation was subsequently confirmed by a retrospective legislative clarification, the validity of which was upheld by the Madras High Court in Verizon Communications Singapore Pte. Ltd. v. ITO. A large part of the Court's 50-page decision was dedicated to the question whether the comma, appearing after the word 'process', changed the interpretation of the term 'royalties' for the purposes of the tax treaty.[85]

In contrast to the previous scenarios, a comparison of texts would have provided for a quicker route to resolve the issue because the Dutch text uses the expression *een geheim recept of een geheime werkwijze*, that is, the adjective 'secret' is used twice to explicitly qualify both nouns 'formula' and 'process'. This is necessary in Dutch for proper idiomatic phrasing because

---

[84] *Director of Income Tax v New Skies Satellite BV*, ITA 473/2012, 2016.
[85] Dhruv Sanghavi, 'Found in Translation: The Correct Interpretation of "Secret Formula or Process" in India's Tax Treaties', *British Tax Review*, no. 4 (2016): 411–12.

nouns have a gender and here two nouns of different genders are combined: the neuter *recept* and the gender *werkwijze.*[86]

Even without consulting the Dutch text it seems obvious that with respect to the enumeration of 'any …, secret formula or process, or' the adjective 'secret' relates to both nouns, as this is standard idiomatic phrasing in English. The alternative meaning the court was led to contemplate by its reference to domestic law requires a different wording to really be manifest, for example, 'any …, secret formula, process, or'. That the Dutch text uses the adjective twice is merely incidental for purely syntactic reasons. If both nouns had the same gender, the enumeration would follow the same logic of using the adjective only once to apply it to both subjects, which is the ordinary idiomatic phrasing for such enumerations.

Using the adjective twice in English would be foolproof formulation recommendable for legal drafting, but not doing so hardly renders the text ambiguous. The proper ordinary meaning that this is an enumeration and the adjective applies to both subjects is manifest from its ordinary grammatical phrasing, whereas the alternative meaning considered by the court requires additional reasoning to become manifest. In view of the Dutch text it becomes abundantly clear that the adjective 'secret' is intended to qualify both 'formula' and 'process', and there can be no notion that the English text remains ambiguous or that there would be a difference between the texts. Thus, recourse neither to Article 33(4) nor supplementary means is needed. The case, however, raises the question of how the feature of tax treaties to refer to domestic law affects interpretation in plurilingual scenarios.

4.5. Special Considerations concerning Tax Treaties

Tax treaties commonly feature *renvoi* clauses modelled on Article 3(2) of the OECD and UN Model Conventions.[87] This introduces an additional layer of complexity to the issue at hand, because such clauses implement a situation in which the meanings of terms in the treaty intentionally have an asymmetric scope depending on the domestic laws of the treaty partners,

---

[86]See ibid., 413–14.

[87]Henceforth, 'Article 3(2)' will be used to refer to both *renvoi* clauses in Model Conventions and corresponding provisions in actual treaties.

attributable to the need to connect two different tax systems and ensure that domestic taxation and treaty relief are equally matched to effectively implement the treaty's object and purpose of avoiding double taxation.[88]

The interaction between Article 3(2) and final clauses granting equal authenticity to several texts requires the texts to make Article 3(2) compatible with Article 33 and integrate potentially asymmetrical meanings of treaty terms introduced by the referral to domestic law.[89] Under Article

---

[88]See Avery Jones, 'Treaty Interpretation', s. 7.1 [4.3.1]; Edwardes-Ker, *Tax Treaty Interpretation*, 173, s. 12.01. This asymmetry is mostly confined to terms concerning types of income that need to connect the different domestic tax systems at the treaty level, whereas in respect of other terms contextual meanings will usually apply because of the need for a symmetrical common meaning, see Avery Jones, 'Treaty Interpretation', s. 8.2.4.2.1 [5.1.2.4.2.1]. Much has been written about Article 3(2). Its interpretation is a fiercely discussed topic, as it is a rule of interpretation directly contained in all important Model Conventions and most effective tax treaties, wherefore it must be considered in addition to the VCLT. Its application is of high impact both on the contracting states with respect to the balance of effective taxing rights implemented by the treaty through reciprocal double tax relief via exemption and credit, and the taxpayer in respect of how much tax he has to pay where and overall. The debate about Article 3(2) has been intense and fruitful in the sense that a consensus to follow the qualification of the source state in case of qualification conflicts has been adopted by the OECD, see OECD, *Model Tax Convention*, 2017, Commentary on Articles 23A and 23B, paras. 32.1–32.7; for a summary of the underlying argument see Avery Jones, 'Treaty Interpretation', s. 7.6.1 [4.7.1]. The debate is continuing in view of the practical relevance, see, e.g., Seminar D: Article 3(2) and the Scope of Domestic Law, 66th IFA Congress in Boston, 2012. Much will continue to be written also in view of the not diminishing number of cases in which its application plays a role, see Mónica Sada Garibay, 'An Analysis of the Case Law on Article 3(2) of the OECD Model (2010)', *Bulletin for International Taxation* 65, no. 8 (2011). An extensive consideration of all arguments concerning Article 3(2) is way beyond the scope of this study, which will focus as much as possible on the limited issue of its interaction with Article 33 and assume familiarity of the reader with the overall debate including the most relevant literature and case law.

[89]See Wassermeyer, *Doppelbesteuerung: Kommentar zu allen deutschen Doppelbesteuerungsabkommen*, MA, Vor Art. 1, 37, para. 47. Article 3(2) must not be understood to simply override the principles of interpretation codified in the VCLT, by way of the principle *specialia generalibus derogant* (the specific derogates from the general), see Edwin van der Bruggen, 'Unless the Vienna Convention Otherwise Requires: Notes on the Relationship between Article 3(2) of the OECD Model Tax Convention and Articles 31 and 32 of the Vienna Convention on the Law of Treaties', *European Taxation* 43, no. 5 (2003): 142–56, 154–155; John F. Avery Jones et al., 'The Interpretation of Tax Treaties

3(2), the contracting states may interpret the treaty differently according to the meaning of terms in their domestic laws 'unless the context otherwise requires'; however, each contracting state must in principle be able to depart from any text because of the principle of unity and the equal authority of the texts. If country A interprets term X as F while country B interprets it as G, and this is so intended by the treaty, that is, the context does not require otherwise, X must allow for both F and G to be included in the expressed agreement, as each country must be able to interpret either text to reach the intended meaning. The principle of unity is preserved in this situation by the stipulation to follow the qualification of the source state in a qualification conflict.[90] Country A may not interpret term X as F based on one text and as G based on another, but country A must be able to interpret X as F while country B must be able to interpret X as G, based on either text. Thus, term X in either text must allow to be construed both as F and G.

This is embodied also in the concept of context as implied by Article 3(2), which differs from that employed by Article 31.[91] The meaning of the latter is relatively narrow and intended to differentiate authentic from supplementary means, attributing different weights to them for their use in the interpretative process. In contrast, the meaning of the former is intended to establish whether an existing domestic law meaning of a term should not be applied. Therefore, it is much broader and does not attribute different weights to different interpretative means, which remains an exercise left to the interpreter. Basically, it includes any material relevant and, certainly, all material listed in the VCLT, including all texts.[92] Consequently, Article 3(2) does not contrast domestic law and context as opposites,[93] but its concept

---

with Particular Reference to Art. 3(2) of the OECD Model – II', *British Tax Review*, no. 2 (1984): 104.

[90] See OECD, *Model Tax Convention*, 2017, Commentary on Articles 23A and 23B, paras. 32.1–32.7.

[91] See Avery Jones et al., 'The Interpretation of Tax Treaties with Particular Reference to Art. 3(2) of the OECD Model – II', 104.

[92] See van der Bruggen, 'Unless the Vienna Convention Otherwise Requires', 155; Avery Jones, 'Treaty Interpretation', ss. 6.2 [4.2] and 8.1 [5.1.1].

[93] Domestic law meanings represent definitions of terms incorporated by reference of Article 3(2) into the treaty. As part of the text, they are within the context definition of Article 31(2). Since the concept of context under Article 3(2) is broader and includes all interpretative means included in the VCLT definition of context, it also necessarily

of context includes the domestic law meanings of both contracting states,[94] while domestic law itself may be the only context necessary to decide that it should not be applied.[95]

In essence, many terms of a tax treaty are intended as conceptual abstractions that are comprehensive enough to allow for asymmetric interpretation according to the domestic laws of both contracting states.[96] Yet, we may not conceive of Article 3(2) as splitting the treaty in two, with separate texts in the official languages of the contracting states for terms that are to have the meaning they have under their respective domestic laws, as this would be in direct contradiction to the principle of unity and the final clause declaring all texts as equally authentic. Rather, Article 3(2) is intended to complete the treaty where it remains indistinct conceptually.

Since many terms in a treaty are intended as conceptual abstractions to be determined either symmetrically via an autonomous interpretation or asymmetrically via domestic law in order to connect two different tax systems and ensure that domestic taxation and treaty relief are equally matched, both to implement the treaty's object and purpose of avoiding double taxation, the wording of Article 3(2) has to be understood as having such conceptual scope. Avery Jones notes the following in this respect:

> It is relevant that domestic law may not use the precise expression used in the OECD Model. For instance, UK tax law refers to 'land' rather than 'immovable property', does not use 'profits of an enterprise', uses 'disposal' rather than 'alienation' in relation to capital gains, and 'earnings' rather than 'salaries, wages and other similar remuneration' in relation to employment income. It would be contrary to the purpose of the OECD Model (and a tax treaty based on it) not to apply the equivalent domestic law in such cases. This suggests that 'term' in article 3(2) of the OECD Model should be given a wide meaning, not restricted to identical words, but, rather, to the equivalent domestic law concept. ...The width of the meaning of 'term' can be even more extreme where a tax treaty provides that, in cases of different

---

includes both domestic law definitions.

[94] See Avery Jones, 'Treaty Interpretation', ss. 6.2 [4.2], 8.1 [5.1.1], and 8.2.2.1 [5.1.2.2.1]; OECD, *Model Tax Convention*, 2014, Commentary to Article 3, para. 12.

[95] See Avery Jones, 'Treaty Interpretation', ss. 8.2.2.3 [5.1.2.2.3] and 8.2.4 [5.1.2.4].

[96] See Gaja, 'The Perspective of International Law', 99–100; Wim Wijnen, 'Some Thoughts on Convergence and Tax Treaty Interpretation', *Bulletin for International Taxation*, no. 11 (2013): 575.

meanings of two language texts, a third language version is to prevail or where the only official version of a tax treaty is in a third language (*see* section 3.5.2.). As domestic law will not be written in the third (or sole other) language, there will never be an identical word in domestic law and so it is essential to give a meaning to "term" that conveys the equivalent concept.[97]

Crucially, the same understanding has to be applied when – deliberately or incidentally – actual domestic law terms are used in the respective language texts of a treaty. Such may frequently happen (particularly for terms denoting types of income) because domestic law technical terms may be simply what OECD Model terms literally translate to in the languages of the treaty partners, treaty negotiators discuss treaty provisions using their domestic law technical language with the laws of their countries in mind (and particularly with respect to their understanding of what certain types of income imply), or the treaty is indeed intended to apply asymmetrically concerning the point in question.[98]

The pitfall of this is that – especially if only the text in the own language is consulted – the seemingly obvious reference to domestic law may trick the interpreter into overlooking the term in question to constitute first and foremost a general abstraction that, of course, may default to its domestic law meaning if so intended, which can however be determined only when analysed against the background of both contexts implied by Articles 3(2) and 31(2), or else mismatches in qualification may result that lead to double taxation or double non-taxation unintended by the treaty.[99]

---

[97] Avery Jones, 'Treaty Interpretation', s. 7.2.1 [4.3.2.1].

[98] See Wassermeyer, *Doppelbesteuerung: Kommentar zu allen deutschen Doppelbesteuerungsabkommen*, MA, Vor Art. 1, 37, para. 47.

[99] See Klaus Vogel, 'Conflicts of Qualification: The Discussion is not Finished', *Bulletin for International Taxation*, no. 2 (2003): 41–44, Case 2, 43–43; John F. Avery Jones, 'Conflicts of Qualification: Comment on Prof. Vogel's and Alexander Rust's Articles', *Bulletin for International Taxation*, no. 5 (2003): 184–86, Response by Prof. Vogel, 186. Vogel discusses this as a 'conflict of qualification' not resolved by the application of the OECD approach to interpret the method article, laid out in the OECD Commentary on Article 23A and 23B, paras. 32.1–32.7. I use a different terminology, i.e., 'mismatch', because the OECD Commentary seems to reserve the terminology 'conflict of qualification' to cases in which taxation or non-taxation by the source state and the resulting double taxation or double non-taxation is (otherwise) 'in accordance with the provisions of the Convention', whereas I view Vogel's case as one in which the 'divergence is based

Vogel devises such a case between Austria and Germany with respect to a taxpayer being an Austrian national who alternates between both countries (sometimes on the same day, so accumulating stays in each exceeding six months) without having a permanent home in either.[100] The case is based on the tax treaty Austria-Germany (2000), which is unilingual in German and contains the wording *gewöhnlicher Aufenthalt* in the residence tie-breaker provision 4(2)(b).[101] This is not only a literal translation of the OECD Model wording 'habitual abode', but also a defined concept in both the domestic laws of Austria and Germany resulting in unlimited tax liability.

Crucially, however, both domestic law concepts differ from the habitual abode concept in the OECD Model and each other. In particular, German domestic tax law contains a fiction of any stay with a duration of more than six months automatically constituting an habitual abode,[102] whereas the OECD conception does not implement any such fiction concerning a specific length of time.[103] Austrian domestic law, on the other hand, specifies that whenever unlimited tax liability depends on the taxpayer's habitual abode, he will become subject to unlimited tax liability if he stays longer than six months in Austria whether or not he actually establishes an habitual abode, which will depend entirely on factual circumstances.[104]

---

not on different interpretations of the provisions of the Convention but on different provisions of domestic law', ultimately being a case of treaty misapplication to be distinguished from a 'conflict of qualification' as understood by the OECD Commentary (see below).

[100] Vogel, 'Conflicts of Qualification: The Discussion is not Finished', Case 2, 43–43.

[101] Article 4 of the treaty is modelled on Article 4 of the OECD Model.

[102] Article 9(2) AO. The AEAO to Article 9 AO, para. 1, asserts an 'irrefutable presumption' in this respect. The duration of more than six months does not have to be uninterrupted or contained in a single tax year but must not be merely transitory. Interrupted stays are to be evaluated as to whether they still constitute a single stay overall, interrupted only by short absence (attributable, e.g., to vacation) and connected by the intention to continue the stay as embodied in the factual circumstances. Merely private stays with a duration of less than one year are not taken into account, as well as cases in which the taxpayer only works in Germany but lives abroad and does not regularly stay overnight, see Article 9(1)–(2) AO in combination with AEAO to Article 9 AO, paras. 1–2.

[103] OECD, *Model Tax Convention*, 2014, Commentary on Article 4, para. 19, replaced by paras. 19–19.1 in 2017.

[104] Article 26(2) BAO in combination with Article 66(2) JN.

4. Practical Implications and Additional Issues

In Vogel's fictional scenario the taxpayer becomes subject to unlimited tax liability both in Austria and Germany under their respective domestic laws. In Austria because of his stay of more than six months, however, without establishing an habitual abode, and in Germany as a result of establishing an habitual abode because of his stay of more than six months. The taxpayer receives dividend and interest income from third countries, which ultimately falls under Article 21 of the treaty, requiring the tie-breaker rule to decide residence for treaty purposes.

Despite acknowledging that the context seems to require an autonomous interpretation of the OECD Model and treaty term 'habitual abode',[105] Vogel nevertheless suggests an interpretation ultimately based on domestic law:

> [S]ubparagraph b) does not specify the time of a stay which would qualify it as being 'habitual', and they merely add that the length of this time must be 'sufficient'. Thus, though the core of the term 'habitual abode' can be determined by autonomous interpretation, its 'boundaries' remain indistinct. To this extent, therefore, the reference to domestic law provided by Art. 3(2) persists.[106]

In consequence, Article 4 in combination with Article 3(2) would cause Austria to consider the taxpayer resident in Germany for treaty purposes because he has an habitual abode in Germany but not in Austria under the assumed factual circumstances, whereas Germany would consider the taxpayer resident in Austria for treaty purposes because he has an habitual abode in both states according to the six months fiction, wherefore residence is ultimately decided based on nationality under Article 4(2)c. The result is double non-taxation of the dividend and interest income.[107]

The question is whether the interpretation of Article 4 in combination with Article 3(2) applied by Vogel – which he himself admits to be controversial[108] – is really correct, or whether this is a case for which the context

---

[105]For conclusive argument in this respect, see Vogel and Lehner, *Doppelbesteuerungsabkommen der Bundesrepublik Deutschland auf dem Gebiet der Steuern vom Einkommen und Vermögen: Kommentar auf der Grundlage der Musterabkommen*, 440–41, paras. 203–206; Wassermeyer, *Doppelbesteuerung: Kommentar zu allen deutschen Doppelbesteuerungsabkommen*, MA, Art. 4, 55–59, paras. 74–77.

[106]Vogel, 'Conflicts of Qualification: The Discussion is not Finished', 42.

[107]See ibid., 42–43.

[108]See ibid., 43.

requires otherwise. Avery Jones rejects Vogel's view, pointing to the pitfall outlined above Vogel falls victim to:

> I suggest that the fact that Germany uses an identical expression (or rather an identical expression in the German translation of the OECD Model) in its internal law is insufficient to cause Art. 3(2) to apply internal law, particularly in light of the Commentary, when the result of doing so is that both Austria and Germany would resolve the dual residence in favour of the other state, leaving the taxpayer a resident of neither, which is not exactly in accordance with the object and purpose of the treaty. The case for using internal law to define a type of income is much stronger because the result is that the treaty exemption or relief corresponds exactly to the internal law tax charge; for other expressions, there is a much stronger argument for the term to mean the same in both states. Dual residence would not be resolved in the same way in all states if one state happens to use one of the expressions in Art. 4(2) in its internal law. If there is a conflict between the two states' interpretations, it has to be resolved by the mutual agreement article.[109]

In light of all the aforesaid I strongly agree with Avery Jones. What may be added to his analysis is that the concept of *gewöhnlicher Aufenthalt* in German tax law not only differs from the OECD habitual abode concept as regards the six months fiction, but also in other respects and in terms of its context.[110] Crucially, according to the OECD Model, the taxpayer may have an habitual abode at the same time in both contracting states, whereas under German tax law the taxpayer can have only a single habitual abode at any point in time.[111] Therefore, domestic law itself may be the only context necessary to decide that it should not be applied, because the conclusion that the taxpayer has his habitual abode both in Austria and Germany is at the same time based on domestic law and precluded by it, that is, applying the German domestic law definition is self-contradicting.

---

[109] Avery Jones, 'Conflicts of Qualification: Comment on Prof. Vogel's and Alexander Rust's Articles', 186.

[110] See Vogel and Lehner, *Doppelbesteuerungsabkommen der Bundesrepublik Deutschland auf dem Gebiet der Steuern vom Einkommen und Vermögen: Kommentar auf der Grundlage der Musterabkommen*, 440, para. 203.

[111] AEAO to Article 9 AO, para. 3; see BFH, 'I 244/63' (BStBl 1966 III, February 1966); BFH, 'I R 241/82' (BStBl 1984 II, August 1983).

4. Practical Implications and Additional Issues

In summary, when applying Article 3(2), it is crucial to bear in mind that most treaty terms are first and foremost general abstractions even if terminology identical to domestic law is used. Neither do treaty terms identical to domestic law terminology imply they should be interpreted according to domestic law,[112] nor treaty terms different from domestic law terminology that they should not be interpreted according to it.[113]

Under a contextual interpretation of habitual abode – in this particular case considering specifically the domestic laws of both contracting states and the treaty object and purpose – the correct outcome of Vogel's fictional scenario should be one of the following, depending on the particular facts and circumstances assumed:

(a) The taxpayer has an habitual abode in either Austria or Germany.
(b) He has an habitual abode both in Austria and Germany.
(c) He does not have an habitual abode in either of them.

In other words, there should be a common interpretation concerning the length of time to be sufficient for qualifying a stay as habitual. As a result, residence for treaty purposes would be attributed by both Austria and Germany to the same state based on either the habitual abode criterion or the nationality of the taxpayer. The outcome suggested by Vogel does not constitute a 'conflict of qualification' as defined by the OECD Commentary but represents a treaty misapplication attributable to a mismatch in interpretation caused by mistakenly applying domestic law definitions because the treaty text incidentally featured terminology identical to domestic law, which should be resolved via a mutual agreement procedure.[114]

---

[112]See Wassermeyer, *Doppelbesteuerung: Kommentar zu allen deutschen Doppelbesteuerungsabkommen*, MA, Art. 4, 55–56, para. 74.

[113]See Avery Jones, 'Treaty Interpretation', s. 7.2.1 [4.3.2.1].

[114]The 2017 OECD Model and Commentary update addresses such scenario: 'Under paragraph 3, the competent authorities can, in particular, enter into a mutual agreement to define a term not defined in the Convention, or to complete or clarify the definition of a defined term, where such an agreement would resolve difficulties or doubts arising as to the interpretation or application of the Convention. Such circumstances could arise, for example, where a conflict in meaning under the domestic laws of the two States creates difficulties or leads to an unintended or absurd result. As expressly recognised in paragraph 2 of Article 3, an agreement reached under paragraph 3 concerning the

Unfortunately, confusing treaty concepts with domestic law ones is a mistake easy to make, as tax treaties will for a variety of reasons often feature terminology identical to domestic law.[115] Therefore, Article 3(2) provides an additional argument for an obligation to compare texts: in order to define any treaty term X according to domestic law, one first has to establish the exact term X to be defined, for which it is necessary to compare all texts. Since the different language texts may translate treaty term X as F or G in the languages of the contracting states – which may be terms borrowed from their respective domestic laws (either deliberately because their domestic law meanings may indeed be intended, or incidentally although a contextual meaning may be intended) – one runs the risk of interpreting X as not-X according to the domestic law meaning of either F or G if only the text in the own language is looked at.

Hence, for any decision whether a domestic law meaning is to be applied, both contexts as implied by Article 3(2) and Article 31 including the domestic laws of both contracting states and the other language texts need to be considered. Ellis notes in this respect against the background of specific case law on capital gains:

> There are States that, in their national tax systems, do not differentiate between capital gains and ordinary income. There is case law in which the

---

meaning of a term used in the Convention prevails over each State's domestic law meaning of that term', OECD, *Model Tax Convention*, 2017, Commentary on Article 25, para. 6.1.

[115] The true lesson of Vogel's thought experiment is that treaty negotiators are setting courts up for committing this type of error if they use domestic law terms too indiscriminately, see, by analogy, Bernhard Grossfield, 'Language and the Law', *Journal of Air Law and Commerce* 50 (1985): 793–803, 801: 'If the structure of a particular language plays an important role in defining our thinking, it may well be that a particular language can only express certain legal ideas and that the limits of our particular language are the limits of our legal reasoning.' Vogel's case illustrates that the same applies if the treaty is in a shared official language of the contracting states. As Kuner has pointed out, 'The interrelation between legal terminology and the legal system in which it is used is so strong that substantial differences in usage exist even among States that (supposedly) share a common language', Kuner, 'The Interpretation of Multilingual Treaties', 957. Hence, treaty negotiators should make an effort to restrict use of terms with a defined domestic law meaning to cases when an asymmetrical application of the treaty is indeed intended.

courts of such States have been called upon to interpret the expression 'capital gain' laid down in tax treaties and, in order to do so, reverted to Article 3(2) of the treaty. The courts in these cases decided to interpret the treaty on the basis of the text drafted in the foreign domestic language since the difference between the concept of 'income' and that of 'capital gain' in the other language was perceivable. In order to reach such conclusions, the courts first considered Article 3(2) but then affirmed that the context overrides the principle under which the meaning of a term or expression shall be based on the domestic law of the State applying the treaty – and certainly the other language of the treaty is a part of the context. The text of the treaty drafted in the foreign authentic language has therefore been considered relevant to understanding the contextual meaning of a given expression.[116]

Vogel's fictional scenario is particularly problematic because the treaty at its base is unilingual in German and contains no definition of *gewöhnlicher Aufenthalt*, which makes it hard for any judge not to resort to domestic law:

> Regarding Art. 4(2), *gewöhnlicher Aufenthalt* is not only the German translation of the OECD Model; rather, it is the wording of all of Germany's current tax treaties (and of Austria's treaties, and maybe Switzerland's treaties, as well). With respect to Germany's treaties with Austria and Switzerland, there is not even a version in another language on which one could base an interpretation which differs from the German domestic one. I have not yet met a German judge who, in this situation, would be prepared to accept an interpretation which differs from German domestic law. And where should he find a criterion to choose between one of the two possible interpretations?[117]

How can we reply? Although there is no English text available reading 'habitual abode', it is obvious that *gewöhnlicher Aufenthalt* is intended to mean habitual abode as understood by the OECD Commentary, not as defined under domestic law.[118] This is only obscured by *gewöhnlicher Aufenthalt* in-

---

[116]Gaja, 'The Perspective of International Law', Appendix, Intervention by Prof. Maarten Ellis; see cases quoted by Avery Jones, 'Treaty Interpretation', s. 8.1 [5.1.1].

[117]Avery Jones, 'Conflicts of Qualification: Comment on Prof. Vogel's and Alexander Rust's Articles', Response by Prof. Vogel, 186.

[118]See Vogel and Lehner, *Doppelbesteuerungsabkommen der Bundesrepublik Deutschland auf dem Gebiet der Steuern vom Einkommen und Vermögen: Kommentar auf der Grundlage der Musterabkommen*, 440–41, para. 203–206; Wassermeyer, *Doppelbesteuerung: Kommentar zu allen deutschen Doppelbesteuerungsabkommen*, MA, Art. 4, 55–59, paras. 74–77.

cidentally being the literal translation of 'habitual abode' while also being a defined legal concept under domestic law.[119] Both Austria and Germany are members of the OECD since 1961 (the same applies to Switzerland), and neither has placed a reservation or observation in the OECD Commentary concerning the interpretation of Article 4. Hence, it seems reasonable to assume that whenever their treaties are modelled on the OECD Model reading 'habitual abode', an autonomous interpretation along the lines of Avery Jones as quoted above is implied.

Probably for all plurilingual treaties of Austria and Germany with a residence tie-breaker rule modelled on the OECD Model the German text reads *gewöhnlicher Aufenthalt* where the English text reads 'habitual abode'.[120] Therefore, it is unreasonable to assume that the meaning should be any different when there is only a German text reading *gewöhnlicher Aufenthalt* unless the treaty itself or its particular context would provide further indication to the contrary. Granted, such line of reasoning is generally problematic because of the bilateral nature of tax treaties. In this particular case, however, a multilateral perspective based on the treaty policy embodied in the treaty networks of both countries seems warranted for said reasons.

---

[119]See Wassermeyer, *Doppelbesteuerung: Kommentar zu allen deutschen Doppelbesteuerungsabkommen*, MA, Vor Art. 1, 37, para. 47.

[120]See, e.g, Austria-Bulgaria (2010) or Germany-China (2014). Noteworthy, the French texts of both Austria-France (1993) and Germany-France (1959) use the wording *séjourne de façon habituelle* in the residence tie-breaker where the German texts read *gewöhnlicher Aufenthalt*, which is equivalent to the wording of Article 4(2)b of the French text of the OECD Model, see OECD, *Modèle de convention fiscale concernant le revenu et la fortune* (Paris: OECD Publishing, 2010).

5. Reliance on the Prevailing Text

5.1. Research Question

The previous chapters may have left the reader with unease. If we subscribe to the arguments refuting the routine interpretation approach, we are at the same time presented with the real life practical challenges involved in a comparison of all texts. The situation may look particularly bleak for tax treaties because disputes about their application have to be decided by national courts of various levels that may not be sufficiently equipped to compare all texts.[1] While the number of different language texts most commonly amounts only to two or three per treaty,[2] the problem increases with the expansion of a country's treaty network and the addition of languages. Whereas getting hold of the texts in the other languages may no longer pose much of a problem in today's world,[3] the expertise to illuminate their meaning may not be so readily available.[4]

Even if the judges interpreting the treaty are generally familiar with the other languages, it may be difficult for them to establish the exact meaning of any specific expression, in which case recourse to dictionaries, translators, and legal experts may become necessary.[5] Thus, Waldock's suggestion that from a pragmatic perspective an obligatory comparison of all texts seems unreasonable in view of the needed resources and countries being unequally equipped to follow such prescription in practice remains a fair

---

[1] See Gaja, 'The Perspective of International Law', 98.

[2] Exact statistics in his respect will be presented in Chapter 8, s. 8.2.1.

[3] For a counterexample, see *Kiliç İnşaat İthalat İhracat Sanayi ve Ticaret Anonim Şirketi v Turkmenistan*, paras. 7.8–7.11.

[4] See Philip Baker, 'Recent Developments in the Interpretation and Application of Double Taxation Conventions', *Fiscalidade – Revista de Direito e Gestao Fiscal*, no. 4 (2000): 24.

[5] See, e.g., *Fothergill v Monarch Airlines Ltd.*, 273–74, 286–87, 293–94, 300–301; *Buchanan (James) & Co. Ltd. v Babco Forwarding and Shipping (UK) Ltd.*, [1978] AC 141, HL, 152–53; *Kiliç İnşaat İthalat İhracat Sanayi ve Ticaret Anonim Şirketi v Turkmenistan*, paras. 1.38, 1.58, 1.60.

point.[6] This leaves us with an obvious dilemma.

What if we just stick to the routine interpretation approach, tacitly accept its shortcomings, and hope for the best – no plaintiff, no judge? Even so the problem does not change in substance but only in degree: the issue remains how to deal with the practical problems associated with a comparison once ambiguities arise or divergences between the texts have been pointed out. Given the potential for divergences[7] together with the ever-increasing globalisation of commercial and investment activities[8] likely accompanied by respective international tax issues and growing taxpayer awareness out of self-interest, it is more than likely that the number of cases in which divergences will play a role and put judges in the predicament outlined above will grow in the future.[9] This sets us back to the practical problems involved in a comparison of texts whether or not we agree with the arguments presented before or continue to adhere to the routine interpretation approach.

---

[6]See ILC, *Summary Records of the Eighteenth Session, 4 May – 19 July 1966*, I, Part II:211, para. 35.

[7]Linguistic and juridical concordance between legal texts in different languages is hard to achieve in practice even in case of the most careful drafting, see Rosenne, 'The Meaning of "Authentic Text" in Modern Treaty Law', 416–23, concerning the efforts spent on UNCLOS III.

[8]See Peter Dicken, *Global Shift: Mapping the Changing Contours of the World Economy*, 7th ed. (Thousand Oaks, CA: Sage Publications Ltd., 2014), passim.

[9]In the aftermath of the *Natexis* case, *SA Natixis* (formerly *SA Natexis Banques Populaires*) filed for tax sparing credits under the French tax treaties with Argentina, China, India, Indonesia, and Turkey. The French tax administration denied these claims again based on the argument that the respective treaty clauses should not be read as tax sparing but matching credit provisions, concerning which a matching credit for income completely exempt from withholding tax must be explicitly provided for by the wording of the treaty. Otherwise, the actual payment of at least some (if only minimal) withholding tax is required for a credit to be granted. The French Administrative Court of Appeal confirmed this view, basing itself on the decision of the Conseil d'État in *Natexis*. The case went again in front of the Conseil d'État, which decided that under the treaty with China the credit was not conditional upon taxation there. The other treaties, however, contained different language to the effect that the income, if completely exempt, had to be so by virtue of special domestic incentive measures for the promotion of economic development. Since *SA Natixis* did not prove such had been the case, the Conseil d'État denied the credit, see Conseil d'État, *9ème et 10ème sous-sections réunies, 25/02/2015, 366680, Inédit Au Recueil Lebon*, 2015.

In summary, comparing all language texts is correct but inconvenient, whereas the routine interpretation approach is convenient but incorrect.[10] And even if it were correct, it would remain convenient only to the extent no ambiguities arise and nobody raises a divergence, that is, it is no solution in principle. In order to solve the problem posed by plurilingual form in a truly pragmatic fashion, this chapter argues the case for an alternative approach that avoids the necessity of a comparison, is consistent with the VCLT principles, and is readily available in practice, namely, automatic recourse to and sole reliance on the prevailing text when such exists,[11] which is the case for the majority of plurilingual tax treaties.[12] In addition, the lim-

---

[10] It has been suggested that the routine interpretation approach is motivated predominantly by considerations of practical convenience and political expediency, see Kuner, 'The Interpretation of Multilingual Treaties', 962; Hilf, *Die Auslegung mehrsprachiger Verträge*, 75; Tabory, *Multilingualism in International Law and Institutions*, 199; Germer, 'Interpretation of Plurilingual Treaties', 413.

[11] Henceforth shortened to sole reliance on the prevailing text.

[12] Chapter 8 will analyse the global tax treaty network to account for all cases for which this solution is available, all cases for which it is not necessary because of unilingual form, and all cases for which a comparison of texts remains obligatory. The solution of sole reliance on the prevailing text is discussed and submitted here on a theoretical basis for academic purposes. It may be resorted to in practice; however, given the reality that it is for a variety of reasons customary for courts to rely on their own language text (at least initially), such suggestion may be dismissed by the practitioner as an academic ivory tower proposal. Hence, the following modified approach is suggested in practice: instead of direct recourse to the prevailing text, the text in the own language is relied on together with recourse to the prevailing text to gauge the result. The other language text(s) may then be ignored – at least most of the times (see below). Given that countries tend to choose a language for the prevailing text they have a high level of familiarity with (and for which Model Conventions coupled with Commentaries exist that, depending on the circumstances, may be drawn on for purposes of interpretation), together with a largely uniform choice of prevailing language over the entire global tax treaty network reducing the amount of third party resources needed (Chapters 8 and 9 will put exact numbers to these claims), such approach seems practicable, neither overburdening states nor taxpayers. Indeed, this may come close to what is practice already, at least by some courts. In 'I R 48/12', para. 13, the German BFH employed this approach in a decision concerning the status of S-Corporations under the Germany-US (1989) tax treaty in order to establish the exact point in time when the 2006 protocol would start to take effect. Although the treaty does not feature a prevailing text – this being an example of the court merely consulting the other text – the approach suggested here would be analogous concerning method and in the case of a prevailing text

itations to such approach will be outlined as well. The fundamental research question underlying this chapter is whether and to what extent courts are required to compare the other authentic texts when they have one designated as prevailing at their disposal, and the hypothesis put forward in this respect is threefold: (1) The VCLT permits automatic recourse to the prevailing text. (2) Sole reliance on it is justified as long as its interpretation under Article 31 neither leaves its meaning ambiguous or obscure nor leads to a result that is manifestly absurd or unreasonable. (3) The contrary view currently supported by many scholars rests on an erroneous interpretation of Article 33.

5.2. Framing the Issue

The discussion about the use of prevailing texts to date has been framed by the way in which the drafters of the VCLT have posed the question in the VCLT Commentary:

> The application of provisions giving priority to a particular text in case of divergence may raise a difficult problem as to the exact point in the interpretation at which the provision should be put into operation. Should the 'master' text be applied automatically as soon as the slightest difference appears in the wording of the texts? Or should recourse first be had to all, or at any rate some, of the normal means of interpretation in an attempt to reconcile the texts before concluding that there is a case of 'divergence'?[13]

Given this pretext, scholars have commonly discussed the issue along the same lines, namely, at which point in the interpretative process recourse

---

all the more warranted. The court interpreted the German text and then confirmed its interpretation by reference to the English text. Although the formulation of the English text happened to be more precise concerning the specific point in time supporting the conclusion of the court, there was no suggestion that the German text had been ambiguous. The practitioner may mentally insert this modified approach every time I talk about sole reliance on the prevailing text. Shelton discusses various alternatives from returning to unilingual treaties in Latin to simultaneous negotiation and drafting by the negotiators in the various languages (as done in the UNCLOS III procedure), see Shelton, 'Reconcilable Differences? The Interpretation of Multilingual Treaties'. Since they are all either less feasible or less effective than the solution proposed here, they will not be discussed.

[13]ILC, *Draft Articles on the Law of Treaties with Commentaries*, II:224, para. 4.

must be had to an existing prevailing text, and up to what point efforts to reconcile divergent texts should be sustained before the prevailing text is to be invoked. From its beginning until today the focal point of the discussion has been whether the slightest difference in expression between the texts suffices to justify recourse to the prevailing text or whether it would be necessary to first establish a difference in meaning between the texts that cannot otherwise be reconciled.[14]

Framing the issue this way somewhat suggests itself in respect of disputes about tax treaties, in which it is custom for the national courts presiding to rely on their own language text (at least initially). At the same time, however, framing the issue this way is unfortunate because it conceives of the prevailing text in terms of a problem rather than a solution, and this mode of thinking has invisibly guided the discussion of the issue to date and the answers given. To some extent this is unsurprising because the drafters of the VCLT failed to provide a definitive answer to their question but remained indecisive in view of the varied jurisprudence on the issue:

> The question is essentially one of the intention of the parties in inserting the provision in the treaty, and the Commission doubted whether it would be appropriate for the Commission to try to resolve the problem in a formulation of the general rules of interpretation. Accordingly, it seemed to the Commission sufficient in paragraph 1 to make a general reservation of cases where the treaty contains this type of provision.[15]

Two important preliminary observations may be made about this. First, it appears that both approaches are in line with the VCLT – neither is ruled out by the ILC. Second, it is important for the interpreter to determine the intention of the contracting parties on this point in order to resolve the issue on a case-by-case basis. Concerning the first observation, if we presume that the intention behind introducing a prevailing text is to ease interpretation rather than to encumber it, the issue in question may be posed differently, namely, the other way around. Given the principle of unity and equal authenticity, the interpreter is free to start with any text, which could equally

---

[14]See, e.g., Hardy, 'The Interpretation of Plurilingual Treaties by International Courts and Tribunals', 123 et seq.; Arginelli, *The Interpretation of Multilingual Tax Treaties*, 325 et seq.

[15]ILC, *Draft Articles on the Law of Treaties with Commentaries*, II:224, para. 4.

be the one additionally declared as prevailing and by no means has to be the one in the official language of the country where the case is being decided. Thus, the question important to answer is whether and under what circumstances the interpreter is obliged to have recourse to the other texts if there is one designated as prevailing at his disposal. This is the way the question should be posed. Rather than constituting an additional variable increasing complexity for the interpreter, the prevailing text should be conceived of as a tool to avoid or at least significantly reduce additional complexity induced by plurilingual form. How exactly this approach fits with the principles enshrined in the VCLT will be the topic of this chapter. Concerning the second observation, given the special focus of this study on tax treaties, an empirical analysis evaluating their factual situation with respect to the theoretical solution submitted is necessary, which will be provided by Chapter 8.

5.3. The Contrary Positions

5.3.1. The Permissive Approach

The essence of the permissive approach advocated by me is to conceive of the prevailing text as a tool to reduce complexity of plurilingual treaty interpretation into a situation of quasi-unilinguality, based on the hypothesis that the VCLT framework of interpretation allows for sole reliance on the prevailing text, which has been practised by international courts in several cases.[16] At the same time, it does not rule out reconciliatory comparative interpretation of all texts as an alternative as long as the result converges to the meaning of the prevailing text. Reconciliatory comparative interpretation of all texts may still become necessary under certain circumstances, for example, when an interpretation of the prevailing text under Article 31

---

[16] See, e.g., *Treaty of Neuilly (Bulgaria v Greece)*, PCIJ (Publications of the Permanent Court of International Justice 1922–1946, 1924), 3–10, as referenced by ILC, *Draft Articles on the Law of Treaties with Commentaries*, 224, para. 4; *Aron Kahane Successeur v Francesco Parisi and the Austrian State*, Romanian-Austrian Mixed Arbitral Tribunal (Recueil des décisions des tribunaux arbitraux mixtes institués par les traités de paix, 1929), as discussed by Arginelli, *The Interpretation of Multilingual Tax Treaties*, 327–328.

leaves the meaning ambiguous or obscure, or leads to a result that is manifestly absurd or unreasonable.

The permissive approach is based on what may be called the *logical argument*.[17] The core of the logical argument is that it does not matter whether there is a divergence, because the prevailing text can be relied on in any case; the other texts must be interpreted always to have the same meaning as the prevailing text, which makes recourse to them unnecessary if the meaning of the prevailing text is manifest. Either the prevailing text has the same meaning as the other texts, in which case it may be relied on same as the others, or it has a different meaning, in which case it must be relied on while the other texts must be interpreted to concord to its meaning.[18] In the words of Lord Roskill (by analogy but nevertheless pertinent):

> I think, like my noble and learned friends, that those writings point strongly to the conclusion which all your Lordships have reached, that 'avarie' in this context includes 'partial loss'. Either therefore 'damage' in the English text must be construed so as to include 'partial loss', or there is an inconsistency and the French text as I would interpret it in the light of those writings must prevail. *I do not think it matters by which route that conclusion is reached.*[19]

The complete hypothesis submitted here is comprised of two propositions and the conclusions drawn from them. First, although it is custom for national courts to have recourse to their own language text initially, they may in principle have initial recourse to any text. Second, the prevailing text is at minimum equally authoritative when there is no divergence. When there is one, it is super-authoritative in the sense that it prevails over the other texts whatever they may say: a clear meaning of the prevailing text must be regarded as the one true meaning of the treaty, and a reconciliatory comparative interpretation of the other texts is no longer necessary because its outcome may not depart from the established meaning of the

---

[17]Implying that, logically, both methods (interpretation of the prevailing text and reconciliatory comparative interpretation of all texts) should lead to the same result.

[18]See Engelen, *Interpretation of Tax Treaties under International Law*, 380; Hardy, 'The Interpretation of Plurilingual Treaties by International Courts and Tribunals', 126, with reference to *Foreign Relations of the United States* (1923), vol. 2, 1166, 1171.

[19]*Fothergill v Monarch Airlines Ltd.*, 301 (emphasis added).

prevailing text. Hence, automatic recourse to the prevailing text is permitted, and courts may rely on the prevailing text alone as long as its meaning is clear. On the other hand, they are not prevented from reconciliatory comparative interpretation as long as the outcome does not deviate from the clear meaning of the prevailing text, and they have to engage in reconciliatory comparative interpretation if the meaning of the prevailing text remains unclear otherwise.

The first proposition will not be subject to extensive discussion, as it must be considered uncontroversial. To deny it would mean to deny the principle of unity and the authentic status of all texts explicitly declared by the treaty's final clause. It is uncontroversial even if only the own language text is given effect in law through incorporation into domestic legislation, because by the final clause contained in that same text all texts of the treaty are declared authentic; therefore, equal recourse to them is warranted under domestic legislation via the incorporated one.[20]

The validity of the second proposition and the conclusions drawn from both will be the main subject of discussion in this chapter. For this purpose, a notional standard final clause is assumed that, based on the wordings of Article 33(1) and (4), declares several texts as authentic and one of them as prevailing in case of divergence,[21] as for example implemented in Armenia-United Arab Emirates (2002):

> Done in Abu Dhabi on April 20, 2002, in two originals, in the Armenian, Arabic and English languages, all texts being equally authentic. In case of divergence the English text shall prevail.

5.3.2. The Restrictive Approach

Contrary to the permissive approach advocated by me, the restrictive approach currently supported by many scholars and most comprehensively argued by Arginelli rules out sole reliance on the prevailing text.[22] Recourse

---

[20]See *Buchanan (James) & Co. Ltd. v Babco Forwarding and Shipping (UK) Ltd.*, 152; Avery Jones, 'Treaty Interpretation', s. 3.7.1.8.

[21]Specific issues with respect to the actual wordings of tax treaty final clauses in practice will be discussed in detail in Chapter 8, s. 8.3.

[22]See Arginelli, *The Interpretation of Multilingual Tax Treaties*, 333 et seq. His arguments will be subject to in-depth considerations in Chapter 6, s. 6.4.

to it is permitted only as a limited solution for cases in which a reconciliation of texts in the course of a comparative interpretation has proven impossible. At the core of the restrictive approach lies a particular interpretation of the term 'divergence'. According to this view, a divergence warranting recourse to the prevailing text under Article 33 is given only when a difference in meaning between the texts persists after the application of Articles 31 and 32 to all texts, otherwise the prevailing text cannot be taken to prevail. In consequence, decisive recourse to the prevailing text requires the interpreter to conduct a reconciliatory comparative interpretation first in order to establish whether the condition of a divergence is fulfilled and the meaning of the prevailing text may be applied as prevailing.

This view rejects the logical argument, on grounds of Hardy's supposition that the interpretation most compatible with all texts is not necessarily the one suggested by the prevailing text in isolation.[23] Based on the assumption that all texts were always intended to mean the same, the existence of a divergence warranting decisive recourse to the prevailing text is practically ruled out,[24] and Arginelli goes as far as to advocate reconciliatory comparative interpretation to the point that it ought to be conducted instead of decisive recourse to the prevailing text even if reconciliation is possible only with the help of supplementary means or by granting decisive weight to the original text, because such renders recourse to the prevailing text 'superfluous'.[25]

The restrictive approach may be traced back to a decision by the Polish supreme court.[26] The court's reasoning rests on two propositions. First, the fact that the contracting parties have decided to authenticate more than one language text must be interpreted as intended to have some legal consequence, namely, that of attributing legal authority to each text.[27] Second,

---

[23]See Hardy, 'The Interpretation of Plurilingual Treaties by International Courts and Tribunals', 126, 133–34. This argument will be discussed in depth in Chapter 6, s. 6.2.

[24]See Engelen, *Interpretation of Tax Treaties under International Law*, 394; Arginelli, *The Interpretation of Multilingual Tax Treaties*, 103, 232, 333–38, 241.

[25]Arginelli, *The Interpretation of Multilingual Tax Treaties*, 333.

[26]*Archdukes of the Habsburg-Lorraine House v The Polish State Treasury, Annual Digest of Public International Law Cases (1929–1930), Case No. 235*, Supreme Court Poland (Cambridge University Press, 1930).

[27]Concerning this proposition, Arginelli observes that the court only respected the prin-

the status of the prevailing text is superior only once the existence of a material divergence has been established, and such material divergence may not be said to exist solely because of a mere difference in wording, but its existence can be established only with the help of all available means of interpretation attributing all possible meanings to all texts. The court concluded that since the final clause of the treaty has to be interpreted as meaning that all three texts are authentic and therefore relevant for interpretative purposes, the superior status of the prevailing text comes into play only in case the existence of a material divergence is established. Consequently, any common meaning of all texts always prevails, and a text may be disregarded only insofar as none of its possible meanings may be attributed also to the text designated as prevailing.[28]

Several preliminary observations may be made concerning this reasoning. The court is of course right to suggest that the plurilingual form of the treaty must have been intended to have some legal consequence, namely, that of all texts being authentic. Along the same lines, however, the declaration of one text as prevailing must have been intended to have some legal consequence as well, namely, that of granting that text prevailing status. In this respect we will have to discuss the meaning of 'prevailing'; however, we may note already that the principle of effectiveness equally applies to the clause establishing one text as prevailing. Consequently, the court may have made a mistake in following an interpretation that renders this clause ineffective and, thereby, may have violated the expressed intentions of the contracting parties. Such contention will hinge on what is covered by the term 'divergence'.

The English text of the treaty subject to the case reads 'The present Treaty, in French, in English, and in Italian, shall be ratified. In case of divergence the French text shall prevail'.[29] Thus, it merely speaks of divergence, without

---

ciple of effectiveness, as in his view a contrary contention would imply that the contracting parties, by declaring one text as prevailing in case of divergence, nullified their own intentions expressed by authenticating several texts, see Arginelli, *The Interpretation of Multilingual Tax Treaties*, 329.

[28] See ibid., 329–30.

[29] *Treaty of Peace between the Allied and Associated Powers and Austria*; Protocol, Declaration and Special Declaration (St. Germain-en-Laye, 10 September 1919). The prevailing French text is equivalent and reads '*Le présent Traité, rédigé en français, en anglais et*

any further qualification. We will have to see whether the interpretation of divergence as material divergence the court as well as Arginelli and others subscribe to, that is, a difference in meaning that cannot be reconciled with any interpretation of the prevailing text, is truly in line with the VCLT. In the previous chapter we saw already that any meaning common to all texts may not necessarily turn out to be the treaty meaning under Article 33(4) in case of a divergence – such would grant the *Mavrommatis* approach the status of a general principle, which it has been denied by the ILC.[30]

5.4. Interpretation of Article 33(1) and (4)

5.4.1. The Meaning of Prevailing

The Oxford Dictionary defines to prevail as to 'Prove more powerful or superior', stemming from the Latin *praevalere* (to have greater power). Hence, the meaning of the prevailing text must be considered more authoritative than the meaning of any other text or all others combined, otherwise we cannot make sense of the notion of it prevailing. According to the wording of Article 33(1), the prevailing text does not prevail by default but only conditional upon the existence of a divergence. From this situation originates the problem of 'when to apply the prevailing text'.[31] As has been convincingly established by Engelen,[32] however, this limitation may be the result of 'infelicitous drafting' not intended to create a peremptory norm,[33] but the intention of the contracting parties expressed in the wording of the ac-

---

en italien, sera ratifié. En cas de divergence, le texte français fera foi.'

[30] See ILC, *Draft Articles on the Law of Treaties with Commentaries*, II:225–26, para. 8; Gaja, 'The Perspective of International Law', 93–94.

[31] ILC, *Draft Articles on the Law of Treaties with Commentaries*, II:224, para. 4; see Hardy, 'The Interpretation of Plurilingual Treaties by International Courts and Tribunals', 123 et seq.; Arginelli, *The Interpretation of Multilingual Tax Treaties*, 325 et seq.

[32] See Engelen, *Interpretation of Tax Treaties under International Law*, 376–79.

[33] Defined by the VCLT as follows: 'For the purposes of the present Convention, a peremptory norm of general international law is a norm accepted and recognized by the international community of States as a whole as a norm from which no derogation is permitted and which can be modified only by a subsequent norm of general international law having the same character', UN, *Vienna Convention on the Law of Treaties*, Article 53.

tual treaty final clause remains decisive while Article 33(1) is intended only as a general reservation of such clauses.[34]

In essence, the prevailing text may be considered super-authoritative as a kind of *primus inter pares* (first among equals) even under the VCLT wording: as authentic text it is at minimum equally authoritative but of higher authority when circumstances are such that it ought to be regarded as prevailing. Hence, the existence of a prevailing text may be viewed as creating a new category of interpretative means in form of the non-prevailing texts, because the notion of one text to prevail in case of divergence is just another way of saying that the other texts can only confirm but not contest a clear meaning of the prevailing one. In relation to the prevailing text the others may be viewed akin to supplementary means: recourse to them is permissible but not mandatory unless an interpretation of the prevailing text leaves its meaning unclear, in which case recourse to the other texts becomes mandatory again to determine the meaning of the treaty.[35] Versus supplementary means, however, they retain their status as authentic means and the corresponding higher weight, constituting 'text' and therefore 'context' under Article 31(2).

In summary, when the prevailing text has a clear meaning, that meaning qualifies as the definitive treaty meaning. Either the other texts say exactly the same, or there is a divergence and their meanings must be reinterpreted to concur to the meaning of the prevailing text, which constitutes the one true meaning of the treaty. Hence, the prevalence of the prevailing text may be regarded as not conditional but quasi-absolute, that is, not really dependent on the de facto existence of any divergence.

This is congruent with the particular object and purpose of Article 33 to establish a relationship of comparative authority between the authentic texts: looking into the genesis of Article 33, we find that Special Rapporteur Sir Humphrey Waldock explicitly stated in the ILC's 770th meeting that 'article 74 dealt with the texts or versions which could be consulted for the purposes of interpretation, whereas article 75 was concerned with the

---

[34]See ILC, *Draft Articles on the Law of Treaties with Commentaries*, II:224, para. 4.
[35]See ILC, *Documents of the Sixteenth Session Including the Report of the Commission to the General Assembly*, II:65, para. 10.

comparative authority of texts.'[36] The VCLT Commentary speaks in this respect of the 'master text',[37] which paraphrases this property of supremacy.

It is congruent also with the overall wording and systematic of Article 33, which states in paragraph (1) that each text is equally authoritative 'unless' circumstances are such that one text prevails, and in paragraph (4) that 'Except where' one text prevails, the further prescribed operation shall be performed. The syntactic placement of the 'Except where' condition at the beginning of paragraph (4) makes clear that what follows applies only if the condition is not fulfilled.

5.4.2. The Meaning of Divergence

The peculiar term 'divergence' in Article 33(1) instead of 'difference' like in Article 33(4) should attract attention because the debate revolves around when it can be presumed that the condition of a divergence is fulfilled. The Oxford Learner's Dictionary defines divergence as 'the process or fact of separating or becoming different …from what is expected, planned'. Consequently, divergence is a dynamic concept, whereas difference is a static one. The underlying idea of departing and unintentionally deviating from an initial situation of equivalence fits with the axiom of the principle of unity as stipulated by Article 33(1) and (3), and suggests a dynamic meaning of 'divergence' in Article 33, encompassing all possible states of difference from slightly deviating expressions to complete opposites.

Article 33(1) itself only speaks of divergence in general without providing any further explicit qualification. In particular, its wording does not specify whether the term refers to differences in wording or meaning (or both). In the absence of any such explicit delimitation it is reasonable to start out with the assumption that the term is used in its broadest sense, encompassing all differences in wording and meaning whether only *prima facie* or material. Such proposition is congruent with the wording of Article 33(1) having 'texts' as its implied subject, which allows for the inference that 'divergence' serves as a predicate for the subject 'texts'. The concept

---

[36] ILC, *Summary Records of the Sixteenth Session, 11 May – 24 July 1964*, I:319, para. 60. Articles 74 and 75 were combined later into one article, which in its final version was included as Article 33 in the VCLT.

[37] ILC, *Draft Articles on the Law of Treaties with Commentaries*, II:224, para. 4.

of text, however, encompasses both its wording and meaning and not only one of those two more narrow subsets.

In fact, the wording 'in case of divergence, a particular text shall prevail' is synonymous to the wording 'in case of divergence *between the texts*, a particular text shall prevail'. Our addition *between the texts* does not change the meaning and is superfluous if 'divergence' relates as a predicate to 'texts'. In other words, it may be left out as done by the English text. The Russian text of Article 33(1) explicitly includes the implied subject and literally translates to 'divergence between these texts'.[38] Like the English one, the Chinese, French, and Spanish texts lack the repeated reference to the subject; however, this divergence does not constitute an irreconcilable difference in meaning between them and the Russian text or render all others ambiguous, because the subject 'texts' may not be explicitly reiterated but is still clearly implied. Any interpretation to the contrary is much less manifest and would require additional evidence to impose itself.

In order to support an interpretation of divergence as material divergence, we would need to insert *in meaning* instead of *between the texts*. This would introduce an additional subject, namely, the meaning of texts, which is only a more narrow subset of 'texts'. In consequence, the overall meaning would be enriched: *in meaning* could not be deleted without changing the sense of the whole paragraph. The fact that nothing in this respect is added to the texts of Article 33(1) makes clear that the intention is not to delimit the meaning of divergence to material divergences in meaning and exclude mere differences in expression, even in case the Russian text would not contain the more precise formulation.

The VCLT Commentary confirms this interpretation by explicitly stating that 'a plurilingual treaty may provide that in the event of *divergence between the texts* a specified text is to prevail.'[39] The wording of the French Commentary is equivalent and reads '*Deuxièmement, un traité plurilingue peut disposer qu'en cas de divergence entre les textes, un texte déterminé l'emportera.*'[40] Therefore, the VCLT is an instance of the hypothetical scen-

---

[38] Translation with the kind help of Ksenia Levushkina.
[39] Ibid., II:224, para. 3 (emphasis added).
[40] ILC, *Projet d'articles sur le droit des traites et commentaires 1966. Texte adopté par la Commission à sa dix-huitième session, en 1966, et soumis à l'Assemblée générale dans le cadre*

ario considered in the previous chapter: the formulations of the Chinese, English, French, and Spanish texts do not imply anything different from the Russian one but are grammatically slightly imprecise, which makes a less manifest additional interpretation possible, whereas the Russian text employs the grammatically precise formulation by explicitly repeating the otherwise implicit subject. The precise meaning is chosen under Article 31 and then confirmed via Article 32$_1$.

Article 33(4) may be consulted to deliberate this interpretation because of its direct reference and systematic connection to Article 33(1).[41] It does not explicitly echo the term 'divergence' but implicitly distinguishes between three different situations that refer to cases of divergence via the wording of 'difference in meaning' in combination with the existence or non-existence of a prevailing text, linking it to Article 33(1): First, a prevailing text exists, in which case we are referred back to Article 33(1). Second, no prevailing text exists and there are differences in meaning that can be reconciled by a comparative application of Articles 31 and 32$_1$ to all texts,[42] in which case the problem has been solved already. And third, no prevailing text exists and there are differences in meaning that cannot be reconciled by a comparative application of Articles 31 and 32$_1$ to all texts, for which a further *modus operandi* (mode of operation) is needed and provided by Article 33(4) itself.

Although Article 33(4) concerns itself in substance only with the latter case by providing an additional interpretative instruction for cases when Articles 31 and 32$_1$ fail to reconcile differences in meaning between the texts in the absence of a prevailing one, it does not contain any notion that the term divergence should be delimited to this particular scenario. On the contrary, its connection to Article 33(1) by direct reference encompasses all differences in meaning irrespective of whether they are reconcilable by Articles 31 and 32$_1$, that is, any divergence, whether material or only apparent.

Such understanding is not impaired by the fact that Article 33(4) explicitly only references 'a difference of meaning which the application of art-

---

de son rapport sur les travaux de ladite session, vol. II, Annuaire de la Commission du droit international 1966 (United Nations, 1967), 244, para. 3.

[41]See Mössner, 'Die Auslegung mehrsprachiger Staatsverträge', 300.

[42]In line with the analysis conducted in the previous chapter, the reference to Article 32 must be understood to refer to Article 32$_1$ only.

icles 31 and 32 does not remove',[43] as this must be interpreted in the context of the provision merely providing a specific instruction for a particular case. By explicitly mentioning only the particular case of an irreconcilable difference in meaning, the general case of reconcilable differences in meaning is presupposed. Since all reconcilable differences have been reconciled along the way by an application of Article 33(1) in combination with Articles 31 and 32_1 before the specific instruction contained in Article 33(4) comes into play, there is no need to explicitly repeat any instructions applying to them. Both reconcilable differences as well as their reconciliation are implied to have been the case and taken place already. Therefore, the concept of material difference in meaning explicitly described by Article 33(4) entails both: itself as operand of the second part of the entire operation (the specific *modus operandi* contained in paragraph (4) of Article 33), and the concept of merely *prima facie* difference in meaning as operand of the initial part of the operation (reconciliatory comparative interpretation under Articles 31 and 32_1). The entire operation consists in the two *modi operandi* reconciliatory comparative interpretation under Articles 31 and 32_1 and application of the interpretative rule contained in Article 33(4), whereas the operand itself (the divergence) retains its identity and only changes its character over the course of the entire operation from merely apparent into material.

The wording 'when' of Article 33(4) instead of 'if' or 'in case' is indicative in this respect: it does not talk about an imaginable scenario of the interpreter encountering a divergence, but about the definite case that he has encountered one. As soon as the normal way to handle it (reconciliatory comparative interpretation under Articles 31 and 32_1) has failed, he needs to implement the particular operation prescribed by Article 33(4). Implementing that special operation presupposes that, beforehand, reconciliatory comparative interpretation under Articles 31 and 32_1 has failed and, in consequence, that a divergence, necessitating such reconciliatory comparative interpretation under Articles 31 and 32_1, has been present.

In summary, the systematic composition of Article 33 suggests that paragraph (4) employs the disjunctive standard form of definitions regarding the

---

[43]Contra: Arginelli, *The Interpretation of Multilingual Tax Treaties*, 335, discussed in more detail in Chapter 6, s. 6.4.

concept of divergence introduced in paragraph (1).[44] That is to say, it combines all conditions that are by themselves each sufficient but not necessary to establish a case of divergence. Thus, a divergence is either a material difference (not reconcilable by the comparative application of Articles 31 and 32_1) or a merely apparent one (reconcilable by the comparative application of Articles 31 and 32_1), that is, not a difference in meaning but a mere difference in expression. Both are covered by the combined wordings of Article 33(1) and (4), which together provide a definition *per genus proximum et differentiam specificam*[45] (definition per category and specific difference) for the *definiendum* 'divergence' through the *definientia* reconcilable and irreconcilable 'difference of meaning'.

Commentators seem to be confused in this respect because of the equivocational use of the term 'difference of meaning', namely, both as a persistent (material) and reconcilable (not material) difference in meaning, that is, a de facto difference in meaning as well as a mere difference in expression. This fosters imprecise and inconsistent reasoning because persistent and reconcilable differences in meaning are not only an equivocation but by definition also mutually exclusive concepts.

The words used by the texts could also be equivalent in the different languages (for example, 'control' in English and *contrôle* in French) but with their meaning being different, as in the case brought forward by Mr Bartos in the ILC's 770th meeting.[46] From this follows also that the term divergence cannot be restricted to either 'difference of expression' or 'differ-

---

[44]X is F if X is G *or* X is H, see Pfister, *Werkzeuge des Philosophierens*, 68. This may escape the eye because paragraph (4) does not explicitly echo the term 'divergence' but only relates to it via its systematic connection to paragraph (1); however, this only conforms to the requirement of *terminus definitus non debet ingredi definitionem* (a term may not be defined through itself) for any proper definition, with the violation of this requirement also known as fallacy *idem per idem* (explaining the same through the same).

[45]A conception first developed by Aristotle, see Aristotle, *Topics*, Book IV, Part 1; Aristotle, *Prior Analytics*, Book II, parts 2–3; Pfister, *Werkzeuge des Philosophierens*, 66.

[46]See ILC, *Summary Records of the Sixteenth Session, 11 May – 24 July 1964*, I:319, para. 65. For some more examples, see Claudio Sacchetto, 'The Italian Experience', in *Multilingual Texts and Interpretation of Tax Treaties and EC Tax Law*, ed. Guglielmo Maisto (Amsterdam: IBFD, 2005), 63–78, 70–73; Shelton, 'Reconcilable Differences? The Interpretation of Multilingual Treaties', 4–5. For a comprehensive discussion of this issue, see Cao, *Translating Law*, 54–60.

ence of meaning', as the expression could be equivalent but the meaning different and vice-versa. This may explain why 'divergence' is used in Article 33(1) and neither 'difference of meaning' nor 'difference of expression': both types of differences needed to be addressed in a way that even cases of equivalent terms having different connotations in their respective languages would be covered.

For Article 33(4) to distinguish between three different situations is only logical. When no prevailing text exists, Article 33(1) only tells us that all texts are equally authoritative. Hence, we need further guidance for all situations when (a) any kind of difference appears and (b) the difference persists, that is, when Articles 31 and 32_1 fail to produce a clear meaning common to all texts in the face of (a). Article 33(4) presumes a comparison of all texts has been undertaken in order to resolve any problems between them and only provides an additional instruction what to do in case such has failed. For cases that fall under (a) but not (b) no additional instruction is needed; Articles 31 and 32_1 apply (and resolve the case) in line with the dictum that the fundamental principles of interpretation are not to be different for plurilingual treaties than they are for unilingual ones.[47]

Article 33(1) in combination with Articles 31 and 32_1 is sufficient also when a prevailing text exists: for a quasi-unilingual situation no further interpretative instruction on top of the general rule is needed because the VCLT assumes that a contextual interpretation of a single text in the light of its object and purpose can always be found,[48] unless the text remains ambiguous or obscure, or the result of its interpretation is absurd or unreasonable. Concerning this, the only difference between a unilingual treaty and a plurilingual one with prevailing text is that in the latter case the other texts are available as additional context to help resolve any residual problems of the prevailing one and recourse to them takes precedence over recourse to supplementary means in their active role (see below).

This understanding is consistent with the wording of Article 33(4) starting out with the condition that 'Except where a particular text prevails in accordance with paragraph 1', which implies that what follows is relevant only in such case. Thus, Article 33(4) merely completes Article 31 for pluri-

---

[47] See ILC, *Draft Articles on the Law of Treaties with Commentaries*, II:225, para. 7.
[48] See Avery Jones, 'Treaty Interpretation', s. 8.2.2.6 [5.1.2.2.6].

lingual treaties without prevailing text in order to avoid a gap in the general rule of interpretation identified by the ILC during the drafting period of the VCLT.[49] It is an extension to adapt the general rule to plurilingual scenarios, not a distinct rule in its own right, which again is implicit in the dictum that, fundamentally, the same principles apply whether the treaty is unilingual or plurilingual.[50]

For unilingual treaties the rule as provided in Article 31 is complete and suffices unless the meaning remains unclear. In principle, because of Article 33(1) in combination with the 'Except where' condition in Article 33(4), the same applies to the quasi-unilingual case of a plurilingual treaty with prevailing text unless the meaning of the prevailing text turns out to be unclear. Treaties without prevailing text, however, require a supplementation of the general rule to extend it to the scenario of multiple texts, which is provided by Article 33(4) via Article 33(1) and its connection to Article 31(2) by way of the shared reference to the text.

5.4.3. Application of the Permissive Approach

Read like this, paragraphs (1) and (4) of Article 33 together suggest the following approach when a prevailing text exists: Interpret the prevailing text and treat its manifest meaning as authoritative. If the prevailing text is unclear, engage in a reconciliatory comparison of all texts and ensure that the result corresponds to the meaning of the prevailing text. Alternatively, do the latter straight away. In view of the otherwise equal authenticity, the interpreter can rely on the prevailing text and does not have to bother about the others as long as he arrives at a clear meaning. On the other hand, he is not prevented from engaging in a reconciliatory comparison of all texts

---

[49]See UN, *United Nations Conference on the Law of Treaties, First Session Vienna, 26 March – 24 May 1968, Official Records, Summary Records of the Plenary Meetings and of the Meetings of the Committee of the Whole*, 188–89, paras. 39–43.

[50]See ILC, *Draft Articles on the Law of Treaties with Commentaries*, II:225, para. 7. The singular employed by the title of Article 31 is indicative: it makes clear that there is only one combined general rule of interpretation. Article 33(4) merely adapts the rule to multiple texts. As a corollary, the meaning of 'object and purpose' in Articles 31 and 33(4) is the same. The latter only provides for a different application as sole decider, not a teleological expansion, see Chapter 4, s. 4.3.2.

from the start as long as he makes sure the result equals the meaning of the prevailing one.

What precisely has to happen if the interpreter chooses the first option and Article 31 does not lead to a clear meaning of the prevailing text (optionally confirmed under Article 32$_1$)? Even if the prevailing text happens to be ambiguous or obscure, it cannot be put aside, because being ambiguous or obscure does not revoke its status as an equally authentic and, in case of a divergence, prevailing text.[51] Therefore, the court must have recourse to the other texts to see whether a reconciliatory comparative interpretation leads to a clear meaning of the treaty under Article 31. Such clear meaning may then be confirmed but not contested by supplementary means, as supplementary means may be used to derive the meaning only in case a comparative interpretation of the texts also fails to provide a clear result.[52] In terms of the comparison, the ambiguous or obscure prevailing text may not be left out of the equation but continues to prevail in the sense that the meaning determined with the help of the other texts must fit within the overall scope of meanings covered by the ambiguous or obscure wording of the prevailing text and cannot lie outside.[53]

If the overall result remains ambiguous or obscure, Article 32(a) may be invoked. In practice, this boils down to a reconciliatory comparative interpretation of all texts that may either be viewed as such or, alternatively, as a clarification of the prevailing text with the help of the others. It is clear in this context that invoking Article 32(a) before considering the other texts as context would upset the fundamental principle of different weights to be attributed to authentic and supplementary means. Such course of action would erroneously attempt to derive the treaty meaning from supplementary means before all authentic means to be considered in order to establish the ordinary meaning have been exhausted, confusing an ambiguity in one text for a fundamental ambiguity of the treaty.

Conceptually, the same does not apply to the extent the prevailing text

---

[51]UN, *Vienna Convention on the Law of Treaties*, Article 10 in combination with Article 33(1).

[52]See Chapter 4, s. 4.4.2.

[53]See ILC, *Documents of the Sixteenth Session Including the Report of the Commission to the General Assembly*, II:65, paras. 9–10.

turns out to be manifestly absurd or unreasonable, as then such suggestion would be self-contradicting: one cannot declare the absurd and unreasonable as a standard for the sensible and reasonable. In such case the interpreter must heal the absurdity or unreasonableness of the prevailing text with the help of the others and supplementary means, as otherwise he is left with the impasse that there is an obvious divergence that forces him to apply the prevailing text.[54] The prevailing text may not be discarded because its status as authentic and prevailing text granted by Article 10 VCLT and the treaty final clause is not revoked by the mere fact of its interpretation leading to an absurd or unreasonable result. Here the prevailing text has an unequivocal, albeit manifestly absurd or unreasonable, meaning. Unlike the first scenario, which could be viewed as a reconciliatory comparative interpretation of all texts for which all meanings attributable to the ambiguous or obscure prevailing text provided the scope, this case requires that the defects of the unequivocal meaning of the prevailing text are healed with recourse to the other texts and supplementary means; however, the distinction is merely conceptual – an outside observer of the process will not notice any difference.[55]

Let us briefly return to the *New Skies* case introduced in the previous chapter. There it was discussed as if all texts had been equally authoritative, however, the Netherlands-India (1988) tax treaty declares the English text as prevailing.[56] Hence, we may use *New Skies* as a case study to test the approach submitted here. The court relied solely on the prevailing English text, which would be permitted as long as its meaning is clear. As argued

---

[54]Once more it must be asked how the meaning of a single text can possibly turn out absurd or unreasonable under Article 31 if teleological reasoning is to be excluded. As argued in the previous chapter, such cases must be assumed to be restricted to obvious drafting errors rendering the text inconsistent.

[55]In view of the analysis presented in the previous chapter, it is submitted that Article 33(4) should be applied before Article 32(a) or (b) are invoked. Since interpretation of the prevailing text fails to establish a clear meaning, the reconciliatory comparative interpretation of all texts must include consideration of the object and purpose as sole decider before resorting to supplementary means. In both scenarios the outcome is to be supplanted into the prevailing text as constitutive treaty meaning.

[56]The fact that the final clause declares the English text as prevailing only in case the Dutch and Hindi texts diverge shall be ignored for the moment. This particular type of wording will be subject of in-depth considerations in Chapter 8, s. 8.3.3.

in the previous chapter, the meaning of 'secret formula or process' is clear: the adjective 'secret' applies to both nouns 'formula' and 'process' enumerated before the comma as a matter of standard phrasing. The conjured up ambiguity is to a large extent not an inherent property of the text but the result of the court referring to domestic law.

The case nicely exemplifies that the prevailing text does not need to be unequivocal to be relied on, but that it is enough for it to have a manifest meaning. Notwithstanding, what matters is that the court considered the text ambiguous. We can see that the approach proposed here works well as a corrective in such case. As next step the court should have consulted the other texts, which would have instantly resolved the problem via the Dutch one. Instead it continued to disregard them in favour of going to the bottom of domestic law, considerations of general context in terms of double taxation, balancing taxing rights between contracting states, India's position on the OECD Commentary, and so forth.

In the end the court arrived at the right conclusion, but the case still illustrates how relying on a single text while interpreting the meaning of terms not defined in the treaty via domestic law can go wrong even when applied to the prevailing text. The VCLT context includes grammar and phrasing, that is, how things are expressed in all texts. One must distinguish in this respect between single terms and entire phrases: 'any secret formula or process' is not a term but an entire phrase that makes a particular sense in the way it is used in English. If one considers the phrase ambiguous, one must conduct a comparison with all other texts even under the approach submitted here. Looking immediately to domestic law may go wrong, imposing a domestic law meaning on the actually intended treaty meaning: if the judge would draw the erroneous conclusion that the phrase is no longer ambiguous but clarified simply by recourse to the domestic law meaning, the result is a misapplication of the treaty.

Hence, we have to attach a big warning sign to the approach of sole reliance on the prevailing text submitted here, because this is a mistake easy to make in the case of tax treaties. When interpreting a tax treaty, we must not lose sight of most of its terms being intended first and foremost as general abstractions subject to an interpretation in light of the two contexts under Article 3(2) and Article 31 even if the treaty uses terminology identical to domestic law. If one considers the meaning of the prevailing text ambiguous (whether or not such judgement is justified in the eye of the observer), one must have recourse to the other texts as part of the VCLT context before or at least while going to domestic law to first establish the actual treaty term to be defined beyond doubt. Otherwise, one may erroneously transgress the intended treaty meaning by imposing domestic law.

5.4.4. Evaluation of the Restrictive Approach

The proponents of the restrictive approach promote a less broad meaning of the term divergence,[57] limited to cases of material differences in meaning, that is, differences not reconcilable by a comparison of all texts under Articles 31 and 32. Their interpretation is based on a different reading of Article 33(4), essentially conceiving it to distinguish only between two not three situations: cases where differences in meaning either can or cannot be reconciled by a comparison of texts under application of Articles 31 and 32.[58] Hence their suggested approach in case of a divergence differs from the one proposed here. It may be summarised as follows: Disregard any prevailing text status and conduct a reconciliatory comparison of all texts.[59] In the course of this, establish whether the divergence is only *prima facie* or material. If the latter is the case, adopt 'the meaning which best reconciles the texts, having regard to the object and purpose of the treaty'. Alternatively, adopt the meaning of an existing prevailing text.

Although at first sight such reading seems possible, it is inconclusive. It reads Article 33(4) as if the 'Except where' condition were placed at the end of the provision after 'shall be adopted', which could suggest treating the meaning of the prevailing text as a mere alternative to be used over the method proposed in paragraph (4) for cases without prevailing texts. But,

---

[57]See, e.g., Arginelli, *The Interpretation of Multilingual Tax Treaties*, 333–38; Engelen, *Interpretation of Tax Treaties under International Law*, 394.

[58]Since most of them fail to properly distinguish explicitly between the two different functions of Article 32, they end up promoting recourse to supplementary means over Article 33(4) to resolve divergences.

[59]Some authors seem to imply that it is sufficient to only compare the divergent texts in the official languages of the contracting states. This view will be discussed in more detail in Chapter 6, s. 6.4.

the condition is placed at the beginning, which suggests that what follows regulates only what is supposed to happen when there is no prevailing text.

Moreover, the prevailing text is referenced in paragraph (1) already, establishing its general prevalence over the other texts whenever there is a divergence, and neither paragraph (1) nor (4) expressly delimit 'divergence' to exclude any particular types. The substantive interpretation rule in paragraph (4) is intended and needed only for cases when no prevailing text exists. If the intention were different, that is, if the prevailing text were to be invoked only as a prevailing alternative to the specific *modus operandi* provided by paragraph (4) for cases without prevailing text when differences in meaning cannot be resolved by the application of Articles 31 and 32_1, then the reference to a prevailing text should equally have been confined to paragraph (4) and not extend to the main clause in paragraph (1). Since the intention behind agreeing on one text as prevailing is to establish a fundamental comparative order of authority between the texts as stated by Waldock,[60] the prevailing text may not be viewed as a mere alternative to the particular interpretative *modus operandi* of Article 33(4), to be applied only after it has been established that this *modus operandi* would indeed have to be applied if there were no prevailing text.

As regards the general object and purpose of Article 33, such must be considered to consist in aiding the 'Interpretation of treaties authenticated in two or more languages', as is provided by its heading. Generally, any rule of interpretation must be considered to be intended to facilitate and not hinder interpretation of a treaty,[61] which must itself be considered to be intended to provide legal certainty not uncertainty. As a corollary, the introduction of a prevailing text must be considered to be intended to foster interpretation and legal certainty, not to encumber it. Although both the broad and the narrow understanding of the term 'divergence' are in line with this object and purpose, the broad understanding suggested here eases interpretation to a greater extent by allowing exclusive reliance on the prevailing text in any case (as long as it is clear), without going through the more complex comparative interpretation of all texts in order to establish a

---

[60] See ILC, *Summary Records of the Sixteenth Session, 11 May – 24 July 1964*, I:319, para. 60.
[61] The Oxford Dictionary defines interpretation as 'The action of explaining the meaning of something.'

case of material divergence first.[62]

It seems rather obvious that the intention behind a prevailing text must be to avoid having to grind through a comparative interpretation of all texts, and not to use it only once that grind proves unfruitful. One must not forget in this context that the 'different genius of languages'[63] will require more than literal word-for-word translations of expressions.[64] A proper translation must accurately reflect the complete sense of the translated,[65] which may demand an extensive linguistic effort.[66] For this reason, different language versions of a text will often differ in phrasing and expression precisely out of the need to convey the same meaning, that is, *prima facie* differences between texts will be common, which has been recognised by the drafters of the VCLT.[67] Hence, even if one would not subscribe to the argument that a comparison of all texts is obligatory for any serious effort to interpret a treaty in good faith in the absence of a prevailing text, it is clear that the potential need for such comparison may be rather large in practice.

---

[62]Clearly, the proponents of the restrictive approach prescribe a narrower interpretation than intended by the drafters of the VCLT, who remained agnostic about the matter, see ILC, *Draft Articles on the Law of Treaties with Commentaries*, II:224, para. 4.

[63]Ibid., II:225, para. 6.

[64]Such may even be impossible because of the lack of equivalent terms. The DARS serve as an example. The French text of Article 1 reads '*Tout fait internationalement illicite de l'État engage sa responsabilité internationale*' while the English text reads 'Every internationally wrongful act of a State entails the international responsibility of that State.' The French terminology *fait internationalement illicite* was chosen for two reasons: to avoid any terminology that had a special meaning under internal law, and to remain unequivocal about encompassing wrongfulness resulting from omissions by using *fait* instead of *acte*. For the same reason the Spanish text uses the expression *hecho internacionalmente ilícito*. Since there is no exact equivalent for the French *fait* in English, the English text resorts to 'act', which is however intended to also encompass omissions. This is obvious from the text of the DARS, as Article 2 reads 'conduct consisting of an action or omission'. In the absence of such obvious context, however, an interpretation of the English text alone could lead to the conclusion that omissions are excluded from the scope, see ILC, *Draft Articles on Responsibility of States for Internationally Wrongful Acts*, 34, para. 8; 35, para. 4.

[65]The Oxford Dictionary defines translate as to 'Express the sense of (words or text) in another language.'

[66]See Cao, *Translating Law*, Chs. 2, 4 and 7; *Kiliç İnşaat İthalat İhracat Sanayi ve Ticaret Anonim Şirketi v Turkmenistan*, paras. 8.4–8.9.

[67]See ILC, *Draft Articles on the Law of Treaties with Commentaries*, II:225, para. 6.

What would be the purpose then of having a prevailing text if not to assist the judge in his difficult task and relieve him as much as possible from the burden of a reconciliatory comparative interpretation? It seems an odd suggestion in the presence of a prevailing text that the judge should still be required to first compare all texts in order to find out whether he ought to rely on the prevailing one, because that would be tantamount to saying the judge must conduct a reconciliatory comparative interpretation in order to establish whether such was necessary in the first place. To borrow Bertrand Russell's words, the restrictive approach 'is one of those views which are so absurd that only very learned men could possibly adopt them.'[68]

5.4.5. Comparison of All VCLT Texts

The VCLT has English, French, Chinese, Russian, and Spanish texts, none of which is designated as prevailing.[69] Hence, all texts have to be compared to ensure correct interpretation.[70] As discussed and explicitly transcribed by the Russian text, the VCLT intends 'divergence' to mean 'divergence between texts'. Although there are some additional differences between the texts, none of them are material in terms of the interpretation submitted here. The crucial syntax of Article 33(4) with the 'Except where' condition at the beginning, which supports the interpretation that what follows applies only to situations when no prevailing text exists, is the same for all.

Besides the addition 'between these texts', the Russian text shows no significant deviations from the English one. The Russian expressions for 'divergence' and 'prevailing' are equivalent, and the wordings of paragraphs (2) and (3) also correspond to their English counterparts. The same goes for the Chinese text: the translation is complete and accurate, and the expressions for the English 'divergence' and 'prevailing' are equivalent. Some minor syntactic differences attributable to linguistic customs exist in paragraph

---

[68]Bertrand Russell, *My Philosophical Development*, 1st ed. (New York: Simon and Schuster, 1959), 148.

[69]UN, *Vienna Convention on the Law of Treaties*, Article 85.

[70]The comparison in this subsection has been conducted with the kind help of Ksenia Levushkina, Roberto Bernales, Ridha Hamzaoui, Antoine Reillac, and Tian Xu, all native speakers in the respective languages of the other texts as well as experts in the field of international tax law.

(2), but the crucial syntax of paragraph (4) remains the same.

The French text shows a slight difference in paragraph (1): '*son texte fait foi dans chacune de ces langues*' literally translates to 'the text is authoritative in each language', that is, the word 'equally' is not transcribed.[71] But, this does not change the overall meaning of the paragraph: if each language text is authoritative and none is specified as either more or less authoritative, then all are equally authoritative, that is, the additional 'equally' in the English text is merely pleonastic. Apart from that, the same terminology of *divergence* and *différence* is employed, while *l'emporter* is to be translated with 'to prevail'. Some dictionaries translate it with 'to win' or 'to have the upper hand', which does not differ in substance.

Regarding the Spanish text, the use of *discrepancia* instead of 'divergence' is curious. According to the Oxford Dictionary, the English 'discrepancy' would imply an 'illogical or surprising lack of compatibility or similarity between two or more facts', which inspires an interpretation in terms of a contradiction, that is, necessarily a material divergence. But, according to the Dictionary of the Royal Academy of the Spanish Language, which has the authority to establish the definition of concepts in Spanish, *discrepancia* merely implies diversity or disagreement, not necessarily a contradiction. Therefore, not only material divergences are implied. As for the other terminology, *prevalecer* translates to 'to prevail', and *hará fe*, although not a literal translation for 'authoritative', implies the same meaning.

5.4.6. Recourse to the VCLT Commentary

The VCLT Commentary may be consulted to confirm but not contest the interpretation submitted. There are several paragraphs in the Commentary that directly refer to situations of divergence.[72] Paragraph 3 on page 224 speaks of 'divergence between texts', which in the absence of any explicit delimitation may imply differences both in expression and meaning because the ordinary meaning of the word 'text' encompasses both its wording and meaning, same as the word 'treaty' (the word 'text' stands for) encompasses

---

[71]The English text reads 'the text is *equally* authoritative in each language' (emphasis added).

[72]See ILC, *Draft Articles on the Law of Treaties with Commentaries*, II:224–25, paras. 3–4, 6–8.

both the expressed intentions of the contracting parties as well as the expressions expressing them.

Paragraph 4 on page 224 seems to contrast differences in expression to differences in meaning and raises the question of where to draw the line for an 'actual divergence' to exist. Arginelli suggests that the paragraph clearly distinguishes between differences in wording and meaning, providing the context for his contention that only a material difference in meaning qualifies as a divergence.[73] But, it is not entirely clear from the paragraph whether 'actual divergence' refers to a material divergence in meaning or a mere divergence in expression or both, as it deals with a case in which the tribunal applied the prevailing text without even investigating the potential occurrence of any divergence. Hence, the paragraph could be read to merely differentiate differences in expression that require more thought than cases of 'slightest difference' from those that do not pose real problems, without implying material differences in meaning. As the case may be, although it states that the VCLT rules do not stipulate any obligation to go immediately to the prevailing text upon the slightest difference in wording, it does not rule out the option to do so either.

The wording 'appear to diverge' of paragraph 6 on page 225 first and foremost refers to merely apparent differences of expression, but the terminology gets extended to a 'discrepancy between the texts' and 'discrepancies in the meaning of the texts'. Especially the latter seems to extend the scope to material differences in meaning; however, the overall wording ('result in minor or even major discrepancies') makes clear that it refers to a continuum ranging from slightest differences in expression to material differences in meaning, focussing on the first. In order to make the paragraph apply to material differences in meaning only, we would need to add something to the wording to limit its scope, for example, 'Few plurilingual treaties containing more than one or two articles are without some discrepancy between *the meanings of* the texts' (emphasised text added). This would suggest that the principle of unity is broken regularly; however, without doubt, the intention behind the entire paragraph is to primarily address differences in expression that imply differences in meaning resolvable via interpretative means, with material differences in meaning being

---

[73]See Arginelli, *The Interpretation of Multilingual Tax Treaties*, 336.

the absolute exception.

Paragraph 7 on page 225 is peculiar versus the others. It may be read to employ the expression 'difference between the texts' as referring to material differences in meaning not resolvable by the comparative application of Articles 31 and 32, contrasting it to mere differences in expression; however, it does not draw any conclusions as to whether only one or the other or both are cases of divergence, because it is not so much concerned with how to define a divergence than where to locate the reasons for it: in the ambiguity of one text or a divergence between the texts. Moreover, it does not concern itself with prevailing texts but deals exclusively with scenarios of equal authority. Concerning these it concludes that 'every reasonable effort should first be made to reconcile the texts and to ascertain the intention of the parties by recourse to the normal means of interpretation' before 'preferring one text to another'.

Paragraph 8 on page 225 only talks about differences in expression, not meaning. Indeed, it may not be too sensible to speak of differences in meaning in the first place. The distinction between *prima facie* and material divergences is artificial: obviously, any divergence is at first merely *prima facie* before a full interpretative comparison has been conducted, apart from the most obvious cases of outright contradictions. To distinguish between *prima facie* and material divergences before such comparison and suggest a different treatment based on such distinction concerning whether a comparison is to be conducted is based on circular reasoning and therefore nonsensical.

Based on the principle of unity, the meaning ought to be presumed to be the same even if expressions diverge unless a difference persists. If the latter happens, the treaty may be defective if there is no prevailing text and the situation cannot be resolved by application of the interpretative rule in Article 33(4). Hence, the principal understanding of divergence must be one of merely apparent differences that can be reconciled in the course of an interpretative comparison including recourse to the object and purpose as sole decider, because the true intention of the parties can be identified, wherefore a choice between the texts can be made.[74] Divergences that can-

---

[74]See Hardy, 'The Interpretation of Plurilingual Treaties by International Courts and Tribunals', 132.

not be resolved in this way must be considered to lie outside the scope of the VCLT for cases without prevailing text unless one agrees with the reasoning brought forward in the previous chapter that they constitute absurd or unreasonable results subject to a further application of Article 32(b) before the treaty must be considered defective.

In summary, the VCLT Commentary employs varied terminology to discuss a continuum of situations from mere differences in expression to material differences in meaning, contemplated in various contexts from equal authority to cases with prevailing text. Nowhere does it contain any explicit or implicit suggestion that the notion of divergence should be restricted to mean only material differences in meaning and courts should rely on the prevailing text only after having engaged in a reconciliatory comparison without success. At best, the VCLT Commentary remains indecisive about the matter: it issues no recommendation but leaves it up to the contracting parties,[75] that is, neither reconciliatory comparative interpretation of all texts nor sole reliance on the prevailing one are ruled out in principle. This confirms the interpretation submitted here.

5.5. Limitations to the Permissive Approach

The permissive approach is subject to three limitations. First, if the meaning of the prevailing text remains unclear, recourse to the other texts and supplementary means must be had to establish the treaty meaning. Second, the reasoning presented assumed a final clause modelled on Article 33(1), that is, a final clause declaring several texts as authentic and, in addition, one of them as prevailing in case of divergence; however, Article 33(1) is not intended to constitute a peremptory norm, but the intentions of the contracting parties take precedence. Third, the analysis and conclusions presented are based on the VCLT. Hence, strictly speaking, the VCLT needs to be implemented by the contracting states for them to apply. The first limitation I have discussed at length above. Concerning practical applicability, actual formulations of individual treaty final clauses will have to be examined to establish whether the permissive approach is covered by them, which will

---

[75] See ILC, *Draft Articles on the Law of Treaties with Commentaries*, II:224, para. 4.

be the topic of Chapter 8. The following briefly considers applicability of the VCLT concerning actual treaty relationships.

The VCLT was adopted on 22 May 1969, opened for signature on 23 May 1969, and entered into force on 27 January 1980. To date, 116 states have implemented it by way of accession, succession, or ratification, and 15 states have signed but not implemented it (a complete list is provided in Appendix A.2). The VCLT itself stipulates non-retroactivity of its rules:

> Without prejudice to the application of any rules set forth in the present Convention to which treaties would be subject under international law independently of the Convention, the Convention applies only to treaties which are concluded by States after the entry into force of the present Convention with regard to such States. ...

> Unless a different intention appears from the treaty or is otherwise established, its provisions do not bind a party in relation to any act or fact which took place or any situation which ceased to exist before the date of the entry into force of the treaty with respect to that party.[76]

Notwithstanding, most states and their courts subscribe to the view that the VCLT rules of interpretation stipulate what is valid customary international law,[77] for example, Australia, Germany, and the UK.[78] To a certain extent, this view is shared by states not being signatories, for example, France and India.[79] The situation in the US seems to be ambivalent, caught up in

---

[76]UN, *Vienna Convention on the Law of Treaties*, Articles 4 and 28.

[77]See Vogel and Prokisch, 'Interpretation of Double Taxation Conventions', 66–67; Richard Crawford Pugh, Oscar Schachter, and Hans Smit, *International Law: Cases and Materials*, ed. Louis Henkin, 3rd edition (St. Paul, Minn: West Group, 1993), 416; Avery Jones, 'Treaty Interpretation', s. 3.1.

[78]See Bjorge, '"Contractual" And "Statutory" Treaty Interpretation in Domestic Courts? Convergence Around the Vienna Rules', 64; Alexander Rust, 'Germany', in *Courts and Tax Treaty Law* (Amsterdam: IBFD, 2007), s. 11.2.1; *Thiel v Federal Commissioner of Taxation*, 356; FG Köln, 'II K 223/85' (EFG 1987, December 1986); *Czech Republic v European Media Ventures SA*, [2007] EWHC 2851 (Comm), 15.

[79]See Martin, 'Courts and Tax Treaties in Civil Law Countries', s. 4.3.2.2; Kanwar, 'Treaty Interpretation in Indian Courts', passim; *Ram Jethmalani v Union of India*, para. 60, states that 'While India is not a party to the Vienna Convention, it contains many principles of customary international law, and the principle of interpretation, of Article 31 of the Vienna Convention, provides a broad guideline as to what could be an appropriate manner of interpreting a treaty in the Indian context also.'

a historical struggle between internationalist and nationalist paradigms.[80] Many lower federal and state courts regularly appeal to the VCLT rules of interpretation as binding rules of customary international law,[81] but the US Supreme Court hardly ever refers to them.[82] Several of its decisions stretch the VCLT textual approach in favour of making liberal use of extraneous materials,[83] its decision in *O'Connor* is based on unilateral material not part of the official *travaux préparatoires*,[84] and in *Alvarez-Machain* it arguably decided the case in violation of Article 31(3)c.[85]

The ICJ has repeatedly recognised 'The existence of identical rules in international treaty law and customary law'.[86] It is settled case law to apply the VCLT to cases in which one or even both parties have not implemented

---

[80]See Evan J. Criddle, 'The Vienna Convention on the Law of Treaties in U.S. Treaty Interpretation', *Virginia Journal of International Law* 44, no. 2 (2004): 431–500, passim. The US Department of State positions itself as follows: 'Is the United States a party to the Vienna Convention on the Law of Treaties? No. The United States signed the treaty on April 24, 1970. The U.S. Senate has not given its advice and consent to the treaty. The United States considers many of the provisions of the Vienna Convention on the Law of Treaties to constitute customary international law on the law of treaties', http://www.state.gov/s/l/treaty/faqs/70139.htm.

[81]See, e.g., *Fujitsu Ltd. v Federal Exp. Corp.*, 247 F.3d 423 (2d Cir. 2001), 433.

[82]See Criddle, 'The Vienna Convention on the Law of Treaties in U.S. Treaty Interpretation', 433–34.

[83]See, e.g., *Air France v Sacks*, 470 U.S. 392 (1985), 396; *Volkswagenwerk Aktiengesellschaft v Schlunk*, 486 U.S. 694 (1988), 700; *Eastern Airlines, Inc., Petitioner v Rose Marie Floyd, et vir., et al.*, 499 U.S. 530 (1991), 535; *Itel Containers Int'l Corp. v Huddleston*, 507 U.S. 60 (1993), 84.

[84]See *O'Connor v United States*, 479 U.S. 27 (1986), 31; Criddle, 'The Vienna Convention on the Law of Treaties in U.S. Treaty Interpretation', 453.

[85]See *United States v Alvarez-Machain*, 504 U.S. 655 (1992), 668–69, para. 15; Criddle, 'The Vienna Convention on the Law of Treaties in U.S. Treaty Interpretation', 433; Michael Waibel, 'Principles of Treaty Interpretation: Developed for and Applied by National Courts?', in *The Interpretation of International Law by Domestic Courts: Uniformity, Diversity, Convergence*, ed. Helmut Philipp Aust and Georg Nolte (Oxford; New York: Oxford University Press, 2016), 21.

[86]*Nicaragua v United States of America – Military and Paramilitary Activities in and Against Nicaragua*, ICJ (Annual Reports of the International Court of Justice, 1986), 95, para. 177; see also *North Sea Continental Shelf (Federal Republic of Germany/Denmark; Federal Republic of Germany/Netherlands)*, ICJ (Annual Reports of the International Court of Justice, 1969), 38–39, para. 63; *Avena and Other Mexican Nationals (Mexico v USA)*, ICJ (Annual Reports of the International Court of Justice, 2004), 48, para. 83.

it, on grounds that the VCLT articles reflect customary international law.[87] The same rationale has been applied, for example, by the High Court of Australia concerning the tax treaty between Australia and Switzerland:

> Those rules [of interpretation recognised by international lawyers] have now been codified by the Vienna Convention on the Law of Treaties to which Australia, but not Switzerland, is a party. Nevertheless, because the interpretation provisions of the Vienna Convention reflect the customary rules for the interpretation of treaties, it is proper to have regard to the terms of the Convention in interpreting the Agreement, even though Switzerland is not a party to that Convention.[88]

With extensive reference to case law of the ICJ, the ITLOS, the WTO Appellate Body, the ECHR, the Inter-American Court of Human Rights, the ECJ, and the ICSID, the ILC has confirmed that Articles 31–32 'apply as customary international law'.[89] Although it found 'significant indications in the case law that article 33, in its entirety, indeed reflects customary international law', the ILC did not pass a final verdict but left the issue open to be addressed in the future because some courts to date have dealt only with parts of Article 33 in terms of reflecting customary international law, whereas others have explicitly stated that it reflects customary international law as a whole.[90] For example, despite the stipulated non-retroactivity, the ECHR has applied the VCLT principles of interpretation even before the convention's entry into force, based on the recognition that 'its Articles 31 to 33 enunciate in essence generally accepted principles of international law, to which the Court has already referred on occasion.'[91]

---

[87] See *Territorial Dispute (Libyan Arab Jamahiriya/Chad)*, 19–22, para. 41; *Arbitral Award of 31 July 1989 (Guinea Bissau v Senegal)*, ICJ (Annual Reports of the International Court of Justice, 1991), 69–70, para. 48; *LaGrand (Germany v United States of America)*, 501–2, paras. 99, 101; *Kasikili/Sedudu Island (Botswana/Namibia)*, ICJ (Annual Reports of the International Court of Justice, 1999), 1059, para. 18, 1075, para. 48; *Sovereignty over Pulau Litigan and Pulau Sipidan (Indonesia v Malaysia)*, ICJ (Annual Reports of the International Court of Justice, 2002), 645, para. 37.

[88] *Thiel v Federal Commissioner of Taxation*, 356.

[89] ILC, 'Report of the International Law Commission on the Sixty-fifth Session, 6 May – 7 June and 8 July – 9 August 2013', 13, Conclusion 1(5), and 14–15, para. 4.

[90] See ibid., 15–16, paras. 5–6.

[91] *Golder v United Kingdom*, European Court of Human Rights (Application no. 4451/70, 1975), 10, para. 29.

5. Reliance on the Prevailing Text

The VCLT itself does not intend its stipulation of non-retroactivity to constitute a peremptory norm but considers the intentions of the parties decisive,[92] as is explicitly stated by Article 28 VCLT; however, adoption of the VCLT by itself may not necessarily be taken to count as having 'otherwise established' such intention, as domestic constitutional law may preclude such assumption. For example, while stressing that the VCLT rules of interpretation did not preclude its own view in the particular case decided, the BFH expressed a strict position concerning the VCLT's non-retroactivity, attributable to the relationship between international and constitutional law under the German legal system:

> It is true that since the entry into force of the Assent Act of 3 August 1985 …the VCLT has been directly applicable national law. But, Article 4 thereof only applies to contracts concluded after the entry into force of the Convention, and the tax treaty with Italy was concluded on October 31, 1925, long before the VCLT came into force. Therefore, the VCLT cannot apply to the wages paid by X to the applicant for the period from 1 January 1980 to 31 December 1982. …International customary law cannot invalidate Article 59(2) sentence 1 GG, according to which the content of an international treaty relating to subjects of federal legislation becomes part of the domestic legal system only on the basis of a statute passing consent. According to Article 25 GG, customary international law can only be part of the national legal system insofar as it does not contradict constitutional law. …A rule of interpretation of international law relating to an international treaty can by no means change domestic law without a formal statute of approval pursuant to Art. 59(2) sentence 1 GG.[93]

In summary, as regards the reach of the VCLT, the limitation to the applicability of the permissive approach is not strictly demarcated. If indeed to be considered customary international law, Article 33 should be regarded as applicable without restriction;[94] however, domestic legal systematics may

---

[92]See Sinclair, *The Vienna Convention on the Law of Treaties*, 85.

[93]BFH, 'I R 74/86' (BStBl 1990 II, February 1989), *Entscheidungsgründe*; see also BFH, 'I R 20/87' (BStBl 1989 II, March 1989), s. II, para. 3.

[94]See Vogel and Prokisch, 'Interpretation of Double Taxation Conventions', 66–67; Klaus Vogel, 'Double Tax Treaties and Their Interpretation', *International Tax & Business Lawyer* 4, no. 1 (1986): 15; Engelen, *Interpretation of Tax Treaties under International Law*, 48–57; Tanja Bender and Frank Engelen, 'The Final Clause of the 1987 Netherlands Model Tax Convention and the Interpretation of Plurilingual Treaties', in *A Tax Glob-*

interfere. A deeper analysis of this point apart from the few general observations presented here lies outside the scope of this study; the interested reader is referred to the cited sources as a suitable point of departure.

---

alist: Essays in Honour of Maarten J. Ellis, ed. H. P. A. M. van Arendonk, F. A. Engelen and Sjaak Jansen (Amsterdam: IBFD, 2005), 3; Sinclair in Avery Jones, 'Interpretation of Tax Treaties', 75–76.

6. The Restrictive Approach: A Critical Review

6.1. Research Topic

This chapter examines the counterarguments to sole reliance on the prevailing text brought forward by the most adamant advocates of the restrictive approach in detail. Before commencing with a comprehensive review, it is useful to first discuss the most important point they have in common, which has been made initially by Hardy and is relied on without much scrutiny by other scholars, most prominently Arginelli and Engelen.[1]

6.2. The Attack on the Logical Argument

This core argument of the restrictive approach, which Hardy repeats twice in his study, rests on the idea that 'the interpretation most compatible with all texts is not necessarily the one suggested by the authentic text viewed separately'.[2] The first is the outcome of a selective comparison during which the interpretations of all texts are 'hedged' against each other and errors are corrected by cross-examination, whereas the latter is a one-dimensional exercise by the judge without such corrective 'hedge'.[3] This argument implies the presumption that as long as there is a common meaning to all texts, no divergence can be said to exist, in which case any meaning of the prevailing text not in congruence with the common meaning does not prevail.

Immediately, the question arises why and under what circumstances it would be necessary for the interpretation of the prevailing text to be hedged

---

[1] See Arginelli, *The Interpretation of Multilingual Tax Treaties*, 337; Engelen, *Interpretation of Tax Treaties under International Law*, 380–81.

[2] Hardy, 'The Interpretation of Plurilingual Treaties by International Courts and Tribunals', 133–34. By 'authentic text' he means the prevailing text (see below).

[3] See ibid., 126.

within the limits of the others. The suggestion seems in friction with the property of it prevailing, which rather suggests the opposite, namely, that the interpretations of the other texts are to be hedged within the limits of the prevailing one. In order to make sense of Hardy's argument, we must examine its theoretical foundations. In essence, it rests on the following two premises: (1) The notion of divergence is subjective, that is, the existence of a divergence, which is the precondition for the prevalence of the prevailing text, can be established only after a close objective examination. (2) Texts lend themselves to several interpretations, and they may be so 'obscure or vague' that they lend themselves 'either to no constructions or a virtually unlimited number.'[4]

Consequently, if the prevailing text is equivocal, any particular interpretation chosen by the judge may be in conflict with an interpretation arrived at by a concordant interpretation of all texts after a comparison. Given this, no interpretation of the prevailing text may be chosen as the prevailing one without establishment of a divergence, because it may not prevail over any other interpretation that happens to be in concordance with the other texts, in which case no real divergence can be said to exist. Therefore, the interpreter must always engage in reconciliatory comparative interpretation and can rely on the prevailing text only when such turns out fruitless, that is, only when no single common meaning can be established. Accordingly, the prevailing text is a device of last resort only, to be applied as a prevailing alternative to the *modus operandi* provided by Article 33(4) for cases in which no text is designated as prevailing.

To some extent, this construction is owed to the timing of Hardy's study in combination with his inductive method, applied in the absence of the principles codified in the VCLT (see below). It has become clear from the analysis in the previous chapter that any delimitation of the term divergence to narrow criteria is not in line with the ordinary meaning of Article 33. Hardy's argument relies on contrasting the interpretation suggested by the prevailing text to an interpretation compatible with all texts, and it implies the notion that all texts considered together constitute the treaty versus each text representing it. As discussed in Chapter 3, this suggestion makes sense for plurilingual treaties without prevailing text because of the

---

[4]Ibid., 82.

otherwise residual indeterminacy of the treaty meaning; however, here we are considering the case of a quasi-unilingual treaty, as one text is designated as prevailing. When there is a clear meaning of the prevailing text, the principle of unity in combination with Article 31 demands that this meaning is the undivided meaning of the treaty. For cases without prevailing text the previous chapters followed Hardy's argument because of the failure of clarity of a single text as a criterion to resolve the inherent indeterminacy. When there is a prevailing text with a clear meaning, however, there is no longer any indeterminacy; clarity of the prevailing text becomes sufficient as a criterion, or else we cannot make sense of the notion of it to prevail. In summary, Hardy's argument is valid only for cases in which no prevailing text exists or cases in which its meaning remains unclear.

It is not necessary for the prevailing text to have only a single meaning to be clear. When one of its possible meanings is manifest under Article 31, it constitutes the treaty meaning – much alike the case of a unilingual treaty, in which it is precisely the task of interpretation to establish the one true meaning out of all possible ones. If text X means A and text Y (prevailing) can be read to mean either A or B, B prevails as meaning of the treaty if such conclusion is manifest according to an interpretation of Y under Article 31 (optionally confirmed under Article 32_1). To suggest otherwise, that in this case there would be no divergence and A, common to both texts, needs to be regarded as the meaning of the treaty, runs counter to the VCLT principles: if a consideration of the ordinary wording of the text in good faith in light of the context and object and purpose establishes a meaning, such meaning should be regarded as the meaning of the treaty (bearing in mind that such meaning of the prevailing text is of decisive authority in case the interpretations of the other texts depart from it).

It is easy to see how a suggestion to the contrary would go wrong when applied to our example based on the *Natexis* case. Suppose that the text saying liable to tax would have been declared as prevailing, and an interpretation of it under the VCLT general rule would establish that the effective payment of a tax would not be necessary for granting a tax sparing credit. Since liable to tax means both subject to tax and liable but not subject to tax, following Hardy's argument would mean that the meaning of the text saying subject to tax as the common meaning would have to be given preference every time instead of the different manifest meaning of the prevailing text.

In summary, a common interpretation unequal to the manifest meaning of the prevailing text constitutes a case of divergence, and the manifest meaning of the prevailing text prevails. To suggest that such would not constitute a case of divergence and *any* common meaning of all texts supersedes a different meaning of the prevailing one even though the latter has been established as manifest under Article 31 runs counter to the intention of the contracting parties declaring one text as prevailing and contradicts the interpretative principles enshrined in the VCLT general rule of interpretation. In essence, such suggestion would implement the *Mavrommatis* approach as a general rule, which has been explicitly rejected by the ILC.[5] Thus, Hardy's counterargument is only partially valid for cases in which the prevailing text has no clear meaning, that is, when text X means A while text Y (prevailing) may mean either A or B and neither can be established as manifest under application of Article 31.

One a side note, the unquestioned reliance on Hardy's argument by scholars like Arginelli and Engelen is somewhat curious, as it is inconsistent to agree with Hardy's argument for cases in which a prevailing text exists but deny it for cases without prevailing text. The core of Hardy's argument is that the meaning of the treaty is the one common to all texts, not any one of a single text considered in isolation. It is based on the view that all texts together constitute the text, which is the essential implication of Hardy's argument. If one agrees with it, then it is precisely an argument for comparing all texts and a counterargument against the routine interpretation approach for plurilingual treaties without prevailing text, endorsed by the quoted scholars.[6] In order to be consistent, those advocating Hardy's argument for cases with prevailing text would at the same time have to reject the routine interpretation approach for cases without.

Hardy's argument may be agreed with partially, but only for cases when there is no prevailing text or the prevailing text remains unclear. The exist-

---

[5] See ILC, *Draft Articles on the Law of Treaties with Commentaries*, II:225–26, para. 8; Gaja, 'The Perspective of International Law', 93–94.

[6] See Engelen, *Interpretation of Tax Treaties under International Law*, 388–91; Arginelli, *The Interpretation of Multilingual Tax Treaties*, 250–51, 337.

ence of a prevailing text creates a situation of quasi-unilinguality that allows for a limited routine interpretation approach in the sense of allowing sole reliance on the prevailing text as long as an interpretation under Article 31 leads to a manifest meaning. Advocating Hardy's argument for cases with prevailing text while denying it for cases without is self-contradicting, and the unquestioned reliance on it by Arginelli and Engelen seems to boil down to a mere *argumentum ad verecundiam* without critical examination for its consistency with their otherwise advocated positions.

6.3. Hardy's Search for a Middle Ground

Hardy's seminal study of 1962 is still one of the most influential works on the subject of plurilingual treaty interpretation. The joint dissenting opinion in the *Young Loan Arbitration*, which has been supported by Sinclair in his Commentary to the VCLT drawn on by many other scholars for their own positions concerning the weight of the original text, based itself on his research.[7] This warrants a comprehensive review of his views, on top of the selected arguments already considered.

Starting from the premiss that the primary objective of treaty interpretation is to ascertain the common intention of the contracting parties, the focus of Hardy's research is on illuminating the practice of international courts when texts differ.[8] He does, however, not stop at the modest goal of cataloguing the attitudes displayed by international judges, but his project is to infer technical rules of interpretation via induction:

> Rather than apply deductive processes of abstract logic, the decisions of international courts and tribunals were scrutinized in order to determine whether in this matter there existed, if not legal rules, at least some relevant methods of interpretation – which might be regarded as technical rules – recognized as proper.[9]

---

[7]See *Young Loan Arbitration*, 111 et seq; Sinclair, *The Vienna Convention on the Law of Treaties*, 152.

[8]See Hardy, 'The Interpretation of Plurilingual Treaties by International Courts and Tribunals', 73.

[9]Ibid., 73–74.

6. The Restrictive Approach: A Critical Review

From the pre–VCLT perspective of 1962, this may have seemed like a valid project proposal. One may argue that he was only trying to anticipate the work of the ILC, that is, to observe and formulate what the drafters of the VCLT had not yet codified. Judged from a post–VCLT perspective against the background of the principles enshrined in it, however, the problems inherent in his approach become apparent. First and foremost, his goal of deriving proper technical rules is fundamentally in friction with the VCLT approach of supplying only a few general consensus 'principles of logic and good sense', not technical rules suitable for mechanical application.[10] His inductive approach in this respect proves problematic methodologically.[11] The particularities of case law plus the element of subjectivity employed by judges considerably blur the picture and make distillation of general principles difficult – a comparative evaluation of the reasoning employed by judges in particular cases is itself an interpretative exercise prone to controversy, introducing elements of variance in the absence of pre-established general principles on the basis of which the decisions can be evaluated.

In addition, courts always need to decide the particular case at hand, and different facts and circumstances may lead to different conclusions. From observations that courts in a set of particular cases favoured the clearer or more narrow text or the text in the original language of drafting, one may not necessarily draw the conclusion that this should be a general principle. The courts may have made this choice for particular reasons found in the facts of the case; if the facts would have been different, so would have been the conclusions. Although this is not necessarily an argument in principle, one must still acknowledge the fundamental difficulty of deriving generally applicable rules from the judgements of different national and international courts in an international environment in which general consensus principles on the basis of which these judgements could be evaluated had not been established yet.

Moreover, since courts always only need to judge the particular case at

---

[10]See ILC, *Draft Articles on the Law of Treaties with Commentaries*, II:218–19, paras. 4–5.

[11]An extensive discussion of the problems of induction in general lies outside the scope of this study; the interested reader is referred to John Vickers, 'The Problem of Induction', in *The Stanford Encyclopedia of Philosophy*, ed. Edward N. Zalta, Spring ed. (Stanford University, 2016). For purposes of the current discussion, concentrating on particular observations concerning Hardy's work is sufficient.

hand, their reasoning may leave a lot to be desired for drawing general conclusions. Compare in this respect Hardy's own evaluation of the *Mavrommatis* decision:

> [T]he Court did not, despite appearances, interpret the words at all; it confined itself to proving that, whether the French or the English version was taken as a basis, the grant of the concessions to Rutenberg came within the powers therein defined. Its interpretation was in effect merely a highly logical piece of reasoning, and the assertion of certain authors that the Court endorsed 'limited interpretation' as a rule for solving discrepancies between authentic texts is accordingly erroneous.[12]

Indeed, the question remains how helpful the reasoning of the court is to establish which text gives the right meaning from a general perspective – the decision itself stops short of delivering in this respect.

Unsurprisingly, in an international environment made up of different legal systems without a common hierarchically structured judiciary, a common law approach looking for precedent is unhelpful in establishing a definitive rule in the face of varied case law. The expectable outcome indeed arrived at by the ILC is a truism: it depends on the intentions of the parties – unless a clear preference is transcribed in the treaty, neither approach is off-limits since both are customary.[13] Depending on ones perspective, one may find this to be either a prime example of commonsensical practicality or the 'English habit of muddling along', favouring case by case pragmatism over general principle.[14] In any case, it follows that in posing the question as it has been posed traditionally – that is, whether one has to automatically apply the prevailing text or conduct a comparison to establish the existence of a divergence first – the bulk of academic commentators is barking up the wrong tree: one *has to* either way only if the treaty itself lays down a

---

[12]Hardy, 'The Interpretation of Plurilingual Treaties by International Courts and Tribunals', 80.

[13]See ILC, *Draft Articles on the Law of Treaties with Commentaries*, II:224, para. 4.

[14]For an extensive discussion of the strengths and weaknesses of the common law pragmatic tradition, see Atiyah, *Pragmatism and Theory in English Law*, Chs. 2–3, verbatim quotation by Andrew Ashworth, *Sentencing and Penal Policy* (1983), 448, at 130, also referenced at 4, 43, and 90. The differences of the common and civil law traditions with respect to the topic of this study will be discussed in Chapter 7.

definite rule in this respect, otherwise one simply has the option.[15]

When judging Hardy's conclusions, it must be taken into account that especially in pre–VCLT times courts may have gone into a wrong direction when judged against the later established VCLT principles.[16] The interpretation of 'divergence' as material divergence by the Polish supreme court may be viewed as such a case.[17] Unlike the constant laws of nature, the laws of men are evolutionary, and so is case law.[18] This means that in order to be of any lasting value, inductive generalisations must be evolutionary, too.[19]

The case examples on pages 82–83 of Hardy's study illustrate how he arrives at problematic conclusions based on court decisions not in line with the principles of the VCLT (*Venezuelan Bond* and *German Reparations*). It is obvious that both decisions may easily come into conflict with the principle of using the object and purpose as single decisive criterion under Article 33(4) if their conclusions are generalised as technical rules of interpretation. The resulting idea that always the more narrow meaning of a term should prevail bears a great danger of going wrong in the context of international treaties, which employ terms in the role of broader abstractions.[20]

The idea is exceptionally prone to error in the case of tax treaties because of the interaction between Articles 33 and 3(2). The consequence may be an overuse of domestic law definitions not intended by the contracting states, for example, when there is a domestic law meaning of a term in one of the states but none in the other – a situation in which the context is likely to re-

---

[15]This stance of the ILC implies their conviction that both approaches must lead to a correct interpretation of the treaty, i.e., that the existence of an actual divergence is not a necessary precondition for reliance on the prevailing text, or else a definite rule of interpretation would have been called for. Thus, the ILC implicitly submits to the logical argument and rejects Hardy's reasoning against it. This coincides with Engelen's conclusion that Article 33(1) is not intended as a peremptory norm, and the requirement of a divergence to exist the outcome of 'infelicitous drafting', see Engelen, *Interpretation of Tax Treaties under International Law*, 376–379.

[16]For a brief summary of the practice of the PCJI and ICJ before the adoption of the VCLT, see Eden, 'Plurilingual Treaties', 5–10.

[17]*Archdukes of the Habsburg-Lorraine House v The Polish State Treasury.*

[18]See *Fothergill v Monarch Airlines Ltd.*, 298–99, per Lord Roskill.

[19]See von Kirchmann, 'Die Werthlosigkeit der Jurisprudenz als Wissenschaft', 23.

[20]See *Buchanan (James) & Co. Ltd. v Babco Forwarding and Shipping (UK) Ltd.*, 160, per Lord Salmon.

quire otherwise.[21] Although there are national courts who have recognised this, the danger is great that a given court may not pay attention to the other country's legal situation when judging a case under its domestic law that contains a definition of the term, resulting in a misapplication of the treaty (as in Vogel's hypothetical case discussed in Chapter 4, s. 4.5).

Another problem of Hardy's reasoning is its imprecise categorisation of prevailing texts,[22] which does not properly distinguish between authenticity and authority but defines the prevailing text as the 'authentic text'. This use of terminology is misleading, as it may create the idea that the authenticity of texts is variable. All texts that qualify as authentic under the VCLT remain so irrespective of one being designated in addition as prevailing, because authenticity is established by the procedures codified in Article 10 VCLT. Therefore, all texts are equally authoritative in case of concordance, but the prevailing text is super-authoritative: it prevails over the others if there is a divergence, however, the others still remain authentic in such case – they only lose their relative authority versus the prevailing text, not versus supplementary means.

When applying the proper VCLT categorisation to Hardy's example,[23] the English and Italian texts do not cease to be authentic, and the French text does not only become authentic when the others differ. This is important to remember, and some misconceptions by later scholars implying that the prevailing text needs to be consulted in an overall comparison only after a comparison of the other texts has resulted in a divergence seem to be rooted in Hardy's imprecise categorisation (see below).

Hardy's analysis then starts out from the assumption that 'final clauses

---

[21]See Avery Jones, 'Treaty Interpretation', ss. 8.1 [5.1.1] and 8.2.4 [5.1.2.4].

[22]See Hardy, 'The Interpretation of Plurilingual Treaties by International Courts and Tribunals', 125.

[23]The formulation employed by Hardy derives from the wording of the clause he uses as example, which does not explicitly define the texts as authentic, unlike the majority of final clauses in tax treaties today (see Chapter 8). As acknowledged by Hardy himself, however, such explicit definition is not essential: in the absence of a specific provision, authenticity derives from the mere fact that an instrument has been concluded in a particular language, see ibid., 74, with reference to Arnold D. McNair, *The Law of Treaties* (Oxford: The Clarendon Press, 1961), 60. This principle is laid out also in the VCLT Commentary, see ILC, *Draft Articles on the Law of Treaties with Commentaries*, 224, para. 2.

are nearly always drawn up somewhat automatically' and, therefore, are 'more or less stereotyped formulas which are still accepted in diplomatic parlance but which the courts do not take into consideration because they have lost their true meaning', the wording 'in case of divergence' being such a formula.[24] In addition, he asserts that the employed notion of 'divergence' is a 'relatively hazy and subjective' one.[25] Both assumptions raise doubts in his view concerning the interpretation of such clauses in a 'rigid' way,[26] and 'The provisions must therefore generally be construed less on the basis of the text than in the light of diplomatic practice and, here, as elsewhere, case law affords the surest guidance in the matter.'[27]

In consequence, Hardy finds it difficult to define the exact point in the interpretative process when efforts to reconcile the various texts are to be abandoned and the prevailing text is to be invoked as decisive. He struggles with the reasoning employed by the Polish supreme court because it weakens the authority of the prevailing text, wherefore he emphasises the necessity to define its limits because, 'when the texts can only be reconciled by reference to the preparatory work, a refusal to apply the authentic text would render the relevant final clauses wholly meaningless and constitute a flagrant disregard of the will of the contracting parties.'[28] Nevertheless, based on his rejection of the logical argument discussed above, he rejects sole reliance on the prevailing text without first establishing that there actually exists a divergence.

In order to resolve the ambivalence and strike a middle ground between the two antagonistic approaches applied by courts in practice as observed by him, he resorts to teleological reasoning by proceeding from the assumption that the intention behind the agreement of parties on a prevailing text must be considered to be 'above all, to eliminate any uncertainty that might arise from the plurality of texts and to provide the judge with a sure and rapid means of settling any dispute on the subject', from which he concludes that 'to require of a judge that he constantly keep comparing the

---

[24]See Hardy, 'The Interpretation of Plurilingual Treaties by International Courts and Tribunals', 124, 132–33.

[25]See ibid., 132.

[26]See ibid., 132.

[27]Ibid., 124.

[28]Ibid., 131–32.

texts and only as a last resort recognize that the authentic text must prevail would seem contrary to that intention.'[29] Consequently, he finally pleads for a relatively broad understanding of 'divergence', which encompasses mere differences in wording as long as they prove somehow problematic, allowing judges to resort to the prevailing text 'as soon as a comparison of the texts no longer suffices to reconcile them' on grounds that 'the only type of divergence which the contracting parties would normally have in mind is a purely verbal or *prima facie* divergence, for the much more complex notion of a discrepancy which cannot be solved except by the most subtle process of construction can only be grasped after exhaustive study of the relevant case law.'[30]

Arginelli criticises Hardy for not supplying much argumentative support for the suggestion that the intention behind final clauses providing for a prevailing text is to provide courts with a sure and rapid means to settle disputes.[31] To counter Hardy, he suggests that it would be equally plausible to assume that the intention of the contracting parties consists in providing 'the interpreter with a single and clear means to construe the multilingual treaty where no (other) reconciliation appears possible, i.e., where no single reasonable meaning may be attributed to all authentic texts when they are interpreted in good faith and the light of the overall context.'[32] Maybe Hardy thought his proposition would be sufficiently self-evident and not require further reasoning – it certainly appears commonsensical. In any case, it does not follow from any of his premises but is itself a premiss. Nonetheless, Hardy's suggestion is correct, and it has been one of the objectives of the current study to provide conclusive arguments in its favour on the basis of the VCLT.

In summary, Hardy's research and evaluation of the relevant case law leads him to advocate a somewhat permissive application of the prevailing text, with some moderation. Although he rejects sole reliance on the prevailing text from a conceptual point of view,[33] he accepts it as a 'second best'

---

[29]Ibid., 132.

[30]Ibid., 132.

[31]See Arginelli, *The Interpretation of Multilingual Tax Treaties*, 332.

[32]Ibid., 332.

[33]See Hardy, 'The Interpretation of Plurilingual Treaties by International Courts and Tribunals', 126, 133–34.

pragmatic solution because 'This method, which has received tacit approval from the International Court, has one practical advantage which should suffice to ensure its adoption: it is simple, rapid and sure.'[34] Hence, it is a bit misplaced to categorise Hardy as an advocate of the restrictive approach. He rather seems to want to occupy a middle ground, without being able to pin-point the exact spot.

The problem of his approach is that he does not arrive at a definite solution, stating himself that setting an exact limit in the interpretative process when it would be time to stop trying reconciliation of all texts and resorting to the prevailing one 'would be somewhat arbitrary'.[35] In consequence, his implicit 'first best' solution remains elusive because applying the supposedly right amount of moderation and finding this limit remains an exogenous variable – he can only tell when one has gone too far, namely, when reconciliation of texts is effected by recourse to supplementary means over application of the prevailing text. Thus, Hardy fails his own project of identifying clear-cut technical rules,[36] falling victim to his inductive approach in the face of antagonistic case law. His common sense pulls him towards the right conclusions, but he fails to provide a sufficient base of arguments for them while providing arguments in support of the opposite position. On the whole, he makes two steps forward but one step back.

6.4. Arginelli's Position

Arginelli's thesis is the most comprehensive study on plurilingual tax treaty interpretation to date. At the same time, it provides the most extensive reasoning representative of the restrictive approach, which warrants a critical examination of all his points in addition to those already considered. In essence, Arginelli pleads for decisive recourse to the prevailing text only as a method of last resort after all interpretative efforts fail to establish a meaning common to all texts:

> The author submits that, unless some decisive evidence to the contrary is
> available, final clauses providing for a prevailing text in the case of diver-

---

[34]Ibid., 133–34.
[35]Ibid., 132.
[36]See ibid., 73–74.

gences should be construed as requiring the interpreter to compare the *prima facie* divergent authentic texts in light of all the available elements and items of evidence, in order to determine whether a reconciliation is possible by applying the rules of interpretation enshrined in Articles 31 and 32 VCLT, before relying exclusively on the prevailing text. The apparently divergent authentic texts, therefore, should be construed in light of the overall context and compared with each other in the quest for a common meaning. Only where, at the end of the interpretative process, no common meaning may be reasonably said to exist should preference be given to the meaning of the prevailing text.[37]

In order to support his view, he fields seven arguments. His first and core argument is that because the only possible meaning of any text for interpretative purposes would be the meaning established by applying Articles 31 and 32, no divergence in meaning between the texts may be said to exist beforehand, that is, the prevailing text can be said to prevail only after the application of Articles 31 and 32 to all texts has established a divergence.[38] In essence, this echoes the reasoning of the Polish supreme court outlined above and delimits 'divergence' to material divergences in meaning that cannot be reconciled by a comparative application of Articles 31 and 32 to all texts. As we have seen, however, this is neither supported by the wording of Article 33 nor its context and object and purpose. If one has to take it to suggest that the comparative application of Articles 31 and 32 to all texts includes giving preference to supplementary means over the prevailing text under Article 32(a) and (b), it is in flagrant violation of the VCLT framework of interpretation and the expressed intentions of the contracting parties declaring one text as prevailing.

As a second argument, he contends that his conclusion fits the VCLT system of interpretation best because the requirement to compare the *prima facie* diverging texts and construe their meaning on the basis of Articles 31 and 32 before applying the prevailing text preserves as much as possible the unity of the treaty. This would again be supported by the mere fact of the prevailing text being relevant only in the case of an actual divergence.[39] In order to support the contention, he lists three quotes derived

---

[37] Arginelli, *The Interpretation of Multilingual Tax Treaties*, 333.
[38] See ibid., 334.
[39] See ibid., 334–35.

from paragraphs 6 and 7 on page 225 of the VCLT Commentary. The quotes, however, do not support his argument because all three refer to situations in which none of the texts is designated as prevailing. Concerning this situation his contention that the texts should be compared before accepting any interpretation based on a single one would indeed be correct – ironically, however, he rejects it for such scenario by supporting the routine interpretation approach. Here we deal with a situation in which one text prevails, and 'prevailing' implies a special property distinguishing the prevailing text from the others not sharing that property, which consists in its prevalence over them, rendering it more authoritative in comparison. The treaty remains one in law, but the prevailing text represents its one true meaning with final, overriding authority. Therefore, the existence of a prevailing text renders the treaty quasi-unilingual, that is, the interpretations of the other texts must converge to the manifest meaning of the prevailing text. If they do not, they must be reinterpreted to conform to it.[40]

Arginelli's suggestion that the prevailing text is relevant only in the case of a material divergence and his proposed solution to require the interpreter to compare the potentially divergent texts and establish their meaning first on the basis of Articles 31 and 32 make little sense. To compare only the other texts without the prevailing one in order to find out whether the divergence between them is material would be an odd suggestion, not consistent with the requirements of Article 33(1) and (4) even if we would disregard its prevailing nature.[41] The prevailing text is still at minimum equally authentic; therefore, if a comparison is enacted, all texts including the prevailing one must be compared, otherwise the outcome is not definitive. Article 33(4) explicitly speaks of a 'comparison of the authentic texts', which unequivocally implies *all* texts. To conclude that there is no divergence when the other texts besides the prevailing one are interpreted to have the same meaning

---

[40]See, by analogy, *Fothergill v Monarch Airlines Ltd.*, 301, per Lord Roskill.

[41]Thus, the ICSID noted in Kiliç: 'Moreover, the tribunal's reasoning in that case seems to have disregarded the Turkish text. ...It is not immediately apparent to the Tribunal in the present case that the *Rumeli* tribunal's reliance on the English and Russian versions alone is consistent with the requirements of Articles 33(1) and (4) of the VCLT. It may be that the *Rumeli* tribunal had a reasoned basis for excluding the Turkish text, but it does not appear to have set out that reasoning in its award', *Kiliç İnşaat İthalat İhracat Sanayi ve Ticaret Anonim Şirketi v Turkmenistan*, para. 9.9.

would be premature; their common meaning could still diverge from the meaning of the prevailing text.

Yet, this is a suggestion sometimes made in the tax treaty context concerning the standard case of two texts in the official languages of the contracting states and a prevailing one in a third language. The implied elevation of the two other texts over the prevailing one may be caused by two intertwined thoughts. First, the assumption that each country's courts will use the country's official language in legal proceedings and, therefore, rely on the text in this language as a matter of custom (at least initially). Second, an implicit extension of the view that a comparison of texts is not required for cases of routine interpretation. The argument by extension then seems to be that when problems surface in form of a divergence between the two texts in the official languages of the contracting states, the third may be disregarded in good faith if the divergence can be resolved by a comparative interpretation of the first two.

Although there may be good reasons to refer to the text in the official language of the proceedings first, this practice is in the international law context mere custom, not obligation; the judge may have recourse initially to any text declared as authentic by the treaty's final clause. Now, even if one does not subscribe to the argument refuting the routine interpretation approach for plurilingual treaties without prevailing text submitted in Chapter 3, which could be extended in an analogous way here, one has to concede that if a problem urging the interpreter to engage in a comparison surfaces, the case can no longer be regarded as one of 'routine interpretation'. Hence, for consistency reasons, even the proponents of the routine interpretation approach would have to concede that a comparison of all texts as part of the context under Article 31(2) becomes obligatory in such case, not only of two out of three – all the more so when the third one has been awarded prevailing status by the contracting states.

In summary, when one text is declared as prevailing, the routine interpretation approach gains force as an argument in terms of supporting sole reliance on it because when c_1 is true for the prevailing text, it is immaterial whether c_2 is true or false, that is, instead of being merely a necessary condition as in the case without prevailing text, c_1 is both a necessary and sufficient condition for applying the routine interpretation approach to the prevailing text. Conversely, the routine interpretation approach completely loses its persuasiveness to support sole reliance on any or all other texts.

Arginelli's third argument is a compound of several related points. First, the submission that his view does not conflict with Article 33(1) and (4) because paragraph (1) does not state that the other texts are not authoritative for interpretative purposes but simply provides an option for the contracting parties to declare one text as prevailing in case of divergence, while paragraph (4) only 'establishes a rule of interpretation for cases where (i) an otherwise irreconcilable divergence exists and (ii) the parties did not agree that a specific text is to prevail in the case of divergence. ...Article 33(4) VCLT does not state anything on the interpretative process that should be followed where the parties agreed that, in the case of divergence, a specific text is to prevail.'[42]

Second, the suggestion that neither the wording nor context of Article 33 would support an 'a contrario reasoning', that is, from Article 33(4) explicitly requiring an interpretative comparison between divergent texts when there is no prevailing one while remaining silent on the case there is one, it may not be concluded that when a prevailing text exists, sole reliance on it should be had instead of an interpretative comparison.[43]

Third, another variation of the 'divergence equals material divergence' argument, namely, that one could not reasonably argue for the term divergence to include a 'difference of meaning resulting before the authentic texts are interpreted according to Articles 31 and 32' on the basis of assuming the wording 'a difference of meaning which the application of Articles 31 and 32 does not remove' to imply for such a difference to exist before a comparative interpretation under Articles 31 and 32 has established so. To support this contention, he lists the following three pieces of evidence:

(i)   the terminology used is different, 'difference' v. 'divergence';

(ii) in paragraph 8 of the commentary to Article 29 of the 1966 Draft, the ILC used the term 'divergence' as a synonym for 'difference of meaning which the application of Articles 27 and 28 does not remove', which would actually point to the opposite conclusion;

(iii) paragraph 4 of the commentary to Article 29 of the 1966 Draft is clear enough in denying the existence, under Article 33 VCLT, of any oblig-

---

[42] Arginelli, *The Interpretation of Multilingual Tax Treaties*, 335.

[43] See ibid., 335.

ation for the interpreter to apply the prevailing text as soon as a prima
facie difference between the various authentic texts is put forward.[44]

Several observations may be made concerning these points. If it were
really true that his view would not be in conflict with Article 33(1) and (4),
this alone would not render it applicable in view of other available options
that may be more manifest. Although it is true that Article 33(1) does not
explicitly state the other texts are not authoritative for interpretative purposes if one text is declared as prevailing, it must not be omitted that when
a prevailing text exists, its meaning is of higher authority, overruling the
interpretations of the other texts in case they diverge.[45] It is also true that
Article 33(4) does not explicitly prescribe a particular interpretative process
in case a prevailing text exists; however, such is not necessary: Article 31
applies in line with the dictum that fundamentally no different principles
should apply to the interpretation of plurilingual treaties than to unilingual
ones.[46]

Article 33(4) does not remain entirely silent concerning prevailing texts.
While distinguishing implicitly between three scenarios as discussed in the
previous chapter, Article 33(4) in substance only concerns itself with the
third one, that is, scenarios in which no prevailing text exists and there
are differences in meaning that cannot be reconciled by the application of
Articles 31 and 32_1, in which case a further *modus operandi* is needed and
provided by Article 33(4) itself. When there is a prevailing text, however,
it is Article 31 that applies in combination with Article 33(1) referred to
by Article 33(4) via the initial 'Except where' condition. As a result, sole
reliance on the prevailing text becomes optional in the sense that applying
Article 31 to the super-authoritative prevailing text will be sufficient as long
as its meaning is clear. At the same time, the interpreter is of course still free
to compare all texts from the outset, as long as the final outcome converges
to the interpretation of the prevailing text.

Arginelli simply falls victim to a false dichotomy by considering only

---

[44]Ibid., 335.

[45]Concerning the clear intention of the drafters of the VCLT for Article 33 to establish a
comparative authority between texts, see ILC, *Summary Records of the Sixteenth Session,
11 May – 24 July 1964*, I:319, para. 60.

[46]See ILC, *Draft Articles on the Law of Treaties with Commentaries*, II:225, para. 7.

the two opposed alternatives of mandatory sole reliance on the prevailing text versus mandatory reconciliatory comparative interpretation of all texts, while excluding the third option of both being optional as long as they lead to the same result. As conducted in the previous chapter, a comprehensive analysis of the wording, context, and object and purpose of Article 33 together with a consideration of supplementary means in form of the VCLT Commentary leads to an understanding of 'divergence' that is opposed to Arginelli's narrow conception. Paragraph 4 of the Commentary to Article 29 of the 1966 Draft Articles he quotes as third piece of evidence precisely rejects the false dichotomy purported by him. As he rightly observes, it denies the existence of an obligation for the interpreter to apply the prevailing text as soon as a *prima facie* difference between the texts is put forward; however, such approach is also not ruled out by it.

Arginelli's fourth argument is in essence another variation of the 'divergence equals material divergence' contention. Its target is Hardy's suggestion that contracting parties would first and foremost have mere verbal differences in mind when drafting final clauses, which would justify recourse to the prevailing text already upon identification of such verbal differences. What is curious this time around is Arginelli's justification for dismissing Hardy's proposition:

> That, in turn, would entail the extremely recurrent exclusive recourse to the prevailing text. In such a way, as a matter of fact, any interested party could unilaterally invoke and obtain the right to rely exclusively on the prevailing text, whenever it would appear more favourable for it than the other authentic texts, by simply highlighting a *prima facie* dictionary divergence. In this respect, the final clause would be transformed into a mere procedural tool in the hands of interested parties. However, since treaties should be interpreted and applied in good faith, it seems reasonable that the prevailing text is to be preferred to the other authentic texts only insofar the existence of a divergence between the provisional utterance meanings of those texts have been ascertained in accordance with the rules of interpretation enshrined in Articles 31 and 32 VCLT, not sufficing in that respect that an interested party merely put forward a presumed difference of meanings in order to rely on the potentially more favourable prevailing text.[47]

---

[47] Arginelli, *The Interpretation of Multilingual Tax Treaties*, 336–37.

First and foremost, any interested party may at any point in time rely on any of the texts designated as authentic by the treaty. That includes the one designated as prevailing unless the treaty would specify otherwise. A contention to the contrary would deny the equal authenticity codified in the treaty and question the principle of unity. Second, the principle *in dubio mitius* (more leniently in case of doubt) is not codified among the VCLT interpretative principles. The VCLT interpretative framework aims to resolve all doubts concerning the meaning of the treaty, so the category of 'more or less favourable' does not fit here. How could one text be more favourable if the texts are supposed to mean the same because of the principle of unity, and how could such be an argument to deny recourse to it? If the prevailing text would indeed mean something more or less favourable, that is, different, one would need to apply it under the VCLT rules. Any notion of a possibility of abuse of the prevailing text as a procedural tool by an interested party putting a lid on its right to refer to any text to argue its position is simply misplaced.

As fifth argument, Arginelli maintains the 'second best' solution proposed by Hardy is not coherent with the VCLT framework of interpretation because his argument is based on the relevance of purely verbal differences, whereas the VCLT framework is based on a textual not literal approach. This point is merely another variation of Arginelli's argument that a reconciliatory comparative interpretation has to be conducted first to establish the existence of a material divergence, and he refers again to his earlier suggestion that Hardy provides insufficient evidence for the assertion that parties would normally have verbal divergences in mind. In his opinion, it would be equally plausible for the contracting parties to have only material divergences in mind.[48] In addition, Arginelli suggests Hardy to be wrong in concluding that when reconciliation of the texts is possible only with recourse to supplementary means, giving such reconciliation preference over application of the prevailing text would render the final clause providing for a prevailing text in case of divergence meaningless; in his view, it would merely render recourse to the prevailing text 'superfluous'.[49]

There are several problems with this line of reasoning. As outlined above,

---

[48]See ibid., 332–33.
[49]Ibid., 333.

recourse to any text being part of the context under Article 31(2) and therefore carrying more relative weight than supplementary means may not be regarded a superfluous exercise in case of a divergence or inclarity without violating the general rule of interpretation and the fundamental weight distribution between authentic and supplementary means implemented by the VCLT.[50] Such recourse is superfluous only when the interpreted text is the prevailing text, in which case the other texts lose their authority relative to it if they say something different and, therefore, lose their interpretative weight as context under Article 31(2) as long as the prevailing text can be attributed a clear meaning. Otherwise, all texts should at all times be compared when there is no prevailing text, because of the residual indeterminacy of plurilingual tax treaties.

When there is a prevailing text, it is not conclusive to suggest that only the other texts should be compared first and supplementary means should be consulted to actively reconcile divergences or resolve any ambiguity before recourse is had to the prevailing text. Article 33(4) reads 'a comparison of the authentic texts', which unequivocally refers to *all* texts. Arginelli's approach effectively tries to replace the prevailing text by supplementary means, which conflicts with Articles 31 and 32: apart from exceptional cases, supplementary means may be consulted only to confirm but not contest a meaning arrived at by a textual interpretation under Article 31. Arginelli's mistake in this respect is somewhat derivative from the view I have refuted in Chapter 4 that Article 32 in its entirety including letters (a) and (b) prevails over application of the *modus operandi* in Article 33(4) to invoke the object and purpose as sole decider. Of course, if one contends subsequently that the prevailing text is only an alternative to the latter, one must follow through and reason that application of Article 32(a) and (b) prevails over sole reliance on the prevailing text in order to remain consistent.

Arginelli's suggestion to restrict the relevance of the prevailing text to cases 'where the intention of the parties is to provide the interpreter with a

---

[50] Arginelli fails to make clear in what way he considers 'superfluous' distinct from 'meaningless' for purposes of the principle of effectiveness. The Oxford Dictionary defines meaningless as 'Having no meaning or significance' or 'Having no purpose or reason', while superfluous is defined as 'Unnecessary, especially through being more than enough'. As regards the principle of effectiveness, the two concepts are synonymous in the sense of Article 33(4) being rendered an empty provision, never to apply.

single and clear means to construe the multilingual treaty in case no reconciliation appears possible in light of the ordinary rules of interpretation'[51]
is purely speculative and not supported by the wording of Article 33. Because of the placement of the 'Except where' condition at the beginning of
paragraph (4) and its direct reference to paragraph (1), comparative reconciliation as necessity comes into play only when there is no prevailing text.
Whatever the other texts may say individually or combined has in the end
no bearing if it deviates from an existing prevailing text.

Arginelli bases his view on a particular reading of Article 33(4), with the
'Except where' condition implied to only qualify its *modus operandi*, as if it
were placed at the end of the paragraph after 'shall be adopted' and not at
the beginning. His argument, in essence reading Article 33(4) as implying a
conjunctive not disjunctive definition of divergence in the sense of a divergence to exist only if there is a difference in meaning *and* that difference
cannot be resolved by comparative interpretation,[52] rests on circular reasoning and is therefore nonsensical: it suggests that only a material divergence
necessitates comparative interpretation or reliance on the prevailing text,
whereas it is necessary to perform a comparative interpretation to establish the existence of a material divergence in the first place.

As his sixth argument, Arginelli proclaims that comparative interpretation is more reliable than interpretation of a single text, even when that text
is designated as prevailing. With reference to Hardy's counterargument to
the logical argument he maintains that if an apparent divergence has been
identified, the lower reliability of single text interpretation would no longer
be acceptable even when that text is designated as prevailing, whereas if no
apparent divergence has been identified, the lower reliability of single text
interpretation of any text would be acceptable because of the presumption
in Article 33(3).[53]

As pointed out previously, Hardy's counterargument to the logical argument Arginelli relies on is valid only when the prevailing text remains
unclear, not when it has a clear meaning. In the latter case, a comparison
with the other texts is no longer necessary to arrive at a reliable result, as

---

[51]Ibid., 333.

[52]See Pfister, *Werkzeuge des Philosophierens*, 68.

[53]See Arginelli, *The Interpretation of Multilingual Tax Treaties*, 337.

the essence of a prevailing text is that it prevails, that is, that it overpowers the other texts if they depart from its meaning. Once it is established that the prevailing text has a clear meaning, Article 33(3) precisely demands that the other texts must be interpreted to concord to it.

With his suggestion that reliance on any single text would be acceptable when there is no alleged divergence but reliance on an existing prevailing text would not be acceptable when there is one, Arginelli obviously tries to make his views compatible with the routine interpretation approach he supports for cases without prevailing text. As already pointed out, it is self-contradicting to support the routine interpretation approach for plurilingual treaties without prevailing text but deny it for the quasi-unilingual situation of a prevailing text.

Arginelli's seventh and final argument is not another substantive point but only a suggestion that unless there would be a strong indication otherwise in the treaty considered, the slightly different forms of existing treaty final clauses do not affect his conclusions because final clauses are nearly always drawn up automatically, containing a number of more or less stereotypical formulas that courts and tribunals do not really take into consideration because they have lost their true meaning.[54]

Two points speak against this view. First, Hardy's contention repeated by Arginelli is merely speculative and not self-evident. It does not necessarily follow from the mere fact that a clause is drawn up automatically without much contemplation that its intention is less clear to the contracting parties. On the contrary, the opposite proposition – that is, the more automatically drawn up clauses are, the more clear and in agreement the contracting parties are about their intention – seems much more compelling because one may not reasonably consider contracting parties to lightheartedly put things into a contract they are unsure of. One may compare the case of severability clauses (also known as *salvatorius* clauses).[55] Many contracts feature such clauses by default, and their formulation in practice is fairly standardised. To suggest that because of this the contracting parties

---

[54]See ibid., 338.

[55]A clause providing that it does not nullify the entire contract if any of its clauses is not in compliance with applicable law, but the clauses in compliance with applicable law remain in force.

have no clear vision of what exactly is implied and the clauses themselves do not clearly express their intentions would be nonsense.

Second, Arginelli's suggestion is in opposition to the VCLT's prescribed textual approach and the principle of effectiveness. As regards the particular form of final clauses inserted in treaties, the VCLT Commentary stresses the importance of the intentions of the contracting parties as expressed.[56] Hence, although it may be true that the set of formulations in actual tax treaties does not show much variance in intention and effect, the different wordings must still be considered carefully to establish the truth of such contention.[57] Arginelli's emphasis on the condition that the existence of a material divergence must be established first in order to invoke the prevailing text, in combination with his assertion that his interpretation applies irrespective of the exact final clause wording, is in friction with Article 33(1) not being intended as a peremptory norm.

---

[56]See ILC, *Draft Articles on the Law of Treaties with Commentaries*, II:226, para. 4.
[57]This will be done in Chapter 8, s. 8.3.3.

7. The View from Domestic Law

7.1. Research Question

So far I have discussed the issue at hand from the perspective of international law. My conclusion has been that the VCLT requires courts to either compare all texts of a plurilingual tax treaty or, as a pragmatic solution, rely on the prevailing text if there is one. The situation of tax treaties being interpreted by domestic courts applying domestic procedures raises the question of how this requirement and solution may be operated in practice from the perspective of the respective jurisdiction.

7.2. Civil versus Common Law

A detailed discussion of all the world's jurisdictions is well beyond the scope and means of this study; however, they may be grouped according to general traits they share despite the fact that the particular ways in which their institutions, rules, and procedures operate may vary. In order to allow general observations, it is necessary to distinguish between legal systems and traditions. According to Merryman and Perez-Perdomo, a legal system may be defined as 'an operating set of legal institutions, procedures, and rules', whereas a legal tradition may be defined as a 'set of deeply rooted, historically conditioned attitudes about the nature of law, about the role of law in the society and the polity, about the proper organization and operation of a legal system, and about the way law is or should be made, applied, studied, perfected, and taught.'[1] The two main legal traditions considered here are civil and common law, as they predominate the legal systems around the globe.[2]

---

[1] John Merryman and Rogelio Perez-Perdomo, *The Civil Law Tradition: An Introduction to the Legal Systems of Europe and Latin America* (Stanford University Press, 2007), 1–2.

[2] The common law tradition prevails in the Commonwealth of Nations and North America, while the civil law tradition prevails throughout Europe, Latin and Middle America,

7. The View from Domestic Law

Concerning the following discussion from a birds-eye view, the reader should bear a few things in mind. First, it would be wrong to conceive of something like a unified civil or common law tradition in view of the differences within the families of legal systems. Even though the common law tradition may appear more unified because of the shared heritage of the British Commonwealth, there are significant deviations between different common law countries.[3] Second, the distinction between the two traditions may be less pronounced in practice than drawn in the abstract – their differences may to some extent lie in more elusive cultural factors and philosophical perspectives,[4] whereas their substantive laws are both rooted in Roman law, albeit in different periods.[5] In addition, there is an element of convergence attributable to mutual influences on each other over the course of history.[6] In consequence, many countries today have mixed systems.[7] In summary, the intention behind the following paragraphs is to briefly sketch fundamental differences relevant to the issue at hand while stressing the point at

and the Commonwealth of Independent States. Traditions based on religious or customary law will not be discussed here; they are found mainly in the Middle East and Asia, while Africa is a mix. The University of Ottawa World Legal Systems Research Group has undertaken a global classification of legal systems and drawn a respective world map, see http://www.juriglobe.ca/eng/index.php.

[3] See Neil MacCormick, Robert S. Summers, and D. Neil MacCormick, *Interpreting Precedents: A Comparative Study* (Aldershot: Dartmouth Publishing Co. Ltd., 1997), 3–4.

[4] See Klaus F. Röhl, *Allgemeine Rechtslehre. Ein Lehrbuch* (Köln: Heymanns Verlag GmbH, 1995), s. 70; Lord Macmillan, 'Two Ways of Thinking', 79.

[5] See Franz Wieacker, 'The Importance of Roman Law for Western Civilization and Western Legal Thought', *Boston College International and Comparative Law Review* 4, no. 2 (1981): 257–61; Watson, Alan, 'Legal Change: Sources of Law and Legal Culture', *University of Pennsylvania Law Review* 131, no. 5 (1983): 1121–57; Cecilia Siac, 'Mining Law: Bridging the Gap Between Common Law and Civil Law Systems', *Mineral Resources Engineering* 11, no. 2 (2002): 217–18.

[6] See Vivienne O'Connor, 'Practitioner's Guide: Common Law and Civil Law Traditions' (International Network to Promote the Rule of Law, March 2012), 33–35; Berkeley School of Law (Boat Hall), 'The Robbins Collection: The Common Law and Civil Law Traditions' (University of California at Berkeley), 4; Jerome N. Frank, 'Civil Law Influences on the Common Law – Some Reflections on "Comparative" and "Contrastive" Law', *University of Pennsylvania Law Review* 104, no. 7 (1956): 887–926; Röhl, *Allgemeine Rechtslehre. Ein Lehrbuch*, s. 70.

[7] See World Legal Systems Research Group, 'JuriGlobe' (University of Ottawa); O'Connor, 'Practitioner's Guide', 33.

the expense of oversimplification. Such necessarily superficial review must suffice for the purpose of the current study.

In order to contrast the crucial differences between the two traditions, it is necessary to view them in the context of their historical formation.[8] Civil law had several influences, although the main one has been Roman law in form of the *Corpus Juris Civilis*, a collection of imperial enactments, textbooks, and writings of Roman lawyers compiled by order of Emperor Justinian I of Constantinople from A.D. 529 to A.D. 534. Additional influences came from local customs, canon law developed by the Christian church and taught by medieval scholars alongside Roman law, and commercial law emerging in Italy to regulate European trade.[9] The political and economic environment on the European continent of scattered territories, unifying states, and growing trade fuelled initiatives of scholars educated in Roman law to rationalise and systematise the law during the early modern period. Growing together politically and economically required a more uniform law, and such could only come from abstract legal theory, not any existing legal system based on local customs, of which there were too many because of territorial fragmentation. As a result, the role of local customs gradually diminished in favour of general principles borrowed from Roman law.[10]

Another important historical influence on civil law has been the French Revolution, which provided a strong impetus to the formation of public law codifying the rights of the individual versus the state.[11] Based on the ideas

---

[8]Based on this historical approach, emphasis is given to the common law in England. As said, there are differences between common law countries, and the US in particular has diverged more from English law than, say, Australia or Canada. For example, the US Supreme Court has a more liberal approach to using extraneous materials in interpretation, see Criddle, 'The Vienna Convention on the Law of Treaties in U.S. Treaty Interpretation', passim.

[9]See Encyclopedia Britannica, 'Code of Justinian'; O'Connor, 'Practitioner's Guide', 9–10; Merryman and Perez-Perdomo, *The Civil Law Tradition*, 13; Berkeley School of Law (Boat Hall), 'The Robbins Collection', 2.

[10]See Berkeley School of Law (Boat Hall), 'The Robbins Collection', 2; Röhl, *Allgemeine Rechtslehre. Ein Lehrbuch*, s. 70; van Caenegem, *Judges, Legislators and Professors*, 100 et seq.

[11]See O'Connor, 'Practitioner's Guide', 10; Merryman and Perez-Perdomo, *The Civil Law Tradition*, 14.

of Montesquieu and Rousseau, the social contract became considered the source of all rights, and legal codes the primary source of law.[12]

During the enlightenment period the scholarly aspirations to unify the law amalgamated with corresponding desires of rulers, which led to comprehensive codification of principles into systematic collections of laws, for example, the Prussian civil code of 1794 and the French *Code Napoléon* of 1804,[13] however, not without slightly deviating underlying rationales influencing the codes of different systems in their particularities until today, like the French ideal of being accessible to ordinary citizens versus the German focus on legal precision and comprehensiveness as well as logically coherent structure.[14] Zweigert *et al.* describe the French *Code civil* as 'a masterpiece from the point of view of style and language',[15] whereas of the German BGB they say the following:

> In language, method, structure, and concepts the BGB is the child of the deep, exact, and abstract learning of the German Pandectist School with all the advantages and disadvantages which that entails. Not for the BGB the simple common sense of the Austrian General Civil Code, the clear and popular style of the Swiss Code, or the sprung diction of the *Code civil*, instinct with the ideal of equality and freedom among citizens. The BGB is not addressed to the citizen at all, but rather to the professional lawyer; it deliberately eschews easy comprehensibility and waives all claims to educate its reader; instead of dealing with particular cases in a clear and concrete manner it adopts throughout an abstract conceptual language which the layman, and often enough the foreign lawyer as well, finds largely incomprehensible, but which the trained expert, after many years of familiarity, cannot help admiring for its precision and rigour of thought.[16]

For common law the historical and philosophical genesis has been different.[17] After the Norman conquest of England in 1066, William the Con-

---

[12] See William Tetley QC, 'Mixed Jurisdictions: Common Law vs Civil Law (Codified and Uncodified)', *Uniform Law Review*, no. 3 (1999): 616.

[13] See Berkeley School of Law (Boat Hall), 'The Robbins Collection', 2; O'Connor, 'Practitioner's Guide', 10.

[14] See O'Connor, 'Practitioner's Guide', 10.

[15] Konrad Zweigert and Hein Kötz, *An Introduction to Comparative Law*, trans. Tony Weir, 3rd revised ed. (Oxford; New York: Clarendon Press, 1998), 91.

[16] Ibid., 144.

[17] See van Caenegem, *Judges, Legislators and Professors*, 114 et seq.; Röhl, *Allgemeine Rechtslehre. Ein Lehrbuch*, s. 70; Lord Macmillan, 'Two Ways of Thinking', 79.

queror and particularly Henry II[18] established a corps of judges to adjudicate local disputes and uphold legal order. Juries were introduced to represent the local interests of the populace in order to ensure their obedience.[19] In contrast to the continent, England always had a centralised legal system with a king's high court since the middle ages. Correspondingly, there was no comparable need to unify locally fragmented legal systems. The point of departure for the development of law was the king's judiciary (to which all common law judges belonged), not necessarily abstract principles, so the essential quest has been to guard the coherence of adjudication, not to unify differing local legal systems and adjudication by independent provincial courts.[20]

Consequently, rather than formulating generally applicable legal principles in a comprehensive code, the traditional focus of common law has been to resolve the dispute at hand on a case-by-case basis,[21] which in spirit may be traced back to the medieval 'system of writs, or royal orders, each of which provided a specific remedy for a specific wrong.'[22] The idea of limiting the power of judges to a mere application of law, stemming from the French Revolution, did not influence common law,[23] which as fundamentally judge-made law retained its feudalistic heritage.[24] Rather than by the ideas of Montesquieu and Rousseau of the state and social contract being the source of all rights, common law has been influenced by Hobbes's idea of the individual forfeiting certain rights to the state.[25]

---

[18]Reigned 1154–1189.

[19]See O'Connor, 'Practitioner's Guide', 11; Berkeley School of Law (Boat Hall), 'The Robbins Collection', 3.

[20]See Röhl, *Allgemeine Rechtslehre. Ein Lehrbuch*, s. 70; van Caenegem, *Judges, Legislators and Professors*, 4–6.

[21]See O'Connor, 'Practitioner's Guide', 13–14.

[22]Berkeley School of Law (Boat Hall), 'The Robbins Collection', 3.

[23]To the contrary, 'the profoundly English belief that an independent judiciary, and a judiciary with the power to issue practical orders, was more important than any number of grand theoretical declarations about the Rights of Man …gained redoubled force after the French Revolution when a series of constitutions proclaiming the Rights of Man were seen by the pragmatic Englishman as so much useless theoretical clutter which had no practical results', Atiyah, *Pragmatism and Theory in English Law*, 22.

[24]See van Caenegem, *Judges, Legislators and Professors*, 6 et seq., 154.

[25]See Tetley, 'Mixed Jurisdictions', 616.

How are the anatomies of civil and common law systems today shaped by these historical influences and philosophical underpinnings? In civil law, the principal source of law is hierarchically structured legislation intended to comprehensively codify all areas of law in a logical and systematic manner according to general principles.[26] According to O'Connor, 'This reliance on codes and laws is a central characteristic of the civil law. At the heart of the civil law lies a belief in codification as a means to ensure a rational, logical, and systematic approach to law.'[27] Case law on the other hand does not function as a primary source of law; judges are supposed to apply not create law, based on the strict separation of powers between legislature and judicature.[28] Cases are to be decided based on legislation not preced-

---

[26] See O'Connor, 'Practitioner's Guide', 11–14; Joseph Dainow, 'The Civil Law and the Common Law: Some Points of Comparison', *The American Journal of Comparative Law* 15, no. 3 (1966–1967): 424; Siac, 'Mining Law', 217.

[27] O'Connor, 'Practitioner's Guide', 11–12.

[28] See Tetley, 'Mixed Jurisdictions', 613, as for example in Germany, see Nigel Foster, *German Legal System and Laws*, 2nd ed. (London: Blackstone Press, 1996), 4; Detlev J. Piltz, 'Macht im Steuerrecht', in *Unternehmen Steuern: Festschrift für Hans Flick zum 70. Geburtstag*, ed. Franz Klein et al. (Köln: Dr. Otto Schmidt Verlag KG, 1997), 506. Nevertheless, as the German Federal Constitutional Court has pointed out, 'The traditional binding of the judge to the law, which is an integral part of the principle of separation of powers, and thus of the rule of law, has in any case been modified in accordance with the wording of the GG to "law and justice" (Article 20, para. 3). According to general opinion, this implies the rejection of a narrow legal positivism. The formula maintains the awareness that law and justice generally coincide as a matter of fact, but do so neither necessarily nor always. Justice is not identical with the sum of all written laws. Given the circumstances, there may exist a surplus in terms of justice vis-à-vis the positive statutes, which has its source in the sense-total of the constitutional legal order and may act as a corrective with regard to the written law; to establish it and bring it to bear in decisions is the task of courts. The GG does not require the judge to apply legislative directives to the individual case within the limits of the possible word-sense. Such a view would presuppose the total gaplessness of the positive legal order, a state which is justifiable as a fundamental postulate of legal certainty but unattainable in practice. Judicial activity consists not only in recognising and expressing decisions of the legislature. The task of courts may require particularly that values immanent in the constitutional legal order but not or only imperfectly expressed in the texts of the written laws are revealed and implemented in decisions in an act of evaluative knowledge not completely lacking wilful elements. In doing so, the judge must rid himself of arbitrariness; his decision must be based on rational reasoning. It must

ent; previous case law is generally non-binding and courts are only bound by statutes.[29]

In common law, judicial opinions are (or at least traditionally were) the principal source of law. Although judges are bound by statutes, they have the power to make law.[30] Statutes only serve as secondary sources of law: they are not used to codify complete branches of law and implement general principles but merely to address particular issues,[31] implement uniformity, and complement or correct judge-made law.[32] Their number has increased over time, however, common law is dominated by case law and must be characterised as uncodified.[33] Dainow provides a good general account of the difference between codes and statutes:

> A code is not a list of special rules for particular situations; it is, rather, a body of general principles carefully arranged and closely integrated. A code achieves the highest level of generalization based upon a scientific structure of classification. A code purports to be comprehensive and to encompass the entire subject matter, not in the details but in the principles, and to provide answers for questions which may arise. ...[S]tatutes are usually not formulated in terms of general principles but consist rather of particular rules intended to control certain fact situations specified with considerable detail.[34]

---

be made clear that the written law does not fulfil its function of solving a legal problem justly. The judicial decision then closes this gap according to the standards of practical reason and the "established general vision of justice of the community" (BVerfGE 9, 338 [349])', BVerfG, '1 BvR 112/65', C, IV, 1. Hence, depending on the legal system in question and the factual circumstances, the situation may be more complex in practice than suggested by the oversimplified dichotomy between applying and creating the law.

[29]See O'Connor, 'Practitioner's Guide', 11–12; Dainow, 'The Civil Law and the Common Law', 426; Mellinghoff, 'The German Federal Fiscal Court', s. 4.5.

[30]See O'Connor, 'Practitioner's Guide', 23; Siac, 'Mining Law', 218.

[31]Compare, e.g., the law of partnerships in the UK Partnership Act of 1890.

[32]See O'Connor, 'Practitioner's Guide', 14, 23; Dainow, 'The Civil Law and the Common Law', 425; Tetley, 'Mixed Jurisdictions', 614.

[33]See Atiyah, *Pragmatism and Theory in English Law*, 28 et seq.; van Caenegem, *Judges, Legislators and Professors*, 39. Certain areas of law have remained constituted almost entirely by case law, e.g., the law of contracts in the UK, see Siac, 'Mining Law', 217 et seq.

[34]Dainow, 'The Civil Law and the Common Law', 424–25.

This has a profound impact on the way courts interpret the law and decide cases. Civil law codes require a liberal interpretation, which applies the underlying principles to actual fact patterns.[35] The civil law judge 'reasons from principles to instances, ...silently asking himself as each new problem arises: "What should we do this time?"'[36] He applies the law by way of subsuming the facts of a case under the codified principles with the help of syllogisms, and his point of departure will be the search for the fundamental principle governing the subject matter.[37] In this context, the *travaux préparatoires* traditionally play a significant role as an indispensable source to help clarify the principles enshrined in the codes.[38]

In contrast, traditionally, a strict interpretation has been called for in common law, as common law statutes compile specific instructions:[39]

> A statute is the will of legislature, and the fundamental rule of interpretation, to which all others are subordinate, is, that a statute is to be expounded, according to the intent of those who made it. ...The fundamental maxim of sound interpretation is: *ita scriptum est*, and it is not the business of courts to be wiser than the laws and to mould them with judicial views of what is just or unjust. The letter of the law is the law itself.[40]

Consequently, investigations into preliminary materials beyond the letter of the law are discouraged;[41] the *travaux préparatoires* have little relevance

---

[35] See ibid., 424.

[36] Thomas Mackay Cooper, 'The Common and the Civil Law – A Scot's View', *Harvard Law Review* 63, no. 3 (1950): 470.

[37] See Zweigert and Kötz, *An Introduction to Comparative Law*, 259; John F. Avery Jones, 'Tax Treaties: The Perspective of Common Law Countries', in *Courts and Tax Treaty Law* (Amsterdam: IBFD, 2007), s. 3.1.7; Dainow, 'The Civil Law and the Common Law', 431.

[38] See Dainow, 'The Civil Law and the Common Law', 424. In Germany, e.g., clarification of the legislator's intentions is part of the historical and teleological methods of interpretation, for which recourse to preparatory materials may be had, see Foster, *German Legal System and Laws*, 64; Ekkehart Reimer, 'Tax Treaty Interpretation in Germany', in *Tax Treaty Interpretation*, ed. Michael Lang (Wien: Linde Verlag Ges.m.b.H., 1998), 125–27.

[39] See Röhl, *Allgemeine Rechtslehre. Ein Lehrbuch*, s. 70.

[40] Peter Benson Maxwell and Gilbert H. B. Jackson, *The Interpretation of Statutes*, 9th ed. (London: Sweet and Maxwell, 1946), 1.

[41] The disregard of preparatory materials partly has historical reasons: common law judges

and, as a recent development, may only be used within strict limits, when the interpretation of a statute otherwise remains ambiguous or obscure, or leads to an unreasonable or absurd result.[42] Contrary to their civil law counterparts, common law judges frown upon syllogistic logic but reason 'from instances to principles …asking aloud in the same situation: "What did we

---

have guarded their law making powers versus parliament by way of denying value to the *travaux préparatoires* and adopting strict methods of statutory interpretation in order to minimise parliamentary infringement on their stewardship of the law, see Dainow, 'The Civil Law and the Common Law', 426.

[42]See *Pepper v Hart*, [1993] AC 593, 617, per Lord Griffiths, and 634, per Lord Browne-Wilkinson; van Caenegem, *Judges, Legislators and Professors*, 17; Avery Jones, 'Tax Treaties', s. 3.3.3. As in civil law, the intentions of the drafters are decisive, however, the perspective on their transposition is different: according to the civil law view, the intentions behind the principles enshrined in the legal text may be investigated via preparatory materials, whereas the English common law view requires the interpreter to consider the intentions as expressed in the written text only and to disregard the preparatory materials as far as possible. It is clear how this follows from common law statutes being a set of specific instructions, not a codification of general principles. Once it is time to enact specific instructions, the process of reflecting on the principles behind them has already been concluded; it is only necessary to establish what exactly the specific instructions instruct, so reference to preparatory materials is justified only in case the instructions turn out to be ambiguous, obscure, unreasonable, or absurd. Concerning treaty interpretation, however, English courts have increasingly recognised and adopted a more purposive approach as implemented by the VCLT, see Bjorge, '"Contractual" And "Statutory" Treaty Interpretation in Domestic Courts? Convergence Around the Vienna Rules', 62–69. In the same vein, the Supreme Court of Canada has stated that 'In interpreting a treaty, the paramount goal is to find the meaning of the words in question. This process involves looking to the language used and the intentions of the parties', *The Queen v Crown Forest Industries Ltd. et al*, 5393. And, 'Contrary to an ordinary taxing statute a tax treaty must be given a liberal interpretation with a view of implementing the true intentions of the parties. A literal or legalistic interpretation must be avoided when the basic object of the treaty might be defeated or frustrated insofar as the particular item under consideration is concerned', *Gladden v Her Majesty the Queen*, 5191. As pointed out earlier, the US approach resembles that of civil law, see, e.g., *Maximov v United States*, 299 F.2d 565 (2d Cir. 1962), 568: 'The basic aim of treaty interpretation is to ascertain the intent of the parties who have entered into agreement, in order to construe the document in a manner consistent with that intent. …And to give the specific words of a treaty a meaning consistent with the genuine shared expectations of the contracting parties, it is necessary to examine not only the language, but the entire context of agreement. We must therefore examine all available evidence of the shared expectations of the parties to this Convention.'

do last time?" '[43] Their point of departure will be the search for a similar previous case unless a statute applies the text of which is clear, requiring the judge to give effect to it.[44]

The VCLT implements a compromise: although its approach to the use of supplementary means is more permissive than the common law one, it is at the same time more restrictive than the civil law approach.[45] The VCLT Commentary to Draft Article 28 reiterates and stresses the primacy of textual interpretation,[46] and it almost seems as if the drafters of the VCLT would have preferred to deny recourse to the *travaux préparatoires* altogether unless interpretation under Article 31 would lead to an ambiguous, obscure, unreasonable, or absurd result.[47] They only conceded a more permissive use in view of varied international practice, which made such restrictiveness feel 'unrealistic and inappropriate',[48] however, not without limiting the more permissive use at the same time to a merely confirmatory role concerning the meaning arrived at under a textual interpretation, subject only to limited exceptions, while emphasising the subordinate character of 'supplementary' means.[49] Thus, it may be fair to say that the VCLT conception concerning use of supplementary means, although being more permissive, gravitates towards a common law approach, and recourse to them should be handled more restrictively than the average civil lawyer would be inclined to have, as has been argued at length in Chapter 4.

Doctrine as developed by legal scholars plays an important role in civil

---

[43]Cooper, 'The Common and the Civil Law – A Scot's View', 470.

[44]See Zweigert and Kötz, *An Introduction to Comparative Law*, 259; Avery Jones, 'Tax Treaties', 11; Dainow, 'The Civil Law and the Common Law', 431; Atiyah, *Pragmatism and Theory in English Law*, 10–13.

[45]Avery Jones suggests that 'This makes little difference in practice since supplementary materials hardly exist in relation to tax treaties', Avery Jones, 'Tax Treaties', s. 3.3.1.

[46]Draft Article 28 became Article 32 in the VCLT.

[47]It is noteworthy that all four special rapporteurs on the law of treaties came from a common law background – only Hersch Lauterpacht had received some of his legal training in Lviv and Vienna, see Waibel, 'Principles of Treaty Interpretation', 11.

[48]ILC, *Draft Articles on the Law of Treaties with Commentaries*, II:223, para. 18.

[49]See ibid., II:223, para. 19. A proposal against implementation of this strict hierarchy of means in the VCLT in favour of a more liberal use of supplementary means made by the US chief delegate was decisively rejected by the Vienna Conference, see Criddle, 'The Vienna Convention on the Law of Treaties in U.S. Treaty Interpretation', 441–442.

law systems, especially in areas the law is unsettled, because of the weight given to the logical and systematic structure of legislation. For every code there exist regularly updated commentaries by scholars that summarise doctrine and case law, and it is common for courts to cite the opinions of academics.[50] Historically, doctrine is inextricably interwoven with the formation of civil law and, although not a source of law, has retained its influence on the development of legal systems through its role in legal education and recourse by lawyers, judges, and legislators.[51]

Conversely, case law as principal source of law creates precedents and has led to the principle of *stare decisis* in common law:[52] higher court decisions are binding for lower courts,[53] which guards legal certainty through a uniform basis of case law rather than codification with a focus on comprehensiveness as well as logical and systematic structure.[54] In the words of Lord Porter, 'The common law is a historical development rather than a logical whole, and the fact that a particular doctrine does not logically accord with another or others is no ground for its rejection.'[55]

In consequence, scholarly commentators do not have the same role and importance in common law as they do in civil law. Rather than to theorise about legislation on the basis of general principles, the role of doctrine in common law is to track the evolution of law by way of compiling, classifying, and analysing case law.[56] Common law is genetically judge-made law by the royal judiciary, whereas, traditionally, the role of academic research

---

[50]See O'Connor, 'Practitioner's Guide', 14, 22.

[51]See ibid., 30–31; Dainow, 'The Civil Law and the Common Law', 428; Wolfgang Schön, 'Tax Law Scholarship in Germany and the United States', *Max Planck Institute for Tax Law and Public Finance Working Paper*, May 2016, passim.

[52]Short for *stare decisis et non quieta movere* (to stand by decisions and not to disturb settled matters).

[53]See Avery Jones, 'Tax Treaties', ss. 3.1.1 and 3.1.7; David A. Ward, 'Use of Foreign Court Decisions in Interpreting Tax Treaties', in *Courts and Tax Treaty Law* (Amsterdam: IBFD, 2007), s. 7.3.

[54]See O'Connor, 'Practitioner's Guide', 14; Dainow, 'The Civil Law and the Common Law', 424–25; Tetley, 'Mixed Jurisdictions', 614; Schön, 'Tax Law Scholarship in Germany and the United States', passim.

[55]*Best v Samuel Fox & Co. Ltd.*, [1952] AC 716, 727.

[56]See O'Connor, 'Practitioner's Guide', 13–14; Dainow, 'The Civil Law and the Common Law', 428.

and theory has been marginal.[57] The historical development as such may be half the story: beneath it lies a strong cultural sentiment in favour of pragmatism over principle – in particular concerning law, which is considered a practical affair and domain of the practitioner.[58]

The image of strict reliance on precedent in common law versus complete disregard for it in civil law is of course an oversimplification. Depending on the legal system in question, the situation today is a lot more complex.[59] In Germany, for example, decisions by courts including the BFH only bind the parties to the particular dispute.[60] Nevertheless, BFH decisions published in the federal fiscal gazette establish a persuasive 'ruling opinion', which is generally followed by the lower courts to avoid the risk of being overruled.[61] Fundamental changes of well established views in case law by the BFH that lead to a disadvantage for the taxpayer may for reasons of protecting legitimate expectations only apply non-retroactively to facts that have arisen after publication in the federal fiscal gazette.[62] It is the primary mandate of the BFH in this respect to preserve unity in the application of law, that is, to ensure legal correctness and certainty through consistency and continuity of case law, together with the development of law by adapting its jurisprudence to improved legal knowledge.[63] In addition to this role of

---

[57] See van Caenegem, *Judges, Legislators and Professors*, 53; Atiyah, *Pragmatism and Theory in English Law*, 34 et seq., 131 et seq.

[58] See Lord Macmillan, 'Two Ways of Thinking', 80; Atiyah, *Pragmatism and Theory in English Law*, 1–42.

[59] For a comparative study of several civil and common law countries, see MacCormick, Summers, and MacCormick, *Interpreting Precedents*.

[60] Article 110(1) FGO; see Deutscher Bundestag, 'Drucksache 15/4549, Nichtanwendungserlasse im Steuerrecht' (Bundesanzeiger Verlagsgesellschaft mbH, January 2005), 1.

[61] See Ward, 'Use of Foreign Court Decisions in Interpreting Tax Treaties', s. 7.4.2; Vogel, 'Über Entscheidungsharmonie', 1055–6.

[62] See Mellinghoff, 'The German Federal Fiscal Court', s. 4.5.

[63] See ibid., ss. 2.2–2.3, 3.2, 3.4, 4.5. The BMF may limit the application of a BFH decision beyond the particular dispute by issuing an explicit non-application decree once the BFH has issued its decision for publication in the federal fiscal gazette; however, it can do so only to avert legal uncertainty and safeguard the uniformity of taxation with respect to the interplay of the BFH decision with other tax laws, and not for purely fiscal reasons, see Deutscher Bundestag, 'Drucksache 15/4549, Nichtanwendungserlasse im Steuerrecht', 1; Wissenschaftliche Dienste des Deutschen Bundestages, 'Der Nichtanwendungserlass im Steuerrecht, Ausarbeitung WD 4–3000–

the BFH,[64] the decisions of the BVerfG bind all courts, including the BFH, by law.[65]

Conversely, one must not underestimate the readiness of common law judges to distinguish new cases from previously decided ones whenever they see fit, even if the facts appear to be similar.[66] Such is not necessarily seen as contradicting the principle of *stare decisis*, but naturally flows from the common lawyer's focus on pragmatic solutions concerning the concrete facts and issue at hand rather than general principle.[67] In the words of Lord Halsbury, 'A case is only authority for what it actually decides. I entirely deny that it can be quoted for a proposition that may seem to follow logically from it. …[T]he law is not always logical at all.'[68]

080/09' (Fachbereich Haushalt und Finanzen, 2009).

[64]Decisions of the BFH cannot be appealed against but may be challenged by way of constitutional complaints at the BVerfG, which may overrule them if it considers them to be in conflict with constitutional law, see Mellinghoff, 'The German Federal Fiscal Court', s. 4.5.

[65]Article 31(1) BVerfGG. The BVerfG itself is not entirely free in its decisions, but its mandate is to apply the German constitution (GG), i.e., concerning taxes, the review of tax laws and decisions of the BFH in terms of their compatibility with the GG, see Piltz, 'Macht im Steuerrecht', 503. Like the BFH in Germany, the French Conseil d'Etat will equally rely on principles as developed by precedent in line with its mandate to foster consistency of case law, and the lower courts will treat its decisions as binding, see Martin, 'The French Supreme Administrative Tax Court', s. 3; Martin, 'Courts and Tax Treaties in Civil Law Countries', s. 4.3.4.2; Avery Jones, 'Tax Treaties', s. 3.1.7; Ward, 'Use of Foreign Court Decisions in Interpreting Tax Treaties', s. 7.4.1. In Italy, too, precedent plays a considerable role in practice concerning the development of law although in theory not being binding – the decisions of the Corte di Cassazione establish a 'prevalent view' generally followed by lower courts, which are obliged to comprehensively justify any deviation, see Ward, 'Use of Foreign Court Decisions in Interpreting Tax Treaties', s. 7.4.3. A more comprehensive survey of country practices in this respect lies beyond the scope of this study.

[66]See Avery Jones, 'Tax Treaties', s. 3.1.7; Zweigert and Kötz, *An Introduction to Comparative Law*, 269. Historically speaking, binding precedent between hierarchically structured courts is a modern development in common law. In the middle ages all common law judges in England were members of the king's unified judiciary; the question of binding precedent between higher and lower courts could not even arise and was more an issue of striking the balance between flexibility and coherence of adjudication, see Röhl, *Allgemeine Rechtslehre. Ein Lehrbuch*, s. 70.

[67]See Atiyah, *Pragmatism and Theory in English Law*, 26 et seq.

[68]*Quinn v Leatham*, [1901] AC 45, 506. See also Oliver Wendell Holmes in *Lochner v New*

7. The View from Domestic Law

Together with the powerful role of judges as law makers, this may be fuelled by the methods employed in legal education. Law classes in common law countries are based on interactively discussing case law in small groups, and students are encouraged to critically reason:

> In the common law educational system, a key learning objective is to demonstrate to students that there can be more than one answer to a particular question or that there may be no one 'right' answer at all. It is important to contrast this with the civil law system where it is presumed that the codes and doctrine provide clear guidance and an answer can be easily extracted without the need for judicial interpretation or creativity in the process. The common law educational system thus rewards creative and novel interpretations of laws and cases.[69]

This is mirrored by the practice of lengthy decisions in which the individual judges extensively outline their arguments under their own name and dissenting opinions are recorded, whereas in civil law systems the individual judges are commonly anonymous, dissenting opinions are not allowed or published, and styles vary from being short and declaratory to longer and more argumentative but in any case more abstract and less detailed than in common law countries.[70]

All in all, neither does the common law judge refrain entirely from reasoning based on principles nor the civil law one from taking previous case law into account; the difference is rather one of point of departure and way of thinking, which may result in a different appreciation of similar factual situations between jurisdictions of the two traditions.[71] Practicalities also play a role. Tax appeals above the First-tier Tribunal require 'permission of either the court appealed from or to' in the UK, and the House of Lords is very selective of what it will hear.[72] The number of relevant cases

---

York, 198 U.S. 45 (1905), 76: 'General propositions do not decide concrete cases.'

[69] O'Connor, 'Practitioner's Guide', 32.

[70] See Michael Kirby, 'Judicial Dissent – Common Law and Civil Law Traditions', *Law Quarterly Review*, July 2007, passim; Avery Jones, 'Tax Treaties', ss. 3.1.8–3.1.9; Rust, 'Germany', s. 11.1.1; Atiyah, *Pragmatism and Theory in English Law*, 30.

[71] See Dainow, 'The Civil Law and the Common Law', 432; Röhl, *Allgemeine Rechtslehre. Ein Lehrbuch*, s. 70; Lord Macmillan, 'Two Ways of Thinking', 67–101; Atiyah, *Pragmatism and Theory in English Law*, passim.

[72] See Avery Jones, 'Tax Treaties', s. 3.1.2.

is much smaller in consequence, which makes consideration of precedent more feasible in comparison to civil law countries such as Germany, where the requirement for all courts to fully reason their decisions leads to a proliferation of reasoned judgements, which cannot all be taken into account because of sheer numbers alone.[73] As enumerated by Avery Jones, the total number of tax appeals at the House of Lords amounted to six direct tax and three indirect tax cases in 2005.[74] In comparison, the eleven senates of the BFH concluded 2,721 procedures in 2015, while 1,857 remained pending.[75] As of 2015, a total of 68,000 decisions of the BFH had been recorded in the *juris* database.[76]

Civil law systems usually feature a sharp separation between private and public law, which has a profound impact on the structure of the judiciary. Typically, separate court structures of specialised and hierarchically organised courts subject to different procedural rules exist for all different areas of law.[77] For common law systems, the distinction is traditionally less marked and may boil down to merely different types of remedies being involved, while the courts and procedural rules may be the same for all areas of law.[78] In the UK, for example, tax law falls entirely under ordinary not administrative law. The First-tier Tribunal (Tax) cannot grant administrative remedies at all, so starting a separate action is necessary when a case concerns an administrative remedy as well as interpretation of law.[79] Although there is

---

[73]See Röhl, *Allgemeine Rechtslehre. Ein Lehrbuch*, s. 70.

[74]See Avery Jones, 'Tax Treaties', s. 3.1.2.

[75]See BFH, 'Jahresbericht 2015', 17.

[76]See ibid., 10. The civil law countries France, Germany, Italy, and the Netherlands together have in total almost six times more tax cases than the common law countries Australia, Canada, and the United States combined (roughly 246,000 versus roughly 42,000), despite having only half the population, and whereas the numbers differ considerably between the individual civil law countries, differences between the common law countries never exceed a factor of 1.5, see Wim Wijnen, 'No Taxation without Litigation – How Tax Courts Survive This Adage', in *Obra Conmemorativa*, Perspectivas Actuales de la Justicia Fiscal y Administrativa en Iberoamérica (Mexico City: 80 Aniversario de la Promulgación de la Ley de Justicia Fiscal, 2016), ss. 4.1–4.3.

[77]See O'Connor, 'Practitioner's Guide', 15–16; Merryman and Perez-Perdomo, *The Civil Law Tradition*, 85; Tetley, 'Mixed Jurisdictions', 618.

[78]See Siac, 'Mining Law', 217 et seq.; Tetley, 'Mixed Jurisdictions', 618.

[79]See Avery Jones, 'Tax Treaties', ss. 3.1.1 and 3.1.3.

an administrative court as part of the High Court, the distinction between administrative law and ordinary law is less marked; in consequence, the entire court structure is generally more unified in common law systems with one appeals and one supreme court for all areas of law, whereas lower courts may be organised by subject matter.[80] This difference is mirrored by the different legal career systems: whereas in civil law countries a differentiated system prepares for different career paths, the common law approach is more holistic and lawyers may easily switch legal roles over the lifetime of their careers.[81]

The role of the common law judge is that of an umpire; although he has the power to raise issues of law, it is for the parties to the dispute to do so, whereas the judge will usually restrict himself to the points submitted.[82] He 'is not treated as knowing the law', but 'It is a professional duty of representatives to produce relevant cases whether or not they are in favour of the party producing them.'[83] The focus is not on rights but on remedies.[84] In the UK, for example, the taxpayer must formally claim treaty benefits for the court to be able to give effect to the treaty.[85] It is plain how this follows from the historical role of the judge to decide the dispute at hand: whatever is not raised by the parties may not be considered under dispute and therefore needs no adjudication. This also affects the burden of proof, which is

---

[80]See O'Connor, 'Practitioner's Guide', 17; Merryman and Perez-Perdomo, *The Civil Law Tradition*, 88.

[81]See O'Connor, 'Practitioner's Guide', 32–33. Since there are no career judges, this almost always involves a one-way switch; switching between barristers and solicitors, although possible, is far less common. Appointing judges from the best practitioners serves as a way of keeping up standards in the UK, whereas in Germany the final mark in the bar exam is decisive.

[82]See A. Giussani, 'Some Comparative Notes on Tax Litigation', in *Courts and Tax Treaty Law* (Amsterdam: IBFD, 2007), 1; Avery Jones, 'Tax Treaties', s. 3.1.1, s. 3.1.7; R. Fentiman, 'Foreign Law in English Courts', *Law Quarterly Review* 108 (1992): 144; Rainer Hausmann, 'Pleading and Proof of Foreign Law – a Comparative Analysis', 5–6; O'Connor, 'Practitioner's Guide', 24.

[83]Avery Jones, 'Tax Treaties', s. 3.1.7.

[84]See Tetley, 'Mixed Jurisdictions', 618. Historically, English law proceeds from duties, from which rights based on obtainable remedies flow in turn, not the other way around, see Atiyah, *Pragmatism and Theory in English Law*, 18 et seq.

[85]See Avery Jones, 'Tax Treaties', s. 3.3.2.

entirely on the parties; the court may not find the facts itself.[86]

In civil law systems, the judge occupies the central role in legal procedure; it is his duty to apply the law *ex officio*, that is, he does not rely on the submissions of the parties, but all issues of fact and law are his domain while parties do not have to call for any points of law at all.[87] It is plain again how this corresponds to the historical role of the judge to apply the law as codified: contrary to his common law counterpart, he has to know the law and apply it to every situation brought before him.[88] This again affects the burden of proof. In Germany, for example, it is for the court to inquire the facts; issues of burden of proof for the taxpayer or tax administration only arise when the facts remain in doubt.[89]

In contrast to civil law systems where written form prevails, proceedings and evidence tend to be predominantly oral in common law systems. Although it is now usual for there to be written skeleton arguments and witness statements, witnesses are normally cross-examined on the contents of their statements.[90] The reason for this may lie in the historic roots: in the beginning of common law, local juries were made up of mostly illiterate people, which necessitated oral proceedings.[91]

In order to examine how these general traits of the civil and common law traditions affect the issue of multiple language texts, the particular legal systems of the UK[92] and Germany will be compared by the following sections.

---

[86]In the UK, the burden of proof in tax cases is normally on the taxpayer because all relevant facts reside with him, see ibid., ss. 3.1.1, 3.1.4.

[87]See Martin, 'Courts and Tax Treaties in Civil Law Countries', s. 4.1.1; Mellinghoff, 'The German Federal Fiscal Court', s. 3.4; Giussani, 'Some Comparative Notes on Tax Litigation', 1; O'Connor, 'Practitioner's Guide', 18.

[88]Together with the focus on general principle, this may explain the traditional anonymity of judges in written decisions and the restrictive attitude towards dissenting opinions. The court only administers the law but does not make it, and in such role there is little place for self-standing dissent of individual judges.

[89]See Rust, 'Germany', s. 11.1.2; Mellinghoff, 'The German Federal Fiscal Court', s. 3.4.

[90]See Avery Jones, 'Tax Treaties', s. 3.1.7; Siac, 'Mining Law', 217.

[91]See O'Connor, 'Practitioner's Guide', 11.

[92]When referring to the UK, it must be borne in mind that Scotland may be considered a mixed system featuring elements of civil law, not in terms of codification but concerning legal thinking, see Lord Macmillan, 'Two Ways of Thinking', passim; Atiyah, *Pragmatism and Theory in English Law*, 9; Tetley, 'Mixed Jurisdictions', 592–93.

7.3. Common Law: United Kingdom[93]

A submission by a party to a tax appeal that the equally authoritative text in another language had a different meaning from the English text would normally need to be supported by expert evidence, which is possible because that issue would be classified as a question of fact. As was said by Lord Scarman in Fothergill, 'the court may receive expert evidence directed not to the questions of law which arise in interpreting the convention, but to the meaning, or possible meanings (for there will often be more than one), of the French. It will be for the court, not the expert, to choose the meaning which it considers should be given to the words in issue.'[94] Although, as Lord Wilberforce said, 'If a judge has some knowledge of the relevant language, there is no reason why he should not use it: this is particularly true of the French or Latin languages, so long languages of our courts. ...In all cases he will have in mind that ours is an adversary system: it is for the parties to make good their contentions. ...They may call evidence of an interpreter, if the language is one unknown to the court, or of an expert if the word or expression is such as to require expert interpretation'.[95]

There is no example that can be quoted in relation to tax treaties, although it is fair to say that there has been little litigation on tax treaties anyway.[96] The nearest example is a non-tax treaty case concerning whether a tax was prohibited by the 1944 Chicago Convention on International Civil Aviation,

---

[93] I claim no knowledge of common law or its procedures; in preparing this section I have relied on the case quoted and comments by one of my supervisors, Prof. Dr. Avery Jones, who would like to acknowledge helpful comments made by Julian Ghosh QC.

[94] *Fothergill v Monarch Airlines Ltd.*, 293. *Fothergill* is an unusual case in which the only authentic text of the treaty was French, which had been legislated in UK law together with a non-authentic English translation and a statement that the French text prevailed. The French text was undoubtedly law in the UK but the quoted statements indicate that its meaning was a fact thus enabling expert evidence to be given, although there was none in the case.

[95] Ibid., 273–74. It is probably the case today that a judge would be less likely to use his own knowledge than at the time of that case.

[96] About seventeen cases since the year 2000 of which eleven concerned treaties in English only. Most of the remainder did not have much scope for considering the other language, being either factual or dealing with treaty language such as 'place of effective management' or 'not less favourably levied'.

which has equally authoritative texts in English, French, Spanish, and Russian.[97] The judge recorded:

> Mr Haddon-Cave [counsel for the Claimants] placed strong reliance on the French, Spanish and Russian texts of Article 15 as supporting the Claimants' interpretation of 'fees, dues or other charges'. The French is '*droits, taxes ou autres redevances*'; the Spanish is '*derechos, impuestos u otros grávemenes*'. (I have omitted the Russian text because of the difficulty of inserting the Cyrillic letters.) I said during Mr Haddon-Cave's opening submissions that the French *taxes* seemed to me to point clearly to taxes being within the prohibition. This led to the evidence of Richard Littlewood, the Head of Translation and Interpreting at the Foreign and Commonwealth Office, being belatedly put in by the Treasury. His evidence is based on his professional knowledge of French and Spanish, and on the advice of colleagues in relation to Russian. His view is that *taxe* in the French text is used in the strict sense of 'a compulsory levy of the same nature as a tax but intended to finance a particular public service and payable only by the users of the service' (see Cornu, *Vocabulaire juridique*); and that if it had been intended to denote a tax in the English sense, *impôt* would have been used. On this basis, the French text does not refer to taxes in the English sense. He accepted, however, that *taxe* often means 'tax', as in *taxe à la valeur ajoutée*. However, both the Spanish and the Russian texts use words that unequivocally translate as 'taxes'.[98]

The procedure is not typical of a tax appeal first, because this was a judicial review case in which witness evidence is uncommon.[99] Secondly, it would be more common for each party to produce its own expert if there was a language issue and for the judge to decide which he preferred and why. Here it was the judge's remark during the hearing that led to the Treasury, which was a party to the appeal, producing a witness from the Foreign and Commonwealth Office at short notice.[100] The evidence suited the claimant, as can be seen from the first sentence of the quotation, and so it would not have wanted to produce contrary expert evidence.

---

[97] The first three are the original languages; Russian was added by a 1977 Protocol.

[98] *R (on the Application of) Federation of Tour Operators v HM Treasury*, [2007] EWHC 20622 (Admin), 52.

[99] It should be emphasised that tax is not classified as administrative law in common law, as outlined above.

[100] This is unusual as normally expert evidence required a direction from the court as part of the preparation of the case and the evidence has to be served on the other party.

But what is typical is that, having raised the language issue, the judge allowed expert witness evidence followed by giving the parties the opportunity of making submissions about how the different language texts should be resolved. A judge would never decide a language issue from his own knowledge of the language without giving the parties the opportunity to disagree with his interpretation and without allowing them to make submissions on how any differences should be resolved.

The judge first tried to reconcile the texts with the aid of subsequent practice,[101] finding substantial evidence that was inconsistent with the claimant's contention. He also considered the *travaux préparatoires* although saying that this was strictly unnecessary, and noted that they contained nothing against this conclusion. Finally, he considered a Belgian Conseil d'Etat case in favour of the claimant's contention, finding the reasoning unclear,[102] particularly as to whether it had considered the English text or subsequent practice; and a Swiss case in which the point had not been argued from which he derived no assistance. The judge therefore did not need to consider Article 33 VCLT.

It is difficult to judge whether in many cases the other language is just ignored. Because treaty cases often involve large sums they tend to be well prepared and both parties are quite likely to have considered the possibility and rejected it. This is particularly the case for the tax authority which may well have been in contact with the other state's tax authority in connection with the case during which a language difference may well be considered.

Lord Diplock said of the Vienna Convention in Fothergill:

> By ratifying that Convention, Her Majesty's Government has undertaken an international obligation on behalf of the United Kingdom to interpret future treaties in this manner and since under our constitution the function of interpreting the written law is an exercise of judicial power and rests with the courts of justice, that obligation assumed by the United Kingdom falls to be performed by those courts.[103]

On the basis concluded above that the VCLT requires a state, and hence a judge, to consider all language texts, the question arises how this might

---

[101] Article 31(3)(b).

[102] Part of the problem was caused by the typically highly-condensed reasoning of the Court which was unfamiliar to an English court.

[103] *Fothergill v Monarch Airlines Ltd.*, 283.

be achieved in a common law system in which the judges perform a more passive role than a civil law judge. A judge will therefore need to rely on the parties assisting him in doing so.[104] It is suggested that first, it should be understood that all language texts should be before the judge. Secondly, the tax authority, which also has a role as part of the state in complying with international obligations, should be expected to make submissions on the meaning of the other language texts. Both suggestions would have to rely on custom rather than on any provision of law.

7.4. Civil Law: Germany

In theory, as it is the duty of the court to apply the law and inquire all facts *ex officio* subject to the principle *iura novit curia*, issues of the other language texts having a different meaning from the German text would not need to be submitted and evidenced by a party to a tax appeal. The parties are consulted and obliged to provide all statements of fact truthfully and in full; they may submit particular evidence such as expert opinions on the other language texts, but the court is in its considerations neither obliged to follow their submissions nor limited to a consideration of them.[105]

Since it is the responsibility of the court to inquire the facts, neither the taxpayer nor the tax administration has the burden of proof; however, the party that would benefit if a certain fact would be evidenced loses the case when that fact remains unproven.[106] Therefore, each party has a strong in-

---

[104] A practical point which makes it less likely for the parties or the judge to raise language issues is that the other language version of a tax treaty is unlikely to be in the papers before the judge because, although presented to Parliament for information in a treaty series, Parliament gives effect in domestic law only to the English language version and other language versions are not reproduced in any of the normal tax sources.

[105] Article 76(1) FGO; see Rust, 'Germany', s. 11.1.2; Mellinghoff, 'The German Federal Fiscal Court', s. 3.4. The tax administration as locus of assessment and first instance of appeal is subject to a similar obligation as the court to inquire all facts under Article 88(1) AO, whereas the taxpayer is obliged again under Article 90(1) AO to answer all requests of the tax administration truthfully and in full; see Rust, 'Germany', s. 11.1.1.

[106] For example, the taxpayer has the burden of proof that he satisfies the requirements for a tax treaty's application, because such is favourable to him, see Rust, 'Germany', s. 11.1.4.

centive to provide as much evidence as possible.[107] In general, a court will request and review all relevant documents irrespective of their language, and only in case not all judges understand the language will a translator be hired.[108]

Given that Germany has a system of specialised tax courts at all levels of the judiciary, a high familiarity of judges with the issues of tax treaty interpretation as a result of multiple language texts must be presupposed. Hence, on the basis of all the aforesaid, one would assume that the other language texts are regularly referred to by judges in practice whether or not the issue is raised by any party to the dispute.

Indeed, it is not uncommon for the other language texts to be referenced.[109] That this is done on initiative of the court is obvious in some cases. For example, in 'I R 369/83' the BFH referred to the Italian text to confirm its interpretation that the taxpayer did not have a fixed base in Italy through which he provided his consultancy services.[110] The Italian text of the treaty translated the German wording *fester Mittelpunkt*[111] with *sede fissa*,[112] not the literal *punto centrale* or *centro*. Whereas the latter would simply indicate a geographical location not necessarily at the disposal of the taxpayer, *sede fissa* implies the holding of that location by him. For its reasoning the court had recourse to a dictionary.[113]

In another example the FG Cologne as court of first instance referred to the English text of the treaty protocol in order to confirm its interpretation of the German text and contradict the interpretation submitted by the taxpayer.[114] In contrast to the German wording of its Article XVII para. 5, the English text of the protocol leaves no doubt as to the point in time when it takes effect. The BFH confirmed the reasoning.[115]

---

[107]See ibid., s. 11.1.2.

[108]See ibid., s. 11.2.5.

[109]See Ekkehart Reimer, 'Germany: Interpretation of Tax Treaties', *European Taxation*, December 1999, 465; Reimer, 'Tax Treaty Interpretation in Germany', 128.

[110]BFH, 'I R 369/83' (BStBl 1988 II, February 1988).

[111]Literally 'fixed centre', meaning fixed base.

[112]Article 7, Germany-Italy (1925), replaced since by Germany-Italy (1989).

[113]E. Bidoli – G. Cosciani, 1957, Italienisch-Deutsch, 817.

[114]FG Köln, '2 K 3928/09' (EFG 1853, April 2012), para. 56, concerning Germany-US (1989), protocol of 1 June 2006.

[115]BFH, 'I R 48/12' (BStBl 2014 II, June 2013), para. 13. For a summary of the case, see Resch,

In other cases it is not entirely obvious on whose initiative the other language text is referred to. For example, in BFH 'I R 63/80' it seems the initial reference to the Spanish text came originally from the tax administration to support its contention that the employment income of the taxpayer did not satisfy the condition of Article 15(2)b of the tax treaty Germany-Spain (1966),[116] rendering the compensation he received for his secondment to a Spanish company taxable in Germany because the German not the Spanish company should be regarded as the employer. It is possible, however, that the initial reference to the Spanish text came from the BMF, which joined the appeal proceedings to side with the taxpayer against the tax administration.[117] Its intervention that Germany's right to tax was successfully limited because Article 15(2)c qualified the term *persona* used by Article 15(2)b in terms of who counts as employer is the first reference to the Spanish text in the decision. The BFH picked up the argument to decide in favour of the taxpayer, upholding the initial decision by the court of first instance.[118]

Although there are several cases in which the other language texts have been considered, this is not true consistently for all case law on tax treaties. The reason for the omission, whether the other language texts are just ignored or have been consulted but found irrelevant and therefore not been further elaborated on, is difficult to judge and quantify. One imaginable reason could be the strong influence of doctrine in Germany.[119] With the

---

'Case Closed'.

[116]Replaced since by Germany-Spain (2011).

[117]The BMF as well as the Ministries of Finance of the individual federal states may join appeal proceedings at the BFH as party upon own initiative or invitation by the BFH, in order to provide considerations important to the case at hand or the interpretation and application of tax law in general, see Mellinghoff, 'The German Federal Fiscal Court', s. 2.5.

[118]BFH, 'I R 63/80' (BStBl 1986 II, August 1985); FG Düsseldorf, 'VII 484/77' (EFG 1980, January 1980).

[119]See Rust, 'Germany', s. 11.1.1. It is common practice of the BFH to cite opinions by academics, see, e.g., BFH, 'I R 48/12'. In addition, university professors are authorised to attend proceedings at the BFH in support of a party 'if this is relevant to a case and there is a need for this in the circumstances of an individual case', Mellinghoff, 'The German Federal Fiscal Court', s. 3.2; their statements are regarded as pleadings of the party they accompany unless they are immediately withdrawn or corrected by the party under Article 62(7) FGO. Several current BFH judges have academic résumés

routine interpretation approach in place as prevailing view, judges without foreign language proficiency could simply feel comfortable in discarding the necessity to look at the other texts until they are confronted with an ambiguity or divergence, whereas for judges having the respective language skills, checking the other language texts by default may be the natural course of action. A change in doctrine should bring about a more consistent practice.

7.5. Comparison per Type of Dispute

How may the different systems be expected to perform in terms of plurilingual tax treaties? In order to evaluate the situation, we may distinguish between disputes in which either one or both parties have recourse to the other language text(s), and those in which neither party does.

Concerning the first type of dispute, both systems may be viewed as performing well albeit in different ways. In Germany, the court does not depend on the submissions of the parties. Theoretically, this could mean that the other language text gets ignored even if a party pleads it, but since the duty of the court is to apply the law *ex officio*, such is not conceivable in practice if the points raised are relevant. Although the court is not limited in terms of investigating all sources of evidence it sees fit,[120] it may in practice rely on its own knowledge of the foreign language or the help of dictionaries.

In the UK, the meaning of foreign language texts seems to be treated as fact not law, somewhat analogous to foreign law.[121] Although there is no

---

and hold appointments as honorary professors, see Mellinghoff, 'The German Federal Fiscal Court', ss. 5.5–5.6. Also in cases involving private international law it is common for judges to resort to academic expert opinions concerning evidence on foreign law, see Rainer Hausmann, 'Pleading and Proof of Foreign Law – a Comparative Analysis', 8.

[120] Articles 81 and 155 FGO (in combination with Article 293 ZPO, which is to be applied correspondingly).

[121] Concerning the treatment of foreign law, see Avery Jones, 'Tax Treaties', s. 3.1.4; Rainer Hausmann, 'Pleading and Proof of Foreign Law – a Comparative Analysis', 2–3, in terms of the historical genesis: 'The fact doctrine is based on the old distinction between the courts of admiralty and the courts of common law. While the former had jurisdic-

clear principle stated to this effect, it may be inferred from expert evidence concerning the meaning of the foreign language text being allowed, which would not be the case if it would be considered an issue of law.[122] Facts have to be proven to the judge by the parties pleading them,[123] for which the testimony of competent experts is required;[124] the other party is not obliged to bring by experts of their own, but will regularly do so if the issue is contested.[125]

The judge will decide based on the evidence provided and will not consider any questions of fact or law not pleaded by the parties.[126] The advantage of this approach is that because of having expert testimony, the quality of evidence provided should be high, that is, the system is well geared towards dealing with a problem of language appropriately once set in motion. On the other hand, if the meaning of the foreign language text would indeed be regarded strictly as a matter of fact, the role of the court as umpire operating under the assumption of ignorance prevents it from investigating any evidence not put forward.[127] Consequently, divergences between the texts will not be considered in the second kind of dispute when they have not been raised.[128]

---

tion in matters with a foreign element, the latter decided on purely domestic issues. When the Common Law Courts extended their jurisdiction to matters with a foreign element in the 18th century they were bound to treat foreign law as fact because the only "law" they could apply was English common law', 10n.

[122] See *Fothergill v Monarch Airlines Ltd.*, 274, 293, per Lords Wilberforce and Scarman. For an example, refer to *R (on the Application of) Federation of Tour Operators v HM Treasury*, 52, as quoted above.

[123] In tax litigation the burden of proof is on the taxpayer, so in an appeal procedure it is for him to prove his case in fact and law; 'an assessment "stands good" unless displaced by evidence.' Avery Jones, 'Tax Treaties', s. 3.1.4.

[124] The question of competence is for the court to decide; what matters is practical experience, not necessarily qualification.

[125] See Rainer Hausmann, 'Pleading and Proof of Foreign Law – a Comparative Analysis', 13; Hartley, 'Pleading and Proof of Foreign Law', 283–84.

[126] See Rainer Hausmann, 'Pleading and Proof of Foreign Law – a Comparative Analysis', 6, 13.

[127] See ibid., 13; Avery Jones, 'Tax Treaties', s. 3.1.4.

[128] For Canada the practice may differ because of the constitutional equality of English and French, i.e., the court may compare the French text of the treaty on its own account, see, e.g., *Conrad M. Black v Her Majesty the Queen*, [2014] TCC 12, para. 25.

Not all is well in Germany either. In principle, the German system is better equipped for dealing with disputes of the second type, because the court applies the law *ex officio* subject to the principle *iura novit curia* and, therefore, may consider other language texts on its own initiative irrespective of any ambiguity in the German text; however, such does not happen consistently in all cases. The routine interpretation approach as prevailing view in doctrine may be responsible. On the whole, the outcome may not be that much better than in the UK: divergences may be overlooked on a larger scale because interpreting the German text alone may be considered sufficient by courts.

The practice to look at other language texts may be less common in other civil law countries to begin with. For example, although the Austrian VwGH has occasionally looked at other language texts,[129] it regularly refers to the German text only.[130] The same seems to apply for Spain.[131] For purposes of the current study, it is sufficient to appreciate the problem in principle; a comprehensive survey of country practices in this respect lies beyond the scope of this study and is left to future research.

7.6. Evaluation of the Status Quo

From all the aforesaid it becomes clear that domestic procedural law plays a pivotal role in litigation involving tax treaties. In combination with the routine interpretation approach as orthodoxy, it curbs proper application of tax treaties by establishing specific procedural prerequisites for the consideration of all texts in form of a requirement for the parties to plead them. Furthermore, procedural law determines to what extent and by which

---

[129]VwGH, '2210/60 VwSlg 2707 F/1962' (RIS, September 1962), as quoted by Johannes Heinrich and Helmut Moritz, 'Austria: Interpretation of Tax Treaties', *European Taxation*, April 2000, 142–52, 148, 50n; more recently: VwGH, '2013/15/0266' (RIS, June 2015), as discussed by Michael Lang, 'Austria: Entertainers under Article 17', in *Tax Treaty Case Law around the Globe 2016*, ed. Eric Kemmeren et al. (Amsterdam: IBFD, 2017).

[130]See Michael Lang, 'Tendenzen in der Rechtsprechung des österreichischen Verwaltungsgerichtshofs zu den Doppelbesteuerungsabkommen', *IFF Forum Für Steuerrecht*, 2012, 38.

[131]See José Calderón and Dolores Piña, 'Spain: Interpretation of Tax Treaties', *European Taxation*, October 1999, 381.

means a judge will examine the content of foreign language texts.[132]

For the UK and most other common law countries, this means that since in tax litigation the burden of proof is almost always on the taxpayer, failure of him or his advisers to appreciate the foreign language text and raise a divergence in his favour will lead to it not being considered by the court and the revenue winning the case on improper grounds.[133] Effectively, this levies a 'tax on the dumb'.[134]

In addition, there are economic disincentives to pleading foreign language texts, as such may increase the costs of an already costly procedure[135] via retaining expert witnesses and incurring additional advisory expenses for an uncertain benefit.[136] According to Wijnen, the higher costs associated with tax proceedings in common law countries are one reason for the considerably lower number of cases in comparison to civil law countries.[137]

Moreover, interpretation of treaties and foreign language texts can be a subtle affair, and a provisional evaluation by oneself or ones advisers may lead to the erroneous conclusion that there is nothing to be gained from in-

---

[132]See, by analogy, Rainer Hausmann, 'Pleading and Proof of Foreign Law – a Comparative Analysis', 1.

[133]See Avery Jones, 'Tax Treaties', s. 3.1.4.

[134]See, by analogy, Gerd Rose, 'Über die Entstehung von "Dummensteuern" und ihre Vermeidung', in *Die Steuerrechtsordnung in der Diskussion: Festschrift für Klaus Tipke zum 70. Geburtstag*, ed. Joachim Lang (Köln: Dr. Otto Schmidt Verlag KG, 1995), 153–64. Rose defines taxes on the dumb as 'tax expenses that would not have arisen if the taxpayer would have achieved the same economic goal under a smart application of existing [legal] planning opportunities differently', 153 (he excludes illegal conduct explicitly as not acceptable means). In particular, he distinguishes between two types of taxes on the dumb: those of a simple order, being the result of ignorance or a lack of information, and those of a higher order, being the result of lacking strategic deliberation, see Rose, 'Über die Entstehung von "Dummensteuern" und ihre Vermeidung' 154 et seq. Therefore, failure to appreciate the other language texts and raise a corresponding divergence may be classified as a simple tax on the dumb. Of course, the legislator does not intend to tax lack of intelligence; however, this is what results from its conduct, which seems intolerable in the context of tax equality as a fundamental goal, see Klaus Tipke, *Die Steuerrechtsordnung, Bände 1–3*, 1st ed. (Köln: Otto Schmidt Verlag, 1993), Bd. 3, 1370, as referred to by Rose, 153–154.

[135]See Avery Jones, 'Tax Treaties', s. 3.1.10.

[136]See, by analogy, Rainer Hausmann, 'Pleading and Proof of Foreign Law – a Comparative Analysis', 6.

[137]Wijnen, 'No Taxation without Litigation – How Tax Courts Survive This Adage', s. 4.1.

voking the other language text(s).[138] Not everybody eligible for the benefits granted by a tax treaty is a multinational enterprise with abundant financial resources and access to the best and most experienced advisers.

Finally, pleading the other language text(s) by default to secure all options may appear as a potentially dangerous strategy, because there is no prohibition of *reformatio in peius* (change to the worse) in UK procedural law, that is, the court is not prevented from increasing the tax assessment if its evaluation of the evidence suggests so.[139]

One's evaluation of this situation may be a matter of perspective. Tipke's view cited above, that taxes on the dumb are intolerable in respect of tax equality as a general goal, may be a natural position to assume from a civil law perspective with focus on general principle, codified rights, and courts applying the law *ex officio* subject to the principle *iura novit curia*. From a common law perspective of judge-made law resolving the dispute at hand in a pragmatic fashion based on precedent with the court functioning as umpire granting remedies, the position that a point not raised by a party needs no remedy may seem equally natural.

Looking at it from the position of the taxpayer may be the wrong perspective altogether. For the other state, which is the actual party to the treaty but not the dispute, the outcome may be that the reciprocal sharing of taxing rights as intended by the treaty is upset. This raises the issue of state responsibility.

Hilf develops an elaborate formulation of the routine interpretation approach based entirely on this question.[140] Although he acknowledges that it amounts to a violation of the treaty when a state tentatively applies an interpretation of a single text that does not correspond to the treaty's true content, he frames the issue in terms of the question what parties can expect from each other. For him the issue boils down to a question of responsibility

---

[138]Effectively turning a simple into a higher order tax on the dumb.

[139]See Avery Jones, 'Tax Treaties', s. 3.1.4. In Germany, the risk is less prevalent because the court is forbidden to worsen the assessment, see Rust, 'Germany', s. 11.1.2. Nevertheless, if the tax authority has issued its assessment under reservation of reconsideration on the basis of Article 164 AO, it may change the assessment within a grace period of four years for direct taxes under Article 164(2) and (4) AO in combination with Article 169(2)2 AO.

[140]See Hilf, *Die Auslegung mehrsprachiger Verträge*, 76–83.

and compensation in case the party that has relied on a single text sees itself confronted with a claim for remedy and fulfilment of its treaty obligations retroactively.[141]

He starts from the premiss that the agreement of parties on equally authentic texts expresses their trust in each correctly reflecting the full content of the treaty.[142] From this he concludes that reliance on a single text is justified as long as the meaning of it is clear and the state organ applying the treaty 'does not stumble on or is not confronted with a divergence', because in his opinion such conduct is not 'culpable' in the sense of not incurring any state responsibility itself, notwithstanding the responsibility to remedy actual violations of the treaty should they result, which he regards as a separate matter.[143]

Thus, he splits the issue in two by viewing it through the lens of state responsibility: the conduct of interpreting a single text in isolation and the conduct after the fact, once it has turned out that this has established a result in violation of the treaty for which the other party claims remedy. In his view, the first would not incur any state responsibility as long as done 'bona fide', that is, does not constitute a violation of any substantive treaty obligation under the condition that no inclarity or divergence has arisen and purposefully been ignored,[144] whereas the latter incurs state responsibility in case of failure to successively remedy a treaty violation being a factual situation under objective criteria.[145] Crucial to his view is the assumption that the trust of each party in each single text correctly reflecting the full content of the treaty is justified as long as there is no inclarity and no divergence has arisen in 'whatever way', or else it would be justified to attribute the risk of treaty misapplication to the parties and hold them responsible if

---

[141]See ibid., 77–79.

[142]See ibid., 80.

[143]See ibid., 82. The expressions he uses in German are *nicht vorwerfbar* and *kein vorwerfbares Verhalten*, which literally translate to 'not blameable' and 'no blameable conduct'.

[144]Despite the toned down language of 'no blameable conduct', this is what he implies.

[145]See ibid., 79, 82. This echoes Hardy's view that 'since the texts are presumed to agree, each party is justified in following its own version as long as the application of the treaty gives rise to no dispute between the parties', Hardy, 'The Interpretation of Plurilingual Treaties by International Courts and Tribunals', 117.

they stick to relying on a single text regardless,[146] which is then picked up by Engelen to formulate his own view.[147]

The rules of state responsibility had been selected already as one of the subjects of the codification conference held in The Hague in 1930 under the auspices of the League of Nations.[148] After the second world war, the matter was picked up by the ILC in 1949 as one of their fourteen provisional topics selected for codification.[149] Since then the work of the ILC has lead to the Draft Articles on Responsibility of States for Internationally Wrongful Acts with Commentaries,[150] which were noted, welcomed, and commended by the General Assembly to the attention of states in 2001.[151] The recommendation has been repeated,[152] however, without resulting in a diplomatic convention and binding treaty to date. Therefore, customary international law applies;[153] however, the DARS may be considered as its crystallisation,[154] as they heavily draw on case law of international courts and, despite their non-binding status *'ad referendum'* (subject to agreement by other parties),

---

[146]See Hilf, *Die Auslegung mehrsprachiger Verträge*, 80.

[147]See Engelen, *Interpretation of Tax Treaties under International Law*, 390–91.

[148]See Hunter Miller, 'The Hague Codification Conference', *The American Journal of International Law* 24, no. 4 (1930): 675.

[149]See ILC, *Summary Records and Documents of the First Session Including the Report of the Commission to the General Assembly*, Yearbook of the International Law Commission 1949 (United Nations, 1956), 281, para. 16.

[150]For a concise overview of the historical background, development, and content, see James Crawford, 'Articles on Responsibility of States for Internationally Wrongful Acts', *United Nations Audiovisual Library of International Law*, 2012.

[151]UN, 'General Assembly Resolution 56/83', Doc. A/56/589 & Corr. 1 (United Nations, December 2001).

[152]UN, 'General Assembly Resolution 59/35', Doc. A/59/505 (United Nations, December 2004), UN, 'General Assembly Resolution 62/61', Doc. A/62/446 (United Nations, December 2010), UN, 'General Assembly Resolution 65/19', Doc. A/65/463 (United Nations, December 2010).

[153]According to Rosenne, customary international law is comprised of 'rules of law derived from the consistent conduct of States acting out of the belief that the law required them to act that way', Shabtai Rosenne, *Practice and Methods of International Law* (Oceana Publications, 1984), 55.

[154]For purposes of the discussion at hand, they are treated as such; a more comprehensive approach lies beyond the scope of this study, for which a few general observations must suffice. The interested reader is referred to James Crawford, *State Responsibility: The General Part* (Cambridge: Cambridge University Press, 2013).

are widely approved of and drawn on in turn, also by the ICJ.[155]

The notion of wilfully risking treaty misapplication as a condition implied by Hilf and Engelen carries the suggestion of intent being necessary to constitute a violation of ones international obligations, which raises the question whether such qualifies as a general rule. The DARS deny such suggestion – what matters is the objective content of the obligation at stake:[156]

> Thus there is no exception to the principle stated in article 2 that there are two necessary conditions for an internationally wrongful act – conduct attributable to the State under international law and the breach by that conduct of an international obligation of the State. The question is whether those two necessary conditions are also sufficient. It is sometimes said that international responsibility is not engaged by conduct of a State in disregard of its obligations unless some further element exists, in particular, 'damage' to another State. But whether such elements are required depends on the content of the primary obligation, and there is no general rule in this respect. ...

> A related question is whether fault constitutes a necessary element of the internationally wrongful act of a State. This is certainly not the case if by "fault" one understands the existence, for example, of an intention to harm. In the absence of any specific requirement of a mental element in terms of the primary obligation, it is only the act of a State that matters, independently of any intention.[157]

---

[155] Crawford, 'Articles on Responsibility of States for Internationally Wrongful Acts', 2, for example in *Gabčíkovo-Nagymaros Project (Hungary/Slovakia)*, ICJ (Annual Reports of the International Court of Justice, 1997), 38–55, paras. 46, 50, 79, 83 (referencing an earlier version of the DARS). The ICJ defines customary international law on the basis of which it decides disputes as 'international custom, as evidence of a general practice accepted as law', UN, 'Statute of the International Court of Justice', June 1945, Article 38(1)(b). Thus, the two substantive constituents of customary international law are 'the actual practice and *opinio juris* [opinion of law] of States', *Continental Shelf (Libyan Arab Jarnahiriya/Malta)*, ICJ (Annual Reports of the International Court of Justice, 1985), 29, para. 27; see also *Legality of the Threat or Use of Nuclear Weapons, Advisory Opinion*, ICJ (Annual Reports of the International Court of Justice, 1996), 253, para. 64; *North Sea Continental Shelf (Federal Republic of Germany/Denmark; Federal Republic of Germany/Netherlands)*, 44, para. 77.

[156] See Hans Pijl, 'State Responsibility in Taxation Matters', *Bulletin for International Taxation*, no. 1 (2006): 42–43.

[157] ILC, *Draft Articles on Responsibility of States for Internationally Wrongful Acts*, II, Part 2:36, paras. 9–10.

The extent to which good faith implies such 'specific requirement of a mental element' justifying the suggestion of intent as a necessary precondition is debatable. Supposedly, the argument would be that Article 33(3) warrants the belief that one has done everything required to fulfil ones obligations in all honesty, fairness, and reasonableness as long as no problem of ambiguity has appeared and no divergence has been raised when interpreting a single text in isolation.[158] Effectively, this treats reliance on Article 33(3) as a surrogate for conduct in good faith and a waiver of the obligation to consider all of the context under Article 31(2); however, it seems not justified to claim that one has put all treaty obligations into effect in their spirit as well as according to their letter and to the best of ones abilities if one at the same time knowingly accepts that actual divergences stay undetected because they are not raised by anyone in the process, resulting in a misapplication of the treaty in violation of Articles 31 and 26 VCLT. Certainly not if undetected divergences are systemic as argued in Chapter 3, but arguably neither if they were a mere contingency (thus, Hilf and Engelen may not even have a point to begin with).

The approach by Hilf to distinguish between obligations of conduct and result, with only a failure of the latter counting as a violation in the absence of wilful neglect because of Article 33(3), is unfounded. Article 12 DARS states that 'There is a breach of an international obligation by a State when an act of that State is not in conformity with what is required of it by that obligation, regardless of its origin or character', and with reference to case law of the ICJ and the ECHR its Commentary makes clear that any distinctions between obligations of conduct and result are neither 'exclusive' nor 'determinative'.[159] Rather, parties may be considered to have accepted a multitude of obligations of conduct and result in order to achieve the objectives of a treaty.[160] Even in cases in which the obligation is identified as primarily being one of the latter, the conduct cannot be separated from the result as a basis for determining whether there is a breach of obligation:

---

[158] See Hilf, *Die Auslegung mehrsprachiger Verträge*, 77.

[159] ILC, *Draft Articles on Responsibility of States for Internationally Wrongful Acts*, II, Part 2:56–57, para. 11.

[160] *Gabčíkovo-Nagymaros Project (Hungary/Slovakia)*, 77, para. 135.

'But, in order to decide whether there had been a breach of the Convention in the circumstances of the case, it [the ECHR] did not simply compare the result required...with the result practically achieved....Rather, it examined what more Italy could have done to make the applicant's right 'effective'.[161]

The question therefore remains whether reliance on a single text in isolation may be considered in good faith because of Article 33(3), not whether state responsibility is invoked concerning the actual outcome in hindsight. The approach of Hilf to confine the matter to the issue of invoked state responsibility must be rejected because state responsibility is only a secondary concern.[162] What matters is whether there is a breach of a primary obligation under the treaty, which depends entirely on the terms of the obligation itself:

> In every case, it is by comparing the conduct in fact engaged in by the State with the conduct legally prescribed by the international obligation that one can determine whether or not there is a breach of that obligation. The phrase 'is not in conformity with' is flexible enough to cover the many different ways in which an obligation can be expressed, as well as the various forms which a breach may take.[163]

The VCLT Commentary makes clear that Article 33(3) is not intended as a waiver of the obligation to compare texts but to assure that the principle of unity is observed in all cases. It presumes the terms of a treaty to have the same meaning in all texts in order to stress that the interpreter is not justified 'in simply preferring one text to another' but required to undertake 'every reasonable effort' in order to ascertain the common intentions of the

---

[161]ILC, *Draft Articles on Responsibility of States for Internationally Wrongful Acts*, II, Part 2:57, para. 11. The ECHR itself notes the following: 'The Italian authorities, relying on no more than a presumption ..., inferred from the status of "latitante" which they attributed to Mr. Colozza that there had been such a waiver. In the Court's view, this presumption did not provide a sufficient basis....It is difficult to reconcile the situation found by the Court with the diligence which the Contracting States must exercise in order to ensure that the rights guaranteed...are enjoyed in an effective manner', *Colozza v Italy*, European Court of Human Rights (Application no. 9024/80, 1985), 10, para. 28. Thus, negligence is ruled out on top of intent.

[162]See Pijl, 'State Responsibility in Taxation Matters', 39.

[163]ILC, *Draft Articles on Responsibility of States for Internationally Wrongful Acts*, II, Part 2:55, para. 2.

parties, that is, the one true meaning of the treaty, not of any single text.[164] The Commentary makes these observations mainly concerning cases of ambiguities, but they must be understood as generally applicable because of what is demanded by the principle of unity being a presumption of law.[165] In the face of q and r_2, this implies that 'every reasonable effort' must be understood to exclude relying on a single text in isolation,[166] at least in the

---

[164]See ILC, *Draft Articles on the Law of Treaties with Commentaries*, II:225, paras. 6–8. The same follows directly from the wording of the general rule in Article 31. The interpreter has to interpret the treaty 'in accordance with the ordinary meaning to be given to the terms of the treaty in their context and in the light of its object and purpose.' It can hardly be claimed that he has done so if he arrives at a wrong result when relying on a single text, see Kuner, 'The Interpretation of Multilingual Treaties', 963, 73n.

[165]Noteworthy, paragraph 7 on page 225 of the Commentary reads 'A term of the treaty may be ambiguous or obscure because it is so in all the authentic texts, or because it is so in one text only but it is not certain whether there is a difference between the texts, or because on their face the authentic texts seem not to have exactly the same meaning. But whether the ambiguity or obscurity is found in all the texts or arises from the plurilingual form of the treaty, the first rule for the interpreter is to look for the meaning intended by the parties to be attached to the term by applying the standard rules for the interpretation of treaties.' Hence, what is talked about is indeterminacy as a result of a divergence between texts and fundamental ambiguity as a result of terms being equally ambiguous in all texts, not ambiguity of a single text in isolation.

[166]In this respect, the WTO Appellate Body has stated the following: 'As we have observed previously, in accordance with the customary rule of treaty interpretation reflected in Article 33(3) of the Vienna Convention ..., the terms of a treaty authenticated in more than one language – like the WTO Agreement – are presumed to have the same meaning in each authentic text. It follows that the treaty interpreter should seek the meaning that gives effect, simultaneously, to all the terms of the treaty, as they are used in each authentic language. ...We also note that, in discussing the draft article that was later adopted as Article 33(3) of the *Vienna Convention*, the International Law Commission observed that the "presumption [that the terms of a treaty are intended to have the same meaning in each authentic text] requires that every effort should be made to find a common meaning for the texts before preferring one to another"', *United States – Final Countervailing Duty Determination with Respect to Certain Softwood Lumber From Canada*, WT/DS257/AB/R (Report of the WTO Appellate Body, 2004), 22, para. 59, 50n, square brackets in the original. And: 'We agree, however, that the Panel's description of "price suppression" in paragraph 7.1277 of the Panel Report reflects the ordinary meaning of that term, particularly when read in conjunction with the French and Spanish versions of Article 6.3(c)1, as required by Article 33(3) of the Vienna Convention', *United States – Subsidies on Upland Cotton*, WT/DS267/AB/R (Report of the WTO Appellate Body, 2005), 159, para. 424.

case of tax treaties, as has been argued at length in Chapter 3. As is admitted by its proponents, the routine interpretation approach sanctions a standard of tentative interpretation possibly in violation of treaty obligations and subject to retroactive correction.[167] Articles 31–33 in combination with Article 26 VCLT, however, require the interpreter to give effect to the common intentions of the parties.

In other words: divergences do not 'arise' – they either exist or not. If they exist, they are either detected or not, and they can be detected only by comparing all texts. Treaties are to be interpreted 'in good faith in accordance with the ordinary meaning to be given to the terms of the treaty in their context and in the light of its object and purpose'.[168] By looking only at one language text, the interpreter may fail on all three accounts: he may fail to appreciate the true object and purpose, he may fail to appreciate the full context, and he may fail to appreciate the intended wording, which may be misrepresented by the text looked at. In consequence, he may violate Article 26 VCLT. In its strong form, the currently prevailing view rests on circular reasoning: it proclaims that looking at a single text is sufficient as long as there is no divergence, whereas the establishment of a divergence requires a comparison of texts. Therefore, it is disproven by means of a *reductio ad absurdum*.[169] The weaker form in essence suggests that divergences do not matter as long as they are not raised by anyone, that is, as long as they remain undetected. Such contention must be rejected in view of the VCLT principles: what matters is that the common intention of the contracting states as expressed by the treaty is observed, not whatever

---

[167] See Hilf, *Die Auslegung mehrsprachiger Verträge*, 78; Engelen, *Interpretation of Tax Treaties under International Law*, 391.

[168] UN, *Vienna Convention on the Law of Treaties*, Article 31(1).

[169] Defined by the American Heritage Dictionary of the English Language as 'Disproof of a proposition by showing that it leads to absurd or untenable conclusions'. Its theoretical foundation and terminology is commonly attributed to Aristotle, see Nicholas Rescher, 'Reductio ad Absurdum', in *The Internet Encyclopedia of Philosophy*, ed. James Fieser and Bradley Dowden, 2018, s. 1, however, use of similar techniques can be traced back to Socrates, Zeno of Elea, Xenophanes of Colophon, and Parmenides of Elea, see Susanne Bobzien, 'Ancient Logic', in *The Stanford Encyclopedia of Philosophy*, ed. Edward N. Zalta, Winter ed. (Stanford University, 2016), s. 1.2; Daigle, Robert W., *The Reductio ad absurdum argument prior to Aristotle* (San Jose, C.A.: SJSU ScholarWorks, 1991), passim.

may be expressed by any single text considered in isolation, which may be at variance. Consequently, what matters is not that divergences remain undetected but that they are excluded, that is, that they are either ascertained not to exist or resolved by way of interpretation to arrive at the one true meaning of the treaty implementing the common intention of the contracting states. If this may be precluded by looking at one text alone as has been shown for tax treaties, interpretation in good faith requires consideration of all texts as long as they must be considered equally authoritative under Article 10 VCLT and the treaty final clause, and Article 33(3) may not be interpreted as a waiver of that obligation, as otherwise divergences may go unnoticed and the treaty may be misapplied in violation of Articles 31–33 and 26 VCLT.

In case the outcome of a court decision relying on a single text in isolation violates the common intentions of the parties concerning the reciprocal sharing of taxing rights, state responsibility may be invoked by the affected state, any other state, groups of states, or the international community as a whole for the protection of collective interests.[170] But, is such likely in tax cases, which must be considered off the radar in this respect? Maybe in a case like *Natexis*, in which not only the taxpayer loses his tax sparing credit but also a loss of billions of foreign direct investment must be feared as a result.[171] The taxpayer may provoke remedy in individual cases via mutual agreement procedures; however, they are focussed on resolving the single issue at hand and commonly remain unpublished, so they neither create precedent nor foster development of treaty interpretation in general.[172]

In summary, with the routine interpretation approach in place and not challenged and replaced by the international community, the status quo is

---

[170]ILC, *Draft Articles on Responsibility of States for Internationally Wrongful Acts*, Articles 42–48 with Commentaries.

[171]Instead of invoking state responsibility, however, it is more likely for the other state to simply change its domestic law in order to counteract the effect, e.g., by levying 0.1% of tax instead of 0% in the *Natexis* scenario, see Arruda Ferreira and Trindade Marinho, 'Tax Sparing and Matching Credit', 402–3.

[172]See Kees van Raad, 'International Coordination of Tax Treaty Interpretation and Application', in *International and Comparative Taxation: Essays in Honour of Klaus Vogel*, ed. Paul Kirchhof et al., Series on International Taxation 26 (Kluwer Law International, 2002), 26.

an invitation for states to favour their own language text and for taxpayers to game the system, that is, to only raise divergences whenever they are favourable and remain silent otherwise. The losers are states and taxpayers who, unwittingly, suffer the losses of treaty misapplication in consequence. I harbour doubts whether my arguments will convince the average common lawyer, to whom my approach and methodology based on axiomatic-deductive reasoning may seem 'beyond the pale';[173] however, there is no denying that divergences between the texts of a treaty are common and will not necessarily disclose themselves if not raised by a party to the dispute.[174] Therefore, an element of arbitrariness in tax assessments and court decisions is the inevitable outcome of the status quo, especially in common law countries for said reasons. With respect to this I shall close my personal evaluation with a quotation by David Hume that, although written with poll taxes in mind, I find nevertheless fitting:

> But the most pernicious of all taxes are the arbitrary. They are commonly converted, by their management, into punishments on industry; and also, by their unavoidable inequality, are more grievous, than by the real burden which they impose. It is surprising, therefore, to see them have place among any civilized people.[175]

7.7. Solutions

How can the problems introduced by domestic procedural law be remedied? Even if the approach to rely on the prevailing text is generally adopted,

---

[173] Atiyah, *Pragmatism and Theory in English Law*, 13.

[174] As happened, e.g., in *Foster & Elam v Neilson*, 27 U.S. (2 Pet.) 253 (1829), in which the US Supreme Court had recourse only to the English text and later had to correct itself after a discrepancy with the Spanish text was raised, employing a rather symptomatic excuse: 'The Spanish part of the treaty was not then brought to our view, and we then supposed that there was no variance between them. We did not suppose that there was even a formal difference of expression in the same instrument, drawn up in the language of the other party', see Kuner, 'The Interpretation of Multilingual Treaties', 958, with reference to Henry P. de Vries, 'Choice of Language', *Virginia Journal of International Law* 3 (1963), 32–33, and *United States v Percheman*, 32 U.S. (7 Pet.) 51 (1833).

[175] David Hume, 'Of Taxes', in *Essays: Moral, Political, and Literary* (Indianapolis: Liberty Fund, Inc., 1987), II.VIII.7.

882 plurilingual (734 bilingual) tax treaties without prevailing text remain currently in place, which (besides France) are mainly treaties of the major common law countries (see next chapter). For civil law countries such as Germany, the problem may resolve automatically given the conditions – a change in the prevailing view abandoning the routine interpretation approach may be sufficient to bring about consistent practice because of the strong influence of doctrine; however, in the case of common law countries such as the UK, a change in doctrine will hardly bring about a change in practice, because the function of doctrine is different and its influence on practice marginal. In consequence, action will be required. As suggested, the intended result could be achieved by an extension of the professional duty of the representatives or the revenue to always compare the other texts and raise issues regardless of whether they are in favour of their own position.[176] This makes sense from the perspective of state responsibility because Article 4 DARS, which attributes the acts or omissions of organs of a state to that state according to the principle of its unity, conceives of such organs in the broadest possible sense, including federal as well as municipal tax authorities.[177]

---

[176]In the UK, an extension of the professional duty could be achieved by the professional bodies or a practice direction by the judges, who could for example say that all language texts should be put before the judge. In Germany, the tax administration as first instance of appeal is under Article 88(1) AO already subject to the requirement to inquire all the facts irrespective of the submissions of the taxpayer, see Rust, 'Germany', s. 11.1.1. A change in the prevailing view abandoning the routine interpretation approach should therefore bring about consideration of the other language text(s) already at the level of assessment. A sure way to implement this would be via a circular from the BMF.

[177]ILC, *Draft Articles on Responsibility of States for Internationally Wrongful Acts*, Article 4 and Commentary, 40–42, paras. 1–13.

8. Applicability of the Permissive Approach

8.1. Research Question

The previous chapters raise the question to what extent the complexities of plurilingual interpretation can be avoided with respect to actual tax treaties. This question may be subdivided into the following three research questions: First, how many tax treaties avoid the problem altogether by being unilingual? Second, how many plurilingual tax treaties provide for a prevailing text the final clause of which allows for sole reliance on it? Third, how many plurilingual tax treaties do not provide for a prevailing text or provide for one but the final clause does not allow for sole reliance on it? In addition to answering these questions, this chapter begins to contemplate how policies of individual countries affect the global landscape, and what general policy recommendations may be deduced from these observations.[1]

---

[1]Policy choices of individual countries as well as cooperative global policy choices or even mere emerging patterns are subject to a complex mix of national and international political and historical factors that are hard to discern in terms of their influence on observable outcomes. Quantifiable patterns in the treaty network of an individual country provide some clues concerning the underlying policy choices; however, the global tax treaty network is made up of bilateral relationships in which the policies of the treaty partners affect each other. The result depends on a mix of political goals, historical influences, asymmetric bargaining power, economic trade-offs, and reciprocal concessions. The line between what may serve as a clear indication for a certain policy and what is mere speculation is blurry and sometimes hard to draw. A comprehensive analysis considering all relevant factors in individual cases lies well beyond the scope and means of this study, which will for the most part limit itself to presenting the clues given by the investigated data.

8.2. Use of Prevailing Texts

8.2.1. Global Analysis

When we look at the entire sample, we find that roughly one-quarter of all treaties is unilingual while three-quarters are plurilingual; however, almost 60% of the plurilingual ones have a prevailing text.[2] Hence, only roughly 30% of all treaties are plurilingual without prevailing text,[3] while 70% are either unilingual or have a prevailing text.

Table (8.1): All Treaties

Treaties	No.	w PT	w/o PT	%global	w PT %PL	w/o PT %PL
global	3844					
UL	967			25.16%		
PL	2877	1700	1170	74.84%	59.09%	40.67%

Regarding the number of authentic languages employed by the 2,877 plurilingual treaties, we find the following: roughly 40% have two texts, only about 15% of which designate one as prevailing; roughly 57% have three texts, about 88% of which designate one as prevailing; only about 3% have four texts, about 94% of which designate one as a prevailing; and less than 1% have five texts, all of which designate one as prevailing. Thus, the standard scenario for plurilingual tax treaties is either two or three texts. Instances with more than three texts are few, and no tax treaty has more than

---

[2] Three Tunisian treaties in force provide for two (English and French) prevailing texts instead of one: Pakistan (1996), Malta (2000), and Iran (2001). The first two have three authentic texts (English, French, Arabic) while the latter has four (English, French, Arabic, Persian). These treaties will be commented on in more detail below; for the purpose of the figures presented in this section they are not separately accounted for but lumped together with treaties featuring one prevailing text. Seven treaties provide for a MAP in case of divergence; they are not accounted for as either with or without prevailing text but will be dealt with separately later.

[3] Henceforth, whenever the addition 'plurilingual' is superfluous because of the context, it is omitted in order to condense the text. The phrase 'treaties without prevailing text' always implies plurilingual treaties only; unilingual treaties will be mentioned separately when referred to.

five texts. Whereas the vast majority of bilingual treaties has no prevailing text, the relation is almost exactly reverse for trilingual treaties, most of which feature a prevailing text. Moreover, almost all treaties with more than three texts feature a prevailing text. From this we may conclude that the main function of additional language texts is to provide for a prevailing text and the problem of additional interpretational complexity is mostly confined to bilingual treaties.

Table (8.2): Number of Authentic Languages (All Plurilingual Treaties)

AL	No.	w PT	w/o PT	%global	w PT %AL	w/o PT %AL
2	1138	169	966	39.56%	14.85%	84.89%
3	1628	1426	198	56.59%	87.59%	12.16%
4	94	88	6	3.27%	93.62%	6.38%
5	17	17	0	0.59%	100.00%	0.00%

When we subtract all terminated treaties from the sample, 3,358 treaties in force or yet to come into force remain. The proportions of unilingual and plurilingual treaties relative to all treaties hardly change, whereas the proportion of treaties with prevailing text as percentage of all plurilingual treaties increases by almost 5%. This is attributable to two factors: (1) a decreased proportion of bilingual treaties versus an increased proportion of trilingual ones, and (2) increases in both the proportions of bilingual and trilingual treaties with prevailing text.

Table (8.3): Global Tax Treaty Network

Treaties	No.	w PT	w/o PT	%total	w PT %PL	w/o PT %PL
Total	3358					
UL	847			25.22%		
PL	2511	1622	882	74.78%	64.60%	35.13%

Hence, we may conclude that the policy to implement a prevailing text has become more popular over the decades. In total, almost three-quarters of all treaties in force or yet to come into force are either unilingual or have a prevailing text, that is, the problem of additional interpretational complexity attributable to plurilingual form is confined to roughly one-quarter of today's global tax treaty network.

Table (8.4): Number of Authentic Languages (Global Tax Treaty Network)

AL	No.	w PT	w/o PT	%total	w PT %AL	w/o PT %AL
2	905	168	734	36.04%	18.56%	81.10%
3	1496	1349	143	59.58%	90.17%	9.56%
4	93	88	5	3.70%	94.62%	5.38%
5	17	17	0	0.68%	100.00%	0.00%

The numbers for terminated treaties reveal that between January 1960 and August 2016 a total of 486 treaties have been terminated, roughly one-quarter of which has been unilingual and three-quarters plurilingual. This corresponds to the overall averages, that is, nothing has changed in terms of the relative potential to conclude unilingual treaties. Out of the terminated plurilingual ones, however, only roughly one in five had a prevailing text.

Table (8.5): Terminated Treaties

Treaties	No.	w PL	w/o PL	%total	w PT %PL	w/o PT %PL
Total	486					
UL	120			24.69%		
PL	366	78	288	75.31%	21.31%	78.69%

Almost 85% of all terminated treaties have been replaced by new treaties of the same type between the same countries. Out of the not replaced plurilingual treaties, only one out of ten had a prevailing text. As regards replaced treaties, roughly 27% have been unilingual and 73% plurilingual. Out of the originally unilingual ones, roughly 46% have been replaced by plurilingual treaties and the rest by unilingual ones. Almost 90% of all originally unilingual treaties replaced by plurilingual ones have been replaced by treaties with prevailing text, whereas out of the originally plurilingual ones, less than 10% have been replaced by unilingual treaties. The vast majority (almost 80%) of plurilingual treaties replaced by unilingual ones had no prevailing text, same as roughly three-quarters of those replaced again by plurilingual ones. Almost half of the treaties originally without prevailing text have been replaced by ones with prevailing text, while only one treaty with prevailing text has been replaced by one without, which has been replaced by a unilingual treaty in turn.[4]

Table (8.6): Not Replaced Terminated Treaties

Treaties	No.	%total/term/PL
total	72	14.81%
UL	8	11.11%
PL	64	88.89%
PL w/o PT	58	90.63%
PL w PT	6	9.38%

Table (8.7): Terminated and Replaced Treaties

Treaties	No.	%term/total/UL/PL
total	414	85.19%
UL	112	27.05%
UL NC	60	53.57%
UL to PL	52	46.43%
UL to PL w PT	46	88.46%
UL to PL w/o PT	6	11.54%
PL	302	72.95%
PL to UL	29	9.60%
PL w/o PT to UL	23	79.31%
PL w PT to UL	6	20.69%
PL NC	273	90.40%
PL NC w/o PT	207	75.82%
PL NC w PT	66	24.18%
PL w/o PT to w PT	103	49.76%
PL w/o PT NC	104	50.24%
PL w PT to w/o PT	1	1.52%

---

[4]Belgium-Norway (1967).

8.2.2. Time-Series Analysis

Although the above analysis contains a dynamic perspective with respect to the effects of termination, the overall picture at this point is still fairly static. A time-series analysis is required to evaluate the global development.[5] This shows that from the 1960s throughout the 1990s, the number of tax treaties has more than doubled per decade. The absolute number of treaties concluded per decade remained high in the 2000s, but the high growth rates of the previous decades slowed down: the number of treaties per decade no longer doubled but only equalled the number of the 1990s.

Table (8.8): Treaties per Decade

Decade	PD w term	PD w/o term	CM w term	CM w/o term
1960-69	176	92	176	92
1970-79	345	225	521	317
1980-89	671	413	1192	730
1990-99	995	975	2187	1705
2000-09	1048	1044	3235	2749
2010-16	609	609	3844	3358

As revealed by the data, the major expansion of the global tax treaty network has been taking off as late as the 1990s: roughly 80% of all tax treaties in force today have been concluded since 1990. The 1970s and especially 1980s may be viewed as a first wave of expansion in which most of the initial 20% of today's global tax treaty network has been concluded; therefore, almost all treaties concluded by OECD members, amounting to roughly two-thirds of the entire global tax treaty network, are within the ambit of some version of the OECD Model.[6]

---

[5]Decades have been chosen as suitable time interval. From now on, all figures exclude terminated treaties unless specified otherwise, in order to represent the global tax treaty network as is.

[6]In total 590 treaties between OECD members and 1,689 treaties between OECD members and non-members, amounting to 17.57% and 50.30% of the global tax treaty network, respectively. Appendix C provides some insight concerning treaties by OECD members concluded before the OECD Models.

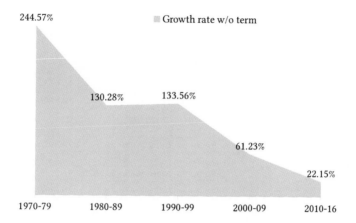

Figure (8.1): Per Decade Treaty Growth Rate

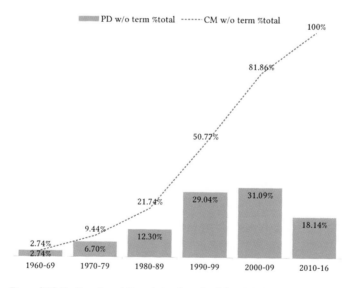

Figure (8.2): Per Decade and Cumulative Growth of the Global Tax Treaty Network

Although the number of unilingual treaties has continued to grow in absolute terms throughout the decades, they have been vastly outgrown by plurilingual ones. Treaties before 1960 were mostly unilingual, but the situation reversed as early as 1960, and the gap between unilingual and plurilingual treaties has continued to widen since in favour of the latter. Noteworthy, the gap has increased in leaps along the waves of expansion. During the initial wave the gap widened steadily from 60:40 to 65:35, whereas along the major wave in the 1990s it leaped to roughly 78:22. The gap narrowed during the 2000s and, based on the numbers of 2010 to August 2016, has widened again to roughly 80:20. The cumulative figures suggest that the numbers logarithmically approach a relation of 75:25, whereas the leap in the per decade numbers from 1990 onwards seems to indicate that the potential for unilingual treaties is approaching exhaustion faster than the potential for plurilingual ones, that is, unilingual treaty growth may not continue in the same proportion.

In summary, conclusion of treaties without prevailing text has been a policy choice mainly of the beginning periods of the global tax treaty network. It reached its peak in the 1990s and has declined since: per decade conclusions of treaties without prevailing text exceeded those with for the last time in the 1980s. In the wake of the major expansion of the global tax treaty network during the 1990s, concluding treaties with prevailing text became the predominant policy choice. This is visible also from the predominant choice for treaties without prevailing text to be terminated and the fact that almost all treaties terminated to date have been concluded up to 1990. During the 1990s per decade conclusions of treaties with prevailing text already exceeded those without by a factor of 2:1, which increased to a factor of 3:1 in the 2000s. In cumulative terms, treaties with prevailing text started to outnumber those without by the 1990s, and their total number doubled to almost twice of the latter in the 2000s.

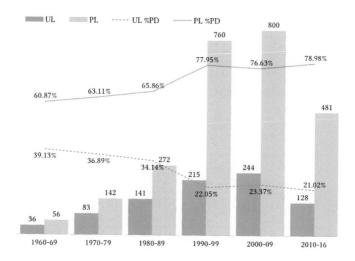

Figure (8.3): Per Decade Growth of Unilingual and Plurilingual Treaties

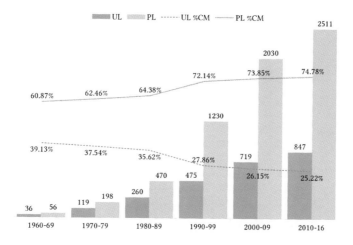

Figure (8.4): Cumulative Growth of Unilingual and Plurilingual Treaties

8. Applicability of the Permissive Approach

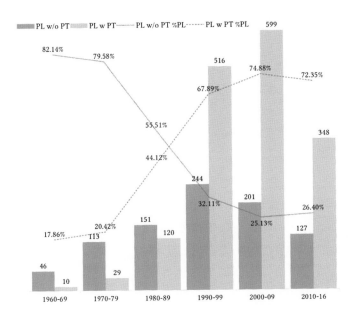

Figure (8.5): Per Decade Growth of Plurilingual Treaties with/without Prevailing Text

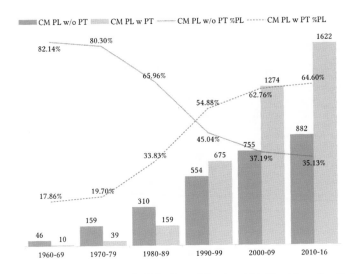

Figure (8.6): Cumulative Growth of Plurilingual Treaties with/without Prevailing Text

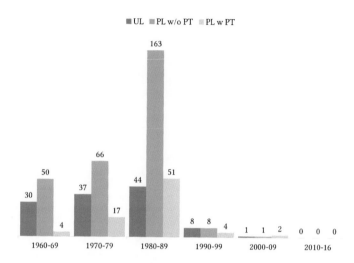

Figure (8.7): *Per Decade Terminated Treaties*

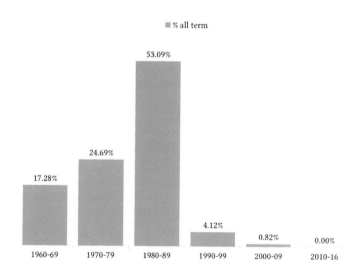

Figure (8.8): *Per Decade Terminated Treaties as Percentage of All Terminated Treaties*

8.2.3. Group Analysis

The preceding analysis allows us to draw general conclusions concerning the global development; however, not every treaty is of equal importance. In order to arrive at a balanced view, we have to examine the policy of individual countries, regions, and political groupings.[7] Treaties without prevailing text are not evenly spread out, but roughly two-thirds (581) of them are concentrated in the treaty networks of nine countries: France, Canada, the UK, Luxembourg, Germany, the US, Switzerland, Ireland, and South Africa. Almost 85% (748) of them are concentrated in the treaty networks of fourteen countries, that is, the previous nine plus Spain, Italy, Malta, Belgium, and Australia.

Table (8.9): Concentration of Plurilingual Treaties without Prevailing Text

Country	Treaties	UL	PL	PL w/o PT	PL w/o PT %PL
Canada	97	0	97	97	100.00%
France	139	34	105	104	99.05%
United States	77	23	54	53	98.15%
Australia	55	24	31	29	93.55%
United Kingdom	132	43	89	81	91.01%
Luxembourg	85	17	68	60	88.24%
South Africa	86	36	50	40	80.00%
Ireland	78	25	53	42	79.25%
Malta	74	24	50	32	64.00%
Germany	108	5	103	56	54.37%

[7] This section will mainly look at aggregate data for certain groups. In order to gauge the effects of the identified group policies, a count of the number of treaties for each group in total and as a percentage of the global tax treaty network is provided in Appendix D.1. The categorisation into groups featured in this section is meaningful only to a certain extent, and all conclusions drawn have to be taken with a grain of salt. All groups will to some extent remain heterogeneous because they bundle countries with different policies. In order to calibrate the picture developed in this section, each country has to be analysed on its own merits. This will be done within limits in the following section. In this section, policies of individual countries will be referenced only to gauge aggregated group data concerning certain key observations. Missing percentage points after the comma in some groups concerning the numbers of treaties without prevailing text are attributable to a few treaties that implement a different mechanism to treat divergences in form of a MAP. These few treaties are not included here in the count of treaties without prevailing text and will be considered separately later.

Country	Treaties	UL	PL	PL w/o PT	PL w/o PT %PL
Belgium	102	38	64	30	46.88%
Spain	99	16	83	38	45.78%
Switzerland	119	14	105	48	45.71%
Italy	109	7	102	38	37.25%

Not all of these countries have the same policy. Canada, France, the US, Australia, the UK, Luxembourg, South Africa, and Ireland all seem to have a dominant policy of not concluding treaties with prevailing text irrespective of their treaty partner.[8] The motivations behind the numbers may still differ for each country. At the same time, the overall outcome comprised of bilateral relationships will be influenced by the policies of their respective treaty partners. The assumed preference of the listed countries not to conclude treaties with prevailing text may be only one side of the coin: their treaty partners may share the sentiment or want to avoid granting linguistic advantages.

Given that the native tongues of most countries in this list are either English or French, the political potential for agreeing on prevailing texts may exhaust itself to some extent in the conclusion of unilingual treaties. France, the US, the UK, and Australia all have sizeable proportions of unilingual treaties: the UK and US of roughly 30%, France of roughly 25%, and Australia of well over 40%.

For countries like Canada and Luxembourg, on the other hand, the availability of multiple official legal languages domestically may strongly influence their policies concerning treaties. This is particularly obvious in the case of Canada, which completely rejects the option of concluding unilingual treaties even when sharing an official language with the treaty partner, whereas Luxembourg has concluded a proportion of 20%. Canada's policy

---

[8]Noteworthy, however, the UK has eight fairly recent treaties with English prevailing text, i.e., Uzbekistan (1993), India (1993), Latvia (1996), Malaysia (1996), Taiwan (2002), Bahrain (2010), Tajikistan (2014), and the United Arab Emirates (2016). Not all of them are with countries having English as official language, and three of them are fairly recent. The prevailing texts may be attributable to policies of the respective treaty partners or indicate a recent policy change on the side of the UK to implement English prevailing texts when politically feasible. Whether the latter proves to be true remains to be seen.

is attributable to domestic law: its constitution provides that English and French have equal status; all federal laws must be adopted in both languages, and each language version is to be equally authoritative, while its Official Languages Act stipulates that all international treaties should be authenticated in both official languages.[9]

Concerning the others, Ireland and South Africa have a strong general policy in disfavour of prevailing texts but display a propensity of roughly 20% to agree to them depending on their treaty partner. Noteworthy again are the sizeable proportions of over 30% unilingual treaties in the case of Ireland and over 40% in the case of South Africa. Malta displays a disfavour of prevailing texts, too, but already with a higher propensity to agree to them in roughly one-third of all cases. In addition, it has a relatively high share of over 30% unilingual treaties.

Although each features a sizeable absolute number of treaties without prevailing text, Germany, Belgium, Spain, Switzerland, and Italy seem not to have a predominant policy either way but to conclude treaties with or without prevailing text on a roughly equal basis depending on the treaty partner. Germany appears to be tilted in disfavour of prevailing texts; however, it recently published its own Model Convention with a final clause providing for one,[10] that is, Germany's own policy is shifting in favour of prevailing texts if it ever was different to begin with.

For the other four, the numbers are reverse. Italy is most clearly in favour of implementing prevailing texts. Like Germany, it has a relatively low propensity of about 5–6% to conclude unilingual treaties. Switzerland has with almost 12% the highest propensity among the three, which may be attributable to the availability of several domestic official languages: twelve of Switzerland's fourteen unilingual treaties are with German, French, or Italian speaking countries in German, French, or Italian, while only two are in English with Norway (1987) and Taiwan (2007). With over 16%, Spain has a higher propensity to conclude unilingual treaties as a consequence of the

---

[9]Constitution Act, 1982, 16 and 18(1), Official Languages Act, 1985, 10(1); see Sasseville, 'The Canadian Experience', 36.

[10]BMF, *Basis for Negotiation for Agreements for the Avoidance of Double Taxation and the Prevention of Fiscal Evasion with Respect to Taxes on Income and on Capital* (Germany: Bundesministerium der Finanzen, 2013), henceforth referred to as German Model.

shared native tongue with all of Latin America except Brazil: fourteen of the sixteen unilingual treaties in its tax treaty network are unilingual in Spanish with Latin American countries; the remaining two are with Morocco (1978) and Tunisia (1982) in French.

The high proportion of almost 40% unilingual treaties in Belgium's tax treaty network is not attributable to its ability to draw on several domestic official languages, as thirty-seven of its thirty-eight unilingual treaties are in English with countries not sharing a common language, while only the treaty with France (1964) is in French. Together with the lower proportion of treaties without prevailing text versus those with, this indicates that Belgium has a preference against plurilingual treaties without prevailing text. It issued its own Model Convention in 2007, which features a final clause codifying a unilingual treaty.[11] This shows that Belgium itself favours unilingual form; prevailing texts appear to be its second choice when feasible, while it accommodates the policies of its treaty partners not to implement one.

Almost all of these fourteen countries are big players in the global economy and international tax system: their treaties cover large cross-border flows of capital, goods, and services, and their policies reverberate throughout the global tax treaty network. When we look at all treaties concluded between OECD members, we see that the ratio of unilingual to plurilingual ones roughly conforms to the global average, whereas the ratio of treaties with prevailing text to those without is roughly 44:56. For treaties between members and non-members, this ratio is more than reversed to roughly 62:38 in favour of prevailing texts. Treaties between non-members show a ratio of roughly 80:20 in favour of prevailing texts. The proportions of unilingual versus plurilingual treaties are almost the same for all three groups, roughly conforming to the global averages of one-quarter versus three-quarters, that is, the potential for unilingual treaties is not influenced by member status and does not bias the potential for treaties with prevailing text. Generally speaking, this means that non-members have a higher propensity to implement prevailing texts, and this policy remains dominant

---

[11]The Kingdom of Belgium, *Belgian Draft Convention for the Avoidance of Double Taxation and the Prevention Of Fiscal Evasion with Respect to Taxes on Income and on Capital,* 2007, henceforth referred to as Belgian Model.

even when concluding treaties with members, whereas within the OECD the policy against prevailing texts dominates. In this context, a comparison with the countries that participate as active key partners in the work of OECD bodies (Brazil, China, India, Indonesia, and South Africa) is illustrative: they show a clear preference for prevailing texts, which would be even more decisive if South Africa would be subtracted from the list.

Table (8.10): OECD, NOECD, and OECDKP Treaties

Treaties	UL	PL	PL w PT %PL	PL w/o PT %PL
OECD-OECD	24.07%	75.93%	43.75%	56.03%
OECD-NOECD	26.23%	73.77%	61.80%	37.72%
OECD any	25.67%	74.33%	57.02%	42.56%
NOECD-NOECD	24.28%	75.72%	80.29%	19.71%
OECDKP-OECD	18.59%	81.41%	67.72%	32.28%
OECDKP-NOECD	16.97%	83.03%	76.24%	23.76%

The G20 countries display a similar pattern: for treaties between them the ratio of treaties with prevailing text versus those without is roughly 43:57, however, the propensity to conclude unilingual treaties is with roughly 10% significantly below the global average. The proportion of treaties with prevailing text increases between G20 members and non-members, but only to roughly equal the proportion of those without, while the proportion of unilingual treaties remains below the global figure, despite doubling. This may be attributable to the group's composition including many countries with a dominant policy against prevailing texts, and a reduced willingness of countries to grant linguistic advantages to economically powerful treaty partners.

Table (8.11): G20 Treaties

Treaties	UL	PL	PL w PT %PL	PL w/o PT %PL
G20-G20	10.24%	89.76%	42.95%	57.05%
G20-NG20	20.50%	79.50%	52.00%	47.80%
G20 any	19.28%	80.72%	50.80%	49.02%

As regards the tax treaty network of the CW,[12] the proportion of unilingual treaties is with over 60% between members high in comparison, while the ratio of treaties with prevailing text versus those without is 50:50. This means that the problem of plurilingual form does not arise much within the CW because of the potential for unilingual treaties (most countries in the CW are either native English-speaking or have English as official language), while half of the plurilingual ones provide for a prevailing text. For treaties between CW and third countries, the proportion of treaties without prevailing text rises to almost 60%, while the proportion of unilingual treaties decreases to less than a quarter. This points again to a strong policy preference of the leading CW countries against prevailing texts, in addition to a possible reluctance of states to grant linguistic advantages. India, an important player in the global economy and international tax system, has a diametrically opposed policy to the other CW countries: out of its one hundred tax treaties, only four are unilingual and 93% of the plurilingual ones feature a prevailing text.

Table (8.12): CW Treaties

Treaties	UL	PL	PL w PT %PL	PL w/o PT %PL
CW-CW	61.26%	38.74%	50.00%	50.00%
CW-NCW	23.96%	76.04%	41.45%	58.29%
CW any	30.57%	69.43%	42.30%	57.47%

As regards all treaties between countries of the European Union including EFTA members but excluding France, Ireland, Malta, and the UK,[13] the proportions of unilingual and plurilingual treaties roughly correspond to the global averages. For treaties between members and non-members, the propensity to conclude unilingual treaties is below the global average, whereas the propensity to conclude plurilingual ones is above. The proportions of treaties without prevailing text versus those with are close to the global averages for both groups, however, the preference for the latter

---

[12]Commonwealth of Nations including former members, prospective members, and other former British colonies that have not been members.
[13]Henceforth abbreviated as EU.

is stronger between EU countries. Thus, in contrast to the excluded ones, the overall policy for the rest of the EU countries is clearly in favour of prevailing texts.

Table (8.13): EU Treaties

Treaties	UL	PL	PL w PT %PL	PL w/o PT %PL
EU-EU	25.75%	74.25%	72.69%	26.57%
EU-NEU	22.04%	77.96%	65.17%	34.49%
EU any	22.77%	77.23%	66.60%	32.98%

Countries of the Commonwealth of Independent States including former members and associate states (CIS) display a dominant policy in favour of prevailing texts. There are hardly any unilingual treaties both between CIS countries and between CIS and third countries, and treaties with prevailing text outnumber those without by roughly 4:1.

Table (8.14): CIS Treaties

Treaties	UL	PL	PL w PT %PL	PL w/o PT %PL
CIS-CIS	0.00%	100.00%	81.08%	18.92%
CIS-NCIS	2.38%	97.62%	78.28%	21.72%
CIS any	2.23%	97.77%	78.46%	21.54%

The Arab World (AW) has a clear preference for prevailing texts. All treaties between AW countries are unilingual, while roughly 80% of all treaties with third countries feature a prevailing text. As regards the treaty networks of all AW countries, roughly 15% treaties without prevailing text remain.

Table (8.15): AW Treaties

Treaties	UL	PL	PL w PT %PL	PL w/o PT %PL
AW-AW	100.00%	0.00%	0.00%	0.00%
AW-NAW	9.95%	90.05%	80.08%	19.33%
AW any	20.90%	79.10%	80.08%	19.33%

Three quarters of all treaties between Latin American countries excluding CARICOM members (LA) are unilingual in Spanish, while the remaining are plurilingual without prevailing text, all with Brazil. The latter does not display a decisive policy with respect to prevailing texts: treaties with prevailing text versus those without are divided roughly 53:47 in its treaty network. As for treaties between LA and third countries, treaties with prevailing text make up almost two-thirds of all plurilingual treaties, corresponding roughly to the global average, whereas the proportion of unilingual treaties remains much lower overall. In summary, LA countries favour prevailing texts once the potential for concluding unilingual treaties in Spanish is exhausted.

Table (8.16): LA Treaties

Treaties	UL	PL	PL w PT %PL	PL w/o PT %PL
LA-LA	75.00%	25.00%	0.00%	100.00%
LA-NLA	8.26%	91.74%	64.93%	35.07%
LA any	14.57%	85.43%	63.13%	36.87%

Over 80% of all treaties between African countries excluding the Arab World (AF) are unilingual, while the remaining ones are all without prevailing text. Concerning treaties with third countries, still a higher proportion than globally is unilingual while roughly two-thirds of the others lack a prevailing text. This high proportion of unilingual treaties and the clear policy against prevailing texts may be attributable to the widespread use of English and French as official languages and the British and French influence.

Table (8.17): AF Treaties

Treaties	UL	PL	PL w PT %PL	PL w/o PT %PL
AF-AF	80.49%	19.51%	0.00%	100.00%
AF-NAF	42.31%	57.69%	32.82%	67.18%
AF any	46.44%	53.56%	31.53%	68.47%

The remaining Asian countries that were neither considered as part of CW, CIS, EU, AF, or AW (AS)[14] display an overwhelming policy preference for treaties with prevailing text. Between AS countries almost 30% of all treaties are unilingual and 90% of all plurilingual ones feature a prevailing text. For treaties with third countries, these percentages drop to roughly 20% and 80%, respectively.

Table (8.18): AS Treaties

Treaties	UL	PL	PL w PT %PL	PL w/o PT %PL
AS-AS	29.82%	70.18%	90.00%	10.00%
AS-NAS	21.34%	78.66%	79.35%	20.65%
AS any	22.04%	77.96%	80.15%	19.85%

8.2.4. Per Country Analysis

This section drills down a bit further into the global tax treaty network in order to obtain a more detailed view with respect to individual countries. It must be borne in mind, however, that every bilateral treaty is the result of a reciprocal trade-off between the interests and policies of the contracting states. In consequence, the aggregate data of actual treaty outcomes examined here will never mirror the policy of any particular country in pure form. A much broader and deeper investigation into all linguistic, legal, political, economic, and historical factors influencing the outcome for every particular treaty would be necessary in order to develop a complete understanding of every country's policy and motivations. For purposes of this study, an aggregated data analysis is sufficient to further gauge the results of the previous sections, with the necessary caution in mind.

In general, the more treaties a country has in its network and the stronger the results lash out in either direction, the more robust the conclusions drawn concerning that country's policy will be. Therefore, the countries analysed have been divided into three groups: all countries with 60 or more

---

[14]China, Indonesia, Iran, Israel, Japan, Korea (Dem. People's Rep.), Korea (Rep.), Laos, Mongolia, Myanmar, Nepal, Philippines, Taiwan, Thailand, Turkey, and Vietnam.

treaties (G1), all countries with 30 or more but fewer than 60 treaties (G2), and all countries with 15 or more but fewer than 30 treaties (G3). Countries with fewer than 15 treaties are not considered. Furthermore, each of the three groups is divided into two sub-groups: countries that have English as official language versus countries that do not.

Almost all countries of G1 that do not have English as official language display a predominant policy in favour of prevailing texts well above the global average. Russia, Poland, Norway, Sweden, Austria, Italy, and Denmark are near the global average, which is still almost two-thirds in favour of prevailing texts. Switzerland, Belgium, Spain, and (to some extent) Germany seem not to have a decisive policy but happy to accommodate the preference of their treaty partners.[15] Only Luxembourg and France display a clear policy against prevailing texts.

Table (8.19): G1 NEOL Treaties

Country	PL w PT %PL	Treaties	PL
Egypt	91.89%	66	37
Indonesia	90.91%	69	44
Estonia	89.80%	60	49
United Arab Emirates	87.69%	80	65
Korea (Rep.)	86.49%	90	74
Croatia	85.96%	63	57
Slovenia	85.71%	60	56
Kuwait	85.48%	70	62
Thailand	85.37%	66	41
Ukraine	80.82%	73	73
Morocco	80.39%	67	51
Turkey	80.00%	83	65
Vietnam	80.00%	72	65
Romania	79.76%	90	84
Hungary	78.95%	82	57
Belarus	78.79%	69	66
Czech Republic	77.59%	91	58
Cyprus	76.92%	64	39
Japan	76.32%	68	38
Bulgaria	76.19%	71	63

[15] As already mentioned, the German Model stipulates a policy in favour of prevailing texts while the Belgian one stipulates a policy in favour of unilingual treaties.

8. Applicability of the Permissive Approach

Country	PL w PT %PL	Treaties	PL
Portugal	76.06%	78	71
China	75.47%	108	106
Slovak Republic	72.88%	69	59
Netherlands	72.46%	99	69
Finland	71.11%	80	45
Qatar	69.23%	74	65
Russia	68.13%	91	91
Poland	67.07%	88	82
Norway	66.67%	94	42
Sweden	65.79%	92	38
Austria	64.00%	93	75
Italy	62.75%	109	102
Denmark	60.98%	81	41
Switzerland	54.29%	119	105
Belgium	53.13%	102	64
Spain	46.99%	99	83
Germany	44.66%	108	103
Luxembourg	11.76%	85	68
France	0.00%	139	105

The situation differs for G1 countries having English as official language. Canada, the US, and the UK have a strict policy against prevailing texts. Conversely, India and Malaysia display a dominant policy in favour. All the others range in the middle but well below the global average. Singapore and Pakistan may be considered not to have a decisive policy of their own but to settle with the preference of their treaty partners. The same seems to apply to Malta, whereas both South Africa and Ireland range so far below the global average that it rather seems they agree to prevailing texts only as a concession to particular circumstance.

Table (8.20): G1 EOL Treaties

Country	PL w PT %PL	Treaties	PL
India	96.88%	100	96
Malaysia	85.53%	83	76
Singapore	47.06%	88	51
Pakistan	44.44%	64	36
Malta	36.00%	74	50

Country	PL w PT %PL	Treaties	PL
Ireland	20.75%	78	53
South Africa	20.00%	86	50
United Kingdom	8.99%	132	89
United States	1.85%	77	54
Canada	0.00%	97	97

For G2 countries not having English as official language, the situation is similar to the equivalent sub-group of G1. Almost all display a strong preference in favour of prevailing texts well above the global average. Mexico, Turkmenistan, and Chile still decisively favour prevailing texts, while Brazil and Algeria seem to have no clear-cut policy. Only Mauritius seems to disfavour prevailing texts.

Table (8.21): G2 NEOL Treaties

Country	PL w PT %PL	Treaties	PL
Greece	95.12%	58	41
Syria	94.74%	32	19
Bahrain	94.44%	42	36
Iran	93.88%	50	49
Latvia	92.16%	59	51
Bosnia and Herzegovina	92.00%	38	25
Serbia and Montenegro	90.00%	38	30
Georgia	88.68%	55	53
Macedonia (FYR)	88.00%	52	50
Uzbekistan	86.27%	53	51
Israel	85.42%	57	48
Kazakhstan	85.37%	43	41
Albania	85.29%	43	34
Lithuania	85.19%	54	54
Lebanon	83.33%	33	12
Azerbaijan	82.98%	48	47
Jordan	81.82%	33	22
Armenia	80.43%	46	46
Saudi Arabia	79.41%	38	34
Oman	79.31%	36	29
Moldova	76.09%	47	46
Tajikistan	75.86%	31	29

Country	PL w PT %PL	Treaties	PL
Iceland	72.73%	47	33
Taiwan	71.43%	30	21
Venezuela	70.00%	34	30
Mexico	66.67%	58	48
Turkmenistan	65.00%	40	40
Chile	64.00%	33	25
Tunisia	58.06%	55	31
Brazil	53.13%	33	32
Algeria	50.00%	35	22
Mauritius	36.36%	52	22

As regards G2 countries with English as official language, the situation is divided. Sri Lanka, Bangladesh, and Hong Kong seem to be strongly in favour of prevailing texts, whereas Australia has a strict policy against them. The Philippines, New Zealand, and Barbados display a less strict policy but still disfavour prevailing texts.

Table (8.22): G2 EOL Treaties

Country	PL w PT %PL	Treaties	PL
Sri Lanka	87.23%	47	47
Bangladesh	86.67%	32	15
Hong Kong	66.67%	35	18
Philippines	30.43%	43	23
New Zealand	26.09%	49	23
Barbados	20.00%	32	20
Australia	6.45%	55	31

For G3 countries the sample sizes are small, so the conclusions drawn should be viewed with extra caution. Nevertheless, for G3 countries not having English as official language, the situation seems comparable to the respective sub-groups of G1 and G2. Most countries of this sub-group have a preference for prevailing texts well above the global average, while Libya and Argentina are in its close proximity. Only Senegal and to some extent Ecuador have a strong preference against prevailing texts.

Table (8.23): G3 NEOL Treaties

Country	PL w PT %PL	Treaties	PL
San Marino	87.50%	21	16
Mongolia	86.96%	28	23
Uruguay	81.25%	20	16
Kyrgyzstan	80.00%	25	25
Liechtenstein	80.00%	19	10
Panama	78.57%	16	14
Serbia	78.26%	26	23
Libya	66.67%	16	12
Argentina	56.25%	20	16
Ecuador	25.00%	16	12
Senegal	0.00%	17	11

As regards G3 countries with English as official language, Sudan and Seychelles are clearly in favour of prevailing texts, while most others are decisively in disfavour. Only Ethiopia and Nigeria display no clear preference. Given the small sample sizes, however, part of the numbers may be coincidental or depending on the treaty partners rather than pointing to a country's own policy.

Table (8.24): G3 EOL Treaties

Country	PL w PT %PL	Treaties	PL
Sudan	100.00%	18	5
Seychelles	66.67%	29	12
Ethiopia	50.00%	20	12
Nigeria	50.00%	16	6
Isle of Man	40.00%	22	5
Kenya	33.33%	16	6
Jersey	28.57%	25	7
Guernsey	20.00%	22	5
Botswana	20.00%	16	5
Zimbabwe	18.18%	19	11
Zambia	9.09%	27	11
Trinidad and Tobago	9.09%	16	11

8.3. Types of Wording

Now that we have a clear view to what extent sole reliance on prevailing texts is available in principle (and to what extent the problem does not arise in the first place because of unilingual form), we need to establish to what extent the permissive approach may be applied to actual tax treaties, that is, to what extent formulations of treaty final clauses in the global tax treaty network permit sole reliance on existing prevailing texts. As Article 33(1) does not constitute a peremptory norm in this regard,[16] such investigation into the intentions of the contracting states as expressed in their treaties is necessary.

8.3.1. TOW Classification

The final clauses used in the global tax treaty network can be classified into nine different types of wording, which I have labelled numerically from TOW1 to TOW9. TOW1 represents the case of plurilingual treaties without prevailing text. In its most basic form the treaty is simply concluded, signed, and sealed in two or more copies and languages without its final clause specifying its linguistic properties, as for example in Norway-Switzerland (1956), having German and Norwegian texts:[17]

> In witness whereof, the plenipotentiaries of the two States have signed this Convention and thereto affixed their seals. Done at Oslo, 7 December 1956.

Strictly speaking, mentioning the linguistic properties is not necessary because, in the absence of a specific clause, authenticity derives from the mere fact that an instrument has been concluded in a particular language.[18] Therefore, each signed and sealed text must be treated as equally authentic.

---

[16]See ILC, *Draft Articles on the Law of Treaties with Commentaries*, II:224, para. 4; Engelen, *Interpretation of Tax Treaties under International Law*, 376–79.

[17]Unless otherwise indicated, English wordings of non-English final clauses are taken from unofficial English translations provided by the IBFD *Tax Treaties Database*.

[18]UN, *Vienna Convention on the Law of Treaties*, Article 10; see ILC, *Draft Articles on the Law of Treaties with Commentaries*, II:224, para. 2; Hardy, 'The Interpretation of Plurilingual Treaties by International Courts and Tribunals', 74, with reference to McNair, *The Law of Treaties*, 60.

This basic form is no longer common but still exists in a handful of older treaties. A more elaborate variety of the basic form references the languages but without specifically commenting on their authenticity, as for example in South Africa-United States (1947):

> Done at Cape Town, in duplicate, in the English and Afrikaans languages, the tenth day of April, 1947.

In general, that is, applicable to all types of wording and all different forms of each, the number of signed and sealed copies does not necessarily need to equal the number of language texts, as for example in Costa Rica-Romania (1991):

> Done in quadruplicate at San José, Costa Rica, on 12 day July 1991, in the Spanish and Romanian languages, both texts being equally authentic.

The standard form of TOW1 used most widely today does not only mention the number of texts and languages but also explicitly comments on equal authenticity in a variety of marginally different but in substance equivalent formulations, for example, 'both texts being equally authoritative',[19] 'both texts being equally authentic',[20] 'each text being equally authentic',[21] 'all three texts being equally authentic',[22] or 'the two texts having equal authenticity'.[23]

In a few special cases the treaty is concluded only in one language, but the final clause specifies that a translation in the language of the other contracting state shall be made, agreed on, and then be treated with equal authority, as for example in Belarus-United Kingdom (1995):

> Done in duplicate at London this 7th day of March 1995 in the English language. A translation of the Convention into the Byelorussian language shall be made and agreed by the Contracting States before ratification, that text having the same authority as the English text.

---

[19]See, e.g., United Kingdom-Greece (1953), having English and Greek texts.
[20]See, e.g., Germany-France (1959), having German and French texts.
[21]See, e.g., Ireland-Switzerland (1966), having English and French texts.
[22]See, e.g., Belgium-Bulgaria (1988), having French, Dutch, and Bulgarian texts.
[23]See, e.g., Luxembourg-United States (1996), having English and French texts.

In some of these cases the final clause outlines the process by which the latter translation is to gain equal authenticity, as for example in Kazakhstan-United States (1993):

> Done at Almaty this 24th day of October 1993, in duplicate, in the Russian and English languages, both texts being equally authentic. A Kazakh language text shall be prepared, which shall be considered equally authentic upon an exchange of diplomatic notes confirming its conformity with the English language text.[24]

TOW2 is the first case of treaties designating one text as prevailing. Its most basic form lists the number of copies and authentic languages, and mimics the wording of Article 33(1) concerning its condition to designate one text as prevailing, as for example in Armenia-United Arab Emirates (2002):

> Done in Abu Dhabi on April 20, 2002, in two originals, in the Armenian, Arabic and English languages, all texts being equally authentic. In case of divergence the English text shall prevail.

Almost all treaties with TOW2 final clauses add 'any' or 'between texts' or both to the wording,[25] for example, 'In case of any divergence, the English text shall prevail',[26] 'In case of divergence between texts, the English text shall prevail',[27] or 'In case of divergence between any of the texts, the English text shall prevail'.[28] These wordings explicitly heal the slight imprecision in the formulation of Article 33 (with exception of the Russian text) on which TOW2 is based and which induces the proponents of the restrictive approach to mistakenly equate 'divergence' with the more narrow concept of material divergence. The first wording makes clear that *any*

---

[24]Noteworthy, conformity only with the English text has to be confirmed, which seems to confer more importance on it despite the equal authenticity of the Russian text. Hence, this might be a rare case in which a court could plausibly reason to give preference to the English text on the basis of the treaty itself pointing to this intention of the contracting parties.

[25]Only three additional TOW2 treaties are without such qualifier: China-Russia (1994), Hungary-Qatar (2012), and Russia-Vietnam (1993).

[26]See, e.g., Czech Republic-Lebanon (1997), having Arabic, Czech, and English texts.

[27]See, e.g., Albania-India (2013), having Albanian, English, and Hindi texts.

[28]See, e.g., Denmark-Slovenia (2001), having English, Danish, and Slovenian texts.

divergence is sufficient to trigger the condition, obviously including mere differences in expression. The latter two explicitly add the subject 'texts' of the predicate 'divergence', which is only implicit in the wording of Article 33(4) via its link to Article 33(1).[29] This makes clear that 'divergence' means divergence between texts, which can be any kind of divergence, that is, a difference in expression as well as a difference in meaning.

There exist a few minor variations of TOW2 formulations that, however, do not change the meaning in substance. Some use the term 'divergency' instead of 'divergence',[30] while others use different ways to designate one text as prevailing by using the term 'authoritative',[31] denoting one text as the 'operative one',[32] stipulating that divergences 'shall be resolved in accordance with' or 'on the basis of', or that 'the interpretation shall be given in accordance with' a particular text.[33]

TOW3 is the second case of treaties designating one text as prevailing. The major difference from TOW2 is the explicit reference to interpretation. The most basic form lists again the number of copies and authentic texts, designating one as prevailing in case of divergence of (or in) interpretation, as for example in Finland-Switzerland (1991):[34]

> Done in duplicate at Helsinki this 16th day of December 1991, in the Finnish, German and English languages, all three texts being equally authentic. In the case of divergence of interpretation the English text shall prevail.

The majority again adds 'any' or 'between texts' to the wording to read 'In case of any divergence of interpretation' or 'In case of divergence in inter-

---

[29]Only as far as the Chinese, English, French, and Spanish texts are concerned, i.e., most treaties with a TOW2 final clause implement the more precise wording of the Russian text by explicitly repeating the subject.

[30]See, e.g., Kuwait-Sri Lanka (2002), having Arabic, English, and Sinhala texts with the English one prevailing.

[31]See, e.g., Cameroon-Tunisia (1999), having Arabic and French texts with the French one prevailing.

[32]See, e.g., India-Mauritius (1982), having Hindi and English texts with the English one prevailing.

[33]See, e.g., Kuwait-Spain (2008), having Arabic, English, and Spanish texts with the English one prevailing, Libya-Serbia (2009), having Arabic, English, and Serbian texts with the English one prevailing, and Indonesia-Russia (1999), having English, Indonesian, and Russian texts with the English one prevailing.

[34]See, e.g., Bulgaria-Lebanon (1999) for a case of 'divergence in interpretation'.

pretation between texts',[35] or otherwise varies the wording without affecting its meaning in substance by using 'divergency' or 'differences' instead of 'divergence',[36] or by paraphrasing the concept of prevailing.[37]

A handful of treaties extends the wording to the effect of broadening the scope, for example, 'In case of divergence on interpretation or application, the English text shall prevail',[38] 'In the case of divergence of interpretation or of any inconsistency the English text shall prevail',[39] or 'In case of any divergence between any of the texts and in the interpretation, the English text shall prevail'.[40] The first wording is not much different from the standard TOW3 form, but the latter two may be viewed as cases of TOW2 and TOW3 combined because of their formulations.

Three treaties with TOW3 wordings deviate from the standard formulation by referring to a divergence or difference in meaning between the texts instead of a divergence or difference in interpretation.[41] As cited above, three treaties of Tunisia designate two texts as prevailing instead of one. Finally, there exist a handful of treaties that are concluded in English but stipulate that translations in the official languages of the contracting states shall be made and exchanged through diplomatic channels.[42]

---

[35] See, e.g., Brazil-China (1991), having English, Portuguese, and Chinese texts with the English one prevailing, and Albania-China (2004), having English, Albanian, and Chinese texts with the English one prevailing, respectively.

[36] See, e.g., Poland-Sweden (2004), having English, Polish, and Swedish texts with the English one prevailing, and Algeria-Turkey (1994), having French, Arabic, and Turkish texts with the English one prevailing, respectively.

[37] See, e.g., Armenia-Malaysia (1987): 'In case of any divergence of interpretation, the interpretation shall be made in accordance with the English text'; Denmark-Russia (1996): 'In case of any divergence of interpretation, the English text shall be used as a reference'; Iceland-Spain (2002): 'In case of any divergence of interpretation, it shall be resolved in accordance with the English text'; Kazakhstan-Macedonia (2012): 'In case of any divergence of interpretation of this Agreement the Contracting States refer to the text in English'; Kazakhstan-Russia (1996): 'In the case of emergence of deviations in the interpretation of this text, the Russian text shall override.'

[38] Italy-Syria (2000).

[39] Estonia-Latvia (2002).

[40] Serbia and Montenegro-Slovenia (2003).

[41] New Zealand-Taiwan (1996), Taiwan-United Kingdom (2002), and Israel-Turkey (1996).

[42] United Kingdom-Uzbekistan (1993), Iran-Syria (1996), Pakistan-Tunisia (1996), Iran-Tajikistan (1998), Malta-Tunisia (2000), Tunisia-Iran (2001). According to their word-

TOW4 is the third instance of treaties designating one text as prevailing, being a variation of both TOW2 and TOW3 in the sense that all texts are declared as equally authentic while in case of divergence (of interpretation) between the first two or three the third or forth, respectively, shall prevail,[43] as for example in Estonia-Germany (1996):[44]

> Done at Tallinn this 29th day of November 1996 in two originals, each in the Estonian, German and English languages, all three texts being authentic. In the case of divergent interpretation of the Estonian and the German texts the English text shall prevail.

The Netherlands-India (1988) treaty subject of the *New Skies* decision discussed previously is another example of TOW4, using the wording 'shall be the operative one' instead of 'shall prevail'.

TOW5 represents the case of unilingual treaties. In its standard form it references the treaty's language and the number of copies, as for example in Egypt-India (1969):

> Done in duplicate at Cairo this twentieth day of February, 1969, in the English language.

Analogous to TOW1, there still exist a few treaties that do not explicitly declare the language, for example, Australia-United States (1982):

> Done in duplicate at Sydney this sixth day of August 1982.

TOW6 is the fourth instance of treaties declaring one text as prevailing.[45] In contrast to TOW2, TOW3, and TOW4, it does not refer to cases of divergence but to cases of doubt, as for example in Thailand-Vietnam (1992):

---

ings, the later translations shall be treated as equally authentic, while in case of divergence of interpretation the English text shall prevail.

[43] Again with a small number of minor variations in formulation that have no effect in substance, e.g., use of 'divergency' instead of 'divergence'.

[44] Kyrgyzstan-Switzerland (2001) is an example of four equally authentic languages (German, English, Kyrgyz, and Russian), with the English text prevailing in case of a divergence of interpretation between the other three.

[45] Australia-India (1991) is the only example of a TOW6 final clause that paraphrases 'prevailing text' with 'operative text'.

> Done in duplicate at Hanoi on this 23rd day of December, one thousand nine hundred and ninety-two Year of the Christian Era, each in the Thai, Vietnamese and English languages, all texts being equally authoritative, except in the case of doubt when the English text shall prevail.

TOW7 is a special case of plurilingual treaties not designating one text as prevailing but instead prescribing application of the treaty MAP as an alternative solution to cases of divergence, as for example in Germany-Spain (2011):

> Done in duplicate in Madrid on the 2nd day of June 2010, in the English and Spanish languages, both texts being equally authentic. In case of divergence of interpretation between any of the texts, it shall be resolved in accordance with the procedure regulated under Article 24 of this Convention.

TOW8 is another special case of treaties designating one text as prevailing, with the defining criterion being a dispute in the interpretation and/or application of the treaty, as for example in Iran-Malaysia (1992):

> Done in duplicate at Tehran this 11th day of November 1992, each in Bahasa Malaysia, Persian and the English languages, the three texts being equally authentic. In the event of there being a dispute in the interpretation and the application of this Agreement, the English text shall prevail.

Finally, TOW9 is a substantive variation of TOW4 in which only the first two texts are declared authentic, whereas the text designated as prevailing in case of divergence is not, as for example in Germany-Japan (1966):

> Done at Bonn this 22nd day of April 1966, in six originals, two each in the German, Japanese and English languages. The German and Japanese texts are equally authentic and, in case there is any divergence of interpretation between the German and Japanese texts, the English text shall prevail.

Two treaties with TOW9 final clauses show a significant variation regarding their formulation to paraphrase prevalence, namely, Hungary-Uruguay (1988) and Poland-Uruguay (1991):

> [B]oth texts being equally authentic and existing a third text in English, which, in case of interpretation of this Convention, shall be taken into consideration as a reference.

8.3.2. TOW Use

Now that we have classified all types of final clause wordings in the global tax treaty network, we can take stock and proceed to quantify the extent of actual use for each type. An examination of our entire sample shows that there are three main wordings in use: TOW5, TOW1, and TOW3. The first two are each implemented by roughly a quarter of the global tax treaty network, while the third is implemented by almost 29%. The remaining 20% are unevenly distributed between the six other types of wording. TOW2 and TOW4 cover a seizable number of treaties each, so they are relevant from a practical perspective. TOW2 is the more important, implemented in about 10% of all treaties, while TOW4 is implemented only by roughly 6%. TOW6 and TOW8, which cover seventy-five and twenty-nine treaties, respectively, still have some practical relevance, while TOW7 and TOW9 together are implemented only by ten treaties, that is, less than half a percent of the global tax treaty network.

Table (8.25): TOW Distribution

TOW	No. w term	%global (w term)	No. w/o term	%total (w/o term)
1	1170	30.44%	882	26.27%
2	374	9.73%	355	10.57%
3	992	25.81%	963	28.68%
4	216	5.62%	197	5.87%
5	967	25.16%	847	25.22%
6	84	2.19%	75	2.23%
7	7	0.18%	7	0.21%
8	30	0.78%	29	0.86%
9	4	0.10%	3	0.09%

In line with the previous findings, we see that TOW1 has suffered most from termination of treaties in proportional terms, whereas TOW3 has seen the largest gain. All other types of wording have only been marginally affected by termination. For the first five types of wording, the development over time from the 1960s to the 2000s[46] shows that TOW1 and TOW5 have

---

[46]For the 2010s, all curves slope downwards because they represent the numbers only up to the cut-off date, i.e., slightly more than half a decade.

steadily increased in absolute terms until the end of the 1990s; however, whereas TOW5 treaties continued to increase per decade throughout the 2000s (albeit with a slowed down growth rate), TOW1 treaties peaked in the 1990s and declined in the 2000s.

TOW3 had outgrown all other types of wording by the end of the 1980s and surged in popularity by the 1990s, steeply outgrowing all others. The growth rate has decreased over the 2000s but remains steeper than for all other types of wording. TOW2 shows steady growth as well but lags behind TOW3 in popularity. It made a major leap in the 1990s along the general wave of expansion of the global tax treaty network, but its growth rate has not been as steep as that for TOW3 and decreased over the 2000s. TOW4 has made a small jump in the 1990s but started to stagnate in terms of treaties per decade throughout the 2000s.

The percentage numbers of all treaties per decade show the steady proportional decline of TOW1 and TOW5 since the 1970s. Whereas TOW5 has flattened out at a percentage share of roughly 20% during the 2000s, TOW1 has continued its decline. If the numbers for 2010 to August 2016 may be taken as an indication of the further trend, TOW1 will stabilise its percentage share throughout the 2010s at roughly 20%.

TOW2 and especially TOW3 have increased largely in percentage share of treaties per decade from the 1980s onward (TOW3 to a roughly 35% share and TOW2 to a roughly 13% share), together accounting for almost half of all treaties concluded in the 2000s. If the numbers for January 2010 to August 2016 may be taken as an indication of the further trend, TOW3 stabilises at its 35% share while TOW2 manages to further increase towards the 15% mark throughout the 2010s. TOW4 peaked in the 1990s and has decreased towards a percentage share of roughly 6% to date.

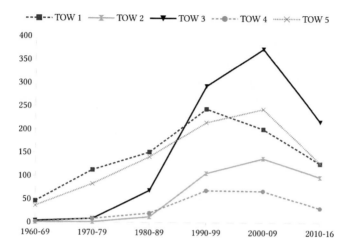

Figure (8.9): TOW of Treaties per Decade

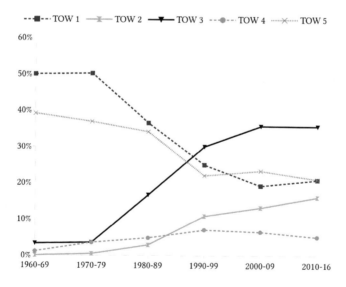

Figure (8.10): TOW as Percentage of Treaties per Decade

255

8.3.3. TOW Interpretation

Now that we have a complete measure of all types of wording used by treaties in the global tax treaty network, we need to examine their suitability in terms of sole reliance on the prevailing text. As TOW1 represents plurilingual treaties without prevailing text and TOW5 represents unilingual treaties, they are not relevant here. TOW2 does not need to be discussed in detail because it corresponds to the wording of Article 33(1), that is, the previous discussion applies. In short, the conclusion is that the permissive approach is applicable and we may resort to sole reliance on the prevailing text for all treaties featuring a TOW2 final clause, subject to the outlined limitations. TOW7 is a special case: instead of implementing a prevailing text, the contracting states agree to use the treaty MAP in cases of divergence.[47] TOW7 appeared for the first time in the treaty France-United Arab Emirates (1989) and remained a singular instance for two decades. In recent years, it has been implemented by Spain in six instances.[48] Whether this marks a sustainable new direction in Spain's treaty policy that will manage to influence other countries remains to be seen. In summary, the types of wording to be considered here are TOW3, TOW4, TOW6, TOW8, and TOW9.

The first impulse of any court may be to initially refer to the text in the country's official legal language; however, such is by no means mandatory. The equal authenticity of all texts implies that the judge may choose any of them as initial reference, including the one designated as prevailing. Hence, concerning sole reliance on the prevailing text the crucial two questions to ask are not whether the judge is allowed to automatically go to the prevailing text and whether he is allowed to rely on it exclusively, but whether the wording of the particular treaty final clause contains anything that prevents

---

[47] In line with the general purpose of MAPs, the conception of 'divergence' employed by TOW7 must be considered one of material divergence, limited to cases when problems persist after exhaustion of all interpretative means provided by the VCLT, that is, when no common meaning of the texts can be established under application of Articles 31–33, leading to taxation not in accordance with the common intentions of the contracting states, see OECD, *Model Tax Convention*, 2017, Commentary on Article 25, paras. 1–3, 7, by analogy. Otherwise, TOW7 would lead to a proliferation of MAP cases given the likelihood of divergences in expression.

[48] Albania (2010), Cyprus (2013), Germany (2011), Oman (2014), Pakistan (2010), Qatar (2015).

him from taking the prevailing text as initial reference and, if not, whether the meaning he arrives at by interpreting the prevailing text alone is such that he can spare himself from comparing it to the others.

The first question I shall now answer for all types of final clauses identified, whereas the second is one that courts may need to answer on a case by case basis. I have already answered it in principle, that is, the court has to refer to the other texts only if the interpretation of the prevailing text under Article 31 leads to a meaning which is either ambiguous or obscure, or must be considered an absurd or unreasonable result. In all other cases, the court may rely on the prevailing text alone.

TOW3 is less broad than TOW2 because it refers to divergence in/of interpretation instead of (any) divergence (between texts) in general. That seems to imply not every difference in expression is a reason to rush headlong into action as long as it does not lead to differing interpretations. This raises the question of what is meant by 'divergence in interpretation': Does it mean any different interpretation brought forward by any party interpreting the treaty, different interpretations the texts *prima facie* lend themselves to in general, or different meanings of the texts arrived at by the court under its authoritative interpretation?

Without doubt, the proponents of the restrictive approach would have it to mean the latter; however, the question is irrelevant because there is nothing in TOW3 that prevents the court from initial reference to the prevailing text. Once a manifest meaning of the prevailing text has been established, such cannot be challenged by any different interpretation on the basis of any or all other texts. As we have seen previously, Hardy's counter-argument to the logical argument does not hit home. It follows that for all treaties featuring a TOW3 final clause, the court may resort to sole reliance on the prevailing text.

This even applies to the few treaties that use the more narrow 'divergence in meaning' formulation. Although this implies a material divergence in the sense suggested by the proponents of the restrictive approach, because 'meaning' may be understood not to be any interpretation by anyone but the final authoritative interpretation by the court, there is otherwise nothing in TOW3 that prevents the court from resorting to the prevailing text as equally authentic in the first place. In consequence, the logical argument applies and whether a divergence of another text from the prevailing one is material or not is irrelevant in this respect.

The conclusion is not different also for the particular TOW3 formulations that paraphrase 'prevailing', because all of them establish a comparative authority of texts. The only exception are the three Tunisian treaties designating two texts as prevailing. Essentially, this transforms TOW3 into a TOW1 situation of two equally authoritative texts, necessitating a comparison of them to arrive at the one true meaning of the treaty.

TOW4 appeared for the first time in the treaty Germany-Iran (1968) and is the preferred policy choice of Germany (82.61% of all treaties with prevailing text), the Netherlands (80% of all treaties with prevailing text), and Switzerland (56.14% of all treaties with prevailing text). It is fairly popular also in a few other countries, for example, Oman, Chile, Russia, and Syria. In absolute terms, the Netherlands have the most TOW4 treaties (40), followed by Germany (38), Switzerland (32), and Russia (21). Both the Netherlands and Germany have TOW4 as final clause in their Model Conventions.[49]

TOW4 is the most equivocal and difficult to interpret of the nine types. Using the final clause in the treaty Netherlands-Russia (1996) as example, Bender and Engelen provide a comprehensive discussion of TOW4.[50] In es-

---

[49]De Regering van het Koninkrijk der Nederlanden, *Nederlands Standaardverdrag*, 1987, henceforth referred to as Dutch Model; BMF, *German Model*.

[50]Bender and Engelen, 'The Final Clause of the 1987 Netherlands Model Tax Convention and the Interpretation of Plurilingual Treaties', 13 et seq. They quote the clause as follows (emphasis added): 'DONE at Moscow this 16th day of December 1996, in duplicate, in the Netherlands, Russian and English language, the three texts being equally authentic. In case there is any divergence of interpretation between the Netherlands and Russian texts, the English text *shall prevail*.' The originally signed English copy, however, reads as follows (emphasis added): 'Done at Moscow, on 16 December 1996, in duplicate, in the Dutch, Russian and English languages, the three texts being equally authentic. In case there is any divergence of interpretation between the Dutch and Russian texts, the English text *shall be operative*.' The difference is not material but curious. It may be a consequence of Bender and Engelen translating from the Dutch text: '*GEDAAN te Moskou, de 16e december 1996, in tweevoud, in de Nederlandse, Russische en Engelse taal, zijnde de drie teksten gelijkelijk authentiek. Ingeval de Nederlandse en de Russische tekst verschillend kunnen worden uitgelegd, is de Engelse tekst beslissend.*' The literal English translation of the Dutch *beslissend* seems to be 'decisive'. In any case, this exemplifies that the two wordings 'shall prevail' and 'shall be operative' are equivalent.

sence, their conclusion boils down to TOW4 implementing the restrictive approach. Since the final clause in question states that the English text only prevails in case the Netherlands and Russian texts diverge, they argue that the logical argument does not apply, as a result of which the English text may only be resorted to as decisive after it has been established that the other two diverge from each other. Sanghavi arrives at the same conclusion in his discussion of *New Skies*.[51] Bender and Engelen's argument reads as follows:

> However, this reasoning [the logical argument] cannot be applied here without hesitation, since the final clause of the Netherlands-Russian tax treaty does not invest the English text with a decisive authority in each and every case of divergence between the texts, but only in case there is a divergence of interpretation between the Netherlands and Russian texts. In other words, there is no legal presumption in favour of the English text in case there is a divergence of interpretation between this text on the one hand, and the Netherlands and Russian texts on the other. Therefore, it would not be correct to presume that the English text is decisive from the very outset. Disregarding the Netherlands and Russian texts in this way would clearly not be in accordance with the intention of the parties in designating the all [sic] three texts as equally authentic, and thus authoritative for purposes of interpretation. In fact, the presumption that each text has the same meaning implies that the burden of proof lies on the party invoking the rule that the English text prevails. In other words, in the absence of any evidence to the contrary, the Netherlands, Russian and English texts are presumed to concord; therefore, in order to activate the supremacy of the English text, it must first be shown that the Netherlands and Russian texts are divergent.[52]

This reasoning is not compelling in terms of the clause analysed, that is, TOW4.[53] Being part of the treaty, the final clause must be interpreted in accordance with its ordinary wording, context, and object and purpose,[54] and the context consists first and foremost in the entire text.[55] Therefore, the

---

[51] See Sanghavi, 'Found in Translation', 414.

[52] Bender and Engelen, 'The Final Clause of the 1987 Netherlands Model Tax Convention and the Interpretation of Plurilingual Treaties', 15.

[53] Instead, it applies to TOW9 (see below).

[54] UN, *Vienna Convention on the Law of Treaties*, Article 31(1).

[55] Ibid., Article 31(2).

second sentence of the final clause designating the English text as prevailing in case the Netherlands and Russian texts diverge must be interpreted in the context of its first sentence declaring all three as equally authentic. As Bender and Engelen themselves stress, this implies that all three texts are first and foremost equally authoritative and usable for purposes of interpretation without restriction.[56]

The wording of the provision is misleading in this respect. When the prevailing condition in the second sentence is read out of context, that is, not in light of the first sentence, it may be misunderstood in the sense that only the Netherlands and Russian texts need to concur, and whatever then the situation of the English text is in such case may be disregarded, whereas in reality the interpretations of all three texts have to concur because of their equal authority declared in the first sentence of the provision. Otherwise, the English text would be treated as being of lesser authority when the two other texts are equal in meaning but of superior authority when they diverge. Such is incompatible with the principle of unity and the wording of TOW4 declaring all texts as equally authentic. Article 33(4) is unequivocal in this respect: the double reference to *the* texts clearly implies *all* texts.

Imagine the crucial scenario that the Russian and Netherlands texts are indeed concordant but their unified meaning diverges from the English text. Bender and Engelen reason that because all three texts are from the start equally authoritative and the prevailing condition fails to render the English text superior in case the Netherlands and Russian texts concur, this scenario is equivalent to a treaty with two language texts that diverge but are equally authoritative. In consequence, the principles of Articles 31–33 should be applied analogous to such case minus what to do when there is a text declared as prevailing, as the case is not one in which the English text may be regarded as such.[57] Therefore, a comparison should be enacted first under Article 31. If that fails, the interpretative rule of Article 33(4) implementing the object and purpose as sole decider should be invoked.

Let us examine this case in some more detail. For this purpose, let us denote the English text as E, the Netherlands text as N, and the Russian

---

[56] See Bender and Engelen, 'The Final Clause of the 1987 Netherlands Model Tax Convention and the Interpretation of Plurilingual Treaties', 14.

[57] See ibid., 17.

text as R. Let us further suppose for the moment that the one true meaning of the treaty is A. The principle of unity and equal authenticity of all three texts declared in the first sentence imply N=R=E=A as point of departure. So, obviously, if N says A, R says A, and E says A, then A. The prevailing condition for E in the second sentence of the clause implies that if N says A, R says B, and E says A, then A. Similarly, if N says B, R says C, and E says A, then A. Hence, in any of these cases, any text that says something different from whatever E says is to be reinterpreted to mean what E says.

Now, if N says B, R says B, and E says A, then, possibly, B? This does not register as a particularly sensible suggestion, but the conclusion should be A again. Of course, we do not know beforehand that the one true meaning of the treaty is A; however, in all cases but the last the one true meaning gravitates to whatever E says. If both N and R say B, then E should say B for it to be the one true meaning of the treaty. If the meaning of E is different, there must be something wrong: we cannot rely on N=R=B to conclude N=R=E=B in the face of E=A, since E is at the very least equally authentic.

Do we really need a comparison of all texts to decide this case as Bender and Engelen suggest? The English text is clearly identified as always prevailing in terms of a divergence between the others, that is, the English text must be presumed to better represent the parties' intentions than the other two. If we assume that the general intention of the final clause is to ease interpretation rather than to complicate it, while it cannot be its intention to ever confer lesser weight on the English text than the others because of its first sentence, it seems not sensible to suggest that the English text prevails in some cases but is subordinated in others, that is, that the outcome of any comparative interpretation under Articles 31 or 33(4) could ever turn out to establish E=B because of N=R=B instead of N=R=A because of E=A.

Looked at from the other way around, there is nothing in TOW4 that prevents the court from initially looking at the English text, since it is declared as equally authentic. It seems not sensible to suggest that the contracting parties, whose common intention must be assumed to be making interpretation easier not more complicated, would agree that the English text prevails for all scenarios except for one, which would make it impossible for any court to rely on the prevailing text without first excluding that said scenario in every case to be decided.

8. Applicability of the Permissive Approach

From a purely practical perspective, it does not seem to be in line with the object and purpose of designating a third text in a well-known third language as prevailing if that text cannot be relied on before the text in the unfamiliar language of the other country is consulted.[58] Coined to our example of Netherlands-Russia (1996), such would imply that the judge on either side would be obliged to compare either the Dutch or Russian text to the one in his own language before being able to rely on the English text; however, it must be assumed that the idea behind introducing a prevailing third text in English in the first place has been to avoid having to deal with the (from each other's perspective) arcane language of the treaty partner in all day to day applications of the treaty.

Given all these considerations, it is submitted that TOW4 must be interpreted contextually in the sense that although factored out by the literal formulation of its second sentence viewed in isolation, the case of the other texts concurring while saying something different from the one declared as prevailing is equally implied by TOW4 as a case of divergence invoking the prevailing condition. As a corollary, TOW4 is only a complicated variation in formulation but not in substance from TOW2 and TOW3, and sole reliance on the prevailing text is available for all treaties with TOW4 final clauses as well.

TOW6 appeared for the first time in the treaty Germany-India (1959), which has been terminated since.[59] In the beginning, TOW6 has been popular with Germany, Italy, and Israel: for roughly a decade from 1959 to 1968, the first ten treaties implementing TOW6 were all by them. Germany has changed its policy since to implement mainly TOW4, but still has four treaties implementing TOW6. Israel still has five treaties with TOW6.[60] Only Italy has with twenty-nine treaties still a sizeable proportion of its treaty network implementing TOW6 (45.31% of its treaties with prevailing text). Otherwise, TOW6 seems modestly popular with Greece and Thailand, which have twelve and eleven treaties implementing TOW6 (30.77% and 31.43% of their treaties with prevailing text), respectively, while the most

---

[58]See Arginelli, *The Interpretation of Multilingual Tax Treaties*, 132–33, 386n, albeit wrongly applied to an example of TOW9.

[59]Germany-India (1995) implements TOW4 instead.

[60]Israel now mostly favours TOW3 (53.66% of all treaties with prevailing text).

recent specimen were concluded not too long ago in the 2000s.[61]

TOW6 is even broader than TOW2 and TOW3. Given the likelihood of differences between different language texts already discussed at length, every case constitutes a case of doubt. Whether the clause is intended to apply only to cases of actual doubt arising with the court interpreting the particular treaty at hand for a specific factual reason is again an irrelevant question. There is nothing in TOW6 that would forbid the court to go directly to the prevailing text, and all other texts have to be interpreted to converge to its meaning if they say something different. Therefore, also all treaties with TOW6 final clauses lend themselves to sole reliance on the prevailing text.

The same conclusion applies to TOW8. Once a case has reached court, it is fairly safe to assume that there is a dispute about the interpretation and application of the treaty.[62] Again, however, this is irrelevant. There is nothing in TOW8 preventing the court from directly referring to the prevailing text, and all interpretations of the other texts must converge to its meaning. Therefore, also all treaties with TOW8 final clauses lend themselves to sole reliance on the prevailing text.

TOW8 is represented only marginally in the global tax treaty network. It appeared first in the treaty India-Kenya (1985). Since then it has been mostly used by Malaysia, which is the only country with a significant number of treaties with TOW8 final clauses (23), amounting to 35.38% of all its treaties with prevailing text. The only other country having more than one treaty featuring a TOW8 final clause is Myanmar.[63]

Finally, TOW9 is a peculiar scenario in that only the texts in the official languages of the treaty partners are declared authentic, whereas the text prevailing in case of them diverging from each other is not. In consequence, the court may not go to the prevailing text from the outset, since it is not equally authentic and therefore of lesser authority than the others. Only once the other texts are found to diverge may the prevailing text be invoked.

---

[61] Greece-Malta (2006) and Bahrain-Thailand (2001).

[62] Disputes about the interpretation and application of tax treaties arise mostly between taxpayers and contracting states, not between the contracting states themselves. Hence, it is unreasonable to assume that the term 'dispute' as used in TOW8 would be intended to apply only to the latter, not the former or rather any dispute.

[63] Thailand (2002), Malaysia (1998), Korea (Rep.) (2002).

8. Applicability of the Permissive Approach

The way this can be done also differs for the two variations of TOW9. The original wording of TOW9, which first appeared in the treaty Germany-Japan (1966), is equivalent to TOW4, however, without the prevailing text being declared as equally authentic. To this wording the whole argumentation of Bender and Engelen concerning TOW4 quoted above applies. Indeed, the entire restrictive approach discussed at length in Chapters 5 and 6 may be viewed as a particular interpretation of Article 33(4) applying in practice only to this particular variation of TOW9, at least as far as tax treaties are concerned.[64]

In order to find out whether there really is a divergence, the court cannot spare itself the comparison of the texts in the languages of the two contracting states declared as authentic, because the prevailing text only becomes authoritative when they diverge. In terms of the example developed in the case of TOW4, if E=A and either N=A and R=B or N=B and R=C, then N=R=E=A. When N=R=A, however, it is immaterial whether E=A or E=B, but the one true meaning of the treaty remains A. Thus, regarding TOW9, the prevailing text functions only as an alternative to the special *modus operandi* of Article 33(4) using the object and purpose criterion as sole decider.

This line of reasoning depends on whether the prevailing text has been subject to signature, ratification, or any authentication procedure stipulated by the treaty same as the other texts at the time of conclusion, because authentic status is bestowed on any text by the conditions specified in Article 10 VCLT. As interpreted, TOW9 suggests that the prevailing text is not an authenticated text but merely an official version prepared at the time of conclusion of the treaty, or the negotiated and initially drafted version kept as a reference without being authenticated. Otherwise, failure of TOW9 to explicitly label the prevailing text as authentic may be considered a drafting error, that is, TOW9 is merely a wrongly formulated TOW4 and the inter-

---

[64] The final clause of the 1930 arbitration treaty between the United States and China constitutes an example of TOW9 outside the tax treaty world. It features equally authoritative English and Chinese texts but a French prevailing text in case of divergence between the other two, see Hardy, 'The Interpretation of Plurilingual Treaties by International Courts and Tribunals', 126–27, with reference to *Treaties, Conventions, International Acts, Protocols and Agreements between the United States of America and other Powers, 1923–1937*, Vol. 4, 4022.

pretation submitted above in respect of TOW4 applies. That there is only one treaty in force with this wording of TOW9 and only two others with a variation of it suggests the latter.[65] Whatever is the case is not investigated here, but TOW9 is simply upheld as a genuine wording and available policy choice for countries, while the factual conditions necessary for it are assumed as given.

For the latter variation of TOW9 implemented in Hungary-Uruguay (1988) and Poland-Uruguay (1991), the process of interpretation is different conceptually. In the original variation the prevailing text 'prevails' over the others once they are found to diverge. Consequently, the other texts would have to be reinterpreted to converge to the meaning of the one declared as prevailing, that is, the exercise is very much one of interpreting the prevailing text and then attributing the outcome to the others. In the latter variation, however, the third text 'shall be taken into consideration as a reference.' Consequently, the third text has more or less only the status of an additional text, not that of one truly prevailing, that is, the exercise is one of augmenting the context used to interpret the other texts in light of the meaning of the third. This fits better with the interpretation of TOW9 as a genuine wording and policy alternative than the original wording, which appears more like a drafting error.

In summary, courts may not resort to sole reliance on the prevailing text for treaties with a TOW9 final clause, subject to the condition that TOW9 is not a drafting error. As the case may be, out of the entire global tax treaty network only three treaties employ TOW9.

8.4. Summary Observations

The preceding analysis has shown that, since the 1990s, prevailing texts have emerged as predominant global standard, while almost all final clause wordings implementing a prevailing text allow for sole reliance on it. Today, additional interpretational complexity induced by plurilingual form is confined to merely one-quarter of all tax treaties in force. Three-quarters of

---

[65]Japan-Netherlands (1970) did also employ a TOW9 final clause of the original variation but has been terminated and replaced by Japan-Netherlands (2010), which is unilingual in English.

8. Applicability of the Permissive Approach

today's global tax treaty network do not pose a problem because of uni-lingual form or existing prevailing texts in combination with final clauses allowing for sole reliance on them. The residual quarter being plurilingual without prevailing text is not evenly distributed over the global tax treaty network but concentrated in the treaty networks of a handful of countries, which are however almost all big players in the global economy and inter-national tax system, so their policies continue to weigh against the global trend and affect large portions of the global flows of capital, goods, and services. Therefore, coordination at the multilateral level may be necessary to eliminate remaining additional interpretational complexity induced by plurilingual form, together with its associated economic cost.

9. English as Lingua Franca of Tax Treaties

9.1. Research Topic

Tax treaties have their roots before the second and even first world war.[1] In their magnitude, however, they are a post–second world war phenomenon: their growth in numbers did not take off until the 1960s after the adoption of the OECD Model, and their big expansion only happened by the 1990s

---

[1] The first tax treaties recorded in the IBFD database were concluded between the German Empire and states of the Austro-Hungarian Empire before the first world war. Their roots can be traced back to the Prussian industrial code of 1845, see *Preußische Gesetzessammlung* 1845, 41, in which the German term for PE (*Betriebsstätte*) first appeared, indicating the total space used for the conduct of a business. The terminology was introduced into tax law in 1885, see *Preußische Gesetzessammlung* 1885, 327, in order to distribute the taxing rights between Prussian municipalities, eliminate double taxation, and decrease the administrative burden on local tax authorities. This led to the Law of the North-German Federation to Eliminate Double Taxation in 1870, see *Gesetz wegen Beseitigung der Doppelbesteuerung, Bundesgesetzblatt des Norddeutschen Bundes* 1870, 119. The tax treaty Prussia-Austria/Hungary (1899) for the first time mentioned criteria defining a PE, structured as a positive list with a generic catch-all clause at the end. It was followed domestically by the German Double Tax Law of 1909, see *Doppelsteuergesetz, Reichsgesetzblatt* 1909, 332, and internationally by several treaties before and after the first world war, see Richard Xenophon Resch, 'The Taxation of Profits without a Permanent Establishment', in *Permanent Establishments in International Tax Law*, ed. Michael Lang, Mario Züger, and Hans-Jörgen Aigner, vol. 29, Schriftenreihe Zum Internationalen Steuerrecht (Wien: Linde Verlag Ges.m.b.H., 2003), 475–500; Joachim Dieter Kolck, *Der Betriebsstättenbegriff im nationalen und im internationalen Steuerrecht* (Münster: Universität, Fachbereich Rechtswissenschaft, Dissertation, 1974), passim; Wassermeyer, *Doppelbesteuerung: Kommentar zu allen deutschen Doppelbesteuerungsabkommen*, MA, Vor Art. 1, 41–44, paras. 71–80; Christian von Roenne, 'The Very Beginning – The First Tax Treaties', in *History of Tax Treaties: The Relevance of the OECD Documents for the Interpretation of Tax Treaties*, ed. Thomas Ecker and Gernot Ressler (Vienna: Linde, 2011), 19–39. For a compilation of all the historical documents drafted in preparation of the OECD Model Convention of 1963 and the older convention drafted under the auspices of the League of Nations after the second world war, see http://www.taxtreatieshistory.org.

alongside the growing interdependence of the world's national economies and their integration into a globalised economy.[2] Today's global tax treaty network has emerged in the era of 'linguistic nationalism', in which it has become custom to conclude international instruments in several languages instead of universally accepted ones such as Latin and French for the preceding eras;[3] however, like other bilateral treaties, they show a higher tendency than multilateral ones to employ a particular third language as lingua franca in form of a prevailing text.[4] In some cases linguistic nationalism is fully overcome and unilingual treaties are concluded in a universally accepted lingua franca.

The present chapter investigates the use of English (and French) as lingua franca for tax treaties. This is of relevance in the current context because English and French are the official languages of the OECD Model Convention and Commentary, which may provide an additional argument for sole reliance on existing English or French prevailing texts.[5] In addition, the official languages of the contracting states and their general proficiency in English (or French) may be factors that influence their policy choice. Therefore, an investigation into these factors may help to shed some more light on the observations made so far.

9.2. Global Analysis

Most treaties (83.92%) in the global tax treaty network have English as language of at least one of their texts, whereas French only plays a limited role (7.68%). The proportion of treaties with neither English nor French texts is equally marginal (8.40%). Termination of treaties over time has affected the overall composition to the effect that the proportion of treaties with neither English nor French texts has decreased by almost a quarter, which has been absorbed entirely by a proportional increase of treaties with an English text,

---

[2] See Dicken, *Global Shift*, passim.

[3] See Hardy, 'The Interpretation of Plurilingual Treaties by International Courts and Tribunals', 72; de Vries, 'Choice of Language', 26.

[4] See Gamble and Ku, 'Choice of Language in Bilateral Treaties', 241 et seq.

[5] An in-depth appraisal of this argument would warrant a separate study; in order not to reproduce the work of others already engaged with the topic, the reader is referred to Lang, 'The Interpretation of Tax Treaties and Authentic Languages'.

while the proportion of treaties with a French text has remained roughly the same. This indicates an increasing tendency towards the already widespread use of English as authentic language, whereas French is stagnating in relative terms at its marginal level.

When we consider only all plurilingual treaties without prevailing text, we see that still over 70% have English, 16% have French, and slightly over 12% have neither as authentic language. This points again to the conclusion that a relatively high proportion of English-speaking countries have a policy of not implementing a prevailing text. In addition, it suggests that English receives a boost once prevailing texts are implemented.

Table (9.1): *Treaties with English or French Texts*

Treaties	eng AL	fre AL	neither
Global No. w term	3135	304	405
Total No. w/o term	2818	258	282
%global w term	81.56%	7.91%	10.54%
%total w/o term	83.92%	7.68%	8.40%
+/-	2.36%	-0.23%	-2.14%
PL w/o PT w/o term	631	148	110
%PL w/o PT w/o term	70.98%	16.65%	12.37%

The language distribution for all unilingual treaties shows that roughly three-quarters of them are in English. Other languages most used are Arabic and French with shares of 8.97% and 7.56%, respectively. Behind Spanish and German with shares of 3.90% and 1.42%, respectively, the combined share of the remaining seven languages is merely 1.53%.

Table (9.2): *Language Distribution of Unilingual Treaties*

lang	lang UL	lang %UL
eng	649	76.62%
ara	76	8.97%
fre	64	7.56%
spa	33	3.90%
ger	12	1.42%
por	5	0.59%

lang	lang UL	lang %UL
chi	2	0.24%
ita	2	0.24%
dut	1	0.12%
gre	1	0.12%
kor	1	0.12%
rum	1	0.12%

A look at the treaties for each individual language reveals that, apart from the English ones, they merely exhaust the potential of sharing a native tongue or official language, that is, none of the other languages is used as true diplomatic language. The seventy-three Arabic treaties are all between members of the AW, the twenty-nine Spanish treaties between Spanish-speaking LA countries and Spain, and the twelve German treaties between Germany, Austria, Switzerland, Liechtenstein, and Luxembourg. As for the sixty-four French treaties, the situation slightly differs but essentially leads to the same conclusion. Roughly two-thirds of them are between countries in which French is either the native or official language, or used as lingua franca (most of them being members of the *Organisation internationale de la Francophonie*). The remaining are all between such countries and third countries, with the only exception of Greece-Italy (1964),[6] that is, only in the case of one treaty is French used as true diplomatic language.

For unilingual treaties in English, the situation is different. Matching them to the countries having English as official language shows that English unilingual treaties between them only amount to 25% of all English unilingual treaties, while almost 40% are between countries having English as official language and countries that do not, and almost 35% are between countries not having English as official language. This means that there is a considerable number of countries not having English as official language that use English as true diplomatic language between themselves and/or accept it as diplomatic language with English-speaking treaty partners, that is, when conceding a hypothetical linguistic advantage.

---

[6]It may be worth mentioning in this context that Greece joined the *Organisation internationale de la Francophonie* in 2004, while Italy seems to have retained a policy of using French as diplomatic language to a certain degree (see below).

Table (9.3): Distribution of English Unilingual Treaties

Treaties	%eng UL	%UL	%total
UL w/o eng		23.38%	5.90%
eng UL		76.62%	19.33%
eng UL EOF	25.89%	19.83%	5.00%
eng UL EOF-NEOF	39.91%	30.58%	7.71%
eng UL NEOF	34.21%	26.21%	6.61%

The numbers for treaties with prevailing text reveal that the overwhelming majority (almost 95%) of them use English as language for the prevailing text. The remaining percentage points are mostly distributed between forty-seven treaties with a French prevailing text and thirty-six with a Russian prevailing text. Three treaties constitute a special case of two prevailing texts (English and French) each. The residual two treaties are one treaty with a Croatian and one with a Portuguese prevailing text.[7] The thirty-six treaties with a Russian prevailing text are all treaties between CIS members or between them and Germany or Poland. As far as the forty-seven treaties with a French prevailing text are concerned, ten are between countries in which French is either the native or official language or generally used as lingua franca, while twenty-six are between such countries and third countries. The remaining eleven are all between third countries.[8]

---

[7]Bosnia and Herzegovina-Croatia (2004) and Portugal-Timor Leste (2011). Noteworthy, the Portugal-Timor Leste treaty has both an English and a Portuguese text but declares the latter as prevailing. The Bosnia and Herzegovina-Croatia treaty has no English text but three texts in Serbian, Bosnian, and Croatian.

[8]Germany-Iran (1968), Hungary-Italy (1977), Italy-Spain (1977), Argentina-Italy (1979), Italy-Portugal (1980), Italy-Sweden (1980), Italy-Slovak Republic (1981), Czech Republic-Italy (1981), Bulgaria-Italy (1988), Italy-Netherlands (1990), Italy-Venezuela (1990). Noteworthy, ten of those eleven treaties are Italian ones, and they all have been concluded before the beginning of the major expansion of the global tax treaty network in the 1990s. Thus, it seems as if Italy had retained a policy of using French as lingua franca up to 1990.

Table (9.4): Language Distribution of Prevailing Texts

lang	PL w lang PT	lang PT %PL w PT
eng	1534	94.57%
fre	47	2.90%
rus	36	2.22%
eng/fre	3	0.18%
por	1	0.06%
cro	1	0.06%

In summary, almost two-thirds of all treaties in the global tax treaty network are either unilingual in English or have an English prevailing text. The share of French is marginal, and its use as true diplomatic language even more so. All other languages are used as unilingual or prevailing language only to a limited extent, confined to certain linguistic, geographical, or political regions, that is, they merely exhaust the potential for unilingual treaties attributable to a shared native or official language. Even French is more important as a language for unilingual treaties than as a prevailing language for plurilingual ones.

An exception to this is Russian, which is used as a prevailing language by CIS members, where Russian is still official language of several countries and regions. Other than that there has been no tendency of Russia as a super power to extend the reach of Russian as diplomatic language to its entire sphere of influence, neither before nor after the cold war. This finding for tax treaties is consistent with the research of Gamble and Ku for other bilateral treaties.[9] Noteworthy, seven of the thirty-six treaties with a Russian prevailing text are treaties between CIS members and either Germany or Poland.[10] This is striking because CIS members have a high propensity to

---

[9]See Gamble and Ku, 'Choice of Language in Bilateral Treaties', 261–62. Only the multilateral COMECON treaties were unilingual in Russian, see Council for Mutual Economic Assistance, *Income and Capital Tax Treaty (Individuals)* (IBFD, 1977); Council for Mutual Economic Assistance, *Income and Capital Tax Treaty (Companies)* (IBFD, 1978). During its existence from 1949 to 1991, Albania, Bulgaria, Cuba, Czechoslovakia, East Germany, Hungary, Mongolia, Poland, Romania, the Soviet Union, and Vietnam were members of the COMECON.

[10]Poland-Uzbekistan (1995), Germany-Uzbekistan (1999), Poland-Georgia (1999), Poland-

use English for prevailing texts with third countries (see below), so it seems that Germany and Poland have been accommodating in granting linguistic advantages. Given that these treaties are all fairly recent, this may indicate a current bargaining strategy in treaty negotiations.[11]

Table (9.5): Language Distribution of Unilingual Treaties and Prevailing Texts

lang	lang (UL+PL w PT) %total
eng	65.01%
fre	3.31%
ara	2.26%
rus	1.07%
spa	0.98%
ger	0.36%
por	0.18%
eng/fre	0.09%
chi	0.06%
ita	0.06%
dut	0.03%
gre	0.03%
kor	0.03%
rum	0.03%
cro	0.03%

Termination of treaties has increased the total share of English as language for unilingual treaties and prevailing texts from roughly 61% to 65%. This increase is attributable to a proportional increase in treaties with prevailing text, caused mainly by a large number of replaced treaties originally without prevailing text, which even overcompensates a slight reduction in the relative proportion of English unilingual treaties. In contrast, French increased its relative share only marginally and plays no truly significant role from a global perspective.

Tajikistan (2003), Germany-Azerbaijan (2004), Germany-Kyrgyzstan (2005), Germany-Georgia (2006).

[11] Owing to the historical context, the availability of human resources proficient in Russian may play a role.

Table (9.6): Changes through Termination

Treaties	eng UL/PT	fre UL/PT
w term total	2,364	127
w/o term total	2,186	114
+/- total	-178	-13
%total w term	61.50%	3.30%
%total w/o term	65.10%	3.40%
UL w term	754	72
UL w/o term	649	64
+/- UL	-105	-8
%UL w term	77.97%	7.45%
%UL w/o term	76.62%	7.56%
PL w term	1,610	55
PL w/o term	1,537	50
+/- PL	-73	-5
%PL w term	55.96%	1.91%
%PL w/o term	61.21%	1.99%

9.3. Time-Series Analysis

Given the overwhelming choice for English as language for prevailing texts, the numbers over time hardly surprise. The share of English prevailing texts has with roughly 79% been lowest in the 1970s and equal or over 90% during all other decades, slowly increasing towards 98%. Nevertheless, we need to be cautious with conclusions concerning the trend character of the data. Each treaty has been concluded at one point in time subject to an individual linguistic and political context. Hence, the data provides no indication of the likelihood that treaties currently with a French prevailing text would be replaced by treaties with an English one if terminated and renegotiated.

As regards changes through termination, the numbers show that the percentage change from no prevailing text to an English prevailing one has been highest with 38.74%, followed by no change in having no prevailing text (33.11%) and no change in having an English prevailing text (21.19%). All other changes are only marginal. As far as replaced unilingual treaties are concerned, the percentage shares of unchanged English unilingual treaties and of English unilingual treaties replaced by treaties with English prevailing text are dominant with 46.43% and 40.18%, respectively. All other changes are only marginal. In particular, the numbers concerning changes from French into English are too minuscule to draw any significant conclusions, apart from the observation that such change is not common.

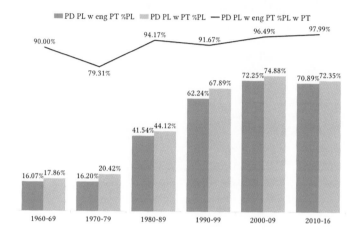

Figure (9.1): English Prevailing Texts as Percentage of All Prevailing Texts per Decade

Table (9.7): Terminated and Replaced Unilingual Treaties

lang	R UL	%R UL
eng UL to eng UL	52	46.43%
eng UL to PL w eng PT	45	40.18%
eng UL to PL w/o PT	4	3.57%
fre UL to fre UL	3	2.68%
fre UL to eng UL	1	0.89%
fre UL to PL w eng PT	1	0.89%
fre UL to PL w/o PT	1	0.89%

Table (9.8): Terminated and Replaced Plurilingual Treaties

lang	R PL	%R PL
eng to eng PT	64	21.19%
eng to n PT	6	1.99%
fre to fre PT	3	0.99%
fre to eng PT	2	0.66%
PL w/o PT NC	100	33.11%
PL w/o PT to eng PT	117	38.74%
PL w/o PT to fre PT	3	0.99%

Concerning the growth of English unilingual treaties and prevailing texts over time versus the cumulative growth of all treaties, we see that the relations have exactly reversed over the decades. In the 1960s and 1970s, English unilingual treaties and prevailing texts made up roughly 35% of the global tax treaty network. By the 2010s their share increased to roughly 65%. The development has been swift. When the first wave of expansion kicked into gear in the 1980s, the share of English unilingual treaties and prevailing texts already increased to almost 50%.

The figures for unilingual treaties alone show that the share of English treaties quickly jumped to over three-quarters by the 1980s and remained at this level in a stable fashion over the decades. The per decade figures of English unilingual treaties as percentages of all cumulative treaties per decade and all cumulative unilingual treaties per decade display a big leap from roughly 58% in the 1960s to roughly 68% in the 1970s and over 87% in the 1980s. Their share decreased again to roughly 78% by the 1990s, bottomed out at roughly 72% in the 2000s, and increased again to almost 79% in the 2010s. This may indicate that the potential for English unilingual treaties is reaching saturation; the residual quarter is comprised mostly of unilingual treaties between countries sharing a common native or official language other than English.

Concerning the combined figure of English unilingual treaties and English prevailing texts, which models the entire use of English as lingua franca by tax treaties, the per decade figure jumps from roughly 37% during the 1970s to roughly 57% during the 1980s, then starts to logarithmically approach a percentage share of roughly 73% by the 2010s. This seems to indicate that the potential for English unilingual and quasi-unilingual treaties is approaching exhaustion if no major policy impetus happens globally, that is, the remaining relative growth potential for English as lingua franca is located with the pool of treaties without prevailing text because of the past policy choice of certain countries for such treaties.

On the whole, we can identify a widespread and increasing use of English as lingua franca for tax treaties, albeit slowing down. The figures confirm the trend observed by Gamble and Ku for other bilateral treaties concerning the reversal of significance between English and French by the 1960s,[12] and show a swift emergence of English as dominant lingua franca for tax treaties since.

---

[12]See Gamble and Ku, 'Choice of Language in Bilateral Treaties', 245 et seq.

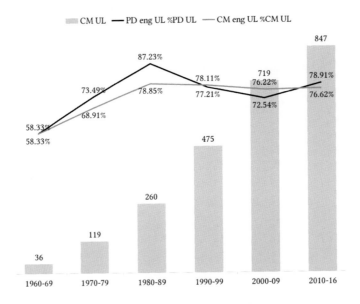

Figure (9.2): Growth of English Unilingual Treaties

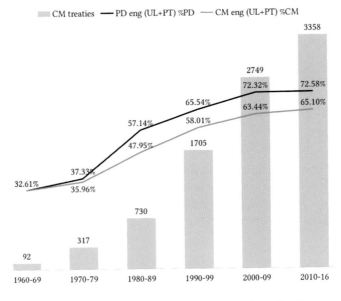

Figure (9.3): Growth of English Unilingual Treaties and Prevailing Texts

9.4. Group Analysis

In order to acquire a balanced view, we have to group the data again. Treaties between OECD members display large proportions of English unilingual treaties (83.80%) and treaties with English prevailing text (95.41%). Nevertheless, the combined share of English unilingual and quasi-unilingual treaties is with 51.86% relatively low. This is attributable to the large number of plurilingual treaties without prevailing text. Noteworthy, however, almost two-thirds (66.14%) of all intra–OECD plurilingual treaties without prevailing text have English as one of their authentic languages. For countries that otherwise accept English as language for prevailing texts, a comparison of texts in cases of treaties without prevailing text has to be considered less of a difficulty if the other text is in English. In consequence, although not used as lingua franca for treaties without prevailing text, the otherwise general use of English as lingua franca still reduces overall interpretational complexity, albeit only for countries the official languages of which are the languages of the other (non-English) texts.

For treaties between OECD members and third countries, the figures almost equal the figures for treaties between OECD members, although the combined share of English unilingual and quasi-unilingual treaties is with 65.13% significantly larger, owing to the reduced number of treaties without prevailing text. In addition, the proportion of treaties without prevailing text having English as authentic language is increased to roughly 70%.

As regards treaties between non-members of the OECD, the proportion of English unilingual treaties is reduced but still at almost two-thirds, while the proportion of English prevailing texts is with over 90% roughly as large as for the previous two groups. The combined share of English unilingual and quasi-unilingual treaties is with over 70% increased compared to the previous groups, again owing to a reduced number of treaties without prevailing text. In addition, the proportion of treaties without prevailing text having English as authentic language is increased to roughly 80%.

In summary, English is used as lingua franca roughly half of the time between OECD members. In addition, it is an authentic language in almost two-thirds of all other cases because of the strong impact of the English-speaking countries, which for the most part have a strict policy in disfavour of prevailing texts. For treaties with third countries their impact decreases, and use of English as lingua franca increases to almost two-thirds of all treaties. The use of English as lingua franca is more widespread in the non-OECD world, encompassing almost three-quarters of all treaties, while English is still an authentic language of four out of five treaties without prevailing text. As far as the OECD key partners are concerned, the proportions of English unilingual treaties are roughly 95% for treaties both with OECD members and third countries, while all prevailing texts are in English. Their use of English as lingua franca amounts to almost three-quarters for treaties with OECD members and almost 80% for treaties with third countries.

Table (9.9): English Unilingual Treaties and Prevailing Texts (OECD)

Treaty	eng %UL	eng PL %PL w PT
OECD-OECD	83.80%	95.41%
OECD-NOECD	81.72%	95.84%
NOECD-NOECD	64.12%	92.84%
OECDKP-OECD	96.55%	100.00%
OECDKP-NOECD	94.59%	100.00%

Table (9.10): English as Treaty Lingua Franca and Authentic Language (OECD)

Treaty	eng (UL+PL w PT) %total	eng AL %PL w/o PT
OECD-OECD	51.86%	66.14%
OECD-NOECD	65.13%	70.43%
NOECD-NOECD	72.01%	80.12%
OECDKP-OECD	73.08%	75.61%
OECDKP-NOECD	79.36%	93.02%

The situation of treaties between G20 countries resembles that of treaties between OECD countries, as many of the countries heavily weighing on the intra–OECD figures also influence the G20 ones. The others increase the figures in favour of English, which is almost exclusively the language of choice for unilingual treaties and prevailing texts. The overall use of English as lingua franca is with 47.59% lower than in the OECD case, owing to the larger number of treaties without prevailing text. The same is true for treaties between G20 members and third countries. The shares for unilingual treaties and prevailing texts resemble those for treaties between OECD members and non-members, while the overall use of English as lingua franca is with 54.84% again significantly lower. Combined with the large number of treaties without prevailing text having English as authentic language, this may point to the conclusion that, on top of the strong policy preference of some English-speaking countries against prevailing texts, countries are reluctant to grant linguistic advantages to economically powerful treaty partners.

Table (9.11): English Unilingual Treaties and Prevailing Texts (G20)

Treaty	eng %UL	eng PL %PL w PT
G20-G20	94.12%	98.44%
G20-NG20	75.40%	95.28%

Table (9.12): English as Treaty Lingua Franca and Authentic Language (G20)

Treaty	eng (UL+PL w PT) %total	eng AL %PL w/o PT
G20-G20	47.59%	75.29%
G20-NG20	54.84%	73.45%

Unsurprisingly, the numbers for the CW are more homogeneous. Intra–CW all unilingual treaties and prevailing texts are in English, while the use of English as diplomatic language is slightly above 80%. In addition, all treaties without prevailing text have English as one of their authentic languages. Thus, the number of cases in which a comparison of texts could be necessary is limited from the outset, while there is always an English text available. This may influence the general attitude of common lawyers towards the importance of comparing texts. For treaties between CW members and third countries, the use of English for unilingual treaties and prevailing texts is both still close to 100%, indicating that the rest of the world accepts English as lingua franca when making the choice for one, while the comparably lower overall share of 53.64% for all English unilingual treaties and prevailing texts combined points to the policy of CW countries to conclude treaties without prevailing text, together with a general reluctance of countries to grant linguistic advantages.

Table (9.13): English Unilingual Treaties and Prevailing Texts (CW)

Treaty	eng %UL	eng PL %PL w PT
CW-CW	100.00%	100.00%
CW-NCW	93.52%	99.08%

Table (9.14): English as Treaty Lingua Franca and Authentic Language (CW)

Treaty	eng (UL+PL w PT) %total	eng AL %PL w/o PT
CW-CW	80.63%	100.00%
CW-NCW	53.64%	98.91%

The figures for treaties between EU countries and between them and third countries are roughly in the same ballpark, except for the percentages concerning treaties without prevailing text having English as an authentic language. Although this percentage is roughly 70% for the latter group, it is with roughly 11% exceptionally low for the first group, indicating greater linguistic diversity. The use of English as lingua franca is around 70% of all treaties for both groups.

Table (9.15): English Unilingual Treaties and Prevailing Texts (EU)

Treaty	eng %UL	eng PL %PL w PT
EU-EU	81.91%	94.42%
EU-NEU	85.02%	95.76%

Table (9.16): English as Treaty Lingua Franca and Authentic Language (EU)

Treaty	eng (UL+PL w PT) %total	eng AL %PL w/o PT
EU-EU	72.05%	11.11%
EU-NEU	67.39%	71.68%

Unsurprisingly, given the linguistic, historical, and political context, CIS members do not use English as lingua franca between themselves but almost exclusively conclude treaties with Russian prevailing texts.[13] Concerning treaties with third countries, however, CIS members show little reluctance to use English as lingua franca. English is used almost exclusively for prevailing texts, as well as for almost 85% of all unilingual treaties. In total, English is used as lingua franca for three-quarters of all treaties.

Table (9.17): English Unilingual Treaties and Prevailing Texts (CIS)

Treaty	eng %UL	eng PL %PL w PT
CIS-CIS	0.00%	3.33%
CIS-NCIS	84.62%	97.85%

Table (9.18): English as Treaty Lingua Franca and Authentic Language (CIS)

Treaty	eng (UL+PL w PT) %total	eng AL %PL w/o PT
CIS-CIS	2.70%	0.00%
CIS-NCIS	76.78%	58.62%

The AW figures resemble those for the CIS. Between AW countries, Arabic is used exclusively. For treaties between AW and third countries, however, the percentages for English unilingual treaties (64.29%) and prevailing texts (92.36%) are lower than in the CIS case, which is attributable to the use of French in North Africa. The multilateral agreements both between

---

[13]Russian is still either official or second state language in Belarus, Kazakhstan, Kyrgyzstan, and Tajikistan, as well as in several regions in Georgia, Moldova, and Ukraine.

the the members of the Arab Economic Union[14] and the members of the Arab Maghreb Union[15] are unilingual in Arabic,[16] while for the latter an unofficial French translation is provided by the Tunisian authorities.

Table (9.19): English Unilingual Treaties and Prevailing Texts (AW)

Treaty	eng %UL	eng PL %PL w PT
AW-AW	0.00%	0.00%
AW-NAW	64.29%	92.36%

Table (9.20): English as Treaty Lingua Franca and Authentic Language (AW)

Treaty	eng (UL+PL w PT) %total	eng AL %PL w/o PT
AW-AW	0.00%	0.00%
AW-NAW	73.00%	68.37%

LA countries do not use English as lingua franca when concluding treaties between themselves but rely exclusively on Spanish or, as in the case of Portuguese-speaking Brazil, do not conclude treaties with prevailing text with their fellow LA countries. They use English almost exclusively for prevailing texts in the case of treaties with third countries but resort to Spanish for unilingual treaties whenever possible. Fifteen out of the nineteen unilingual treaties with third countries are in Spanish, all but one of them

---

[14] Algeria, Bahrain, Egypt, Iraq, Jordan, Kuwait, Lebanon, Libya, Morocco, Oman, Palestine, Qatar, Saudi Arabia, Sudan, Syria, Tunisia, United Arab Emirates, Yemen.

[15] Algeria, Libya, Mauritania, Morocco, Tunisia.

[16] Arab Economic Union Council, *Agreement for the Avoidance of Double Taxation and Prevention of Tax Evasion between the States of the Arab Economic Union Council* (Cairo: Council of Arab Economic Unity, 1973); Arab Maghreb Union, *Convention relative à la non double imposition et l'application des règles de coopération d'échange dans le domaine des impôts sur les revenus entre les pays de l'UMA* (Rabat: Arab Maghreb Union Secretariat, 1990).

with Spain.[17] One of them is in Portuguese,[18] two in English,[19] and one in French.[20] The use of English as lingua franca is with roughly 60% compar- ably low overall because of fewer and almost exclusively Spanish unilin- gual treaties, combined with a comparably large share of treaties without prevailing text.[21]

Table (9.21): English Unilingual Treaties and Prevailing Texts (LA)

Treaty	eng %UL	eng PL %PL w PT
LA-LA	0.00%	0.00%
LA-NAL	10.53%	98.54%

Table (9.22): English as Treaty Lingua Franca and Authentic Language (LA)

Treaty	eng (UL+PL w PT) %total	eng AL %PL w/o PT
LA-LA	0.00%	0.00%
LA-NAL	59.57%	55.41%

Regarding treaties between AF countries, the overall use of English as lingua franca is with 78% relatively high, owing to a large share of English unilingual treaties. This is attributable to many AF countries having English as official language and being part of the CW. Also the ratified but not yet

---

[17]Sweden-Venezuela (1993).

[18]Brazil-Portugal (2000).

[19]Cuba-Lebanon (2001) and Chile-Japan (2016).

[20]France-St. Martin (2010).

[21]On a side note, the policy of the CARICOM countries (which are not included in the LA group) differs. They have relatively few tax treaties in total, which are dominated by the CARICOM official languages English, French, and Dutch, whereas the Intra–Regional Double Taxation Agreement between some of the CARICOM members (Antigua and Barbuda, Belize, Dominica, Guyana, Grenada, Jamaica, Montserrat, St. Kitts and Nevis, St Lucia, St. Vincent and the Grenadines, Trinidad and Tobago) is unilingual in English, see Caribbean Community, *Intra-Regional Double Taxation Agreement* (Georgetown: CARICOM Secretariat, 1994).

in force East African Community[22] income tax treaty of 2010 is unilingual in English.[23] The same was true for the 1997 version.[24] Treaties between AF and third countries feature high percentages for both unilingual treaties and prevailing texts, but the overall use of English as lingua franca is comparably low (48.82%) because of a large number of treaties without prevailing text and a few countries tending to French. Also the West African Economic and Monetary Union[25] tax treaty is unilingual in French.[26]

Table (9.23): English Unilingual Treaties and Prevailing Texts (AF)

Treaty	eng %UL	eng PL %PL w PT
AF-AF	96.97%	0.00%
AF-NAF	79.02%	81.25%

Table (9.24): English as Treaty Lingua Franca and Authentic Language (AF)

Treaty	eng (UL+PL w PT) %total	eng AL %PL w/o PT
AF-AF	78.05%	100.00%
AF-NAF	48.82%	82.44%

Finally, both treaties between AS countries and between AS and third countries show a high propensity to use English almost exclusively for unilingual treaties and prevailing texts. The use of English as lingua franca is

---

[22]Burundi, Kenya, Rwanda, South Sudan, Tanzania, and Uganda.

[23]East African Community, *Agreement between the Governments of the Republics of Kenya, Uganda, Burundi, Rwanda and the United Republic of Tanzania for the Avoidance of Double Taxation and the Prevention of Fiscal Evasion with Respect to Taxes on Income* (Arusha: East African Community, 2010).

[24]East African Community, *Agreement between the Governments of the Republic of Kenya, the United Republic of Tanzania and the Republic of Uganda for the Avoidance of Double Taxation and the Prevention of Fiscal Evasion with Respect to Taxes on Income* (Arusha: East African Community, 1997).

[25]Benin, Burkina Faso, Cote d'Ivoire, Guinea-Bissau, Mali, Niger, Senegal, and Togo.

[26]West African Economic and Monetary Union, *Income Tax Treaty* (Bamako: UEMOA, 2008).

below 90% only for treaties between AS and third countries because of a small number of treaties without prevailing text. This policy is reflected in the multilateral income tax and mutual assistance treaty of the South Asian Association for Regional Cooperation,[27] which is unilingual in English.[28]

Table (9.25): *English Unilingual Treaties and Prevailing Texts (AS)*

Treaty	eng %UL	eng PL %PL w PT
AS-AS	94.12%	100.00%
AS-NAS	98.51%	99.49%

Table (9.26): *English as Treaty Lingua Franca and Authentic Language (AS)*

Treaty	eng (UL+PL w PT) %total	eng AL %PL w/o PT
AS-AS	91.23%	100.00%
AS-NAS	83.12%	86.27%

It remains difficult to pinpoint the exact motivations for a particular language choice without an in-depth analysis of the entire background for each case, which is not the purpose of this study. Several factors may influence the outcome, for example, a country's official language and linguistic policy, the official language and linguistic policy of the treaty partner, the entire historical and political background behind the current treaty relationship, and the willingness to grant perceived linguistic advantages. Factors that affect bargaining power such as relative economic size, asymmetric economic interests, and the availability of human resources proficient in certain third languages may also play a role. Even sentiments such as linguistic nationalism translating into domestic socio-political forces may have a considerable impact.

---

[27]Bangladesh, Bhutan, India, Maldives, Nepal, Pakistan, and Sri Lanka.
[28]South Asian Association for Regional Cooperation, *SAARC Limited Multilateral Agreement on Avoidance of Double Taxation and Mutual Administrative Assistance in Tax Matters* (Kathmandu: SAARC Secretariat, 2005).

The relative weight of all these factors is hard to discern by simply observing the outcome from a birds-eye view; however, we may zoom in a little on the observations most relevant in the current context by analysing the data for certain groups and individual countries. For example, the data shows that out of all treaties between countries having English as official language, roughly two-thirds are unilingual and one-third is plurilingual. Unsurprisingly, English is the language of all unilingual treaties and prevailing texts. Yet, only roughly half of all plurilingual treaties feature a prevailing text to begin with. Hence, some English-speaking countries have a policy of not concluding treaties with prevailing text even when English is available as a shared official language.

Roughly a quarter of treaties between countries having English as official language and countries that do not is comprised of unilingual treaties, over 95% of which are in English. Only about 40% of their plurilingual treaties have prevailing texts, but almost all of them are in English. When we compare that to treaties concluded by countries both having other official languages, we see that the overall proportions of unilingual and plurilingual treaties are roughly in the same ballpark, but only about half of the unilingual treaties are in English, while roughly 80% of the plurilingual ones have prevailing texts, almost 90% of which are in English.

Table (9.27): English as Treaty Lingua Franca in Relation to Official Language

Treaties	EOL-EOL	EOL-NEOL	NEOL-NEOL
No.	262	1129	1967
UL %total	64.12%	23.91%	20.79%
eng %UL	100.00%	95.93%	54.28%
PL %total	35.88%	76.09%	79.21%
PL w PT %PL	48.94%	39.12%	79.59%
eng PT %PL w PT	100.00%	99.40%	87.58%
eng (UL+PT) %total	81.68%	52.52%	66.50%

From all this we may conclude that there exists a considerable number of countries willing to agree to English as language for unilingual treaties or prevailing texts even when English is the official language of the treaty partner and not theirs, that is, when granting a linguistic advantage. Nevertheless, countries with official languages other than English have a much higher propensity (roughly 2:1) to conclude treaties with English prevailing text with each other than with countries having English as official language. This may be attributable to two factors, that is, the policy preference of some English-speaking countries against prevailing texts and the greater willingness of countries to use English as lingua franca when no concession of a linguistic advantage is involved. All in all, the propensity to use English as lingua franca in the non-English-speaking world (as in not having English as official language) is almost exactly at two-thirds, whereas there remains a gap of roughly 14% that mixed treaties (between countries that have English as official language and countries that do not) lag behind in using English as diplomatic language.

Another telling angle to look at the data is from the perspective of English proficiency.[29] Two-thirds of the thirty treaties between the native English-speaking countries are unilingual in English. The remaining nine plurilingual without prevailing text are treaties of Canada, which has a strict policy of only concluding treaties with texts in both domestic official languages English and French, none of which is to be designated as prevailing.

The treaties between native English-speaking countries and countries with very good to very low English proficiency show relatively low figures regarding English unilingual treaties and treaties with English prevailing text. Nevertheless, non-English-speaking countries display a limited propensity (close to a quarter on average) to agree to English as diplomatic language when concluding treaties with native English-speaking countries, with the exception of countries with low and very low English proficiency, which fall with roughly 16% short in this respect.

---

[29]Following the classification of the UK government for native English-speaking countries (Antigua and Barbuda, Australia, The Bahamas, Barbados, Belize, Canada, Dominica, Grenada, Guyana, Ireland, Jamaica, New Zealand, St Kitts and Nevis, St Lucia, St Vincent and the Grenadines, Trinidad and Tobago, United Kingdom, United States of America), together with the EF English Proficiency Index (http://www.ef.de/epi) for countries the native tongue of which is not English. The EF EPI indexes only 70 countries, so (together with the 18 native English-speaking countries) the total sample size is with 1,916 treaties much smaller than the global sample. In consequence, the respective statistics and conclusions presented in this section are somewhat less robust.

Table (9.28): *English as Treaty Lingua Franca for Native English-speaking Countries*

Treaties	n-n	n-vg/g	n-m	n-l/vl
No.	30	155	69	108
UL %total	66.67%	16.77%	14.49%	8.33%
eng %UL	100.00%	100.00%	100.00%	100.00%
PL %total	33.33%	83.23%	85.51%	91.67%
PL w PT %PL	0.00%	8.53%	10.17%	8.08%
eng PT %PL w PT	0.00%	100.00%	100.00%	100.00%
eng (UL+PT) %total	66.67%	23.87%	23.19%	15.74%

For the treaty networks of all countries with good and very good English proficiency, most figures concerning treaties between themselves, them and countries with medium English proficiency, and them and countries with low or very low English proficiency are roughly in the same ballpark; however, the first two groups have a much higher propensity to conclude unilingual treaties than the third, whereas the latter two have a much higher propensity to conclude plurilingual treaties with prevailing text. The overall propensity to use English as true diplomatic language and lingua franca is relatively high for all three groups, while lowest for the first group and highest for the group comprising countries with medium English proficiency.

Table (9.29): *English as Treaty Lingua Franca for Countries with Very Good and Good English Proficiency*

Treaties	vg-g	vg/g-m	vg/g-l/vl
No.	203	223	336
UL %total	25.62%	25.56%	13.10%
eng %UL	84.62%	96.49%	75.00%
PL %total	74.38%	74.44%	86.90%
PL w PT %PL	64.24%	78.31%	80.82%
eng PT %PL w PT	97.94%	95.38%	94.49%
eng (UL+PT) %total	68.47%	80.27%	76.19%

For the treaty networks of all countries with medium English proficiency, most figures concerning treaties between themselves, them and countries with very good or good English proficiency, and them and countries with low or very low English proficiency are again roughly in the same ballpark; however, the first and third groups have a much lower propensity to conclude unilingual treaties than the second one, while they have a higher propensity to conclude plurilingual treaties with prevailing text. The overall propensity to use English as true diplomatic language and lingua franca is high. Treaties between countries with medium English proficiency display the comparably highest propensity while treaties with low or very low English proficiency countries display the comparably lowest.

Table (9.30): *English as Treaty Lingua Franca for Countries with Medium English Proficiency*

Treaties	m-m	m-vg/g	m-l/vl
No.	52	223	204
UL %total	15.38%	25.56%	11.76%
eng %UL	87.50%	96.49%	50.00%
PL %total	84.62%	74.44%	88.24%
PL w PT %PL	86.36%	78.31%	83.89%
eng PT %PL w PT	94.74%	95.38%	86.09%
eng (UL+PT) %total	82.69%	80.27%	69.61%

For the treaty networks of all countries with low or very low English proficiency, the figures for treaties between themselves, them and countries with medium English proficiency, and them and countries with very good or good English proficiency deviate the most. Although the first group has a higher propensity to conclude unilingual treaties than the global average of roughly 25%, the propensities of the latter two to do so are significantly lower. Only about 16% of the unilingual treaties concluded by the first group are in English. This number increases to half for the second, and three-quarters for the third group. Overall, the lower propensities to conclude English unilingual treaties are mostly compensated by plurilingual treaties with English prevailing text. Consequently, the overall propensity to use English as lingua franca increases to levels close to the previous groupings, with only the first group falling short at 52.82%.

Table (9.31): English as Treaty Lingua Franca for Countries with Low and Very Low English Proficiency

Treaties	l-vl	l/vl-m	l/vl-vg/g
No.	195	204	336
UL %total	28.72%	11.76%	13.10%
eng %UL	16.07%	50.00%	75.00%
PL %total	71.28%	88.24%	86.90%
PL w PT %PL	71.22%	83.89%	80.82%
eng PT %PL w PT	94.95%	86.09%	94.49%
eng (UL+PT) %total	52.82%	69.61%	76.19%

All in all, the propensity of non-English-speaking countries to use English as lingua franca is fairly high and does not diminish significantly with the level of English proficiency when concluding treaties with each other, apart from treaties between countries that have a low or very low English proficiency, which fall short by almost 20% but still remain over 50%. This may not be surprising because the country level of English proficiency may not be overly representative of the level of English proficiency of the human resources involved in the negotiation, interpretation, and application of tax treaties.

Strikingly, however, the correlation is not linear. The countries with medium levels of English proficiency – not the ones with the highest levels – display the most extensive use of English as lingua franca. The countries with good and very good English proficiency come in second by 10% short, while the countries with low and very low English proficiency come in almost 20% behind countries with good and very good English proficiency and almost 30% behind countries with medium English proficiency. Again, however, this is not true across the board but only concerning the treaties of these countries with each other.

For treaties between countries of low and very low English proficiency with countries with very good, good, and medium English proficiency, these numbers increase by almost 20–25%. Hence, the lower level of using English as lingua franca is not necessarily attributable to a lack of readiness to do so on their part, but rather caused by two factors: the slightly higher levels of plurilingual treaties without prevailing text and the significantly lower number of unilingual treaties in English together with a higher number of unilingual treaties in other languages, that is, rather attributable to a lack of opportunity because their treaty partners prefer not to implement prevailing texts, in addition to a larger opportunity to use languages other than English for unilingual treaties because of other shared native or official languages.

In contrast, the 5–10% higher propensity of countries with good and very good English proficiency to use English as lingua franca when concluding treaties with countries of medium, low, or very low English proficiency compared to treaties with countries of their own group is attributable almost entirely to a lower propensity to conclude treaties with prevailing text because the percentages of unilingual English treaties for treaties between themselves and with countries of medium English proficiency do barely deviate from the global average. Thus, this group contains more countries that have a policy not to implement prevailing texts when concluding plurilingual treaties.

The picture is entirely reversed when native English-speaking countries are involved. Their treaties with all other countries show a low propensity to use English as diplomatic language, which is represented both by less English unilingual treaties and less treaties with prevailing text, that is, this group contains mostly countries that have a strong policy not to implement prevailing texts. In addition, the low figures may contain an element of reluctance on the part of other countries to grant linguistic advantages to native English-speaking countries, which is highest for countries with low and very low English proficiency.

9.5. Per Country Analysis

Analogous to the previous chapter, this section performs a per country analysis of the use of English as lingua franca and (true) diplomatic language. The sub-group of G1 countries that do not have English as official language shows a high acceptance of English as lingua franca in general. Noteworthy, several of them have a large number of English unilingual treaties, for example, all the Nordic countries, Belgium, the Czech Republic, Japan, and the Netherlands, together with a few others with slightly smaller but still sizeable amounts relative to the total number of their treaties. These countries have a stronger than average acceptance of English as true diplomatic language.[30] Despite having a policy to conclude unilingual treaties in English as codified in its Model Convention, Belgium ranges in the midfield concerning its overall score. This is attributable to a relatively large number of treaties without prevailing text or with a French prevailing text.

France and Luxembourg virtually do not accept English as lingua franca for tax treaties. In the case of France this may be rooted in the historical context of French having played a dominant role as (true) diplomatic language from the times of Louis XIV until the beginning of the 20th century, whereas for Luxembourg the reasons may lie in the domestic linguistic context of having three official languages: French, German, and Luxembourgish. Noteworthy, Luxembourg has a handful of unilingual treaties in English.[31] The newer ones with the English-speaking Channel Islands and the Czech Republic (showing itself a strong propensity in favour of using English as true diplomatic language and lingua franca) are fairly recent. It remains to be seen whether they mark a change in Luxembourg's policy for the future. For the older ones, the motivation may have been rather to avoid the impasse of being faced with equally authentic texts in from a European perspective arcane languages, together with respective policy preferences of the treaty partners.

Table (9.32): English as Treaty Lingua Franca G1 NEOL

Country	eng (UL+PT) %total	treaties	eng UL
Indonesia	94.20%	69	25
Estonia	91.67%	60	11
Thailand	90.91%	66	25
Korea (Rep.)	87.78%	90	15
Japan	86.76%	68	30
Slovenia	86.67%	60	4
Croatia	85.71%	63	6

---

[30]Nevertheless, the Nordic Convention between the Scandinavian countries has Danish, Faroese, Finnish, Icelandic, Norwegian, and Swedish texts, all being equally authoritative, see Denmark, Faroe Islands, Finland, Iceland, Norway, Sweden, *Income and Capital Tax Treaty* (Amsterdam: IBFD, 1996).

[31]Czech Republic (2013), Guernsey (2013), Isle of Man (2013), Japan (1992), Jersey (2013), Korea (Rep.) (1984), Singapore (2013), Taiwan (2011), and Turkey (2003).

Country	eng (UL+PT) %total	treaties	eng UL
Cyprus	84.38%	64	24
Czech Republic	83.52%	91	32
Turkey	83.13%	83	18
Finland	82.50%	80	35
Vietnam	81.94%	72	7
Hungary	80.49%	82	24
Sweden	79.35%	92	49
Denmark	79.01%	81	39
United Arab Emirates	78.75%	80	6
Norway	78.72%	94	46
Bulgaria	77.46%	71	8
Kuwait	77.14%	70	1
Netherlands	76.77%	99	29
Romania	76.67%	90	5
China	74.07%	108	0
Slovak Republic	73.91%	69	9
Egypt	71.21%	66	13
Belarus	69.57%	69	3
Ukraine	68.49%	73	0
Belgium	64.71%	102	37
Portugal	64.10%	78	1
Poland	63.64%	88	6
Russia	62.64%	91	0
Austria	62.37%	93	12
Qatar	62.16%	74	1
Italy	50.46%	109	4
Switzerland	49.58%	119	2
Spain	38.38%	99	0
Germany	37.04%	108	0
Morocco	35.82%	67	0
Luxembourg	21.18%	85	10
France	0.00%	139	0

In the case of Morocco, the low percentage is an outcome of the large proportions of treaties with a French prevailing text and unilingual treaties in Arabic. Nevertheless, Morocco still has a sizeable number of treaties with English prevailing texts. Thus, generally speaking, Morocco seems to be open to use English, French, or Arabic depending on the preferences of its treaty partners.

The situation is somewhat similar for Germany. Given the larger number of plurilingual treaties without prevailing text, the overall propensity to use English is only at roughly 37%. Nevertheless, Germany seems to be fairly happy to accept English as lingua franca for tax treaties, while not being a driving force in this respect.[32] Noteworthy, Germany has four treaties with a prevailing text in Russian;[33] hence, given that the treaty partners in all these cases are themselves fairly happy to use English for prevailing texts, Germany seems to be open to accommodate its treaty partners in terms of their native tongue or official language as a bargaining strategy.[34]

Spain also appears open to use English as lingua franca depending on the treaty parter, while the relatively low score overall is attributable to the larger amount of plurilingual treaties without prevailing text plus the sizeable amount of Spanish unilingual treaties with LA countries.

All prevailing texts of Switzerland's treaties are in English; however, out of the one hundred and five plurilingual treaties in total, only roughly half have a prevailing text to begin with. Therefore, the overall propensity to use English as lingua franca for tax treaties remains with 49.58% comparably low versus the global average because Switzerland's unilingual treaties are distributed over English, French, German, and Italian, the latter three being official languages domestically. On the whole, it seems that Switzerland, too, is willing to use English as lingua franca for tax treaties, depending on the preferences of its treaty partners.

The same goes for Italy, but with the peculiarity that it seems to have retained a certain willingness to use French as lingua franca at least up to the 1990s, embodied in 13 treaties with a French prevailing text and one French unilingual treaty.[35]

---

[32]However, the final clause of the German Model published for the first time in 2013 implements an English prevailing text (see next section), so it seems that German treaty policy has shifted if it ever was different.

[33]Uzbekistan (1999), Azerbaijan (2004), Kyrgyzstan (2005), and Georgia (2006). It has to be noted in this context that, for historical reasons, Germany disposes of a sizeable amount of human resources proficient in Russian.

[34]Germany also has two treaties with a French prevailing text, namely, Iran (1968) and Algeria (2007).

[35]Greece (1964 – unilingual), Morocco (1972), Spain (1977), Hungary (1977), Tunisia (1979), Argentina (1979), Sweden (1980), Portugal (1980), Slovak Republic (1981), Czech Repub-

When we look at the numbers for all G1 countries with English as official language, we see again that Canada has a strict policy not to use English as lingua franca – a policy rooted in its domestic law.[36] For the other countries in this sub-group, the use of English exhausts itself largely in unilingual treaties with fellow English-speaking countries, with the exception of India and Malaysia, which both display a strong policy to use English as lingua franca for tax treaties.

Table (9.33): English as Treaty Lingua Franca G1 EOL

Country	eng (UL+PT) %total	treaties	eng UL
India	97.00%	100	4
Malaysia	86.75%	83	7
Singapore	69.32%	88	37
Pakistan	68.75%	64	28
Malta	56.76%	74	24
South Africa	53.49%	86	36
Ireland	46.15%	78	25
United Kingdom	38.64%	132	43
United States	31.17%	77	23
Canada	0.00%	97	0

Overall, the sub-group of G2 countries not having English as official language shows a high propensity to use English as lingua franca. Mexico, Jordan, Brazil, Chile, Turkmenistan, and Lebanon make up the midfield open to use English depending on the treaty parter. Only Tunisia and Algeria show little propensity to accept English. Noteworthy, only few countries have significant amounts of English unilingual treaties.

---

lic (1981), Bulgaria (1988), Netherlands (1990), Venezuela (1990), Mozambique (1998).
[36]See Gamble and Ku, 'Choice of Language in Bilateral Treaties', 249–53; Sasseville, 'The Canadian Experience', 36.

Table (9.34): English as Treaty Lingua Franca G2 NEOL

Country	eng (UL+PT) %total	treaties	eng UL
Latvia	93.22%	59	8
Bosnia and Herzegovina	92.11%	38	13
Serbia and Montenegro	92.11%	38	8
Iran	92.00%	50	1
Macedonia (FYR)	88.46%	52	2
Albania	88.37%	43	9
Greece	87.93%	58	14
Israel	87.72%	57	9
Lithuania	85.19%	54	0
Bahrain	80.95%	42	0
Iceland	80.85%	47	14
Georgia	78.18%	55	2
Armenia	76.09%	46	0
Azerbaijan	75.00%	48	1
Kazakhstan	72.09%	43	2
Uzbekistan	71.70%	53	1
Saudi Arabia	71.05%	38	0
Mauritius	67.31%	52	27
Moldova	65.96%	47	0
Syria	65.63%	32	3
Oman	63.89%	36	0
Venezuela	58.82%	34	0
Tajikistan	58.06%	31	2
Mexico	55.17%	58	0
Jordan	54.55%	33	0
Brazil	51.52%	33	0
Chile	51.52%	33	1
Turkmenistan	47.50%	40	0
Lebanon	45.45%	33	5
Algeria	17.14%	35	0
Tunisia	16.36%	55	0

Use of English for G2 countries with English as official language largely follows their preference for and against prevailing texts. While Bangladesh, Sri Lanka, and Hong Kong show a high propensity to use English as diplomatic language, the numbers for New Zealand, Philippines, Barbados, and Australia are lower but still around 50-65% because of the high number of English unilingual treaties.

Table (9.35): English as Treaty Lingua Franca G2 EOL

Country	eng (UL+PT) %total	treaties	eng UL
Bangladesh	93.75%	32	17
Sri Lanka	87.23%	47	0
Hong Kong	80.00%	35	16
New Zealand	65.31%	49	26
Philippines	62.79%	43	20
Barbados	50.00%	32	12
Australia	47.27%	55	24

For both G3 sub-groups, one has to be careful with conclusions because of the small sample sizes. Concerning the sub-group of countries not having English as official language, the majority shows a high propensity to use English as lingua franca. Libya and Argentina may be categorised as belonging to the indifferent group, whereas Ecuador and in particular Senegal are the only countries showing reluctance to use English.

Table (9.36): English as Treaty Lingua Franca G3 NEOL

Country	eng (UL+PT) %total	treaties	eng UL
Mongolia	89.29%	28	5
San Marino	85.71%	21	4
Serbia	80.77%	26	3
Panama	68.75%	16	0
Uruguay	65.00%	20	0
Kyrgyzstan	64.00%	25	0
Liechtenstein	57.89%	19	3
Libya	50.00%	16	0
Argentina	40.00%	20	0
Ecuador	18.75%	16	0
Senegal	0.00%	17	0

Regarding the G3 sub-group of countries with English as official language, the generally high percentages seem to be based mostly in a larger number of English unilingual treaties with fellow English-speaking countries. Sudan and Zimbabwe seem to be in the indifferent category. Trinidad and Tobago and Guernsey are the only countries showing reluctance to use English as diplomatic language. Alternatively, the numbers may be attributable to their treaty partners not being prepared to concede a linguistic advantage; however, the sample sizes may be too small for robust conclusions.

Table (9.37): English as Treaty Lingua Franca G3 EOL

Country	eng (UL+PT) %total	treaties	eng UL
Isle of Man	86.36%	22	17
Seychelles	86.21%	29	17
Nigeria	81.25%	16	10
Jersey	80.00%	25	18
Botswana	75.00%	16	11
Kenya	75.00%	16	10
Ethiopia	70.00%	20	8
Zambia	62.96%	27	16
Sudan	55.56%	18	5
Zimbabwe	52.63%	19	8
Trinidad and Tobago	37.50%	16	5
Guernsey	4.55%	22	0

If we look at all countries with twenty or more unilingual treaties not having English as official language, we see that most of them have a high acceptance of English as true diplomatic language. Only France and Tunisia do not accept English at all. Lebanon and Egypt accept English, but most of their unilingual treaties are in Arabic and French. Almost all the others display an implementation rate of English as true diplomatic language above 90% up to 100%. Only Norway falls slightly below 90%.

Table (9.38): English as Treaty True Diplomatic Language for Countries with Twenty or More Unilingual Treaties

Country	UL	eng %UL
Finland	35	100.00%
Indonesia	25	100.00%
Japan	30	100.00%
Thailand	25	100.00%
Denmark	40	97.50%

Country	UL	eng %UL
Belgium	38	97.37%
Czech Republic	33	96.97%
Netherlands	30	96.67%
Cyprus	25	96.00%
Hungary	25	96.00%
Sweden	54	90.74%
Mauritius	30	90.00%
Norway	52	88.46%
Egypt	29	44.83%
Lebanon	21	23.81%
France	34	0.00%
Tunisia	24	0.00%

For countries with ten or more but fewer than twenty unilingual treaties, the picture is more varied. Bosnia and Herzegovina, Estonia, Iceland, Turkey, Korea (Rep.), the Slovak Republic, and Greece range at the top with more than 80% up to 100% English unilingual treaties. Algeria, Jordan, Mexico, Morocco, and Spain have none at all. Syria, Yemen, and Switzerland accept English at least to some extent, while Austria, Luxembourg, and the UAE range the midfield.

Table (9.39): *English as Treaty True Diplomatic Language for Countries with Ten or More but Fewer than Twenty Unilingual Treaties*

Country	UL	eng %UL
Bosnia and Herzegovina	13	100.00%
Estonia	11	100.00%
Iceland	14	100.00%
Turkey	18	100.00%
Korea (Rep.)	16	93.75%
Slovak Republic	10	90.00%
Greece	17	82.35%
Austria	18	66.67%
Luxembourg	17	58.82%
United Arab Emirates	15	40.00%
Syria	13	23.08%
Yemen	12	16.67%
Switzerland	14	14.29%

Country	UL	eng %UL
Algeria	13	0.00%
Jordan	11	0.00%
Mexico	10	0.00%
Morocco	16	0.00%
Spain	16	0.00%

Finally, most of the countries that do not have a single English unilingual treaty or prevailing text in their treaty network have merely one or two treaties. Only France and Canada have larger treaty networks. Senegal, Ivory Coast, and Gabon are the only three other countries with more than five treaties. If we subtract France and Canada, the sum of all treaties of the remaining countries amounts to less than 3% of the global tax treaty network.

Table (9.40): Countries with Zero English Unilingual Treaties and Prevailing Texts

Country	treaties
France	139
Canada	97
Senegal	17
Ivory Coast	10
Gabon	9
Cameroon	5
Congo (Rep.)	4
Guinea	4
Mali	4
Burkina Faso	3
Congo (Dem. Rep.)	3
Belize	2
Benin	2
Cape Verde	2
Dominican Republic	2
Grenada	2
Guinea-Bissau	2
Sao Tome and Principe	2
Togo	2
Anguilla	1
Antigua and Barbuda	1

Country	treaties
Central African Republic	1
Dominica	1
El Salvador	1
Guatemala	1
Liberia	1
Madagascar	1
Mauritania	1
Mayotte	1
Montserrat	1
New Caledonia	1
Niger	1
Quebec	1
Sierra Leone	1
St. Lucia	1
St. Martin	1
St. Pierre and Miquelon	1
St. Vincent and the Grenadines	1
Timor-Leste	1

9.6. Model Convention Final Clauses

Model Conventions provide additional insight into the policies of (groups of) countries. Although the work of the OECD is done mainly in English,[37] the Model itself contains no final provision implementing a policy in this respect: both the English and French versions of the Model and Commentary are equally official. The same is true for the OECD Estate and Inheritance Tax Model Convention.[38] Hence, regarding tax treaties, the OECD makes no policy suggestion with respect to linguistic form but leaves the matter to the contracting states.[39] The recent Exchange of Information Convention Model, however, features the following final clause:

---

[37] Sasseville, 'The OECD Model Convention and Commentaries', 130.

[38] OECD, 'Recommendation of the Council Concerning the Avoidance of Double Taxation with Respect to Taxes on Estates and Inheritances and on Gifts' (Paris: OECD Publishing, June 1982).

[39] The new multilateral instrument resulting from the BEPS project contains a final clause declaring its English and French texts as equally authentic without declaring one as prevailing, see OECD, *Multilateral Convention to Implement Tax Treaty Related Meas-*

Signed in duplicate in (…..) on (…..).[40]

This seems to suggest a policy of unilingual form to the extent exchange of information treaties are concerned. The placeholder does not necessarily have to represent a single language but could be intended equally for any number of languages to be inserted; however, the fact that the clause contains no language concerning authenticity rather points to the conclusion that it is indeed intended to implement a unilingual treaty – otherwise it would represent an odd implementation of a historical form of final clause not explicitly stipulating the authenticity of texts, which hardly exists any more in actual treaties in force. To find out whether countries use this final clause in practice would necessitate an investigation of all exchange of information treaties, which has been excluded from the scope of this study.

Like the OECD Model, the UN Model contains no final clause suggesting any policy concerning lingual form; however, in a recent publication concerning the negotiation of tax treaties, a paragraph has been included that may be read as a recommendation:

> A treaty may be negotiated in the English language even if the two countries are non-English-speaking countries. To avoid a problem with translation errors, they may agree to have the treaty signed in the English language only and have two unofficial translations. Alternatively, they may agree to have three official languages where the English language shall prevail in case of differences of interpretation.[41]

The Andean[42] Model contains a final clause implementing plurilingual form without prevailing text:

> In witness whereof, the respective plenipotentiaries sign and stamp this agreement. Signed in (…..) on the (…..) of (…..) in (…..) copies (…..) in the

---

ures to Prevent Base Erosion and Profit Shifting (Paris: OECD Publishing, 2016), Article 39. This policy and its consequences are discussed separately in the Annex.

[40] OECD, *Standard for Automatic Exchange of Financial Account Information in Tax Matters, Model Competent Authority Agreement* (Paris: OECD Publishing, 2014).

[41] UN, *Papers on Selected Topics in Negotiation of Tax Treaties for Developing Countries* (New York: United Nations, 2014), 130.

[42] The current members of the Andean Community are Bolivia, Colombia, Ecuador, and Peru. Argentina, Brazil, Paraguay, and Uruguay are associate members.

(.....) language and (.....) copies in the (.....) language, the (.....) and (.....) copies being equally authentic.[43]

The SADC[44] Model features a final clause implementing unilingual form:

DONE at (.....) in duplicate, this (.....) day of (.....) 20(..).[45]

Although no specific language is specified in the Model, the observations made above point to the conclusion that mainly English would be implied, while French or Portuguese would be used alternatively when shared by the contracting states as common official language. Given that the wording contains no explicit formulation concerning authenticity, it is flexible enough to cover plurilingual form without prevailing text just by the mere fact that the signed texts could be in different languages; however, that would amount to implementing a type of final clause hardly in use any more. Moreover, Article 5 of the Memorandum of Understanding on Co-operation in Taxation and Related Matters of SADC regulates that 'Member States will develop a common policy for the negotiation of tax treaties between or amongst themselves or with countries outside the Community.'[46] One may infer that unilingual form has been intended and implemented in the Model as common policy.

The ASEAN[47] Model features a final clause implementing plurilingual form modelled on TOW6, explicitly implementing English as prevailing text language:

---

[43] Andean Community, *Standard Agreement to Avoid Double Taxation Between Member Countries and States Outside the Subregion* (Lima: Andean Community General Secretariat, 1971), official English translation provided by the Andean Community General Secretariat.

[44] Current members of the SADC are Angola, Botswana, Democratic Republic of Congo, Lesotho, Madagascar, Malawi, Mauritius, Mozambique, Namibia, Seychelles, South Africa, Swaziland, United Republic of Tanzania, Zambia, and Zimbabwe.

[45] Southern African Development Community, *Agreement for the Avoidance of Double Taxation and the Prevention of Fiscal Evasion with Respect to Taxes on Income* (Gaborone: SADC Secretariat, 2013).

[46] Southern African Development Community, *Memorandum of Understanding on Co-Operation in Taxation and Related Matters* (Gaborone: SADC Secretariat, 2002), para. 1.

[47] Members of the ASEAN signatory to the Model are Brunei, Cambodia, Indonesia, Laos, Malaysia, Myanmar (Birma), Philippines, Singapore, Thailand, and Vietnam.

> Done in duplicate at (.....) this (.....) day of (.....) One thousand nine hundred and ninety (.....), each in (.....) and the English language, both texts being equally authoritative, except in the case of doubt when the English text shall prevail.[48]

Although the curious TOW6 does not necessarily reflect the dominant policy of the ASEAN countries concerning final clauses in their bilateral tax treaties, the opposite is true for the explicit stipulation of English as prevailing text language. This may be seen as evidence for TOW6 generally being regarded as equivalent to TOW3 and TOW2.

A few countries have issued Model Tax Conventions of their own, the most prominent being the US Model. All incarnations of the Model to date (1981, 1996, 2006, and 2016) feature the same final clause implementing plurilingual form without prevailing text:

> Done at (.....) in duplicate, in the English and (.....) languages, the two texts having equal authenticity, this (.....) day of (.....).

The same is true for the US inheritance and gift tax and FATCA Models.[49] Hence it is safe to say that the US has a strong policy in favour of concluding treaties without prevailing text. Noteworthy, however, it has one treaty with an English prevailing text, namely, with India (1989). At the same time, it has twenty-three English unilingual treaties, some of which with countries not having English as official language: Egypt (1980), Cyprus (1984), Netherlands Antilles (1986), Aruba (1986), Indonesia (1988), Sweden (1994), Thailand (1996), Denmark (1999), and Belgium (2006). Some of those countries have close historical ties to English while others have a policy of using English as true diplomatic language, for example, the Nordic ones and Belgium.

The Netherlands, Germany, Russia, and Belgium also have their own Models. The Dutch and German ones feature TOW4 final clauses explicitly implementing English as language of the prevailing text:

---

[48] Association of Southeast Asian Nations, *Intra-Asean Model Double Taxation Convention* (Jakarta: The ASEAN Secretariat, 1987).

[49] United States, *Estates, Inheritances, Gifts, and Generation-Skipping Transfers Model Convention*, 1980; United States, *Model Intergovernmental Agreement to Improve Tax Compliance and to Implement FATCA*, 2012.

GEDAAN in tweevoud te (.....) de (.....) in de Nederlandse, de (.....) en de Engelse taal, zijnde de drie teksten gelijkelijk authentiek. In geval de Nederlandse en de (.....) tekst verschillend kunnen worden uitgelegd, is de Engelse tekst beslissend.[50]

Done at [place] on [date], in duplicate, in the German, [foreign language] and [English] languages, each text being authentic. In case of divergent interpretations of the German and [foreign language] texts, the English text shall prevail.[51]

Thus, for both countries having an English prevailing text is official policy. Whereas Germany is not a driving force in this respect to date, the case is different for the Netherlands with almost 70% of its treaties being plurilingual, roughly 72% of which implement prevailing texts, 94% of which in turn are in English. Noteworthy about the German text are the square brackets around 'English', indicating a placeholder as for 'place', 'date', and 'foreign language'. Consequently, the policy of Germany seems to be to implement a prevailing text preferably in English, but other prevailing language preferences of treaty partners may be accommodated.

The final clause of the Russian Model employs a TOW3 clause with English designated as language of the prevailing text. It translates to:[52]

Executed in the city of (.....) on (.....) in two originals, each one in the Russian, (.....) and English languages, all texts having equal force. In case of any discrepancies in interpretation the English text will be used.[53]

Finally, Belgium implements English as true diplomatic language in its Model Convention final clause:

SIGNED in duplicate at (.....), this (.....), in the English language.[54]

---

[50]De Regering van het Koninkrijk der Nederlanden, *Dutch Model.*

[51]BMF, *German Model* (the BMF has published an English text alongside the German), square brackets in the original.

[52]Translation with the kind help of Ksenia Levushkina.

[53]Russia, *Income and Capital Model Convention* (Amsterdam: IBFD, 2010).

[54]The Kingdom of Belgium, *Belgian Model.* The 2010 update features the same wording.

9.7. Summary Observations

The preceding analysis has shown that, since the 1990s, the paradigm of linguistic nationalism has been largely transcended and replaced by a new paradigm of English as predominant lingua franca for tax treaties: two-thirds of today's global tax treaty network are made up of treaties unilingual in English or with an English prevailing text. Paradoxically, aside France, mainly the major English-speaking countries have resisted this trend. Concluding plurilingual treaties without English prevailing text is a political anachronism that should be overcome to cut its economic cost and increase consistency of treaty interpretation. The politics involved may require a multilateral approach to close the residual gap. The best forum to tackle the problem would be the OECD because mostly OECD members have failed to catch up with the global developments while they are already engaged there in a project to increase consistency of treaty interpretation in form of the OECD Model Convention and Commentary.

10. Conclusions

10.1. Synopsis

This chapter aggregates the conclusions of the previous chapters and discusses them from a macro perspective. In addition, it assumes the perspective of a technical strategy paper and, on the basis of all findings, issues policy recommendations how to best close the residual gap and eliminate remaining additional interpretational complexity induced by plurilingual form, together with its associated economic cost.

10.1.1. Theoretical Analysis

The fundamental propositions on which the VCLT principles concerning the interpretation of plurilingual treaties are based, that is, p and q, can in the absence of a prevailing text only be reconciled with each other if (1) the texts are de facto identical, that is, q does not hold, or (2) divergences between the texts can be reconciled by way of interpretation, that is, q is proven to be immaterial.

The thought experiment based on the *Natexis* case has shown that r_2 holds for tax treaties. Hence, all texts must be compared for purposes of interpreting the treaty in good faith, as the presumption contained in Article 33(3) must be considered rebutted until proven otherwise; courts may not rely in good faith on a single text of a tax treaty in the absence of a prevailing one but are required to compare all texts to correctly apply the VLCT rules.

The routine interpretation approach is a *petitio principii* and therefore invalid. Its fundamental proposition implies its requirement c_2 to be fulfilled, whereas establishment of c_2 abandons reliance on a single text by definition. Consequently, the fundamental proposition of the routine interpretation approach in its stronger form is disproven by means of a *reductio ad absurdum*. In addition, it has been shown that assuming c_2 to be fulfilled is not sound for tax treaties, but the set of cases for which the routine interpretation approach may be considered applicable because c_2 would be safe to assume is an empty set, that is, the routine interpretation approach in its weaker form must be considered unsound. When c_2 cannot be safely assumed, c_1 by itself fails to be sufficient to justify reliance on a single text that is not designated as prevailing. Consequently, the routine interpretation approach does not apply to plurilingual tax treaties without prevailing text.

Tax treaties may not be special in this regard, but the conclusion may be reformulated as a general principle: *If the object and purpose of a treaty covers conflicting interpretations, then clarity of a single text considered in isolation does not satisfy the VCLT principles of interpretation and the set of cases to which the routine interpretation approach may be applied in good faith is an empty set.* The thought experiment on which the proof of this point is essentially based has been conducted only in the context of tax treaties in line with the scope of this study. Therefore, this conclusion must be restricted to tax treaties as a matter of scientific rigour. To the extent no similar thought experiments are conducted or actual cases are observed for other types of treaties to test its applicability, the principle remains a hypothesis in their context.

Notwithstanding, it seems more likely than not that the principle applies to all plurilingual treaties because differences in scope and procedure may not necessarily affect the object and purpose as we have seen in the *Kiliç* case. A current example may be CETA in terms of the text 'made public exclusively for information purposes', which 'is not binding under international law and will only become so after the entry into force of the Agreement'.[1] CETA has equally authoritative texts in the Bulgarian, Croatian, Czech, Danish, Dutch, English, Estonian, Finnish, French, German, Greek, Hungarian, Italian, Latvian, Lithuanian, Maltese, Polish, Portuguese, Romanian, Slovak, Slovenian, Spanish, and Swedish languages.[2] The English and German texts diverge with respect to the members of the CETA court:

---

[1] European Commission, 'Comprehensive Economic and Trade Agreement (CETA) between Canada, of the One Part, and the European Union, of the Other Part (Non-Binding Text Made Public Exclusively for Information Purposes)' (European Commission, 2016).

[2] Ibid., Article 30.11.

the English text of Article 8.27(4) reads 'The Members of the Tribunal shall possess the qualifications required in their respective countries for appointment to judicial office, or be jurists of recognised competence', whereas the German text employs the wording 'jurists of recognised *excellent* competence',[3] which implies a stricter selection process.[4]

Given all the additional language texts, there should be no problem to come to a conclusive interpretation that reconciles the divergence; however, if only the English and German texts existed, we would face a problem if they were the final texts in force, because the more narrow set of jurists of 'recognised excellent competence' and the wider set of jurists of mere 'recognised competence' are mutually exclusive for jurists that are of mere recognised but not recognised excellent competence. This difference hardly affects the object and purpose of free trade and having an international tribunal instead of national ones presiding. If there are no further clues in the text itself, neither Article 31 nor 33(4) should be of much help to reconcile the divergence.

The German newspaper *Süddeutsche Zeitung* has asked the European Commission as responsible organ about the reason for the divergence,[5] and it appears the Commission has recycled formulations of the Treaty of Lisbon that display the same divergence between the English and German texts.[6] Generally speaking, it seems sensible to economise and reuse well-established formulations; however, one has to pay attention to the context, which is not necessarily transplanted at the same time. The requirements for the appointment of ECJ judges are much stricter, which is obvious also from the text of Article 253 itself:

---

[3]Europäische Kommission, 'Vorschlag für einen Beschluss des Rates über die Unterzeichnung im Namen der Europäischen Union des umfassenden Wirtschafts- und Handelsabkommens zwischen Kanada einerseits und der Europäischen Union und ihren Mitgliedstaaten andererseits' (Germany: Bundesministerium für Wirtschaft und Energie, 2016), Article 8.27(4) (emphasis added).

[4]Trade agreement expert Manfred Spengler, as quoted in Silvia Liebrich, 'Im Ceta-Vertrag stecken kuriose Wortspiele', *Süddeutsche Zeitung*, 6 October 2016.

[5]Ibid.

[6]European Union, 'Consolidated Versions of the Treaty on European Union and the Treaty on the Functioning of the European Union', *Official Journal of the European Union* 51, no. C 115 (May 2008), Article 253.

> The Judges and Advocates-General of the Court of Justice shall be chosen from persons whose independence is beyond doubt and who possess the qualifications required for appointment to the highest judicial offices in their respective countries or who are jurisconsults of recognised competence; they shall be appointed by common accord of the governments of the Member States for a term of six years, after consultation of the panel provided for in Article 255.[7]

The initial part of the sentence makes clear that appointment to the ECJ requires exceptional qualifications fit for 'highest judicial offices'. The same does not apply to the CETA formulation, which only requires 'qualifications ...for appointment to judicial office'. Also the procedure concerning appointment is much stricter: whereas ECJ judges are appointed 'by common accord of the governments of the Member States', the CETA court judges are appointed by the CETA Joint Committee.[8] It seems reasonable to conclude that in the case of the Treaty of Lisbon the formulation of 'recognised competence' would default to the meaning implied by the German text under a reconciliatory comparative interpretation of both, whereas the opposite would be true for CETA.

As the case may be, for tax treaties the above defined general principle may be violated in a wide variety of ways by the routine interpretation approach, not only in terms of liable versus subject to tax, but also for all issues of personal and material scope that may affect the reciprocal sharing of taxing rights between the contracting states in ways not intended but undetected because the court fails to look into the other text(s) and realise the false meaning projected by the seemingly clear text looked at, mistakenly taking clarity of one text for clarity of the treaty meaning.

For other types of treaties, the problem is of somewhat less significance. Treaty interpretation developed in the field of international law with states arguing in front of an international court. One may assume that in such context the court is naturally informed about any language differences between the treaty texts. Tax treaty interpretation is different in that it typically involves an argument between one of the states which is party to the treaty and one of the contracting states' taxpayers. Consequently, the other language version is not necessarily argued.

---

[7]Ibid., Article 253. The German text, again, reads 'recognised excellent competence'.
[8]European Commission, 'CETA', Article 8.27(2) in combination with Article 26.1.

Although it is a particular anatomic feature of the institutional architecture of international tax law that national courts preside over the application of tax treaties, those courts have to apply international law as if they were a proxy for an international court, that is, to the extent the issues at stake are governed by international law, their guiding line has to be a consideration of the correct principles of interpretation to be applied by an international tax court, assuming such existed.[9] *Fothergill* states in this respect per Lord Diplock:

> By ratifying that convention, Her Majesty's government has undertaken an international obligation on behalf of the United Kingdom to interpret future

---

[9]See, by analogy, *Penhallow et al. v Doane's Administrators*, 3 U.S. 54 (1795) (Dallas's Reports), 36: 'A prize court is, in effect, a court of all the nations of the world, because all persons in every part of the world are concluded by its sentences, in cases clearly coming within its jurisdiction' (a prize court is a 'municipal (national) court in which the legality of captures of goods and vessels at sea and related questions are determined', Encyclopedia Britannica, 'Prize Court'; see also Manley O. Hudson, *The Permanent Court of International Justice 1920–1942* (New York: The Macmillan Company, 1943), 71–79); *Rose v Himeley*, 8 U.S. 241 (1808), 277, concerning the 'principle that the law of nations is the law of all tribunals in the society of nations, and is supposed to be equally understood by all'; *TWA v Franklin Mint Corp.*, 466 U.S. 243 (1984), 262–263, Justice Stevens (dissenting): 'The great object of an international agreement is to define the common ground between sovereign nations. Given the gulfs of language, culture, and values that separate nations, it is essential in international agreements for the parties to make explicit their common ground on the most rudimentary of matters. The frame of reference in interpreting treaties is naturally international, and not domestic. Accordingly, the language of the law of nations is always to be consulted in the interpretation of treaties. …Constructions of treaties yielding parochial variations in their implementation are anathema to the *raison d'etre* of treaties, and hence to the rules of construction applicable to them'; *Buchanan (James) & Co. Ltd. v Babco Forwarding and Shipping (UK) Ltd*, 152, per Lord Wilberforce, concerning interpretation of a treaty 'unconstrained by technical rules of English law, or by English legal precedent, but on broad principles of general acceptation'; *Memec Plc v Inland Revenue Comissioners*, [1996] STC 1336, 1349, per Robert Walker J., in terms of treaties to be construed in an 'international, not exclusively English' way; *R v Secretary for the Home Department, Ex Parte Adan*, [2001] AC 477, 515–517, per Lord Steyn: 'In principle therefore there can only be one true interpretation of a treaty. …In practice it is left to national courts, faced with a material disagreement on an issue of interpretation, to resolve it. But in doing so it must search, untrammelled by notions of its national legal culture, for the true autonomous and international meaning of the treaty. And there can only be one true meaning.'

treaties in this manner and, since under our constitution the function of interpreting the written law is an exercise of judicial power and rests with the courts of justice, that obligation assumed by the United Kingdom falls to be performed by those courts.[10]

The common law judge may be trying to come to the same answer as an international court, but if in doing so he obstinately adheres to the domestic litigation traditions in terms of relying on one text alone when the parties do not raise a divergence, he will not be able to come to that answer and, in consequence, violate Articles 26 and 27 VCLT. Domestic procedural rules do not have to be abandoned, but they have to be transcended to ensure proper observance of obligations under international law, because with respect to tax treaties it is not the law as argued by the parties to the dispute that is at stake, but the terms of the deal struck between the contracting states.[11] In practice, such may only be achieved in common law countries via an extension of the duties of parties to put all texts before the judge.

The routine interpretation approach has frequently claimed heritage of Waldock's arguments. It is true that Waldock may be interpreted to have argued its case; however, he may also be understood to have been primarily concerned with how a comparison is to be conducted, that is, the point in

---

[10] *Fothergill v Monarch Airlines Ltd.*, 283. As Waibel notes, although the VCLT is not incorporated into UK domestic law, 'there is widespread agreement about the customary character of the VCLT interpretative principles' and English courts 'refer to the VCLT with some regularity, and when they do so seem to apply the VCLT as international law', Waibel, 'Principles of Treaty Interpretation', 20–21.

[11] Noteworthy, the principle of *iura novit curia* has been recognised and applied by international courts such as the PCIJ, the ICJ, the Inter-American Court of Human Rights, the ECHR, and the WTO adjudicating bodies, see Matthias Oesch, *Standards of Review in WTO Dispute Resolution* (Oxford; New York: Oxford University Press, 2003), 50 et seq.; Federico Ortino, *The WTO Dispute Settlement System, 1995–2003* (The Hague: Kluwer Law International, 2004), 167 et seq.; Jo M. Pasqualucci, *The Practice and Procedure of the Inter-American Court of Human Rights* (Cambridge; New York: Cambridge University Press, 2003), 154 et seq.; *Nicaragua v United States of America – Military and Paramilitary Activities in and Against Nicaragua*, 14 and 29; *Fisheries Jurisdiction (United Kingdom v Iceland)*, ICJ (Annual Reports of the International Court of Justice, 1974), 9, para. 17; *Hilaire, Constantine and Benjamin et al. v Trinidad and Tobago*, Inter-American Court of Human Rights, 2002, para. 107. Thus, it may be regarded as a principle to be applied in proceedings concerned with issues of international law.

time *when* to best compare the texts, and not with denying the need for a comparison in general.[12]

When not understood in the sense of excluding a comparison altogether, the idea to first contemplate every text on its own merit in order to avoid additional confusion may to some extent be sensible because the judge cannot consider everything all at once but has to work his way forward through the materials. Because of the remaining indeterminacy of a single text interpreted in isolation, the question is then not whether but at what point

---

[12]If he were to be understood otherwise, his overall position would have to be qualified as inconsistent. As pointed out by him in the ILC's 874th meeting, the defects of the initially drafted text may be the source of the problem rather than the solution, so any notion that the initially drafted text should necessarily prevail must be rejected, see ILC, *Summary Records of the Eighteenth Session, 4 May – 19 July 1966*, I, Part II:210–11, para. 33. This contradicts interpretation of his conceptual argument against adding a comparison among the principal means of interpretation along the lines of the routine interpretation approach, which presupposes an ultimate security of the individual texts when interpreted in isolation. Here Waldock concedes that the contrary is true: there is no ultimate security based on any individual text if the result is not confirmed by the others, even when the text considered is the original one. Hence, his argument against a comparison in order not to undermine the 'security of the individual texts' by transplanting 'concepts of one language into the interpretation of a text in another language', ILC, *Documents of the Second Part of the Seventeenth Session and of the Eighteenth Session Including the Reports of the Commission to the General Assembly*, 100, para. 23, may be understood only as implying a provisional procedural measure intended to safeguard interpretation of each text according to its own idiomatic construction, while the outcomes remain subject to verification under a consecutive comparison. Otherwise he would have to be considered to contradict himself. As construed by the proponents of the routine interpretation approach, his argument would not be very convincing in the first place because he fails to provide sufficient reason why comparing terms during the process of interpretation should result in distortion rather than clarification. Such contention is merely speculative, while the opposite appears much more plausible. In view of the need to preserve the unity of the treaty, the purposive constructions of the texts ought to be reconciled regardless of their individual idiomatic constructions unless such proves impossible, in which case the treaty must be considered defective. This is the essence of Article 33(1), (3), and (4), and Waldock provides no good reason why in order to achieve this goal a comparison of terms should prove more harmful than helpful, see Kuner, 'The Interpretation of Multilingual Treaties', 958. Certainly, his contention as understood by the proponents of the routine interpretation approach would not find support among the prominent hermeneutic theorists of all eras, some of whom forcefully rejected analogous ideas explicitly, see Chapter 3, s. 3.5.

in time to conduct a comparison. The VCLT is tacit as to this point in terms of explicit imperative language. According to Waldock as understood here, the interpreter should first appreciate each text separately and then venture to interpret them in light of each other. The approach to adopt may be summarised as per Lord Wilberforce (by analogy but nevertheless pertinent):

> So, in the present case the process of interpretation seems to involve (1) interpretation of the English text, according to the principles on which international conventions are to be interpreted, (2) interpretation of the French text according to the same principles but with additional linguistic problems, (3) comparison of these meanings. Moreover, if the process of interpretation leaves the matter in doubt, the question may have to be faced whether *travaux preparatoires* may be looked at in order to resolve the difficulty.[13]

It is submitted here that (3) includes a consideration of the object and purpose as sole decider under Article 33(4) as final authentic means to establish the ordinary meaning on the basis of the text before supplementary means may be used in their active role to determine the treaty meaning. Concerning this, the ambiguous reference to Article 32 in Article 33(4) must be interpreted as referring only to the passive confirmatory role of Article 32, excluding the second part of its sentence. Otherwise, the fundamental hierarchy implemented by the VCLT principles between authentic and supplementary means, limiting use of the latter, would be upset. To the extent the omission of letters (a) and (b) in the reference to Article 32 by Article 33(4) may be seen as deliberate in view of the context and object and purpose of Article 32 as merely permissive aid to be used in its active role only in limited situations, this coincides with a super-literal interpretation. The quasi-literal interpretation, understanding the ambiguous reference to Article 32 as a reference to the entire article including letters (a) and (b), leads to an inconsistent back and forth between authentic and supplementary means and a crowding out of Article 33(4) in practice, rendering it an empty provision never to apply, which violates the principle of effectiveness.

'Ambiguous', 'obscure', 'absurd', and 'unreasonable' in Article 32 must be understood as intended to apply only to problems of the treaty meaning, not to problems between texts, to which 'divergence' and Article 33(4) are

---

[13] *Fothergill v Monarch Airlines Ltd.*, 272. Noteworthy, recourse to supplementary means is understood to come after a comparison of texts, not before.

intended to apply, that is, Article 33(4) must be understood as a mere extension of Article 31, augmenting it to close a gap in terms of plurilingual form, whereas Article 32 must be understood to be supplementary to both. To suggest otherwise and interpret 'ambiguous', 'obscure', 'absurd', and 'unreasonable' in a wider colloquial sense collapses the conceptual demarcations between them and 'divergence', effectively rendering divergence an empty concept. To the extent that problems between texts are classified as an ambiguity to be treated by reference to supplementary means, Article 33(4) is bypassed, violating the intentions of the parties to the VCLT expressed by including it.

Such understanding is consistent with the dictum that in principle plurilingual form of a treaty should not entail a different system of interpretation than codified in the general rule, that is, Article 33 should only augment the general rule of interpretation for plurilingual scenarios but not alter it. The only alteration comes in the form of multiple texts, which are however intended to have the same meaning, that is, they constitute the same treaty, and this construction has to be made compatible in a sensible way with the general rule of interpretation devised for interpreting one treaty, whether embodied in a single text or equally expressed in multiple language texts.

An important corollary of the relationship between Article 33(4) and Article 32(a) and (b) as suggested is that contradictions between texts do not render the treaty immediately defective once Article 33(4) fails, but Article 32(b) allows for a final resort after the last resort in that the interpreter may have recourse to supplementary means to overcome the contradiction before he must finally regard the treaty as defective if such is again not possible. Such final resort after the last resort makes sense given that there is a treaty, which implies that the parties actually intended to agree. Thus, Article 33(4) is not a rule of ultimate last resort but only a rule of last resort in terms of establishing the ordinary meaning with the help of all authentic means before recourse to supplementary means may be had in their exceptional active role to establish the treaty meaning.

Even in such case, however, there can be no notion that the interpreter *must* choose one text if he cannot find decisive arguments on the basis of supplementary means fitting into the VCLT framework, but the evidence used from supplementary means must still orientate itself on the criteria considered adequate by the VCLT, that is, either the intentions concerning the meaning of the contradictory worded provisions in question are unequivocally represented in form of a stated understanding on their interpretation, or their object and purpose can be deduced without doubt. Caution needs to be applied because the preparatory materials of a treaty may be far from clear in this respect but may be a collage of all positions taken by the contracting parties during the negotiation phase, which may be misleading. What matters is the final compromise that made it into the text. If the adopted compromise is not obvious from the supplementary means with some decisive force, the conclusion must be that the treaty meaning cannot be determined under Article 32(a) or (b) as well.

In summary, Article 32(a) and (b) only extends the *modi operandi* of Articles 31 and 33(4) by method of recourse to supplementary means but does not allow for an expansion beyond their scope. Even if we suffer the predicament that the meaning arrived at according to an interpretation of the treaty under Articles 31 and 33(4) remains ambiguous, obscure, absurd, or unreasonable, which allows recourse to supplementary means in order to determine the meaning under Article 32(a) and (b), such determination must be conducted within the framework of the principles provided by Articles 31 and 33(4), that is, Article 32 does not provide for a distinct method of interpretation but only defines additional means to be used according to the methods provided by Articles 31 and 33(4). Whereas the latter two contain both legal rules and means, Article 32 only provides auxiliary means in case the authentic means prove insufficient. For its application in substance, Article 32(a) and (b) requires recourse to the rules codified in Articles 31 and 33(4) as a legal basis. This understanding is contained in the ordinary meaning of 'supplementary means of interpretation' as intended by the VCLT: 'The word "supplementary" emphasizes that article 28 does not provide for alternative, autonomous, means of interpretation but only for means to aid an interpretation governed by the principles contained in article 27.'[14]

The routine interpretation approach transforms Waldock's concern with the point in time when to compare the texts effectively to *never*, because it suggests that such comparison must be conducted only in case a problem

---

[14]ILC, *Draft Articles on the Law of Treaties with Commentaries*, II:223, para. 19. Draft Articles 27 and 28 became Articles 31 and 32 in the final text of the VCLT.

arises, which does however not happen automatically with tax treaties under consideration of a single text in isolation, that is, the problems defined
by the routine interpretation approach as conditions legitimately limiting
its application, if present, are partly ignored as a consequence of its application. Thus, its claim to validity is a result of it being applied and not of all
the conditions granting legitimacy to its application being fulfilled, that is,
in the context of tax treaties, the routine interpretation approach is not a scientific but a reflexive theory.[15] It concludes that it is safe to ignore q as long
as nobody raises a divergence; in consequence, it damages the principle of
unity and impairs proper application of the *pacta sunt servanda* principle
enshrined in Article 26 VCLT.

Although the VCLT rules may not explicitly stipulate any obligation for
a comparison of texts in all cases, such obligation must be construed from
the context and object and purpose of the VCLT principles in the case of
tax treaties. The VCLT rules were drawn up with disputes between states
in mind, for which issues of divergent texts would be raised automatically
by the conflicting parties when existent. For tax treaties, the problems of
multiple texts are less likely to be raised automatically while they are not
less likely to exist, which necessarily leads to an undetected number of cases
in breach of Article 26 VCLT. To implicitly sanction each state to give preference to the text in its own language may be pragmatically opportune in
view of the number of international tax cases, but effectively promotes divergence rather than uniformity of interpretation and may lead to fragmented jurisprudence.

Abandoning the routine interpretation approach escalates the practical
problems and resource demands implied by a comparison of texts. The natural reflex of the judge may be to look to the original text, that is, the text
of initial negotiation and drafting. Without explicit support by the treaty,
however, such preference is in violation of Article 10 VCLT establishing authenticity of texts, Article 33, and the treaty final clause declaring all texts
as equally authoritative. The fact that treaties are concluded with multiple
language texts declared as authentic implies the common intention of the
parties not to consider the text in the language of negotiation and draft-

---

[15]Conducting all tests that might refute a theory is an essential element of any scientific
approach, see Popper, *The Logic of Scientific Discovery*, passim.

ing of higher relevance for interpretative purposes, regardless of what the process of authentication in detail entails.

The VCLT is drafted in the way it is out of political considerations, precisely because countries may not want to give precedence to a text in the language of one of the treaty partners. The way the issue is posed by Rosenne, 'whether the word "authentic" possesses any juridical content or whether it is merely descriptive to serve a political purpose',[16] asks the wrong question, and his arguments in favour of 'linguistic concordance' are of little relevance to the matter. The term 'authentic' possesses a particular formalistic juridical content because of the political purpose it is intended to serve, and the VCLT is drafted the way it is to implement that formalistic juridical content.

Thus, there is nothing 'normal' or 'natural' about the original text to be preferred, such contention is merely speculative and without legal basis. If an implicit pre-eminence of the original text were to be naturally assumed, such should have been codified in the VCLT. What all the authors in support of granting decisive weight to the original text are basically saying is that the VCLT principles should be ignored to a large extent because everybody simply *knows* the text initially drawn up provides the proper meaning. They do not interpret the VCLT rules but revise them. The ethically charged language of their suggestions like 'unfair', 'natural', or 'normal' shows the difficulty to base their view on the VCLT principles other than through a loose reference to the principle of good faith.

It remains difficult to appreciate and delineate the scope of good faith in its application as a legal principle, because its substance rests on the broader and less tangible moral concepts of honesty, fairness, and reasonableness. According to the ILC, the principle of interpretation in good faith is an essential component of the rule *pacta sunt servanda* enshrined in Article 26 VCLT, and also embodies the principle of effectiveness to the extent that 'Properly limited and applied, the maxim [*ut res magis valeat quam pereat*] does not call for an "extensive" or "liberal" interpretation in the sense of an interpretation going beyond what is expressed or necessarily to be implied in the terms of the treaty.'[17] Understood in this way, good faith rejects any

---

[16]Rosenne, 'The Meaning of "Authentic Text" in Modern Treaty Law', 399.

[17]ILC, *Draft Articles on the Law of Treaties with Commentaries*, II:219, para. 6.

disposition in favour of the initially drafted text not decisively based on the wording, context, and object and purpose of the treaty.

In order to overcome the problem of additional interpretational complexity induced by plurilingual form, contracting parties may explicitly confer special authority to one text for purposes of interpretation by designating it as prevailing. Thereby, the practical and resource problems implied by comparing texts can be reduced because the VCLT framework of interpretation allows for sole reliance on the prevailing text by the interpreter as long as interpretation of the prevailing text under Article 31 establishes a clear meaning.[18] If such clear meaning cannot be established, recourse must first be had to the other texts to clarify the meaning of the treaty via a comparative application of Article 31 to all texts. If that remains unsuccessful, then Article 33(4) must be applied, that is, the object and purpose criterion should be invoked as sole decider. If all these efforts based on authentic means remain unfruitful to establish the treaty meaning, the interpreter may have recourse to supplementary means to determine it under Article 32(a) or (b). If that fails as well, the treaty must be regarded as defective. Alternatively, the interpreter may engage in a reconciliatory comparison of all texts from the start; however, such may turn out to be a moot exercise in view of the prevailing text having a clear meaning under Article 31. Hence, from a pragmatic point of view, it is always preferable to begin with the prevailing text and only resort to the others when it does not provide a clear meaning.

The view that sole reliance on the prevailing text is permitted only once a comparison of texts in the face of an apparent divergence fails to reconcile their meaning, submitted by the advocates of the restrictive approach, is not in line with the VCLT principles. In particular, it rests on a misinterpretation of the term 'divergence' (as used by Article 33) in the light of its ordinary wording, context, and object and purpose. As a result, it is accompanied by a conglomerate of erroneous theories prescribing excessive use of supplementary means or comparing only the texts in the two languages of the contracting states while ignoring an existing prevailing text in a third language until the others cannot be reconciled, which are all in violation of the principles codified in Articles 31–33 and 26 VCLT. Contrary to their view, a divergence as referred to by Article 33(1) can be any divergence,

---

[18]Optionally, such may be confirmed but not contested by supplementary means.

that is, a mere difference in expression as well as differences in meaning that can or cannot be reconciled by a comparison of the texts under Article 31 and, optionally, Article 32 in its passive confirmatory role. This notion fits with the fundamental axiom of the unity of the treaty in the sense that any problem of difference between texts, even if only a different choice of words or equivalent words with different connotations, must be addressed by interpretative means to ensure equivalence in meaning.

As a corollary, Article 33 allows for sole reliance to the prevailing text but does not prescribe it. In principle, recourse to the prevailing text becomes mandatory only in case the interpreter would otherwise depart from its meaning. This implies, however, that the prevailing text must be checked always and can never be left out of the equation. Because the meaning of the prevailing text prevails in all cases the other texts diverge from it, the one true meaning of the treaty defaults to its meaning in any case, that is, the existence of a prevailing text creates a situation of quasi-unilinguality. This is confirmed by the VCLT Commentary, as it contains no conclusive evidence that the meaning of 'divergence' should be delimited to material differences in meaning, but employs terminology suggesting a continuum from mere differences in expression to material differences in meaning.

The conclusion should hardly come as a surprise, since the VCLT Commentary is relatively explicit in implying it in paragraph 4 on page 224, in which the drafters of the VCLT express their indecisiveness with respect to prescribing a definite rule when the interpreter has to resort to the prevailing text, apart from prohibiting cases of departure from its meaning. Therefore, the wording supplied by the VCLT, if not expressly delimited by the contracting parties in their actual treaties, must be considered flexible enough to allow for sole reliance on the prevailing text as a tool to decrease the complexity of interpreting plurilingual treaties, because either there is a divergence prescribing reliance on it, or there is no divergence, allowing reliance on it. At the same time, the VCLT wording does not compel sole reliance on the prevailing text, but the court may compare all texts instead as long as it does not depart from the meaning of the prevailing text.

10.1.2. Empirical Analysis

Regarding the applicability of the permissive approach to treaties with prevailing text in practice, an analysis of the global tax treaty network establishes the following:

1. With respect to one-quarter (25.22%), there is no problem of plurilingual interpretation because of unilingual form.

2. Almost two-thirds (64.60%) of the remaining three-quarters feature a prevailing text, amounting to almost half (48.30%) of the global tax treaty network.

3. Apart from a small handful of exceptions, the wordings of all actual tax treaty final clauses implementing a prevailing text allow for sole reliance on it.

4. Sole reliance on prevailing texts is unavailable for roughly one-third (35.13%) of all plurilingual tax treaties not providing for one, amounting to roughly one-quarter (26.27%) of the global tax treaty network. In addition, it remains unavailable for a small handful of treaties that provide for either TOW7, TOW9, or two prevailing texts.

5. English dominates as widely accepted lingua franca for tax treaties: About three-quarters (76.62%) of all unilingual treaties as well as the overwhelming majority (94.57%) of all prevailing texts are in English. In total, almost two-thirds (65.01%) of the global tax treaty network use English as language for unilingual treaties and prevailing texts, whereas for French that share is confined to 3.31%. English is used in numerous cases as (true) diplomatic language for unilingual treaties by countries that do not have English as official language. In contrast, French is confined to a marginal role with only 7.56% of all unilingual treaties and 2.90% of all prevailing texts. Apart from a few exceptions, French is hardly used as (true) diplomatic language.

6. English permeates the global tax treaty network as authentic language up to 83.92%, whereas French remains marginal with only a

7.68% share. An equally marginal 8.40% of all tax treaties use neither English nor French as authentic language.

7. France and Canada are the only countries with major treaty networks that have not concluded a single treaty unilingual in English or with an English prevailing text. Apart from them, the total number of all treaties of countries to which the same applies accounts for less than 3% of the global tax treaty network. Moreover, they are distributed over countries with only one or two treaties in total plus a few French-speaking countries with small treaty networks.

In summary, we may conclude that, since the 1990s, prevailing texts have emerged as the standard device to address the difficulties of plurilingual interpretation whenever the linguistic and political potential for unilingual form has been exhausted. In total, almost three-quarters of today's global tax treaty network do not pose a problem by being either unilingual or providing for a prevailing text in combination with a final clause allowing for sole reliance on it. Additional interpretational complexity induced by plurilingual form remains a residual problem of only one-quarter of all tax treaties in force today that is plurilingual but lacks prevailing texts.

A bit of caution must be applied when concluding a general trend from the magnitude of the numbers because treaties without prevailing text in force today may be replaced again by treaties without prevailing text in the future, depending on the policies of the particular countries in question. Notwithstanding, the numbers concerning terminated treaties show that the fraction of plurilingual treaties without prevailing text has reduced over time in favour of prevailing texts.

With respect to the overall composition of the global tax treaty network concerning unilingual and plurilingual form, the trend for newer treaties to predominantly feature a prevailing text has been supported by a trend for older treaties without prevailing text to be terminated and replaced by newer versions with prevailing text, while the proportion of unilingual treaties has remained stable.

Table (10.1): Lingual Form of All Treaties

Treaties	UL %total	PL w/o PT %total	PL w PT %total
global	25.16%	30.44%	44.22%
w/o term	25.22%	26.27%	48.30%

Finally, it must not be omitted that tax treaties look back at quite a success story. To date, only about 13% of all treaties concluded since 1960 have been terminated, and less than 2% have been terminated and not replaced by later treaties on the same subject between the same countries.

Although the global tax treaty network grew steadily from the 1960s throughout the 1980s, its major wave of expansion took off as late as the 1990s. Three-quarters of all tax treaties in force today have been concluded since 1990, and over 95% of all tax treaties concluded by OECD members in force today had some version of the OECD Model available to draw on. This may provide yet another argument for sole reliance on the prevailing text, because the official versions of the OECD Model and Commentary are in English and French (while the actual work is done in English with the French version being a translation), and almost all texts designated as pre-vailing by treaties in the global tax treaty network are in English.

The slow-down in growth since the 1990s may indicate a certain satura-tion starting to set in. In principle, the total potential for bilateral tax treat-ies is only limited by the number of countries. To date almost two hundred countries have concluded tax treaties with each other. Nevertheless, the average number of treaties concluded per country is only 33.77, while the standard deviation of 33.98 is fairly wide in comparison. In combination with the slow-down in growth between the 1990s and 2000s, this may in-dicate that in the context of the current global economy and its distribution of capital, goods, and services, the global tax treaty network may be starting to mature regarding its extension versus the economic needs of the coun-tries involved.

This development may be only at the beginning: growth has still been going strong from 2010 to August 2016, with the number of treaties con-cluded already exceeding the total per decade numbers for the 1970s and 1980s and half of the per decade numbers for the 1990s and 2000s, which suggests that by the end of the decade a number roughly equal to the 1990s and 2000s will again be reached unless a major slow-down in growth will set in beforehand. Of course, the economic circumstances and policies of countries may change over time, so countries that today only have a few treaties may expand their treaty networks heavily in the future.

Whether the pattern of expansion since the 1990s has been driving or itself been driven by the growing structural interdependence and integration of the world economy that took off after the Reagan and Thatcher years is a topic for another study, but in itself the synchronicity is striking.

10.2. Policy Recommendations

10.2.1. Mission Statement

Issuing policy recommendations in a thesis raises the question of perspective. I have discussed the subject of this study mainly as a technical issue from a technical point of view; matters of policy have been considered only to the extent I perceived them to impact on the technical issues. Policy makers have to adopt a broader perspective than technical experts, consider more variables, and weigh courses of action applying a broader measure. In line with the previous chapters, the following sections are written from a technical perspective. When employing normative language in terms of what should and should not be done, I assume the perspective of a consultant providing recommendations on a specific issue in order to engineer a system within a narrow framework of specifications that include political aspects only to the extent they affect implementation of the technical recommendations. Overall, a simple policy goal of improving the system in respect of the issues identified in the preceding analysis is assumed.

10.2.2. General Considerations

Plurilingual treaties without a prevailing text are manifested mainly as bilingual treaties, about 81% of which have no prevailing text. Already for treaties having a third authentic language, the percentage implementing a prevailing text surges to over 90%. Hence, it may be concluded that the primary motivation behind adding an additional text on top of the texts in the official languages of the contracting states has been to provide for a prevailing text.

If we look at the treaties with more than two texts none of which prevails, we can see that the overwhelming majority of them (about 80%) are treaties of Belgium, Canada, and Luxembourg, that is, mostly treaties of countries that domestically have more than one official legal language in place, in combination with a policy to not implement prevailing texts (at least as far as Canada and Luxembourg are concerned). The addition of texts in these cases may be attributable rather to a policy of extending the domestic use of multiple official legal languages to international instruments.

Additional texts reduce the residual problem of unresolved additional interpretational complexity induced by plurilingual form even if they are not designated as prevailing, because the more language texts there are, the more context is available for interpretation, which will help to resolve the problem (as in *New Skies*, had the court looked). Hence, application of Article 33(4) using the object and purpose criterion as sole decider in case of divergence and absence of a prevailing text will mainly be an issue for bilingual treaties because of two equally authentic texts saying different things. Notwithstanding, almost 70% of bilingual tax treaties without prevailing text have an English authentic text, and English is otherwise widely used as lingua franca. Therefore, in respect of resource demands, the global costs involved in a comparison of texts may be considered reduced, at least with respect to the countries having the other languages as official language.

In order to properly evaluate the residual policy choice against prevailing texts, we have to view it against the background of English as emerging lingua franca in the world of tax treaties. The numbers show that tax treaties have already largely transcended the period of linguistic nationalism, which has characterised treaty making after the second world war. Remaining plurilingual treaties without prevailing text are not evenly distributed over the global tax treaty network but concentrated in the treaty networks of a few countries with strong policies in disfavour of prevailing texts such as Canada, France, the UK, and the US; however, as these handful of countries are among the most influential in the global economy, the global political system, and intergovernmental organisations that shape the international tax law regime like the OECD, UN, and G20, their policy choice remains a strong force at the core of the global tax treaty network.

Nevertheless, the use of either English unilingual treaties or English prevailing texts is already the preferred policy of the vast majority of countries to the effect of covering roughly two-thirds of all tax treaties. More than three-quarters of all unilingual treaties and almost 95% of all prevailing texts are in English, but there still remains a gap of roughly 14% that mixed bilingual treaties (between countries that have English as official language and countries that do not) lag behind in using English as diplomatic language compared to the non-English speaking world. This gap is attributable to the strong policy preferences of the same handful of countries referred to above, which have a large impact because of their political influence, economic weight, and importance in the world of tax treaties. Their effect is amplified by some other English-speaking countries such as Ireland, South Africa, and Australia, combined with larger shares of treaties without prevailing text in the treaty networks of a few more countries that themselves however are not policy drivers in this respect, such as Germany and Switzerland. The only strong driver not being English-speaking is France. Luxembourg may be added but displays a somewhat less strict policy.

In summary, the fact that use of English as lingua franca is not even more wide-spread in the world of tax treaties than it already is today is except for France (and Luxembourg) largely attributable to the policy choices of a few native English-speaking countries that do not exhaust the potential, whereas the rest of the world largely accepts and uses English as lingua franca in form of English prevailing texts. Several countries (such as the Nordic ones) have even gone a step further by using English as true diplomatic language for unilingual treaties. This almost schizophrenic seeming result is all the more striking because the same English-speaking countries must be considered the biggest losers of this situation in terms of resource efficiency. With recourse to an English prevailing text being unavailable, they will have to compare texts in (from their perspective) arcane languages, whereas their treaty partners will only need to compare the other text in English, used by them already as lingua franca in most other treaty relationships.

What might be the reasons for the paradoxic persistence of this gap? One argument traditionally put forward is that countries may be reluctant to concede linguistic advantages, as Arginelli concludes from his observations on the Maisto sample.[19] There are documented cases of this sentiment in practice: when acceding to the Treaty of Rome, Denmark would concede to restricting the number of languages to English and French only if in turn the English-speaking members would exclusively use French and vice-versa.[20] The numbers concerning English as official language confirm a certain potential for this problem to show resilience, as roughly 87% of all bilingual treaties without prevailing text having English as one authentic language are between a country having English as official language and one that does not (the rest is largely attributable to Canada not implementing prevailing texts even if English is available as shared native tongue).

Moreover, the major English-speaking countries themselves may have little incentive to change.[21] With the routine interpretation approach in place as dominant doctrine, they are not necessarily the biggest losers as diagnosed by me, but may be regarded as the biggest beneficiaries because they can tacitly favour their own language text in bilingual situations, and when more languages are involved, the English text will almost without exception have prevailing status. As Lord Diplock has put it, 'Machiavellism is not extinct at international conferences.'[22] On the other hand, it is only understandable if they simply want to avoid accusations of imperialism. Tax treaties are ultimately based on economic reciprocity and thus subject to sensitive trade-offs between individual and mutual benefits. It might not exactly be opportune to suggest one's own language as prevailing in such bargaining situation even though it may be the obvious choice for various good reasons – a double bind.[23] Overall, however, the numbers concerning the groups of countries investigated seem to suggest that this is much less a

---

[19]See Arginelli, *The Interpretation of Multilingual Tax Treaties*, 133; Gaja, 'The Perspective of International Law', 92.

[20]See Leigh Oakes, 'Multilingualism in Europe: An Effective French Identity Strategy?', *Journal of Multilingual and Multicultural Development* 23, no. 5 (2002): 375.

[21]As pointed out previously, the UK shows signs of a shift in policy, depending probably on the readiness of the treaty partner. It would be interesting to know which side has put the topic on the table in the negotiations.

[22]*Fothergill v Monarch Airlines Ltd.*, 283.

[23]Defined by the Oxford Dictionary as 'A situation in which a person is confronted with two irreconcilable demands or a choice between two undesirable courses of action.'

problem in the relationship between economically powerful and economically less powerful countries, but rather one between economically powerful countries themselves.

Finally, domestic constitutional law may interfere with the policy to designate one text as prevailing, as in the case of Canada. As for France being the only major country outside the English-speaking world that has resisted the global trend, the reasons may be rooted in history with French having once played a dominant role as lingua franca and even true diplomatic language for a prolonged period, as well as national political doctrine.[24]

How can these issues be addressed? From a purely theoretical perspective, the 'linguistic advantage' argument makes little sense. According to the principle of unity there is only one treaty with one set of terms, irrespective of the language in which they are expressed. Hence, it remains elusive what the conjured up linguistic advantage or disadvantage should exactly consist in. Reserving a kind of linguistic sovereignty in the sense of reserving the right to arrive at different results depending on one's own language text goes against the very idea of the unity of the treaty and must be discarded as a motivation not in good faith to begin with.

The numbers concerning general English proficiency on the other hand show that it has little impact on a country's propensity to conclude treaties with an English prevailing text, that is, lack of general English proficiency is for the most part not viewed as a disadvantage by countries that would impede their conclusion of treaties with English prevailing texts.

Any argument in favour of texts in equally authentic languages without English prevailing text in order to facilitate interpretation and application of tax treaties by taxpayers, national authorities, and courts, 'who might not be familiar with other languages, not even French or English, but are generally very familiar with the technical language of domestic tax law',[25] is equally unconvincing. Tax treaties are necessarily formulated in terms of general abstractions connecting the tax systems of two countries. Consid-

---

[24]See Henrik Uterwedde, 'Frankreich – Grundlagen der Grandeur', in *Außenpolitik in der Wirtschafts– und Finanzkrise* (Walter de Gruyter, 2012); Günter Haensch, 'Frankreich: Politik, Gesellschaft, Wirtschaft', in *Außenpolitik in der Wirtschafts– und Finanzkrise* (Walter de Gruyter, 2012).

[25]Arginelli, *The Interpretation of Multilingual Tax Treaties*, 134.

erations of domestic law technical language are an important component in their interpretation under Article 3(2); however, interpretation primarily according to domestic law technical language is not the guiding principle and may lead down a dangerous path to treaty misapplication (as discussed in the context of the *New Skies* case and Vogel's fictional scenario).

Moreover, English is without doubt the language of global trade and business, permeating also all other social dimensions such as diplomacy and science as global lingua franca.[26] As *The Economist* has pointed out already at the beginning of this century:

> It [English] is everywhere. Some 380 million people speak it as their first language and perhaps two-thirds as many again as their second. A billion are learning it, about a third of the world's population are in some sense exposed to it and by 2050, it is predicted, half the world will be more or less proficient in it. It is the language of globalization – of international business, politics and diplomacy.[27]

For taxpayers who need to evoke the protection of tax treaties for their cross-border transactions, it is more than likely that they already conduct their cross-border business in English or have no problem in doing so. If they should really lack the proficiency, their legal advisers, who should be accustomed to dealing with tax treaties and clients with cross-border activities, will not. On the other hand, taxpayers should obviously welcome the extra legal certainty that comes with a prevailing text, especially since otherwise they, too, need to compare texts in all other languages for their purposes.

As far as authorities and courts are concerned, the numbers in terms of treaties concluded unilingual in English or with English prevailing text show that general English proficiency of a country has little effect, which implies that the required English proficiency of the human resources involved in the negotiation, interpretation, and application of treaties must

---

[26]See, e.g., David Crystal, *English as a Global Language*, 2nd ed. (Cambridge; New York: Cambridge University Press, 2012); Anne Johnson, 'The Rise of English: The Language of Globalization in China and the European Union', *Macalester International* 22 (2009): 131–68; Tsedal Neeley, 'Global Business Speaks English', *Harvard Buisness Review* 90, no. 5 (May 2012).

[27]The Economist, 'A World Empire by Other Means: The Triumph of English', 22 December 2001.

be assumed as a given. It is not necessarily the countries with lower English proficiency that show a low tendency to conclude treaties with English prevailing texts, but the native English-speaking countries plus France and Luxembourg and a few others with a generally high level of English proficiency. The policy against prevailing texts in English seems even less reasonable in the context of where it is most widespread, namely, the OECD, G20, and EU, where English is the de facto working language on a multilateral level.[28]

In essence, aside a self-defeating policy not to provide for a prevailing text, the arguments in favour of plurilingual form without prevailing text seem to boil down to nothing more than a costly concession to national sentiment.[29] In the absence of an artificial universal language like Esperanto, which despite some support by the UN never gained critical mass,[30] English prevailing texts in addition to texts in the official languages of the contracting states are the next best thing to balance these sentiments with political and economic interests, because of the de facto global reach of English.[31]

All national sentiment aside,[32] the gap of plurilingual treaties without

---

[28] According to Sasseville, 'The practical reality is that, nowadays, the OECD work on tax treaties is primarily carried on in English and the French version is usually a translation', Sasseville, 'The OECD Model Convention and Commentaries', 130; according to Dor, 'Ninety nine per cent of European institutions cite English as their working language', Daniel Dor, 'From Englishization to Imposed Multilingualism: Globalization, the Internet, and the Political Economy of the Linguistic Code', *Public Culture* 16, no. 1 (2004): 103.

[29] Costly not only in terms of the resource costs involved but also because of the inherent indeterminacy of tax treaties as a result of which reliance on a single text may lead to treaty misapplication bilaterally and fragmented jurisprudence domestically.

[30] See John King Gamble, Lauren Kolb, and Casey Graml, 'Choice of Official Text in Multilateral Treaties: The Interplay of Law, Politics, Language, Pragmatism and (Multi)-Nationalism', *Santa Clara Journal of International Law* 12, no. 2 (May 2014): 31–32.

[31] This is not to say that English is necessarily also the most suitable language given its intrinsic properties. Especially in the past there has been much argument in favour of French because of certain of its characteristics, see ibid., 36 et seq. Although this may be a valid discussion from a linguistic point of view, such is moot for purposes of this study in view of the realities.

[32] This is not intended to denounce national sentiment per se, and especially not as love for and devotion to one's own native tongue. The present author is far from free of it, loving his native tongue German for its capability to organically create and relate concepts;

English prevailing text constitutes a costly impediment to economic activities in a global economy the de facto operating language of which is English, and an anachronism in times of 'harmonization' being identified as a policy goal on many levels.[33]

In view of all this, it is submitted that the policy to conclude plurilingual treaties without prevailing text should be reconsidered and abandoned to close the residual gap. One may point particularly to the Asian (but also CIS, AW, and LA) countries as setting a good example in this respect. Their economic success over the past decades may be attributable to a multitude of different factors, however, considering the observed data, pragmatism certainly appears to be one of them.

Of course, it would be naive to think national sentiment would simply wane when confronted with its dead-weight loss. In bilateral scenarios all sorts of additional historical and political factors may weigh in, so success may vary. In order to take the sting out of the issue, the topic should be discussed at the multilateral level. The best forum to achieve real progress in this respect would be the OECD, as most of the countries clinging to the policy choice of plurilingual treaties without prevailing text are OECD members, while they are at the same time engaged there in a project to achieve conformity of interpretation via the OECD Model and Commentary, carried on primarily in English.

---

however, tax treaties are not works of philosophy, poetry, or literature, essential for defining cultural identity, but international legal tools to facilitate cross-border trade, business, and investment. Hence it seems sensible to give the devil his due, at least from a purely pragmatic perspective. There are of course drawbacks of such choice in general to moan about, see Minae Mizumura, *The Fall of Language in the Age of English*, trans. Mari Yoshihara and Juliet Winters Carpenter, Tra (New York: Columbia University Press, 2015), passim, however, the question remains whether tax treaties are really the proper area to make a stand.

[33] Although the gap of easily available potential not exhausted only amounts to 14%, it represents a much larger share of global economic activity with respect to flows of capital, goods, and services. This is obvious from the countries involved and the sizes of their economies. As this study is not focussed on economics, I refrain from matching the data in order to put an exact number to this assertion. For purposes of the discussion at hand, it is sufficient to appreciate the economic weight of the issue in principle.

10.2.3. Specific Recommendations

Unilingual treaties (TOW5) are the optimal solution for avoiding additional complexity of interpretation induced by plurilingual form, but the option may not be available for many countries because of domestic legal reasons requiring the existence of an authentic text in the country's official language. The proportion of unilingual treaties has remained stable over the decades, which suggests that the relative potential for them is exhausted, at least with respect to non-English unilingual treaties. For treaties with an English prevailing text, there might exist a certain potential for transformation into unilingual treaties, but this is hard to quantify from a bird's-eye view. In any case, quasi-unilingual form through prevailing texts is suitable to successfully reduce most of the extra complexity of plurilingual interpretation and its economic cost in practice, so a wide-spread move to TOW5 apart from countries that do so on their own initiative needs no push-start.

The practice of bilingual treaties with TOW1 clauses, however, should be discontinued. Such treaties have a major disadvantage versus all other forms. They may in principle be defective if all means provided by the VCLT exhaust without success. Such cases may be limited in practice, but they do occur. Moreover, the effort required from courts to properly interpret cases of *prima facie* divergence is generally more burdensome for such treaties even if a solution in line with the VCLT principles can eventually be found and discarding the treaty as defective on the point under dispute is averted. Treaties with a prevailing text may never be defective because of their quasi-unilinguality. The VCLT principles leave no gap but assume that the meaning of a single text can always be found. For cases in which the prevailing text remains unclear if interpreted in isolation, the possibility that a comparison of all texts should not bring resolution seems remote and confined to serious drafting errors in all texts that have remained undetected and cannot even be resolved via the *travaux preparatoires*.

Even trilingual treaties without prevailing texts perform better in this respect because of the additional context provided by the third text, which should help to resolve the issue in most cases. Bilingual treaties with TOW1 final clauses are the real problem because of two equally authentic texts stating different things, which may have the judge at a loss, clutching at straws. The resulting wasteful interpretation effort entailed in evaluating all supplementary means may in the worst case lead to just *any* meaning not in line with the VCLT principles and the true intentions of the contracting parties. If the routine interpretation approach is applied by the judge and the difference between the texts is not paid attention to in the first place, correct treaty application becomes a question of chance.

Concerning the actual drafting of treaty final clauses, the UN Handbook is instructive in stressing the importance of precision:

> In general, the final clauses of a treaty relate to procedural aspects rather than to substantive aspects of the treaty. However, well-drafted final clauses allow for the easy operation of the treaty and facilitate implementation by the parties and the depositary. They can have a significant impact on substance as well. Accordingly, precision in drafting the final clauses becomes important.[34]

In this regard, countries have several commonly used formulations at their disposal when implementing prevailing texts. Although TOW2, TOW3, TOW4, TOW6, and TOW8 all allow for sole reliance on the prevailing text and therefore may be chosen indiscriminately, TOW3 has solidified its position as main standard. TOW4 is a complicated wording that requires a contextual interpretation to be applied correctly. It may mislead courts and lead to varying practice. Given the number of alternatives available, TOW4 is redundant and should be depreciated in favour of a more precise wording. Countries using it at the moment should move to either TOW3 or any other more straightforward alternative, or implement TOW9 if the intention is indeed to discourage sole reliance on the prevailing text. This is especially relevant for the Netherlands and Germany, which both have TOW4 implemented as policy standard in their Model Conventions.

Although TOW9 in its original form installs a prevailing text, such takes precedence over the object and purpose as sole decider only if a divergence persists after a comparative interpretation of the texts in the languages of the contracting states. In its more modern form, an additional text is given status as a reference to be taken into consideration, providing additional context to help resolve problematic situations. The original form, having a non-authentic text suddenly prevail, appears somewhat in friction with the

---

[34]UN, *Final Clauses of Multilateral Treaties: Handbook*, E.04.V.3 (United Nations, 2003), 1.

general construction of the VCLT. Implementation in a sound way requires careful consideration to manage the interplay between Article 10 and Article 33(1), (2), and (4) VCLT. Therefore, it should be discarded as an option. The more modern form, however, appears usable if one really wants to rule out sole reliance on the prevailing text. In reality, it is likely that a treaty is negotiated in English and later translated into the individual languages of the contracting states; hence, such English text could be used as additional context given decisive weight via the formulation of the final clause. This would explicitly implement the 'original text rationale', which otherwise cannot be applied in view of the VCLT principles.

TOW7 heals material divergences with the help of the treaty MAP clause instead of leaving it to the national courts, that is, TOW7 is an alternative for countries that want to have a mechanism in place in case a material divergence between the treaty texts surfaces, but do not want to rely on the courts of the other country deciding such case. Whether TOW7 is suitable from a pragmatic perspective remains to be seen. Although theoretically appealing because of its emphasis on the reciprocal character of treaties, it trades speed of decision for having a direct reciprocal means available to resolve cases of material divergence. Mutual agreement procedures take time, which is never a good thing for the taxpayer engaged in economic activities requiring financial liquidity and certainty. Prevailing texts are preferable in this respect. After all, countries should know what they agree on at the time they strike the deal and make the effort to arrive at a text that correctly expresses their common intention. In the worst case, more common use of TOW7 may serve to justify a practice of sloppy drafting and translation.

Considering the options, what can be done about the 734 bilingual treaties without prevailing text currently in place amounting to 21.86% of the global tax treaty network? It depends on their individual make-up. The best solution would be to declare one text as prevailing. Almost always this should default to the English text, as English will already be used as lingua franca in other treaty relationships by the country not having English as official language. In most cases, it will be the text of initial negotiation and drafting that, based on a Model Convention with Commentary, implements respective standardised phrasing and therefore fosters consistency of interpretation.

If there is no English text, however, the proposal to declare one text as prevailing is not conclusive. Even when there is one, there may be reservations on the side of the country not having English as official language because of a reluctance to grant linguistic advantages. Although the argument per se is flawed because the terms of the treaty are the terms of the treaty irrespective of the language in which they are transcribed, and any wilful deviation from that principle must be regarded as bad faith, such does not prevent it from having political force. What can be done in such case is to propose the more modern form of TOW9. Given an existing English text, the explicit status as additional reference decisive in cases of doubt seems within reach of acceptance if that English text has been the text of initial negotiation and drafting. If such proposal fails, one may consider TOW7 as a last resort. Even Canada and France might find it useful to have a mechanism in place for tricky cases, and TOW7 does not interfere with constitutional requirements or the preference for not having an English prevailing text. TOW7 may also be the choice when no English text of initial negotiation and drafting is available.

The bilateral way to roll this out would be via requests for memoranda of understanding. That way the openness of the treaty partner can be tested and idle potential eliminated. Such approach allows for different roll-out speeds, and individual countries can take action concerning their treaties on a case-by-case basis without waiting for a global solution. Following the same rationale, there is also a limited potential for France to suggest French instead of English. Yet, the bilateral approach may remain underachieving because of individual political issues in bilateral relationships. Therefore, it may be helpful to discuss the issue simultaneously at a multilateral level to pave the way. Once a global consensus is reached, implementation at the bilateral level will be easier and future policy choices by individual countries will be more consistent.

Based on all the aforesaid, the most suitable way to handle the issue efficiently would be for the OECD to implement recommendations for final clauses in the OECD Model or at least the Commentary. The two primary options recommended as main standard should be a TOW5 clause for countries wanting to agree on a unilingual treaty, and a TOW3 clause for plurilingual treaties.[35] The formulation should follow the example of the German Model in putting English in square brackets as unilingual language and language for the prevailing text recommending it as default, but two countries with another shared language may of course replace it accordingly while still following the recommendation for type of wording.

The main supplementary recommendation should be a modern type TOW9 clause for countries that do not want to declare one text as prevailing, serving as lowest common denominator. As a final restricted recommendation, TOW7 should be added for countries that cannot even agree on TOW9, cases for which no lingua franca text is available, or when constitutional law forbids all other options. Nevertheless, use of TOW7 should be discouraged beyond cases in which it is the only option available for material reasons. In order to prevent excessive proliferation of MAP cases, the Commentary should include a restrictive interpretation of the meaning of 'divergence' as material divergence concerning its use in TOW7 clauses.

Finally, for any remainder of plurilingual treaties without prevailing text, Waldock's argument concerning the practical difficulties and extra burden of a comparison of texts in respect of resource gaps between countries remains a fair point. Depending on the countries and languages involved, the sourcing of expert witnesses may be difficult and expensive, while use of mere language experts may not be sufficient in respect of interpreting tax treaties, which involve a lot of technical language and domestic law concepts.[36] As Hilf has pointed out, some treaty terms require scientific mono-

---

[35] In order to address the reality of already existing treaties, TOW2, TOW6, and TOW8 may be listed as alternatives in the Commentary, together with a paragraph concerning the correct interpretation of TOW4 as equivalent; however, use of TOW4 should be discouraged by the Commentary for said reasons, and countries should clarify its meaning for their existing treaty relationships to create legal certainty, either by accepting the suggested Commentary formulation concerning its interpretation without reservation or issuing a reservation in combination with bilateral memoranda of understanding in case their intentions deviate for individual treaty relationships.

[36] With regard to foreign law expertise, the US Supreme Court has noted that 'Because the only authentic text of the Warsaw Convention is in French, the French text must guide our analysis. ...We must consider the "French legal meaning" of "*lesion corporelle*" for guidance as to the shared expectations of the parties to the Convention because the Convention was drafted in French by continental jurists', *Eastern Airlines, Inc., Peti-*

graphs rather than dictionaries to elucidate their proper meaning.[37] In the words of Lord Wilberforce:

> In a case, such as I think the present is, when one is dealing with a nuanced expression, a dictionary will not assist and reference to an expert might also be unhelpful, for the expert would have to direct his evidence to a two-text situation rather than simply to the meaning of words in his own language, so that he would be in the same difficulty as the court.[38]

Concerning this, I would like to submit a modified version of a proposal initially put forward by van Raad, namely, the creation of an advisory body of independent tax treaty experts, however, not as an additional institutional pillar but as a discretionary scientific service provided by the OECD.[39] The service should be accessible for taxpayers and tax authorities from the beginning of its creation, while its composition should reflect all relevant languages in tax treaty scenarios. Barring taxpayers and authorities from access to the service, even if only initially, would defeat its purpose in common law countries as long as their courts would consider themselves not in the position to acquire evidence from the advisory body on their own initiative. Although it is not unusual for civil law courts to have recourse to expertise of academic institutions, for example, concerning questions of foreign law in private international law cases, introduction of the service may help to improve the evidence situation in civil law countries in which courts may habitually tend to rely on their own language skills and dictionaries despite having the option to investigate any sources they see fit, that is, the mere existence of the service would suggest its use in the eyes of

---

tioner v Rose Marie Floyd, et vir., et al., paras. 6 and 11.

[37] See Hilf, *Die Auslegung mehrsprachiger Verträge*, 23.

[38] *Buchanan (James) & Co. Ltd. v Babco Forwarding and Shipping (UK) Ltd.*, 153. Fantozzi notes in this respect that 'one could say that the interpreter of a DTC deals with fluid concepts and therefore translation needs, necessarily, to be coupled with classification', Augusto Fantozzi, 'Conclusions', in *Multilingual Texts and Interpretation of Tax Treaties and EC Tax Law*, ed. Guglielmo Maisto (Amsterdam: IBFD, 2005), 129–34, 338.

[39] See van Raad, 'International Coordination of Tax Treaty Interpretation and Application', 219–20, 225–30. For obvious reasons, the language issue discussed in this study suggests itself to be added to the list of issues 'why a particular tax treaty provision may be interpreted and/or applied differently by the two countries involved', outlined by van Raad at 220–225.

courts. Van Raad discusses all relevant operational, compositional, and in-stitutional issues in detail, accompanied by relevant proposals. I agree on all accounts without any additions of myself apart from the broader access and composition in terms of language, so I simply refer the reader to the original source concerning these matters.[40]

With these observations I conclude my study.

— *Richard Xenophon Resch*

---

[40]See ibid., 225–30.

11. Annex: The BEPS Multilateral Instrument

11.1. Research Question

The previous analysis revealed that the paradigm of linguistic nationalism, which had shaped treaty making since the second world war, has been largely transcended and replaced by a new paradigm of English as dominant lingua franca for tax treaties. Since the conclusion of my study, the OECD has issued the BEPS multilateral instrument,[1] which modifies a large number of treaties. As of 27 September 2018, eighty-four countries have signed the MLI and six more have expressed their intent to do so.[2] The MLI turns out to be a bilingual treaty with equally authentic English and French texts:

> In witness whereof the undersigned, being duly authorised thereto, have signed this Convention. Done at Paris, the 24th day of November 2016, in English and French, both texts being equally authentic, in a single copy which shall be deposited in the archives of the Organisation for Economic Co-operation and Development.[3]

On the face of it, this appears as a compromise solution in view of the linguistic heterogeneity of the global tax treaty network; however, the question arises whether it really implements the optimal policy available given the linguistic and political realities and, if not, what can be done to improve it. This Annex will evaluate the MLI final clause on the basis of the research presented in the previous chapters. In the course of this, possible ways to remedy its deficiencies will be discussed.

---

[1]OECD, *Multilateral Convention to Implement Tax Treaty Related Measures to Prevent Base Erosion and Profit Shifting.* Henceforth referred to as MLI.

[2]See http://www.oecd.org/tax/treaties/beps-mli-signatories-and-parties.pdf.

[3]Ibid., Article 39. The French text is equivalent and reads '*Fait à Paris, le 24ème jour de novembre 2016, en anglais et français, les deux textes faisant également foi, en un exemplaire unique qui sera déposé aux archives de l'Organisation de coopération et de développement économiques.*' OECD, *Convention multilatérale pour la mise en œuvre des mesures relatives aux conventions fiscales pour prévenir le BEPS* (Paris: OECD Publishing, 2016), Article 39.

11.2. The Optimal Policy

In view of all the aforesaid, it is clear that a unilingual MLI in English or one with an English prevailing text would constitute the optimal policy: additional interpretational complexity induced by plurilingual form would be reduced, and countries that currently have treaties without prevailing text would be encouraged to designate existing English texts as prevailing.[4] The question is whether such policy would be feasible and, if not, what would be the best alternative given the circumstances.

Before publication of the MLI, Austry et al. discussed the particular language issues involved in detail,[5] considering several alternatives on the basis of two different envisaged routes to implement the MLI substantive provisions: by way of directly inserting them into individual treaties or by keeping them separate in their own multilateral treaty to be considered alongside the bilateral ones when applying them.[6] The OECD has opted for the latter path, which avoids the pitfalls of a 'multitude of official language versions of the amendments made by the MLI, with the corresponding risks of differences in meaning.'[7]

Austry et al. still identify a problem of such approach, namely, that it 'results in some modifications being made to a tax treaty in a language different from the rest of the treaty'.[8] Obviously, this problem is not only relevant for unilingual treaties but also for plurilingual ones having neither English nor French texts or having texts in other languages while their English or French text is not designated as prevailing. A plurilingual MLI having a prevailing text does not resolve this:

> There is also the middle way of using the original language (if not English or French) versions for the modifications made by the MLI, but insisting on the English or French version of those amendments prevailing in the event of a conflict. While a prevailing version of part of a tax treaty is probably unique, it would be important to ensure consistency of interpretation and

---

[4] See Austry et al., 'The Proposed OECD Multilateral Instrument Amending Tax Treaties', s. 3.

[5] See ibid., ss. 3–4.

[6] See ibid., s. 1.

[7] Ibid., s. 3.

[8] Ibid., s. 3.

might be accepted in preference to the two extremes. ...The middle way of requiring an English or French prevailing text of the modifications made by the MLI might be attractive, however unusual it would be to have a prevailing version of part of a tax treaty, as the price to ensure consistency of interpretation.[9]

Would such really constitute a problem as (seemingly) implied by Austry et al. and other authors?[10] The maybe perplexing because counter-intuitive answer to this question is no: language ought to be considered an immaterial factor of treaties, which is the very essence of the principle of unity. That treaties have (multiple) texts consistently in one language (each) is merely a sensible convention in view of the linguistic and political anatomy of the world. For all that matters from a purely legal perspective, treaty texts could be written provision for provision in different languages. Such would not change the fact that 'in law there is only one treaty'.[11]

This is counter-intuitive only because of the way we relate to language as persons and use it to express (legal) content, which makes it difficult for us to separate language as in any particular language to be considered an immaterial factor in terms of treaty content from language in the abstract as a tool to convey meaning.[12] In principle, however, there is no problem with

---

[9]Ibid., s. 3.

[10]See, Schuch and West, 'Authentic Languages and Official Translations of the Multilateral Instrument and Covered Tax Agreements', 67–68, 81.

[11]ILC, *Draft Articles on the Law of Treaties with Commentaries*, II:225, para. 6. In this respect I assume the reader to agree with me that the OECD Commentary is relevant for the interpretation of all texts of treaties modelled in content on the OECD Model, not only for texts incidentally in English or French. The contrary would imply that the OECD Commentary could be relevant only for the English or French texts of plurilingual tax treaties and not in an equal way for their other authentic texts in third languages, which is precluded by the principle of unity, i.e., a self-contradicting proposition.

[12]This consideration is not only relevant in the context of plurilingual treaties but also concerning unilingual ones, which should be obvious already from the fact that countries conclude unilingual treaties not only in their native tongues but also in the native tongue of only one contracting state or in third languages. It is implicit also in the textual approach prescribed by the VCLT. Most treaty terms are conceptual abstractions subject to a contextual interpretation; since connotations of words together with syntax function as building blocks of language, this re-introduces language as a potentially material factor in a derivative way because of the way we use it, which to some extent we cannot escape unless we resort to a completely formal language like mathematics

a unilingual multilateral agreement or a plurilingual one with a prevailing text resulting in partial modifications of existing bilateral treaties.[13] Newly introduced prevailing parts of a treaty originally in different languages are no different from agreeing (retroactively) on a prevailing text for the whole treaty; the difference is merely a matter of degree. That this appears as a novelty is attributable to the fact that in the past no good reason existed for such practice, because of the given linguistic and political circumstances. The MLI now brings with it a good reason, namely, 'to ensure consistency of interpretation' of a multilateral agreement devised to augment a large number of bilateral tax treaties in various languages currently in place.[14]

What about the French treaties and all the others having neither English nor French (prevailing) texts? They might be fewer in numbers, but that does not mean we can simply ignore them when devising a multilateral agreement modifying them.[15] As already pointed out, in what particular (prevailing) language they are amended does not matter because language ought to be considered an immaterial factor based on the principle of unity. Notwithstanding, the parties to those treaties might not want to use English for good reasons, or else they would have done so in the first place.

Although the point is valid in principle, it remains exaggerated as submitted by Austry et al., because of being considered from the wrong per-

---

or computer code, defined by convention to help us abstract and sharpen language's blurred lines. In consequence, treaties can be clear only after (not before) interpretation, and concerning plurilingual treaties the idiosyncrasies of all authentic languages combined result in the problem of divergences that necessitates a comparison of all texts if they are equally authoritative and none of them is designated as prevailing, because of the otherwise residual indeterminacy.

[13] A similar position is taken by Lang, according to whom the issue of different authentic languages being authoritative for different parts of a treaty provision modified by the MLI should not be exaggerated in importance: 'For the language question is, of course, only relevant to the text of a provision; however, the text is only the starting point of interpretation, not its end. In addition to its wording, the context, object and purpose, and legal development are to be used to determine the content of a provision. Concerning this it makes no difference which language is considered authentic', Michael Lang, 'Die Auslegung des multilateralen Instruments', *Steuer- und Wirtschaft International*, no. 1 (2017): 22–23.

[14] See Austry et al., 'The Proposed OECD Multilateral Instrument Amending Tax Treaties', s. 3.

[15] See ibid., s. 3.

spective: it is not really the number of treaties in languages other than English we need to consider but the actual policies of individual countries in this respect. The perspective from which we need to evaluate the issue is whether there are countries that have a strict policy not to agree to English unilingual treaties or prevailing texts and, if so, why. The crucial question is whether there are any hard legal reasons for such policy, as otherwise nothing speaks against an English unilingual multilateral agreement or a plurilingual one with an English prevailing text, apart from lacking capacities in terms of English speaking human resources. In short, when contemplating a policy for a multilateral agreement, we should adopt a truly multilateral perspective and not an essentially bilateral one that merely considers the properties of individual treaties in an aggregated yet unsystematic fashion.

The first observation to make in this context is that 83.92% of all treaties in the global tax treaty network have an English text, only 7.68% have a French one, and only 8.40% have neither. Thus, the previously counted two-thirds of all treaties either unilingual in English or with an English prevailing text under-represent the actual potential for agreement to an English unilingual MLI or one with an English prevailing text: there exist a lot of treaties without prevailing text that feature an English text attributable to English being the official language of one treaty partner while the other might in principle be available to agree to English unilingual treaties or prevailing texts and has done so in other treaty relationships. The gap concerning the particular treaty relationship constellation between countries having English as official language and those that do not is merely attributable to both the reluctance of English-speaking countries to implement prevailing texts and the reluctance of non-English-speaking countries to grant potential linguistic advantages. As I have argued at length before, the former is a costly and ultimately self-defeating policy while the latter does not rest on sound argument.

Now, the mere numbers concerning treaties with either French but no English texts or only texts in neither English nor French alone tell us nothing about whether the particular countries party to those treaties reject English as language for unilingual treaties or prevailing texts. If we look at all countries without a single English unilingual treaty or prevailing text and subtract France and Canada for the moment, we see that the remainder amounts to less than 3% of the global tax treaty network and is made up mostly of countries with one to five treaties in total, except for Senegal, Ivory Coast, and Gabon, which have slightly larger but nonetheless small treaty networks below the global average. If we take a closer look at all these jurisdictions, we can immediately eliminate Anguilla, Antigua and Barbuda, Belize, Dominica, Grenada, Liberia, Montserrat, Sierra Leone, St. Lucia, and St. Vincent and the Grenadines from the list because they all have English as official language domestically and their 'own' text of plurilingual treaties is the English one, so it is unreasonable to assume they would anything but welcome an MLI unilingual in English or with an English prevailing text.

Besides France, bilingual Canada, and all countries having French unilingual treaties or treaties with a French prevailing text, this leaves us only with Cape Verde, Dominican Republic, El Salvador, Guatemala, and Timor-Leste, that is, five countries with seven treaties in total, belonging to the Portuguese- and Spanish-speaking world. As of now, they are not signatories to the MLI and have not expressed their interest to become so. In any case, rather than to accommodate them with additional Portuguese and Spanish texts of a multilateral agreement that would increase interpretational complexity and economic cost of treaty application on a global scale, the obvious solution would be to pool a fraction of the costs saved in order to fund capacity building programs in terms of English language skills for human resources of those countries in case such capacity would really constitute a problem for them, which might also have other positive spill-over effects in terms of economic development.

In summary, the only substantial argument against a unilingual MLI in English or a plurilingual one with an English prevailing text rests with a handful of French-speaking countries.[16] If we again disregard France and Canada for the moment, the small treaty networks of the remaining countries do not allow for the conclusion that all of them would be categorically opposed to agreeing at least to an English prevailing text. In any case, given

---

[16] Arabic, Spanish, and Russian, the other three only marginally represented but still relevant languages in terms of unilingual treaties or prevailing texts, do not pose the same problem because all AW, LA, and CIS countries have treaties with either English or French prevailing texts in their respective treaty networks and to a large extent display a preference for English as lingua franca.

the small number of treaties involved, it would rather make sense to add these countries to the group receiving capacity building measures than to accommodate them with a separate French text that increases interpretational complexity for everybody.

Hence, it comes down to Canada and France, and here the problem becomes difficult to resolve because of their economic importance, political weight, large and important treaty networks in terms of flows of capital, goods, and services covered, possibly strong cultural preferences, and (at least in the case of Canada) strict domestic law requirements.[17] Although it seems not reasonable that global policy should be taken hostage by the cultural preferences and domestic law idiosyncrasies of a few countries to the detriment of everybody else, one cannot demand of countries to renounce their constitutional principles or sacrifice their cultural preferences if they are not inclined to do so by themselves. Thus, unfortunately, although preferable on many accounts, introducing an English unilingual MLI or a plurilingual one with an English prevailing text seems to remain a bridge too far in terms of its political feasibility.

11.3. The OECD Solution

As outlined at the beginning, the MLI is a bilingual treaty with equally authentic English and French texts, none of which is designated as prevailing. This implements a political anachronism on a global scale, ignoring the reality that the vast majority of tax treaties (92.32%) does not feature French texts and the world at large prefers and implements English as treaty lingua franca. In fact, it outright counteracts the globally predominant policy of countries to implement English prevailing texts (and unilingual treaties)

---

[17]Judging from the observed data, the problem posed by domestic constitutional law seems to be limited to Canada and, possibly, a few others for which the data remains indeterminate in this respect. Most countries seem to have no problem in accepting prevailing texts in another language if at least an authentic text in their official language is available, while some even accept unilingual treaties in a third language. For many countries the issue does not arise because English as the language of choice for the MLI is already their official one. Canada's case is peculiar because of the strict requirement of treaty bilinguality under domestic law. Other bilingual countries such as Belgium, Luxembourg, and Switzerland do not follow the example.

and condemns all who have done so to suddenly compare an additional French text, even if their treaties do not feature one.[18]

The MLI qualifies as a subsequent agreement under Article 31(3)(a) VCLT. Therefore, its own final clause applies with respect to the modifications it introduces, that is, even if the modified treaty originally designates its English text as prevailing, the court has to compare the French text of the MLI concerning the introduced modifications.[19] Consequently, instead of reducing complexity and global economic costs of tax treaty interpretation and application versus the current state of affairs, the solution chosen by the OECD for the MLI inflates them. In the words of Austry et al.:

> If the OECD were to produce the MLI and its Explanatory Statements in English and French versions that are equally authoritative, which might be the natural way to proceed, this would have a disadvantage because it would introduce a French official version of a modification to a tax treaty that was only in English, which would have to be considered in case there was a divergence of meaning (and similarly for a tax treaty only in French).[20]

Unfortunately, although the OECD realised that 'Drafting a multilateral instrument in a number of languages would increase its cost, the risk of conflict between versions in different languages and practical challenges in its administration',[21] it chose the worst option available in this respect, namely, TOW1, which increases the interpretative burden in case of divergences to the comparably largest extent.[22] In principle, it may even lead to the treaty being defective because of two texts stating the opposite and no

---

[18]This conclusion is largely independent of whether or not one agrees with me that in respect of treaties with all equally authoritative texts courts may not rely on a single text in isolation. As pointed out earlier, the routine interpretation approach does not provide a solution in principle because (by its own standards) it has to be abandoned as soon as an ambiguity or divergence arises. It is not to be expected that with the MLI substantially modifying a large number of tax treaties currently in place, the number of contested cases will be small in practice.

[19]See Schuch and West, 'Authentic Languages and Official Translations of the Multilateral Instrument and Covered Tax Agreements', 83.

[20]Austry et al., 'The Proposed OECD Multilateral Instrument Amending Tax Treaties', s. 3.

[21]OECD, *Developing a Multilateral Instrument to Modify Bilateral Tax Treaties, Action 15 – 2015 Final Report* (Paris: OECD Publishing, 2015), 22.

[22]Like many authors on the subject (e.g., Schuch and West, 'Authentic Languages and Of-

further text being available as additional context to decide the matter; however, via its Article 32(1), the MLI emulates a TOW7 final clause because a divergence between the English and French texts of the MLI certainly qualifies as a 'question arising as to the interpretation or implementation of provisions of a Covered Tax Agreement as they are modified by this Convention'.[23] Hence, treaty MAPs alleviate the problem; however, as argued earlier, TOW7 is suitable only as a method of last resort if none of the other options is available for material reasons. In comparison to what had already been achieved at large in terms of legal certainty through (English) prevailing texts and unilingual treaties, TOW1+7 as a new global standard constitutes a regression.

11.4. Solutions

How can this problem be solved while adequately addressing the outlined political impediments? Austry et al. provide the silver bullet, namely, allowing countries to subscribe to either the English or French text of the MLI as prevailing:

> A possible way of avoiding the problem caused by introducing an equally authoritative French version into a tax treaty in English only (and vice versa), with the MLI and its Explanatory Statements being in both English and French, might be for it to provide that states could adopt the modifications to existing tax treaties and the Explanatory Statements either in English only,

---

ficial Translations of the Multilateral Instrument and Covered Tax Agreements', 69, 80, 86; Shelton, 'Reconcilable Differences? The Interpretation of Multilingual Treaties', 20), the OECD fails to appreciate that the correlation between additional interpretational complexity and the number of equally authoritative language texts is not linear. While lowest for unilingual treaties, it is highest for two texts and decreases with the number of languages added because of the additional context. In consequence, although the drafting and administrative costs may be slightly lower for two language texts than for three or more, the costs incurred by the international community as a whole with respect to the interpretation and application of tax treaties in practice are incomparably higher for two texts versus any other number and, of course, most versus a unilingual MLI or one with a prevailing text.

[23] See Schuch and West, 'Authentic Languages and Official Translations of the Multilateral Instrument and Covered Tax Agreements', 83.

or French only, or both (which Canada would adopt for constitutional reasons) in which case both versions would have equal authority. Regardless of which version a state adopted, the English version would apply to modify a treaty solely in English or with a prevailing English text (and similarly with French). If the tax treaty being modified is between two states that have adopted the English version, that version of the modifications and Explanatory Statements would apply. If the tax treaty being modified is between two states that have adopted different versions, both versions would apply and be equally authoritative (this would automatically apply in Canada). However, states could, when signing the MLI, agree to use a different one of those languages in relation to a particular tax treaty, so that two countries both adopting the English version could modify a treaty in two Romance languages in French.[24]

Such approach, which is supported by the present author, would remove all French-speaking countries from the problem-country list. At the same time, it would allow Canada to continue walking its self-chosen path without everybody else being forced to incur the damaging costs of extra interpretational complexity induced by plurilingual form. Effectively, the issue would be condensed to the five countries with currently seven treaties listed above belonging to the Portuguese- and Spanish-speaking world, which are not yet signatories of the MLI but could be supported via targeted English language capacity building programs once they decide to join and face problems in this respect.

It almost seems as if the MLI final clause is intended to implement this approach despite its wording. Concerning its application, the Explanatory Statement to the MLI says the following:

> The final clause of the Convention provides the authentic languages of the Convention are English and French. Accordingly, where questions of interpretation arise in relation to Covered Tax Agreements concluded in other languages or in relation to translations of the Convention into other languages, it may be necessary to refer back to the English *or* French authentic texts of the Convention.[25]

---

[24] Austry et al., 'The Proposed OECD Multilateral Instrument Amending Tax Treaties', s. 3.

[25] OECD, *Explanatory Statement to the Multilateral Convention to Implement Tax Treaty Related Measures to Prevent Base Erosion and Profit Shifting* (Paris: OECD Publishing, 2016), para. 317 (emphasis added). The French text of the Explanatory Statement is equivalent, reading *ou* in place of the English 'or'.

The rather inconspicuous final 'or' seems to suggest an interpretation and application of the clause along the lines of the solution proposed by Austry et al. and supported here, that is, instead of implementing two equally authentic texts, the MLI could be considered to implement two equally authentic alternatives for countries to choose from as prevailing concerning their bilateral treaties.[26]

Unfortunately, under the textual approach to interpretation prescribed by the VCLT, the plain words of the MLI cannot be ignored and teleologically re-interpreted because of an Explanatory Statement that is not even very explicit; in view of the MLI final clause wording and the overall content and composition of the VCLT with respect to Articles 10 and 31–33, the Explanatory Statement formulation as it stands is too indistinct to provide enough traction for an application along the lines suggested here; the final clause wording itself should be different in order to explicitly implement such application.

What can be done to save the day? Several routes remain open. Under Article 33(1) MLI, 'Any Party may propose an amendment to this Convention by submitting the proposed amendment to the Depositary.' For the proposal to be considered by a 'Conference of the Parties', it will be necessary for the corresponding request to be 'supported by one-third of the Parties within six calendar months of the communication by the Depositary of the request'.[27] Given the global preference for English, this should pose no problem. The French speaking countries may prefer the same solution, which would allow them to treat the French text as prevailing. At the same time, the option of treating both texts as equally authoritative may be preserved for countries that want to do so. Hence, general consent at the conference leading to a respective amendment of the MLI final clause seems within reach.

Alternatively, presupposing agreement of all parties, the wording of the final clause could be qualified as a drafting error and corrected under Article 79 VCLT, explicitly implementing the approach hinted at by the Explanat-

---

[26]The VCLT would not stand in the way of such approach because Article 33(1) does not constitute a peremptory norm but ultimately leaves the matter to the actual intentions of the parties.

[27]Article 33(2) MLI in combination with 31(3) MLI.

ory Statement. Such errors constitute defects of the text in its property to correctly convey the intentions of the treaty partners; their correction does not imply a change or amendment of the treaty in substance, but the corrected text applies *ab initio* under Article 79(4) VCLT. Once more this would have to be instigated by a party under Article 31(3) MLI or all parties under Article 31(1) MLI.

Yet another possibility would be to expand the context concerning the interpretation and application of the final clause by a subsequent agreement of the parties under Article 31(3)(a) VCLT. In theory, this could be done by any two parties concerning their 'Covered Tax Agreement' on the basis of Article 32(1) MLI in combination with the treaty MAP.

Concerning the approach proposed here in general, issues of linguistic concordance between the English and French texts of the MLI gain in importance. Since both would remain equally authentic but applied asymmetrically as prevailing by different countries, special care has to be taken to ensure equivalence in order to prevent a schism between the English and French speaking worlds. This may require the OECD to adjust its now common practice of working predominantly in English, giving more attention again to French via simultaneous drafting of all further agreements and commentaries on the MLI.[28] There are signs of such approach having been adopted in respect of the MLI itself,[29] which seem to confirm the OECD's earlier statement that 'The multilateral instrument is being negotiated in English and French'.[30]

---

[28]Discrepancies remaining regardless may be healed subsequently under Article 33(2) and (3) MLI as soon as they are raised.

[29]See ibid., para. 80.

[30]OECD, *Public Discussion Draft, BEPS Action 15: Development of a Multilateral Instrument to Implement the Tax Treaty related BEPS Measures, 31 May – June 30* (Paris: OECD Publishing, 2016), 3, para. 9; see Schuch and West, 'Authentic Languages and Official Translations of the Multilateral Instrument and Covered Tax Agreements', 85.

Appendices

A. Vienna Convention on the Law of Treaties

A.1. Articles 31–33

Article 31

General rule of interpretation

1. A treaty shall be interpreted in good faith in accordance with the ordinary meaning to be given to the terms of the treaty in their context and in the light of its object and purpose.
2. The context for the purpose of the interpretation of a treaty shall comprise, in addition to the text, including its preamble and annexes:

    (a) any agreement relating to the treaty which was made between all the parties in connection with the conclusion of the treaty;
    (b) any instrument which was made by one or more parties in connection with the conclusion of the treaty and accepted by the other parties as an instrument related to the treaty.

3. There shall be taken into account, together with the context:

    (a) any subsequent agreement between the parties regarding the interpretation of the treaty or the application of its provisions;
    (b) any subsequent practice in the application of the treaty which establishes the agreement of the parties regarding its interpretation;
    (c) any relevant rules of international law applicable in the relations between the parties.

4. A special meaning shall be given to a term if it is established that the parties so intended.

A. Vienna Convention on the Law of Treaties

Article 32

Supplementary means of interpretation

Recourse may be had to supplementary means of interpretation, including the preparatory work of the treaty and the circumstances of its conclusion, in order to confirm the meaning resulting from the application of article 31, or to determine the meaning when the interpretation according to article 31:

   (a) leaves the meaning ambiguous or obscure; or
   (b) leads to a result which is manifestly absurd or unreasonable.

Article 33

Interpretation of treaties authenticated in two or more languages

1. When a treaty has been authenticated in two or more languages, the text is equally authoritative in each language, unless the treaty provides or the parties agree that, in case of divergence, a particular text shall prevail.
2. A version of the treaty in a language other than one of those in which the text was authenticated shall be considered an authentic text only if the treaty so provides or the parties so agree.
3. The terms of the treaty are presumed to have the same meaning in each authentic text.
4. Except where a particular text prevails in accordance with paragraph 1, when a comparison of the authentic texts discloses a difference of meaning which the application of articles 31 and 32 does not remove, the meaning which best reconciles the texts, having regard to the object and purpose of the treaty, shall be adopted.

A.2. Parties

Vienna Convention on the Law of Treaties.
Entry into force: 27 January 1980, in accordance with article 84(1).
Registration: 27 January 1980, No. 18232.
Signatories: 45.
Parties: 116.
Status: 02.06.2018.
Text: United Nations, *Treaty Series*, vol. 1155, p. 331.
Source: United Nations Treaty Collection, Chapter XXIII, Law of Treaties.

Table (A.1): Parties to the VCLT

Participant	Signature	Accession(a), Succession(d), Ratification
Afghanistan	23 May 1969	
Albania		27 Jun 2001 a
Algeria		8 Nov 1988 a
Andorra		5 Apr 2004 a
Argentina	23 May 1969	5 Dec 1972
Armenia		17 May 2005 a
Australia		13 Jun 1974 a
Austria		30 Apr 1979 a
Azerbaijan		11 Jan 2018 a
Barbados	23 May 1969	24 Jun 1971
Belarus		1 May 1986 a
Belgium		1 Sep 1992 a
Benin		2 Nov 2017 a
Bolivia	23 May 1969	
Bosnia-Herz.		1 Sep 1993 d
Brazil	23 May 1969	25 Sep 2009
Bulgaria		21 Apr 1987 a
Burkina Faso		25 May 2006 a
Cambodia	23 May 1969	
Cameroon		23 Oct 1991 a
Canada		14 Oct 1970 a
Central African Republic		10 Dec 1971 a
Chile	23 May 1969	9 Apr 1981
China		3 Sep 1997 a
Colombia	23 May 1969	10 Apr 1985
Congo	23 May 1969	12 Apr 1982

A. Vienna Convention on the Law of Treaties

Participant	Signature	Accession(a), Succession(d), Ratification
Costa Rica	23 May 1969	22 Nov 1996
Côte d'Ivoire	23 Jul 1969	
Croatia		12 Oct 1992 d
Cuba		9 Sep 1998 a
Cyprus		28 Dec 1976 a
Czech Republic		22 Feb 1993 d
Dem. Rep. Congo		25 Jul 1977 a
Denmark	18 Apr 1970	1 Jun 1976
Dominican Republic		1 Apr 2010 a
Ecuador	23 May 1969	11 Feb 2005
Egypt		11 Feb 1982 a
El Salvador	16 Feb 1970	
Estonia		21 Oct 1991 a
Ethiopia	30 Apr 1970	
Finland	23 May 1969	19 Aug 1977
Gabon		5 Nov 2004 a
Georgia		8 Jun 1995 a
Germany	30 Apr 1970	21 Jul 1987
Ghana	23 May 1969	
Greece		30 Oct 1974 a
Guatemala	23 May 1969	21 Jul 1997
Guinea		16 Sep 2005 a
Guyana	23 May 1969	15 Sep 2005
Haiti		25 Aug 1980 a
Holy See	30 Sep 1969	25 Feb 1977
Honduras	23 May 1969	20 Sep 1979
Hungary		19 Jun 1987 a
Iran (Islamic Republic of)	23 May 1969	
Ireland		7 Aug 2006 a
Italy	22 Apr 1970	25 Jul 1974
Jamaica	23 May 1969	28 Jul 1970
Japan		2 Jul 1981 a
Kazakhstan		5 Jan 1994 a
Kenya	23 May 1969	
Kiribati		15 Sep 2005 a
Kuwait		11 Nov 1975 a
Kyrgyzstan		11 May 1999 a
Lao People's Dem. Rep.		31 Mar 1998 a
Latvia		4 May 1993 a
Lesotho		3 Mar 1972 a
Liberia	23 May 1969	29 Aug 1985

Participant	Signature	Accession(a), Succession(d), Ratification
Libya		22 Dec 2008 a
Liechtenstein		8 Feb 1990 a
Lithuania		15 Jan 1992 a
Luxembourg	4 Sep 1969	23 May 2003
Madagascar	23 May 1969	
Malawi		23 Aug 1983 a
Malaysia		27 Jul 1994 a
Maldives		14 Sep 2005 a
Mali		31 Aug 1998 a
Malta		26 Sep 2012 a
Mauritius		18 Jan 1973 a
Mexico	23 May 1969	25 Sep 1974
Mongolia		16 May 1988 a
Montenegro		23 Oct 2006 d
Morocco	23 May 1969	26 Sep 1972
Mozambique		8 May 2001 a
Myanmar		16 Sep 1998 a
Nauru		5 May 1978 a
Nepal	23 May 1969	
Netherlands		9 Apr 1985 a
New Zealand	29 Apr 1970	4 Aug 1971
Niger		27 Oct 1971 a
Nigeria	23 May 1969	31 Jul 1969
Oman		18 Oct 1990 a
Pakistan	29 Apr 1970	
Panama		28 Jul 1980 a
Paraguay		3 Feb 1972 a
Peru	23 May 1969	14 Sep 2000
Philippines	23 May 1969	15 Nov 1972
Poland		2 Jul 1990 a
Portugal		6 Feb 2004 a
Republic of Korea	27 Nov 1969	27 Apr 1977
Republic of Moldova		26 Jan 1993 a
Russian Federation		29 Apr 1986 a
Rwanda		3 Jan 1980 a
Saudi Arabia		14 Apr 2003 a
Senegal		11 Apr 1986 a
Serbia		12 Mar 2001 d
Slovakia		28 May 1993 d
Slovenia		6 Jul 1992 d
Solomon Islands		9 Aug 1989 a

A. Vienna Convention on the Law of Treaties

Participant	Signature	Accession(a), Succession(d), Ratification
Spain		16 May 1972 a
St. Vincent / Grenadines		27 Apr 1999 a
State of Palestine		2 Apr 2014 a
Sudan	23 May 1969	18 Apr 1990
Suriname		31 Jan 1991 a
Sweden	23 Apr 1970	4 Feb 1975
Switzerland		7 May 1990 a
Syrian Arab Republic		2 Oct 1970 a
Tajikistan		6 May 1996 a
Macedonia		8 Jul 1999 d
Timor-Leste		8 Jan 2013 a
Togo		28 Dec 1979 a
Trinidad and Tobago	23 May 1969	
Tunisia		23 Jun 1971 a
Turkmenistan		4 Jan 1996 a
Ukraine		14 May 1986 a
UK and Northern Ireland	20 Apr 1970	25 Jun 1971
United Republic of Tanzania		12 Apr 1976 a
United States of America	24 Apr 1970	
Uruguay	23 May 1969	5 Mar 1982
Uzbekistan		12 Jul 1995 a
Viet Nam		10 Oct 2001 a
Zambia	23 May 1969	

B. Article 32(b) Case Law

The ILC cites two cases that, in its view, led to manifestly absurd or unreasonable results in respect of an interpretation under Article 31, mandating an 'exception to the rule that the ordinary meaning must prevail' in favour of an alternative meaning established with the help of supplementary means.[1] In my view, these two cases are not compelling as examples.

B.1. Netherlands Workers Delegate

In *Netherlands Workers Delegate* the court clearly established the ordinary meaning of Article 389(3) of the Treaty of Versailles via a textual interpretation under Article 31,[2] and there can be no suggestion that an 'absurd or unreasonable character of the "ordinary" meaning is manifest',[3] which would warrant departure from it in favour of an alternative meaning to be determined by recourse to supplementary means under Article 32(b). There is, of course, an implied assumption that the interpretation brought forward by the Netherlands government in support for its nomination of a single workers' delegate from the multitude of labour unions, namely, that the plural employed by the provision in question would refer to both one representative of the employers and one of the workers, is unreasonable; however, this unreasonableness is established by the court's interpretation of the ordinary wording of the provision in the light of its context and object and purpose. That the interpretation arrived at by the Netherlands government is unreasonable in view of the interpretation arrived at by the court is another matter that does not establish a case of Article 32(b); the Netherlands

---

[1] See ILC, *Documents of the Sixteenth Session Including the Report of the Commission to the General Assembly*, II:57, para. 16; ILC, *Draft Articles on the Law of Treaties with Commentaries*, II:223, para. 19.

[2] *Netherlands Workers Delegate to the ILO*, PCIJ (Publications of the Permanent Court of International Justice, 1922).

[3] ILC, *Draft Articles on the Law of Treaties with Commentaries*, II:223, para. 19.

government as party to the dispute was simply wrong in its interpretation of the ordinary wording of the provision given its context and object and purpose. Summary quote:

> The obligation is, that the persons nominated should have been chosen in agreement with the organisations most representative of employers or work people, as the case may be. There is no definition of the word 'representative' in the Treaty. The most representative organisations for this purpose are, of course, those organisations which best represent the employers and the workers respectively. What these organisations are, is a question to be decided in the particular case, having regard to the circumstances in each particular country at the time when the choice falls to be made. Numbers are not the only test of the representative character of the organisations, but they are an important factor; other things being equal, the most numerous will be the most representative. ...The view maintained by the Netherlands Confederation is not sufficiently supported by the text of the Article, and it is at all events obvious that the ideas inspiring the provisions of paragraph 3 clearly demonstrate that the only possible construction that can be given to the word 'organisations' is that the plural refers as well to employers' as to workers' organisations. ...The only object of the intervention of industrial organisations, in connection with the selection of delegates and technical advisers, is to ensure, as far as possible, that the Governments should nominate persons whose opinions are in harmony with the opinions of employers and workers respectively. If, therefore, in a particular country there exist several industrial organisations representing the working classes, the Government must take all of them into consideration when it is proceeding to the nomination of the workers' delegate and his technical advisers. Only by acting in this way can the Government succeed in choosing persons who, having regard to the particular circumstances, will be able to represent at the Conference the views of the working classes concerned. ...The following example will show how widely the view maintained by the Netherlands Confederation of Trades Unions differs from the spirit of Article 389 of the Treaty of Versailles. In a given country there are six organisations of workers, one with 110,000 members, and five others each with a membership of 100,000. According to the view of the objectors to the nomination made in the present case, the candidate proposed by the five last organisations jointly would have to be discarded in favour of the candidate of the first. One hundred and ten thousand workers would dictate to five hundred thousand. ...The Court confines itself to observing that no suggestion to the effect that only one organisation should be represented is anywhere to be found in the Treaty, which, on the contrary, expressly refers, in the first paragraph of Article 389, to there presentation of the workers of each particular country.

…Even admitting that such an interpretation is reconcilable with the letter of paragraph 3 of Article 389, it is clearly inadmissible. In order to realise this, it will suffice to point out that the construction in question would make it possible for one single organisation, in opposition to the wishes of the great majority of workers, to prevent the reaching of an agreement.[4]

B.2. South West Africa (Ethiopia v South Africa)

The second case cited by the ILC seems to be closer to the mark.[5] Article 7 of the Mandate of 17 December 1920 for South West Africa regarding Article 80(1) of the United Nations Charter read 'the Mandatory agrees that, if any dispute whatever should arise between the Mandatory and another Member of the League of Nations relating to the interpretation or the application of the provisions of the Mandate, such dispute shall be submitted to the Permanent Court of International Justice'. As the League of Nations ceased to exist on 19 April 1946, the objection was raised that there could no longer be 'another Member of the League of Nations'. Accordingly, 'no State had "*locus standi*" or was qualified to invoke the jurisdiction of the court in any dispute with the Respondent as Mandatory.'[6] The court dismissed this objection with reference to the agreement of the league members to continue their mandates despite the dissolution of the league.

It may be disputed again whether this is really a case 'where the absurd or unreasonable character of the "ordinary" meaning is manifest'.[7] Clearly, under a literal interpretation, the term 'Member of the League of Nations' had lost its reference in a technical sense of the word,[8] however, not necessarily its meaning under a textual interpretation. The case seems to be rather one of Article 31(3)(a) than Article 32(b): the court established the ordinary meaning of the term referring to its context and object and purpose with the help of a 'subsequent agreement between the parties regarding the

---

[4] *Netherlands Workers Delegate to the ILO.*

[5] *South West Africa (Ethiopia v South Africa)*, ICJ (Annual Reports of the International Court of Justice, 1962).

[6] Ibid.

[7] ILC, *Draft Articles on the Law of Treaties with Commentaries*, II:223, para. 19.

[8] 'Reference is a relation that obtains between certain sorts of representational tokens (e.g. names, mental states, pictures) and objects', Reimer and Michaelson, 'Reference'.

interpretation of the treaty or the application of its provisions' that must be read into the treaty,[9] and this ordinary meaning boiled down to 'former member of the League of Nations continuing its mandate'. Summary quote:

> The third reason for concluding that Article 7 with particular reference to the term 'another Member of the League of Nations' continues to be applicable is that obviously an agreement was reached among all the Members of the League at the Assembly session in April 1946 to continue the different Mandates as far as it was practically feasible or operable with reference to the obligations of the Mandatory Powers and therefore to maintain the rights of the Members of the League, notwithstanding the dissolution of the League itself. This agreement is evidenced not only by the contents of the dissolution resolution of 18 April 1946 but also by the discussions relating to the question of Mandates in the First Committee of the Assembly and the whole set of surrounding circumstances which preceded, and prevailed at, the session. Moreover, the Court sees no valid ground for departing from the conclusion reached in the Advisory Opinion of 1950 to the effect that the dissolution of the League of Nations has not rendered inoperable Article 7 of the Mandate. Those States who were Members of the League at the time of its dissolution continue to have the right to invoke the compulsory jurisdiction of the Court, as they had the right to do before the dissolution of the League. That right continues to exist for as long as the Respondent holds on to the right to administer the territory under the Mandate. ...Manifestly, this continuance of obligations under the Mandate could not begin to operate until the day after the dissolution of the League of Nations and hence the literal objections derived from the words 'another Member of the League of Nations' are not meaningful, since the resolution of 18 April 1946 was adopted precisely with a view to averting them and continuing the Mandate as a treaty between the Mandatory and the Members of the League of Nations.[10]

---

[9] UN, *Vienna Convention on the Law of Treaties*, Article 31(3)(a); see ILC, *Draft Articles on the Law of Treaties with Commentaries*, II:221, para. 14.

[10] *South West Africa (Ethiopia v South Africa)*.

C. Pre–Model OECD Member Treaties

C.1. 1963 Model (Income and Capital)

From the time before the adoption of the OECD Model on 30 July 1963, the IBFD records thirty-eight income tax treaties of OECD members as still in force,[1] thirteen between OECD members and twenty-five between OECD members and non-members:

Table (C.1): OECD Income Tax Treaties pre–OECD Model

Treaty	Conclusion
Antigua and Barbuda-United Kingdom	1947
Austria-Egypt	1962
Austria-Japan	1961
Austria-Luxembourg	1962
Austria-Sweden	1959
Belize-United Kingdom	1947
Brunei-United Kingdom	1950
Cyprus-Norway	1955
France-French Polynesia	1957
France-Germany	1959
France-Lebanon	1962
France-Luxembourg	1958
France-Monaco	1963
France-Spain	1961
Germany-Israel	1962
Germany-Netherlands	1959
Greece-Sweden	1961
Greece-United Kingdom	1953
Greece-United States	1950
Grenada-United Kingdom	1949
Guernsey-United Kingdom	1952
Isle of Man-United Kingdom	1955

---

[1] *Tax Treaties Database*, 2016.

Treaty	Conclusion
Israel-Sweden	1959
Israel-United Kingdom	1962
Jersey-United Kingdom	1952
Kiribati-United Kingdom	1950
Malawi-Switzerland	1961
Malawi-United Kingdom	1955
Montserrat-United Kingdom	1947
Myanmar-United Kingdom	1950
Namibia-United Kingdom	1962
Norway-Sierra Leone	1955
Pakistan-United States	1957
Sierra Leone-United Kingdom	1947
Solomon Islands-United Kingdom	1950
St. Kitts and Nevis-United Kingdom	1947
Switzerland-Zambia	1961
Tuvalu-United Kingdom	1950

C.2. 1982 Model (Estates, Inheritances, and Gifts)

From the time before the OECD Model on inheritance taxes,[2] the IBFD records sixty-four inheritance and gift tax treaties as still in force,[3] forty-one between OECD members and twenty-three between OECD members and non-members:

Table (C.2): OECD Inheritance Tax Treaties pre–OECD Inheritance Tax Model

Treaty	Conclusion
Australia-United States	1953
Australia-United States	1953
Austria-Liechtenstein	1955
Austria-Sweden	1962
Belgium-France	1959
Belgium-Sweden	1956
Benin-France	1975

---

[2] OECD, 'Recommendation of the Council Concerning the Avoidance of Double Taxation with Respect to Taxes on Estates and Inheritances and on Gifts'.

[3] *Tax Treaties Database*, 2016.

C.2. 1982 Model (Estates, Inheritances, and Gifts)

Treaty	Conclusion
Burkina Faso-France	1965
Cameroon-France	1976
Central African Republic-France	1969
Denmark-Italy	1966
Denmark-Switzerland	1973
Faroe Islands-Switzerland	1978
Finland-France	1958
Finland-Netherlands	1954
Finland-Switzerland	1956
Finland-United States	1952
France-Ivory Coast	1966
France-Kuwait	1982
France-Lebanon	1962
France-Mali	1972
France-Mauritania	1967
France-Mayotte	1970
France-Monaco	1950
France-Niger	1965
France-Saudi Arabia	1982
France-Senegal	1974
France-Spain	1963
France-Switzerland	1953
France-Switzerland	1979
France-Togo	1971
France-Tunisia	1973
France-United Kingdom	1963
France-United States	1978
Germany-Greece	1910
Germany-Switzerland	1978
Germany-United States	1980
Greece-Italy	1964

C. Pre–Model OECD Member Treaties

Fifteen of them are coupled with income tax treaties:

Table (C.3): OECD Mixed Tax Treaties pre–OECD Inheritance Tax Model

Treaty	Conclusion
Benin-France	1975
Burkina Faso-France	1965
Cameroon-France	1976
Central African Republic-France	1969
France-Ivory Coast	1966
France-Kuwait	1982
France-Lebanon	1962
France-Mali	1972
France-Mauritania	1967
France-Mayotte	1970
France-Niger	1965
France-Saudi Arabia	1982
France-Senegal	1974
France-Togo	1971
France-Tunisia	1973

D. Treaty and TOW Distributions

D.1. Treaties per Group

Table (D.1): Global Tax Treaty Network per Group

Treaty	No.	%total
OECD-OECD	590	17.57%
OECD-NOECD	1689	50.30%
NOECD-NOECD	1079	32.13%
OECDKP-OECD	156	4.65%
OECDKP-NOECD	218	6.49%
G20-G20	166	4.94%
G20-NG20	1229	36.60%
CW-CW	222	6.61%
CW-NCW	1031	30.70%
EU-EU	365	10.87%
EU-NEU	1484	44.19%
CIS-CIS	37	1.10%
CIS-NCIS	547	16.29%
AW-AW	78	2.32%
AW-NAW	563	16.77%
LA-LA	24	0.71%
LA-NAL	230	6.85%
AF-AF	41	1.22%
AF-NAF	338	10.07%
AS-AS	57	1.70%
AS-NAS	628	18.70%

D. Treaty and TOW Distributions

Table (D.2): Global Tax Treaty Network per Group with One or Both Group Members per Treaty

Treaty	No.	%total
OECD any	2279	67.87%
OECDKP any	374	11.14%
G20 any	1395	41.54%
CW any	1253	37.31%
EU any	1849	55.06%
CIS any	584	17.39%
AW any	641	19.09%
LA any	254	7.56%
AF any	379	11.29%
AS any	685	20.40%

D.2. Per Country TOW Distribution

The following table displays the TOW use of countries with twenty or more plurilingual treaties with prevailing text. TOW9 is omitted since only three treaties in the global tax treaty network implement it. TOW8 is omitted because it is only relevant in the case of Malaysia (35.38% of all its treaties with prevailing text). The special case of TOW7 is only used by Spain in six instances and France-UAE (1989).

Table (D.3): TOW Distribution for Countries with Twenty or more Plurilingual Treaties

Country	PL w PT	TOW2	TOW3	TOW4	TOW6
India	93	38.71%	50.54%	4.30%	5.38%
China (People's Rep.)	80	6.25%	80.00%	6.25%	6.25%
Romania	67	8.96%	83.58%	4.48%	2.99%
Malaysia	65	3.08%	56.92%	4.62%	0.00%
Italy	64	4.69%	43.75%	4.69%	45.31%
Korea (Rep.)	64	7.81%	84.38%	4.69%	1.56%
Russia	62	27.42%	38.71%	33.87%	0.00%
Ukraine	59	20.34%	64.41%	11.86%	3.39%
Switzerland	57	7.02%	28.07%	56.14%	8.77%
United Arab Emirates	57	29.82%	56.14%	10.53%	3.51%
Poland	55	9.09%	76.36%	9.09%	3.64%
Portugal	54	7.41%	79.63%	3.70%	7.41%
Kuwait	53	75.47%	18.87%	5.66%	0.00%
Belarus	52	15.38%	76.92%	5.77%	1.92%
Turkey	52	53.85%	30.77%	11.54%	1.92%
Vietnam	52	9.62%	78.85%	5.77%	3.85%
Netherlands	50	6.00%	14.00%	80.00%	0.00%
Croatia	49	8.16%	63.27%	28.57%	0.00%
Austria	48	18.75%	70.83%	8.33%	2.08%
Bulgaria	48	6.25%	81.25%	10.42%	0.00%
Slovenia	48	62.50%	29.17%	6.25%	2.08%
Georgia	47	25.53%	61.70%	8.51%	4.26%
Latvia	47	12.77%	82.98%	4.26%	0.00%
Germany	46	0.00%	6.52%	82.61%	8.70%
Iran	46	13.04%	76.09%	8.70%	0.00%
Lithuania	46	4.35%	89.13%	6.52%	0.00%
Czech Republic	45	48.89%	24.44%	24.44%	2.22%
Hungary	45	11.11%	68.89%	13.33%	2.22%
Qatar	45	71.11%	26.67%	2.22%	0.00%

D. Treaty and TOW Distributions

Country	PL w PT	TOW2	TOW3	TOW4	TOW6
Estonia	44	15.91%	81.82%	2.27%	0.00%
Macedonia (FYR)	44	18.18%	65.91%	13.64%	2.27%
Uzbekistan	44	20.45%	68.18%	9.09%	2.27%
Slovak Republic	43	9.30%	74.42%	13.95%	0.00%
Israel	41	19.51%	53.66%	14.63%	12.20%
Morocco	41	4.88%	82.93%	7.32%	2.44%
Sri Lanka	41	7.32%	82.93%	4.88%	2.44%
Indonesia	40	12.50%	57.50%	25.00%	2.50%
Azerbaijan	39	23.08%	69.23%	7.69%	0.00%
Greece	39	15.38%	43.59%	7.69%	30.77%
Spain	39	46.15%	35.90%	7.69%	7.69%
Armenia	37	16.22%	75.68%	8.11%	0.00%
Kazakhstan	35	37.14%	57.14%	2.86%	2.86%
Moldova	35	31.43%	60.00%	5.71%	2.86%
Thailand	35	17.14%	28.57%	20.00%	31.43%
Bahrain	34	35.29%	50.00%	2.94%	8.82%
Belgium	34	52.94%	47.06%	0.00%	0.00%
Egypt	34	11.76%	61.76%	14.71%	11.76%
Finland	32	3.13%	96.88%	0.00%	0.00%
Mexico	32	37.50%	56.25%	6.25%	0.00%
Cyprus	30	16.67%	53.33%	23.33%	6.67%
Albania	29	44.83%	34.48%	13.79%	3.45%
Japan	29	0.00%	86.21%	10.34%	0.00%
Norway	28	17.86%	57.14%	21.43%	3.57%
Saudi Arabia	27	11.11%	88.89%	0.00%	0.00%
Serbia and Montenegro	27	7.41%	81.48%	11.11%	0.00%
Turkmenistan	26	50.00%	50.00%	0.00%	0.00%
Denmark	25	28.00%	52.00%	4.00%	16.00%
Sweden	25	32.00%	52.00%	0.00%	16.00%
Iceland	24	12.50%	75.00%	4.17%	12.50%
Singapore	24	37.50%	62.50%	0.00%	0.00%
Bosnia and Herzegovina	23	13.04%	69.57%	13.04%	0.00%
Oman	23	8.70%	47.83%	43.48%	0.00%
Tajikistan	22	40.91%	54.55%	4.55%	0.00%
Venezuela	21	38.10%	33.33%	28.57%	0.00%
Kyrgyzstan	20	30.00%	55.00%	10.00%	0.00%
Mongolia	20	30.00%	55.00%	10.00%	0.00%

E. Sample

The sample consists of all tax treaties concluded between 1 January 1960 and 15 August 2016 insofar as they have been recorded in the IBFD tax treaties database, independent of their status, that is, not only treaties in force but also terminated treaties and treaties not yet in force but still to be ratified are included. Treaties reported as merely initialed, under negotiation, or abandoned are excluded. The same goes for mere exchanges of notes, memoranda of understanding, dominion double taxation relief rules, and agreements concerning the provisional abolition of double taxation prior to a treaty. All types of tax treaties are included, that is, mainly income and capital and inheritance and gift tax treaties, whether separate or in combination, or only covering specific types of income. Not included are exchange of information treaties, transport agreements, social security treaties, economic relations treaties, FATCA agreements, friendship and fiscal co-operation agreements, friendship and commerce treaties, and mutual assistance agreements unless they are not stand-alone but coupled with a tax treaty in one single instrument. In addition, one hundred and forty-six treaties satisfying the above criteria have been excluded because either their texts could not be retrieved or their final clause type of wording could not be established beyond doubt. They are listed below as excluded treaties. The sample comprises 3,844 tax treaties in total: 3,358 in force (or yet to come into force) and 486 terminated.

E.1. Excluded Treaties

Table (E.1): Treaties Excluded from the Sample

Treaty	Conclusion
Austria-Iceland	2016
Algeria-India	2001
Algeria-Mali	1999
Algeria-Mauritania	2011
Algeria-Niger	1998
Algeria-Saudi Arabia	2013
Algeria-Vietnam	1999
Andorra-Luxembourg	2014
Andorra-Portugal	2015
Andorra-United Arab Emirates	2015
Armenia-Belarus	2000
Armenia-Georgia	1997
Armenia-Germany	2016
Armenia-Moldova	2002
Armenia-Ukraine	1996
Azerbaijan-Belarus	2001
Azerbaijan-Kuwait	2009
Azerbaijan-Moldova	1997
Azerbaijan-Poland	1997
Azerbaijan-Tajikistan	2007
Azerbaijan-Uzbekistan	1996
Bahrain-Egypt	2016
Bangladesh-Kuwait	2014
Bangladesh-Myanmar	2008
Bangladesh-United Arab Emirates	2011
Belarus-Ecuador	2016
Belarus-Korea (Dem. People's Rep.)	2006
Belize-United Arab Emirates	2015
Benin-Kuwait	2009
Benin-United Arab Emirates	2013
Bosnia and Herzegovina-Egypt	1998
Botswana-Lesotho	2010
Botswana-Malawi	2016
Brunei-Korea (Rep.)	2014
Brunei-Qatar	2012
Brunei-Tajikistan	2010

E. Sample

Treaty	Conclusion
Brunei-United Arab Emirates	2013
Cape Verde-Guinea-Bissau	2015
China (People's Rep.)-Paraguay	1994
China (People's Rep.)-Romania	2016
China (People's Rep.)-Taiwan	2015
Colombia-Panama	2016
Comoros Islands-United Arab Emirates	2015
Costa Rica-Mexico	2014
Curaçao-Netherlands	2013
Djibouti-Kuwait	2009
Egypt-Kuwait	2014
Egypt-Serbia and Montenegro	1987
Egypt-Sri Lanka	2000
Egypt-Tunisia	1989
Eritrea-Qatar	2000
Ethiopia-Iran	2005
Ethiopia-Korea (Dem. People's Rep.)	2012
Ethiopia-Korea (Rep.)	2016
Ethiopia-Qatar	2013
Ethiopia-Saudi Arabia	2013
Ethiopia-United Arab Emirates	2015
Gabon-Mauritius	2013
Gabon-Saudi Arabia	2015
Georgia-Kazakhstan	1997
Georgia-Russia	1999
Greece-Spain	1919
Guyana-Kuwait	2010
Hong Kong-Pakistan	2015
India-Kenya	2016
Indonesia-Laos	2011
Indonesia-Papua New Guinea	2003
Iran-Italy	2005
Iran-Kenya	2009
Iran-Senegal	2010
Iran-Sri Lanka	1997
Iran-Yemen	2004
Ivory Coast-Turkey	2016
Jamaica-Mexico	2016
Jordan-Kuwait	2001
Jordan-United Arab Emirates	2005
Kazakhstan-Kyrgyzstan	1997

Treaty	Conclusion
Kazakhstan-Moldova	1999
Kazakhstan-Saudi Arabia	2011
Kazakhstan-Slovenia	2016
Kazakhstan-Tajikistan	1999
Kenya-Korea (Rep.)	2014
Kenya-Kuwait	2013
Kenya-Nigeria	2013
Kenya-Qatar	2014
Kenya-Seychelles	2014
Korea (Dem. People's Rep.)-Macedonia (FYR)	1997
Korea (Dem. People's Rep.)-Malaysia	1998
Korea (Dem. People's Rep.)-Vietnam	2002
Korea (Rep.)-Sudan	2004
Korea (Rep.)-Tajikistan	2013
Korea (Rep.)-Turkmenistan	2015
Kosovo-United Arab Emirates	2016
Kuwait-Lithuania	2013
Kuwait-Mauritania	2009
Kuwait-Russia	2010
Kuwait-Senegal	2007
Kuwait-Syria	1997
Kuwait-Tajikistan	2013
Kyrgystan-Qatar	2014
Kyrgyzstan-Moldova	2004
Kyrgyzstan-Poland	1998
Kyrgyzstan-Tajikistan	1998
Kyrgyzstan-United Arab Emirates	2014
Kyrgyzstan-Uzbekistan	1996
Libya-Syria	2007
Libya-Tunisia	1978
Madagascar-Mauritius	1994
Malawi-Seychelles	2012
Malaysia-Ukraine	2016
Malta-Vietnam	2016
Mauritania-Qatar	2003
Mauritania-Senegal	1971
Mauritania-Sudan	2009
Mauritania-Tunisia	1986
Mauritania-United Arab Emirates	2015
Mauritius-Swaziland	2014
Mexico-Philippines	2015

E. Sample

Treaty	Conclusion
Mexico-Saudi Arabia	2016
Moldova-Poland	1994
Moldova-Tajikistan	2002
Montenegro-Portugal	2016
Montenegro-Serbia	2011
Morocco-Tunisia	1974
Netherlands-St. Maarten	2014
Nigeria-Poland	1999
Nigeria-United Arab Emirates	2016
Palestine-Sudan	2013
Palestinian Autonomous Areas-United Arab Emirates	2012
Philippines-Sri Lanka	2000
Philippines-Taiwan	2002
Romania-Sudan	1979
Romania-Syria	2008
Romania-Syria	1987
Romania-Tajikistan	2007
Saudi Arabia-Tajikistan	2014
Saudi Arabia-Turkmenistan	2016
Senegal-Turkey	2015
Senegal-United Arab Emirates	2015
Singapore-South Africa	2015
Somalia-Turkey	2016
Spain-Syria	2008
Sudan-Syria	2001
Turkmenistan-Uzbekistan	1996
Uganda-United Arab Emirates	2015
United Arab Emirates-Uruguay	2014

E.2. Global Tax Treaty Network

Table (E.2): Treaties In Force or Yet to Come Into Force

Treaty	Conclusion	AL	UL/PT	TOW
Albania–Austria	2007	eng;alb;ger	eng	3
Albania–Belgium	2002	eng	eng	5
Albania–Bosnia and Herzegovina	2008	eng;alb;bos;ser;cro	eng	3
Albania–Bulgaria	1998	eng;alb;bul	eng	3
Albania–China (People's Rep.)	2004	eng;alb;chi	eng	3
Albania–Croatia	1994	eng	eng	5
Albania–Czech Republic	1995	eng	eng	5
Albania–Egypt	2005	eng;alb;ara	eng	3
Albania–Estonia	2010	eng;est;alb	eng	3
Albania–France	2002	fre;alb		1
Albania–Germany	2010	eng;ger;alb	eng	4
Albania–Greece	1995	eng	eng	5
Albania–Hungary	1992	eng	eng	5
Albania–Iceland	2014	eng	eng	5
Albania–India	2013	eng;hin;alb	eng	2
Albania–Ireland	2009	eng;alb		1
Albania–Italy	1994	eng;alb;ita	eng	6
Albania–Korea (Rep.)	2006	eng;alb;kor	eng	2
Albania–Kosovo	2004	eng;alb	eng	2
Albania–Kosovo	2014	eng;alb	eng	2
Albania–Kuwait	2010	eng;ara;alb	eng	2
Albania–Latvia	2008	eng;alb;lat	eng	2
Albania–Luxembourg	2009	fre;alb		1
Albania–Macedonia (FYR)	1998	eng;alb;mac	eng	3
Albania–Malaysia	1994	eng;alb;may	eng	8
Albania–Malta	2000	eng;alb	eng	2
Albania–Moldova	2002	eng;alb;mol	eng	2
Albania–Morocco	2015	eng;ara;alb	eng	3
Albania–Netherlands	2004	eng;alb;dut	eng	4
Albania–Norway	1998	eng	eng	5
Albania–Poland	1993	eng;alb;pol	eng	3
Albania–Qatar	2011	eng;ara;alb	eng	2
Albania–Romania	1994	eng;alb;rum	eng	2
Albania–Russia	1995	eng;alb;rus	eng	2
Albania–Serbia and Montenegro	2004	eng;alb;ser	eng	3
Albania–Singapore	2010	eng;alb	eng	2
Albania–Slovenia	2008	eng;alb;slv	eng	2
Albania–Spain	2010	eng;spa;alb	map	7
Albania–Sweden	1998	eng	eng	5
Albania–Switzerland	1999	eng;alb;ger	eng	4
Albania–Turkey	1994	eng	eng	5
Albania–United Arab Emirates	2014	eng;ara;alb	eng	4
Albania–United Kingdom	2013	eng;alb		1
Algeria–Austria	2003	fre;ara;ger	fre	3
Algeria–Bahrain	2000	ara	ara	5
Algeria–Belgium	1991	fre;ara;dut		1

E. Sample

Treaty	Conclusion	AL	UL/PT	TOW
Algeria–Bosnia and Herzegovina	2009	eng;bos;ser;cro;ara	eng	3
Algeria–Bulgaria	1998	eng;ara;bul	eng	3
Algeria–Canada	1999	eng;fre;ara		1
Algeria–China (People's Rep.)	2006	eng;ara;chi	eng	3
Algeria–Egypt	2001	ara	ara	5
Algeria–France	1999	fre;ara		1
Algeria–Germany	2007	fre;ara;ger	fre	4
Algeria–Indonesia	1995	ara;ind		1
Algeria–Iran	2008	eng;ara;per	eng	3
Algeria–Italy	1991	fre;ara;ita		1
Algeria–Jordan	1997	ara	ara	5
Algeria–Korea (Rep.)	2001	eng;ara;kor	eng	3
Algeria–Kuwait	2006	ara	ara	5
Algeria–Lebanon	2002	ara	ara	5
Algeria–Libya	1988	ara	ara	5
Algeria–Morocco	1990	ara	ara	5
Algeria–Oman	2000	ara	ara	5
Algeria–Poland	2000	fre;ara;pol		1
Algeria–Portugal	2003	fre;ara;por	fre	3
Algeria–Qatar	2008	fre	fre	5
Algeria–Romania	1994	fre;ara;rum		1
Algeria–Russia	2006	fre;ara;rus	fre	2
Algeria–South Africa	1998	eng;ara		1
Algeria–Spain	2002	eng;ara;spa	eng	2
Algeria–Switzerland	2006	fre;ara		1
Algeria–Syria	1997	ara	ara	5
Algeria–Tunisia	1985	ara	ara	5
Algeria–Turkey	1994	fre;ara;tur	fre	3
Algeria–Ukraine	2002	fre;ara;ukr		1
Algeria–United Arab Emirates	2001	ara	ara	5
Algeria–United Kingdom	2015	eng;ara		1
Algeria–Yemen	2002	ara	ara	5
Andorra–France	2013	fre;cat		1
Andorra–Liechtenstein	2015	eng;ger;cat	eng	3
Andorra–Spain	2015	spa;cat		1
Anguilla–Switzerland	1963	eng;fre		1
Antigua and Barbuda–Switzerland	1963	eng;fre		1
Argentina–Australia	1999	eng;spa;rus		1
Argentina–Belgium	1996	eng;fre;spa;dut	eng	2
Argentina–Bolivia	1976	spa	spa	5
Argentina–Brazil	1980	por;spa		1
Argentina–Canada	1993	eng;fre;spa		1
Argentina–Chile	2015	spa	spa	5
Argentina–Denmark	1995	eng;spa;den	eng	2
Argentina–Finland	1994	eng;spa;fin	eng	3
Argentina–France	1979	fre;spa		1
Argentina–Germany	1978	spa;ger		1
Argentina–Italy	1979	fre;spa;ita	fre	3
Argentina–Mexico	2015	spa	spa	5
Argentina–Netherlands	1996	eng;spa;dut	eng	4
Argentina–Norway	1997	eng;spa;nor	eng	3
Argentina–Russia	2001	eng;spa;rus	eng	2

Treaty	Conclusion	AL	UL/PT	TOW
Argentina–Spain	2013	spa	spa	5
Argentina–Sweden	1995	eng;spa;swe	eng	3
Argentina–Switzerland	2014	eng;fre;spa	eng	4
Argentina–United Kingdom	1996	eng;spa		1
Argentina–United States	1981	eng;spa		1
Armenia–Austria	2002	eng;arm;ger	eng	3
Armenia–Belgium	2001	eng;fre;arm;dut	eng	3
Armenia–Bulgaria	1995	eng;arm;bul	eng	3
Armenia–Canada	2004	eng;fre;arm		1
Armenia–China (People's Rep.)	1996	eng;arm;chi	eng	3
Armenia–Croatia	2009	eng;arm;cro	eng	3
Armenia–Cyprus	2011	eng;arm;gre	eng	4
Armenia–Czech Republic	2008	eng;arm;cze	eng	2
Armenia–Denmark	1986	rus;dan		1
Armenia–Egypt	2005	eng;arm;ara	eng	3
Armenia–Estonia	2001	eng;arm;est	eng	3
Armenia–Finland	2006	eng;arm;fin	eng	3
Armenia–France	1997	fre;arm		1
Armenia–Germany	1981	ger;rus		1
Armenia–Greece	1999	eng;arm;gre	eng	3
Armenia–Hungary	2009	eng;arm;hun	eng	3
Armenia–India	2003	eng;arm;hin	eng	3
Armenia–Indonesia	2005	eng;arm;ind	eng	3
Armenia–Iran	1995	eng;arm;per	eng	3
Armenia–Ireland	2011	eng;arm		1
Armenia–Italy	2002	eng;arm;ita	eng	3
Armenia–Japan	1986	eng;rus;jap	eng	3
Armenia–Kuwait	2009	eng;arm;ara	eng	2
Armenia–Latvia	2000	eng;arm;lat	eng	3
Armenia–Lebanon	1998	eng;arm;ara	eng	3
Armenia–Lithuania	2000	eng;arm;lit	eng	3
Armenia–Luxembourg	2009	eng;fre;arm		1
Armenia–Malaysia	1987	eng;rus;may	eng	3
Armenia–Netherlands	2001	eng;arm;dut	eng	4
Armenia–Poland	1999	eng;arm;pol	eng	3
Armenia–Qatar	2002	eng;arm;ara	eng	2
Armenia–Romania	1996	eng;arm;rum	eng	3
Armenia–Russia	1996	rus;arm		1
Armenia–Serbia	2014	eng;ser;arm	eng	3
Armenia–Slovak Republic	2015	eng;arm;slo	eng	3
Armenia–Slovenia	2010	eng;arm;slo	eng	2
Armenia–Spain	2010	eng;arm;spa	eng	2
Armenia–Sweden	2016	eng;swe;arm	eng	3
Armenia–Switzerland	2006	eng;arm;ger	eng	4
Armenia–Syria	2005	eng;arm;ara	eng	3
Armenia–Tajikistan	2005	rus;tgk;arm	rus	3
Armenia–Thailand	2001	eng;arm;tha	eng	3
Armenia–Turkmenistan	1997	arm;tkm;rus	rus	3
Armenia–United Arab Emirates	2002	eng;arm;ara	eng	2
Armenia–United Kingdom	2011	eng;arm		1
Armenia–United States	1973	eng;rus		1
Aruba–Australia	2009	eng	eng	5

E. Sample

Treaty	Conclusion	AL	UL/PT	TOW
Aruba–United States	1986	eng	eng	5
Australia–Austria	1986	eng;ger		1
Australia–Belgium	1977	eng;fre;dut		1
Australia–British Virgin Islands	2008	eng	eng	5
Australia–Canada	1980	eng;fre		1
Australia–Chile	2010	eng;spa		1
Australia–China (People's Rep.)	1988	eng;chi		1
Australia–Cook Islands	2009	eng	eng	5
Australia–Czech Republic	1995	eng;cze		1
Australia–Denmark	1981	eng	eng	5
Australia–Fiji	1990	eng	eng	5
Australia–Finland	2006	eng;fin		1
Australia–France	2006	eng;fre		1
Australia–Germany	1972	eng;ger		1
Australia–Germany	2015	eng;ger		1
Australia–Guernsey	2009	eng	eng	5
Australia–Hungary	1990	eng;hun		1
Australia–India	1991	eng;hin	eng	6
Australia–Indonesia	1992	eng	eng	5
Australia–Ireland	1983	eng	eng	5
Australia–Isle of Man	2009	eng	eng	5
Australia–Italy	1982	eng;ita		1
Australia–Japan	2008	eng;jap		1
Australia–Jersey	2009	eng	eng	5
Australia–Kiribati	1991	eng	eng	5
Australia–Korea (Rep.)	1982	eng;kor		1
Australia–Malaysia	1980	eng;may		1
Australia–Malta	1984	eng	eng	5
Australia–Marshall Islands	2010	eng	eng	5
Australia–Mauritius	2010	eng	eng	5
Australia–Mexico	2002	eng;spa		1
Australia–Netherlands	1976	eng;dut		1
Australia–New Zealand	2009	eng	eng	5
Australia–Norway	2006	eng	eng	5
Australia–Papua New Guinea	1989	eng	eng	5
Australia–Philippines	1979	eng	eng	5
Australia–Poland	1991	eng;pol		1
Australia–Romania	2000	eng;rum		1
Australia–Russia	2000	eng;rus		1
Australia–Samoa	2009	eng	eng	5
Australia–Singapore	1969	eng	eng	5
Australia–Slovak Republic	1999	eng;slv		1
Australia–South Africa	1999	eng	eng	5
Australia–Spain	1992	eng;spa		1
Australia–Sri Lanka	1989	eng;sin		1
Australia–Sweden	1981	eng	eng	5
Australia–Switzerland	1980	eng;ger		1
Australia–Switzerland	2013	eng;ger		1
Australia–Taiwan	1996	eng;chi	eng	3
Australia–Thailand	1989	eng;tha		1
Australia–Turkey	2010	eng;tur		1
Australia–United Kingdom	2003	eng	eng	5

Treaty	Conclusion	AL	UL/PT	TOW
Australia–United States	1982	eng	eng	5
Australia–Vietnam	1992	eng;vts		1
Austria–Azerbaijan	2000	eng;ger;aze	eng	2
Austria–Bahrain	2009	eng;ger;ara	eng	3
Austria–Barbados	2006	eng;ger		1
Austria–Belarus	2001	eng;ger;bel	eng	3
Austria–Belgium	1971	fre;ger;dut		1
Austria–Belize	2002	eng;ger		1
Austria–Bosnia and Herzegovina	2010	eng;ger;bos;ser;cro	eng	3
Austria–Brazil	1975	ger;por		1
Austria–Bulgaria	2010	eng;ger;bul	eng	3
Austria–Canada	1976	eng;fre;ger		1
Austria–Chile	2012	eng;ger;spa	eng	3
Austria–China (People's Rep.)	1991	eng;ger;chi	eng	3
Austria–Croatia	2000	eng;ger;cro	eng	3
Austria–Cuba	2003	eng;ger;spa	eng	3
Austria–Cyprus	1990	eng;ger;gre	eng	6
Austria–Czech Republic	1996	eng	eng	5
Austria–Czech Republic	2006	eng	eng	5
Austria–Denmark	2007	ger;dan		1
Austria–Egypt	1962	eng	eng	5
Austria–Estonia	2001	eng;ger;est	eng	3
Austria–Faroe Islands	1967	ger;dan		1
Austria–Finland	2000	ger;fin		1
Austria–France	1993	fre;ger		1
Austria–France	1993	fre;ger		1
Austria–Georgia	2005	eng;ger;geo	eng	4
Austria–Germany	2000	ger	ger	5
Austria–Greece	2007	eng	eng	5
Austria–Hong Kong	2010	eng	eng	5
Austria–Hungary	1975	ger;hun		1
Austria–India	1999	eng;ger;hin	eng	2
Austria–Indonesia	1986	eng	eng	5
Austria–Iran	2002	eng;ger;per	eng	2
Austria–Ireland	1966	eng;ger		1
Austria–Israel	1970	eng	eng	5
Austria–Italy	1981	ger;ita		1
Austria–Japan	1961	eng	eng	5
Austria–Kazakhstan	2004	eng;ger;rus;kaz	eng	2
Austria–Korea (Rep.)	1985	eng	eng	5
Austria–Kuwait	2002	eng;ger;ara	eng	2
Austria–Kyrgyzstan	2001	eng;ger;rus;kyr	eng	3
Austria–Latvia	2005	eng;ger;lat	eng	3
Austria–Liechtenstein	1969	ger	ger	5
Austria–Liechtenstein	2013	ger	ger	5
Austria–Lithuania	2005	eng;ger;lit	eng	3
Austria–Luxembourg	1962	ger	ger	5
Austria–Macedonia (FYR)	2007	eng;ger;mac	eng	3
Austria–Malaysia	1989	eng;ger;may	eng	3
Austria–Malta	1978	eng;ger		1
Austria–Mexico	2004	eng;ger;spa	eng	3
Austria–Moldova	2004	eng;ger;mol	eng	3

E. Sample

Treaty	Conclusion	AL	UL/PT	TOW
Austria–Mongolia	2003	eng;ger;mol	eng	3
Austria–Montenegro	2014	eng;ger;mtg	eng	3
Austria–Morocco	2002	fre;ger;ara	fre	3
Austria–Nepal	2000	eng	eng	5
Austria–Netherlands	1970	ger;dut		1
Austria–Netherlands	2001	ger;dut		1
Austria–New Zealand	2006	eng;ger	eng	3
Austria–Norway	1995	eng;ger;nor	eng	4
Austria–Pakistan	2005	eng	eng	5
Austria–Philippines	1981	eng;ger		1
Austria–Poland	2004	eng;ger;pol	eng	3
Austria–Qatar	2010	eng;ger;ara	eng	2
Austria–Romania	2005	eng;ger;rum	eng	3
Austria–Russia	2000	eng;ger;rus	eng	4
Austria–San Marino	2004	eng;ger;ita	eng	3
Austria–Saudi Arabia	2006	eng;ger;ara	eng	3
Austria–Serbia	2010	eng;ger;ser	eng	3
Austria–Singapore	2001	eng;ger		1
Austria–Slovak Republic	1978	ger;cze		1
Austria–Slovenia	1997	eng;ger;slv	eng	2
Austria–South Africa	1996	eng;ger		1
Austria–Spain	1966	ger;spa		1
Austria–Sweden	1962	ger;swe		1
Austria–Switzerland	1974	ger	ger	5
Austria–Taiwan	2014	eng;ger;chi	eng	3
Austria–Tajikistan	2011	eng;ger;tgk	eng	3
Austria–Thailand	1985	eng	eng	5
Austria–Tunisia	1977	fre	fre	5
Austria–Turkey	2008	eng;ger;tur	eng	3
Austria–Turkmenistan	1981	ger;rus		1
Austria–Turkmenistan	2015	eng;ger;rus;tkm	eng	2
Austria–Ukraine	1997	eng;ger;ukr	eng	3
Austria–United Arab Emirates	2003	eng;ger;ara	eng	2
Austria–United Kingdom	1969	eng;ger		1
Austria–United States	1982	eng;ger		1
Austria–United States	1996	eng;ger		1
Austria–Uzbekistan	2000	eng;ger;uzb	eng	3
Austria–Venezuela	2006	eng;ger;spa	eng	4
Austria–Vietnam	2008	eng;ger;vts	eng	3
Azerbaijan–Belgium	2004	eng;fre;aze;dut	eng	2
Azerbaijan–Bosnia and Herzegovina	2012	eng;aze;bos;ser;cro	eng	3
Azerbaijan–Bulgaria	2007	eng;aze;bul	eng	3
Azerbaijan–Canada	2004	eng;fre;aze		1
Azerbaijan–China (People's Rep.)	2005	eng;aze;chi	eng	3
Azerbaijan–Croatia	2012	eng;aze;cro	eng	3
Azerbaijan–Cyprus	1982	eng;rus		1
Azerbaijan–Czech Republic	2005	eng;aze;cze	eng	4
Azerbaijan–Estonia	2007	eng;aze;est	eng	3
Azerbaijan–Finland	2005	eng;aze;fin	eng	3
Azerbaijan–France	2001	fre;aze		1
Azerbaijan–Georgia	1997	rus;aze;geo	rus	3
Azerbaijan–Germany	2004	ger;aze;rus	rus	4

Treaty	Conclusion	AL	UL/PT	TOW
Azerbaijan–Greece	2009	eng;aze;gre	eng	3
Azerbaijan–Hungary	2008	eng;aze;hun	eng	3
Azerbaijan–India	1988	eng;rus;hin	eng	2
Azerbaijan–Iran	2009	eng;aze;per	eng	3
Azerbaijan–Italy	2004	eng;aze;ita	eng	3
Azerbaijan–Jordan	2008	eng;aze;ara	eng	3
Azerbaijan–Kazakhstan	1996	rus;aze;kaz	rus	3
Azerbaijan–Korea (Rep.)	2008	eng;aze;kor	eng	3
Azerbaijan–Latvia	2005	eng;aze;lat	eng	3
Azerbaijan–Lithuania	2004	eng;aze;lit	eng	3
Azerbaijan–Luxembourg	2006	fre;aze		1
Azerbaijan–Macedonia (FYR)	2013	eng;mac;aze	eng	3
Azerbaijan–Malaysia	1987	eng;rus;may	eng	3
Azerbaijan–Malta	2016	eng;aze		1
Azerbaijan–Montenegro	2013	eng;aze;mtg	eng	3
Azerbaijan–Netherlands	2008	eng;aze;dut	eng	4
Azerbaijan–Norway	1996	eng;aze;nor	eng	3
Azerbaijan–Pakistan	1996	eng;aze	eng	2
Azerbaijan–Qatar	2007	eng;aze;ara	eng	2
Azerbaijan–Romania	2002	eng;aze;rum	eng	2
Azerbaijan–Russia	1997	rus;aze		1
Azerbaijan–San Marino	2015	eng;ita;aze	eng	3
Azerbaijan–Saudi Arabia	2014	eng;aze;ara	eng	3
Azerbaijan–Serbia	2010	eng;aze;ser	eng	3
Azerbaijan–Slovenia	2011	eng;aze;slv	eng	2
Azerbaijan–Spain	2014	eng;spa;aze	eng	2
Azerbaijan–Sweden	2016	eng;aze;swe	eng	3
Azerbaijan–Switzerland	2006	eng;ger;aze	eng	3
Azerbaijan–Turkey	1994	aze;tur		1
Azerbaijan–Ukraine	1999	rus;aze;ukr	rus	3
Azerbaijan–United Arab Emirates	2006	eng;aze;ara	eng	2
Azerbaijan–United Kingdom	1994	eng	eng	5
Azerbaijan–United States	1973	eng;rus		1
Azerbaijan–Vietnam	2014	eng;aze;vts	eng	3
Bahrain–Bangladesh	2015	eng;ara	eng	3
Bahrain–Barbados	2012	eng;ara	eng	3
Bahrain–Belarus	2002	eng;ara;rus	eng	6
Bahrain–Belgium	2007	eng;ara;fre;dut	eng	2
Bahrain–Bermuda	2010	eng;ara	eng	2
Bahrain–Brunei	2008	eng;ara;may	eng	2
Bahrain–Bulgaria	2009	eng;ara;bul	eng	3
Bahrain–China (People's Rep.)	2002	eng;ara;chi	eng	3
Bahrain–Cyprus	2015	eng;ara;gre	eng	3
Bahrain–Czech Republic	2011	eng;ara;cze	eng	2
Bahrain–Egypt	1997	ara	ara	5
Bahrain–Estonia	2012	eng;ara;est	eng	2
Bahrain–France	1993	fre;ara		1
Bahrain–Georgia	2011	eng;ara;geo	eng	2
Bahrain–Hungary	2014	eng;ara;hun	eng	3
Bahrain–Iran	2002	eng;ara;per	eng	3
Bahrain–Ireland	2009	eng;ara	eng	2
Bahrain–Isle of Man	2011	eng;ara	eng	2

E. Sample

Treaty	Conclusion	AL	UL/PT	TOW
Bahrain–Jordan	2000	ara	ara	5
Bahrain–Korea (Rep.)	2012	eng;ara;kor	eng	3
Bahrain–Lebanon	2003	ara	ara	5
Bahrain–Luxembourg	2009	eng;ara;fre		1
Bahrain–Malaysia	1999	eng;ara;may	eng	8
Bahrain–Malta	2010	eng;ara	eng	3
Bahrain–Mexico	2010	eng;ara;spa	eng	2
Bahrain–Morocco	2000	ara	ara	5
Bahrain–Netherlands	2008	eng;ara;dut	eng	4
Bahrain–Pakistan	2005	eng;ara	eng	6
Bahrain–Philippines	2001	eng;ara	eng	3
Bahrain–Portugal	2015	eng;por;ara	eng	3
Bahrain–Seychelles	2010	eng;ara	eng	3
Bahrain–Singapore	2004	eng;ara	eng	3
Bahrain–Sri Lanka	2011	eng;ara;sin	eng	3
Bahrain–Syria	2000	ara	ara	5
Bahrain–Tajikistan	2014	eng;ara;tgk	eng	2
Bahrain–Thailand	2001	eng;ara;tha	eng	6
Bahrain–Turkey	2005	eng;ara;tur	eng	2
Bahrain–Turkmenistan	2011	eng;ara;tkm	eng	2
Bahrain–United Kingdom	2010	eng;ara	eng	3
Bahrain–Uzbekistan	2009	eng;ara;uzb	eng	3
Bangladesh–Belarus	2013	eng;rus;ben	eng	3
Bangladesh–Belgium	1990	eng;fre;dut;ben	eng	3
Bangladesh–Canada	1982	eng;fre;ben		1
Bangladesh–China (People's Rep.)	1996	eng;chi;ben	eng	3
Bangladesh–Denmark	1996	eng	eng	5
Bangladesh–France	1987	eng;fre;ben		1
Bangladesh–Germany	1990	eng;ger;ben	eng	3
Bangladesh–India	1991	eng;hin;ben	eng	3
Bangladesh–Indonesia	2003	eng	eng	5
Bangladesh–Italy	1990	eng;ita;ben	eng	6
Bangladesh–Japan	1991	eng	eng	5
Bangladesh–Korea (Rep.)	1983	eng	eng	5
Bangladesh–Malaysia	1983	eng;may;ben	eng	3
Bangladesh–Mauritius	2009	eng	eng	5
Bangladesh–Netherlands	1993	eng	eng	5
Bangladesh–Norway	2004	eng	eng	5
Bangladesh–Pakistan	1981	eng	eng	5
Bangladesh–Philippines	1997	eng	eng	5
Bangladesh–Poland	1997	eng	eng	5
Bangladesh–Romania	1987	eng;rum;ben	eng	3
Bangladesh–Saudi Arabia	2011	eng;ara;ben	eng	3
Bangladesh–Singapore	1980	eng	eng	5
Bangladesh–Sri Lanka	1986	eng;ben;sin	eng	3
Bangladesh–Sweden	1982	eng	eng	5
Bangladesh–Switzerland	2007	eng;ger;ben	eng	3
Bangladesh–Thailand	1997	eng	eng	5
Bangladesh–Turkey	1999	eng;tur;ben	eng	3
Bangladesh–United Kingdom	1979	eng	eng	5
Bangladesh–United States	1980	eng	eng	5
Bangladesh–United States	2004	eng	eng	5

Treaty	Conclusion	AL	UL/PT	TOW
Bangladesh–Vietnam	2004	eng	eng	5
Barbados–Botswana	2005	eng	eng	5
Barbados–Canada	1980	eng;fre		1
Barbados–China (People's Rep.)	2000	eng;chi		1
Barbados–Cuba	1999	eng;spa		1
Barbados–Czech Republic	2011	eng;cze		1
Barbados–Finland	1989	eng;fin		1
Barbados–Ghana	2008	eng	eng	5
Barbados–Iceland	2011	eng;ice		1
Barbados–Italy	2015	eng;ita		1
Barbados–Luxembourg	2009	eng;fre		1
Barbados–Malta	2001	eng	eng	5
Barbados–Mauritius	2004	eng	eng	5
Barbados–Mexico	2008	eng;spa	eng	2
Barbados–Netherlands	2006	eng	eng	5
Barbados–Norway	1990	eng;nor		1
Barbados–Panama	2010	eng;spa	eng	2
Barbados–Portugal	2010	eng;por		1
Barbados–Qatar	2012	eng;ara		1
Barbados–Rwanda	2014	eng	eng	5
Barbados–San Marino	2012	eng	eng	5
Barbados–Seychelles	2007	eng	eng	5
Barbados–Singapore	2013	eng	eng	5
Barbados–Slovak Republic	2015	eng;slo		1
Barbados–Spain	2010	eng;spa		1
Barbados–Sweden	1991	eng	eng	5
Barbados–Switzerland	1963	eng;fre		1
Barbados–United Arab Emirates	2014	eng;ara	eng	2
Barbados–United Kingdom	2012	eng	eng	5
Barbados–United States	1984	eng	eng	5
Barbados–Venezuela	1998	eng;spa		1
Belarus–Belgium	1995	eng	eng	5
Belarus–Bulgaria	1996	eng;bel;bul	eng	3
Belarus–Canada	1985	eng;rus;fre		1
Belarus–China (People's Rep.)	1995	eng;bel;chi	eng	3
Belarus–Croatia	2003	eng;bel;cro	eng	3
Belarus–Cyprus	1998	eng;rus;gre	eng	3
Belarus–Czech Republic	1996	eng;bel;cze	eng	3
Belarus–Denmark	1986	rus;dan		1
Belarus–Egypt	1998	eng;rus;ara	eng	3
Belarus–Estonia	1997	eng;bel;est	eng	3
Belarus–Finland	2007	eng;rus;fin	eng	3
Belarus–France	1985	fre;rus		1
Belarus–Georgia	2015	eng;rus;geo	eng	2
Belarus–Germany	2005	ger;bel		1
Belarus–Hungary	2002	eng;bel;hun	eng	3
Belarus–India	1997	eng;bel;hin	eng	2
Belarus–Indonesia	2013	eng;ind;bel	eng	3
Belarus–Iran	1995	eng;bel;per	eng	3
Belarus–Ireland	2009	eng;rus		1
Belarus–Israel	2000	eng;bel;heb	eng	3
Belarus–Italy	2005	eng;bel;ita	eng	4

E. Sample

Treaty	Conclusion	AL	UL/PT	TOW
Belarus–Japan	1986	eng;rus;jap	eng	3
Belarus–Kazakhstan	1997	rus;kaz;bel	rus	3
Belarus–Korea (Rep.)	2002	eng;bel;kor	eng	3
Belarus–Kuwait	2001	eng;rus;ara	eng	3
Belarus–Kyrgyzstan	1997	rus;bel;kyr	rus	3
Belarus–Laos	2013	eng;rus;lao	eng	3
Belarus–Latvia	1995	eng;bel;lat	eng	3
Belarus–Lebanon	2001	eng;bel;ara	eng	3
Belarus–Libya	2008	eng;rus;ara	eng	2
Belarus–Lithuania	1995	eng;bel;lit	eng	3
Belarus–Macedonia (FYR)	2005	eng;rus;mac	eng	3
Belarus–Malaysia	1987	eng;rus;may	eng	3
Belarus–Moldova	1994	rus;bel;mol	rus	3
Belarus–Mongolia	2001	eng;bel;mon	eng	3
Belarus–Netherlands	1996	eng;bel;dut	eng	4
Belarus–Norway	1980	rus;nor		1
Belarus–Oman	2007	eng;ara;rus	eng	4
Belarus–Pakistan	2004	eng;bel		1
Belarus–Poland	1992	pol;bel		1
Belarus–Qatar	2007	eng;rus;ara	eng	3
Belarus–Romania	1997	eng;bel;rum	eng	3
Belarus–Russia	1995	rus;bel		1
Belarus–Saudi Arabia	2009	eng;rus;ara	eng	3
Belarus–Serbia and Montenegro	1998	eng;bel;ser	eng	3
Belarus–Singapore	2013	eng;rus	eng	2
Belarus–Slovak Republic	1999	eng;bel;slo	eng	3
Belarus–Slovenia	2010	eng;rus;slv	eng	2
Belarus–South Africa	2002	eng;bel		1
Belarus–Spain	1985	rus;spa		1
Belarus–Sri Lanka	2013	eng;rus;sin	eng	3
Belarus–Sweden	1994	eng;bel;swe	eng	3
Belarus–Switzerland	1999	eng;bel;ger	eng	3
Belarus–Syria	1998	eng	eng	5
Belarus–Tajikistan	1999	rus;bel;tgk	rus	3
Belarus–Thailand	2005	eng;rus;tha	eng	3
Belarus–Turkey	1996	eng;bel;tur	eng	2
Belarus–Turkmenistan	2002	rus;bel;tkm	rus	3
Belarus–Ukraine	1993	rus;ukr;bel	rus	2
Belarus–United Arab Emirates	2000	eng;bel;ara	eng	3
Belarus–United Kingdom	1985	eng;rus		1
Belarus–United Kingdom	1995	eng;bel		1
Belarus–United States	1973	eng;rus		1
Belarus–Uzbekistan	1994	rus;uzb;bel	rus	2
Belarus–Venezuela	2007	eng;rus;spa	eng	3
Belarus–Vietnam	1997	eng	eng	5
Belgium–Bosnia and Herzegovina	1980	eng	eng	5
Belgium–Brazil	1972	fre;dut;por		1
Belgium–Bulgaria	1988	fre;dut;bul		1
Belgium–Canada	2002	eng;fre;dut		1
Belgium–Chile	2007	eng;fre;dut;spa	eng	2
Belgium–China (People's Rep.)	2009	eng;fre;chi;dut	eng	3
Belgium–Congo (Dem. Rep.)	2007	fre;dut	fre	3

Treaty	Conclusion	AL	UL/PT	TOW
Belgium–Croatia	2001	eng;fre;dut;cro	eng	2
Belgium–Cyprus	1996	eng	eng	5
Belgium–Czech Republic	1996	eng	eng	5
Belgium–Denmark	1969	fre;dut;dan		1
Belgium–Ecuador	1996	fre;dut;spa		1
Belgium–Egypt	1991	eng;fre;dut;ara	eng	3
Belgium–Estonia	1999	eng;fre;dut;est	eng	3
Belgium–Finland	1976	eng	eng	5
Belgium–France	1964	fre	fre	5
Belgium–Gabon	1993	fre;dut		1
Belgium–Georgia	2000	eng	eng	5
Belgium–Germany	1967	fre;dut;ger		1
Belgium–Ghana	2005	eng	eng	5
Belgium–Greece	2004	fre;dut;gre	fre	3
Belgium–Hong Kong	2003	eng	eng	5
Belgium–Hungary	1982	fre;dut;hun	fre	3
Belgium–Iceland	2000	eng	eng	5
Belgium–India	1993	eng;fre;dut;hin	eng	3
Belgium–Indonesia	1997	eng	eng	5
Belgium–Ireland	1970	eng;fre;dut;iri		1
Belgium–Isle of Man	2009	eng	eng	5
Belgium–Israel	1972	eng	eng	5
Belgium–Italy	1983	fre;dut;ita		1
Belgium–Ivory Coast	1977	fre;dut		1
Belgium–Japan	1968	eng	eng	5
Belgium–Kazakhstan	1998	eng;fre;dut;rus;kaz	eng	2
Belgium–Korea (Rep.)	1977	eng	eng	5
Belgium–Kuwait	1990	eng;fre;dut;ara	eng	2
Belgium–Kyrgyzstan	1987	fre;dut;rus		1
Belgium–Latvia	1999	eng;fre;dut;lat	eng	3
Belgium–Lithuania	1998	eng;fre;dut;lit	eng	3
Belgium–Luxembourg	1970	fre;dut		1
Belgium–Macau	2006	eng;fre;dut;chi;por	eng	2
Belgium–Macedonia (FYR)	2010	eng;fre;dut;mac	eng	2
Belgium–Malaysia	1973	eng	eng	5
Belgium–Malta	1974	eng	eng	5
Belgium–Mauritius	1995	eng;fre;dut		1
Belgium–Mexico	1992	fre;dut;spa		1
Belgium–Moldova	1987	fre;dut;rus		1
Belgium–Moldova	2008	eng;fre;dut;mol	eng	2
Belgium–Mongolia	1995	eng	eng	5
Belgium–Morocco	2006	fre;ara;dut	fre	3
Belgium–Netherlands	2001	fre;dut		1
Belgium–New Zealand	1981	eng;fre;dut		1
Belgium–Nigeria	1989	eng	eng	5
Belgium–Norway	1988	eng	eng	5
Belgium–Norway	2014	eng	eng	5
Belgium–Oman	2008	eng;fre;dut;ara	eng	2
Belgium–Pakistan	1980	eng	eng	5
Belgium–Philippines	1976	eng	eng	5
Belgium–Poland	2001	fre;dut;pol		1
Belgium–Portugal	1969	fre;dut;por		1

E. Sample

Treaty	Conclusion	AL	UL/PT	TOW
Belgium–Qatar	2007	eng;fre;dut;ara	eng	2
Belgium–Romania	1996	fre;dut;rum	fre	2
Belgium–Russia	1995	fre;dut;rus		1
Belgium–Russia	2015	eng;fre;rus;dut	eng	2
Belgium–Rwanda	2007	eng	eng	5
Belgium–San Marino	2005	eng	eng	5
Belgium–Senegal	1987	fre;dut		1
Belgium–Serbia and Montenegro	1980	eng	eng	5
Belgium–Seychelles	2006	eng	eng	5
Belgium–Singapore	2006	eng	eng	5
Belgium–Slovak Republic	1997	eng;fre;dut;slo	eng	3
Belgium–Slovenia	1998	eng;fre;dut;slv	eng	2
Belgium–South Africa	1995	eng	eng	5
Belgium–Spain	1995	fre;dut;spa		1
Belgium–Sri Lanka	1983	eng;fre;dut;sin	eng	3
Belgium–Sweden	1991	fre;dut;swe		1
Belgium–Switzerland	1978	fre;dut		1
Belgium–Taiwan	2004	eng	eng	5
Belgium–Tajikistan	1987	fre;dut;rus		1
Belgium–Tajikistan	2009	eng;fre;dut;tgk	eng	2
Belgium–Thailand	1978	eng	eng	5
Belgium–Tunisia	2004	eng;fre;ara	eng	3
Belgium–Turkey	1987	eng	eng	5
Belgium–Turkmenistan	1987	fre;dut;rus		1
Belgium–Uganda	2007	eng	eng	5
Belgium–Ukraine	1996	eng;fre;dut;ukr	eng	2
Belgium–United Arab Emirates	1996	eng	eng	5
Belgium–United Kingdom	1987	eng;fre;dut		1
Belgium–United States	2006	eng	eng	5
Belgium–Uruguay	2013	eng;fre;spa;dut	eng	2
Belgium–Uzbekistan	1996	eng	eng	5
Belgium–Venezuela	1993	eng;fre;dut;spa	eng	3
Belgium–Vietnam	1996	eng	eng	5
Belize–Switzerland	1963	eng;fre		1
Benin–France	1975	fre	fre	5
Benin–Norway	1979	fre	fre	5
Bermuda–Denmark	2009	eng	eng	5
Bermuda–Finland	2009	eng	eng	5
Bermuda–Iceland	2009	eng	eng	5
Bermuda–Japan	2010	eng;jap		1
Bermuda–Netherlands	2009	eng	eng	5
Bermuda–Norway	2009	eng	eng	5
Bermuda–Qatar	2012	eng;ara		1
Bermuda–Sweden	2009	eng	eng	5
Bermuda–United States	1986	eng	eng	5
Bhutan–India	2013	eng;hin;dzo	eng	3
Bolivia–Colombia	2004	spa	spa	5
Bolivia–France	1994	fre;spa		1
Bolivia–Germany	1992	spa;ger		1
Bolivia–Spain	1997	spa	spa	5
Bolivia–Sweden	1994	eng;spa;swe	eng	3
Bolivia–United Kingdom	1994	eng;spa		1

Treaty	Conclusion	AL	UL/PT	TOW
Bosnia and Herzegovina–China (People's Rep.)	1988	eng;scr;chi	eng	3
Bosnia and Herzegovina–Croatia	2004	bos;ser;cro	cro	3
Bosnia and Herzegovina–Cyprus	1985	eng	eng	5
Bosnia and Herzegovina–Czech Republic	2007	eng	eng	5
Bosnia and Herzegovina–Denmark	1981	eng	eng	5
Bosnia and Herzegovina–Finland	1986	eng	eng	5
Bosnia and Herzegovina–France	1974	fre;scr		1
Bosnia and Herzegovina–Germany	1987	eng;scr;ger	eng	4
Bosnia and Herzegovina–Greece	2007	eng;bos;ser;cro;gre	eng	8
Bosnia and Herzegovina–Hungary	1985	eng	eng	5
Bosnia and Herzegovina–Ireland	2009	eng	eng	5
Bosnia and Herzegovina–Italy	1982	eng	eng	5
Bosnia and Herzegovina–Jordan	2007	eng;ara;cro;ser;bos	eng	3
Bosnia and Herzegovina–Kuwait	2008	eng;ara;bos;ser;cro	eng	2
Bosnia and Herzegovina–Macedonia (FYR)	2013	eng;mac;bos;ser;cro	eng	3
Bosnia and Herzegovina–Malaysia	2007	eng;may;bos;ser;cro	eng	3
Bosnia and Herzegovina–Moldova	2003	eng;mol;bos;ser;cro	eng	3
Bosnia and Herzegovina–Netherlands	1982	eng;scr;dut	eng	4
Bosnia and Herzegovina–Norway	1983	eng	eng	5
Bosnia and Herzegovina–Pakistan	2004	eng;bos;ser;cro	eng	3
Bosnia and Herzegovina–Poland	1985	eng;scr;pol	eng	4
Bosnia and Herzegovina–Poland	2014	eng;pol;bos;ser;cro	eng	3
Bosnia and Herzegovina–Qatar	2010	eng;ara;bos;ser;cro	eng	2
Bosnia and Herzegovina–Romania	1986	eng;scr;rum	eng	3
Bosnia and Herzegovina–Serbia and Montenegro	2004	eng;bos;ser;cro	eng	3
Bosnia and Herzegovina–Slovak Republic	1981	eng	eng	5
Bosnia and Herzegovina–Slovenia	2006	eng	eng	5
Bosnia and Herzegovina–Spain	2008	eng;spa;bos;ser;cro	eng	2
Bosnia and Herzegovina–Sri Lanka	1985	eng;scr;sin	eng	3
Bosnia and Herzegovina–Sweden	1980	eng	eng	5
Bosnia and Herzegovina–Turkey	2005	eng	eng	5
Bosnia and Herzegovina–United Arab Emirates	2006	eng;ara;bos;ser;cro	eng	3
Bosnia and Herzegovina–United Kingdom	1981	eng;scr		1
Botswana–China (People's Rep.)	2012	eng;chi		1
Botswana–France	1999	eng;fre		1
Botswana–India	2006	eng;hin	eng	3
Botswana–Ireland	2014	eng	eng	5
Botswana–Mauritius	1995	eng	eng	5
Botswana–Mozambique	2009	eng;por		1
Botswana–Namibia	2004	eng	eng	5
Botswana–Russia	2003	eng;rus		1
Botswana–Seychelles	2004	eng	eng	5
Botswana–South Africa	2003	eng	eng	5
Botswana–Swaziland	2010	eng	eng	5
Botswana–Sweden	1992	eng	eng	5
Botswana–United Kingdom	2005	eng	eng	5
Botswana–Zambia	2013	eng	eng	5
Botswana–Zimbabwe	2004	eng	eng	5
Brazil–Canada	1984	eng;fre;por		1
Brazil–Chile	2001	por;spa		1
Brazil–China (People's Rep.)	1991	eng;por;chi	eng	3
Brazil–Czech Republic	1986	eng;por;cze	eng	3

E. Sample

Treaty	Conclusion	AL	UL/PT	TOW
Brazil–Denmark	1974	eng;por;dan	eng	6
Brazil–Ecuador	1983	spa;por		1
Brazil–Finland	1996	eng;por;fin	eng	3
Brazil–France	1971	fre;por		1
Brazil–Hungary	1986	eng;por;hun	eng	4
Brazil–India	1988	eng;hin;por	eng	3
Brazil–Israel	2002	eng;por;heb	eng	3
Brazil–Italy	1978	eng;por;ita	eng	6
Brazil–Japan	1967	eng;por;jap	eng	3
Brazil–Korea (Rep.)	1989	eng;por;kor	eng	4
Brazil–Luxembourg	1978	eng;por		1
Brazil–Mexico	2003	por;spa		1
Brazil–Netherlands	1990	eng;por;dut	eng	3
Brazil–Norway	1980	eng;por;nor	eng	3
Brazil–Peru	2006	spa;por		1
Brazil–Philippines	1983	eng;por		1
Brazil–Portugal	2000	por	por	5
Brazil–Russia	2004	eng;por;rus	eng	3
Brazil–Slovak Republic	1986	eng;por;cze	eng	3
Brazil–South Africa	2003	eng;por		1
Brazil–Spain	1974	spa;por		1
Brazil–Sweden	1975	eng;por;swe	eng	3
Brazil–Trinidad and Tobago	2008	eng;por;tur		1
Brazil–Turkey	2010	eng;por;tur	eng	4
Brazil–Ukraine	2002	eng;por;ukr	eng	4
Brazil–Venezuela	2005	spa;por		1
British Virgin Islands–Denmark	2009	eng	eng	5
British Virgin Islands–Finland	2009	eng	eng	5
British Virgin Islands–Iceland	2009	eng	eng	5
British Virgin Islands–New Zealand	2009	eng	eng	5
British Virgin Islands–Norway	2009	eng	eng	5
British Virgin Islands–Sweden	2009	eng	eng	5
British Virgin Islands–Switzerland	1963	eng;fre		1
British Virgin Islands–United Kingdom	2008	eng	eng	5
Brunei–China (People's Rep.)	2004	eng;may;chi	eng	3
Brunei–Hong Kong	2010	eng	eng	5
Brunei–Indonesia	2000	eng	eng	5
Brunei–Japan	2009	eng	eng	5
Brunei–Kuwait	2009	eng;ara;may	eng	2
Brunei–Laos	2006	eng	eng	5
Brunei–Luxembourg	2015	eng;fre;may	eng	2
Brunei–Malaysia	2009	eng	eng	5
Brunei–Oman	2008	eng;ara;may	eng	4
Brunei–Pakistan	2009	eng	eng	5
Brunei–Singapore	2005	eng;may	eng	3
Brunei–Vietnam	2007	eng;may;vts	eng	3
Bulgaria–Canada	1999	eng;fre		1
Bulgaria–China (People's Rep.)	1989	eng;bul;chi	eng	3
Bulgaria–Croatia	1997	eng;bul;cro	eng	4
Bulgaria–Cyprus	2000	eng;bul;gre	eng	3
Bulgaria–Czech Republic	1998	eng;bul;cze	eng	2
Bulgaria–Denmark	1988	eng	eng	5

Treaty	Conclusion	AL	UL/PT	TOW
Bulgaria–Egypt	2003	eng;bul;ara	eng	3
Bulgaria–Estonia	2008	eng;bul;est	eng	3
Bulgaria–Finland	1985	eng;bul;fin	eng	3
Bulgaria–France	1987	fre;bul		1
Bulgaria–Georgia	1998	eng;bul;geo	eng	3
Bulgaria–Germany	2010	eng;bul;ger	eng	4
Bulgaria–Greece	1991	eng	eng	5
Bulgaria–Hungary	1994	eng	eng	5
Bulgaria–India	1994	eng;bul;hin	eng	4
Bulgaria–Indonesia	1991	eng	eng	5
Bulgaria–Iran	2004	eng;bul;per	eng	3
Bulgaria–Ireland	2000	eng;bul		1
Bulgaria–Israel	2000	eng;bul;heb	eng	3
Bulgaria–Italy	1988	fre;ita;bul	fre	8
Bulgaria–Japan	1991	eng	eng	5
Bulgaria–Jordan	2006	eng;bul;ara	eng	3
Bulgaria–Kazakhstan	1997	eng;bul;kaz;rus	eng	3
Bulgaria–Korea (Dem. People's Rep.)	1999	eng;bul;kor	eng	3
Bulgaria–Korea (Rep.)	1994	eng;kor;bul	eng	3
Bulgaria–Kuwait	2002	eng;bul;ara	eng	3
Bulgaria–Latvia	2003	eng;bul;lat	eng	3
Bulgaria–Lebanon	1999	eng;bul;ara	eng	3
Bulgaria–Lithuania	2006	eng;bul;lit	eng	3
Bulgaria–Luxembourg	1992	fre;bul		1
Bulgaria–Macedonia (FYR)	1999	bul;mac		1
Bulgaria–Malta	1986	eng;bul		1
Bulgaria–Moldova	1998	eng;bul;mol	eng	3
Bulgaria–Mongolia	2000	eng;bul;mon	eng	3
Bulgaria–Morocco	1996	eng;fre;bul;ara	eng	3
Bulgaria–Netherlands	1990	eng;bul;dut	eng	4
Bulgaria–Norway	1988	eng	eng	5
Bulgaria–Norway	2014	eng;bul;nor	eng	3
Bulgaria–Poland	1994	eng;bul;pol	eng	3
Bulgaria–Portugal	1995	eng;bul;por	eng	3
Bulgaria–Qatar	2010	eng;bul;ara	eng	2
Bulgaria–Romania	1994	eng;bul;rum	eng	3
Bulgaria–Romania	2015	eng;bul;rum	eng	3
Bulgaria–Russia	1993	rus;bul		1
Bulgaria–Serbia and Montenegro	1998	eng;bul;ser	eng	3
Bulgaria–Singapore	1996	eng;bul		1
Bulgaria–Slovak Republic	1999	eng;bul;slo	eng	3
Bulgaria–Slovenia	2003	eng;bul;slv	eng	3
Bulgaria–South Africa	2004	eng;bul		1
Bulgaria–Spain	1990	spa;bul		1
Bulgaria–Sweden	1988	eng	eng	5
Bulgaria–Switzerland	2012	eng;ger;bul	eng	4
Bulgaria–Syria	2001	eng;bul;ara	eng	2
Bulgaria–Thailand	2000	eng;bul;tha	eng	3
Bulgaria–Turkey	1994	eng	eng	5
Bulgaria–Ukraine	1995	eng;bul;ukr	eng	3
Bulgaria–United Arab Emirates	2007	eng;bul;ara	eng	3
Bulgaria–United Kingdom	1987	eng;bul		1

E. Sample

Treaty	Conclusion	AL	UL/PT	TOW
Bulgaria–United Kingdom	2015	eng;bul		1
Bulgaria–United States	2007	eng;bul		1
Bulgaria–Uzbekistan	2003	eng;bul;uzb	eng	3
Bulgaria–Vietnam	1996	eng;bul;vts	eng	3
Bulgaria–Zimbabwe	1988	eng;bul		1
Burkina Faso–France	1965	fre	fre	5
Burkina Faso–Morocco	2012	fre;ara		1
Burkina Faso–Tunisia	2003	fre;ara	fre	3
Cambodia–Singapore	2016	eng	eng	5
Cameroon–Canada	1982	eng;fre		1
Cameroon–France	1976	fre	fre	5
Cameroon–Morocco	2012	eng;fre;ara	fre	3
Cameroon–South Africa	2015	eng;fre		1
Cameroon–Tunisia	1999	fre;ara	fre	2
Canada–Chile	1998	eng;fre;spa		1
Canada–China (People's Rep.)	1986	eng;fre;chi		1
Canada–Colombia	2008	eng;fre;spa		1
Canada–Croatia	1997	eng;fre;cro		1
Canada–Cyprus	1984	eng;fre		1
Canada–Czech Republic	2001	eng;fre;cze		1
Canada–Denmark	1997	eng;fre;dan		1
Canada–Dominican Republic	1976	eng;fre;spa		1
Canada–Ecuador	2001	eng;fre;spa		1
Canada–Egypt	1983	eng;fre;ara		1
Canada–Estonia	1995	eng;fre;est		1
Canada–Finland	2006	eng;fre;fin;swe		1
Canada–France	1975	eng;fre		1
Canada–Gabon	2002	eng;fre		1
Canada–Germany	2001	eng;fre;ger		1
Canada–Greece	2009	eng;fre;gre		1
Canada–Guyana	1985	eng;fre		1
Canada–Hong Kong	2012	eng;fre;chi		1
Canada–Hungary	1992	eng;fre;hun		1
Canada–Iceland	1997	eng;fre;ice		1
Canada–India	1996	eng;fre;hin		1
Canada–Indonesia	1979	eng;fre;ind		1
Canada–Ireland	2003	eng;fre		1
Canada–Israel	1975	eng;fre;heb		1
Canada–Italy	2002	eng;fre;ita		1
Canada–Jamaica	1978	eng;fre		1
Canada–Japan	1986	eng;fre;jap		1
Canada–Jordan	1999	eng;fre;ara		1
Canada–Kazakhstan	1996	eng;fre;rus;kaz		1
Canada–Kenya	1983	eng;fre		1
Canada–Korea (Rep.)	2006	eng;fre;kor		1
Canada–Kuwait	2002	eng;fre;ara		1
Canada–Kyrgyzstan	1998	eng;fre;rus		1
Canada–Latvia	1995	eng;fre;lat		1
Canada–Lebanon	1998	eng;fre;ara		1
Canada–Lithuania	1996	eng;fre;lit		1
Canada–Luxembourg	1999	eng;fre		1
Canada–Malaysia	1976	eng;fre;may		1

Treaty	Conclusion	AL	UL/PT	TOW
Canada–Malta	1986	eng;fre		1
Canada–Mexico	2006	eng;fre;spa		1
Canada–Moldova	2002	eng;fre;mol		1
Canada–Mongolia	2002	eng;fre;mon		1
Canada–Morocco	1975	eng;fre		1
Canada–Namibia	2010	eng;fre		1
Canada–Netherlands	1986	eng;fre;dut		1
Canada–New Zealand	1980	eng;fre		1
Canada–New Zealand	2012	eng;fre		1
Canada–Nigeria	1992	eng;fre		1
Canada–Norway	2002	eng;fre;nor		1
Canada–Oman	2004	eng;fre;ara		1
Canada–Pakistan	1976	eng;fre		1
Canada–Papua New Guinea	1987	eng;fre		1
Canada–Peru	2001	eng;fre;spa		1
Canada–Philippines	1976	eng;fre		1
Canada–Poland	2012	eng;fre;pol		1
Canada–Portugal	1999	eng;fre;por		1
Canada–Romania	2004	eng;fre;rum		1
Canada–Russia	1995	eng;fre;rus		1
Canada–Senegal	2001	eng;fre		1
Canada–Serbia	2012	eng;fre;ser		1
Canada–Singapore	1976	eng;fre		1
Canada–Slovak Republic	2001	eng;fre;slo		1
Canada–Slovenia	2000	eng;fre;slv		1
Canada–South Africa	1995	eng;fre		1
Canada–Spain	1976	eng;fre;spa		1
Canada–Sri Lanka	1982	eng;fre;sin		1
Canada–Sweden	1996	eng;fre;swe		1
Canada–Switzerland	1997	eng;fre		1
Canada–Taiwan	2016	eng;fre		1
Canada–Tanzania	1995	eng;fre		1
Canada–Thailand	1984	eng;fre;tha		1
Canada–Trinidad and Tobago	1995	eng;fre		1
Canada–Tunisia	1982	eng;fre;ara		1
Canada–Turkey	2009	eng;fre;tur		1
Canada–Turkmenistan	1985	eng;fre;rus		1
Canada–Ukraine	1996	eng;fre;ukr		1
Canada–United Arab Emirates	2002	eng;fre;ara		1
Canada–United Kingdom	1978	eng;fre		1
Canada–United States	1980	eng;fre		1
Canada–Uzbekistan	1999	eng;fre;uzb		1
Canada–Venezuela	2001	eng;fre;spa		1
Canada–Vietnam	1997	eng;fre;vts		1
Canada–Zambia	1984	eng;fre		1
Canada–Zimbabwe	1992	eng;fre		1
Cape Verde–Macau	2010	por;chi		1
Cape Verde–Portugal	1999	por	por	5
Cayman Islands–Denmark	2009	eng	eng	5
Cayman Islands–Faroe Islands	2009	eng	eng	5
Cayman Islands–Finland	2009	eng	eng	5
Cayman Islands–Greenland	2009	eng	eng	5

E. Sample

Treaty	Conclusion	AL	UL/PT	TOW
Cayman Islands–Iceland	2009	eng	eng	5
Cayman Islands–New Zealand	2009	eng	eng	5
Cayman Islands–Norway	2009	eng	eng	5
Cayman Islands–Sweden	2009	eng	eng	5
Cayman Islands–United Kingdom	2009	eng	eng	5
Central African Republic–France	1969	fre	fre	5
Chad–Libya	2009	eng;fre;ara	eng	3
Chad–Tunisia	2012	fre;ara		1
Chile–China (People's Rep.)	2015	eng;spa;chi	eng	3
Chile–Croatia	2003	eng;spa;cro	eng	3
Chile–Czech Republic	2015	eng;spa;cze	eng	2
Chile–Denmark	2002	eng;spa;dan	eng	4
Chile–Ecuador	1999	spa	spa	5
Chile–France	2004	fre;spa		1
Chile–Ireland	2005	eng;spa		1
Chile–Italy	2015	eng;spa;ita	eng	3
Chile–Japan	2016	eng	eng	5
Chile–Korea (Rep.)	2002	eng;spa;kor	eng	3
Chile–Malaysia	2004	eng;spa;may	eng	4
Chile–Mexico	1998	spa	spa	5
Chile–New Zealand	2003	eng;spa		1
Chile–Norway	2001	eng;spa;nor	eng	4
Chile–Paraguay	2005	spa	spa	5
Chile–Peru	2001	spa	spa	5
Chile–Poland	2000	eng;spa;pol	eng	3
Chile–Portugal	2005	eng;spa;por	eng	3
Chile–Russia	2004	eng;spa;rus	eng	4
Chile–South Africa	2012	eng;spa		1
Chile–Spain	2003	spa	spa	5
Chile–Sweden	2004	eng;spa;swe	eng	2
Chile–Switzerland	2008	eng;fre;spa	eng	4
Chile–Thailand	2006	eng;spa;tha	eng	4
Chile–United Kingdom	2003	eng;spa		1
Chile–United States	2010	eng;spa		1
Chile–Uruguay	2016	spa	spa	5
China (People's Rep.)–Croatia	1995	eng;chi;cro	eng	3
China (People's Rep.)–Cuba	2001	eng;chi;spa	eng	3
China (People's Rep.)–Cyprus	1990	eng;chi;gre	eng	6
China (People's Rep.)–Czech Republic	2009	eng;chi;cze	eng	3
China (People's Rep.)–Denmark	2012	eng;chi;den	eng	6
China (People's Rep.)–Ecuador	2013	eng;chi;spa	eng	3
China (People's Rep.)–Egypt	1997	eng;chi;ara	eng	3
China (People's Rep.)–Estonia	1998	eng;chi;est	eng	3
China (People's Rep.)–Ethiopia	2009	eng;chi		1
China (People's Rep.)–Finland	2010	eng;chi;fin	eng	3
China (People's Rep.)–France	1984	fre;chi		1
China (People's Rep.)–France	2013	fre;chi		1
China (People's Rep.)–Georgia	2005	eng;chi;geo	eng	3
China (People's Rep.)–Germany	1985	chi;ger		1
China (People's Rep.)–Germany	2014	eng;chi;ger	eng	4
China (People's Rep.)–Greece	2002	eng;chi;gre	eng	4
China (People's Rep.)–Hong Kong	2006	chi	chi	5

Treaty	Conclusion	AL	UL/PT	TOW
China (People's Rep.)–Hungary	1992	eng;chi;hun	eng	3
China (People's Rep.)–Iceland	1996	eng;chi;ice	eng	3
China (People's Rep.)–India	1994	eng;chi;hin	eng	2
China (People's Rep.)–Indonesia	2001	eng;chi;ind	eng	3
China (People's Rep.)–Iran	2002	eng;chi;per	eng	3
China (People's Rep.)–Ireland	2000	eng;chi		1
China (People's Rep.)–Israel	1995	eng;chi;heb	eng	3
China (People's Rep.)–Italy	1986	eng;chi;ita	eng	6
China (People's Rep.)–Jamaica	1996	eng;chi		1
China (People's Rep.)–Japan	1983	eng;chi;jap	eng	3
China (People's Rep.)–Kazakhstan	2001	eng;chi;kaz	eng	3
China (People's Rep.)–Korea (Rep.)	1994	eng;chi;kor	eng	3
China (People's Rep.)–Kuwait	1989	eng;chi;ara	eng	2
China (People's Rep.)–Kyrgyzstan	2002	eng;chi;kyr;rus	eng	3
China (People's Rep.)–Laos	1999	eng;chi;lao	eng	3
China (People's Rep.)–Latvia	1996	eng;chi;lat	eng	3
China (People's Rep.)–Lithuania	1996	eng;chi;lit	eng	3
China (People's Rep.)–Luxembourg	1994	eng;chi;fre		1
China (People's Rep.)–Macau	2003	chi	chi	5
China (People's Rep.)–Macedonia (FYR)	1997	eng;chi;mac	eng	3
China (People's Rep.)–Malaysia	1985	eng;chi;may	eng	8
China (People's Rep.)–Malta	2010	eng;chi		1
China (People's Rep.)–Mauritius	1994	eng;chi		1
China (People's Rep.)–Mexico	2005	eng;chi;spa	eng	3
China (People's Rep.)–Moldova	2000	eng;chi;mol	eng	3
China (People's Rep.)–Mongolia	1991	eng;chi;mon	eng	3
China (People's Rep.)–Morocco	2002	eng;chi;ara	eng	3
China (People's Rep.)–Nepal	2001	eng;chi;nep	eng	2
China (People's Rep.)–Netherlands	1987	eng;chi;dut	eng	4
China (People's Rep.)–Netherlands	2013	eng;chi;dut	eng	3
China (People's Rep.)–New Zealand	1986	eng;chi		1
China (People's Rep.)–Nigeria	2002	eng;chi	eng	2
China (People's Rep.)–Norway	1986	eng;chi;nor	eng	4
China (People's Rep.)–Oman	2002	eng;chi;ara	eng	3
China (People's Rep.)–Pakistan	1989	eng;chi		1
China (People's Rep.)–Papua New Guinea	1994	eng;chi		1
China (People's Rep.)–Philippines	1999	eng;chi		1
China (People's Rep.)–Poland	1988	eng;chi;pol	eng	3
China (People's Rep.)–Portugal	1998	eng;chi;por	eng	3
China (People's Rep.)–Qatar	2001	eng;chi;ara	eng	3
China (People's Rep.)–Romania	1991	eng;chi;rum	eng	3
China (People's Rep.)–Russia	1994	eng;chi;rus	eng	3
China (People's Rep.)–Russia	2014	eng;rus;chi	eng	3
China (People's Rep.)–Saudi Arabia	2006	eng;chi;ara	eng	3
China (People's Rep.)–Serbia and Montenegro	1997	eng;chi;ser	eng	3
China (People's Rep.)–Seychelles	1999	eng;chi		1
China (People's Rep.)–Singapore	2007	eng;chi		1
China (People's Rep.)–Slovak Republic	1987	eng;chi;cze	eng	3
China (People's Rep.)–Slovenia	1995	eng;chi;slv	eng	3
China (People's Rep.)–South Africa	2000	eng;chi		1
China (People's Rep.)–Spain	1990	eng;chi;spa	eng	3
China (People's Rep.)–Sri Lanka	2003	eng;chi;sin	eng	3

E. Sample

Treaty	Conclusion	AL	UL/PT	TOW
China (People's Rep.)–Sudan	1997	eng;chi;mac	eng	3
China (People's Rep.)–Sweden	1986	eng;chi;swe	eng	6
China (People's Rep.)–Switzerland	1990	eng;chi;fre	eng	4
China (People's Rep.)–Switzerland	2013	eng;chi;ger	eng	3
China (People's Rep.)–Syria	2010	eng;chi;ara	eng	3
China (People's Rep.)–Tajikistan	2008	eng;chi;tgk	eng	3
China (People's Rep.)–Thailand	1986	eng;chi;tha	eng	6
China (People's Rep.)–Trinidad and Tobago	2003	eng;chi		1
China (People's Rep.)–Tunisia	2002	eng;chi;fre;ara	eng	3
China (People's Rep.)–Turkey	1995	eng;chi;tkm	eng	3
China (People's Rep.)–Turkmenistan	2009	eng;chi;tkm;rus	eng	3
China (People's Rep.)–Uganda	2012	eng;chi		1
China (People's Rep.)–Ukraine	1995	eng;chi;ukr	eng	3
China (People's Rep.)–United Arab Emirates	1993	eng;chi;ara	eng	2
China (People's Rep.)–United Kingdom	2011	eng;chi		1
China (People's Rep.)–United States	1984	eng;chi		1
China (People's Rep.)–Uzbekistan	1996	eng;chi;uzb	eng	3
China (People's Rep.)–Venezuela	2001	eng;chi;spa	eng	3
China (People's Rep.)–Vietnam	1995	eng;chi;vts	eng	3
China (People's Rep.)–Zambia	2010	eng;chi		1
China (People's Rep.)–Zimbabwe	2015	eng;chi		1
Colombia–Czech Republic	2012	eng;spa;cze	eng	2
Colombia–France	2015	fre;spa		1
Colombia–India	2011	eng;spa;hin	eng	3
Colombia–Korea (Rep.)	2010	eng;spa;kor	eng	3
Colombia–Mexico	2009	spa	spa	5
Colombia–Portugal	2010	eng;spa;por	eng	3
Colombia–Spain	2005	spa	spa	5
Colombia–Switzerland	2007	fre;spa		1
Congo (Dem. Rep.)–South Africa	2005	eng;fre		1
Congo (Dem. Rep.)–Zimbabwe	2002	eng;fre		1
Congo (Rep.)–France	1987	fre	fre	5
Congo (Rep.)–Italy	2003	fre;ita		1
Congo (Rep.)–Mauritius	2010	fre	fre	5
Congo (Rep.)–Tunisia	2005	fre;ara		1
Cook Islands–New Zealand	2009	eng	eng	5
Costa Rica–Germany	1993	spa;ger		1
Costa Rica–Germany	2014	eng;spa;ger	eng	4
Costa Rica–Romania	1991	spa;rum		1
Costa Rica–Spain	2004	spa	spa	5
Croatia–Czech Republic	1999	eng;cro;cze	eng	4
Croatia–Denmark	2007	eng;cro;dan	eng	3
Croatia–Egypt	2005	eng;cro;ara	eng	3
Croatia–Estonia	2002	eng;cro;est	eng	3
Croatia–Finland	1986	eng	eng	5
Croatia–France	2003	fre;cro		1
Croatia–Georgia	2013	eng;cro;geo	eng	3
Croatia–Germany	2006	ger;cro		1
Croatia–Greece	1996	eng;cro;gre	eng	4
Croatia–Hungary	1996	eng;cro;hun	eng	4
Croatia–Iceland	2010	eng;cro;ice	eng	3
Croatia–India	2014	eng;cro;hin	eng	3

Treaty	Conclusion	AL	UL/PT	TOW
Croatia–Indonesia	2002	eng;cro;ind	eng	4
Croatia–Iran	2003	eng;cro;per	eng	3
Croatia–Ireland	2002	eng;cro	eng	3
Croatia–Israel	2006	eng;cro;heb	eng	4
Croatia–Italy	1999	eng;cro;ita	eng	3
Croatia–Jordan	2005	eng;cro;ara	eng	3
Croatia–Korea (Rep.)	2002	eng;cro;kor	eng	3
Croatia–Kuwait	2001	eng;cro;ara	eng	3
Croatia–Latvia	2000	eng;cro;lat	eng	3
Croatia–Lithuania	2000	eng;cro;lit	eng	3
Croatia–Luxembourg	2014	eng;fre;cro	eng	3
Croatia–Macedonia (FYR)	1994	eng;cro;mac	eng	3
Croatia–Malaysia	2002	eng;cro;may	eng	4
Croatia–Malta	1998	eng;cro		1
Croatia–Mauritius	2002	eng;cro		1
Croatia–Moldova	2005	eng;cro;mol	eng	3
Croatia–Morocco	2008	eng;cro;ara	eng	3
Croatia–Netherlands	2000	eng;cro;dut	eng	4
Croatia–Norway	1983	eng	eng	5
Croatia–Oman	2009	eng;cro;ara	eng	3
Croatia–Poland	1994	eng;cro;rus	eng	4
Croatia–Portugal	2013	eng;cro;por	eng	3
Croatia–Qatar	2008	eng;cro;ara	eng	2
Croatia–Romania	1996	eng;cro;rum	eng	4
Croatia–Russia	1995	eng;cro;rus	eng	4
Croatia–San Marino	2004	eng;cro;ita	eng	3
Croatia–Serbia and Montenegro	2001	eng	eng	5
Croatia–Slovak Republic	1996	eng;cro;slo	eng	4
Croatia–Slovenia	2005	eng;cro;slv	eng	2
Croatia–South Africa	1996	eng;cro		1
Croatia–Spain	2005	eng;cro;spa	eng	2
Croatia–Sri Lanka	1985	eng;scr;sin	eng	3
Croatia–Sweden	1980	eng	eng	5
Croatia–Switzerland	1999	eng;cro;ger	eng	4
Croatia–Syria	2008	eng;cro;ara	eng	3
Croatia–Turkey	1997	eng	eng	5
Croatia–Turkmenistan	2014	eng;rus;cro;tkm	eng	3
Croatia–Ukraine	1996	eng;cro;ukr	eng	4
Croatia–United Kingdom	1981	eng;scr		1
Croatia–United Kingdom	2015	eng;cro		1
Cuba–Italy	2000	spa;ita		1
Cuba–Lebanon	2001	eng	eng	5
Cuba–Portugal	2000	spa;pro		1
Cuba–Qatar	2006	eng;spa;ara	eng	2
Cuba–Russia	2000	spa;rus		1
Cuba–Spain	1999	spa	spa	5
Cuba–Ukraine	2003	eng;spa;ukr	eng	3
Cuba–Venezuela	2003	spa	spa	5
Cuba–Vietnam	2002	eng;spa;vts	eng	3
Curacao–Malta	2015	eng	eng	5
Cyprus–Czech Republic	2009	eng	eng	5
Cyprus–Denmark	2010	eng	eng	5

E. Sample

Treaty	Conclusion	AL	UL/PT	TOW
Cyprus–Egypt	1993	eng;ara	eng	3
Cyprus–Estonia	2012	eng	eng	5
Cyprus–Ethiopia	2015	eng;gre	eng	3
Cyprus–Finland	2012	eng	eng	5
Cyprus–France	1981	eng;fre		1
Cyprus–Georgia	2015	eng;gre;geo	eng	3
Cyprus–Germany	2011	eng;gre;ger	eng	4
Cyprus–Greece	1968	gre	gre	5
Cyprus–Guernsey	2014	eng;gre		1
Cyprus–Hungary	1981	eng	eng	5
Cyprus–Iceland	2014	eng;gre;ice	eng	4
Cyprus–India	1994	eng;hin	eng	2
Cyprus–Iran	2015	eng;gre;per	eng	3
Cyprus–Ireland	1968	eng	eng	5
Cyprus–Italy	1974	eng;gre;ita	eng	3
Cyprus–Jersey	2016	eng;gre	eng	3
Cyprus–Kuwait	1984	eng	eng	5
Cyprus–Kuwait	2010	eng;gre;ara	eng	2
Cyprus–Kyrgyzstan	1982	eng;rus		1
Cyprus–Latvia	2016	eng;gre;lat	eng	3
Cyprus–Lebanon	2003	eng	eng	5
Cyprus–Lithuania	2013	eng;gre;lit	eng	3
Cyprus–Macedonia (FYR)	1985	eng	eng	5
Cyprus–Malta	1993	eng	eng	5
Cyprus–Mauritius	2000	eng	eng	5
Cyprus–Moldova	2008	eng;gre;mol	eng	3
Cyprus–Norway	2014	eng	eng	5
Cyprus–Poland	1992	eng;gre;pol	eng	3
Cyprus–Portugal	2012	eng;gre;por	eng	3
Cyprus–Qatar	2008	eng;gre;ara	eng	2
Cyprus–Romania	1981	eng;gre;rum	eng	3
Cyprus–Russia	1998	eng;gre;rus	eng	4
Cyprus–San Marino	2007	eng;gre;ita	eng	2
Cyprus–Serbia and Montenegro	1985	eng	eng	5
Cyprus–Seychelles	2006	eng;gre	eng	3
Cyprus–Singapore	2000	eng	eng	5
Cyprus–Slovak Republic	1980	eng	eng	5
Cyprus–Slovenia	1985	eng	eng	5
Cyprus–Slovenia	2010	eng;gre;slv	eng	2
Cyprus–South Africa	1997	eng	eng	5
Cyprus–Spain	2013	eng;gre;spa	map	7
Cyprus–Sweden	1988	eng	eng	5
Cyprus–Switzerland	2014	eng;fre;gre	eng	4
Cyprus–Syria	1992	eng	eng	5
Cyprus–Tajikistan	1982	eng;rus		1
Cyprus–Thailand	1998	eng	eng	5
Cyprus–Turkmenistan	1982	eng;rus		1
Cyprus–Ukraine	2012	eng;gre;ukr	eng	4
Cyprus–United Arab Emirates	2011	eng;gre;ara	eng	4
Cyprus–United Kingdom	1974	eng	eng	5
Cyprus–United States	1984	eng	eng	5
Cyprus–Uzbekistan	1982	eng;rus		1

Treaty	Conclusion	AL	UL/PT	TOW
Czech Republic–Denmark	2011	eng	eng	5
Czech Republic–Egypt	1995	eng	eng	5
Czech Republic–Estonia	1994	eng	eng	5
Czech Republic–Ethiopia	2007	eng	eng	5
Czech Republic–Finland	1994	eng	eng	5
Czech Republic–France	2003	fre;cze		1
Czech Republic–Georgia	2006	eng;cze;geo	eng	4
Czech Republic–Germany	1980	cze;ger		1
Czech Republic–Greece	1986	eng	eng	5
Czech Republic–Hong Kong	2011	eng;cze;chi	eng	2
Czech Republic–Hungary	1993	eng	eng	5
Czech Republic–Iceland	2000	eng	eng	5
Czech Republic–India	1998	eng;cze;hin	eng	2
Czech Republic–Indonesia	1994	eng	eng	5
Czech Republic–Iran	2015	eng;cze;per	eng	4
Czech Republic–Ireland	1995	eng;cze		1
Czech Republic–Israel	1993	eng	eng	5
Czech Republic–Italy	1981	fre;cze;ita	fre	6
Czech Republic–Japan	1977	eng	eng	5
Czech Republic–Jordan	2006	eng;cze;ara	eng	2
Czech Republic–Kazakhstan	1998	eng;cze;kaz;rus	eng	2
Czech Republic–Korea (Dem. People's Rep.)	2005	eng;cze;kor	eng	2
Czech Republic–Korea (Rep.)	1992	eng;cze;kor	eng	3
Czech Republic–Kosovo	2013	eng	eng	5
Czech Republic–Kuwait	2001	eng;cze;ara	eng	2
Czech Republic–Latvia	1994	eng	eng	5
Czech Republic–Lebanon	1997	eng;cze;ara	eng	2
Czech Republic–Liechtenstein	2014	eng	eng	5
Czech Republic–Lithuania	1994	eng;cze;lit	eng	3
Czech Republic–Luxembourg	1991	fre;cze		1
Czech Republic–Luxembourg	2013	eng	eng	5
Czech Republic–Macedonia (FYR)	2001	eng;cze;mac	eng	4
Czech Republic–Malaysia	1996	eng;cze;may	eng	3
Czech Republic–Malta	1996	eng	eng	5
Czech Republic–Mexico	2002	eng;cze;spa	eng	2
Czech Republic–Moldova	1999	eng;cze;mol	eng	2
Czech Republic–Mongolia	1997	eng	eng	5
Czech Republic–Morocco	2001	eng;cze;ara	eng	2
Czech Republic–Netherlands	1974	eng;cze;dut	eng	4
Czech Republic–New Zealand	2007	eng;cze		1
Czech Republic–Nigeria	1989	eng	eng	5
Czech Republic–Norway	2004	eng	eng	5
Czech Republic–Pakistan	2014	eng	eng	5
Czech Republic–Panama	2012	eng;cze;spa	eng	2
Czech Republic–Philippines	2000	eng	eng	5
Czech Republic–Poland	2011	eng;cze;pol	eng	2
Czech Republic–Portugal	1994	eng;cze;por	eng	3
Czech Republic–Romania	1993	eng;cze;rum	eng	3
Czech Republic–Russia	1995	eng;cze;rus	eng	4
Czech Republic–Saudi Arabia	2012	eng;cze;ara	eng	2
Czech Republic–Serbia and Montenegro	2004	eng	eng	5
Czech Republic–Singapore	1997	eng	eng	5

E. Sample

Treaty	Conclusion	AL	UL/PT	TOW
Czech Republic–Slovak Republic	2002	cze;slo		1
Czech Republic–Slovenia	1997	eng;cze;slv	eng	4
Czech Republic–South Africa	1996	eng;cze		1
Czech Republic–Spain	1980	cze;spa		1
Czech Republic–Sri Lanka	1978	eng;cze;sin	eng	3
Czech Republic–Sweden	1979	eng	eng	5
Czech Republic–Switzerland	1995	eng;cze;ger	eng	4
Czech Republic–Syria	2008	eng;cze;ara	eng	4
Czech Republic–Tajikistan	2006	eng;cze;tgk;rus	eng	2
Czech Republic–Thailand	1994	eng	eng	5
Czech Republic–Tunisia	1990	fre	fre	5
Czech Republic–Turkey	1999	eng	eng	5
Czech Republic–Turkmenistan	2016	eng;cze;tkm	eng	2
Czech Republic–Ukraine	1997	eng;cze;ukr	eng	2
Czech Republic–United Arab Emirates	1996	eng;cze;ara	eng	3
Czech Republic–United Kingdom	1990	eng;cze		1
Czech Republic–United States	1993	eng;cze		1
Czech Republic–Uzbekistan	2000	eng;cze;uzb	eng	2
Czech Republic–Venezuela	1996	eng;cze;spa	eng	4
Czech Republic–Vietnam	1997	eng;cze;vts	eng	3
Denmark–Egypt	1989	eng;dan;ara	eng	3
Denmark–Estonia	1993	eng	eng	5
Denmark–Georgia	2007	eng	eng	5
Denmark–Germany	1995	dan;ger		1
Denmark–Ghana	2014	eng	eng	5
Denmark–Greece	1989	eng	eng	5
Denmark–Greenland	1979	dan;gro		1
Denmark–Guernsey	2008	eng	eng	5
Denmark–Hungary	2011	eng;dan;hun	eng	3
Denmark–India	1989	eng;dan;hin	eng	2
Denmark–Indonesia	1985	eng	eng	5
Denmark–Ireland	1993	eng	eng	5
Denmark–Isle of Man	2007	eng	eng	5
Denmark–Israel	2009	eng;dan;heb	eng	2
Denmark–Italy	1966	eng;dan;ita	eng	6
Denmark–Italy	1999	eng;dan;ita	eng	6
Denmark–Jamaica	1990	eng	eng	5
Denmark–Japan	1968	eng	eng	5
Denmark–Jersey	2008	eng	eng	5
Denmark–Kenya	1972	eng	eng	5
Denmark–Korea (Rep.)	1977	eng	eng	5
Denmark–Kuwait	2010	eng;dan;ara	eng	2
Denmark–Kyrgyzstan	1986	dan;rus		1
Denmark–Latvia	1993	eng	eng	5
Denmark–Lithuania	1993	eng;dan;lit	eng	3
Denmark–Luxembourg	1980	fre;dan		1
Denmark–Macedonia (FYR)	2000	eng;dan;mac	eng	3
Denmark–Malaysia	1970	eng	eng	5
Denmark–Malta	1998	eng	eng	5
Denmark–Mexico	1997	eng;dan;spa	eng	3
Denmark–Morocco	1984	fre;dan;ara		1
Denmark–Netherlands	1996	eng	eng	5

Treaty	Conclusion	AL	UL/PT	TOW
Denmark–New Zealand	1980	eng	eng	5
Denmark–Pakistan	1987	eng	eng	5
Denmark–Philippines	1995	eng	eng	5
Denmark–Poland	2001	eng;dan;pol	eng	3
Denmark–Portugal	2000	eng;dan;por	eng	2
Denmark–Romania	1976	eng;dan;rum	eng	3
Denmark–Russia	1996	eng;dan;rus	eng	3
Denmark–Serbia	2009	eng	eng	5
Denmark–Singapore	2000	eng	eng	5
Denmark–Slovak Republic	1982	eng	eng	5
Denmark–Slovenia	2001	eng;dan;slv	eng	2
Denmark–South Africa	1995	eng	eng	5
Denmark–Sri Lanka	1981	eng;dan;sin	eng	3
Denmark–Switzerland	1973	dan;ger		1
Denmark–Switzerland	1973	dan;ger		1
Denmark–Taiwan	2005	eng	eng	5
Denmark–Tanzania	1976	eng	eng	5
Denmark–Thailand	1998	eng	eng	5
Denmark–Trinidad and Tobago	1969	eng	eng	5
Denmark–Tunisia	1981	fre	fre	5
Denmark–Turkey	1991	eng;dan;tur	eng	2
Denmark–Turkmenistan	1986	dan;rus		1
Denmark–Uganda	2000	eng	eng	5
Denmark–Ukraine	1996	eng;dan;ukr	eng	3
Denmark–United Kingdom	1980	eng;dan		1
Denmark–United States	1983	eng;dan		1
Denmark–United States	1999	eng	eng	5
Denmark–Venezuela	1998	eng;dan;spa	eng	3
Denmark–Vietnam	1995	eng;dan;vts	eng	3
Denmark–Zambia	1973	eng;dan		1
Dominica–Switzerland	1963	eng;fre		1
Dominican Republic–Spain	2011	spa	spa	5
Ecuador–France	1989	fre;spa		1
Ecuador–Germany	1982	spa;ger		1
Ecuador–Italy	1984	spa;ita		1
Ecuador–Korea (Rep.)	2012	eng;spa;kor	eng	3
Ecuador–Mexico	1992	spa	spa	5
Ecuador–Qatar	2014	eng;ara;spa	eng	2
Ecuador–Romania	1992	spa;rum		1
Ecuador–Singapore	2013	eng;spa		1
Ecuador–Spain	1991	spa	spa	5
Ecuador–Switzerland	1994	fre;spa		1
Ecuador–Uruguay	2011	spa	spa	5
Egypt–Ethiopia	2011	eng;ara	eng	3
Egypt–Finland	1965	eng	eng	5
Egypt–France	1980	fre;ara		1
Egypt–Georgia	2010	eng;ara;geo	eng	3
Egypt–Germany	1987	eng;ara;ger	eng	4
Egypt–Greece	2004	eng;ara;gre	eng	6
Egypt–Hungary	1991	eng;ara;hun	eng	4
Egypt–India	1969	eng	eng	5
Egypt–Indonesia	1998	eng;ara;ind	eng	3

E. Sample

Treaty	Conclusion	AL	UL/PT	TOW
Egypt–Iraq	1968	ara	ara	5
Egypt–Ireland	2012	eng;ara	eng	3
Egypt–Italy	1979	eng	eng	5
Egypt–Japan	1968	eng	eng	5
Egypt–Jordan	1996	ara	ara	5
Egypt–Korea (Rep.)	1992	eng;ara;kor	eng	3
Egypt–Kuwait	2004	ara	ara	5
Egypt–Lebanon	1996	ara	ara	5
Egypt–Libya	1990	ara	ara	5
Egypt–Macedonia (FYR)	1999	eng;ara;mac	eng	3
Egypt–Malaysia	1997	eng;ara;may	eng	3
Egypt–Malta	1999	eng;ara	eng	3
Egypt–Mauritius	2012	eng;ara	eng	2
Egypt–Morocco	1989	ara	ara	5
Egypt–Netherlands	1999	eng;ara;dut	eng	4
Egypt–Norway	1964	eng	eng	5
Egypt–Oman	2000	ara	ara	5
Egypt–Pakistan	1995	eng;ara		1
Egypt–Palestinian Autonomous Areas	1998	ara	ara	5
Egypt–Poland	1996	eng	eng	5
Egypt–Romania	1979	eng;ara;rum	eng	6
Egypt–Russia	1997	eng;ara;rus	eng	2
Egypt–Saudi Arabia	2016	ara	ara	5
Egypt–Serbia and Montenegro	2005	eng;ara;ser	eng	3
Egypt–Singapore	1996	eng	eng	5
Egypt–Slovak Republic	2004	eng;ara;slo	eng	3
Egypt–Slovenia	2009	eng;ara;slv	eng	2
Egypt–South Africa	1997	eng	eng	5
Egypt–Spain	2005	eng;ara;spa	eng	2
Egypt–Sudan	1970	ara	ara	5
Egypt–Sudan	2001	ara	ara	5
Egypt–Sweden	1994	eng;ara;swe	eng	6
Egypt–Switzerland	1987	eng;ara;fre	eng	6
Egypt–Syria	1991	ara	ara	5
Egypt–Thailand	2006	eng;ara;tha	eng	4
Egypt–Turkey	1993	eng	eng	5
Egypt–Ukraine	1997	eng;ara;ukr	eng	4
Egypt–United Arab Emirates	1994	ara	ara	5
Egypt–United Kingdom	1977	eng	eng	5
Egypt–United States	1980	eng	eng	5
Egypt–Uzbekistan	1999	eng;ara;uzb	eng	3
Egypt–Vietnam	2006	eng;ara;vts	eng	3
Egypt–Yemen	1997	ara	ara	5
El Salvador–Spain	2008	spa	spa	5
Estonia–Finland	1993	eng	eng	5
Estonia–France	1997	fre;est		1
Estonia–Georgia	2006	eng;est;geo	eng	3
Estonia–Germany	1996	eng;est;ger	eng	4
Estonia–Greece	2006	eng;est;gre	eng	3
Estonia–Hungary	2002	eng;est;hun	eng	3
Estonia–Iceland	1994	eng	eng	5
Estonia–India	2011	eng;est;hin	eng	3

Treaty	Conclusion	AL	UL/PT	TOW
Estonia–Ireland	1997	eng;est	eng	3
Estonia–Isle of Man	2009	eng;est	eng	2
Estonia–Israel	2009	eng;est;heb	eng	2
Estonia–Italy	1997	eng;est;ita	eng	3
Estonia–Jersey	2010	eng;est	eng	2
Estonia–Kazakhstan	1999	eng;est;kaz;rus	eng	3
Estonia–Korea (Rep.)	2009	eng;est;kor	eng	3
Estonia–Latvia	2002	eng;est;lat	eng	3
Estonia–Lithuania	2004	eng;est;lit	eng	3
Estonia–Luxembourg	2006	eng;fre;est		1
Estonia–Luxembourg	2014	eng	eng	5
Estonia–Macedonia (FYR)	2008	eng;est;mac	eng	3
Estonia–Malta	2001	eng;est	eng	3
Estonia–Mexico	2012	eng;est;spa	eng	2
Estonia–Moldova	1998	eng;est;mol	eng	3
Estonia–Morocco	2013	eng;est;ara	eng	3
Estonia–Netherlands	1997	eng	eng	5
Estonia–Norway	1993	eng	eng	5
Estonia–Poland	1994	eng;est;pol	eng	3
Estonia–Portugal	2003	eng;est;por	eng	3
Estonia–Romania	2003	eng;est;rum	eng	3
Estonia–Russia	2002	eng;est;rus	eng	3
Estonia–Serbia	2009	eng	eng	5
Estonia–Singapore	2006	eng;est	eng	3
Estonia–Slovak Republic	2003	eng;est;slo	eng	3
Estonia–Slovenia	2005	eng;est;slv	eng	3
Estonia–Spain	2003	eng;est;spa	eng	2
Estonia–Sweden	1993	eng	eng	5
Estonia–Switzerland	2002	eng;est;ger	eng	3
Estonia–Thailand	2012	eng	eng	5
Estonia–Turkey	2003	eng;est;tur	eng	3
Estonia–Turkmenistan	2011	eng;est;tkm	eng	2
Estonia–Ukraine	1996	eng;est;ukr	eng	3
Estonia–United Arab Emirates	2011	eng;est;ara	eng	3
Estonia–United Kingdom	1994	eng;est		1
Estonia–United States	1998	eng;est		1
Estonia–Uzbekistan	2012	eng;est;uzb	eng	3
Estonia–Vietnam	2015	eng;est;vts	eng	3
Ethiopia–France	2006	eng;fre		1
Ethiopia–India	2011	eng;hin	eng	3
Ethiopia–Ireland	2014	eng	eng	5
Ethiopia–Israel	2004	eng;heb	eng	3
Ethiopia–Italy	1997	eng;ita		1
Ethiopia–Kuwait	1996	eng;ara		1
Ethiopia–Netherlands	2012	eng	eng	5
Ethiopia–Poland	2015	eng;pol		1
Ethiopia–Romania	2003	eng;rum	eng	3
Ethiopia–Russia	1999	eng;rus		1
Ethiopia–Seychelles	2012	eng	eng	5
Ethiopia–South Africa	2004	eng	eng	5
Ethiopia–Sudan	2006	eng	eng	5
Ethiopia–Tunisia	2003	eng;ara	eng	3

E. Sample

Treaty	Conclusion	AL	UL/PT	TOW
Ethiopia–Turkey	2005	eng	eng	5
Ethiopia–United Kingdom	2011	eng	eng	5
Falkland Islands–United Kingdom	1997	eng	eng	5
Faroe Islands–Greenland	2000	fao;gro;dan		1
Faroe Islands–Guernsey	2008	eng	eng	5
Faroe Islands–India	1989	eng;dan;hin	eng	2
Faroe Islands–Isle of Man	2007	eng	eng	5
Faroe Islands–Jersey	2008	eng	eng	5
Faroe Islands–Switzerland	1978	dan;ger		1
Faroe Islands–Switzerland	1978	dan;ger		1
Faroe Islands–United Kingdom	2007	eng;fao		1
Fiji–India	2014	eng;hin	eng	3
Fiji–Japan	1970	eng;jap		1
Fiji–Korea (Rep.)	1994	eng;kor	eng	3
Fiji–Malaysia	1995	eng;may	eng	8
Fiji–New Zealand	1976	eng	eng	5
Fiji–Papua New Guinea	1998	eng	eng	5
Fiji–Qatar	2013	eng;ara		1
Fiji–Singapore	2005	eng	eng	5
Fiji–United Arab Emirates	2012	eng;ara	eng	2
Fiji–United Kingdom	1975	eng	eng	5
Finland–France	1970	fre;fin		1
Finland–Georgia	2007	eng;fin;geo	eng	3
Finland–Germany	1979	fin;ger		1
Finland–Germany	2016	ger;fin		1
Finland–Greece	1980	eng	eng	5
Finland–Greece	1995	eng	eng	5
Finland–Guernsey	2008	eng	eng	5
Finland–Hungary	1978	eng	eng	5
Finland–India	2010	eng;fin;swe;hin	eng	3
Finland–Indonesia	1987	eng	eng	5
Finland–Ireland	1992	eng;fin		1
Finland–Isle of Man	2007	eng	eng	5
Finland–Israel	1997	eng	eng	5
Finland–Italy	1981	eng;fin;ita	eng	3
Finland–Japan	1972	eng	eng	5
Finland–Jersey	2008	eng	eng	5
Finland–Kazakhstan	2009	eng;fin;swe;kaz;rus	eng	3
Finland–Korea (Rep.)	1979	eng	eng	5
Finland–Kosovo	1986	eng	eng	5
Finland–Kyrgyzstan	2003	eng;fin;kyr;rus	eng	3
Finland–Latvia	1993	eng	eng	5
Finland–Lithuania	1993	eng;fin;ukr	eng	3
Finland–Luxembourg	1982	fre;fin		1
Finland–Macedonia (FYR)	2001	eng;fin;mac	eng	3
Finland–Malaysia	1984	eng;fin;may	eng	3
Finland–Malta	2000	eng	eng	5
Finland–Mexico	1997	eng;fin;spa	eng	3
Finland–Moldova	2008	eng;fin;mol	eng	3
Finland–Montenegro	1986	eng	eng	5
Finland–Morocco	2006	fre;fin;swe;are	fre	3
Finland–Netherlands	1995	eng	eng	5

Treaty	Conclusion	AL	UL/PT	TOW
Finland–New Zealand	1982	eng	eng	5
Finland–Pakistan	1994	eng	eng	5
Finland–Philippines	1978	eng	eng	5
Finland–Poland	2009	eng;fin;pol	eng	3
Finland–Portugal	1970	eng	eng	5
Finland–Romania	1998	eng;fin;rum	eng	3
Finland–Russia	1996	eng;fin;rus	eng	3
Finland–Serbia	1986	eng	eng	5
Finland–Singapore	2002	eng	eng	5
Finland–Slovak Republic	1999	eng;fin;slo	eng	3
Finland–Slovenia	2003	eng;fin;slv	eng	3
Finland–South Africa	1995	eng	eng	5
Finland–Spain	1967	fin;spa		1
Finland–Spain	2015	spa;fin		1
Finland–Sri Lanka	1982	eng;fin;sin	eng	3
Finland–Switzerland	1991	eng;fin;ger	eng	3
Finland–Tajikistan	2012	eng;fin;tgk	eng	3
Finland–Tanzania	1976	eng	eng	5
Finland–Thailand	1985	eng	eng	5
Finland–Turkey	2009	eng;fin;tur	eng	3
Finland–Ukraine	1994	eng;fin;ukr	eng	3
Finland–United Arab Emirates	1996	eng;fin;ara	eng	3
Finland–United Kingdom	1969	eng;fin		1
Finland–United States	1989	eng;fin		1
Finland–Uruguay	2011	eng;fin;spa	eng	2
Finland–Uzbekistan	1998	eng;fin;uzb	eng	3
Finland–Vietnam	2001	eng;fin;vts	eng	3
Finland–Zambia	1978	eng	eng	5
France–Gabon	1995	fre	fre	5
France–Georgia	2007	fre;geo		1
France–Germany	2006	fre;ger		1
France–Ghana	1993	eng;fre		1
France–Greece	1963	fre	fre	5
France–Guinea	1999	fre	fre	5
France–Hong Kong	2010	eng;fre		1
France–Hungary	1980	fre;hun		1
France–Iceland	1990	fre;ice		1
France–India	1992	eng;fre;hin		1
France–Indonesia	1979	fre;ind		1
France–Iran	1973	fre;per		1
France–Ireland	1968	eng;fre		1
France–Israel	1995	eng;heb		1
France–Italy	1989	fre;ita		1
France–Italy	1990	fre;ita		1
France–Ivory Coast	1966	fre	fre	5
France–Jamaica	1995	eng;fre		1
France–Japan	1995	fre;jap		1
France–Jordan	1984	fre;ara		1
France–Kazakhstan	1998	fre;rus;kaz		1
France–Kenya	2007	eng;fre		1
France–Korea (Rep.)	1979	fre;kor		1
France–Kosovo	1974	fre;scr		1

E. Sample

Treaty	Conclusion	AL	UL/PT	TOW
France–Kuwait	1982	fre;ara		1
France–Kyrgyzstan	1985	fre;rus		1
France–Latvia	1997	fre;lat		1
France–Lebanon	1962	fre	fre	5
France–Libya	2005	fre;ara		1
France–Lithuania	1997	fre;lit		1
France–Macedonia (FYR)	1999	fre;mac		1
France–Madagascar	1983	fre	fre	5
France–Malawi	1963	eng;fre		1
France–Malaysia	1975	fre;may		1
France–Mali	1972	fre	fre	5
France–Malta	1977	eng;fre		1
France–Mauritania	1967	fre	fre	5
France–Mauritius	1980	eng;fre		1
France–Mayotte	1970	fre	fre	5
France–Mexico	1991	fre;spa		1
France–Moldova	1985	fre;rus		1
France–Moldova	2006	fre;mol		1
France–Monaco	1963	fre	fre	5
France–Mongolia	1996	fre;mon		1
France–Morocco	1970	fre	fre	5
France–Namibia	1996	eng;fre		1
France–Netherlands	1973	fre;dut		1
France–New Caledonia	1983	fre	fre	5
France–New Zealand	1979	eng;fre		1
France–Niger	1965	fre	fre	5
France–Nigeria	1990	eng;fre		1
France–Norway	1980	fre	fre	5
France–Oman	1989	fre;ara		1
France–Pakistan	1994	eng;fre		1
France–Panama	2011	fre;spa		1
France–Philippines	1976	eng;fre		1
France–Poland	1975	fre;pol		1
France–Portugal	1971	fre;por		1
France–Portugal	1994	fre	fre	5
France–Qatar	1990	fre;ara		1
France–Quebec	1987	fre	fre	5
France–Romania	1974	fre;rum		1
France–Russia	1996	fre;rus		1
France–Saudi Arabia	1982	fre;ara		1
France–Senegal	1974	fre	fre	5
France–Serbia and Montenegro	1974	fre;scr		1
France–Singapore	1974	eng;fre		1
France–Singapore	2015	eng;fre		1
France–Slovak Republic	1973	fre;cze		1
France–Slovenia	2004	fre;slv		1
France–South Africa	1993	eng;fre		1
France–Spain	1961	fre;spa		1
France–Spain	1963	fre;spa		1
France–Spain	1995	fre;spa		1
France–Sri Lanka	1981	fre;sin		1
France–St. Martin	2010	fre	fre	5

Treaty	Conclusion	AL	UL/PT	TOW
France–St. Pierre and Miquelon	1988	fre	fre	5
France–Sweden	1990	fre	fre	5
France–Sweden	1994	fre	fre	5
France–Switzerland	1966	fre	fre	5
France–Switzerland	1979	fre	fre	5
France–Switzerland	1983	fre	fre	5
France–Switzerland	2013	fre	fre	5
France–Syria	1998	fre;ara		1
France–Taiwan	2010	eng;fre;chi		1
France–Tajikistan	1985	fre;rus		1
France–Thailand	1974	fre;tha		1
France–Togo	1971	fre	fre	5
France–Trinidad and Tobago	1987	eng;fre		1
France–Tunisia	1973	fre	fre	5
France–Turkey	1987	fre;tur		1
France–Turkmenistan	1985	fre;rus		1
France–Ukraine	1997	fre;ukr		1
France–United Arab Emirates	1989	fre;ara	map	7
France–United Kingdom	1963	eng;fre		1
France–United Kingdom	2008	eng;fre		1
France–United States	1978	eng;fre		1
France–United States	1994	eng;fre		1
France–Uzbekistan	1996	fre	fre	5
France–Venezuela	1992	fre;spa		1
France–Vietnam	1993	fre;vts		1
France–Zambia	1963	eng;fre		1
France–Zimbabwe	1993	eng;fre		1
Gabon–Italy	1999	fre;ita		1
Gabon–Korea (Rep.)	2010	eng;fre;kor		1
Gabon–Lebanon	2001	fre	fre	5
Gabon–Morocco	1999	fre;ara	fre	3
Gabon–South Africa	2005	eng;fre		1
Gabon–Tunisia	1986	fre	fre	5
Gambia–Norway	1994	eng	eng	5
Gambia–Qatar	2014	eng;ara		1
Gambia–Sweden	1993	eng	eng	5
Gambia–Switzerland	1963	eng;fre		1
Gambia–Taiwan	1998	eng;chi	eng	2
Gambia–United Kingdom	1980	eng	eng	5
Georgia–Germany	2006	rus;geo;ger	rus	4
Georgia–Greece	1999	eng;geo;gre	eng	6
Georgia–Hungary	2012	eng;geo;hun	eng	3
Georgia–Iceland	2015	eng;geo;ice	eng	3
Georgia–India	2011	eng;geo;hin	eng	3
Georgia–Iran	1996	eng;geo;per	eng	3
Georgia–Ireland	2008	eng;geo		1
Georgia–Israel	2010	eng;geo;heb	eng	2
Georgia–Italy	2000	eng;geo;ita	eng	6
Georgia–Japan	1986	eng;rus;jap	eng	3
Georgia–Korea (Rep.)	2016	eng;kor;geo	eng	3
Georgia–Kuwait	2009	eng;geo;ara	eng	2
Georgia–Latvia	2004	eng;geo;lat	eng	3

E. Sample

Treaty	Conclusion	AL	UL/PT	TOW
Georgia–Liechtenstein	2015	eng;ger;geo	eng	3
Georgia–Lithuania	2003	eng;geo;lit	eng	3
Georgia–Luxembourg	2007	eng;geo;fre		1
Georgia–Malaysia	1987	eng;rus;may	eng	3
Georgia–Malta	2009	eng;geo	eng	2
Georgia–Netherlands	2002	eng;geo;dut	eng	4
Georgia–Norway	2011	eng;geo;nor	eng	3
Georgia–Poland	1999	rus;geo;pol	rus	3
Georgia–Portugal	2012	eng;geo;por	eng	3
Georgia–Qatar	2010	eng;geo;ara	eng	2
Georgia–Romania	1997	eng;geo;rum	eng	3
Georgia–San Marino	2012	eng;geo;ita	eng	3
Georgia–Serbia	2012	eng;geo;ser	eng	3
Georgia–Singapore	2009	eng;geo	eng	2
Georgia–Slovak Republic	2011	eng;geo;slo	eng	3
Georgia–Slovenia	2012	eng;geo;slv	eng	2
Georgia–Spain	2010	eng;geo;spa	eng	2
Georgia–Sweden	2013	eng;geo;swe	eng	2
Georgia–Switzerland	1986	rus;ger		1
Georgia–Switzerland	2010	eng;geo;ger	eng	3
Georgia–Turkey	2007	eng;geo;tur	eng	2
Georgia–Turkmenistan	1997	geo;tkm;rus	rus	3
Georgia–Ukraine	1997	rus;geo;ukr	rus	3
Georgia–United Arab Emirates	2010	eng;geo;ara	eng	2
Georgia–United Kingdom	2004	eng;geo		1
Georgia–United States	1973	eng;rus		1
Georgia–Uzbekistan	1996	rus;geo;uzb	rus	3
Germany–Ghana	2004	eng;ger		1
Germany–Greece	1966	eng;ger;gre	eng	6
Germany–Hungary	2011	eng;ger;hun	eng	4
Germany–Iceland	1971	ger;ice		1
Germany–India	1995	eng;ger;hin	eng	4
Germany–Indonesia	1990	eng;ger;ind	eng	4
Germany–Iran	1968	fre;ger;per	fre	4
Germany–Ireland	2011	eng;ger		1
Germany–Israel	1962	eng;ger;heb	eng	6
Germany–Israel	2014	eng;ger;heb	eng	4
Germany–Italy	1989	ger;ita		1
Germany–Ivory Coast	1979	fre;ger		1
Germany–Jamaica	1974	eng;ger		1
Germany–Japan	1966	eng;ger;jap	eng	9
Germany–Japan	2015	eng;ger;jap	eng	4
Germany–Jersey	2008	eng;ger		1
Germany–Jersey	2015	eng;ger		1
Germany–Kazakhstan	1997	eng;ger;rus;kaz	eng	4
Germany–Kenya	1977	eng;ger		1
Germany–Korea (Rep.)	2000	eng;ger;kor	eng	4
Germany–Kuwait	1999	eng;ger;ara	eng	4
Germany–Kyrgyzstan	2005	rus;ger;kyr	rus	4
Germany–Latvia	1997	eng;ger;lat	eng	4
Germany–Liberia	1970	eng;ger		1
Germany–Liechtenstein	2011	ger	ger	5

410

Treaty	Conclusion	AL	UL/PT	TOW
Germany–Lithuania	1997	eng;ger;lit	eng	4
Germany–Luxembourg	2012	ger	ger	5
Germany–Macedonia (FYR)	2006	eng;ger;mac	eng	4
Germany–Malaysia	2010	eng;ger;may	eng	4
Germany–Malta	2001	eng;ger		1
Germany–Mauritius	2011	eng;ger		1
Germany–Mexico	2008	eng;ger;spa	eng	4
Germany–Moldova	1981	ger;rus		1
Germany–Mongolia	1994	eng;ger;mon	eng	4
Germany–Morocco	1972	fre;ger		1
Germany–Namibia	1993	eng;ger		1
Germany–Netherlands	2012	ger;dut		1
Germany–New Zealand	1978	eng;ger		1
Germany–Norway	1991	ger;nor		1
Germany–Oman	2012	eng;ger;ara	eng	4
Germany–Pakistan	1994	eng;ger		1
Germany–Papua New Guinea	1995	eng;ger		1
Germany–Philippines	1983	eng;ger		1
Germany–Philippines	2013	eng;ger		1
Germany–Poland	2003	ger;pol		1
Germany–Portugal	1980	eng;ger;por	eng	4
Germany–Romania	2001	eng;ger;rum	eng	4
Germany–Russia	1996	ger;rus		1
Germany–Serbia and Montenegro	1987	eng;ger;scr	eng	4
Germany–Singapore	2004	eng;ger		1
Germany–Slovak Republic	1980	ger;cze		1
Germany–Slovenia	2006	eng;ger;slv	eng	4
Germany–South Africa	1973	eng;ger;afr	eng	6
Germany–South Africa	2008	eng;ger		1
Germany–Spain	2011	ger;spa	map	7
Germany–Sri Lanka	1979	eng;ger;sin	eng	3
Germany–Sweden	1992	ger;swe		1
Germany–Switzerland	1971	ger	ger	5
Germany–Switzerland	1978	ger	ger	5
Germany–Syria	2010	eng;ger;ara	eng	4
Germany–Taiwan	2011	eng;ger;chi	eng	4
Germany–Tajikistan	2003	ger;rus		1
Germany–Thailand	1967	eng;ger;tha	eng	6
Germany–Trinidad and Tobago	1973	eng;ger		1
Germany–Tunisia	1975	fre;ger		1
Germany–Turkey	2011	eng;ger;tur	eng	4
Germany–Turkmenistan	1981	ger;rus		1
Germany–Ukraine	1995	eng;ger;ukr	eng	3
Germany–United Arab Emirates	2010	eng;ger;ara	eng	4
Germany–United Kingdom	2010	eng;ger		1
Germany–United States	1980	eng;ger		1
Germany–United States	1989	eng;ger		1
Germany–Uruguay	2010	ger;spa		1
Germany–Uzbekistan	1999	rus;ger;uzb	rus	4
Germany–Venezuela	1995	ger;spa		1
Germany–Vietnam	1995	eng;ger;vts	eng	4
Germany–Zambia	1973	eng;ger		1

E. Sample

Treaty	Conclusion	AL	UL/PT	TOW
Germany–Zimbabwe	1988	eng;ger		1
Ghana–Italy	2004	eng;ita		1
Ghana–Netherlands	2008	eng	eng	5
Ghana–Serbia and Montenegro	2000	eng;ser	eng	3
Ghana–Seychelles	2014	eng	eng	5
Ghana–South Africa	2004	eng	eng	5
Ghana–Switzerland	2008	eng;fre		1
Ghana–United Kingdom	1977	eng	eng	5
Ghana–United Kingdom	1993	eng	eng	5
Greece–Hungary	1983	eng	eng	5
Greece–Iceland	2006	eng;gre;ice	eng	3
Greece–India	1965	eng	eng	5
Greece–Ireland	2003	eng;gre	eng	6
Greece–Israel	1995	eng;gre;heb	eng	3
Greece–Italy	1964	fre	fre	5
Greece–Italy	1987	eng	eng	5
Greece–Korea (Rep.)	1995	eng;gre;kor	eng	3
Greece–Kuwait	2003	eng;gre;ara	eng	2
Greece–Latvia	2002	eng;gre;lat	eng	3
Greece–Lithuania	2002	eng;gre;lit	eng	3
Greece–Luxembourg	1991	eng;fre;gre		1
Greece–Malta	2006	eng;gre	eng	6
Greece–Mexico	2004	eng;gre;spa	eng	3
Greece–Moldova	2004	eng;gre;mol	eng	6
Greece–Montenegro	1997	eng;gre;ser	eng	3
Greece–Morocco	2007	eng;fre;gre;ara	eng	3
Greece–Netherlands	1981	eng;gre;dut	eng	4
Greece–Norway	1988	eng	eng	5
Greece–Poland	1987	eng;gre;pol	eng	3
Greece–Portugal	1999	eng;gre;por	eng	6
Greece–Qatar	2008	eng;gre;ara	eng	2
Greece–Romania	1991	eng;gre;rum	eng	6
Greece–Russia	2000	eng;gre;rus	eng	3
Greece–San Marino	2013	eng;gre;ita	eng	2
Greece–Saudi Arabia	2008	eng;gre;ara	eng	3
Greece–Serbia	1997	eng;gre;ser	eng	3
Greece–Slovak Republic	1986	eng	eng	5
Greece–Slovenia	2001	eng;gre;slv	eng	2
Greece–South Africa	1998	eng;gre	eng	6
Greece–Spain	2000	eng;gre;spa	eng	3
Greece–Sweden	1961	eng	eng	5
Greece–Switzerland	1983	eng;fre;ger	eng	6
Greece–Tunisia	1992	fre;gre;ara	fre	2
Greece–Turkey	2003	eng;gre;tur	eng	2
Greece–Ukraine	2000	eng;gre;ukr	eng	6
Greece–United Arab Emirates	2010	eng	eng	5
Greece–Uzbekistan	1997	eng;gre;uzb	eng	6
Greenland–Guernsey	2008	eng	eng	5
Greenland–Iceland	2002	eng	eng	5
Greenland–Isle of Man	2007	eng	eng	5
Greenland–Jersey	2008	eng	eng	5
Greenland–Norway	2005	nor;gro		1

Treaty	Conclusion	AL	UL/PT	TOW
Grenada–South Africa	1960	eng;afr		1
Grenada–Switzerland	1963	eng;fre		1
Guatemala–Mexico	2015	spa	spa	5
Guernsey–Hong Kong	2013	eng	eng	5
Guernsey–Iceland	2008	eng	eng	5
Guernsey–Ireland	2009	eng	eng	5
Guernsey–Isle of Man	2013	eng	eng	5
Guernsey–Jersey	2013	eng	eng	5
Guernsey–Liechtenstein	2014	eng;ger	eng	3
Guernsey–Luxembourg	2013	eng	eng	5
Guernsey–Malta	2012	eng	eng	5
Guernsey–Mauritius	2013	eng	eng	5
Guernsey–Monaco	2014	eng;fre		1
Guernsey–Norway	2008	eng	eng	5
Guernsey–Poland	2013	eng;pol		1
Guernsey–Qatar	2013	eng;ara		1
Guernsey–Seychelles	2014	eng	eng	5
Guernsey–Singapore	2013	eng	eng	5
Guernsey–Sweden	2008	eng	eng	5
Guinea–Morocco	2014	fre;ara	fre	3
Guinea–Serbia and Montenegro	1996	fre;ser		1
Guinea–Tunisia	1993	fre	fre	5
Guinea-Bissau–Morocco	2015	fre;ara;por	fre	3
Guinea-Bissau–Portugal	2008	por	por	5
Guyana–United Kingdom	1992	eng	eng	5
Hong Kong–Hungary	2010	eng	eng	5
Hong Kong–Indonesia	2010	eng	eng	5
Hong Kong–Ireland	2010	eng	eng	5
Hong Kong–Italy	2013	eng;ita		1
Hong Kong–Japan	2010	eng;chi;jap	eng	3
Hong Kong–Jersey	2012	eng	eng	5
Hong Kong–Korea (Rep.)	2014	eng;chi;kor	eng	3
Hong Kong–Kuwait	2010	eng;chi;ara	eng	2
Hong Kong–Latvia	2016	eng;chi;lat	eng	3
Hong Kong–Liechtenstein	2010	eng	eng	5
Hong Kong–Luxembourg	2007	eng;fre		1
Hong Kong–Malaysia	2012	eng;chi;may	eng	3
Hong Kong–Malta	2011	eng	eng	5
Hong Kong–Mexico	2012	eng;chi;spa	eng	2
Hong Kong–Netherlands	2010	eng	eng	5
Hong Kong–New Zealand	2010	eng	eng	5
Hong Kong–Portugal	2011	eng;chi;por	eng	2
Hong Kong–Qatar	2013	eng;chi;spa	eng	2
Hong Kong–Romania	2015	eng	eng	5
Hong Kong–Russia	2016	eng;rus;chi	eng	3
Hong Kong–South Africa	2014	eng	eng	5
Hong Kong–Spain	2011	eng;spa		1
Hong Kong–Switzerland	2011	eng;chi;ger	eng	3
Hong Kong–Thailand	2005	eng	eng	5
Hong Kong–United Arab Emirates	2014	eng;ara	eng	2
Hong Kong–United Kingdom	2010	eng	eng	5
Hong Kong–Vietnam	2008	eng;vts		1

E. Sample

Treaty	Conclusion	AL	UL/PT	TOW
Hungary–Iceland	2005	eng;hun;ice	eng	3
Hungary–India	2003	eng;hun;hin	eng	2
Hungary–Indonesia	1989	eng	eng	5
Hungary–Iran	2015	eng;hun;per	eng	3
Hungary–Ireland	1995	eng;hun		1
Hungary–Israel	1991	eng	eng	5
Hungary–Italy	1977	fre;hun;ita	fre	6
Hungary–Japan	1980	eng	eng	5
Hungary–Korea (Rep.)	1989	eng;hun;kor	eng	3
Hungary–Kosovo	2013	eng;hun;alb	eng	3
Hungary–Kosovo (FYR)	1985	eng	eng	5
Hungary–Kuwait	1994	eng;hun;ara	eng	2
Hungary–Latvia	2004	eng;hun;lat	eng	3
Hungary–Liechtenstein	2015	eng	eng	5
Hungary–Lithuania	2004	eng;hun;lit	eng	3
Hungary–Luxembourg	1990	eng;fre;hun		1
Hungary–Luxembourg	2015	eng;fre;hun	eng	3
Hungary–Macedonia (FYR)	2001	eng;hun;mac	eng	2
Hungary–Malaysia	1989	eng;hun;may	eng	8
Hungary–Malta	1991	eng	eng	5
Hungary–Mexico	2011	eng;hun;spa	eng	3
Hungary–Moldova	1995	eng;hun;mol	eng	3
Hungary–Mongolia	1994	eng;hun;mon	eng	3
Hungary–Morocco	1991	fre;hun;ara	fre	3
Hungary–Netherlands	1986	eng	eng	5
Hungary–Norway	1980	eng	eng	5
Hungary–Pakistan	1992	eng	eng	5
Hungary–Philippines	1997	eng	eng	5
Hungary–Poland	1992	eng;hun;pol	eng	3
Hungary–Portugal	1995	eng;hun;por	eng	3
Hungary–Qatar	2012	eng;hun;ara	eng	2
Hungary–Romania	1993	eng	eng	5
Hungary–Russia	1994	eng;hun;rus	eng	3
Hungary–San Marino	2009	eng;hun;ita	eng	3
Hungary–Saudi Arabia	2014	eng;hun;ara	eng	3
Hungary–Serbia and Montenegro	2001	eng	eng	5
Hungary–Singapore	1997	eng	eng	5
Hungary–Slovak Republic	1994	eng;hun;slo	eng	4
Hungary–Slovenia	2004	eng;hun;slv	eng	2
Hungary–South Africa	1994	eng;hun		1
Hungary–Spain	1984	eng;hun;spa		1
Hungary–Sweden	1981	eng	eng	5
Hungary–Switzerland	1981	hun;ger		1
Hungary–Switzerland	2013	eng;hun;ger	eng	4
Hungary–Taiwan	2010	eng;hun;chi	eng	3
Hungary–Thailand	1989	eng	eng	5
Hungary–Tunisia	1992	fre	fre	5
Hungary–Turkey	1993	eng	eng	5
Hungary–Turkmenistan	2016	eng;hun;tkm	eng	3
Hungary–Ukraine	1995	eng;hun;ukr	eng	3
Hungary–United Arab Emirates	2013	eng;hun;ara	eng	3
Hungary–United Kingdom	2011	eng;hun		1

Treaty	Conclusion	AL	UL/PT	TOW
Hungary–United States	1979	eng;hun		1
Hungary–United States	2010	eng;hun		1
Hungary–Uruguay	1988	eng;hun;spa	eng	9
Hungary–Uzbekistan	2008	eng;hun;uzb	eng	3
Hungary–Vietnam	1994	eng;hun;vts	eng	3
Iceland–India	2007	eng;ice;hin	eng	3
Iceland–Ireland	2003	eng;ice		1
Iceland–Isle of Man	2007	eng	eng	5
Iceland–Italy	2002	eng;ice;ita	eng	3
Iceland–Jersey	2008	eng	eng	5
Iceland–Korea (Rep.)	2008	eng;ice;kor	eng	3
Iceland–Latvia	1994	eng	eng	5
Iceland–Liechtenstein	2016	eng;ger;ice	eng	2
Iceland–Lithuania	1998	eng;ice;lit	eng	3
Iceland–Luxembourg	1999	eng;fre;ice		1
Iceland–Malta	2004	eng	eng	5
Iceland–Mexico	2008	eng;ice;spa	eng	2
Iceland–Netherlands	1997	eng	eng	5
Iceland–Poland	1998	eng;ice;pol	eng	3
Iceland–Portugal	1999	eng;ice;por	eng	3
Iceland–Romania	2007	eng;ice;rum	eng	3
Iceland–Russia	1999	eng;ice;rus	eng	3
Iceland–Russia	1999	eng;rus;ice	eng	3
Iceland–Slovak Republic	2002	eng;ice;slo	eng	3
Iceland–Slovenia	2011	eng;slv;ice	eng	2
Iceland–Spain	2002	eng;ice;spa	eng	3
Iceland–Switzerland	1988	eng;ice;ger	eng	6
Iceland–Switzerland	2014	eng;ger;ice	eng	6
Iceland–Ukraine	2006	eng;ice;ukr	eng	3
Iceland–United Kingdom	1991	eng;ice		1
Iceland–United Kingdom	2013	eng;ice		1
Iceland–United States	2007	eng;ice		1
Iceland–Vietnam	2002	eng;ice;vts	eng	3
India–Indonesia	1987	eng;hin;ind	eng	3
India–Indonesia	2012	eng;hin;ind	eng	3
India–Ireland	2000	eng;hin	eng	2
India–Israel	1996	eng;hin;heb	eng	3
India–Italy	1993	eng;hin;ita	eng	6
India–Japan	1989	eng;hin;jap	eng	3
India–Jordan	1999	eng;hin;ara	eng	2
India–Kazakhstan	1996	eng;hin;kaz;rus	eng	2
India–Kenya	1985	eng;hin	eng	8
India–Korea (Rep.)	1985	eng;hin;kor	eng	2
India–Korea (Rep.)	2015	eng;hin;kor	eng	3
India–Kuwait	2006	eng;hin;ara	eng	3
India–Kyrgyzstan	1999	eng;hin;kyr;rus	eng	2
India–Latvia	2013	eng;hin;lat	eng	3
India–Libya	1981	eng;hin;ara	eng	6
India–Lithuania	2011	eng;hin;lit	eng	3
India–Luxembourg	2008	eng;fre;hin		1
India–Macedonia (FYR)	2013	eng;mac;hin	eng	3
India–Malaysia	2012	eng;hin;may	eng	3

E. Sample

Treaty	Conclusion	AL	UL/PT	TOW
India–Malta	1994	eng;hin	eng	2
India–Malta	2013	eng;hin	eng	3
India–Mauritius	1982	eng;hin	eng	2
India–Mexico	2007	eng;hin;spa	eng	3
India–Moldova	1988	eng;hin;rus	eng	2
India–Mongolia	1994	eng;hin;mon	eng	2
India–Morocco	1998	eng;fre;hin;ara	eng	3
India–Mozambique	2010	eng;hin;por	eng	3
India–Myanmar	2008	eng;hin;bur	eng	3
India–Namibia	1997	eng;hin	eng	3
India–Nepal	2011	eng;hin;nep	eng	3
India–Netherlands	1988	eng;hin;dut	eng	4
India–New Zealand	1986	eng;hin	eng	2
India–Norway	2011	eng;hin;nor	eng	3
India–Oman	1997	eng;hin;ara	eng	3
India–Philippines	1990	eng;hin	eng	3
India–Poland	1989	eng;hin;pol	eng	4
India–Portugal	1998	eng;hin;por	eng	6
India–Qatar	1999	eng;hin;ara	eng	2
India–Romania	2013	eng;hin;rum	eng	3
India–Russia	1997	eng;hin;rus	eng	2
India–Saudi Arabia	2006	eng;hin;ara	eng	3
India–Serbia and Montenegro	2006	eng;hin;ser	eng	3
India–Singapore	1994	eng;hin	eng	2
India–Slovak Republic	1986	eng	eng	5
India–Slovenia	2003	eng;hin;slv	eng	2
India–South Africa	1996	eng;hin	eng	3
India–Spain	1993	eng;hin;spa	eng	2
India–Sri Lanka	2013	eng;hin;sin	eng	3
India–Sudan	2003	eng;hin;ara	eng	3
India–Sweden	1997	eng;hin;swe	eng	2
India–Switzerland	1994	eng;hin;ger	eng	6
India–Syria	2008	eng;hin;ara	eng	3
India–Taiwan	2011	eng;hin;chi	eng	3
India–Tajikistan	2008	eng;hin;tgk	eng	3
India–Tanzania	2011	eng;hin	eng	3
India–Thailand	1985	eng;hin;tha	eng	2
India–Thailand	2015	eng;hin;tha	eng	3
India–Trinidad and Tobago	1999	eng;hin	eng	2
India–Turkey	1995	eng;hin;tur	eng	2
India–Turkmenistan	1997	eng;hin;tkm	eng	2
India–Uganda	2004	eng;hin	eng	2
India–Ukraine	1999	eng;hin;ukr	eng	2
India–United Arab Emirates	1992	eng;hin;ara	eng	2
India–United Kingdom	1993	eng;hin	eng	2
India–United States	1989	eng;hin	eng	2
India–Uruguay	2011	eng;hin;spa	eng	3
India–Uzbekistan	1993	eng;hin;uzb	eng	2
India–Vietnam	1994	eng;hin;vts	eng	3
India–Zambia	1981	eng	eng	5
Indonesia–Iran	2004	eng;ind;per	eng	3
Indonesia–Italy	1990	eng;ind;ita	eng	6

Treaty	Conclusion	AL	UL/PT	TOW
Indonesia–Japan	1982	eng	eng	5
Indonesia–Jordan	1996	eng;ind;ara	eng	3
Indonesia–Korea (Dem. People's Rep.)	2002	eng;ind;kor	eng	3
Indonesia–Korea (Rep.)	1988	eng	eng	5
Indonesia–Kuwait	1997	eng;ind;ara	eng	2
Indonesia–Luxembourg	1993	eng;fre;ind		1
Indonesia–Malaysia	1991	eng;ind;may	eng	8
Indonesia–Mexico	2002	eng;ind;spa	eng	4
Indonesia–Mongolia	1996	eng;ind;mon	eng	3
Indonesia–Morocco	2008	eng;ind;ara	eng	3
Indonesia–Myanmar	2003	eng	eng	5
Indonesia–Netherlands	2002	eng;ind;dut	eng	4
Indonesia–New Zealand	1987	eng	eng	5
Indonesia–Norway	1988	eng	eng	5
Indonesia–Pakistan	1990	eng	eng	5
Indonesia–Philippines	1993	eng	eng	5
Indonesia–Poland	1992	eng;ind;pol	eng	3
Indonesia–Portugal	2003	eng;ind;por	eng	3
Indonesia–Qatar	2006	eng;ind;ara	eng	2
Indonesia–Romania	1996	eng;ind;rum	eng	3
Indonesia–Russia	1999	eng;ind;rus	eng	2
Indonesia–Serbia	2011	eng;ind;ser	eng	3
Indonesia–Seychelles	1999	eng	eng	5
Indonesia–Singapore	1990	eng	eng	5
Indonesia–Slovak Republic	2000	eng;ind;slo	eng	4
Indonesia–South Africa	1997	eng	eng	5
Indonesia–Spain	1995	eng;ind;spa	eng	3
Indonesia–Sri Lanka	1993	eng;ind;sin	eng	3
Indonesia–Sudan	1998	eng;ind;ara	eng	4
Indonesia–Suriname	2003	eng;ind;dut	eng	4
Indonesia–Sweden	1989	eng	eng	5
Indonesia–Switzerland	1988	eng;fre;ind	eng	4
Indonesia–Syria	1997	eng;ind;ara	eng	4
Indonesia–Taiwan	1995	eng;ind;chi	eng	3
Indonesia–Tajikistan	2003	eng;ind;tgk	eng	3
Indonesia–Thailand	2001	eng	eng	5
Indonesia–Tunisia	1992	eng;ind;ara;fre	eng	3
Indonesia–Turkey	1997	eng;ind;tur	eng	2
Indonesia–Ukraine	1996	eng;ind;ukr	eng	4
Indonesia–United Arab Emirates	1995	eng;ind;ara	eng	3
Indonesia–United Kingdom	1993	eng	eng	5
Indonesia–United States	1988	eng	eng	5
Indonesia–Uzbekistan	1996	eng;ind;uzb	eng	3
Indonesia–Venezuela	1997	eng;ind;spa	eng	2
Indonesia–Vietnam	1997	eng;ind;vts	eng	3
Iran–Iraq	2011	eng;ara;per	eng	3
Iran–Jordan	2003	eng;per;ara	eng	3
Iran–Kazakhstan	1996	eng;per;kaz;rus	eng	2
Iran–Kenya	2012	eng	eng	5
Iran–Korea (Rep.)	2006	eng;per;kor	eng	3
Iran–Kuwait	2008	eng;per;ara	eng	2
Iran–Kyrgyzstan	2002	eng;per;kyr;rus	eng	3

417

E. Sample

Treaty	Conclusion	AL	UL/PT	TOW
Iran–Lebanon	1998	eng;per;ara	eng	3
Iran–Macedonia (FYR)	2000	eng;per;mac	eng	3
Iran–Malaysia	1992	eng;per;may	eng	8
Iran–Morocco	2008	eng;fre;per;ara	eng	3
Iran–Oman	2004	eng;per;ara	eng	4
Iran–Pakistan	1999	eng;per		1
Iran–Poland	1998	eng;per;pol	eng	3
Iran–Qatar	2000	eng;per;ara	eng	3
Iran–Romania	2001	eng;per;rum	eng	3
Iran–Russia	1998	eng;per;rus	eng	4
Iran–Serbia and Montenegro	2004	eng;per;ser	eng	3
Iran–Slovak Republic	2016	eng;slo;per	eng	3
Iran–Slovenia	2011	eng;per;slv	eng	2
Iran–South Africa	1997	eng;per		1
Iran–Spain	2003	eng;per;spa	eng	3
Iran–Sri Lanka	2000	eng;per;sin	eng	3
Iran–Sudan	2004	eng;per;ara	eng	3
Iran–Switzerland	2002	eng;per;ger	eng	3
Iran–Syria	1996	eng;per;ara	eng	3
Iran–Tajikistan	1998	eng;per;tgk	eng	3
Iran–Tunisia	2001	eng;fre;per;ara	eng;fre	3
Iran–Turkey	2002	eng;per;tur	eng	3
Iran–Turkmenistan	1995	eng;per;tkm	eng	2
Iran–Ukraine	1996	eng;per;ukr	eng	3
Iran–Uzbekistan	2002	eng;per;uzb	eng	3
Iran–Venezuela	2005	eng;per;spa	eng	2
Iran–Vietnam	2014	eng;per;vts	eng	3
Iraq–Sudan	2002	ara	ara	5
Iraq–Tunisia	2001	ara	ara	5
Iraq–Yemen	2001	ara	ara	5
Ireland–Isle of Man	2008	eng	eng	5
Ireland–Israel	1995	eng;heb		1
Ireland–Italy	1971	eng;ita		1
Ireland–Japan	1974	eng	eng	5
Ireland–Jersey	2009	eng	eng	5
Ireland–Korea (Rep.)	1990	eng	eng	5
Ireland–Kuwait	2010	eng;ara		1
Ireland–Latvia	1997	eng;lat	eng	2
Ireland–Lithuania	1997	eng;lit		1
Ireland–Luxembourg	1972	eng;fre		1
Ireland–Macedonia (FYR)	2008	eng;mac		1
Ireland–Malaysia	1998	eng;may	eng	8
Ireland–Malta	2008	eng	eng	5
Ireland–Mexico	1998	eng;spa		1
Ireland–Moldova	2009	eng;mol		1
Ireland–Montenegro	2010	eng;mon		1
Ireland–Morocco	2010	eng;ara		1
Ireland–Netherlands	1969	eng;dut		1
Ireland–New Zealand	1986	eng	eng	5
Ireland–Norway	2000	eng;nor		1
Ireland–Pakistan	1973	eng	eng	5
Ireland–Pakistan	2015	eng	eng	5

Treaty	Conclusion	AL	UL/PT	TOW
Ireland–Panama	2011	eng;spa	eng	2
Ireland–Poland	1995	eng;pol		1
Ireland–Portugal	1993	eng;por		1
Ireland–Qatar	2012	eng;ara		1
Ireland–Romania	1999	eng;rum	eng	3
Ireland–Russia	1994	eng;rus		1
Ireland–Saudi Arabia	2011	eng;ara		1
Ireland–Serbia	2009	eng;ser		1
Ireland–Singapore	2010	eng	eng	5
Ireland–Slovak Republic	1999	eng;slo		1
Ireland–Slovenia	2002	eng;slv		1
Ireland–South Africa	1997	eng	eng	5
Ireland–Spain	1994	eng;spa		1
Ireland–Sweden	1986	eng	eng	5
Ireland–Switzerland	1966	eng;fre		1
Ireland–Thailand	2013	eng	eng	5
Ireland–Turkey	2008	eng;tur		1
Ireland–Ukraine	2013	eng;ukr		1
Ireland–United Arab Emirates	2010	eng;ara		1
Ireland–United Kingdom	1976	eng	eng	5
Ireland–United Kingdom	1977	eng	eng	5
Ireland–United States	1997	eng	eng	5
Ireland–Uzbekistan	2012	eng;uzb	eng	3
Ireland–Vietnam	2008	eng;vts		1
Ireland–Zambia	1971	eng	eng	5
Ireland–Zambia	2015	eng	eng	5
Isle of Man–Jersey	2013	eng	eng	5
Isle of Man–Luxembourg	2013	eng	eng	5
Isle of Man–Malta	2009	eng	eng	5
Isle of Man–New Zealand	2009	eng	eng	5
Isle of Man–Norway	2007	eng	eng	5
Isle of Man–Poland	2011	eng;pol		1
Isle of Man–Qatar	2012	eng;ara		1
Isle of Man–Seychelles	2013	eng	eng	5
Isle of Man–Singapore	2012	eng	eng	5
Isle of Man–Slovenia	2011	eng;slv		1
Isle of Man–Sweden	2007	eng	eng	5
Israel–Italy	1968	eng;heb;ita	eng	6
Israel–Italy	1995	eng;heb;ita	eng	6
Israel–Jamaica	1984	eng;heb		1
Israel–Japan	1993	eng	eng	5
Israel–Korea (Rep.)	1997	eng;heb;kor	eng	3
Israel–Latvia	2006	eng;heb;lat	eng	3
Israel–Lithuania	2006	eng;heb;lit	eng	3
Israel–Luxembourg	2004	eng;fre;heb		1
Israel–Macedonia (FYR)	2016	eng;heb;mac	eng	2
Israel–Malta	2011	eng;heb	eng	2
Israel–Mexico	1999	eng;heb;spa	eng	3
Israel–Moldova	2006	eng;heb;mol	eng	3
Israel–Netherlands	1973	eng;heb;dut	eng	4
Israel–Netherlands	1974	eng;heb;dut	eng	4
Israel–Norway	1966	eng	eng	5

E. Sample

Treaty	Conclusion	AL	UL/PT	TOW
Israel–Panama	2012	eng;heb;spa	eng	2
Israel–Philippines	1992	eng;heb	eng	3
Israel–Poland	1991	eng;heb;pol	eng	3
Israel–Portugal	2006	eng;heb;por	eng	3
Israel–Romania	1997	eng;heb;rum	eng	3
Israel–Russia	1994	eng;heb;rus	eng	2
Israel–Singapore	2005	eng;heb	eng	3
Israel–Slovak Republic	1999	eng;heb;slo	eng	3
Israel–Slovenia	2007	eng;heb;slv	eng	2
Israel–South Africa	1978	eng;heb;afr	eng	6
Israel–Spain	1999	eng;heb;spa	eng	3
Israel–Sweden	1962	eng	eng	5
Israel–Switzerland	2003	eng;heb;ger	eng	4
Israel–Taiwan	2009	eng	eng	5
Israel–Thailand	1996	eng;heb;tha	eng	6
Israel–Turkey	1996	eng;heb;tur	eng	3
Israel–Ukraine	2003	eng;heb;ukr	eng	4
Israel–United Kingdom	1962	eng;heb		1
Israel–United States	1975	eng;heb		1
Israel–Uzbekistan	1998	eng;heb;uzb	eng	3
Israel–Vietnam	2009	eng;heb;vts	eng	3
Italy–Ivory Coast	1982	fre;ita		1
Italy–Japan	1969	eng;ita;jap	eng	3
Italy–Jordan	2004	eng;ita;ara	eng	3
Italy–Kazakhstan	1994	eng;ita;kaz;rus	eng	6
Italy–Kenya	1979	eng;ita		1
Italy–Korea (Rep.)	1989	eng;ita;kor	eng	3
Italy–Kuwait	1987	eng;ita;ara	eng	2
Italy–Latvia	1997	eng;ita;lat	eng	3
Italy–Lebanon	2000	eng;ita;ara	eng	3
Italy–Libya	2009	eng;ita;ara	eng	3
Italy–Lithuania	1996	eng;ita;lit	eng	3
Italy–Luxembourg	1981	fre;ita		1
Italy–Macedonia (FYR)	1996	eng;ita;mac	eng	6
Italy–Malaysia	1984	eng;ita;may	eng	3
Italy–Malta	1981	eng;ita		1
Italy–Mauritius	1990	eng;ita		1
Italy–Mexico	1991	ita;spa		1
Italy–Moldova	2002	eng;ita;mol	eng	3
Italy–Mongolia	2003	eng;ita;mon	eng	3
Italy–Morocco	1972	fre;ita;ara	fre	6
Italy–Mozambique	1998	fre;ita;por	fre	3
Italy–Netherlands	1990	fre;ita;dut	fre	4
Italy–New Zealand	1979	eng;ita		1
Italy–Norway	1985	eng;ita;nor	eng	6
Italy–Oman	1998	eng;ita;ara	eng	3
Italy–Pakistan	1984	eng;ita	eng	3
Italy–Panama	2010	eng;ita;spa	eng	2
Italy–Philippines	1980	eng;ita		1
Italy–Poland	1985	eng;ita;pol	eng	6
Italy–Portugal	1980	fre;ita;por	fre	6
Italy–Qatar	2002	eng;ita;ara	eng	3

Treaty	Conclusion	AL	UL/PT	TOW
Italy–Romania	1977	ita;rum		1
Italy–Romania	2015	eng;ita;rum	eng	3
Italy–Russia	1996	eng;ita;rus	eng	4
Italy–San Marino	2002	ita	ita	5
Italy–Saudi Arabia	2007	eng;ita;ara	eng	3
Italy–Senegal	1998	fre;ita		1
Italy–Serbia and Montenegro	1982	eng	eng	5
Italy–Singapore	1977	eng;ita		1
Italy–Slovak Republic	1981	fre;ita;cze	fre	6
Italy–Slovenia	2001	eng;ita;slv	eng	6
Italy–South Africa	1995	eng;ita		1
Italy–Spain	1977	fre;ita;spa	fre	6
Italy–Sri Lanka	1984	eng;ita;sin	eng	3
Italy–Sweden	1980	fre;ita;swe	fre	6
Italy–Switzerland	1976	ita	ita	5
Italy–Syria	2000	eng;ita;ara	eng	3
Italy–Taiwan	2015	ita;chi		1
Italy–Tanzania	1973	eng;ita		1
Italy–Thailand	1977	eng;ita;tha	eng	6
Italy–Trinidad and Tobago	1971	eng;ita		1
Italy–Tunisia	1979	fre;ita	fre	6
Italy–Turkey	1990	eng;ita;tur	eng	6
Italy–Turkmenistan	1985	ita;rus		1
Italy–Uganda	2000	eng;ita		1
Italy–Ukraine	1997	eng;ita;ukr	eng	6
Italy–United Arab Emirates	1995	eng;ita;ara	eng	6
Italy–United Kingdom	1966	eng;ita		1
Italy–United Kingdom	1988	eng;ita		1
Italy–United States	1999	eng;ita		1
Italy–Uzbekistan	2000	eng;ita;uzb	eng	2
Italy–Venezuela	1990	fre;ita;spa	fre	3
Italy–Vietnam	1996	eng;ita;vts	eng	6
Italy–Zambia	1972	eng;ita		1
Ivory Coast–Morocco	2006	fre;ara	fre	3
Ivory Coast–Norway	1978	fre	fre	5
Ivory Coast–Portugal	2015	fre;por		1
Ivory Coast–Switzerland	1987	fre	fre	5
Ivory Coast–Tunisia	1999	fre;ara	fre	3
Ivory Coast–United Kingdom	1985	eng;fre		1
Jamaica–Norway	1991	eng;nor		1
Jamaica–Spain	2008	eng;spa		1
Jamaica–Sweden	1985	eng	eng	5
Jamaica–Switzerland	1994	eng;fre		1
Jamaica–United Kingdom	1973	eng	eng	5
Jamaica–United States	1980	eng	eng	5
Japan–Kazakhstan	2008	eng	eng	5
Japan–Korea (Rep.)	1998	eng	eng	5
Japan–Kuwait	2010	eng;jap;ara	eng	3
Japan–Kyrgyzstan	1986	eng;jap;rus	eng	3
Japan–Luxembourg	1992	eng	eng	5
Japan–Malaysia	1999	eng	eng	5
Japan–Mexico	1996	eng;jap;spa	eng	3

E. Sample

Treaty	Conclusion	AL	UL/PT	TOW
Japan–Moldova	1986	eng;jap;rus	eng	3
Japan–Netherlands	2010	eng	eng	5
Japan–New Zealand	2012	eng;jap		1
Japan–Norway	1992	eng	eng	5
Japan–Oman	2014	eng;jap;ara	eng	3
Japan–Pakistan	2008	eng	eng	5
Japan–Philippines	1980	eng	eng	5
Japan–Poland	1980	eng;jap;pol	eng	3
Japan–Portugal	2011	eng;jap;por	eng	3
Japan–Qatar	2015	eng;ara;jap	eng	3
Japan–Romania	1976	eng	eng	5
Japan–Russia	1986	eng;jap;rus	eng	3
Japan–Saudi Arabia	2010	eng;jap;ara	eng	3
Japan–Singapore	1994	eng	eng	5
Japan–Slovak Republic	1977	eng	eng	5
Japan–South Africa	1997	eng	eng	5
Japan–Spain	1974	eng;jap;spa	eng	4
Japan–Sri Lanka	1967	eng;jap;sin	eng	3
Japan–Sweden	1983	eng	eng	5
Japan–Switzerland	1971	eng;jap;ger	eng	4
Japan–Taiwan	2015	eng	eng	5
Japan–Tajikistan	1986	eng;jap;rus	eng	3
Japan–Thailand	1990	eng	eng	5
Japan–Turkey	1993	eng	eng	5
Japan–Turkmenistan	1986	eng;jap;rus	eng	3
Japan–Ukraine	1986	eng;jap;rus	eng	3
Japan–United Arab Emirates	2013	eng;jap;ara	eng	3
Japan–United Kingdom	2006	eng;jap		1
Japan–United States	2003	eng;jap		1
Japan–Uzbekistan	1986	eng;jap;rus	eng	3
Japan–Vietnam	1995	eng;jap;vts	eng	3
Japan–Zambia	1970	eng;jap		1
Jersey–Luxembourg	2013	eng	eng	5
Jersey–Malta	2010	eng	eng	5
Jersey–New Zealand	2009	eng	eng	5
Jersey–Norway	2008	eng	eng	5
Jersey–Poland	2011	eng;pol		1
Jersey–Qatar	2012	eng;ara		1
Jersey–Rwanda	2015	eng	eng	5
Jersey–Seychelles	2015	eng	eng	5
Jersey–Singapore	2012	eng	eng	5
Jersey–Sweden	2008	eng	eng	5
Jersey–United Arab Emirates	2016	eng;ara		1
Jordan–Korea (Rep.)	2004	eng;ara;kor	eng	3
Jordan–Lebanon	2002	ara	ara	5
Jordan–Malaysia	1994	eng;ara;may	eng	3
Jordan–Malta	2009	eng;ara		1
Jordan–Morocco	2005	ara	ara	5
Jordan–Netherlands	2006	eng;dut;ara	eng	4
Jordan–Pakistan	2006	eng;ara	eng	6
Jordan–Palestinian Autonomous Areas	2011	ara	ara	5
Jordan–Poland	1997	eng;ara;pol	eng	3

Treaty	Conclusion	AL	UL/PT	TOW
Jordan–Qatar	2004	ara	ara	5
Jordan–Romania	1983	eng;ara;rum	eng	3
Jordan–Syria	2001	ara	ara	5
Jordan–Tunisia	1988	ara	ara	5
Jordan–Turkey	1985	eng;ara;tur	eng	4
Jordan–Ukraine	2005	eng;ara;ukr	eng	3
Jordan–United Arab Emirates	2016	ara	ara	5
Jordan–United Kingdom	2001	eng;ara		1
Jordan–Uzbekistan	2010	eng;ara;uzb	eng	3
Jordan–Yemen	1998	ara	ara	5
Kazakhstan–Korea (Rep.)	1997	eng;kaz;kor	eng	3
Kazakhstan–Latvia	2001	eng;kaz;lat;rus	eng	3
Kazakhstan–Lithuania	1997	eng;kaz;lit;rus	eng	3
Kazakhstan–Luxembourg	2008	eng;fre;kaz;rus		1
Kazakhstan–Macedonia (FYR)	2012	eng;kaz;mac;rus	eng	3
Kazakhstan–Malaysia	2006	eng;kaz;may;rus	eng	3
Kazakhstan–Mongolia	1998	eng;kaz;mon;rus	eng	2
Kazakhstan–Netherlands	1996	eng;kaz;dut;rus	eng	3
Kazakhstan–Norway	2001	eng;kaz;nor;rus	eng	2
Kazakhstan–Pakistan	1995	eng;kaz;rus	eng	2
Kazakhstan–Qatar	2014	eng	eng	5
Kazakhstan–Romania	1998	eng;kaz;rum;rus	eng	2
Kazakhstan–Russia	1996	rus;kaz	rus	3
Kazakhstan–Serbia	2015	eng;rus;kaz;ser	eng	2
Kazakhstan–Singapore	2006	eng;kaz;rus	eng	3
Kazakhstan–Slovak Republic	2007	eng;kaz;slo;rus	eng	3
Kazakhstan–Spain	2009	eng;kaz;spa;rus		1
Kazakhstan–Sweden	1997	eng;kaz;swe;rus	eng	2
Kazakhstan–Switzerland	1999	eng;kaz;ger;rus	eng	2
Kazakhstan–Turkey	1995	eng;kaz;tur;rus	eng	2
Kazakhstan–Turkmenistan	1997	rus;kaz;tkm	rus	3
Kazakhstan–Ukraine	1996	rus;kaz;ukr	rus	3
Kazakhstan–United Arab Emirates	2008	eng;kaz;ara;rus	eng	3
Kazakhstan–United Kingdom	1994	eng;kaz;rus		1
Kazakhstan–United States	1993	eng;rus;kaz		1
Kazakhstan–Uzbekistan	1996	rus;kaz;uzb	rus	3
Kazakhstan–Vietnam	2011	eng;vts;rus;kaz	eng	3
Kenya–Mauritius	2012	eng	eng	5
Kenya–Netherlands	2015	eng	eng	5
Kenya–Norway	1972	eng	eng	5
Kenya–South Africa	2010	eng	eng	5
Kenya–Sweden	1973	eng	eng	5
Kenya–Thailand	2006	eng	eng	5
Kenya–United Arab Emirates	2011	eng;ara	eng	3
Kenya–United Kingdom	1973	eng	eng	5
Kenya–Zambia	1968	eng	eng	5
Korea (Dem. People's Rep.)–Korea (Rep.)	2000	kor	kor	5
Korea (Dem. People's Rep.)–Romania	1998	eng;kor;rum	eng	3
Korea (Dem. People's Rep.)–Russia	1997	eng;kor;rus	eng	4
Korea (Dem. People's Rep.)–Serbia and Montenegro	2000	eng;kor;ser	eng	3
Korea (Dem. People's Rep.)–Syria	2000	eng;kor;ara	eng	2
Korea (Rep.)–Kuwait	1998	eng;kor;ara	eng	3

E. Sample

Treaty	Conclusion	AL	UL/PT	TOW
Korea (Rep.)–Kyrgyzstan	2012	eng;kor;rus;kyr	eng	3
Korea (Rep.)–Laos	2004	eng;kor;lao	eng	3
Korea (Rep.)–Latvia	2008	eng;kor;lat	eng	3
Korea (Rep.)–Lithuania	2006	eng;kor;lit	eng	3
Korea (Rep.)–Luxembourg	1984	eng	eng	5
Korea (Rep.)–Malaysia	1982	eng;kor;may	eng	3
Korea (Rep.)–Malta	1997	eng;kor		1
Korea (Rep.)–Mexico	1994	eng;kor;spa	eng	3
Korea (Rep.)–Mongolia	1992	eng;kor;mon	eng	3
Korea (Rep.)–Morocco	1999	eng;kor;ara	eng	3
Korea (Rep.)–Myanmar	2002	eng;kor;bur	eng	8
Korea (Rep.)–Nepal	2001	eng;kor;nep	eng	3
Korea (Rep.)–Netherlands	1978	eng	eng	5
Korea (Rep.)–New Zealand	1981	eng	eng	5
Korea (Rep.)–Norway	1982	eng	eng	5
Korea (Rep.)–Oman	2005	eng;kor;ara	eng	3
Korea (Rep.)–Pakistan	1987	eng	eng	5
Korea (Rep.)–Panama	2010	eng;kor;spa	eng	3
Korea (Rep.)–Papua New Guinea	1996	eng;kor		1
Korea (Rep.)–Peru	2012	eng;kor;spa	eng	3
Korea (Rep.)–Philippines	1984	eng;kor		1
Korea (Rep.)–Poland	1991	eng;kor;pol	eng	3
Korea (Rep.)–Portugal	1996	eng;kor;por	eng	3
Korea (Rep.)–Qatar	2007	eng;kor;ara	eng	2
Korea (Rep.)–Romania	1993	eng;kor;rum	eng	3
Korea (Rep.)–Russia	1992	eng;kor;rus	eng	3
Korea (Rep.)–Saudi Arabia	2007	eng;kor;ara	eng	3
Korea (Rep.)–Serbia	2016	eng;kor;ser	eng	3
Korea (Rep.)–Singapore	1979	eng	eng	5
Korea (Rep.)–Slovak Republic	2001	eng;kor;slo	eng	3
Korea (Rep.)–Slovenia	2005	eng;kor;slv	eng	3
Korea (Rep.)–South Africa	1995	eng;kor		1
Korea (Rep.)–Spain	1994	eng;kor;spa	eng	3
Korea (Rep.)–Sri Lanka	1984	eng;kor;sin	eng	6
Korea (Rep.)–Sweden	1981	eng	eng	5
Korea (Rep.)–Switzerland	1980	eng;kor;ger	eng	4
Korea (Rep.)–Thailand	2006	eng;kor;tha	eng	3
Korea (Rep.)–Tunisia	1988	eng;kor;ara;fre	eng	3
Korea (Rep.)–Turkey	1983	eng;kor;tur	eng	2
Korea (Rep.)–Ukraine	1999	eng;kor;ukr	eng	3
Korea (Rep.)–United Arab Emirates	2003	eng;kor;ara	eng	3
Korea (Rep.)–United Kingdom	1996	eng;kor		1
Korea (Rep.)–United States	1976	eng;kor		1
Korea (Rep.)–Uruguay	2011	eng;kor;spa	eng	3
Korea (Rep.)–Uzbekistan	1998	eng;kor;uzb	eng	3
Korea (Rep.)–Venezuela	2006	eng;kor;spa	eng	2
Korea (Rep.)–Vietnam	1994	eng;kor;vts	eng	3
Kosovo–Macedonia (FYR)	2011	eng;alb;mac	eng	3
Kosovo–Netherlands	1982	eng;scr;dut	eng	4
Kosovo–Slovenia	2013	eng;alb;slv	eng	2
Kosovo–Turkey	2012	eng;alb;tur	eng	3
Kosovo–United Kingdom	2015	eng;alb		1

Treaty	Conclusion	AL	UL/PT	TOW
Kuwait–Kyrgyzstan	2015	eng;rus;ara;kyr	eng	2
Kuwait–Latvia	2009	eng;ara;lat	eng	3
Kuwait–Lebanon	2001	ara	ara	5
Kuwait–Luxembourg	2007	eng;fre;ara		1
Kuwait–Macedonia (FYR)	2012	eng;ara;mac	eng	2
Kuwait–Malaysia	2003	eng;ara;may	eng	2
Kuwait–Malta	2002	eng;ara;mal	eng	3
Kuwait–Mauritius	1997	eng;ara	eng	2
Kuwait–Mexico	2009	eng;ara;spa	eng	2
Kuwait–Moldova	2010	eng;ara;mol	eng	3
Kuwait–Mongolia	1998	eng;ara;mon	eng	2
Kuwait–Morocco	2002	ara	ara	5
Kuwait–Netherlands	2001	eng;ara;dut	eng	4
Kuwait–Pakistan	1998	eng;ara	eng	2
Kuwait–Philippines	2009	eng;ara	eng	2
Kuwait–Poland	1996	eng;ara;pol	eng	2
Kuwait–Portugal	2010	eng;ara;por	eng	3
Kuwait–Romania	1992	eng;ara;rum	eng	2
Kuwait–Russia	1999	eng;ara;rus	eng	4
Kuwait–Serbia and Montenegro	2002	eng;ara;ser	eng	2
Kuwait–Seychelles	2008	eng;ara	eng	2
Kuwait–Singapore	2002	eng;ara		1
Kuwait–Slovak Republic	2012	eng;ara;slo	eng	2
Kuwait–Slovenia	2010	eng;ara;slv	eng	2
Kuwait–South Africa	2004	eng;ara		1
Kuwait–Spain	2008	eng;ara;spa	eng	2
Kuwait–Sri Lanka	2002	eng;ara;sin	eng	2
Kuwait–Sudan	2001	ara	ara	5
Kuwait–Switzerland	1999	eng;ara;ger	eng	2
Kuwait–Thailand	2003	eng;ara;tha	eng	2
Kuwait–Tunisia	2000	ara	ara	5
Kuwait–Turkey	1997	eng;ara;tur	eng	2
Kuwait–Ukraine	2003	eng;ara;ukr	eng	2
Kuwait–United Kingdom	1999	eng;ara		1
Kuwait–Uzbekistan	2004	eng;ara;uzb	eng	2
Kuwait–Venezuela	2004	eng;ara;spa	eng	2
Kuwait–Vietnam	2009	eng;ara;vts	eng	2
Kuwait–Yemen	2001	ara	ara	5
Kuwait–Zimbabwe	2006	eng;ara		1
Kyrgyzstan–Latvia	2006	eng;lat;kyr;rus	eng	3
Kyrgyzstan–Lithuania	2008	eng;rus;lit	eng	3
Kyrgyzstan–Malaysia	1987	eng;rus;may	eng	3
Kyrgyzstan–Malaysia	2000	eng;kyr;rus;may	eng	8
Kyrgyzstan–Mongolia	1999	eng;kyr;rus;mon	eng	2
Kyrgyzstan–Pakistan	2005	eng;kyr;rus	eng	2
Kyrgyzstan–Russia	1999	rus;kyr	rus	3
Kyrgyzstan–Switzerland	2001	eng;kyr;rus;ger	eng	4
Kyrgyzstan–Turkey	1999	eng;kyr;rus;tur	eng	2
Kyrgyzstan–Ukraine	1997	rus;kyr;ukr	rus	2
Laos–Luxembourg	2012	eng;fre;lao		1
Laos–Malaysia	2010	eng;lao;may	eng	3
Laos–Russia	1999	eng;lao;rus	eng	4

E. Sample

Treaty	Conclusion	AL	UL/PT	TOW
Laos–Singapore	2014	eng;lao	eng	3
Laos–Thailand	1997	eng;lao;tha	eng	6
Laos–Vietnam	1996	eng;lao;vts	eng	4
Latvia–Lithuania	1993	eng;lat;lit	eng	2
Latvia–Luxembourg	2004	eng;fre;lat		1
Latvia–Macedonia (FYR)	2006	eng;lat;mac	eng	3
Latvia–Malta	2000	eng;lat	eng	3
Latvia–Mexico	2012	eng;lat;spa	eng	3
Latvia–Moldova	1998	eng;lat;mol	eng	3
Latvia–Morocco	2008	eng;lat;fre;ara	eng	4
Latvia–Netherlands	1994	eng	eng	5
Latvia–Norway	1993	eng	eng	5
Latvia–Poland	1993	eng	eng	5
Latvia–Portugal	2001	eng;lat;por	eng	3
Latvia–Qatar	2015	eng;ara;lat	eng	2
Latvia–Romania	2002	eng;lat;rum	eng	3
Latvia–Russia	2010	eng;lat;rus	eng	3
Latvia–Serbia and Montenegro	2005	eng;lat;ser	eng	3
Latvia–Singapore	1999	eng;lat	eng	3
Latvia–Slovak Republic	1999	eng;lat;slo	eng	3
Latvia–Slovenia	2002	eng;lat;slv	eng	3
Latvia–Spain	2003	eng;lat;spa	eng	2
Latvia–Sweden	1993	eng	eng	5
Latvia–Switzerland	2002	eng;lat;ger	eng	3
Latvia–Tajikistan	2009	eng;lat;tgk;rus	eng	2
Latvia–Turkey	1999	eng;lat;tur	eng	3
Latvia–Turkmenistan	2012	eng;lat;rus;tkm	eng	3
Latvia–Ukraine	1995	eng;lat;ukr	eng	3
Latvia–United Arab Emirates	2012	eng;lat;ara	eng	3
Latvia–United Kingdom	1996	eng;lat	eng	3
Latvia–United States	1998	eng;lat		1
Latvia–Uzbekistan	1998	eng;lat;uzb	eng	3
Lebanon–Malaysia	2003	eng	eng	5
Lebanon–Malta	1999	eng;ara		1
Lebanon–Morocco	2001	ara	ara	5
Lebanon–Oman	2001	ara	ara	5
Lebanon–Pakistan	2005	eng	eng	5
Lebanon–Poland	1999	eng;ara;pol	eng	3
Lebanon–Qatar	2005	ara	ara	5
Lebanon–Romania	1995	eng;ara;rum	eng	3
Lebanon–Russia	1997	eng;ara;rus	eng	4
Lebanon–Senegal	2002	fre	fre	5
Lebanon–Sudan	2004	ara	ara	5
Lebanon–Syria	1997	ara	ara	5
Lebanon–Tunisia	1998	ara	ara	5
Lebanon–Turkey	2004	eng	eng	5
Lebanon–Ukraine	2002	eng;ara;ukr	eng	3
Lebanon–United Arab Emirates	1998	ara	ara	5
Lebanon–Yemen	2002	ara	ara	5
Lesotho–Mauritius	1997	eng	eng	5
Lesotho–South Africa	1995	eng	eng	5
Lesotho–South Africa	2014	eng	eng	5

Treaty	Conclusion	AL	UL/PT	TOW
Lesotho–United Kingdom	1997	eng	eng	5
Libya–Malta	2008	eng;ara		1
Libya–Pakistan	1975	eng;ara		1
Libya–Serbia	2009	eng;ara;ser	eng	2
Libya–Singapore	2009	eng;ara	eng	2
Libya–Slovak Republic	2009	eng;ara;slo	eng	3
Libya–Sudan	1990	ara	ara	5
Libya–Ukraine	2008	eng;ara;ukr	eng	3
Libya–United Arab Emirates	2013	ara	ara	5
Libya–United Kingdom	2008	eng;ara		1
Liechtenstein–Luxembourg	2009	ger	ger	5
Liechtenstein–Malta	2013	eng;ger	eng	2
Liechtenstein–San Marino	2009	eng;ger;ita	eng	2
Liechtenstein–Singapore	2013	eng;ger	eng	3
Liechtenstein–Switzerland	1995	ger	ger	5
Liechtenstein–Switzerland	2015	ger	ger	5
Liechtenstein–United Arab Emirates	2015	eng;ara;ger	eng	3
Liechtenstein–United Kingdom	2012	eng;ger		1
Liechtenstein–Uruguay	2010	eng;spa		1
Lithuania–Luxembourg	2004	eng;fre;lit		1
Lithuania–Macedonia (FYR)	2007	eng;lit;mac	eng	3
Lithuania–Malta	2001	eng;lit		1
Lithuania–Mexico	2012	eng;lit;spa	eng	3
Lithuania–Moldova	1998	eng;lit;mol	eng	3
Lithuania–Morocco	2013	eng;lit;ara	eng	3
Lithuania–Netherlands	1999	eng;lit;dut	eng	4
Lithuania–Norway	1993	eng;lit;nor	eng	3
Lithuania–Poland	1994	eng;lit;por	eng	3
Lithuania–Portugal	2002	eng;por	eng	3
Lithuania–Romania	2001	eng;lit;rum	eng	3
Lithuania–Russia	1999	eng;lit;rus	eng	4
Lithuania–Serbia	2007	eng;lit;ser	eng	3
Lithuania–Singapore	2003	eng;lit		1
Lithuania–Slovak Republic	2001	eng;lit;slo	eng	3
Lithuania–Slovenia	2000	eng;lit;slv	eng	3
Lithuania–Spain	2003	eng;lit;spa	eng	2
Lithuania–Sweden	1993	eng;lit;swe	eng	3
Lithuania–Switzerland	2002	eng;lit;ger	eng	3
Lithuania–Turkey	1998	eng;lit;tur	eng	3
Lithuania–Turkmenistan	2013	eng;lit;tkm	eng	3
Lithuania–Ukraine	1996	eng;lit;ukr	eng	3
Lithuania–United Arab Emirates	2013	eng;ara;lit	eng	3
Lithuania–United Kingdom	2001	eng;lit		1
Lithuania–United States	1998	eng;lit		1
Lithuania–Uzbekistan	2002	eng;lit;uzb	eng	3
Luxembourg–Macedonia (FYR)	2012	eng;fre;mac		1
Luxembourg–Malaysia	2002	eng;fre;may		1
Luxembourg–Malta	1994	eng;fre		1
Luxembourg–Mauritius	1995	eng;fre		1
Luxembourg–Mexico	2001	eng;fre;spa		1
Luxembourg–Moldova	2007	eng;fre;mol		1
Luxembourg–Monaco	2009	fre	fre	5

E. Sample

Treaty	Conclusion	AL	UL/PT	TOW
Luxembourg–Morocco	1980	fre;ara		1
Luxembourg–Netherlands	1968	fre;dut		1
Luxembourg–Norway	1983	fre;nor		1
Luxembourg–Panama	2010	eng;fre;spa		1
Luxembourg–Poland	1995	fre;pol		1
Luxembourg–Portugal	1999	fre;por		1
Luxembourg–Qatar	2009	eng;fre;ara		1
Luxembourg–Romania	1993	fre;rum		1
Luxembourg–Russia	1993	fre;rus		1
Luxembourg–San Marino	2006	eng;fre;ita		1
Luxembourg–Saudi Arabia	2013	eng;fre;ara	eng	3
Luxembourg–Senegal	2016	fre	fre	5
Luxembourg–Serbia	2015	eng;fre;ser	eng	3
Luxembourg–Seychelles	2012	eng;fre		1
Luxembourg–Singapore	1993	eng;fre		1
Luxembourg–Singapore	2013	eng	eng	5
Luxembourg–Slovak Republic	1991	fre;cze		1
Luxembourg–Slovenia	2001	eng;fre;slv		1
Luxembourg–South Africa	1998	eng;fre		1
Luxembourg–Spain	1986	fre;spa		1
Luxembourg–Sri Lanka	2013	eng;fre;sin	eng	3
Luxembourg–Sweden	1996	fre	fre	5
Luxembourg–Switzerland	1993	fre	fre	5
Luxembourg–Taiwan	2011	eng	eng	5
Luxembourg–Tajikistan	2011	eng;fre;tgk	eng	2
Luxembourg–Thailand	1996	eng;fre;tha		1
Luxembourg–Trinidad and Tobago	2001	eng;fre		1
Luxembourg–Tunisia	1996	eng;ara		1
Luxembourg–Turkey	2003	eng	eng	5
Luxembourg–Ukraine	1997	eng;fre;ukr		1
Luxembourg–United Arab Emirates	2005	eng;fre;ara		1
Luxembourg–United Kingdom	1967	eng;fre		1
Luxembourg–United States	1996	eng;fre		1
Luxembourg–Uruguay	2015	eng;fre;spa	eng	3
Luxembourg–Uzbekistan	1997	eng;fre;uzb		1
Luxembourg–Vietnam	1996	eng;fre;vts		1
Macau–Mozambique	2007	chi;por		1
Macau–Portugal	1999	chi;por		1
Macedonia (FYR)–Moldova	2006	eng;mac;mol	eng	3
Macedonia (FYR)–Morocco	2010	eng;mac;ara	eng	2
Macedonia (FYR)–Netherlands	1998	eng;chi;dut	eng	4
Macedonia (FYR)–Norway	1983	eng	eng	5
Macedonia (FYR)–Norway	2011	eng;mac;nor	eng	3
Macedonia (FYR)–Poland	1996	eng;mac;pol	eng	3
Macedonia (FYR)–Qatar	2008	eng;mac;ara		1
Macedonia (FYR)–Romania	2000	eng;mac;rum	eng	3
Macedonia (FYR)–Russia	1997	eng;mac;rus	eng	4
Macedonia (FYR)–Saudi Arabia	2014	eng;ara;mac	eng	3
Macedonia (FYR)–Serbia and Montenegro	1996	eng;mac;ser	eng	3
Macedonia (FYR)–Slovak Republic	2009	eng;mac;slo	eng	3
Macedonia (FYR)–Slovenia	1998	eng;mac;slv	eng	2
Macedonia (FYR)–Spain	2005	eng;mac;spa	eng	4

Treaty	Conclusion	AL	UL/PT	TOW
Macedonia (FYR)–Sri Lanka	1985	eng;scr;sin	eng	3
Macedonia (FYR)–Sweden	1998	eng;mac;swe	eng	2
Macedonia (FYR)–Switzerland	2000	eng;mac;ger	eng	4
Macedonia (FYR)–Taiwan	1999	eng;mac;chi	eng	3
Macedonia (FYR)–Turkey	1995	eng;mac;tur	eng	2
Macedonia (FYR)–Ukraine	1998	eng;mac;ukr	eng	3
Macedonia (FYR)–United Arab Emirates	2015	eng;ara;mac	eng	3
Macedonia (FYR)–United Kingdom	2006	eng;mac		1
Macedonia (FYR)–Vietnam	2014	eng;mac;vts	eng	3
Malawi–Netherlands	2015	eng	eng	5
Malawi–Norway	2009	eng	eng	5
Malawi–South Africa	1971	eng;afr		1
Malawi–Switzerland	1961	eng;fre		1
Malaysia–Malta	1995	eng;may		1
Malaysia–Mauritius	1992	eng;may	eng	8
Malaysia–Moldova	1987	eng;may;rus	eng	3
Malaysia–Mongolia	1995	eng;may;mon	eng	8
Malaysia–Morocco	2001	eng;fre;may;ara	eng	8
Malaysia–Myanmar	1998	eng;may;bur	eng	8
Malaysia–Namibia	1998	eng;may	eng	8
Malaysia–Netherlands	1988	eng;may;dut	eng	3
Malaysia–New Zealand	1976	eng	eng	5
Malaysia–Norway	1970	eng	eng	5
Malaysia–Pakistan	1982	eng;may		1
Malaysia–Papua New Guinea	1993	eng;may	eng	8
Malaysia–Philippines	1982	eng;may		1
Malaysia–Poland	1977	eng;may;pol		1
Malaysia–Poland	2013	eng;may;pol	eng	3
Malaysia–Qatar	2008	eng;may;ara	eng	3
Malaysia–Romania	1982	eng;may;rum	eng	3
Malaysia–Russia	1987	eng;may;rus	eng	3
Malaysia–San Marino	2009	eng;may;ita	eng	3
Malaysia–Saudi Arabia	2006	eng;may;ara	eng	3
Malaysia–Senegal	2010	eng;fre;may		1
Malaysia–Serbia and Montenegro	1990	eng;may;scr	eng	3
Malaysia–Seychelles	2003	eng;may	eng	3
Malaysia–Singapore	2004	eng;may	eng	3
Malaysia–South Africa	2005	eng;may	eng	3
Malaysia–Spain	2006	eng;may;spa	eng	8
Malaysia–Sri Lanka	1997	eng;may;sin	eng	8
Malaysia–Sudan	1993	eng;may;ara	eng	3
Malaysia–Sweden	2002	eng;may;swe	eng	3
Malaysia–Switzerland	1974	may;ger		1
Malaysia–Syria	2007	eng;may;ara	eng	8
Malaysia–Taiwan	1996	eng;may;chi	eng	8
Malaysia–Thailand	1982	eng;may;tha		1
Malaysia–Turkey	1994	eng;may;tur	eng	8
Malaysia–Turkmenistan	2008	eng;may;tkm;rus	eng	2
Malaysia–Ukraine	1987	eng;may;rus	eng	3
Malaysia–United Arab Emirates	1995	eng;may;ara	eng	3
Malaysia–United Kingdom	1996	eng;may	eng	8
Malaysia–Uzbekistan	1997	eng;may;uzb	eng	3

E. Sample

Treaty	Conclusion	AL	UL/PT	TOW
Malaysia–Venezuela	2006	eng;may;spa	eng	3
Malaysia–Vietnam	1995	eng;may;vts	eng	8
Malaysia–Zimbabwe	1994	eng;may	eng	8
Mali–Morocco	2014	fre;ara	fre	3
Mali–Russia	1996	fre;rus		1
Mali–Tunisia	2000	fre;ara		1
Malta–Mauritius	2014	eng	eng	5
Malta–Mexico	2012	eng;spa		1
Malta–Moldova	2014	eng;rum		1
Malta–Montenegro	2008	eng;mtg		1
Malta–Morocco	2001	eng;ara	eng	3
Malta–Netherlands	1977	eng;dut		1
Malta–Norway	2012	eng	eng	5
Malta–Pakistan	1975	eng	eng	5
Malta–Poland	1994	eng;pol		1
Malta–Portugal	2001	eng;por		1
Malta–Qatar	2009	eng;ara		1
Malta–Romania	1995	eng;rum	eng	3
Malta–Russia	2013	eng;rus		1
Malta–San Marino	2005	eng;ita		1
Malta–Saudi Arabia	2012	eng;ara		1
Malta–Serbia	2009	eng;ser		1
Malta–Singapore	2006	eng	eng	5
Malta–Slovak Republic	1999	eng;slo		1
Malta–Slovenia	2002	eng;slv	eng	2
Malta–South Africa	1997	eng	eng	5
Malta–Spain	2005	eng;spa	eng	3
Malta–Sweden	1995	eng	eng	5
Malta–Switzerland	2011	eng;fre		1
Malta–Syria	1999	eng	eng	5
Malta–Tunisia	2000	eng;fre;ara	eng;fre	3
Malta–Turkey	2011	eng;tur		1
Malta–Ukraine	2013	eng;ukr		1
Malta–United Arab Emirates	2006	eng;ara		1
Malta–United Kingdom	1994	eng	eng	5
Malta–United States	2008	eng	eng	5
Malta–Uruguay	2011	eng;spa	eng	2
Marshall Islands–New Zealand	2010	eng	eng	5
Mauritius–Monaco	2013	fre	fre	5
Mauritius–Morocco	2015	eng;ara	eng	3
Mauritius–Mozambique	1997	eng;por		1
Mauritius–Namibia	1995	eng	eng	5
Mauritius–Nepal	1999	eng	eng	5
Mauritius–Nigeria	2012	eng	eng	5
Mauritius–Oman	1998	eng;ara		1
Mauritius–Pakistan	1994	eng	eng	5
Mauritius–Qatar	2008	eng;ara		1
Mauritius–Russia	1995	eng;rus		1
Mauritius–Rwanda	2001	eng	eng	5
Mauritius–Rwanda	2013	eng	eng	5
Mauritius–Senegal	2002	fre	fre	5
Mauritius–Seychelles	2005	eng	eng	5

Treaty	Conclusion	AL	UL/PT	TOW
Mauritius–Singapore	1995	eng	eng	5
Mauritius–South Africa	1996	eng	eng	5
Mauritius–South Africa	2013	eng	eng	5
Mauritius–Sri Lanka	1996	eng;sin	eng	3
Mauritius–Swaziland	1994	eng	eng	5
Mauritius–Sweden	2011	eng	eng	5
Mauritius–Thailand	1997	eng;tha	eng	6
Mauritius–Tunisia	2008	fre;ara		1
Mauritius–Uganda	2003	eng	eng	5
Mauritius–United Arab Emirates	2006	eng;ara	eng	2
Mauritius–United Kingdom	1981	eng	eng	5
Mauritius–Zambia	2011	eng	eng	5
Mauritius–Zimbabwe	1992	eng	eng	5
Mexico–Netherlands	1993	spa;dut		1
Mexico–New Zealand	2006	eng;spa	eng	2
Mexico–Norway	1995	spa;nor		1
Mexico–Panama	2010	spa	spa	5
Mexico–Peru	2011	spa	spa	5
Mexico–Poland	1998	eng;spa;pol	eng	3
Mexico–Portugal	1999	eng;spa;por	eng	3
Mexico–Qatar	2012	eng;spa;ara	eng	2
Mexico–Romania	2000	spa;rum		1
Mexico–Russia	2004	eng;spa;rus	eng	3
Mexico–Singapore	1994	eng;spa	eng	3
Mexico–Slovak Republic	2006	eng;spa;slo	eng	2
Mexico–South Africa	2009	eng;spa	eng	3
Mexico–Spain	1992	spa	spa	5
Mexico–Sweden	1992	eng;spa		1
Mexico–Switzerland	1993	fre;spa		1
Mexico–Turkey	2013	eng;spa;tur	eng	2
Mexico–Ukraine	2012	eng;spa;ukr	eng	3
Mexico–United Arab Emirates	2012	eng;ara;spa	eng	2
Mexico–United Kingdom	1994	eng;spa		1
Mexico–United States	1992	eng;spa		1
Mexico–Uruguay	2009	spa	spa	5
Mexico–Venezuela	1997	spa	spa	5
Moldova–Netherlands	2000	eng;mol;dut	eng	4
Moldova–Oman	2007	eng;ara;mol	eng	4
Moldova–Portugal	2009	eng;mol;por	eng	3
Moldova–Romania	1995	rum	rum	5
Moldova–Russia	1996	rus;mol		1
Moldova–Serbia and Montenegro	2005	eng;ser;mol	eng	3
Moldova–Slovak Republic	2003	eng;mol;slo	eng	3
Moldova–Slovenia	2006	eng;mol;slv	eng	2
Moldova–Spain	2007	eng;mol;spa	eng	2
Moldova–Switzerland	1999	eng;mol;ger	eng	2
Moldova–Turkey	1998	eng;mol;tur	eng	2
Moldova–Turkmenistan	2013	rus;mol;tgk	rus	2
Moldova–Ukraine	1995	rus;mol;ukr	rus	2
Moldova–United Kingdom	2007	eng;mol		1
Moldova–United States	1973	eng;rus		1
Moldova–Uzbekistan	1995	rus;mol;uzb	rus	2

E. Sample

Treaty	Conclusion	AL	UL/PT	TOW
Monaco–Qatar	2009	eng;fre;ara	eng	2
Monaco–Seychelles	2010	eng;fre		1
Monaco–St. Kitts and Nevis	2009	eng;fre		1
Mongolia–Poland	1997	eng;mon;pol	eng	3
Mongolia–Russia	1995	eng;mon;rus	eng	2
Mongolia–Singapore	2002	eng	eng	5
Mongolia–Switzerland	1999	eng;mon;ger	eng	4
Mongolia–Thailand	2006	eng	eng	5
Mongolia–Turkey	1995	eng;mon;tur	eng	2
Mongolia–Ukraine	2002	eng;mon;ukr	eng	3
Mongolia–United Arab Emirates	2001	eng	eng	5
Mongolia–United Kingdom	1996	eng;mon		1
Mongolia–Vietnam	1996	eng;mon;vts	eng	3
Montenegro–United Arab Emirates	2012	eng;mtg;ara		1
Montserrat–Switzerland	1963	eng;fre		1
Morocco–Netherlands	1977	fre;ara;dut	fre	4
Morocco–Norway	1972	fre	fre	5
Morocco–Oman	2006	ara	ara	5
Morocco–Pakistan	2006	eng;fre;ara	eng	3
Morocco–Poland	1994	fre;ara;pol	fre	3
Morocco–Portugal	1997	fre;ara;por	fre	3
Morocco–Qatar	2006	ara	ara	5
Morocco–Qatar	2013	ara	ara	5
Morocco–Romania	2003	fre;ara;rum	fre	3
Morocco–Russia	1997	fre;ara;rus	fre	4
Morocco–Sao Tome and Principe	2016	fre;ara	fre	3
Morocco–Saudi Arabia	2015	ara	ara	5
Morocco–Senegal	2002	fre;ara		1
Morocco–Serbia	2013	eng;fre;ara;ser	eng	3
Morocco–Singapore	2007	eng;fre;ara	eng	3
Morocco–Slovenia	2016	eng;fre;ara;slv	eng	3
Morocco–Spain	1978	fre	fre	5
Morocco–Switzerland	1993	fre;ara		1
Morocco–Syria	2005	ara	ara	5
Morocco–Turkey	2004	eng;ara;tur	eng	3
Morocco–Ukraine	2007	eng;fre;ara;ukr	eng	3
Morocco–United Arab Emirates	1999	ara	ara	5
Morocco–United Kingdom	1981	eng;ara		1
Morocco–United States	1977	eng;fre;ara		1
Morocco–Vietnam	2008	eng;ara;vts	eng	3
Morocco–Yemen	2006	ara	ara	5
Mozambique–Portugal	1991	por	por	5
Mozambique–South Africa	2007	eng;por		1
Mozambique–United Arab Emirates	2003	eng;por;ara	eng	3
Mozambique–Vietnam	2010	eng;por;vts	eng	3
Myanmar–Singapore	1999	eng	eng	5
Myanmar–Thailand	2002	eng;tha;bur	eng	8
Myanmar–Vietnam	2000	eng	eng	5
Namibia–Romania	1998	eng;rum		1
Namibia–Russia	1998	eng;rus		1
Namibia–South Africa	1998	eng	eng	5
Namibia–Sweden	1993	eng	eng	5

Treaty	Conclusion	AL	UL/PT	TOW
Namibia–United Kingdom	1962	eng;afr		1
Nepal–Norway	1996	eng	eng	5
Nepal–Pakistan	2001	eng	eng	5
Nepal–Qatar	2007	eng;nep;ara	eng	2
Nepal–Sri Lanka	1999	eng;nep;sin	eng	3
Nepal–Thailand	1998	eng	eng	5
Netherlands Antilles–Norway	1989	eng	eng	5
Netherlands Antilles–United States	1986	eng	eng	5
Netherlands–New Zealand	1980	eng;dut		1
Netherlands–Nigeria	1991	eng	eng	5
Netherlands–Norway	1990	eng;dut;nor	eng	4
Netherlands–Oman	2009	eng;dut;ara	eng	4
Netherlands–Pakistan	1982	eng;dut		1
Netherlands–Panama	2010	eng;dut;spa	eng	3
Netherlands–Philippines	1989	eng	eng	5
Netherlands–Poland	2002	eng;dut;pol	eng	4
Netherlands–Portugal	1999	eng;dut;por	eng	4
Netherlands–Qatar	2008	eng;dut;ara	eng	2
Netherlands–Romania	1998	eng	eng	5
Netherlands–Russia	1996	eng;dur;rus	eng	4
Netherlands–Saudi Arabia	2008	eng;dut;ara	eng	3
Netherlands–Serbia and Montenegro	1982	eng;dut;scr	eng	4
Netherlands–Singapore	1971	eng;dut		1
Netherlands–Slovak Republic	1974	eng;dut;cze	eng	4
Netherlands–Slovenia	2004	eng;dut;slv	eng	2
Netherlands–South Africa	2005	eng	eng	5
Netherlands–Spain	1971	eng;dut;spa	eng	2
Netherlands–Sri Lanka	1982	eng;dut;sin	eng	4
Netherlands–Suriname	1975	dut	dut	5
Netherlands–Sweden	1991	eng	eng	5
Netherlands–Switzerland	2010	eng;fre;dut	eng	4
Netherlands–Taiwan	2001	eng	eng	5
Netherlands–Tajikistan	1986	eng;dut;rus		1
Netherlands–Thailand	1975	eng;dut;tha	eng	4
Netherlands–Tunisia	1995	fre;dut;ara	fre	3
Netherlands–Turkey	1986	eng	eng	5
Netherlands–Uganda	2004	eng	eng	5
Netherlands–Ukraine	1995	eng;dut;ukr	eng	4
Netherlands–United Arab Emirates	2007	eng;dut;ara	eng	4
Netherlands–United Kingdom	1979	eng;dut		1
Netherlands–United Kingdom	2008	eng;dut		1
Netherlands–United Kingdom	2013	eng	eng	5
Netherlands–United States	1969	eng;dut		1
Netherlands–United States	1992	eng;dut		1
Netherlands–Uzbekistan	2001	eng;dut;uzb	eng	4
Netherlands–Venezuela	1991	eng;dut;spa	eng	4
Netherlands–Vietnam	1995	eng	eng	5
Netherlands–Zambia	1977	eng	eng	5
Netherlands–Zambia	2015	eng	eng	5
Netherlands–Zimbabwe	1989	eng	eng	5
New Zealand–Norway	1982	eng	eng	5
New Zealand–Papua New Guinea	2012	eng	eng	5

E. Sample

Treaty	Conclusion	AL	UL/PT	TOW
New Zealand–Philippines	1980	eng	eng	5
New Zealand–Poland	2005	eng;pol		1
New Zealand–Russia	2000	eng;rus		1
New Zealand–Samoa	2010	eng	eng	5
New Zealand–Samoa	2015	eng	eng	5
New Zealand–Singapore	2009	eng	eng	5
New Zealand–South Africa	2002	eng	eng	5
New Zealand–Spain	2005	eng;spa	eng	2
New Zealand–St. Kitts and Nevis	2009	eng	eng	5
New Zealand–Sweden	1979	eng;swe		1
New Zealand–Switzerland	1980	eng;ger		1
New Zealand–Taiwan	1996	eng;chi	eng	3
New Zealand–Thailand	1998	eng	eng	5
New Zealand–Turkey	2010	eng;tur		1
New Zealand–United Arab Emirates	2003	eng;ara	eng	6
New Zealand–United Kingdom	1983	eng	eng	5
New Zealand–United States	1982	eng	eng	5
New Zealand–Vietnam	2013	eng;vts		1
Nigeria–Pakistan	1989	eng	eng	5
Nigeria–Philippines	1997	eng	eng	5
Nigeria–Qatar	2016	eng;ara		1
Nigeria–Romania	1992	eng;rum	eng	3
Nigeria–Slovak Republic	1989	eng	eng	5
Nigeria–South Africa	2000	eng	eng	5
Nigeria–Spain	2009	eng;spa	eng	3
Nigeria–Sweden	2004	eng	eng	5
Nigeria–United Kingdom	1987	eng	eng	5
Norway–Pakistan	1986	eng	eng	5
Norway–Philippines	1987	eng;nor		1
Norway–Poland	2009	eng;nor;pol	eng	3
Norway–Portugal	2011	eng;por;nor	eng	3
Norway–Qatar	2009	eng;nor;ara	eng	2
Norway–Romania	1980	eng;nor;rum	eng	3
Norway–Romania	2015	eng;nor;rum	eng	3
Norway–Russia	1996	eng;nor;rus	eng	2
Norway–Senegal	1994	fre	fre	5
Norway–Serbia	2015	eng;nor;ser	eng	3
Norway–Serbia and Montenegro	1983	eng	eng	5
Norway–Singapore	1997	eng	eng	5
Norway–Slovak Republic	1979	eng	eng	5
Norway–Slovenia	2008	eng;nor;slv	eng	2
Norway–South Africa	1996	eng	eng	5
Norway–Spain	1999	eng;nor;spa	eng	4
Norway–Sri Lanka	1986	eng;nor;sin	eng	3
Norway–Switzerland	1987	eng	eng	5
Norway–Tanzania	1976	eng	eng	5
Norway–Thailand	2003	eng	eng	5
Norway–Trinidad and Tobago	1969	eng	eng	5
Norway–Tunisia	1978	fre	fre	5
Norway–Turkey	2010	eng;nor;tur	eng	2
Norway–Turkmenistan	1980	nor;rus		1
Norway–Uganda	1999	eng	eng	5

Treaty	Conclusion	AL	UL/PT	TOW
Norway–Ukraine	1996	eng;nor;ukr	eng	3
Norway–United Kingdom	2013	eng;nor		1
Norway–United States	1971	eng;nor		1
Norway–Venezuela	1997	eng;nor;spa	eng	4
Norway–Vietnam	1995	eng;nor;vts	eng	3
Norway–Zambia	1971	eng	eng	5
Norway–Zambia	2015	eng;nor		1
Norway–Zimbabwe	1989	eng	eng	5
Oman–Pakistan	1999	eng;ara	eng	3
Oman–Portugal	2015	eng;por;ara	eng	3
Oman–Russia	2001	eng;ara;rus	eng	4
Oman–Seychelles	2003	eng;ara	eng	3
Oman–Singapore	2003	eng;ara		1
Oman–South Africa	2002	eng;ara	eng	2
Oman–Spain	2014	eng;ara;spa	map	7
Oman–Sudan	2003	ara	ara	5
Oman–Switzerland	2015	eng;fre;ara	eng	3
Oman–Thailand	2003	eng;ara;tha	eng	4
Oman–Tunisia	1997	ara	ara	5
Oman–Turkey	2006	eng;ara;tur	eng	4
Oman–United Kingdom	1998	eng;ara		1
Oman–Uzbekistan	2009	eng;ara;uzb	eng	4
Oman–Vietnam	2008	eng;ara;vts	eng	3
Oman–Yemen	2002	ara	ara	5
Pakistan–Philippines	1979	eng	eng	5
Pakistan–Poland	1974	eng;pol		1
Pakistan–Portugal	2000	eng;por	eng	6
Pakistan–Qatar	1999	eng;ara		1
Pakistan–Romania	1999	eng;rum		1
Pakistan–Saudi Arabia	2006	eng;ara		1
Pakistan–Serbia	2010	eng;ser		1
Pakistan–Singapore	1993	eng	eng	5
Pakistan–South Africa	1998	eng	eng	5
Pakistan–Spain	2010	eng;spa	map	7
Pakistan–Sri Lanka	1981	eng;sin	eng	3
Pakistan–Sweden	1985	eng	eng	5
Pakistan–Switzerland	2005	eng;ger		1
Pakistan–Syria	2001	eng;ara	eng	3
Pakistan–Tajikistan	2004	eng;rus;tgk	eng	3
Pakistan–Thailand	1980	eng	eng	5
Pakistan–Tunisia	1996	eng;fre;ara	eng;fre	3
Pakistan–Turkey	1985	eng	eng	5
Pakistan–Turkmenistan	1994	eng;tkm;rus	eng	2
Pakistan–Ukraine	2008	eng;ukr		1
Pakistan–United Arab Emirates	1993	eng	eng	5
Pakistan–United Kingdom	1986	eng	eng	5
Pakistan–Uzbekistan	1995	eng;uzb		1
Pakistan–Vietnam	2004	eng;vts		1
Pakistan–Yemen	2004	eng	eng	5
Palestinian Autonomous Areas–Serbia	2012	eng;ser;ara	eng	3
Palestinian Autonomous Areas–Sri Lanka	2012	eng;sin	eng	3
Palestinian Autonomous Areas–Venezuela	2014	eng;spa		1

E. Sample

Treaty	Conclusion	AL	UL/PT	TOW
Palestinian Autonomous Areas–Vietnam	2013	eng;ara;vts	eng	3
Panama–Portugal	2010	eng;spa;por	eng	3
Panama–Qatar	2010	eng;spa;ara	eng	2
Panama–Singapore	2010	eng;spa	eng	2
Panama–Spain	2010	spa	spa	5
Panama–United Arab Emirates	2012	eng;spa;ara	eng	2
Panama–United Kingdom	2013	eng;spa		1
Papua New Guinea–Singapore	1991	eng	eng	5
Papua New Guinea–United Kingdom	1991	eng	eng	5
Paraguay–Taiwan	1994	eng;spa;chi	eng	2
Peru–Portugal	2012	eng;spa;por	eng	3
Peru–Spain	2006	spa	spa	5
Peru–Switzerland	2012	eng;fre;spa	eng	4
Philippines–Poland	1992	eng	eng	5
Philippines–Qatar	2008	eng;ara		1
Philippines–Romania	1994	eng;rum		1
Philippines–Russia	1995	eng;rus	eng	2
Philippines–Singapore	1977	eng	eng	5
Philippines–Spain	1989	eng;spa		1
Philippines–Sweden	1998	eng	eng	5
Philippines–Switzerland	1998	eng;ger	eng	3
Philippines–Thailand	1982	eng	eng	5
Philippines–Thailand	2013	eng	eng	5
Philippines–Turkey	2009	eng;tur		1
Philippines–United Arab Emirates	2003	eng;ara	eng	3
Philippines–United Kingdom	1976	eng	eng	5
Philippines–United States	1976	eng	eng	5
Philippines–Vietnam	2001	eng;vts		1
Poland–Portugal	1995	eng;pol;por	eng	3
Poland–Qatar	2008	eng;pol;ara	eng	2
Poland–Romania	1994	eng;pol;rum	eng	3
Poland–Russia	1992	pol;rus		1
Poland–Saudi Arabia	2011	eng;pol;ara	eng	3
Poland–Serbia and Montenegro	1997	eng;pol;ser	eng	3
Poland–Singapore	1993	eng	eng	5
Poland–Singapore	2012	eng;pol		1
Poland–Slovak Republic	1994	eng;pol;slo	eng	3
Poland–Slovenia	1996	eng	eng	5
Poland–South Africa	1993	eng;pol		1
Poland–Spain	1979	pol;spa		1
Poland–Sri Lanka	1980	eng;pol;sin	eng	3
Poland–Sri Lanka	2015	eng;pol;sin	eng	3
Poland–Sweden	2004	eng;pol;swe	eng	3
Poland–Switzerland	1991	eng;pol;ger	eng	4
Poland–Syria	2001	eng;pol;ara	eng	3
Poland–Tajikistan	2003	rus;pol;tgk	rus	3
Poland–Thailand	1978	eng;pol;tha	eng	6
Poland–Tunisia	1993	fre;pol;ara	fre	2
Poland–Turkey	1993	eng;pol;tur	eng	2
Poland–Ukraine	1993	pol;ukr		1
Poland–United Arab Emirates	1993	eng;pol;ara	eng	3
Poland–United Kingdom	2006	eng;pol		1

Treaty	Conclusion	AL	UL/PT	TOW
Poland–United States	1974	eng;pol		1
Poland–United States	2013	eng;pol		1
Poland–Uruguay	1991	pol;spa	eng	9
Poland–Uzbekistan	1995	rus;pol;uzb	rus	3
Poland–Vietnam	1994	eng;pol;vts	eng	3
Poland–Zambia	1995	eng;pol		1
Poland–Zimbabwe	1993	eng;pol		1
Portugal–Qatar	2011	eng;por;ara	eng	3
Portugal–Romania	1997	eng;por;rum	eng	3
Portugal–Russia	2000	eng;por;rus	eng	3
Portugal–San Marino	2010	eng;por;ita	eng	3
Portugal–Sao Tome and Principe	2015	por	por	5
Portugal–Saudi Arabia	2015	eng;ara;por	eng	3
Portugal–Senegal	2014	fre;por		1
Portugal–Senegal	2014	fre;por		1
Portugal–Singapore	1999	eng;por	eng	3
Portugal–Slovak Republic	2001	eng;por;slo	eng	3
Portugal–Slovenia	2003	eng;por;slv	eng	3
Portugal–South Africa	2006	eng;por		1
Portugal–Spain	1993	por;spa		1
Portugal–Sweden	2002	eng;por;swe	eng	2
Portugal–Switzerland	1974	fre;por		1
Portugal–Timor-Leste	2011	eng;por	por	3
Portugal–Tunisia	1999	fre;por;ara	fre	8
Portugal–Turkey	2005	eng;por;tur	eng	3
Portugal–Ukraine	2000	eng;por;ukr	eng	3
Portugal–United Arab Emirates	2011	eng;por;ara	eng	3
Portugal–United Kingdom	1968	eng;por		1
Portugal–United States	1994	eng;por		1
Portugal–Uruguay	2009	eng;por;spa	eng	2
Portugal–Uzbekistan	2001	eng;por;uzb	eng	3
Portugal–Venezuela	1996	eng;por;spa	eng	3
Portugal–Vietnam	2015	eng;por;vts	eng	3
Qatar–Romania	1999	eng;ara;rum	eng	3
Qatar–Russia	1998	eng;ara;rus	eng	4
Qatar–San Marino	2013	eng;ara;ita	eng	2
Qatar–Senegal	1998	fre;ara		1
Qatar–Serbia	2009	eng;ara;ser	eng	3
Qatar–Seychelles	2006	eng;ara	eng	3
Qatar–Singapore	2006	eng;ara	eng	2
Qatar–Slovenia	2010	eng;ara;slv	eng	2
Qatar–South Africa	2015	eng;ara		1
Qatar–Spain	2015	eng;ara;spa	map	7
Qatar–Sri Lanka	2004	eng;ara;sin	eng	2
Qatar–Sudan	1998	ara	ara	5
Qatar–Switzerland	2009	eng;fre;ara	eng	3
Qatar–Syria	2003	ara	ara	5
Qatar–Tunisia	1997	fre	fre	5
Qatar–Turkey	2001	eng;ara;tur	eng	2
Qatar–United Kingdom	2009	eng;ara		1
Qatar–Venezuela	2006	eng;ara;spa	eng	2
Qatar–Vietnam	2009	eng;ara;vts	eng	3

E. Sample

Treaty	Conclusion	AL	UL/PT	TOW
Romania–Russia	1993	eng;rum;rus	eng	3
Romania–San Marino	2007	eng;rum;ita	eng	2
Romania–Saudi Arabia	2011	eng;rum;ara	eng	3
Romania–Serbia and Montenegro	1996	eng;rum;ser	eng	3
Romania–Singapore	2002	eng;rum		1
Romania–Slovak Republic	1994	eng;rum;slo	eng	3
Romania–Slovenia	2002	eng;rum;slv	eng	3
Romania–South Africa	1993	eng;rum;afr	eng	3
Romania–Spain	1979	spa;rum		1
Romania–Sri Lanka	1984	eng;rum;sin	eng	3
Romania–Sudan	2007	eng	eng	5
Romania–Sweden	1976	eng;rum;swe	eng	3
Romania–Switzerland	1993	fre;rum		1
Romania–Thailand	1996	eng;rum;tha	eng	4
Romania–Tunisia	1987	fre;rum	fre	3
Romania–Turkey	1986	eng;rum;tur	eng	3
Romania–Turkmenistan	2008	eng;rum;tkm	eng	3
Romania–Ukraine	1996	eng;rum;ukr	eng	3
Romania–United Arab Emirates	1993	eng;rum;ara	eng	3
Romania–United Arab Emirates	2015	eng;ara;rum	eng	3
Romania–United Kingdom	1975	eng;rum		1
Romania–United States	1973	eng;rum		1
Romania–Uruguay	2012	eng;spa;rum	eng	3
Romania–Uzbekistan	1996	eng;rum;uzb	eng	3
Romania–Vietnam	1995	eng;rum;vts	eng	3
Romania–Zambia	1983	eng;rum	eng	3
Russia–Saudi Arabia	2007	eng;rus;ara	eng	3
Russia–Serbia and Montenegro	1995	eng;rus;ser	eng	2
Russia–Singapore	2002	eng;rus		1
Russia–Slovak Republic	1994	rus;slo		1
Russia–Slovenia	1995	eng;rus;slv	eng	2
Russia–South Africa	1995	eng;rus		1
Russia–Spain	1998	eng;rus;spa	eng	3
Russia–Sri Lanka	1999	eng;rus;sin	eng	2
Russia–Sweden	1993	eng;rus;swe	eng	3
Russia–Switzerland	1995	eng;rus;ger	eng	4
Russia–Syria	2000	eng;rus;ara	eng	4
Russia–Tajikistan	1997	rus;tgk	rus	3
Russia–Thailand	1999	eng;rus;tha	eng	2
Russia–Turkey	1997	eng;rus;tur	eng	2
Russia–Turkmenistan	1998	rus;tkm		1
Russia–Ukraine	1995	rus;ukr		1
Russia–United Arab Emirates	2011	eng;rus;ara	eng	4
Russia–United Kingdom	1994	eng;rus		1
Russia–United States	1992	eng;rus		1
Russia–Uzbekistan	1994	rus;uzb		1
Russia–Venezuela	2003	eng;rus;spa	eng	4
Russia–Vietnam	1993	eng;rus;vts	eng	2
Rwanda–Singapore	2014	eng	eng	5
Rwanda–South Africa	2002	eng	eng	5
San Marino–Seychelles	2012	eng	eng	5
San Marino–Singapore	2013	eng	eng	5

Treaty	Conclusion	AL	UL/PT	TOW
San Marino–Vietnam	2013	eng;vts;ita	eng	3
Saudi Arabia–Singapore	2010	eng;ara		1
Saudi Arabia–South Africa	2007	eng;ara		1
Saudi Arabia–Spain	2007	eng;ara;spa	eng	2
Saudi Arabia–Sweden	2015	eng;ara;swe	eng	3
Saudi Arabia–Syria	2009	ara	ara	5
Saudi Arabia–Tunisia	2010	ara	ara	5
Saudi Arabia–Turkey	2007	eng;ara;tur	eng	3
Saudi Arabia–Ukraine	2011	eng;ara;ukr	eng	3
Saudi Arabia–United Kingdom	2007	eng;ara		1
Saudi Arabia–Uzbekistan	2008	eng;ara;uzb	eng	3
Saudi Arabia–Venezuela	2015	eng;spa;ara	eng	2
Saudi Arabia–Vietnam	2010	eng;ara;vts	eng	3
Senegal–Spain	2006	fre;spa		1
Senegal–Taiwan	2000	eng;fre;chi		1
Senegal–Tunisia	1984	fre	fre	5
Senegal–United Kingdom	2015	eng;fre		1
Serbia and Montenegro–Slovak Republic	2001	eng;ser;slo	eng	3
Serbia and Montenegro–Slovenia	2003	eng;ser;slv	eng	3
Serbia and Montenegro–Sri Lanka	1985	eng;scr;sin	eng	3
Serbia and Montenegro–Sweden	1980	eng	eng	5
Serbia and Montenegro–Switzerland	2005	eng;fre;ser	eng	4
Serbia and Montenegro–Turkey	2005	eng;ser;tur	eng	3
Serbia and Montenegro–Ukraine	2001	eng;ser;ukr	eng	3
Serbia and Montenegro–United Kingdom	1981	eng;scr		1
Serbia and Montenegro–Zimbabwe	1996	eng;ser	eng	3
Serbia–Spain	2009	eng;ser;spa	eng	3
Serbia–Tunisia	2012	fre;ser;ara		1
Serbia–United Arab Emirates	2013	eng;ser;ara	eng	3
Serbia–Vietnam	2013	eng;ser;vts	eng	3
Seychelles–Singapore	2014	eng	eng	5
Seychelles–South Africa	1998	eng	eng	5
Seychelles–Sri Lanka	2011	eng;sin	eng	3
Seychelles–Swaziland	2012	eng	eng	5
Seychelles–Thailand	2001	eng	eng	5
Seychelles–United Arab Emirates	2006	eng;ara	eng	3
Seychelles–Vietnam	2005	eng;vts		1
Seychelles–Zambia	2010	eng	eng	5
Seychelles–Zimbabwe	2002	eng	eng	5
Sierra Leone–South Africa	1960	eng;afr		1
Singapore–Slovak Republic	2005	eng;slo		1
Singapore–Slovenia	2010	eng;slv		1
Singapore–South Africa	1996	eng	eng	5
Singapore–Spain	2011	eng;spa		1
Singapore–Sri Lanka	1979	eng;sin		1
Singapore–Sri Lanka	2014	eng;sin	eng	3
Singapore–Sweden	1968	eng	eng	5
Singapore–Switzerland	2011	eng;ger		1
Singapore–Taiwan	1981	eng;chi		1
Singapore–Thailand	1975	eng	eng	5
Singapore–Thailand	2015	eng;tha	eng	3
Singapore–Turkey	1999	eng;tur		1

E. Sample

Treaty	Conclusion	AL	UL/PT	TOW
Singapore–Ukraine	2007	eng;ukr		1
Singapore–United Arab Emirates	1995	eng;ara	eng	2
Singapore–United Kingdom	1997	eng	eng	5
Singapore–Uruguay	2015	eng;spa	eng	3
Singapore–Uzbekistan	2008	eng;uzb	eng	2
Singapore–Vietnam	1994	eng;vts		1
Slovak Republic–Malaysia	2015	eng;slo;may	eng	3
Slovak Republic–Slovenia	2003	eng;slo;slv	eng	3
Slovak Republic–South Africa	1998	eng;slo		1
Slovak Republic–Spain	1980	spa;cze		1
Slovak Republic–Sri Lanka	1978	eng;cze;sin	eng	3
Slovak Republic–Sweden	1979	eng	eng	5
Slovak Republic–Switzerland	1997	eng;slo;ger	eng	4
Slovak Republic–Syria	2009	eng;slo;ara	eng	4
Slovak Republic–Taiwan	2011	eng;slo;chi	eng	3
Slovak Republic–Tunisia	1990	fre	fre	5
Slovak Republic–Turkey	1997	eng;slo;tur	eng	2
Slovak Republic–Turkmenistan	1996	eng;slo;tkm	eng	2
Slovak Republic–Ukraine	1996	eng;slo;ukr	eng	3
Slovak Republic–United Arab Emirates	2015	eng;ara;slo	eng	3
Slovak Republic–United Kingdom	1990	eng;cze		1
Slovak Republic–United States	1993	eng;slo		1
Slovak Republic–Uzbekistan	2003	eng;slo;uzb	eng	3
Slovak Republic–Vietnam	2008	eng;slo;vts	eng	3
Slovenia–Spain	2001	eng;slv;spa	eng	2
Slovenia–Sweden	1980	eng	eng	5
Slovenia–Switzerland	1996	eng;slv;ger	eng	4
Slovenia–Thailand	2003	eng;slv;tha	eng	2
Slovenia–Turkey	2001	eng;slv;tur	eng	2
Slovenia–Ukraine	2003	eng;slv;ukr	eng	3
Slovenia–United Arab Emirates	2013	eng;slv;ara	eng	2
Slovenia–United Kingdom	2007	eng;slv		1
Slovenia–United States	1999	eng;slv		1
Slovenia–Uzbekistan	2013	eng;slv;uzb	eng	3
South Africa–Spain	2006	eng;spa	eng	3
South Africa–Sudan	2007	eng	eng	5
South Africa–Swaziland	2004	eng	eng	5
South Africa–Sweden	1961	eng;afr;swe		1
South Africa–Sweden	1995	eng	eng	5
South Africa–Switzerland	2007	eng;fre		1
South Africa–Taiwan	1994	eng;chi		1
South Africa–Tanzania	2005	eng	eng	5
South Africa–Thailand	1996	eng;tha	eng	6
South Africa–Tunisia	1999	eng;ara		1
South Africa–Turkey	2005	eng;tur		1
South Africa–Uganda	1997	eng	eng	5
South Africa–Ukraine	2003	eng;ukr		1
South Africa–United Arab Emirates	2015	eng;ara		1
South Africa–United Kingdom	1978	eng;afr		1
South Africa–United Kingdom	2002	eng	eng	5
South Africa–United States	1997	eng	eng	5
South Africa–Zimbabwe	1965	eng;afr		1

Treaty	Conclusion	AL	UL/PT	TOW
South Africa–Zimbabwe	2015	eng	eng	5
Spain–Sweden	1963	spa;swe		1
Spain–Sweden	1976	eng;spa;swe	eng	6
Spain–Switzerland	1966	fre;spa		1
Spain–Tajikistan	1985	spa;rus		1
Spain–Thailand	1997	eng;spa;tha	eng	6
Spain–Trinidad and Tobago	2009	eng;spa		1
Spain–Tunisia	1982	fre	fre	5
Spain–Turkey	2002	eng;spa;tur	eng	2
Spain–Turkmenistan	1985	spa;rus		1
Spain–Ukraine	1985	spa;rus		1
Spain–United Arab Emirates	2006	eng;spa;ara	eng	3
Spain–United Kingdom	1975	eng;spa		1
Spain–United Kingdom	2013	eng;spa		1
Spain–United States	1990	eng;spa		1
Spain–Uruguay	2009	spa	spa	5
Spain–Uzbekistan	2013	eng;spa;uzb		1
Spain–Venezuela	2003	spa	spa	5
Spain–Vietnam	2005	eng;spa;vts	eng	3
Sri Lanka–Sweden	1983	eng;sin;swe	eng	3
Sri Lanka–Switzerland	1983	eng;sin;ger	eng	4
Sri Lanka–Thailand	1988	eng;sin;tha	eng	3
Sri Lanka–United Arab Emirates	2003	eng;sin;ara	eng	3
Sri Lanka–United Kingdom	1979	eng;sin		1
Sri Lanka–United States	1985	eng;sin		1
Sri Lanka–Vietnam	2005	eng;sin;vts	eng	3
St. Kitts and Nevis–San Marino	2010	eng;ita	eng	2
St. Kitts and Nevis–Switzerland	1963	eng;fre		1
St. Lucia–Switzerland	1963	eng;fre		1
St. Vincent and the Grenadines–Switzerland	1963	eng;fre		1
Sudan–Turkey	2001	eng	eng	5
Sudan–United Kingdom	1975	eng	eng	5
Swaziland–Taiwan	1998	eng;chi	eng	3
Swaziland–United Kingdom	1968	eng	eng	5
Sweden–Switzerland	1965	swe;ger		1
Sweden–Switzerland	1979	swe;ger		1
Sweden–Taiwan	2001	eng	eng	5
Sweden–Tanzania	1976	eng	eng	5
Sweden–Thailand	1988	eng	eng	5
Sweden–Trinidad and Tobago	1984	eng	eng	5
Sweden–Tunisia	1981	fre	fre	5
Sweden–Turkey	1988	eng	eng	5
Sweden–Turkmenistan	1981	rus;swe		1
Sweden–Ukraine	1995	eng;swe;ukr	eng	2
Sweden–United Kingdom	1980	eng;swe		1
Sweden–United Kingdom	1983	eng;swe		1
Sweden–United Kingdom	2015	eng	eng	5
Sweden–United States	1994	eng	eng	5
Sweden–Venezuela	1993	spa	spa	5
Sweden–Vietnam	1994	eng;swe;vts	eng	2
Sweden–Zambia	1974	eng	eng	5
Sweden–Zimbabwe	1989	eng	eng	5

E. Sample

Treaty	Conclusion	AL	UL/PT	TOW
Switzerland–Taiwan	2007	eng	eng	5
Switzerland–Tajikistan	2010	eng;ger;tgk;rus	eng	4
Switzerland–Thailand	1996	eng;ger;tha	eng	4
Switzerland–Trinidad and Tobago	1973	eng;fre		1
Switzerland–Tunisia	1994	fre;ara		1
Switzerland–Turkey	2010	eng;fre;tur	eng	2
Switzerland–Turkmenistan	2012	eng;ger;rus;tkm	eng	3
Switzerland–Ukraine	2000	eng;ger;ukr	eng	3
Switzerland–United Arab Emirates	2011	eng;fre;ara	eng	4
Switzerland–United Kingdom	1977	eng;fre		1
Switzerland–United Kingdom	1993	eng;fre		1
Switzerland–United States	1996	eng;ger		1
Switzerland–Uruguay	2010	eng;fre;spa	eng	4
Switzerland–Uzbekistan	2002	eng;ger;uzb	eng	4
Switzerland–Venezuela	1996	eng;fre;spa	eng	4
Switzerland–Vietnam	1996	eng;ger;vts	eng	4
Switzerland–Zambia	1961	eng;fre		1
Syria–Tunisia	1998	ara	ara	5
Syria–Turkey	2004	eng;ara;tur	eng	4
Syria–Ukraine	2003	eng;ara;ukr	eng	3
Syria–United Arab Emirates	2000	ara	ara	5
Taiwan–Thailand	1999	eng;chi;tha	eng	2
Taiwan–United Kingdom	2002	eng;chi	eng	3
Taiwan–Vietnam	1998	eng	eng	5
Tajikistan–Thailand	2013	eng;rus;tgk;tha	eng	2
Tajikistan–Turkey	1996	eng	eng	5
Tajikistan–Turkmenistan	2007	rus;tgk;tgk	rus	2
Tajikistan–Ukraine	2002	rus;ukr;tgk	rus	2
Tajikistan–United Arab Emirates	1995	eng	eng	5
Tajikistan–United Kingdom	2014	eng;tgk	eng	2
Tajikistan–United States	1973	eng;rus		1
Tanzania–Zambia	1968	eng	eng	5
Thailand–Turkey	2002	eng;tha;tur	eng	4
Thailand–Ukraine	2004	eng;tha;ukr	eng	3
Thailand–United Arab Emirates	2000	eng;ara;tha	eng	3
Thailand–United Kingdom	1981	eng;tha		1
Thailand–United States	1996	eng	eng	5
Thailand–Uzbekistan	1999	eng;tha;uzb	eng	3
Thailand–Vietnam	1992	eng;tha;vts	eng	6
Togo–Tunisia	1987	fre	fre	5
Trinidad and Tobago–United Kingdom	1982	eng	eng	5
Trinidad and Tobago–United States	1970	eng	eng	5
Trinidad and Tobago–Venezuela	1996	eng;spa		1
Tunisia–Turkey	1986	eng;fre		1
Tunisia–United Arab Emirates	1996	ara	ara	5
Tunisia–United Kingdom	1982	eng;fre;ara		1
Tunisia–United States	1985	eng;fre		1
Tunisia–Vietnam	2010	eng;ara;vts	eng	3
Tunisia–Yemen	1998	ara	ara	5
Turkey–Turkmenistan	1995	eng;tur;tkm	eng	2
Turkey–Ukraine	1996	eng;tur;ukr	eng	2
Turkey–United Arab Emirates	1993	eng;tur;ara	eng	2

Treaty	Conclusion	AL	UL/PT	TOW
Turkey–United Kingdom	1986	eng;tur		1
Turkey–United States	1996	eng;tur		1
Turkey–Uzbekistan	1996	eng;tur;uzb	eng	2
Turkey–Vietnam	2014	eng;tur;vts	eng	2
Turkey–Yemen	2005	eng	eng	5
Turkmenistan–Ukraine	1998	rus;ukr;tkm	rus	2
Turkmenistan–United Arab Emirates	1998	eng;rus	eng	3
Turkmenistan–United Kingdom	1985	eng;rus		1
Turkmenistan–United Kingdom	2016	eng;tkm		1
Uganda–United Kingdom	1992	eng	eng	5
Uganda–Zambia	1968	eng	eng	5
Ukraine–United Arab Emirates	2003	eng;ara;ukr	eng	3
Ukraine–United Kingdom	1993	eng;ukr		1
Ukraine–United States	1994	eng;ukr		1
Ukraine–Uzbekistan	1994	rus;ukr;uzb	rus	2
Ukraine–Vietnam	1996	eng;ukr;vts	eng	3
United Arab Emirates–United Kingdom	2016	eng;ara	eng	2
United Arab Emirates–Uzbekistan	2007	eng;ara;uzb	eng	3
United Arab Emirates–Venezuela	2010	eng;spa;ara	eng	2
United Arab Emirates–Vietnam	2009	eng	eng	5
United Arab Emirates–Yemen	2001	ara	ara	5
United Kingdom–United States	1978	eng	eng	5
United Kingdom–United States	2001	eng	eng	5
United Kingdom–Uruguay	2016	eng;spa		1
United Kingdom–Uzbekistan	1993	eng;rus	eng	3
United Kingdom–Venezuela	1996	eng;spa		1
United Kingdom–Vietnam	1994	eng;vts		1
United Kingdom–Zambia	1972	eng	eng	5
United Kingdom–Zambia	2014	eng	eng	5
United Kingdom–Zimbabwe	1982	eng	eng	5
United States–Uzbekistan	1973	eng;rus		1
United States–Venezuela	1999	eng;spa		1
United States–Vietnam	2015	eng;vts		1
Uruguay–Vietnam	2013	eng;spa;vts	eng	3
Uzbekistan–Vietnam	1996	eng;uzb;vts	eng	3
Venezuela–Vietnam	2008	eng;spa;vts	eng	2

E.3. Terminated Treaties

Table (E.3): Treaties Concluded and Terminated 1960–2016

Treaty	Conclusion	AL	UL/PT	TOW
Algeria–France	1982	fre;ara		1
Anguilla–Sweden	1972	eng;swe		1
Antigua and Barbuda–Sweden	1972	eng;swe		1
Argentina–Austria	1979	spa;ger		1
Argentina–Chile	1976	spa	spa	5
Argentina–Spain	1992	spa	spa	5
Argentina–Sweden	1962	spa;swe		1
Argentina–Switzerland	1997	eng;fre;spa	eng	4
Armenia–Austria	1981	ger;rus		1
Armenia–Belgium	1987	fre;dut;rus		1
Armenia–Canada	1985	eng;fre;rus		1
Armenia–Cyprus	1982	eng;rus		1
Armenia–Finland	1987	rus;fin		1
Armenia–France	1985	fre;rus		1
Armenia–India	1988	eng;rus;hin	eng	2
Armenia–Italy	1985	ita;rus		1
Armenia–Netherlands	1986	eng;rus;dut		1
Armenia–Norway	1980	rus;nor		1
Armenia–Spain	1985	spa;rus		1
Armenia–Sweden	1981	rus;swe		1
Armenia–Switzerland	1986	ger;rus		1
Armenia–United Kingdom	1985	eng;rus		1
Australia–Finland	1984	eng;fin		1
Australia–France	1976	eng;fre		1
Australia–Japan	1969	eng;jap		1
Australia–New Zealand	1960	eng	eng	5
Australia–New Zealand	1972	eng	eng	5
Australia–New Zealand	1995	eng	eng	5
Australia–Norway	1982	eng	eng	5
Australia–United Kingdom	1967	eng	eng	5
Austria–Azerbaijan	1981	ger;rus		1
Austria–Belarus	1981	ger;rus		1
Austria–Bulgaria	1983	ger;bul		1
Austria–Czech Republic	1978	ger;cze		1
Austria–Denmark	1961	ger;dan		1
Austria–Finland	1963	ger;fin		1
Austria–Georgia	1981	ger;rus		1
Austria–Germany	2008	ger	ger	5
Austria–Greece	1970	eng;ger;gre	eng	6
Austria–India	1963	eng	eng	5
Austria–Kazakhstan	1981	ger;rus		1
Austria–Kyrgyzstan	1981	ger;rus		1
Austria–Moldova	1981	ger;rus		1
Austria–Norway	1960	ger;nor		1
Austria–Pakistan	1970	eng	eng	5
Austria–Poland	1974	ger;pol		1

E. Sample

Treaty	Conclusion	AL	UL/PT	TOW
Austria–Portugal	1970	ger;por		1
Austria–Romania	1976	ger;rum		1
Austria–Russia	1981	ger;rus		1
Austria–Tajikistan	1981	ger;rus		1
Austria–Turkey	1970	ger;tur		1
Austria–Ukraine	1981	ger;rus		1
Austria–Uzbekistan	1981	ger;rus		1
Azerbaijan–Belgium	1987	fre;rus;dut		1
Azerbaijan–Canada	1985	eng;rus;fre		1
Azerbaijan–Denmark	1986	rus;dan		1
Azerbaijan–Finland	1987	rus;fin		1
Azerbaijan–France	1985	rus;fre		1
Azerbaijan–Germany	1981	rus;ger		1
Azerbaijan–Italy	1985	rus;ita		1
Azerbaijan–Japan	1986	eng;rus;jap	eng	3
Azerbaijan–Netherlands	1986	eng;rus;dut		1
Azerbaijan–Norway	1980	rus;nor		1
Azerbaijan–Spain	1985	rus;spa		1
Azerbaijan–Sweden	1981	rus;swe		1
Azerbaijan–Switzerland	1986	ger;rus		1
Azerbaijan–United Kingdom	1985	eng;rus		1
Barbados–United Kingdom	1970	eng	eng	5
Belarus–Belgium	1987	eng;rus;dut		1
Belarus–Cyprus	1982	eng;rus		1
Belarus–Finland	1987	rus;fin		1
Belarus–Germany	1981	rus;ger		1
Belarus–India	1988	eng;rus;hin	eng	3
Belarus–Italy	1985	rus;ita		1
Belarus–Netherlands	1986	eng;rus;dut		1
Belarus–Sweden	1981	rus;swe		1
Belarus–Switzerland	1986	rus;ger		1
Belgium–Canada	1975	eng;fre;dut		1
Belgium–China (People's Rep.)	1985	fre;dut;chi		1
Belgium–Croatia	1980	eng	eng	5
Belgium–Czech Republic	1975	fre	fre	5
Belgium–Georgia	1987	fre;dut;rus		1
Belgium–Greece	1968	fre;dut;gre	fre	2
Belgium–India	1974	eng;fre;dut;hin		1
Belgium–Indonesia	1973	eng	eng	5
Belgium–Italy	1970	fre;dut;ita		1
Belgium–Kazakhstan	1987	fre;dut;rus		1
Belgium–Morocco	1972	fre;dut		1
Belgium–Netherlands	1970	fre;dut		1
Belgium–Norway	1967	fre;dut;nor		1
Belgium–Poland	1976	fre;dut;pol		1
Belgium–Romania	1976	fre;dut;rum	fre	2
Belgium–Russia	1987	fre;dut;rus		1
Belgium–Singapore	1972	eng	eng	5
Belgium–Slovak Republic	1975	fre	fre	5
Belgium–Slovenia	1980	eng	eng	5
Belgium–Spain	1970	fre;dut;spa		1
Belgium–Sweden	1965	fre;dut;swe		1

Treaty	Conclusion	AL	UL/PT	TOW
Belgium–Tunisia	1975	fre;dut;ara	fre	2
Belgium–Ukraine	1987	fre;dut;rus		1
Belgium–United Kingdom	1967	eng;fre;dut		1
Belgium–United States	1970	eng;fre;dut		1
Belgium–Uzbekistan	1987	fre;dut;rus		1
Belize–Sweden	1972	eng;swe		1
Bolivia–Colombia	1971	spa		5
Bosnia and Herzegovina–Czech Republic	1981	eng	spa	5
Botswana–South Africa	1977	eng;afr	eng	5
Botswana–United Kingdom	1977	eng		1
Brazil–Finland	1972	eng;por;fin	eng	5
Brazil–Germany	1975	eng;por;ger	eng	3
Brazil–Portugal	1971	por	eng	4
British Virgin Islands–Japan	1970	eng;jap	por	5
British Virgin Islands–Sweden	1972	eng;swe		1
Bulgaria–Cyprus	1985	eng;bul;gre		1
Bulgaria–Denmark	1977	eng	eng	3
Bulgaria–Germany	1987	ger;bul	eng	5
Bulgaria–Switzerland	1991	fre;bul		1
Canada–Czech Republic	1990	eng;fre;cze		1
Canada–Finland	1990	eng;fre;fin		1
Canada–Georgia	1985	eng;fre;rus		1
Canada–Germany	1981	eng;fre;ger		1
Canada–India	1985	eng;fre;hin		1
Canada–Ireland	1966	eng;fre;iri		1
Canada–Italy	1977	eng;fre;ita		1
Canada–Japan	1964	eng;jap		1
Canada–Kazakhstan	1985	eng;fre;rus		1
Canada–Korea (Rep.)	1978	eng;fre;kor		1
Canada–Kyrgyzstan	1985	eng;fre;rus		1
Canada–Luxembourg	1989	eng;fre		1
Canada–Mexico	1991	eng;fre;spa		1
Canada–Moldova	1985	eng;fre;rus		1
Canada–Norway	1966	eng;fre;nor		1
Canada–Poland	1987	eng;fre;pol		1
Canada–Romania	1978	eng;fre;rum		1
Canada–Russia	1985	eng;fre;rus		1
Canada–Slovak Republic	1990	eng;fre;cze		1
Canada–Sweden	1983	eng;fre;swe		1
Canada–Switzerland	1976	eng	eng	5
Canada–Tajikistan	1985	eng;fre;rus		1
Canada–Trinidad and Tobago	1966	eng;fre		1
Canada–Ukraine	1985	eng;fre;rus		1
Canada–United Kingdom	1966	eng;fre		1
Canada–Uzbekistan	1985	eng;fre;rus		1
China (People's Rep.)–Croatia	1988	eng;chi;scr	eng	3
China (People's Rep.)–Czech Republic	1987	eng;chi;cze	eng	3
China (People's Rep.)–Denmark	1986	eng;chi;dan	eng	6
China (People's Rep.)–Finland	1986	eng;chi;fin	eng	3
China (People's Rep.)–Hong Kong	1998	chi	chi	5
China (People's Rep.)–Macedonia (FYR)	1988	eng;chi;scr	eng	3
China (People's Rep.)–Malta	1993	eng;chi		1

E. Sample

Treaty	Conclusion	AL	UL/PT	TOW
China (People's Rep.)–Serbia and Montenegro	1988	eng;chi;scr	eng	3
China (People's Rep.)–Singapore	1986	eng;chi		1
China (People's Rep.)–Slovenia	1988	eng;chi;scr	eng	3
China (People's Rep.)–United Kingdom	1984	eng;chi		1
Comoro Islands–France	1970	fre	fre	5
Congo (Rep.)–France	1967	fre	fre	5
Croatia–Cyprus	1985	eng	eng	5
Croatia–Czech Republic	1981	eng	eng	5
Croatia–Denmark	1981	eng	eng	5
Croatia–France	1974	fre;scr		1
Croatia–Germany	1987	eng;scr;ger	eng	4
Croatia–Hungary	1985	eng	eng	5
Croatia–Italy	1982	eng	eng	5
Croatia–Netherlands	1982	eng;scr;dut	eng	4
Croatia–Poland	1985	eng;scr;pol	eng	4
Croatia–Romania	1986	eng;scr;rum	eng	3
Croatia–Slovak Republic	1981	eng	eng	5
Cyprus–Czech Republic	1980	eng	eng	5
Cyprus–Denmark	1981	eng	eng	5
Cyprus–Georgia	1982	eng;rus		1
Cyprus–Germany	1974	eng;gre;ger		1
Cyprus–Kazakhstan	1982	eng;rus		1
Cyprus–Moldova	1982	eng;rus		1
Cyprus–Russia	1982	eng;rus		1
Cyprus–South Africa	1960	eng;afr		1
Cyprus–Ukraine	1982	eng;rus		1
Czech Republic–Denmark	1982	eng	eng	5
Czech Republic–Finland	1975	eng	eng	5
Czech Republic–France	1973	fre;cze		1
Czech Republic–India	1986	eng	eng	5
Czech Republic–Macedonia (FYR)	1981	eng	eng	5
Czech Republic–Norway	1979	eng	eng	5
Czech Republic–Poland	1993	eng;cze;pol	eng	3
Czech Republic–Serbia and Montenegro	1981	eng	eng	5
Czech Republic–Slovak Republic	1992	cze	cze	5
Czech Republic–Slovenia	1981	eng	eng	5
Denmark–Faroe Islands	1986	dan;fao		1
Denmark–Georgia	1986	dan;rus		1
Denmark–Germany	1962	dan;ger		1
Denmark–Hungary	1978	eng	eng	5
Denmark–Ireland	1964	eng	eng	5
Denmark–Israel	1966	eng	eng	5
Denmark–Italy	1980	eng;dan;ita	eng	6
Denmark–Kazakhstan	1986	dan;rus		1
Denmark–Macedonia (FYR)	1981	eng	eng	5
Denmark–Malta	1975	eng;dan		1
Denmark–Moldova	1986	dan;rus		1
Denmark–Netherlands Antilles	1960	eng	eng	5
Denmark–Pakistan	1961	eng;dan		1
Denmark–Philippines	1966	eng	eng	5
Denmark–Poland	1976	eng	eng	5
Denmark–Portugal	1972	eng	eng	5

Treaty	Conclusion	AL	UL/PT	TOW
Denmark–Russia	1986	dan;rus		1
Denmark–Serbia and Montenegro	1981	eng	eng	5
Denmark–Singapore	1986	eng	eng	5
Denmark–Slovenia	1981	eng	eng	5
Denmark–Spain	1972	eng;dan;spa	eng	6
Denmark–Tajikistan	1986	dan;rus		1
Denmark–Thailand	1965	eng	eng	5
Denmark–Ukraine	1986	dan;rus		1
Denmark–Uzbekistan	1986	dan;rus		1
Dominica–Sweden	1972	eng;swe		1
Estonia–Latvia	1993	eng	eng	5
Estonia–Lithuania	1993	eng;est;lit	eng	2
Falkland Islands–Switzerland	1963	eng;fre		1
Falkland Islands–United Kingdom	1984	eng	eng	5
Faroe Islands–United Kingdom	1960	eng	eng	5
Fiji–Switzerland	1963	eng;fre		1
Finland–Georgia	1987	fin;rus		1
Finland–India	1983	eng;fin;hin	eng	3
Finland–Ireland	1969	eng	eng	5
Finland–Israel	1965	eng	eng	5
Finland–Kazakhstan	1987	fin;rus		1
Finland–Kyrgyzstan	1987	fin;rus		1
Finland–Macedonia (FYR)	1986	eng	eng	5
Finland–Malta	1975	eng;fin		1
Finland–Moldova	1987	fin;rus		1
Finland–Morocco	1973	fre;fin;ara		1
Finland–Netherlands	1970	fin;dut		1
Finland–Poland	1977	eng	eng	5
Finland–Romania	1977	eng;fin;rum	eng	3
Finland–Russia	1987	fin;rus		1
Finland–Singapore	1981	eng	eng	5
Finland–Slovak Republic	1975	eng	eng	5
Finland–Slovenia	1986	eng	eng	5
Finland–Tajikistan	1987	fin;rus		1
Finland–Turkey	1986	eng;fin;tur	eng	2
Finland–Turkmenistan	1987	fin;rus		1
Finland–Ukraine	1987	fin;rus		1
Finland–United States	1970	eng;fin		1
Finland–Uzbekistan	1987	fin;rus		1
France–Gabon	1966	fre	fre	5
France–Georgia	1985	fre;rus		1
France–India	1969	fre;hin		1
France–Israel	1963	fre;heb		1
France–Japan	1964	fre;jap		1
France–Kazakhstan	1985	fre;rus		1
France–Macedonia (FYR)	1974	fre;scr		1
France–Pakistan	1966	eng;fre		1
France–Panama	1995	fre	fre	5
France–Russia	1985	fre;rus		1
France–Slovenia	1974	fre;scr		1
France–Spain	1973	fre;spa		1
France–Ukraine	1985	fre;rus		1

E. Sample

Treaty	Conclusion	AL	UL/PT	TOW
France–United Kingdom	1968	eng;fre		1
France–United States	1967	eng;fre		1
France–Uzbekistan	1985	fre;rus		1
Gambia–South Africa	1960	eng;afr		1
Georgia–Germany	1981	rus;ger		1
Georgia–India	1988	eng;geo;hin	eng	2
Georgia–Italy	1985	rus;ita		1
Georgia–Netherlands	1986	eng;rus;dut		1
Georgia–Norway	1980	rus;nor		1
Georgia–Spain	1985	rus;spa		1
Georgia–Sweden	1981	rus;swe		1
Georgia–United Kingdom	1985	eng;rus		1
Germany–Hungary	1977	ger;hun		1
Germany–Indonesia	1977	eng;ger;ind	eng	4
Germany–Ireland	1962	eng;ger;iri	eng	6
Germany–Kazakhstan	1981	ger;rus		1
Germany–Korea (Rep.)	1976	eng;ger;kor	eng	6
Germany–Kuwait	1987	eng;ger;ara	eng	2
Germany–Kyrgyzstan	1981	ger;rus		1
Germany–Macedonia (FYR)	1987	eng;ger;scr	eng	4
Germany–Malaysia	1977	eng;ger;may	eng	3
Germany–Malta	1974	eng;ger		1
Germany–Mauritius	1978	eng;ger		1
Germany–Mexico	1993	ger;spa		1
Germany–Poland	1972	ger;pol		1
Germany–Romania	1973	ger;rum		1
Germany–Russia	1981	ger;rus		1
Germany–Singapore	1972	eng;ger		1
Germany–Slovenia	1987	eng;ger;scr	eng	4
Germany–Spain	1966	ger;spa		1
Germany–Tajikistan	1981	ger;rus		1
Germany–Turkey	1985	eng;ger;tur	eng	4
Germany–Ukraine	1981	ger;rus		1
Germany–United Arab Emirates	1995	eng;ger;ara	eng	4
Germany–United Kingdom	1964	eng;ger		1
Germany–Uruguay	1987	ger;spa		1
Germany–Uzbekistan	1981	ger;rus		1
Greece–Italy	1965	eng;gre;ita	eng	6
Grenada–Sweden	1972	eng;swe		1
Hungary–India	1986	eng	eng	5
Hungary–Macedonia (FYR)	1985	eng	eng	5
Hungary–Serbia and Montenegro	1985	eng	eng	5
Hungary–Slovenia	1985	eng	eng	5
Hungary–United Kingdom	1977	eng;hun		1
Iceland–United States	1975	eng;ice		1
India–Italy	1981	eng;hin;ita	eng	6
India–Japan	1960	eng	eng	5
India–Kazakhstan	1988	eng;hin;rus	eng	2
India–Malaysia	1976	eng;hin;may	eng	3
India–Malaysia	2001	eng;hin;may	eng	8
India–Nepal	1987	eng;hin;nep	eng	3
India–Norway	1986	eng;hin;nor	eng	2

450

Treaty	Conclusion	AL	UL/PT	TOW
India–Romania	1987	eng;hin;rum	eng	2
India–Russia	1988	eng;hin;rus	eng	2
India–Singapore	1981	eng	eng	5
India–Sri Lanka	1982	eng;hin;sin	eng	3
India–Sweden	1988	eng	eng	5
India–Syria	1984	eng;hin;ara	eng	2
India–Tajikistan	1988	eng;hin;rus	eng	2
India–Tanzania	1979	eng	eng	5
India–Turkmenistan	1988	eng;hin;rus	eng	2
India–Ukraine	1988	eng;hin;rus	eng	2
India–United Kingdom	1981	eng;hin	eng	2
India–Uzbekistan	1988	eng;hin;rus	eng	2
Indonesia–Mauritius	1996	eng	eng	5
Indonesia–Netherlands	1973	eng;ind;dut	eng	4
Indonesia–Philippines	1981	eng	eng	5
Indonesia–Thailand	1981	eng	eng	5
Indonesia–United Kingdom	1974	eng	eng	5
Ireland–Norway	1969	eng	eng	5
Israel–Italy	1968	eng;heb;ita	eng	6
Israel–Singapore	1971	eng	eng	5
Italy–Kazakhstan	1985	ita;rus		1
Italy–Kyrgyzstan	1985	ita;rus		1
Italy–Macedonia (FYR)	1982	eng	eng	5
Italy–Moldova	1985	ita;rus		1
Italy–Russia	1985	ita;rus		1
Italy–Slovenia	1982	eng	eng	5
Italy–Tajikistan	1985	ita;rus		1
Italy–Ukraine	1985	ita;rus		1
Italy–United Kingdom	1960	eng;ita		1
Italy–United States	1984	eng;ita		1
Italy–Uzbekistan	1985	ita;rus		1
Japan–Kazakhstan	1986	eng;jap;rus	eng	3
Japan–Korea (Rep.)	1970	eng	eng	5
Japan–Malaysia	1970	eng	eng	5
Japan–Montserrat	1970	eng;jap		1
Japan–Netherlands	1970	eng;jap;dut	eng	9
Japan–New Zealand	1963	eng;jap		1
Japan–Norway	1967	eng	eng	5
Japan–Seychelles	1970	eng;jap		1
Japan–Singapore	1971	eng	eng	5
Japan–Thailand	1963	eng	eng	5
Japan–United Kingdom	1969	eng;jap		1
Japan–United States	1971	eng;jap		1
Kazakhstan–Malaysia	1987	eng;rus;may	eng	3
Kazakhstan–Netherlands	1986	eng;rus;dut		1
Kazakhstan–Norway	1980	rus;nor		1
Kazakhstan–Spain	1985	rus;spa		1
Kazakhstan–Sweden	1981	rus;swe		1
Kazakhstan–Switzerland	1986	rus;ger		1
Kazakhstan–United Kingdom	1985	eng;rus		1
Kazakhstan–United States	1973	eng;rus		1
Kenya–Switzerland	1963	eng;fre		1

451

E. Sample

Treaty	Conclusion	AL	UL/PT	TOW
Kiribati–Sweden	1972	eng;swe		1
Korea (Rep.)–Thailand	1974	eng;kor;tha	eng	2
Korea (Rep.)–United Kingdom	1977	eng;kor		1
Kyrgyzstan–Netherlands	1986	eng;rus;dut		1
Kyrgyzstan–Norway	1980	rus;nor		1
Kyrgyzstan–Spain	1985	rus;spa		1
Kyrgyzstan–Sweden	1981	rus;swe		1
Kyrgyzstan–Switzerland	1986	ger;rus		1
Kyrgyzstan–United Kingdom	1985	eng;rus		1
Kyrgyzstan–United States	1973	eng;rus		1
Liberia–Sweden	1969	eng	eng	5
Libya–Malta	1972	eng;ara		1
Luxembourg–Mongolia	1998	fre;mon		1
Luxembourg–Sweden	1983	fre	fre	5
Luxembourg–United States	1962	eng;fre		1
Macedonia (FYR)–Netherlands	1982	eng;scr;dut	eng	4
Macedonia (FYR)–Poland	1985	eng;scr;pol	eng	4
Macedonia (FYR)–Romania	1986	eng;scr;rum	eng	3
Macedonia (FYR)–Slovak Republic	1981	eng	eng	5
Macedonia (FYR)–Sweden	1980	eng	eng	5
Macedonia (FYR)–United Kingdom	1981	eng;scr		1
Malawi–Netherlands	1969	eng;dut		1
Malawi–Norway	1961	eng	eng	5
Malaysia–Singapore	1968	eng	eng	5
Malaysia–Sri Lanka	1972	eng;may;sin	eng	3
Malaysia–Sweden	1970	eng	eng	5
Malaysia–Tajikistan	1987	eng;may;rus	eng	3
Malaysia–Turkmenistan	1987	eng;may;rus	eng	3
Malaysia–United Kingdom	1973	eng	eng	5
Malaysia–Uzbekistan	1987	eng;may;rus	eng	3
Malta–Norway	1975	eng	eng	5
Malta–Sweden	1975	eng	eng	5
Malta–United Kingdom	1962	eng	eng	5
Malta–United States	1980	eng	eng	5
Mauritius–South Africa	1960	eng;afr		1
Mauritius–Sweden	1992	eng	eng	5
Moldova–Netherlands	1986	eng;rus;dut		1
Moldova–Norway	1980	rus;nor		1
Moldova–Spain	1985	rus;spa		1
Moldova–Switzerland	1986	rus;ger		1
Moldova–United Kingdom	1985	eng;rus		1
Mongolia–Netherlands	2002	eng;mon;dut	eng	4
Montserrat–Sweden	1972	eng;swe		1
Morocco–Romania	1981	fre;ara;rum	fre	3
Morocco–Sweden	1961	fre	fre	5
Netherlands–Norway	1966	dut;nor		1
Netherlands–Poland	1979	eng;dut;pol	eng	4
Netherlands–Romania	1979	fre;dut;pol	fre	4
Netherlands–Russia	1986	eng;dut;rus		1
Netherlands–Slovenia	1982	eng;dut;scr	eng	4
Netherlands–South Africa	1971	eng;dut;afr		1
Netherlands–Sweden	1968	dut;swe		1

Treaty	Conclusion	AL	UL/PT	TOW
Netherlands–Turkmenistan	1986	eng;dut;rus		1
Netherlands–Ukraine	1986	eng;dut;rus		1
Netherlands–United Kingdom	1967	eng;dut		1
Netherlands–United Kingdom	1980	eng;dut		1
Netherlands–Uzbekistan	1986	eng;dut;rus		1
New Zealand–Singapore	1973	eng	eng	5
New Zealand–United Kingdom	1966	eng	eng	5
Norway–Poland	1977	eng	eng	5
Norway–Portugal	1970	eng	eng	5
Norway–Russia	1980	nor;rus		1
Norway–Singapore	1966	eng	eng	5
Norway–Singapore	1984	eng	eng	5
Norway–Slovenia	1983	eng	eng	5
Norway–Spain	1963	eng;spa		1
Norway–Sri Lanka	1964	eng	eng	5
Norway–Tajikistan	1980	nor;rus		1
Norway–Thailand	1964	eng	eng	5
Norway–Turkey	1971	eng	eng	5
Norway–Ukraine	1980	nor;rus		1
Norway–United Kingdom	1969	eng;nor		1
Norway–United Kingdom	1985	eng;nor		1
Norway–United Kingdom	2000	eng;nor		1
Norway–Uzbekistan	1980	nor;rus		1
Pakistan–Romania	1978	eng;rum		1
Pakistan–United Kingdom	1961	eng	eng	5
Peru–Sweden	1966	spa;swe		1
Philippines–Sweden	1966	eng	eng	5
Philippines–Sweden	1987	eng	eng	5
Poland–Serbia and Montenegro	1985	eng;pol;scr	eng	4
Poland–Slovenia	1985	eng;pol;scr	eng	4
Poland–Sweden	1975	eng	eng	5
Poland–United Kingdom	1976	eng;pol		1
Portugal–Spain	1968	por;spa		1
Romania–Serbia and Montenegro	1986	eng;rum;scr	eng	3
Romania–Slovenia	1986	eng;rum;scr	eng	3
Russia–Spain	1985	rus;spa		1
Russia–Sweden	1981	rus;swe		1
Russia–Switzerland	1986	rus;ger		1
Russia–United Kingdom	1985	eng;rus		1
Russia–United States	1973	eng;rus		1
Serbia and Montenegro–Slovak Republic	1981	eng	eng	5
Seychelles–South Africa	1960	eng;afr		1
Seychelles–Switzerland	1963	eng;fre		1
Singapore–Switzerland	1975	eng;ger		1
Singapore–United Kingdom	1966	eng	eng	5
Slovak Republic–Slovenia	1981	eng	eng	5
Slovenia–Sri Lanka	1985	eng;scr;sin	eng	3
Slovenia–United Kingdom	1981	eng;scr		1
South Africa–Swaziland	1972	eng;afr		1
South Africa–Switzerland	1967	eng;ger;afr		1
South Africa–Trinidad and Tobago	1960	eng;afr		1
South Africa–United Kingdom	1968	eng;afr		1

E. Sample

Treaty	Conclusion	AL	UL/PT	TOW
Spain–Uzbekistan	1985	spa;rus		1
St. Kitts and Nevis–Sweden	1972	eng;swe		1
St. Lucia–Sweden	1972	eng;swe		1
St. Vincent and the Grenadines–Sweden	1972	eng;swe		1
Swaziland–Sweden	1972	eng;swe		1
Sweden–Tajikistan	1981	rus;swe		1
Sweden–Thailand	1961	eng	eng	5
Sweden–Tuvalu	1972	eng;swe		1
Sweden–Ukraine	1981	rus;swe		1
Sweden–United Kingdom	1960	eng;swe		1
Sweden–United States	1983	eng;swe		1
Sweden–Uzbekistan	1981	rus;swe		1
Switzerland–Tajikistan	1986	ger;rus		1
Switzerland–Tanzania	1963	eng;fre		1
Switzerland–Turkmenistan	1986	ger;rus		1
Switzerland–Ukraine	1986	ger;rus		1
Switzerland–Uzbekistan	1986	ger;rus		1
Switzerland–Yemen	1963	eng;fre		1
Switzerland–Zimbabwe	1961	eng;fre		1
Tajikistan–United Kingdom	1985	eng;rus		1
Ukraine–United Kingdom	1985	eng;rus		1
Ukraine–United States	1973	eng;rus		1
United Kingdom–United States	1975	eng	eng	5
United Kingdom–Uzbekistan	1985	eng;rus		1

References

Air France v Sacks. 470 U.S. 392 (1985).

Ajulo, Sunday Babalola. 'Myth and Reality of Law, Language and International Organization in Africa: The Case of African Economic Community'. *Journal of African Law* 41, no. 1 (1997): 27–42.

Alexy, Robert. *Theorie der juristischen Argumentation*. Frankfurt am Main: Suhrkamp Verlag, 1983.

Ambatielos (Greece v United Kingdom), Preliminary Objection. ICJ. Annual Reports of the International Court of Justice, 1952.

Andean Community. *Standard Agreement to Avoid Double Taxation Between Member Countries and States Outside the Subregion*. Lima: Andean Community General Secretariat, 1971.

Andersen, Hanne, and Brian Hepburn. 'Scientific Method'. In *The Stanford Encyclopedia of Philosophy*, edited by Edward N. Zalta, Summer ed. Stanford University, 2016.

Anglo-Iranian Oil Co. (United Kingdom v Iran). ICJ. Annual Reports of the International Court of Justice, 1952.

Arab Economic Union Council. *Agreement for the Avoidance of Double Taxation and Prevention of Tax Evasion between the States of the Arab Economic Union Council*. Cairo: Council of Arab Economic Unity, 1973.

Arab Maghreb Union. *Convention relative à la non double imposition et l'application des règles de coopération d'échange dans le domaine des impôts sur les revenus entre les pays de l'UMA*. Rabat: Arab Maghreb Union Secretariat, 1990.

Arbitral Award of 31 July 1989 (Guinea Bissau v Senegal). ICJ. Annual Reports of the International Court of Justice, 1991.

Archdukes of the Habsburg-Lorraine House v The Polish State Treasury. Annual Digest of Public International Law Cases (1929–1930), Case No. 235. Supreme Court Poland. Cambridge University Press, 1930.

Arginelli, Paolo. *The Interpretation of Multilingual Tax Treaties*. Leiden: Leiden University Press, 2013.

Aristotle. *Metaphysics*. The Internet Classics Archive, 350 B.C.

Aristotle. *On Interpretation*. The Internet Classics Archive, 350 B.C.

Aristotle. *Prior Analytics*. The Internet Classics Archive, 350 B.C.

Aristotle. *The Organon*. Edited by Harold P. Cooke and Hugh Tredennick. Andesite Press, 2015.

Aristotle. *Topics*. The Internet Classics Archive, 350 B.C.

Arnauld, Antoine, and Pierre Nicole. *Logic or the Art of Thinking*. Translated by Jill Buroker. Cambridge: Cambridge University Press, 1996.

Arnold, Brian J. 'The Interpretation of Tax Treaties: Myth and Reality'. *Bulletin for International Taxation*, no. 1 (2010): 2–15.

Aron Kahane Successeur v Francesco Parisi and the Austrian State. Romanian-Austrian Mixed Arbitral Tribunal. Recueil des décisions des tribunaux arbitraux mixtes institués par les traités de paix, 1929.

Arruda Ferreira, Vanessa, and Anapaula Trindade Marinho. 'Tax Sparing and Matching Credit: From an Unclear Concept to an Uncertain Regime'. *Bulletin for International Taxation* 67, no. 8 (2013): 397–413.

Association of Southeast Asian Nations. *Intra-Asean Model Double Taxation Convention*. Jakarta: The ASEAN Secretariat, 1987.

Atiyah, P. S. *Pragmatism and Theory in English Law*. London: Stevens & Sons, 1987.

Aust, Anthony. *Modern Treaty Law and Practice*. Cambridge; New York: Cambridge University Press, 2000.

Austry, Stéphane, John F. Avery Jones, Philip Baker, Peter Blessing, Robert Danon, Shefali Goradia, Koichi Inoue, et al. 'The Proposed OECD Multilateral Instrument Amending Tax Treaties'. *Bulletin for International Taxation* 70, no. 12 (October 2016).

Avena and Other Mexican Nationals (Mexico v USA). ICJ. Annual Reports of the International Court of Justice, 2004.

Avery Jones, John F. 'Conflicts of Qualification: Comment on Prof. Vogel's and Alexander Rust's Articles'. *Bulletin for International Taxation*, no. 5 (2003): 184–86.

Avery Jones, John F., ed. 'Interpretation of Tax Treaties'. *Bulletin for International Taxation*, no. 2 (1986): 75–86.

Avery Jones, John F. 'Tax Treaties: The Perspective of Common Law Countries'. In *Courts and Tax Treaty Law*. Amsterdam: IBFD, 2007.

Avery Jones, John F. 'Treaty Interpretation'. In *Global Tax Treaty Commentaries*.

IBFD, 2016.

Avery Jones, John F., Charles J. Berg, Henri-Robert Depret, Maarten J. Ellis, Pierre Fontaneau, Raoul Lenz, Toshio Miyatake, et al. 'The Interpretation of Tax Treaties with Particular Reference to Art. 3(2) of the OECD Model – II'. *British Tax Review*, no. 2 (1984): 90–108.

Baker, Philip. *Double Taxation Conventions: A Manual on the OECD Model Tax Convention on Income and on Capital*. Sweet & Maxwell, Limited, 2001.

Baker, Philip. 'Recent Developments in the Interpretation and Application of Double Taxation Conventions'. *Fiscalidade – Revista de Direito e Gestao Fiscal*, no. 4 (2000): 15–27.

Bank of India v Trans Continental Commodity Merchants Ltd. & J. N. Patel. [1982] 1 Lloyd's Rep. 427.

Behrends, Okko, Rolf Knütel, Berthold Kupisch, Hans Hermann Seiler, Peter Apathy, Elmar Bund, Manfred Harder, et al. *Corpus Iuris Civilis II: Digesten 1-10*. 1st ed. Heidelberg: C.F. Müller, 1995.

Bender, Tanja, and Frank Engelen. 'The Final Clause of the 1987 Netherlands Model Tax Convention and the Interpretation of Plurilingual Treaties'. In *A Tax Globalist: Essays in Honour of Maarten J. Ellis*, edited by H. P. A. M. van Arendonk, F. A. Engelen and Sjaak Jansen. Amsterdam: IBFD, 2005.

Berkeley School of Law (Boat Hall). 'The Robbins Collection: The Common Law and Civil Law Traditions'. University of California at Berkeley.

Best v Samuel Fox & Co. Ltd. [1952] AC 716.

Betti, Emilio. *Allgemeine Auslegungslehre als Methodik der Geisteswissenschaften*. Mohr Siebeck, 1967.

BFH. 'I 244/63'. BStBl 1966 III, February 1966.

BFH. 'I R 20/87'. BStBl 1989 II, March 1989.

BFH. 'I R 241/82'. BStBl 1984 II, August 1983.

BFH. 'I R 369/83'. BStBl 1988 II, February 1988.

BFH. 'I R 48/12'. BStBl 2014 II, June 2013.

BFH. 'I R 63/80'. BStBl 1986 II, August 1985.

BFH. 'I R 74/86'. BStBl 1990 II, February 1989.

BFH. 'Jahresbericht 2015'.

Bjorge, Eirik. '"Contractual" And "Statutory" Treaty Interpretation in Domestic Courts? Convergence Around the Vienna Rules'. In *The Interpretation of International Law by Domestic Courts: Uniformity, Diversity, Convergence*, edited by Helmut Philipp Aust and Georg Nolte, 49–71. Oxford; New York: Oxford University Press, 2016.

BMF. *Basis for Negotiation for Agreements for the Avoidance of Double Taxation and the Prevention of Fiscal Evasion with Respect to Taxes on Income and on Capital.* Germany: Bundesministerium der Finanzen, 2013.

Bobzien, Susanne. 'Ancient Logic'. In *The Stanford Encyclopedia of Philosophy*, edited by Edward N. Zalta, Winter ed. Stanford University, 2016.

Böhl, Meinrad, Wolfgang Reinhard and Peter Walter. *Hermeneutik: die Geschichte der abendländischen Textauslegung von der Antike bis zur Gegenwart.* Böhlau Verlag Wien, 2013.

Brown, James Robert, and Yiftach Fehige. 'Thought Experiments'. In *The Stanford Encyclopedia of Philosophy*, edited by Edward N. Zalta, Spring ed. Stanford University, 2016.

Buchanan (James) & Co. Ltd. v Babco Forwarding and Shipping (UK) Ltd. [1978] AC 141, HL.

Bunikowski, Dawid. 'The Origins of Open Texture in Language and Legal Philosophies in Oxford and Cambridge'. *Oxford Journal of Legal Studies*, August 2015, 29.

Burchfield, R. W., ed. *The New Fowler's Modern English Usage.* 3rd ed. Oxford: Oxford University Press, 1996.

Buroker, Jill. 'Port Royal Logic'. In *The Stanford Encyclopedia of Philosophy*, edited by Edward N. Zalta, Spring ed. Stanford University, 2017.

Butcher, Judith. *Butcher's Copy-editing: The Cambridge Handbook for Editors, Copyeditors and Proofreaders.* 3rd ed. Cambridge: Cambridge University Press, 1992.

BVerfG. '1 BvR 112/65'. BVerfGE 34, 269, February 1973.

Calderón, José, and Dolores Piña. 'Spain: Interpretation of Tax Treaties'. *European Taxation*, October 1999, 376–86.

Cao, Deborah. *Translating Law.* Channel View Publications Ltd., 2007.

Caribbean Community. *Intra-Regional Double Taxation Agreement.* Georgetown: CARICOM Secretariat, 1994.

Chappell, Sophie Grace. 'Plato on Knowledge in the Theaetetus'. In *The Stanford Encyclopedia of Philosophy*, edited by Edward N. Zalta, Winter ed. Stanford University, 2013.

Colozza v Italy. European Court of Human Rights. Application no. 9024/80, 1985.

Conditions of Admission of a State to Membership in the United Nations (Article 4 of the Charter), Advisory Opinion. ICJ. Annual Reports of the International Court of Justice, 1948.

Conrad M. Black v Her Majesty the Queen. [2014] TCC 12.

Conseil d'État. *9ème et 10ème sous-sections réunies, 25/02/2015, 366680. Inédit Au Recueil Lebon*, 2015.

Conseil d'État. *Ministre du Budget c Ragazzacci*, 2012.

Conseil d'État. *Société Natexis Banques Populaires v France*, 2006.

Conseil d'État. *Société Schneider Electric*, 2002.

Continental Shelf (Libyan Arab Jarnahiriya/Malta). ICJ. Annual Reports of the International Court of Justice, 1985.

Cooper, Thomas Mackay. 'The Common and the Civil Law – A Scot's View'. *Harvard Law Review* 63, no. 3 (1950): 468–75.

Coste, Daniel, Danièle Moore, and Geneviève Zarate. 'Plurilingual and Pluricultural Competence: Studies Towards a Common European Framework of Reference for Language Learning and Teaching'. Strasbourg: Language Policy Division, Council of Europe, 2009.

Council for Mutual Economic Assistance. *Income and Capital Tax Treaty (Companies)*. IBFD, 1978.

Council for Mutual Economic Assistance. *Income and Capital Tax Treaty (Individuals)*. IBFD, 1977.

Crawford, James. 'Articles on Responsibility of States for Internationally Wrongful Acts'. *United Nations Audiovisual Library of International Law*, 2012.

Crawford, James. *State Responsibility: The General Part*. Cambridge: Cambridge University Press, 2013.

Criddle, Evan J. 'The Vienna Convention on the Law of Treaties in U.S. Treaty Interpretation'. *Virginia Journal of International Law* 44, no. 2 (2004): 431–500.

Crystal, David. *English as a Global Language*. 2nd ed. Cambridge; New York: Cambridge University Press, 2012.

Cuéllar, Sergio Bolaños. 'Equivalence Revisited: A Key Concept in Modern Translation Theory'. *Forma y Función*, no. 15 (August 2010): 60–88.

Czech Republic v European Media Ventures SA. [2007] EWHC 2851 (Comm).

Daigle, Robert W. *The Reductio ad absurdum argument prior to Aristotle*. San Jose, C.A.: SJSU ScholarWorks, 1991.

Dainow, Joseph. 'The Civil Law and the Common Law: Some Points of Comparison'. *The American Journal of Comparative Law* 15, no. 3 (1966–1967): 419–35.

De Regering van het Koninkrijk der Nederlanden. *Nederlands Standaardverdrag*,

1987.

de Vattel, Emer. *The Law of Nations*. Indianapolis, IN: Liberty Fund, Inc., 1797.

de Visscher, Charles. *Problèmes d'interprétation judiciaire en droit international public*. Paris: Pedone, 1963.

de Vries, Henry P. 'Choice of Language'. *Virginia Journal of International Law* 3 (1963).

Denmark, Faroe Islands, Finland, Iceland, Norway, Sweden. *Income and Capital Tax Treaty*. Amsterdam: IBFD, 1996.

Derlén, Mattias. *Multilingual Interpretation of European Union Law*. Kluwer Law International, 2009.

Deutscher Bundestag. 'Drucksache 15/4549, Nichtanwendungserlasse im Steuerrecht'. Bundesanzeiger Verlagsgesellschaft mbH, January 2005.

Dicken, Peter. *Global Shift: Mapping the Changing Contours of the World Economy*. 7th ed. Thousand Oaks, CA: Sage Publications Ltd., 2014.

Director of Income Tax v New Skies Satellite BV. ITA 473/2012, 2016.

Dor, Daniel. 'From Englishization to Imposed Multilingualism: Globalization, the Internet, and the Political Economy of the Linguistic Code'. *Public Culture* 16, no. 1 (2004): 97–118.

East African Community. *Agreement between the Governments of the Republic of Kenya, the United Republic of Tanzania and the Republic of Uganda for the Avoidance of Double Taxation and the Prevention of Fiscal Evasion with Respect to Taxes on Income*. Arusha: East African Community, 1997.

East African Community. *Agreement between the Governments of the Republics of Kenya, Uganda, Burundi, Rwanda and the United Republic of Tanzania for the Avoidance of Double Taxation and the Prevention of Fiscal Evasion with Respect to Taxes on Income*. Arusha: East African Community, 2010.

Eastern Airlines, Inc., Petitioner v Rose Marie Floyd, et vir., et al. 499 U.S. 530 (1991).

Eden, Paul A. 'Plurilingual Treaties: Aspects of Interpretation'. Rochester, NY: Social Science Research Network, March 2010.

Edwardes-Ker, Michael. *Tax Treaty Interpretation*, 1994.

Encyclopedia Britannica. 'Antinomy'.

Encyclopedia Britannica. 'Code of Justinian'.

Encyclopedia Britannica. 'Prize Court'.

Encyclopedia Britannica. 'Treaty of Wichale'.

Engelen, Frank A. *Interpretation of Tax Treaties under International Law: A Study of Articles 31, 32, and 33 of the Vienna Convention on the Law of Treaties and Their*

Application to Tax Treaties. Amsterdam: IBFD, 2004.

Europäische Kommission. 'Vorschlag für einen Beschluss des Rates über die Unterzeichnung im Namen der Europäischen Union des umfassenden Wirtschafts- und Handelsabkommens zwischen Kanada einerseits und der Europäischen Union und ihren Mitgliedstaaten andererseits'. Germany: Bundesministerium für Wirtschaft und Energie, 2016.

European Commission. 'Comprehensive Economic and Trade Agreement (CETA) between Canada, of the One Part, and the European Union, of the Other Part (Non-Binding Text Made Public Exclusively for Information Purposes)'. European Commission, 2016.

European Union. 'Consolidated Versions of the Treaty on European Union and the Treaty on the Functioning of the European Union'. *Official Journal of the European Union* 51, no. C 115 (May 2008).

Fantozzi, Augusto. 'Conclusions'. In *Multilingual Texts and Interpretation of Tax Treaties and EC Tax Law*, edited by Guglielmo Maisto, 129–34. Amsterdam: IBFD, 2005.

Fentiman, R. 'Foreign Law in English Courts'. *Law Quarterly Review* 108 (1992): 142.

FG Düsseldorf. 'VII 484/77'. EFG 1980, January 1980.

FG Köln. '2 K 3928/09'. EFG 1853, April 2012.

FG Köln. 'II K 223/85'. EFG 1987, December 1986.

Fisheries Jurisdiction (United Kingdom v Iceland). ICJ. Annual Reports of the International Court of Justice, 1974.

Fitzmaurice, Malgosia. 'The Practical Working of the Law of Treaties'. In *International Law*, edited by Malcolm D. Evans. Oxford; New York: Oxford University Press, 2003.

Flick, Hans. 'Zur Auslegung von Normen des Internationalen Steuerrechts'. In *Von der Auslegung und Anwendung der Steuergesetze*, edited by Günther Felix, 151 et seq. Festschrift für Armin Spitaler. Stuttgart: C.E. Poeschel, 1958.

Fogg, Keith. 'The United States Tax Court – A Court for All Parties'. *Bulletin for International Taxation* 70, no. 1/2 (December 2015).

Forster, Michael. 'Friedrich Daniel Ernst Schleiermacher'. In *The Stanford Encyclopedia of Philosophy*, edited by Edward N. Zalta, Fall ed. Stanford University, 2017.

Foster & Elam v Neilson. 27 U.S. (2 Pet.) 253 (1829).

Foster, Nigel. *German Legal System and Laws.* 2nd ed. London: Blackstone Press,

1996.

Fothergill v Monarch Airlines Ltd. [1981] AC 251, HL.

Frank, Jerome N. 'Civil Law Influences on the Common Law – Some Reflections on "Comparative" and "Contrastive" Law'. *University of Pennsylvania Law Review* 104, no. 7 (1956): 887–926.

Frege, Gottlob. *Begriffsschrift: Eine der arithmetischen nachgebildete Formelsprache des reinen Denkens.* Halle: Louis Nebert Verlag, 1879.

Frege, Gottlob. *Die Grundlagen der Arithmetik: eine logisch mathematische Untersuchung über den Begriff der Zahl.* Breslau: Verlag von Wilhelm Koebner, 1884.

Frege, Gottlob. 'Über Sinn und Bedeutung'. *Zeitschrift für Philosophie und Philosophische Kritik*, 1892, 25–50.

Fugro Engineering BV v ACIT. TTJ. Vol. 122. Delhi Income Tax Appelate Tribunal, 2008.

Fujitsu Ltd. v Federal Exp. Corp. 247 F.3d 423 (2d Cir. 2001).

Fuller, Steve. 'The Demarcation of Science: A Problem Whose Demise Has Been Greatly Exaggerated'. *Pacific Philosophical Quarterly* 66, nos. 3 – 4: 329–41.

Gabčíkovo-Nagymaros Project (Hungary/Slovakia). ICJ. Annual Reports of the International Court of Justice, 1997.

Gadamer, Hans-Georg. *Truth and Method.* Translated by Joel Weinsheimer and Donald G. Marshall. 2nd ed. London; New York: Continuum, 2004.

Gaja, Giorgio. 'The Perspective of International Law'. In *Multilingual Texts and Interpretation of Tax Treaties and EC Tax Law*, edited by Guglielmo Maisto, 91–102. Amsterdam: IBFD, 2005.

Gamble, John King, and Charlotte Ku. 'Choice of Language in Bilateral Treaties: Fifty Years of Changing State Practice'. *Indiana International and Comparative Law Review* 3 (1993): 233–64.

Gamble, John King, Lauren Kolb, and Casey Graml. 'Choice of Official Text in Multilateral Treaties: The Interplay of Law, Politics, Language, Pragmatism and (Multi)-Nationalism'. *Santa Clara Journal of International Law* 12, no. 2 (May 2014): 29–55.

Gardiner, Richard K. *Treaty Interpretation.* Oxford: Oxford University Press, 2010.

Garibay, Mónica Sada. 'An Analysis of the Case Law on Article 3(2) of the OECD Model (2010)'. *Bulletin for International Taxation* 65, no. 8 (2011).

Germer, Peter. 'Interpretation of Plurilingual Treaties: A Study of Article 33 of the Vienna Convention on the Law of Treaties'. *Harvard International Law Journal* 11 (1970): 400.

Ghyselen, Myriam, and Bernard Peeters. 'The Court of Cassation as the Supreme

Body of the Judiciary in Belgium'. *Bulletin for International Taxation* 70, nos. 1 – 2 (December 2015).

Giussani, A. 'Some Comparative Notes on Tax Litigation'. In *Courts and Tax Treaty Law*. Amsterdam: IBFD, 2007.

Gladden v Her Majesty the Queen. [1985] 85 DTC 5188.

Golder v United Kingdom. European Court of Human Rights. Application no. 4451/70, 1975.

Grossfield, Bernhard. 'Language and the Law'. *Journal of Air Law and Commerce* 50 (1985): 793–803.

Haensch, Günter. 'Frankreich: Politik, Gesellschaft, Wirtschaft'. In *Außenpolitik in der Wirtschafts– und Finanzkrise*. Walter de Gruyter, 2012.

Hardy, Jean. 'The Interpretation of Plurilingual Treaties by International Courts and Tribunals'. *The British Year Book of International Law*, 1961, 73–155.

Hare, Richard M. *The Language of Morals*. Reprint. London; New York: Oxford University Press, USA, 1991.

Harper, Russell David, ed. *The Chicago Manual of Style*. 16th ed. Chicago, IL: University of Chicago Press, 2010.

Hart, Herbert L. A. *Essays in Jurisprudence and Philosophy*. Oxford; New York: Oxford University Press, USA, 1984.

Hart, Herbert L. A. 'Positivism and the Separation of Law and Morals'. *Harvard Law Review* 71, no. 4 (1958): 593–629.

Hart, Herbert L. A. *The Concept of Law*. Oxford: The Clarendon Press, 1961.

Hartley, Trevor C. 'Pleading and Proof of Foreign Law: The Major European Systems Compared'. *International and Comparative Law Quarterly* 45 (1996): 271.

Hegel, Georg Wilhelm Friedrich. *Wissenschaft der Logik*. Berlin: Hofenberg, 2016.

Heidegger, Martin. *Ontology – The Hermeneutics of Facticity*. Translated by John van Buren. Bloomington, IN: Indiana University Press, 1999.

Heidegger, Martin. *Philosophical and Political Writings*. Edited by Manfred Stassen. New York: Continuum, 2003.

Heinrich, Johannes, and Helmut Moritz. 'Austria: Interpretation of Tax Treaties'. *European Taxation*, April 2000, 142–52.

Hilaire, Constantine and Benjamin et al. v Trinidad and Tobago. Inter-American Court of Human Rights, 2002.

Hilf, Meinhard. *Die Auslegung mehrsprachiger Verträge: eine Untersuchung zum Völkerrecht und zum Staatsrecht der Bundesrepublik Deutschland*. Berlin, New York: Springer-Verlag, 1973.

Holmes, Oliver Wendell. *The Common Law*. Edited by Paulo J. S. Pereira and Diego

M. Beltran. 1881 edition. Toronto: University of Toronto Law School Typographical Society, 2011.

Høyesterett. *PGS Geophysical AS v Government of Norway*. 2004–01003–A, (Sak Nr. 2003/1311). Amsterdam: IBFD, *Tax Treaty Case Law Database 2016*, 2004.

Hudson, Manley O. *The Permanent Court of International Justice 1920–1942*. New York: The Macmillan Company, 1943.

Hume, David. 'Of Taxes'. In *Essays: Moral, Political, and Literary*. Indianapolis: Liberty Fund, Inc., 1987.

Ichikawa, Jonathan Jenkins, and Matthias Steup. 'The Analysis of Knowledge'. In *The Stanford Encyclopedia of Philosophy*, edited by Edward N. Zalta, Spring ed. Stanford University, 2014.

ILC. *Documents of the Second Part of the Seventeenth Session and of the Eighteenth Session Including the Reports of the Commission to the General Assembly*. Vol. II. Yearbook of the International Law Commission 1966, A/CN.4/SER. A/1966/Add.1. United Nations, 1967.

ILC. *Documents of the Second Session Including the Report of the Commission to the General Assembly*. Vol. II. Yearbook of the International Law Commission 1950, A/CN. 4/SER.A/1950/Add.1. United Nations, 1957.

ILC. *Documents of the Sixteenth Session Including the Report of the Commission to the General Assembly*. Vol. II. Yearbook of the International Law Commission 1964, A/CN.4/SER.A/1964/Add.1. United Nations, 1965.

ILC. *Draft Articles on Responsibility of States for Internationally Wrongful Acts, with Commentaries; Report of the Commission to the General Assembly on the Work of Its Fifty-Third Session, Document A/56/10*. Vol. II, Part 2. Yearbook of the International Law Commission 2001, A/CN.4/SER.A/2001/Add.1. United Nations, 2001.

ILC. *Draft Articles on the Law of Treaties with Commentaries 1966. Documents of the Second Part of the Seventeenth Session and of the Eighteenth Session Including the Reports of the Commission to the General Assembly*. Vol. II. Yearbook of the International Law Commission 1966, A/CN.4/SER. A/1966/Add.1. United Nations, 1967.

ILC. *Projet d'articles sur le droit des traites et commentaires 1966. Texte adopté par la Commission à sa dix-huitième session, en 1966, et soumis à l'Assemblée générale dans le cadre de son rapport sur les travaux de ladite session*. Vol. II. Annuaire de la Commission du droit international 1966. United Nations, 1967.

ILC. 'Report of the International Law Commission on the Sixty-fifth Session, 6 May – 7 June and 8 July – 9 August 2013'. Doc. A/68/10. United Nations, December

2013.

ILC. *Summary Records and Documents of the First Session Including the Report of the Commission to the General Assembly.* Yearbook of the International Law Commission 1949. United Nations, 1956.

ILC. *Summary Records of the Eighteenth Session, 4 May – 19 July 1966.* Vol. I, Part II. Yearbook of the International Law Commission 1966, A/CN.4/SER.A/1966. United Nations, 1967.

ILC. *Summary Records of the Second Session, 5 June – 29 July 1950.* Vol. I. Yearbook of the International Law Commission 1950, A/CN.4/SER.A/1950. United Nations, 1958.

ILC. *Summary Records of the Sixteenth Session, 11 May – 24 July 1964.* Vol. I. Yearbook of the International Law Commission 1964, A/CN.4/SER.A/1964. United Nations, 1965.

Inland Revenue Commissioners v Commerzbank. [1990] STC 285.

Itel Containers Int'l Corp. v Huddleston. 507 U.S. 60 (1993).

Jankowiak, Ingo. *Doppelte Nichtbesteuerung im internationalen Steuerrecht.* Baden-Baden: Nomos, 2009.

John Paul II. *Encyclical Letter Fides et Ratio,* 1998.

Johnson, Anne. 'The Rise of English: The Language of Globalization in China and the European Union'. *Macalester International* 22 (2009): 131–68.

Johnson v Olson. 92 Kan. 819 142 P. 256 (1914).

Joisten, Karen. *Philosophische Hermeneutik.* Berlin: Akademie Verlag GmbH, 2009.

Kant, Immanuel. *Kritik der reinen Vernunft.* Köln: Anaconda, 2009.

Kant, Immanuel. *Metaphysische Anfangsgründe der Naturwissenschaft.* Riga: Johann Friedrich Hartknoch, 1786.

Kanwar, Vik. 'Treaty Interpretation in Indian Courts: Adherence, Coherence, and Convergence'. In *The Interpretation of International Law by Domestic Courts: Uniformity, Diversity, Convergence,* edited by Helmut Philipp Aust and Georg Nolte, 239–64. Oxford; New York: Oxford University Press, 2016.

Kasikili/Sedudu Island (Botswana/Namibia). ICJ. Annual Reports of the International Court of Justice, 1999.

Kelsen, Hans. *The Law of the United Nations: A Critical Analysis of Its Fundamental Problems.* The Lawbook Exchange, Ltd., 1950.

Kelsen, Hans. 'The Principle of Sovereign Equality of States as a Basis for International Organization'. *The Yale Law Journal* 53, no. 2 (1944): 207–20.

Kemp, Charlotte. 'Defining Multilingualism'. In *The Exploration of Multilingualism: Development of Research on L3, Multilingualism and Multiple Language Acquisi-*

tion. Amsterdam; Philadelphia: John Benjamins Publishing Co., 2009.

Kennard, Fredrick. *Thought Experiments: Popular Thought Experiments in Philosophy, Physics, Ethics, Computer Science & Mathematics*. Lulu.com, 2015.

Kiliç İnşaat İthalat İhracat Sanayi ve Ticaret Anonim Şirketi v Turkmenistan. ICSID, Case No. ARB/10/1. Washington, D.C.: International Centre for Settlement of Investment Disputes, 2012.

Kirby, Michael. 'Judicial Dissent – Common Law and Civil Law Traditions'. *Law Quarterly Review*, July 2007.

Klabbers, Jan. *The Concept of Treaty in International Law*. The Hague: Kluwer Law International, 1996.

Kneale, William, and Martha Kneale. *The Development of Logic*. Revised ed. Oxford; New York: Oxford University Press, USA, 1985.

Kolck, Joachim Dieter. *Der Betriebsstättenbegriff im nationalen und im internationalen Steuerrecht*. Münster: Universität, Fachbereich Rechtswissenschaft, Dissertation, 1974.

Kraus, Emil. *Der Systemgedanke bei Kant und Fichte*. Berlin: Verlag von Reuther & Reichard, 1916.

Kripke, Saul A. 'Identity and Necessity'. In *Identity and Individuation*, edited by Milton K. Munitz, 1st ed. New York: New York University Press, 1971.

Kripke, Saul A. *Naming and Necessity*. Cambridge, Mass: Harvard University Press, 1980.

Kuner, Christopher B. 'The Interpretation of Multilingual Treaties: Comparison of Texts Versus the Presumption of Similar Meaning'. *International & Comparative Law Quarterly* 40, no. 4 (1991): 953–64.

LaGrand (Germany v United States of America). ICJ. Annual Reports of the International Court of Justice, 2001.

Lang, Michael. 'Auslegung von Doppelbesteuerungsabkommen und authentische Vertragssprachen'. *Internationales Steuerrecht* 20, no. 11 (2011): 403–10.

Lang, Michael. 'Austria: Entertainers under Article 17'. In *Tax Treaty Case Law around the Globe 2016*, edited by Eric Kemmeren et al. Amsterdam: IBFD, 2017.

Lang, Michael. 'Die Auslegung des multilateralen Instruments'. *Steuer- und Wirtschaft International*, no. 1 (2017): 11–24.

Lang, Michael. 'Tendenzen in der Rechtsprechung des österreichischen Verwaltungsgerichtshofs zu den Doppelbesteuerungsabkommen'. *IFF Forum Für Steuerrecht*, 2012, 26–41.

Lang, Michael. 'The Interpretation of Tax Treaties and Authentic Languages'. In *Essays on Tax Treaties: A Tribute to David A. Ward*, edited by Guglielmo Maisto,

Angelo Nikolakakis, and John M. Ulmer, 15–30. Amsterdam: IBFD, 2013.

Language Policy Division. 'Common European Framework of Reference for Languages: Learning, Teaching, Assessment'. Strasbourg: Council of Europe.

Larenz, Karl. *Über die Unentbehrlichkeit der Jurispridenz als Wissenschaft.* Vol. 26. Schriftenreihe Der Juristischen Gesellschaft e.V. Berlin: Walter de Gruyter & Co., 1966.

Larenz, Karl, and Claus-Wilhelm Canaris. *Methodenlehre der Rechtswissenschaft.* 3rd ed. Berlin: Springer-Verlag, 1995.

Legality of the Threat or Use of Nuclear Weapons, Advisory Opinion. ICJ. Annual Reports of the International Court of Justice, 1996.

Lehner, Moris, ed. *Doppelbesteuerungsabkommen der Bundesrepublik Deutschland auf dem Gebiet der Steuern vom Einkommen und Vermögen: Kommentar auf der Grundlage der Musterabkommen (begründet von Klaus Vogel).* 6th ed. München: Beck, 2015.

Leibniz, Gottfried Wilhelm. *Metaphysische Abhandlung.* Edited by Ulrich Johannes Schneider. Hamburg: Felix Meiner Verlag, 2002.

Leibniz, Gottfried Wilhelm. *Monadologie.* Translated by Robert Zimmermann. Wien: Braumüller und Seidel, 1847.

Lenz, Raoul. 'Report on the Interpretation of Double Taxation Conventions'. International Fiscal Association, 1960.

Lewin, Kurt. 'Problems of Research in Social Psychology'. In *Field Theory in Social Science; Selected Theoretical Papers,* edited by D. Cartwright. New York: Harper & Row, 1951.

Liebrich, Silvia. 'Im Ceta-Vertrag stecken kuriose Wortspiele'. *Süddeutsche Zeitung,* 6 October 2016.

Linderfalk, Ulf. *On the Interpretation of Treaties: The Modern International Law as Expressed in the 1969 Vienna Convention on the Law of Treaties.* Springer, 2007.

Lochner v New York. 198 U.S. 45 (1905).

Lord Macmillan. 'Two Ways of Thinking'. In *Law and Other Things,* 76–101. Cambridge: Cambridge University Press, 1937.

MacCormick, Neil. *Legal Reasoning and Legal Theory.* Clarendon Press, 1978.

MacCormick, Neil, Robert S. Summers, and D. Neil MacCormick. *Interpreting Precedents: A Comparative Study.* Aldershot: Dartmouth Publishing Co. Ltd., 1997.

Maisto, Guglielmo. *Multilingual Texts and Interpretation of Tax Treaties and EC Tax Law.* Amsterdam: IBFD, 2005.

Mann, Frederick A. 'Fusion of the Legal Professions?' *Law Quarterly Review* 93

(1977): 367 et seq.

Mann, Frederick A. 'Uniform Statutes in English Law'. In *Further Studies in International Law*. Oxford: Clarendon Press, 1990.

Mantzavinos, C. 'Hermeneutics'. In *The Stanford Encyclopedia of Philosophy*, edited by Edward N. Zalta, Fall ed. Stanford University, 2016.

Maritime Delimitation and Territorial Questions between Qatar and Bahrain (Qatar v Bahrain), Jurisdiction and Admissibility. ICJ. Annual Reports of the International Court of Justice, 1994.

Martin, Philippe. 'Courts and Tax Treaties in Civil Law Countries'. In *Courts and Tax Treaty Law*. Amsterdam: IBFD, 2007.

Martin, Philippe. 'The French Supreme Administrative Tax Court'. *Bulletin for International Taxation* 70, no. 1 (2016).

Maximov v United States. 299 F.2d 565 (2d Cir. 1962).

Maxwell, Peter Benson, and Gilbert H. B. Jackson. *The Interpretation of Statutes*. 9th ed. London: Sweet and Maxwell, 1946.

McNair, Arnold D. *The Law of Treaties*. Oxford: The Clarendon Press, 1961.

McNamara, Paul. 'Deontic Logic'. In *The Stanford Encyclopedia of Philosophy*, edited by Edward N. Zalta, Winter ed. Stanford University, 2014.

McRae, Peter. 'The Search for Meaning: Continuing Problems with the Interpretation of Treaties'. *Victoria U. Wellington L. Rev.* 33 (2002): 209.

Mellinghoff, Rudolf. 'The German Federal Fiscal Court: An Overview'. *Bulletin for International Taxation* 70, no. 1/2 (December 2015).

Memec Plc v Inland Revenue Comissioners. [1998] STC 754.

Memec Plc v Inland Revenue Comissioners. [1996] STC 1336.

Merrils, J.G. 'Two Approaches to Treaty Interpretation'. In *Australian Year Book of International Law*, 55–82, 1969.

Merryman, John, and Rogelio Perez-Perdomo. *The Civil Law Tradition: An Introduction to the Legal Systems of Europe and Latin America*. Stanford University Press, 2007.

Miller, Hunter. 'The Hague Codification Conference'. *The American Journal of International Law* 24, no. 4 (1930): 674–93.

Mizumura, Minae. *The Fall of Language in the Age of English*. Translated by Mari Yoshihara and Juliet Winters Carpenter. Tra. New York: Columbia University Press, 2015.

Moore, George Edward. 'A Defense of Common Sense'. In *Contemporary British Philosophy (second series)*, edited by J. H. Muirhead, 192–233. London: George

Allen & Unwin, 1925.

Morgenstern, Oskar. 'Descriptive, Predictive and Normative Theory'. *Kyklos* 25, no. 4 (1972): 699–714.

Mössner, Jörg Manfred. 'Die Auslegung mehrsprachiger Staatsverträge'. *Archiv des Völkerrechts*, Bd. 15, no. 3. H. (1972): 273–302.

Neeley, Tsedal. 'Global Business Speaks English'. *Harvard Buisness Review* 90, no. 5 (May 2012).

Netherlands Workers Delegate to the ILO. PCIJ. Publications of the Permanent Court of International Justice, 1922.

Nicaragua v United States of America – Military and Paramilitary Activities in and Against Nicaragua. ICJ. Annual Reports of the International Court of Justice, 1986.

Nietzsche, Friedrich. *The Gay Science: With a Prelude in Rhymes and an Appendix of Songs*. Translated by Walter Kaufmann. New York: Random House, Inc., 1974.

Nollkaemper, André. 'Grounds for the Application of International Rules of Interpretation in National Courts'. In *The Interpretation of International Law by Domestic Courts: Uniformity, Diversity, Convergence*, edited by Helmut Philipp Aust and Georg Nolte, 34–48. Oxford; New York: Oxford University Press, 2016.

North Sea Continental Shelf (Federal Republic of Germany/Denmark; Federal Republic of Germany/Netherlands). ICJ. Annual Reports of the International Court of Justice, 1969.

O'Connor, Joseph F. *Good Faith in International Trade*. Aldershot: Dartmouth Publishing Co. Ltd., 1991.

O'Connor v United States. 479 U.S. 27 (1986).

O'Connor, Vivienne. 'Practitioner's Guide: Common Law and Civil Law Traditions'. International Network to Promote the Rule of Law, March 2012.

Oakes, Leigh. 'Multilingualism in Europe: An Effective French Identity Strategy?' *Journal of Multilingual and Multicultural Development* 23, no. 5 (2002): 371–187.

Observatoire européen du plurilinguisme. 'Charte européenne du plurilinguisme', June 2015.

OECD. *Convention multilatérale pour la mise en œuvre des mesures relatives aux conventions fiscales pour prévenir le BEPS*. Paris: OECD Publishing, 2016.

OECD. *Developing a Multilateral Instrument to Modify Bilateral Tax Treaties, Action 15 – 2015 Final Report*. Paris: OECD Publishing, 2015.

OECD. *Explanatory Statement to the Multilateral Convention to Implement Tax Treaty Related Measures to Prevent Base Erosion and Profit Shifting*. Paris: OECD

Publishing, 2016.

OECD. *Model Tax Convention on Income and on Capital: Condensed Version*. Paris: OECD Publishing, 2014.

OECD. *Model Tax Convention on Income and on Capital: Condensed Version*. Paris: OECD Publishing, 2017.

OECD. *Modèle de convention fiscale concernant le revenu et la fortune*. Paris: OECD Publishing, 2010.

OECD. *Multilateral Convention to Implement Tax Treaty Related Measures to Prevent Base Erosion and Profit Shifting*. Paris: OECD Publishing, 2016.

OECD. *Public Discussion Draft, BEPS Action 15: Development of a Multilateral Instrument to Implement the Tax Treaty related BEPS Measures, 31 May – June 30*. Paris: OECD Publishing, 2016.

OECD. 'Recommendation of the Council Concerning the Avoidance of Double Taxation with Respect to Taxes on Estates and Inheritances and on Gifts'. Paris: OECD Publishing, June 1982.

OECD. *Standard for Automatic Exchange of Financial Account Information in Tax Matters, Model Competent Authority Agreement*. Paris: OECD Publishing, 2014.

Oesch, Matthias. *Standards of Review in WTO Dispute Resolution*. Oxford; New York: Oxford University Press, 2003.

Oppenheim, L. *Oppenheim's International Law*. Edited by R. Jennings and A. Watts. 9th ed. Harlow: Longman, 1992.

Ortino, Federico. *The WTO Dispute Settlement System, 1995–2003*. The Hague: Kluwer Law International, 2004.

Pasqualucci, Jo M. *The Practice and Procedure of the Inter-American Court of Human Rights*. Cambridge; New York: Cambridge University Press, 2003.

Penhallow et al. v Doane's Administrators. 3 U.S. 54 (1795). Dallas's Reports.

Pepper v Hart. [1993] AC 593.

Perdelwitz, Andreas. 'A Certain Degree of Permanence Between Temporary and Everlasting Business Activities'. In *Taxation of Business Profits in the 21st Century*, edited by Andreas Perdelwitz and Carlos Gutiérrez. Amsterdam: IBFD, 2013.

Pfister, Jonas. *Werkzeuge des Philosophierens*. Stuttgart: Reclam, Philipp, jun. GmbH, Verlag, 2013.

Philipps, Lothar. 'Braucht die Rechtswissenschaft eine Deontische Logik?' In *Rechtstheorie: Beiträge zur Grundlagendiskussion*, edited by Günther Jahr and Werner Maihofer, 352–68. Frankfurt am Main: Vittorio Klostermann, 1971.

Pijl, Hans. 'State Responsibility in Taxation Matters'. *Bulletin for International Tax-*

ation, no. 1 (2006): 38–51.

Piltz, Detlev J. 'Macht im Steuerrecht'. In *Unternehmen Steuern: Festschrift für Hans Flick zum 70. Geburtstag,* edited by Franz Klein, Hans Peter Stihl, Franz Wassermeyer, Detlev J. Piltz, and Harald Schaumburg, 499–518. Köln: Dr. Otto Schmidt Verlag KG, 1997.

Plato. *Republic.* Perseus Digital Library, Tufts University, 380 B.C.

Plato. *Theaetetus.* Perseus Digital Library, Tufts University, 380 B.C.

Polish Postal Service in Danzig. PCIJ. Publications of the Permanent Court of International Justice, 1925.

Popper, Karl R. 'Facts, Standards, and Truth: A Further Criticism of Relativism'. In *Moral Relativism: A Reader,* edited by Paul K. Moser and Thomas L. Carson, 32–52. New York, NY: Oxford University Press, USA, 2000.

Popper, Karl R. *In Search of a Better World: Lectures and Essays from Thirty Years.* London: Routledge, 2012.

Popper, Karl R. *The Logic of Scientific Discovery.* Reprint 2004. Routledge, 2002.

Popper, Karl R. *The Myth of the Framework: In Defence of Science and Rationality.* New York: Routledge, 1994.

Popper, Karl R. *The Open Society and Its Enemies.* London: Routledge, 2011.

Popper, Karl R. 'What is Dialectic?' *Mind* 49, no. 196 (1940): 403–26.

Preuß, Ulrich K. 'Equality of States – Its Meaning in a Constitutionalized Global Order'. *Chicago Journal of International Law* 9, no. 1 (2008): 17–49.

Pugh, Richard Crawford, Oscar Schachter, and Hans Smit. *International Law: Cases and Materials.* Edited by Louis Henkin. 3rd edition. St. Paul, Minn: West Group, 1993.

Putnam, Hilary. 'Meaning and Reference'. *The Journal of Philosophy* 70, no. 19 (August 1973): 699–711.

Pym, Anthony. 'On History in Formal Conceptualizations of Translation'. *Across Languages and Cultures* 8, no. 2 (January 2007): 153–66.

Quinn v Leatham. [1901] AC 45.

Quinton, Anthony. 'The "A Priori" and the Analytic'. *Proceedings of the Aristotelian Society* 64 (1963): 31–54.

R (on the Application of) Federation of Tour Operators v HM Treasury. [2007] EWHC 20622 (Admin).

R v Secretary for the Home Department, Ex Parte Adan. [2001] AC 477.

Rainer Hausmann. 'Pleading and Proof of Foreign Law – a Comparative Analysis'.

The European Legal Forum, Section I, no. 1 (2008): 1–13.

Ram Jethmalani v Union of India. Supreme Court of India, 2011.

Reid, Thomas. *Essays on the Intellectual Powers of Man*. Cambridge: Cambridge University Press, 2011.

Reimer, Ekkehart. 'Germany: Interpretation of Tax Treaties'. *European Taxation*, December 1999, 458–74.

Reimer, Ekkehart. 'Seminar F: Die sog. Entscheidungsharmonie als Maßstab für die Auslegung von Doppelbesteuerungsabkommen'. *Internationales Steuerrecht*, no. 15 (2008): 551–55.

Reimer, Ekkehart. 'Tax Treaty Interpretation in Germany'. In *Tax Treaty Interpretation*, edited by Michael Lang, 119–52. Wien: Linde Verlag Ges.m.b.H., 1998.

Reimer, Ekkehart, and Alexander Rust, eds. *Klaus Vogel on Double Taxation Conventions*. 4th ed. The Netherlands: Wolters Kluwer Law & Business, 2015.

Reimer, Marga, and Eliot Michaelson. 'Reference'. In *The Stanford Encyclopedia of Philosophy*, edited by Edward N. Zalta, Summer ed. Stanford University, 2016.

Resch, Richard Xenophon. 'Case Closed: Tax Treatment of US S–Corporations under the Germany-US Tax Treaty – Treaty Benefits for Hybrid Entities'. *European Taxation* 54, no. 5 (2014): 192–97.

Resch, Richard Xenophon. 'Not in Good Faith – A Critique of the Vienna Convention Rule of Interpretation Concerning Its Application to Plurilingual (Tax) Treaties'. *British Tax Review*, no. 3 (2014): 307–28.

Resch, Richard Xenophon. 'Tax Treatment of US S–Corporations under the Germany-US Tax Treaty'. *European Taxation* 49, no. 3 (2009): 122–28.

Resch, Richard Xenophon. 'The Taxation of Profits without a Permanent Establishment'. In *Permanent Establishments in International Tax Law*, edited by Michael Lang, Mario Züger, and Hans-Jörgen Aigner, 29:475–500. Schriftenreihe Zum Internationalen Steuerrecht. Wien: Linde Verlag Ges.m.b.H., 2003.

Rescher, Nicholas. 'Reductio ad Absurdum'. In *The Internet Encyclopedia of Philosophy*, edited by James Fieser and Bradley Dowden, 2018.

Rescher, Nicholas. *The Logic of Commands*. London: Routledge & Kegan Paul PLC, 1966.

Reuter, Paul. *Introduction to the Law of Treaties*. Kegan Paul Intl, 1995.

Rickert, Heinrich. *Kulturwissenschaft und Naturwissenschaft*. 1st ed. Berlin: Celtis Verlag, 2013.

Ricoeur, Paul. *Interpretation Theory: Discourse and the Surplus of Meaning*. TCU Press, 1976.

Rights of Nationals of the United States of America in Morocco (France v United States of America). ICJ. Annual Reports of the International Court of Justice, 1952.

Ris, Martin. 'Treaty Interpretation and ICJ Recourse to Travaux Préparatoires: Towards a Proposed Amendment of Articles 31 and 32 of the Vienna Convention on the Law of Treaties'. *Boston College International and Comparative Law Review* 14, no. 1 (1991): 111–36.

Ritter, E. M., ed. *The Oxford Style Manual*. Oxford: Oxford University Press, 2003.

Röhl, Klaus F. *Allgemeine Rechtslehre. Ein Lehrbuch*. Köln: Heymanns Verlag GmbH, 1995.

Rose, Gerd. 'Über die Entstehung von "Dummensteuern" und ihre Vermeidung'. In *Die Steuerrechtsordnung in der Diskussion: Festschrift für Klaus Tipke zum 70. Geburtstag*, edited by Joachim Lang, 153–64. Köln: Dr. Otto Schmidt Verlag KG, 1995.

Rose v Himeley. 8 U.S. 241 (1808).

Rosenne, Shabtai. *Practice and Methods of International Law*. Oceana Publications, 1984.

Rosenne, Shabtai. 'The Meaning of "Authentic Text" in Modern Treaty Law'. In *An International Law Miscellany*, 397–429. Leiden; Boston: Martinus Nijhoff Publishers, 1993.

Rühl, Ulli F. H. 'Ist die Rechtswissenschaft überhaupt eine Wissenschaft?' Bremen: Universität Bremen, 2005.

Russell, Bertrand. *My Philosophical Development*. 1st ed. New York: Simon and Schuster, 1959.

Russell, Bertrand. *The Problems of Philosophy*. Oxford: Oxford University Press, 2001.

Russia. *Income and Capital Model Convention*. Amsterdam: IBFD, 2010.

Rust, Alexander. 'Germany'. In *Courts and Tax Treaty Law*. Amsterdam: IBFD, 2007.

Sacchetto, Claudio. 'The Italian Experience'. In *Multilingual Texts and Interpretation of Tax Treaties and EC Tax Law*, edited by Guglielmo Maisto, 63–78. Amsterdam: IBFD, 2005.

Saint Augustine. *On Christian Doctrine: A Select Library of the Nicene and Post-Nicene Fathers of the Christian Church*. Edited by Philip Schaff. Vol. 2. Buffalo: The Christian Literature Company, 1887.

Sanghavi, Dhruv. 'Found in Translation: The Correct Interpretation of "Secret Formula or Process" in India's Tax Treaties'. *British Tax Review*, no. 4 (2016): 411–15.

Sasseville, Jacques. 'The Canadian Experience'. In *Multilingual Texts and Interpretation of Tax Treaties and EC Tax Law*, edited by Guglielmo Maisto, 35–62. Amsterdam: IBFD, 2005.

Sasseville, Jacques. 'The OECD Model Convention and Commentaries'. In *Multilingual Texts and Interpretation of Tax Treaties and EC Tax Law*, edited by Guglielmo Maisto, 129–34. Amsterdam: IBFD, 2005.

Schleiermacher, Friedrich D. E. *Hermeneutik und Kritik: mit besonderer Beziehung auf das Neue Testament*. Berlin: G. Reimer, 1838.

Schön, Wolfgang. 'Tax Law Scholarship in Germany and the United States'. *Max Planck Institute for Tax Law and Public Finance Working Paper*, May 2016.

Schopenhauer, Arthur. *On the Fourfold Root of the Principle of Sufficient Reason*. Translated by E. F. J. Payne. New York: Open Court Classics, 2001.

Schrödinger, Erwin. 'Die gegenwärtige Situation in der Quantenmechanik'. *Die Naturwissenschaften* 23, no. 48 (1935): 807–12.

Schuch, Josef, and Jean-Philippe Van West. 'Authentic Languages and Official Translations of the Multilateral Instrument and Covered Tax Agreements'. In *The OECD Multilateral Instrument for Tax Treaties: Analysis and Effects*, edited by Lang, Michael et. al., 67–87. Wolters Kluwer Law & Business, 2018.

Shelton, Dinah. 'Reconcilable Differences? The Interpretation of Multilingual Treaties'. *Hastings International and Comparative Law Review* 20 (1997): 611–38.

Siac, Cecilia. 'Mining Law: Bridging the Gap Between Common Law and Civil Law Systems'. *Mineral Resources Engineering* 11, no. 2 (2002): 217–29.

Sinclair, Ian. *The Vienna Convention on the Law of Treaties*. Manchester: Manchester University Press, 1984.

Singh Butra v Ebrahim. [1982] 2 Lloyd's Rep. 11, C.A.

Soros, George. *The Alchemy of Finance: Reading the Mind of the Market by George Soros*. Hoboken, New Jersey: John Wiley & Sons, Inc., 1987.

South Asian Association for Regional Cooperation. *SAARC Limited Multilateral Agreement on Avoidance of Double Taxation and Mutual Administrative Assistance in Tax Matters*. Kathmandu: SAARC Secretariat, 2005.

South West Africa (Ethiopia v South Africa). ICJ. Annual Reports of the International Court of Justice, 1962.

Southern African Development Community. *Agreement for the Avoidance of Double Taxation and the Prevention of Fiscal Evasion with Respect to Taxes on Income*. Gaborone: SADC Secretariat, 2013.

Southern African Development Community. *Memorandum of Understanding on Co-Operation in Taxation and Related Matters*. Gaborone: SADC Secretariat, 2002.

Sovereignty over Certain Frontier Land (Belgium v Netherlands). ICJ. Annual Reports of the International Court of Justice, 1959.

Sovereignty over Pulau Litigan and Pulau Sipidan (Indonesia v Malaysia). ICJ. Annual Reports of the International Court of Justice, 2002.

Spagnolo, Lisa. 'Iura Novit Curia and the CISG: Resolution of the Faux Procedural Black Hole'. In *Towards Uniformity: The 2nd Annual MAA Schlechtriem CISG Conference*, edited by Lisa Spagnolo and Ingeborg Schwenzer, 181–221. The Hague: Eleven International Publishing, 2011.

Sportsman v IRC. [1998] STC (SCD) 289.

Steup, Matthias. 'Epistemology'. In *The Stanford Encyclopedia of Philosophy*, edited by Edward N. Zalta, Fall ed. Stanford University, 2016.

Strawson, Peter Frederick. *Introduction to Logical Theory*. London: Methuen, 1952.

Strunk, William Jr. *The Elements of Style*. Edited by White, E.B. 4th ed. Harlow, Essex: Pearson Education Limited, 2014.

Sur, Serge. *L'interprétation en droit international public*. Vol. 75. Paris: Librairie générale de droit et de jurisprudence, 1974.

Tabory, Mala. *Multilingualism in International Law and Institutions*. Alphen aan den Rijn: Sijthoff & Noordhoff, 1980.

Tammelo, Ilmar. *Modern Logic in the Service of Law*. 1st ed. Wien; New York: Springer, 1978.

Tarski, Alfred. *Introduction to Logic: And to the Methodology of Deductive Sciences*. Courier Corporation, 2013.

Tax Treaties Database. Amsterdam: IBFD, 2016.

Tax Treaty Case Law Database. Amsterdam: IBFD, 2016.

Temple of Preah Vihear (Cambodia v Thailand), Preliminary Objections. ICJ. Annual Reports of the International Court of Justice, 1961.

Territorial Dispute (Libyan Arab Jamahiriya/Chad). ICJ. Annual Reports of the International Court of Justice, 1994.

Tetley, William, QC. 'Mixed Jurisdictions: Common Law vs Civil Law (Codified and Uncodified)'. *Uniform Law Review*, no. 3 (1999): 591–618.

The American Law Institute. *Restatement of the Law Third: The Foreign Relations Law of the United States*. Vol. 1, 1987.

The Economist. 'A World Empire by Other Means: The Triumph of English', 22 December 2001.

The Economist. *Style Guide*. 11th ed. London: Profile Books Ltd., 2015.

The Kingdom of Belgium. *Belgian Draft Convention for the Avoidance of Double Taxation and the Prevention Of Fiscal Evasion with Respect to Taxes on Income and on Capital*, 2007.

The Kingdom of Belgium, the French Republic, the Swiss Confederation, the United Kingdom and the United States of America v The Federal Republic of Germany. Arbitral Tribunal for the Agreement on German External Debts. Reports of International Arbitral Awards, 1980.

The Mavrommatis Palestine Concessions. PCIJ. Publications of the Permanent Court of International Justice 1922–1946, 1924.

The Queen v Crown Forest Industries Ltd. et al.

Thiel v Federal Commissioner of Taxation. [1990] 171 CLR 338.

Tipke, Klaus. *Die Steuerrechtsordnung, Bände 1–3.* 1st ed. Köln: Otto Schmidt Verlag, 1993.

Tipke, Klaus. 'Steuerrecht als Wissenschaft'. In *Festschrift für Joachim Lang: Gestaltung der Steuerrechtsordnung*, edited by Roman Seer, Klaus Tipke, Johanna Hey, and Joachim Englisch, 21–56. Köln: Schmidt, Otto, 2010.

Treaty of Neuilly (Bulgaria v Greece). PCIJ. Publications of the Permanent Court of International Justice 1922–1946, 1924.

Tugendhat, Ernst, and Ursula Wolf. *Logisch-semantische Propädeutik.* Stuttgart: Reclam, Philipp, jun. GmbH, Verlag, 1993.

TWA v Franklin Mint Corp. 466 U.S. 243 (1984).

UN. *Charter of the United Nations.* United Nations, 1945.

UN. *Final Clauses of Multilateral Treaties: Handbook.* E.04.V.3. United Nations, 2003.

UN. 'General Assembly Resolution 56/83'. Doc. A/56/589 & Corr. 1. United Nations, December 2001.

UN. 'General Assembly Resolution 59/35'. Doc. A/59/505. United Nations, December 2004.

UN. 'General Assembly Resolution 62/61'. Doc. A/62/446. United Nations, December 2010.

UN. 'General Assembly Resolution 65/19'. Doc. A/65/463. United Nations, December 2010.

UN. *Papers on Selected Topics in Negotiation of Tax Treaties for Developing Countries.* New York: United Nations, 2014.

UN. 'Statute of the International Court of Justice', June 1945.

UN. *United Nations Conference on the Law of Treaties, First and Second Sessions Vienna, 26 March – 24 May 1968 and 9 April – 22 May 1969, Official Records, Documents of the Conference.* A/CONF.39/1 1/Add.2. United Nations, 1970.

UN. *United Nations Conference on the Law of Treaties, First Session Vienna, 26 March – 24 May 1968, Official Records, Summary Records of the Plenary Meetings and of* the Meetings of the Committee of the Whole. A/CONF.39/11. United Nations, 1969.

UN. *United Nations Model Double Taxation Convention Between Developed and Developing Countries.* United Nations, 2011.

UN. *Vienna Convention on the Law of Treaties.* May 23, 1969, Treaty Series I–18232. United Nations, 1980.

United City Merchants v Royal Bank of Canada. [1983] AC 168, HL.

United States. *Estates, Inheritances, Gifts, and Generation-Skipping Transfers Model Convention,* 1980.

United States. *Income and Capital Model Convention,* 2016.

United States. *Model Intergovernmental Agreement to Improve Tax Compliance and to Implement FATCA,* 2012.

United States – Final Countervailing Duty Determination with Respect to Certain Softwood Lumber From Canada. WT/DS257/AB/R. Report of the WTO Appellate Body, 2004.

United States – Subsidies on Upland Cotton. WT/DS267/AB/R. Report of the WTO Appellate Body, 2005.

United States v Alvarez-Machain. 504 U.S. 655 (1992).

United States v Percheman. 32 U.S. (7 Pet.) 51 (1833).

Uterwedde, Henrik. 'Frankreich – Grundlagen der Grandeur'. In *Außenpolitik in der Wirtschafts– und Finanzkrise.* Walter de Gruyter, 2012.

van Caenegem, Raoul Charles. *Judges, Legislators and Professors: Chapters in European Legal History.* Revised ed. Cambridge: Cambridge University Press, 2008.

van der Bruggen, Edwin. 'Unless the Vienna Convention Otherwise Requires: Notes on the Relationship between Article 3(2) of the OECD Model Tax Convention and Articles 31 and 32 of the Vienna Convention on the Law of Treaties'. *European Taxation* 43, no. 5 (2003): 142–56.

van Loon, Hans. 'The Hague Conventions on Private International Law'. In *Further Studies in International Law,* edited by Francis Geoffrey Jacobs and Shelley Roberts, Vol. 7. United Kingdom Comparative Law Series. London: Sweet & Maxwell, 1987.

van Raad, Kees. 'International Coordination of Tax Treaty Interpretation and Application'. In *International and Comparative Taxation: Essays in Honour of Klaus Vogel,* edited by Paul Kirchhof, Moris Lehner, Arndt Raupach, Michael Rodi, and Kees van Raad, 217–30. Series on International Taxation 26. Kluwer Law International, 2002.

Van Schijndel and van Veen v SPF, Opinion of Advocate General Jacobs. Joined Cases

C–430/93 and C–431/93. ECR I–4705, 1995.

Vickers, John. 'The Problem of Induction'. In *The Stanford Encyclopedia of Philosophy*, edited by Edward N. Zalta, Spring ed. Stanford University, 2016.

Villiger, Mark Eugen. *Commentary on the 1969 Vienna Convention on the Law of Treaties*. Leiden; Boston: Martinus Nijhoff Publishers, 2009.

Vogel, Klaus. 'Conflicts of Qualification: The Discussion is not Finished'. *Bulletin for International Taxation*, no. 2 (2003): 41–44.

Vogel, Klaus. 'Double Tax Treaties and Their Interpretation'. *International Tax & Business Lawyer* 4, no. 1 (1986): 4–85.

Vogel, Klaus. *Klaus Vogel on Double Taxation Conventions: A Commentary to the OECD, UN and US Model Conventions for the Avoidance of Double Taxation of Income and Capital; with Particular Reference to German Treaty Practice*. 3rd ed. London: Kluwer, 1997.

Vogel, Klaus. 'Über Entscheidungsharmonie'. In *Unternehmen Steuern: Festschrift für Hans Flick zum 70. Geburtstag*, edited by Franz Klein, Hans Peter Stihl, Franz Wassermeyer, Detlev J. Piltz, and Harald Schaumburg, 1043–56. Köln: Dr. Otto Schmidt Verlag KG, 1997.

Vogel, Klaus, and Moris Lehner, eds. *Doppelbesteuerungsabkommen der Bundesrepublik Deutschland auf dem Gebiet der Steuern vom Einkommen und Vermögen: Kommentar auf der Grundlage der Musterabkommen*. 4th ed. München: Beck, 2003.

Vogel, Klaus, and Moris Lehner, eds. *Doppelbesteuerungsabkommen der Bundesrepublik Deutschland auf dem Gebiet der Steuern vom Einkommen und Vermögen: Kommentar auf der Grundlage der Musterabkommen*. 5th ed. München: Beck, 2008.

Vogel, Klaus, and Rainer Prokisch. 'Interpretation of Double Taxation Conventions'. General Report. Rotterdam: International Fiscal Association, 1993.

Volkswagenwerk Aktiengesellschaft v Schlunk. 486 U.S. 694 (1988).

von Kirchmann, Julius. 'Die Werthlosigkeit der Jurisprudenz als Wissenschaft'. Berlin: Julius Springer, 1848.

von Roenne, Christian. 'The Very Beginning – The First Tax Treaties'. In *History of Tax Treaties: The Relevance of the OECD Documents for the Interpretation of Tax Treaties*, edited by Thomas Ecker and Gernot Ressler, 19–39. Vienna: Linde, 2011.

VwGH. '2013/15/0266'. RIS, June 2015.

VwGH. '2210/60 VwSlg 2707 F/1962'. RIS, September 1962.

Waibel, Michael. 'Principles of Treaty Interpretation: Developed for and Applied by National Courts?' In *The Interpretation of International Law by Domestic Courts:*

Uniformity, Diversity, Convergence, edited by Helmut Philipp Aust and Georg Nolte, 9–33. Oxford; New York: Oxford University Press, 2016.

Wallace, John. 'Only in the Context of a Sentence Do Words Have Any Meaning'. *Midwest Studies in Philosophy* 2, no. 1 (1977): 144–46.

Ward, David A. 'Use of Foreign Court Decisions in Interpreting Tax Treaties'. In *Courts and Tax Treaty Law*. Amsterdam: IBFD, 2007.

Wassermeyer, Franz, ed. *Doppelbesteuerung: Kommentar zu allen deutschen Doppelbesteuerungsabkommen*. Vol. I. München: Beck, 2016.

Watson, Alan. 'Legal Change: Sources of Law and Legal Culture'. *University of Pennsylvania Law Review* 131, no. 5 (1983): 1121–57.

Wattel, Peter J. 'Tax Litigation in Last Instance in the Netherlands: The Tax Chamber of the Supreme Court'. *Bulletin for International Taxation* 70, nos. 1 – 2 (December 2015).

West African Economic and Monetary Union. *Income Tax Treaty*. Bamako: UEMOA, 2008.

Wieacker, Franz. 'The Importance of Roman Law for Western Civilization and Western Legal Thought'. *Boston College International and Comparative Law Review* 4, no. 2 (1981): 257–81.

Wijnen, Wim. 'No Taxation without Litigation – How Tax Courts Survive This Adage'. In *Obra Conmemorativa*. Perspectivas Actuales de la Justicia Fiscal y Administrativa en Iberoamérica. Mexico City: 80 Aniversario de la Promulgación de la Ley de Justicia Fiscal, 2016.

Wijnen, Wim. 'Some Thoughts on Convergence and Tax Treaty Interpretation'. *Bulletin for International Taxation*, no. 11 (2013): 575–79.

Wissenschaftliche Dienste des Deutschen Bundestages. 'Der Nichtanwendungserlass im Steuerrecht, Ausarbeitung WD 4–3000–080/09'. Fachbereich Haushalt und Finanzen, 2009.

Wittgenstein, Ludwig. *Tractatus Logico-Philosophicus*. London: Kegan Paul, 1922.

Wolf v Canada. [2002] 4 F.C. 396.

Wouters, J., and M. Vidal. 'Non-Tax Treaties: Domestic Courts and Treaty Interpretation'. In *Courts and Tax Treaty Law*. Amsterdam: IBFD, 2007.

Zweigert, Konrad, and Hein Kötz. *An Introduction to Comparative Law*. Translated by Tony Weir. 3rd revised ed. Oxford; New York: Clarendon Press, 1998.